PESTS OF HORTICULTURAL CROPS: A GLANCE

D. SAICHARAN
Department of Entomology
Prof. Jayashankar Telangana State Agricultural Univ.
Hyderabad, **Telangana**

G. YASHASWINI
Department of Entomology
Prof. Jayashankar Telangana State Agricultural Univ.
Hyderabad, **Telangana**

D. LAVA KUMAR
Division of Floriculture and Landscaping
Indian Agricultural Research Institute (ICAR)
Pusa, **New Delhi**

U. MAHESH
Department of Plantation, Spices, Medicinal and Aromatic Crops, Dr. YSR Horticultural University
Thadepalligudem, West Godavari, **Andhra Pradesh**

KALYANI PUBLISHERS
LUDHIANA • NEW DELHI • NOIDA (U.P.) • HYDERABAD • CHENNAI
KOLKATA • CUTTACK • GUWAHATI • KOCHI • BENGALURU

KALYANI PUBLISHERS

Head Office

B-3251/B, Street No. 5, Backside Sandhu Tower, Gurdev Nagar, **Ludhiana-**141 001 • Ph : 0161-2760031
E-mail : kalyanibooks@yahoo.co.in **Website :** www.kalyanipublishers.co.in

Administration Office

4779/23, Ansari Road, Daryaganj, **New Delhi-**110 002 • Ph : 011-23271469, 23274393
E-mail : kalyani_delhi@kalyanipublishers.in

Works

B-16, Sector-8, **NOIDA** (U.P.)

Branches

1, Mahalakshmi Street, T. Nagar, **Chennai-**600 017 • Ph : 044-24344684

Gopabandhu Lane, Behind Govt. Bus Stand, Badambadi, **Cuttack-**753 012 (Odisha) • Ph : 0671-2311391

4-3-65/2/A, Behind HVS Public School, Raghunath Bagh

Sultan Bazar, **Hyderabad-**500 095 • Ph : 040-24750368

10/2B, Ramanath Mazumdar Street, **Kolkata-**700 009 • Ph : 033-22416024

Arunalaya, 1st Floor, Saraswati Road, Pan Bazar, **Guwahati-**781 001 • Ph : 0361-2731274

Koratti Parambil House, Convent Road, **Kochi-**682 035 • Ph : 0484-2367189

No. 24 & 25, 1st Floor, Hameed Shah Complex, Cubbonpet Main Road, **Bengaluru-**560 002

T 39407 05 14 + 430 = 444 Pages 20" x 30" 55.5 Forms

PRINTED IN INDIA

At B.B. Press, A-37, Sec.-67, NOIDA-201301

Special Thanks

To

K. Sai Teja (Ph.D. Scholar)
Department of Entomology, RPCAU, Bihar

and

D. Lava Kumar (Ph.D. Scholar)
Division of Floriculture and Landscaping
ICAR-IARI, New Delhi

For their Invaluable Contribution of Beautiful Photos for the Cover page

Foreword

ICAR-Indian Agricultural Research Institute

Pusa, New Delhi-110012

Dr. Markandey Singh
Head
Division of Floriculture & Landscaping
ICAR-Indian Agricultural Research Institute, New Delhi
Ph: 011-25841929
Email ID: singh_markandey@yahoo.com

Date: 01-08-2023

It is with great pleasure and a profound sense of accomplishment that I extend my warmest congratulations to the authors of the book "Pests of Horticultural Crops: A Glance." As a dedicated researcher in the field of Floriculture and Landscaping at ICAR-Indian Agricultural Research Institute, New Delhi, I understand the critical importance of pest management in the successful cultivation of horticultural crops.

Horticulture plays a pivotal role in addressing global challenges such as food security, nutrition, and environmental sustainability. However, the journey towards abundant and healthy harvests is often hindered by the relentless pressure of pests. Insects, diseases, weeds, nematodes, and other harmful organisms can wreak havoc on horticultural crops, leading to reduced yields and compromised crop quality.

In this outstanding compendium, the authors have skilfully condensed a wealth of knowledge, making it an indispensable resource for farmers, researchers, students, and all stakeholders invested in horticulture. The book offers an insightful overview of the diverse array of pests affecting horticultural crops, shedding light on their life cycles, biology, and the specific damage they inflict.

The comprehensive coverage of various types of pests, from the tiniest insects to the most elusive nematodes, reflects the authors' meticulous approach in providing readers with a complete understanding of pest-related challenges in horticulture. Furthermore, this book is enriched with a comprehensive collection of images showcasing all related pests, providing readers with visual aids to aid in easy identification and better understanding of the diverse pest species affecting horticultural crops.

One of the book's most commendable aspects is its emphasis on integrated pest management (IPM). As we collectively strive for sustainable agricultural practices, IPM emerges as a beacon of hope. It encourages a holistic approach to pest control, combining cultural, biological, and chemical methods in a balanced manner. By adopting IPM strategies, farmers can enhance crop resilience while minimizing environmental impacts, promoting biodiversity, and reducing reliance on conventional pesticides.

In a world characterized by rapid changes in climate, global trade, and human demographics, it is essential to stay updated with the latest advancements in pest management technologies and strategies. This book achieves just that, empowering readers with the knowledge to tackle existing pest challenges and prepare for emerging threats.

Throughout the pages of "Pests of Horticultural Crops: A Glance," readers will find a treasure trove of practical insights and research-backed solutions for pest management in horticulture. The authors' dedication to presenting evidence-based practices will undoubtedly resonate with horticulturists, encouraging them to embrace innovative and sustainable approaches.

I extend my heartfelt gratitude to the authors for their painstaking efforts in compiling this invaluable work. Their collective expertise, passion, and dedication are evident in the clarity of content and the relevance of the information provided. I commend their commitment to advancing the frontiers of pest management knowledge and promoting agricultural sustainability.

As the horticulture community embarks on this enlightening journey through **"Pests of Horticultural Crops: A Glance,"** I encourage each reader to absorb its wisdom, internalize its teachings, and apply its insights to cultivate healthier & quality crops and greener landscapes. Together, let us strive for a future where horticulture thrives, and humanity flourishes.

May this seminal work become a cornerstone in the pursuit of sustainable pest management practices, guiding horticulturists and researchers towards resilient and prosperous agricultural systems.

Dr. Markandey Singh

Head, Division of Floriculture & Landscaping
ICAR-Indian Agricultural Research Institute
New Delhi

Acknowledgements

In the completion of this book, we are humbled and deeply grateful for the contributions of many individuals who have played a significant role. We recognize and extend our heartfelt appreciation to each and every one of them.

First and foremost, we offer our profound gratitude to God Almighty for bestowing upon us the protection, guidance, and the ability to undertake this endeavour. Without divine blessings, this achievement would not have been possible.

We are indebted to the authors whose insightful works have provided us with valuable information and knowledge. Their contributions have laid the foundation upon which this book stands, and we acknowledge their significant influence on our work. Our sincere thanks go to the numerous websites that have served as invaluable sources of information. The wealth of knowledge we gathered from these platforms has enriched the content of this book, and we express our gratitude to their creators and maintainers.

We would like to express our heartfelt appreciation to our teachers, friends, students, and family members who have stood by us and supported us throughout the writing process. Their encouragement, guidance, and unwavering belief in our abilities have been instrumental in bringing this book to fruition.

We owe a profound debt of gratitude to the individuals who generously shared their expertise and provided invaluable feedback on one or more chapters. We extend our deepest appreciation to **Dr. V. Anitha** (Dean PGS, PJTSAU, Hyderabad), **Dr. S. Upendar** (Associate Professor, Department of Entomology, PJTSAU, Hyderabad), **Dr. M. S. Sai Reddy** (Assistant Professor, Entomology, RPCAU, Bihar), **Dr. S. S. Karabhantanal** (Principal Scientist, AICSIP, Vijayapur, Karnataka), **Dr. Pavan Kumar P** (Assistant Professor, Floriculture and Landscape Architecture, UHS, Bagalkot, Karnataka), **Dr. Markandey Singh** (Principal Scientist, Floriculture and Landscaping, ICAR-IARI, New Delhi), and **Dr. G. Anitha** (Principal Scientist, AICRP on Biological Control of Crop Pests and Diseases, PJTSAU, Hyderabad). Their valuable insights and constructive comments have immensely enriched the quality and depth of our work.

In the prologue, where we emphasized the importance of gratitude, we acknowledged you, our esteemed reader. Without your engagement and support, our words would be mere echoes. We are truly grateful for your presence and for choosing to embark on this literary journey with us.

We would like to seize this opportunity to express our heartfelt appreciation to Kalyani Publishers in New Delhi. Their dedication, hard work, and commitment to delivering a high-quality publication within the stipulated timeframe have been commendable. It is through their support and encouragement of young and emerging authors that we have been given the chance to realize our aspirations.

While we have made every effort to acknowledge all individuals who have contributed to this book, we recognize that omissions may have unintentionally occurred. We deeply regret any oversights, as they in no way diminish our gratitude for the valuable contributions made by all.

Finally, I (Saicharan) would like to express my heartfelt gratitude to my dear friends Srinivas, Aravind, Venkatesh, Sridhara, Ramakanth, Akash, Chetan, Revanth Reddy and Raghavendra Kiran for being an invaluable source of inspiration and support throughout the journey of creating this book. Thank you for being the pillars of strength, and for believing in me and this project wholeheartedly.

Thank you, one and all, for your unwavering support, guidance, and inspiration throughout this remarkable journey.

2023

D. Saicharan
G. Yashaswini
D. Lava Kumar
U. Mahesh

Preface

Success is Not Instant......

Horticulture, encompassing the cultivation of various crops such as ornamental, plantation, medicinal, and aromatic plants, as well as fruits, vegetables, spices, and condiments, holds immense significance in global agricultural practices. In this realm, India stands as the second-largest producer of fruits and vegetables worldwide, following China. The cultivation of horticultural crops contributes substantially to India's agricultural output, accounting for approximately 28% of the nation's GDP.

The production of horticultural crops involves a multitude of critical stages, from planting to harvesting, packaging to marketing, storage to processing. Throughout these processes, meticulous care must be exercised to ensure optimal growth and safeguard against various challenges. Among these challenges, pest attacks emerge as a prominent factor leading to yield reduction and financial losses.

Understanding the pests that afflict horticultural crops and implementing effective control measures are of paramount importance. Despite the indispensability of this knowledge, a scarcity of comprehensive literature exists that compiles the significant pests associated with horticultural crops. To address this gap and support the academic and research communities, we present "Pests of Horticultural Crops: A Glance."

This book aims to serve as a valuable resource for individuals seeking to comprehend the diverse array of pests that plague horticultural crops. By exploring their economic significance, distribution patterns, life cycles, distinguishing characteristics, and the damage they cause, readers will gain invaluable insights into the management techniques necessary to mitigate these threats effectively.

Unlike existing publications that focus on horticultural crop pests individually, "Pests of Horticultural Crops: A Glance" aims to provide a comprehensive overview of pests across all branches of horticulture in a single volume. The book also includes information on the current area, production, and productivity of the respective crops. In particular, special attention is given to resistant varieties that have been meticulously curated and detailed for each crop discussed within this volume. Our primary goal in creating this book is to alleviate the burden placed on readers who would otherwise have to consult multiple sources to gather information on horticultural crop pests. This resource is particularly useful for individuals preparing for competitive exams such as ICAR-JRF/SRF, ASRB-NET, and others.

As Ph.D. scholars and students, ourselves, we have diligently planned and executed this work, fully cognizant of the challenges faced by readers in navigating the subject matter. Despite our extensive research and data collection, we humbly acknowledge that there may be areas where we fall short of readers' expectations. We take responsibility for any errors that may have inadvertently occurred.

We welcome any suggestions for improving this book, recognizing that the input of our readers is invaluable in refining our work further. Kindly direct feedback and suggestions to **charan.dharavath@gmail.com,** and we will appreciate and consider them with utmost respect.

We extend our sincere gratitude to the researchers, scholars, and experts whose contributions in the field of horticulture and pest management have significantly influenced the content of this book. It is through their collective efforts that we are able to provide a consolidated resource that addresses the pest-related challenges faced by the horticultural industry.

We hope that **"Pests of Horticultural Crops: A Glance"** serves as a valuable reference and companion for all those involved in horticulture, facilitating a deeper understanding of pest management practices and fostering sustainable approaches. May this book contribute to the advancement of horticultural knowledge and propel the industry towards prosperous growth.

Happy reading and fruitful endeavours!

2023

D. Saicharan
G. Yashaswini
D. Lava Kumar
U. Mahesh

Contents

PART C

PESTS OF PLANTATION CROPS

PART D

PESTS OF SPICE CROPS

PART E

PESTS OF MEDICINAL AND AROMATIC CROPS

PART F

PESTS OF FLOWER CROPS

0 Introduction

Horticulture, the art and science of cultivating and managing plants, encompasses a diverse range of practices aimed at harnessing the potential of flora for sustenance, therapeutic applications, and aesthetic pleasure. With a primary focus on food crops, medicinal plants, and ornamental flora, horticulture employs scientific techniques to maximize yield, diversity, and quality. Recognized as a cornerstone of agricultural industries across the globe, horticulture plays a vital role in ensuring food security, enhancing human well-being, and fostering environmental stewardship. By embracing innovative methodologies, horticulturists strive to unlock the full potential of nature's bounty, cultivating an abundant variety of fruits, vegetables, and flowers that enrich our lives and contribute to a sustainable future.

ORIGIN AND EVOLUTION OF HORTICULTURE

The history of horticulture overlaps with the history of agriculture. Whereas, the origin lies in the transition of human communities from a nomadic lifestyle as hunters to civilized societies.

India: In India, horticulture has ancient roots. The Indus Valley Civilization, which existed around 2500 BCE, provides evidence of advanced agricultural practices, including horticulture. The people of this civilization cultivated a variety of crops, including wheat, barley, rice, dates, and melons. The Vedas, ancient Indian texts dating back to around 1500 BCE, mention the cultivation of fruits and vegetables. These texts describe various horticultural practices, such as grafting and plant propagation.

During the Mughal era (1526-1857), horticulture flourished in India. The Mughal emperors had a keen interest in gardens and horticulture, leading to the creation of exquisite gardens like the Shalimar Bagh and Nishat Bagh in Kashmir and the Taj Mahal gardens in Agra. The Mughals introduced new plant species, including fruits like mangoes and citrus.

In the modern era, the development of horticulture in India received attention during the British colonial period. The British introduced new horticultural crops, improved cultivation techniques, and established research institutes. After independence, the Indian government focused on the expansion and development of horticulture as a means to improve agricultural productivity, generate employment, and boost exports. Today, India is one of the world's leading producers of horticultural crops.

World: Horticulture has a global history that is deeply intertwined with the development of civilizations and the exploration of new territories. Here are some notable milestones:

(*a*) Ancient Egypt: The Egyptians practiced horticulture extensively, cultivating crops like wheat, barley, grapes, figs, and dates. They were skilled in irrigation techniques, and the Nile River played a crucial role in supporting their horticultural activities.

(*b*) Ancient Greece and Rome: The Greeks and Romans made significant contributions to horticulture. Greek philosophers, such as Theophrastus, wrote extensively on plant cultivation and classification. The Romans further advanced horticultural practices, introducing new crops, garden designs, and irrigation systems.

(*c*) Islamic Golden Age: During the Islamic Golden Age (8th to 14th centuries), Arab scholars made notable advancements in horticulture. They introduced new crops, developed irrigation techniques, and wrote influential books on agriculture and gardening.

(*d*) European Renaissance: The Renaissance period saw a resurgence of interest in horticulture, inspired by the knowledge of ancient Greek and Roman practices. Gardens became symbols of wealth and power, with prominent examples like the Gardens of Versailles in France.

(*e*) Modern Era: In the 18th and 19th centuries, the exploration and colonization of new territories facilitated the exchange of plants and horticultural knowledge between different regions. The development of botanical gardens and the establishment of agricultural research institutes further contributed to the growth of horticulture worldwide.

Today, horticulture is a thriving industry globally, encompassing diverse practices, technological advancements, and sustainable approaches. It plays a crucial role in food security, economic development, environmental conservation, and human well-being.

HORTICULTURE IN INDIA

India has highly diversified and favourable climate for horticultural crops such as fruits, vegetables, spices, and aromatic plants, among them major part of production comprises from fruits and vegetables. The horticulture sector in India produces around 320 million tons of products and contributes about 33% of the Gross Value Addition (GDA). Apart from that, 10% of the land in horticulture contributes to 33% of Agricultural Value. In India, nearly 40 types of vegetables are cultivated in different parts of the country and because of this it stood second among world countries in vegetable production. Moreover, around 10 per cent of the world's fruits are produced. The favourable climatic conditions facilitate the production of a variety of flowers throughout the year in selected regions of the country. The growing demand for flowers among the upper and middle classes for beautification purposes has helped in the growth of floriculture as a well-developed business. Not only in production, because it is a labour-intensive sector it provides a lot of employment opportunities, especially for the people of rural regions.

The Growth of Horticulture in India

Horticulture production supplies diverse varieties of fruits and vegetables that are a useful source of nutrients as a part of a balanced diet and enhances a healthy lifestyle. So there is a steady increase in demand for these products as people become more concerned about their health and well-being. The increased affluence and trendy lifestyle have also led to a greater requirement for flowers for gift and decoration purposes. The production of horticulture products is economic and convenient as they are more resilient to changing weather conditions. In India, the productivity of horticulture crops has increased by 38% between 2004-05 and 2019-20. The requirement of area, water, and other resources are much less than other agricultural products and hence reduces the chance of failure thereby giving better returns and income opportunities.

As a part of the initiatives taken by the government, the Mission for Integrated Development of Horticulture (MIDH) was implemented in 2014. It is a centrally sponsored scheme with a focus on devising plans and processes to facilitate horticulture production efficiently and cost-effectively.

Government Contribution to Horticulture Development in The Different States (as per MIDH):

- Union Territories – 100%
- North Indian States – 90%
- Other States -60%

THE FUTURE SCENARIO OF HORTICULTURE IN INDIA

The horticulture sector, as a diversified function of the agriculture sector, not only offers promising income opportunities but also contributes to the steady growth of both the sector and the overall economy. India has emerged as a leading producer of horticulture products, providing employment generation, income creation, and export promotion. With better resource allocation, infrastructure development, technological upgrades, and improved policy implementation, India is likely to gain a prominent position in the world forum in terms of horticulture sector development.

To ensure future growth and development in the horticulture sector, it is essential to implement certain initiatives. Importing technologies can greatly improve productivity and skill development in the horticulture sector. The application of organic farming methods can bring environmental and economic benefits to the production process. Standardizing processes in horticulture production can enable farmers to apply their knowledge and skills effectively, leading to improved production. Involving more private firms in the sector can enhance efficiency and create more export opportunities.

The government should play a role in promoting organic horticulture production by incentivizing farms and providing support during the conversion from conventional to organic farming. Encouraging farmers to adopt Good Agriculture Practices (GAP) and providing certifications can lead to the production of fruits and vegetable products with improved quality. This, in turn, will generate more demand from foreign countries and boost export activities.

Overall, by implementing these initiatives and focusing on sustainable practices, the horticulture sector can continue to thrive, contribute to the economy, and establish India as a significant player in the global horticulture market.

EXTENT OF LOSSES CAUSED BY INSECT PESTS IN HORTICULTURAL CROPS

The extent of losses caused by insect pests in horticultural crops can vary depending on several factors, including the type of pest, the crop being affected, geographic location, management practices, and environmental conditions. Insect pests can cause significant damage to horticultural crops, resulting in economic losses for farmers and reduced yields. Some common insect pests in horticulture include aphids, caterpillars, beetles, thrips, mites, and whiteflies, among others. The specific extent of losses caused by insect pests in horticultural crops is difficult to quantify precisely, as it can vary greatly from one situation to another. However, it is estimated that insect pests are responsible for significant crop losses worldwide. In some cases, pest infestations can lead to complete crop failure if left unmanaged.

Insect pests can cause direct damage to horticultural crops by feeding on plant tissues, resulting in the destruction of leaves, stems, flowers, fruits, and even the entire plant. This damage can reduce photosynthesis, stunt plant growth, and make plants more susceptible to diseases. Additionally, insect pests can transmit plant pathogens, further compromising crop health and productivity. Indirectly, the presence of insect pests in horticultural crops can also lead to losses due to increased production costs. Farmers may need to invest in insecticides, insect-resistant varieties, or other pest control measures to mitigate the damage caused by pests. These additional inputs can increase the production expenses and reduce overall profitability.

Furthermore, insect pests can impact the quality and marketability of horticultural crops. They can leave visible damage on the produce, making it less visually appealing and reducing its market value. Consumers often prefer pest-free, high-quality produce, so the presence of insect damage can lead to lower market prices or rejection of the affected crops. To minimize losses caused by insect pests in horticultural crops, integrated pest management (IPM) practices are commonly employed. IPM combines various strategies, such as cultural practices, biological control, chemical control, and monitoring, to manage pest populations effectively while minimizing the environmental impact and ensuring sustainable crop production. It's important to note that specific data on losses caused by insect pests in horticultural crops can vary depending on regional and crop-specific studies. Therefore, for more accurate and up-to-date information, it is advisable to consult local agricultural extension services, research institutions, or relevant agricultural organizations in your specific area.

With this brief introduction, we would like to introduce the book "Pests of Horticultural Crops: A Glance" which goes beyond mere identification and description by offering valuable insights into integrated pest management (IPM) approaches. The authors explore a range of environmentally friendly and sustainable techniques for pest control, including cultural practices, biological control, botanical pesticides, and the judicious use of chemical pesticides when necessary. The book emphasizes the importance of IPM as a holistic approach that minimizes environmental impacts while maintaining crop health and productivity.

With its concise yet informative style, this book serves as an essential guide for horticulturists, agronomists, researchers, and students who seek a comprehensive understanding of the pests that challenge the horticultural industry. Whether you are a novice entering the field or an experienced professional looking to expand your knowledge, "Pests of Horticultural Crops: A Glance" will equip you with the necessary tools to identify, manage, and mitigate the impact of insect pests on horticultural crops.

In conclusion, "Pests of Horticultural Crops: A Glance" is an invaluable resource that offers a comprehensive overview of the pests affecting horticultural crops, providing insights into their biology, management, and sustainable control strategies. This book serves as a guide to empower horticultural practitioners with the knowledge and tools to safeguard their crops, improve productivity, and contribute to the sustainable growth of the horticultural industry.

PART A

PESTS OF VEGETABLE CROPS

D. Saicharan
(Ph.D. Scholar)
Department of Entomology
Professor Jayashankar Telangana State Agricultural University
Rajendranagar, Hyderabad, Telangana-500030

1 Pests of Potato

Scientific Name	*Solanum tuberosum*
Family	Solanaceae
Origin	Peru
Chromosome Number	4n = 48 (Tetraploid)

The potato is a root vegetable that is indigenous to the Americas, a starchy food, and a tuber of the plant Solanum tuberosum. The plant belongs to the nightshade family Solanaceae and is a perennial. The Spanish word for potato is **"patata"** (the name used in Spain). Potatoes are grown in many different countries and regions around the world, with varying levels of production and consumption. As of 2021, the top five potato-producing countries in the world were:

1. China – 99.4 million tonnes
2. India – 52.3 million tonnes
3. Russian Federation – 32.3 million tonnes
4. Ukraine – 22.4 million tonnes
5. United States – 21.6 million tonnes

However, production expanded most quickly in Southern and Eastern Asia during the 21st century, with China and India dominating global production of 376 million tonnes as of 2021. Potatoes can be grown in a variety of soil types and climates, but they generally prefer well-drained soils with moderate levels of fertility and moisture. In some regions, potatoes are grown as a main crop, while in others they are grown as a secondary crop or in rotation with other crops. Potatoes are an important food crop, providing a significant source of carbohydrates and other nutrients for many people around the world. They are used in a wide variety of dishes and culinary traditions, and are an important ingredient in many processed food products.

Potatoes are susceptible to a variety of pests and diseases that can cause significant yield losses if not properly managed. Here are some examples of pests that can cause yield losses in potato crops:

❑ Greasy cutworm: *Agrotis ipsilon* (Hufnagel, 1766)

Common Name	:	Black/Greasy cutworm; Floodplain cutworm, Ipsilon dart; Over flow worm
Scientific Name	:	*Agrotis ipsilon* (Hufnagel, 1766)
Family	:	Noctuidae
Order	:	Lepidoptera

Source: *https://www.insectimages.org*

Distribution and Host Range

There are 26 species of cutworms known to exist in India, but *A. ipsilon* and *A. segetum* are the most widespread species found throughout the country. Cutworms are pests that are polyphagous and eat a variety of field and vegetable crops. Nearly all of the potato-growing regions in North India, which form a continuous belt from Punjab to Bengal, as well as Madhya Pradesh in Central India, have been reported to contain *A. ipsilon*. With almost 41 species listed as hosts, they have a very diverse range of hosts. Vegetables attacked by cutworms include cole crops, radish, turnip, gobhi, sarson, peas, beans, okra, beetroot, cucurbits, onion, brinjal, chilli, tomato, capsicum, spinach and fenugreek. According to reports, the Cole crop pest *A. ipsilon* is extremely prevalent and dominant in the Srinagar area of Jammu and Kashmir. *A. ipsilon* is known to attack nearly all vegetables in the Ladakh desert's frigid climate. Cabbage, cauliflower, and knol khol are frequently attacked by *A. ipsilon* and *A. flammatra* Fabricius in India's North-eastern regions.

Nature and Symptoms of Damage

Surface cutworms consume enough food to topple the seedlings while feeding at or below the soil's surface. Cutworms that climb plants eat the buds, leaves, and fruits, while cutworms that live underground eat the underground stems and roots. Since most of *A. ipsilon*'s feeding takes place at the soil's surface, it is not thought of as a climbing cutworm. The crop is harmed by gram cutworms, which are active during the *Rabi* season. Cutworms also go by the names surface caterpillars and cutworms because they cut the plant into the ground or twist the entire plant like a gram. They discovered that the crops were most vulnerable between November and February.

Life History and Description

An individual life cycle lasts 35 to 60 days. For 3 to 6 days, the egg stage lasts. Eggs are laid in groups by females on low-lying leaves. In the absence of such host plants, the females will lay their eggs on dead plant matter. On bare ground, however, they will not lay eggs. The female can lay one egg or up to 1200-1900 eggs in a group. A larva's life cycle lasts 20-40 days. Cannibalistic larvae range in colour from light creamy to dark brown. Granules cover the entire body, and the head is covered in numerous dark spots. Pupation occurs underground and lasts for 12 to 20 days. When the adults emerge, they will have dark brown wings with greyish patches.

Management

Pupae in hibernation are killed when fields are flooded. Cut worm incidence is decreased by hand-picking larvae and deep summer ploughing. Installing 12 pheromone traps per hectare to draw male moths. Establishing light trap at 1/ha to capture the adults. In the central United States, 60% of larvae are thought to be infected by an entomopathogenic nematode known as *Hexamermis arvalis*.

Larvae parasitized by the parasitoid *Meteorus leviventris* consume 24% less vegetation and remove 36% fewer seedlings. Spray insecticides like neem oil at 3% or chlorpyriphos 20 EC at 1 lit/ha. It is possible to use soil insecticides as a pre-plant treatment, but this may be constrained by the unpredictable distribution of the cutworm population density.

❑ Potato tuber moth: *Phthorimaea operculella* (Zeller, 1873)

Common Name	:	Potato tuber moth; Tobacco split worm
Scientific Name	:	*Phthorimaea operculella* (Zeller, 1873)
Family	:	Gelechiidae
Order	:	Lepidoptera

Source: *https://www.cabidigitallibrary.org*

Distribution and Host Range

Phthorimaea operculella prefers subtropical, tropical, and mediterranean climates. Additionally, frequently encountered in Africa, Asia, Europe, South America, and Oceania are potato tuber moths. More than 90 countries have received reports of the moth overall. The Solanaceae family of plants, which serves as their host, is where the potato tuber moth typically makes its home. They are well known for consuming potato plants' tubers, roots, and leaves, which they mine for leaves (*Solanum tuberosum*). It has been discovered that the potato tuber moth consumes a variety of Solanaceae plants, including bell peppers, tomatoes, tobacco plants, eggplant (*S. melongena*) and chilli (*Capsicum annuum*). According to a study by **P. G. Fenemore** of Massey University, L-glutamic acid, an amino acid found in potatoes, attracts potato tuber moths and is a key factor in the choice of plant for oviposition.

Nature and Symptoms of Damage

It invades fields and storage spaces. Larva burrows into stems, leaves, and tubers. Galleries develop close to tuber eyes. Potato tubers can only be found by larvae if they are exposed or less than 1 cm below the soil's surface. There is no proof that newly hatched larvae would delve deep and use the root system to find tubers. Blotch mines are brown or white spots that the larvae, which primarily feed on the mesophyll in foliage, leave on the leaves.

Life History and Description

Depending on the temperature, generation can take 17 to 125 days, but it usually takes one month. Adults can live up to 10 days; eggs hatch in 2-6 days; larvae last 13-33 days; and pupae last 6-29 days. Each year, several generations might arise. Life cycle of tubers in storage may continue. Over the course of their lifetime, adult female *P. operculella* can lay over 200 eggs on the ground near a preferred host plant, but they are usually laid next to a vein on the leaf, in the space between the bud and the stem, or beneath the stem. Larvae are typically 12-15 mm long, white or yellow in colour, with a brown prothorax and head. The colour of the larvae changes from white to yellow to pink to green as it gets older. Small black spots and bristles can be found on each segment of the thorax, and the larvae typically feed on the host plant for up to two weeks before pupating. The larvae first spend 5-15 minutes walking around the leaves, attaching a silk thread to the surface as it moves, to decide if it wants to mine a particular host plant. The larva occasionally bites the leaf four to five times while walking and makes slight direction changes. The larvae first choose a location to mine, builds a silk roof over it, and then starts to mine downward, placing the leaf fragments to the side of the hole. *P. operculella* pupae are typically 0.5 inches long and have a narrow width. They typically have a white colour and take 10 to 30 days to develop, depending on the surrounding environment. In general, adult potato tuber moths are nocturnal and do not become active until one to two hours after dusk. *P. operculella* usually have a lifespan of 1-2 weeks. The majority of eggs are laid within the first quarter of the female's life, and mating starts about 24 hours after emergence.

Management

Avoid planting tubers in shallow soil. Place the tubers 10 to 15 cm deep when planting them. Use intercropping with peas, onions, or chilies. To prevent female moths from laying eggs on the exposed tubers 60 days after planting, perform earthing up. Sprinkler irrigation is the most effective way to stop the larvae from consuming the tubers because it prevents the adult female moths from ovipositing. Set up 15 pheromone traps per hectare. Pan-water traps can be baited with the PTM pheromone (male-attracting stimulant) to draw in and keep track of adult male PTMs. Release egg larval parasitoid: *Chelonus blackburnii* @30,000/ha twice at 40 and 70 days after planting. The larval parasitoid wasp *Apanteles subandinus* was introduced as a possible strategy to control *P. operculella* infestations. In South Africa, the spider *Selenops radiatus* has proved to be an effective controlling agent for this species. The wasp *Diadegma mollipla*, which exists in South Africa as well, is another parasitoid of the moth's larvae.

In Field

The intensity of the infestation is decreased by timely earthing up of the crop to cover the exposed tubers. The pest can be effectively controlled with two sprays of 0.05% quinalphos or 0.1% carbaryl spaced 15 days apart beginning 60 days after planting. Potato harvest piles should be covered with straw rather than left exposed in the field, and any infected tubers should be discarded before storage. Release an egg-larval parasite, *Copidosoma koehleri* 50,000 adults/ha, and *Chelonius blackbernii* 15,000 adults/ha, to reduce infestation by 50-55%. However, if harvest is postponed and the leaves have senescent, saturate the soil with any one of the following: Runner (methoxyfenozide) 240 SC 600 ml/ha, Indoxacarb 30 WG 130 g/ha, or Lambda cyhalothrin 600 ml/ha.

In Storage

The potatoes should be kept cool and dry, with a temperature Carbon disulphide (CS_2) no higher than 21°C, in areas that are well-ventilated. Before storing the tubers, fumigate them with CS_2 (1 kg/27 cu m) for 48 hours at 700°F or ethyl bromide (1 kg/27 cu m) for at least three hours. It is recommended that tubers be covered with a 1" layer of dry sand as a quick and low-cost pest control measure. Go down walls need to be sprayed with 1% malathion every three months. It has also been claimed that treating seed potato tubers with 5% malathion at a rate of 125 gm/100 kg will provide good protection against the pest. However, potatoes that have been treated in this way shouldn't be eaten. If cold storage facilities are available, the produce can be safely stored for a longer period.

❑ White grubs: *Holotrichia serrata* (Fabricius, 1781), *H. consanguinea* Blanchard, 1850

Common Name	:	Chafer beetles or White-grubs or June beetles
Scientific Name	:	*Holotrichia serrata* (Fabricius, 1781), *H. consanguinea* Blanchard, 1850
Family	:	Scarabaeidae
Order	:	Coleoptera

Source:*https://commons.wikimedia.org/wiki/File:HolotrichiaNearReynaudi*

Distribution and Host Range

Dung beetles of the species ***Holotrichia serrata***, also referred to as the sugarcane white grub or cockchafer grub, are prevalent in Sri Lanka, Bangladesh, and India. The sugarcane beetle, or ***Holotrichea consanguinea***, is a species of beetle in the ***Holotrichia*** genus. In India, it frequently causes issues for those who grow sugarcane. An infestation of the beetle was discovered in Vidarbha, India, in September 2012, in the ecosystems of soybean, cotton, and pigeon pea.

Nature and Symptoms of Damage

In India, white grubs are an important national pest and seriously impede the growth of *Kharif* crops. Grubs gorge themselves on roots and tubers at night. Beetles frequently eat the roots of plants while they are still larvae, which prevents the plant from absorbing water, causing the plant to dry up and die. It's a good idea to have a backup plan in case something goes wrong. It is a significant pest on many vegetables, groundnuts, and coconut in addition to sugarcane.

Life History and Description

White, nearly spherical eggs are laid by adult female ***Holotrichia serrata*** beetles. The first and second instars have a distinctive **'C'** shape and are translucent and whitish-yellow in colour. The third instar is dirty white in colour and ranges in length from 34 to 39 mm on average. Strong mandibles are the main feature of the head's distinctively coloured brownish-orange colour. Long, brown, and slender antennae. A brief pre-pupal period of two days follows the instar period, which lasts for 60 to 70 days. The third instar dug a small earthen cell deep into the ground and prepared it for puberty inside an earthen chamber. The pupal period for this exarate pupa is 13 to 19 days, and it measures between 25 and 27 mm in length. Within three to four days of the start of the rain, beetles emerge. Adult beetles are brown in colour, and the average length is between 23 and 25 mm for females compared to males. In captivity, adults can live for 12 to 26 days.

A beetle of average size called ***Holotrichia consanguinea*** lacks any horns or spines. Adults will dig deep into the ground during the winter. The beetles emerge and mate after the first rainfall of the year, and the female buries the eggs afterwards. The eggs hatch after 7-10 days, and the larvae then begin to eat the roots of sugarcane and grass. The larvae will fully develop and pupate after two months. The beetles will burrow back underground when autumn arrives. Every year, there is only one generation.

Management

Cultural practises like harrowing, hoeing, flooding, fallowing of fields, trap cropping, and crop rotation can also get rid of grubs from the cultivation land. In addition, trap crops like sorghum, maize, and onion, as well as resistant crops like sunflower, can be grown alongside the cultivation. During the monsoon season, set up a light trap at 1 ha between 7 and 9 pm to catch adult beetles. In the morning, manually collect adult beetles. Grubs can be destroyed by using the parasitic fungus *Metarhizium anisopliae* and also by another entomopathogenic fungus, *Beauveria brongniartii*. Apart from that, the bacterium *Paenibacillus popilliae* and some entomopathogenic nematodes such as *Heterorhabditis indica*, *H. bacteriophora*, *Steinernema glaseri* and *S. riobrave* can be used against pupae and adult beetles. The seed extract from *Datura innoxia* and *Thevetia peruviana* also show biopesticide properties against grubs. 10 days after the first summer rain, dust quinalphos 5% @25 kg/ha. In addition, numerous insecticides, including carbofuran, phorate, quinalphos, and chlorpyrifos, are employed for the grub eradication process.

Tobacco caterpillar: *Spodoptera litura* (Fabricius, 1775)

Common Name	:	Tobacco caterpillar; Tobacco cutworm; Cotton leafworm; Leaf eating caterpillar
Scientific Name	:	*Spodoptera litura* (Fabricius, 1775)
Family	:	Noctuidae
Order	:	Lepidoptera

Source: *https://en.wikipedia.org/wiki/File:Spodoptera_litura.jpg*

Distribution and Host Range

In Asia, Oceania, and the Indian subcontinent, ***Spodoptera litura*** is a serious polyphagous pest that was first identified by Johan Christian Fabricius in 1775. Around 87 different host plant species that are infested by *S. litura* are all significant economically. The most prevalent strain in South Asia is *S. litura*. However, its native range includes portions of the Palearctic as well as the Oriental and Australasian regions. *S. litura* is most prevalent in the populations of China, Indonesia, India, Japan, and Malaysia, among other nations. *S. litura*'s vicious eating habits as larvae cause serious harm to their hosts. Some common host plants include but are not limited to: tobacco, cotton, soybean, beet, cabbage, and chickpeas. When the host plant in a particular area is depleted, big groups of larvae will migrate to find a new food source.

Nature and Symptoms of Damage

On the surfaces of leaves, look for scratch marks to identify newly hatched larvae. When the plants are in the larval stage, they attack by eating ferociously and producing patterns, frequently causing the leaves to be completely destroyed. The effects of the moth are quite disastrous, completely reducing some plants' yield and destroying economically significant agricultural crops. Serious efforts to control the pests have been made as a result of their potential impact on the many different cultivated crops and, consequently, the local agricultural economy. Large holes in leaves, damaged stem bases, and leaf discoloration are a few visible external signs of pest activity.

Life History and Description

Every year, *Spodoptera litura* will complete 12 generations.

Egg: The eggs are covered in brown hairs from the mother's body and are laid in groups of 200-300. It takes 3 to 5 days for an egg to mature. Eggs have a flattened, spherical shape. Each egg is about 0.6 mm in diameter and is either pink or orange-brown in colour. Large clusters of these eggs, each containing several hundred eggs, are typically laid on the surface of leaves.

Larvae: Neonate larvae are gregarious and translucent green when they first hatch, with a dark thorax. The young larvae stay and feed collectively. When they get older, though, they scatter so they can each find their own food. The adult larvae have stout, cylindrical bodies with noticeable black spiracles and are green to pale greenish brown or black in colour. There could be longitudinal and transverse grey and yellow bands on the body. The length of mature larvae can reach about 35-40 mm. The larvae curl into a C shape with the head remaining in the middle when they are disturbed. The larval stage lasts between 15 and 30 days. Larvae go through six instars in total.

Pupa: Pupation occurs in the soil, says the pupa. Pupae are reddish brown and shiny. The pupal stage lasts between one and three weeks.

Adult: The adult is a thick-bodied moth with a wing span of roughly 40 mm. The forewings of adults, which are typically brown in colour, have numerous crisscross streaks against a cream or brown background. The hind wings are white with a bordering brown patch. In female moths, the eighth abdominal segment is covered in thick scales. *S. litura* and *S. littoralis* both produce pheromones that are primarily composed of (Z, E)-9, 11-tetradecadienyl acetate (Z9, E11-14: Ac).

Management

Pupae are exposed and killed when the soil is tilled. As a trap crop, grow castor (*Ricinus communis* L.) along the border and irrigation channel. Egg masses of *S. litura* on trap crops such as tomato and castor should be collected and destroyed. Killing grown up larvae by hand selection. To flush out the larvae that are hibernating, flood the field. Place a light trap at 1 hectare. To draw male moths, use pheromone traps (**Pherodin SL**) at a rate of 15 per hectare. These kinds of chemical signals are used by predators like the stink bug *Eocanthecona furcellata* to find and capture prey. Its prey locating behaviour is activated when exposed to two chemical compounds released by *S. litura* larvae. The use of the fungus *Nomuraea rileyi* on this moth's larval stage is the focus of a recent study on eliminating this pest. Spray Sl NPV @ 1.5×10^{12} POBs/ha.

Parasitoids: *Trichogramma chilonis* (egg), *Tetrastichus* spp. (egg), *Telenomus* spp. (egg), *Chelonus blackburni* (egg-larval), *Carcelia* spp. (larval-pupal), *Campoletis chlorideae* (larval), *Eriborus argentiopilosus* (larval), *Microplitis* sp (larval) etc.

Predators: *Chrysoperla carnea*, coccinellids, King crow, common mynah, wasp, dragonfly, spider, robber fly, reduviid bug, praying mantis, fire ants, big eyed bugs (*Geocoris* sp), pentatomid bug (*Eocanthecona furcellata*), earwigs, ground beetles, rove beetles etc. Pesticides are constantly used on the species year-round due to its inclusion in numerous significant agricultural crops. The rapid evolution of pesticide and insecticide resistance in *S. litura* is a result of this. Spray dichlorovos 76 WSC or chlorpyriphos 20 EC 2 lit/ha, respectively.

Poison bait: Rice bran 5 kg + Molasses or Brown sugar 500 g + Carbaryl 50 WP 500 g + 3 lit of water/ha.

❑ Green leaf hopper: *Empoasca kerri* Pruthi

Common Name	:	Green leaf hopper
Scientific Name	:	*Empoasca kerri* Pruthi; *E. facialis* Jacobi; *E. fabae* Harri
Family	:	Cicadellidae
Order	:	Hemiptera

Source:*https://plantwiseplusknowledgebank.org*

Distribution and Host Range

While *E. facialis* and *E. fabae* are both common in the Americas, *E. kerri* is primarily found in Asia. In general, the weather's relative dryness and humidity encourage the growth of leafhopper populations. This family is widespread throughout the globe and contains at least 20,000 described species and is the second-largest hemipteran family. Insects that belong to the **Proconiini** tribe of the **Cicadellinae** subfamily are referred to as **sharpshooters**.

Nature and Symptoms of Damage

By sucking plant sap, the nymphs and adults consume tender leaves and other plant parts. When attacked severely, leaves become dry and brittle. Hopper burn symptoms, such as leaf cupping, appear. Poor growth may result from the plant losing its vigour. Yellow spots on the leaves, followed by crinkling, curling, bronzing (becoming reddish-brown), and drying, appear when several insects sucking the sap from the same leaf. Similar harm is also done to cotton and potatoes by leafhoppers.

Life History and Description

On the underside of leaves they are green insects with an extended, active wedge shape. Eggs are inserted by the female into the leaf veins. The period of incubation lasts 4 to 8 days. Five nymphal instars each last 7-10 days. The antennae's thickened portion is very short and has a bristle at the end (arista). The hind tibiae have one or more distinct keels, each of which has a row of movable spines that can be moved and occasionally has an enlarged base.

Egg: Eggs can be deposited into the petiole or along the midrib and lateral veins of the leaves by the adult females. Without special equipment, the eggs are invisible. One week or so is the egg period.

Nymph: Nymphs lack wings but otherwise resemble adults. Instead, they have wing pads that are slightly extended. They have a light green hue. When disturbed, they often move in an oblique direction. Depending on the temperature, the nymphal period lasts anywhere between two and three weeks.

Adult: The insects' adults are wedge-shaped and light green. They are about 2.5 mm long and have fully developed wings.

Management

Monitor the insects with yellow (570-580 nm) sticky traps placed at random in the field. Okra, sesame, sorghum and pearl millet can be grown as inter-crops in vegetable legume (e.g., mungbean) fields. This reduces the leafhopper damage significantly. Generalist predators such as ladybird beetles and green lacewings are efficient in preying on leafhopper nymphs and adults. Spray 2 ml/lit of dimecron or dimethoate 30 EC. Spray 750 ml of methyl-o-demeton in 700-1000 L of water per hectare on the infested crop. Observe dosage guidelines when using neem-based biopesticides. Neem seed kernel extract (NSKE) @ 5% can also be sprayed if commercial neem formulations are not readily available. Only employ the systemic pesticides that your local extension service has recommended. To prevent insects developing pesticide resistance, avoid using the same compound or pesticide group repeatedly.

❑ Green peach aphid: *Myzus persicae* (Sulzer, 1776)

Common Name	:	Green peach aphid; Green fly; Peach-potato aphid
Scientific Name	:	*Myzus persicae* (Sulzer, 1776)
Family	:	Aphididae
Order	:	Hemiptera

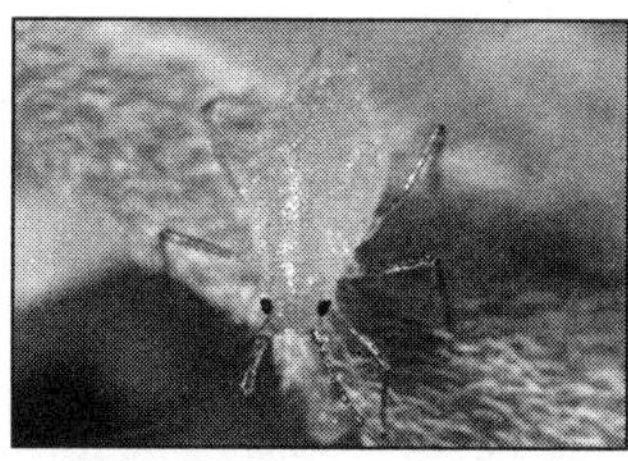

***Source:**https://inpn.mnhn.fr/espece/cd_nom/52046/tab/taxo*

Distribution and Host Range

Despite being widespread, the green peach aphid is probably Asian in origin, just like its main host plant, *Prunus persica*. Extreme heat or humidity are not preferred by this species. Wind and storms can carry these specific aphids over great distances. The introduction of this species into 16 nations or islands. Since it is found in terrestrial habitats, its native range is probably from Asia-Temperate, as was already mentioned.

Over 100 plant species from 40 different families of plants can be colonised by the green peach aphid. This species overwinters on tree hosts from the genus *Prunus*, especially peach and peach hybrid trees, as well as apricot and plum trees. Aphids switch from herbaceous hosts, which include vegetable crops in the Solanaceae, Chenopodiaceae, Compositae, Brassicaceae, and Cucurbitaceae families, to woody tree hosts during the summer. Although the green peach aphid is susceptible to different crops, it most frequently inhabits young, actively growing plants or plant tissue.

Nature and Symptoms of Damage

The most significant aphid pest of peach trees, it stunts growth, causes leaves to shrivel, and kills various tissues. Additionally, it serves as a vehicle for the spread of plant viruses like the tobacco etch virus (TEV), potato virus Y, and cucumber mosaic virus (TEV). Members of the nightshade/potato family (Solanaceae) can contract potato virus Y and potato leafroll virus, and many other food crops can contract various mosaic viruses.

Life History and Description

The green peach aphid's life cycle is temperature-dependent. Over 20 annual generations have been reported in mild climates, with a fully completed generation taking about 10 to 12 days. On Prunus plants, aphids overwinter. When the plants emerge from dormancy, the aphid eggs hatch, and the nymphs begin to feed on the plant's flowers, young foliage, and stems. Nymphs are laid on summer hosts by winged individuals after several generations. Adults in colder climates will return to *Prunus* plants in the fall, where mating takes place and eggs are later laid.

This species' elliptical-shaped eggs are about 0.6 millimetres in size. The eggs start out being green or yellow before turning black. Initially green, the nymphs quickly turn yellowish and resemble the viviparous adults. Pinkish nymphs that develop into winged females can be found. Aphids with wings have a black head, thorax, and abdomen with a noticeable dark dorsal patch. The adult aphids lack wings and are yellow or green in colour, with possible medial and lateral green stripes. Their cornicles are moderately long, the same colour as their skin, and unevenly swollen all the way down. Distinguishing morphological traits from this group include their convergent inner faces of the antennal tubercles in dorsal view.

Management

To lessen the effect, you can change the planting arrangement, the sowing and harvesting times, the winter turning over and deep ploughing, the crop fertilisers used, the timing of the drainage and irrigation, and many other factors. Utilizing the negative taxis that the green peach aphid has; silver-grey film can be hung or silver-grey film nets can be used to cover field crops to prevent their landing and settlement. By taking advantage of adults' preferences for sweet or sour materials, traps can be set up for them. So, to catch and kill them, use a 20:2:1 mixture of water, vinegar, and brown sugar. Lady beetles, soldier beetles, hoverflies, acalyptrate flies, gall midges, flower bugs, leaf bugs, damsel bugs, stink bugs, lacewings, parasitic wasps, mites, fungal pathogens, and other aphids are among the green peach aphid's natural enemies. Insect growth regulators like diflubenzuron and chlorbenzuron, as well as natural pesticides like nicotine and azadirachtin, control the ecology of orchard pests by lowering the population of green peach aphids and the harm they do. Similar to this, applying synthetic insect pheromones like E-farnesene (E-F), the aphid alarm pheromone, can disrupt aphid feeding and location as well as draw a variety of aphids' natural enemies, helping to reduce the aphid population. Cypermethrin, abamectin, chlorpyrifos, methylamine, dimethoate, and imidacloprid are frequently regarded as the first chemical pesticides used to control aphids in the field. Although imidacloprid is an effective insecticide for controlling pests with piercing-sucking mouthparts, repeated use could result in pests developing severe resistance.

❑ White fly: *Bemisia tabaci* (Gennadius, 1889)

Common Name	:	White fly; Sweet potato white fly; Silvery leaf white fly
Scientific Name	:	*Bemisia tabaci* (Gennadius, 1889)
Family	:	Aleyrodidae
Order	:	Hemiptera

Source: *https://www.eurekalert.org/multimedia/650418*

Distribution and Host Range

In tropical and subtropical areas, the whitefly is widely distributed. It is widely distributed throughout the Caribbean Islands, Central and South America, and Mexico. The highly polyphagous *B. tabaci* is known to feed on a variety of vegetables, including field crops, weeds, and legumes as well as tomatoes, eggplant, okra, and other vegetables. *B. tabaci* consumes more than 500 plant species from 74 families, demonstrating its extensive polyphagy. The whitefly thrives in hot, dry conditions, and heavy downpours significantly slow down population growth. This insect is active in the daytime and spends the night on lower leaf surfaces.

Nature and Symptoms of Damage

Both adults and nymphs consume the plant sap, which weakens the plant. The leaves drop off and turn yellow during severe infestations. Large populations produce a lot of honeydew, which encourages the growth of sooty mould on leaf surfaces and lowers the effectiveness of the plants' photosynthetic processes. Infected pods turn yellow and produce shrivelled grains if the infestation takes place during the stage of pod formation. In addition to causing direct harm, *B. tabaci* also serves as a vector for a number of viral diseases that affect crops like mungbean, yard-long bean, common bean, cowpea, and soybean, such as Mungbean Yellow Mosaic Virus (MYMV), Cowpea Mild Mottle Virus (CPMMV), and Bean Golden Yellow Mosaic Virus (BGYMV).

Life History and Description

Egg: On the underside of leaves, the females typically lay their eggs close to the veins. To lay more eggs, they favour leaf surfaces with hairs. In her lifetime, a female can lay about 300 eggs. The pear-shaped, tiny (0.25 mm) eggs are vertically attached to the leaf surface by a pedicel. White eggs are first laid; they later turn brown. The only way to see the eggs is with a magnifying glass or a microscope; they are not visible to the unaided eye. The average egg period varies from 3 to 5 days in the summer to 5 to 33 days in the winter. Nymph: The first instar larva (nymph), after hatching, moves across the leaf surface in search of an appropriate feeding area. It is frequently referred to as a "crawler." Then it places its piercing and sucking mouthpart inside the phloem and starts sucking the plant's sap out. The first instar nymph has three pairs of well-developed legs, three pairs of eyes, and antennae. The nymphs have an oval shape, are flattened, and are coloured greenish yellow. During the following three instars, the legs and antennae deteriorate, and the remaining nymphal stages see them immobile. The eyes of the final nymphal stage are red. Even though insects of this genus do not have a fully developed pupal stage, this stage is occasionally referred to as the puparium (incomplete metamorphosis). Nymphal period is about 9 to 14 days during summer and 17 to 73 days in winter. Adults emerge from puparia through a T-shaped slit, leaving behind empty pupal cases or exuviae.

Adult: The adult whitefly has a soft body and resembles a moth. The body is a light-yellow colour, and the wings are covered in powdery wax. The following are the results of the survey. Male adults are slightly smaller than female adults in size. Adults have a lifespan of 1 to 3 weeks.

Infestations of whiteflies, especially in greenhouses, may occasionally be a mixture of *Bemisia* and *Trialeurodes vaporariorum* (Westwood), the greenhouse whitefly. They can be differentiated at the adult stage based on the position in which the wings are held over the body while alive, close to the body and tent-like in *Bemisia*, and more loosely in *Trialeurodes vaporariorum*.

Management

Plants infected with the Gemini virus can be rogued out and killed during the growing season. To ensure that there is no plant material for numerous whiteflies to carry over the crop-free period, usually the height of summer, crop residue (especially tomato plants) should be removed. Whiteflies themselves have not been found to be particularly resistant to any host plant varieties, but some plant characteristics are not favourites of whiteflies. For instance, ovipositing female *Bemisia* prefer hairy-leaved varieties of cotton and soybean over smooth-leaved varieties. For numerous types of plants, this is true. Glossy (less waxy) crucifers, like collards and broccoli, are less suitable for oviposition than varieties with a typical wax layer. Use yellow sticky traps at the rate of 1-2 traps/50-100 m^2 to trap the whiteflies. Hang the traps slightly above or at the canopy level for better trapping. Plant fast growing crops like maize, sorghum, or pearl millet in the border of the field to act as barriers to reduce whitefly infestations. Reflective and yellow plastic or straw mulches may reduce landing of whiteflies. Many species of insects, mites, and spiders feed on immature and adult whiteflies. Some well-known generalist predators that prey on whiteflies include *Chrysoperla* species larvae (lacewings), *Orius* species (minute pirate bugs), and *Geocoris* species (big eyed bugs). Several coccinellid species are specialist whitefly predators, such as *Delphastus catalinae* (LeConte) and *Nephapsis oculatus* (Blatchely). *Bemisia* populations can be drastically reduced by natural epizootics of entomopathogens. *Beauveria bassiana* and *Verticillium lecanii*, two fungal pathogens with efficacy against *Bemisia* and other insects, have been commercialized and are available for field and greenhouse application against *Bemisia*. Parasitoids: Natural enemies such as *Encarsia sophia* and *E. formosa* are efficient parasitoids of whiteflies. Protect the population of these parasitoids by avoiding the use of broad-spectrum pesticides. Predators: *Dicyphus hesperus*, (mirid bug), dragonfly, spider, robber fly, praying mantis, fire ants, coccinellids, lace wings, big eyed bugs (*Geocoris* sp) etc. Because adults and immatures infest lower leaf surfaces that are challenging to reach with insecticide sprays and because they have evolved resistance to many insecticide chemistries, *Bemisia* is challenging to control with insecticides.

❑ Epilachna beetle: *Henosepilachna viginatioctopunctata* (Fabricius, 1775)

Common Name	:	Epilachna beetle; 28-spotted beetle; Potato ladybird; Hadda beetle
Scientific Name	:	*Henosepilachna viginatioctopunctata* (Fabricius, 1775)
Family	:	Coccinellidae
Order	:	Coleoptera

Source:*https://en.wikipedia.org/wiki/Henosepilachna_vigintioctopunctata*

Distribution and Host Range

Although this species was unintentionally introduced to Australia and New Zealand, it is native to South-eastern Asia, primarily India. It has also been recorded from Brazil and Argentina, beginning in 1996. This species primarily harms crop in the Solanaceae family, particularly potatoes and brinjal, as well as other crops like pumpkin, turnips, radishes, beans, and spinach.

Nature and Symptoms of Damage

Both grub and beetle eat the chlorophyll of the leaf in between the veins and cause characteristic skeletonised patches on leaves. Initially they look like scraping, but as the damage progress they leads to large blotches and entire leaf dries off.

Life History and Description

The adults with the orange and black spots measure 7 to 10 millimetres in length. Short, fine hairs cover the head, prothorax (the first portion of the middle body), and elytra (wing covers). There are 28 spots on the elytra. Only the pairs of spots by the midline of the second and fourth transverse rows may join one another, regardless of the spots' size and shape. The ladybug's underside is orange-brown and black. Three sets of orange-brown legs are present. A set of flying wings are located under the elytra. The tiny head is mostly light orange in colour and has two short antennae in addition to a pair of compound eyes. Antennae are orange-brown in colour.

Near prey infestations, female ladybirds lay clusters of yellow eggs. Each egg gives rise to a larva. Four larval instars are present. The larva moults as it develops. A pale-yellow larva that has just emerged is covered in tubercles and long setae. The tergites, tubercles, setae, and legs remain dark grey while the body remains yellow. Three sets of legs are present. Additionally, larvae use the tip of the abdomen to grasp onto the surface they are walking on. During moulting to a pupa or to a different larval instar, the tip of the abdomen also keeps the larva attached to the surface. The fourth larval instar affixes to a protected area on a plant once it has reached full size. The larva's spiny skin is still affixed to the pupa's base. Black setae cover the pupa's surface. With the exception of the light intersegmental membranes, it is black. There are large, white tubular abdominal spiracles, which are air duct openings (trachea). Pupae develop into adults, who then mate. Each life stage's duration varies with temperature, lasting less time at higher temperatures and *vice-versa*.

Management

Hand packing of grubs and collection of beetles by hand nets during early stages of attack, helps in reducing the intensity of infestation. Shake plants to dislodge grubs, pupae and adults in a pail of kerosene water early in the morning or collect them mechanically and destroy. Conservation and augmentation of natural parasitoids *viz. Pediobius foveolatus, Pleunotrogrus faveolatus* and *Tetrastichus* sp. Application of neem, mahua, ground nut cakes are efficient in suppressing the pest population. Spray malathion 50 EC in 200 liters of water per acre provides up to 82 percent kill of this pest. Mix diflubenzuron invariably with endosulfan 1.5 L or chlorpyriphos 1.0 L/ha and spray on the crop which reduces the population by nearly 95% in field. Emulsify 1 lit of neem oil with 60 g of soap dissolved in $\frac{1}{2}$ L. of water, dilute emulsion by adding 20 lit of water, then mix about 400 g of well crushed garlic and spray.

❑ Colorado potato beetle: *Leptinotarsa decemlineata* Say, 1824

Common Name	:	Colorado potato beetle; Colorado beetle; Ten-striped spearman; The ten-lined potato beetle; The potato bug
Scientific Name	:	*Leptinotarsa decemlineata* Say, 1824
Family	:	Chrysomelidae
Order	:	Coleoptera

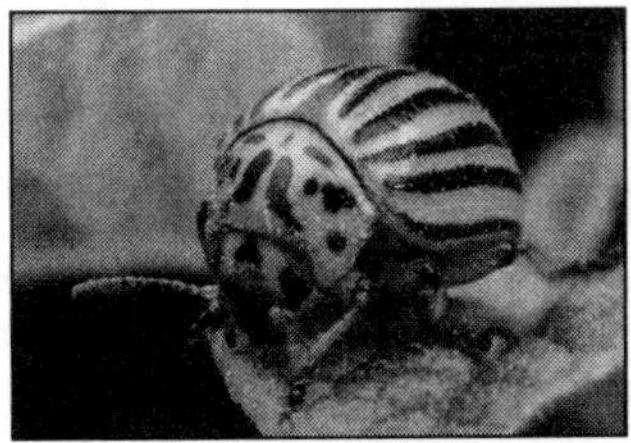

Source: *https://gardenerspath.com/how-to/disease-and-pests/colorado-potato-beetle/*

Distribution and Host Range

The beetle is most likely native to the area between Colorado and Northern Mexico, and was discovered in 1824 by Thomas Say in the Rocky Mountains. It now has a wide distribution across Europe and Asia. *L. decemlineata* has a strong association with plants in the family Solanaceae, particularly those of the genus *Solanum*. It is directly associated with buffalo-bur, black nightshade, eggplant or aubergine, bittersweet nightshade, hairy nightshade, potato, and silverleaf nightshade.

Nature and Symptoms of Damage

Around 1840, *L. decemlineata* adopted the cultivated potato into its host range and it rapidly became a most destructive pest of potato crops. It is today considered to be the most important insect defoliator of potatoes. Larvae may defoliate potato plants resulting in yield losses up to 100% if the damage occurs prior to tuber formation. Larvae may consume 40 cm^2 of potato leaves during the entire larval stage, but adults are capable of consuming 10 cm^2 of foliage per day. So, it can be noted that, both larvae and adults are the damaging stages.

Life History and Description

Colorado potato beetle females are very prolific and are capable of laying over 500 eggs in a 4-5-week period. The eggs are yellow to orange, and are about 1 mm (0.039 in) long. They are usually deposited in batches of about 30 on the underside of host leaves. After 4-15 days, the eggs hatch into reddish-brown larvae with humped backs and two rows of dark brown spots on either side. They feed on the leaves of their host plants. Larvae progress through four distinct growth stages (instars). First instars measure about 1.50 mm (0.059 in) long, and the last (fourth) instars measure 8 mm (0.31 in) in length. The first through third instars each last about 2-3 days duration; the fourth lasts 4-7 days. Upon reaching full size, each fourth instar spends several days as a nonfeeding prepupa, which can be recognized by its inactivity and lighter coloration. The prepupae drop to the soil and burrow to a depth of several inches, then pupate. In 5 to 10 days, the adult beetle emerges to feed and mate. This beetle can thus go from egg to adult in as little as 21 days.

Management

Crop rotation is, however, the most important cultural control of *L. decemlineata*. Rotation may delay the infestation of potatoes and can reduce the build-up of early-season beetle populations because the adults emerging from diapause can only disperse to new food sources by walking. One 1984 study showed that rotating potatoes with nonhost plants reduced the density of early-season adults by 95.8%. Mulching the potato crop with straw early in the growing season may reduce the beetle's ability to locate potato fields, and the mulch creates an environment that favours beetle's predators; Plastic-lined trenches have been used as pitfall traps to catch the beetles as they move toward a field of potatoes in the spring, exploiting their inability to fly immediately after emergence; flamethrowers may also be used to kill the beetles when they are visible at the top of the plant's foliage. Two strains of the bacterium *Bacillus thuringiensis* produce toxins that kill the larvae. *Beauveria bassiana* (Hyphomycetes) is a pathogenic fungus that infects a wide range of insect species, including the Colorado potato beetle. It has shown to be particularly effective as a biological pesticide for *L. decemlineata* when used in combination with *B. thuringiensis*. Feeding can be inhibited by applying antifeedants, products derived from Neem. The steam distillate of fresh leaves and flowers of tansy contains high levels of camphor and umbellulone, and these chemicals are strongly repellent to *L. decemlineata*. The large-scale use of insecticides in agricultural crops effectively controlled the pest until it became resistant to DDT in 1952 and dieldrin in 1958. Insecticides remain the main method of pest control on commercial farms. However, many chemicals are often unsuccessful when used against this pest because of the beetle's ability to rapidly develop insecticide resistance. Different populations in different geographic regions have, between them, developed resistance to all major classes of insecticide, although not every population is resistant to every chemical.

Cold War villain: During the Cold War, some countries in the Warsaw Pact claimed that the beetles had been introduced by the CIA in an attempt to reduce food security by destroying the agriculture of the Soviet Union. A widespread campaign was launched against the beetles; posters were put up and school children were mobilized to gather the pests and kill them in benzene or spirit.

❑ Potato leaf miner: *Liriomyza huidobrensis* (Blanchard, 1926)

Common Name	:	Potato leaf miner; Pea leaf miner
Scientific Name	:	*Liriomyza huidobrensis* (Blanchard, 1926)
Family	:	Agromyzidae
Order	:	Diptera

Source:*https://www.researchgate.net/figure/Female-Liriomyza-huidobrensis*

Distribution and Host Range

The South American continent and Central America were the only places this leaf miner could be found before the 1980s. It was first discovered in Europe in 1987 when a glasshouse in the Netherlands tested positive for it. From there, it spread throughout Europe, primarily in the Mediterranean region and Eastern Europe, the latter of which caught people off guard because cold winters are typically associated with that region. Due to its extreme polyphagous nature, this insect consumes plants from at least fifteen different plant families without showing preference for any one of them. Host plants includes peas, beans, lettuce, celery, spinach, broccoli, onions, and numerous ornamental plants.

Nature and Symptoms of Damage

Older plants have decreased photosynthetic activity and consequently slower growth rates, while young plants can be severely harmed and even die. The crop can become unmarketable if there are even a few mines in the lettuce, celery, or spinach foliage. Cut flowers and ornamental plants' appearance can be impacted by adult females' feeding damage and the puncture holes they make when laying eggs. When it comes to potatoes, the larvae initially only affect the lower part of the plant; however, as the plant matures and its growth slows, the upper parts also become affected, causing the tissues to become necrotic and eventually die.

Life History and Description

The adult female leaf miner deposits eggs individually in the tissues of host plants, usually laying a total of 100 to 120 eggs. When these hatch, the larvae eat their way through the leaf tissue, leaving an intact layer of epidermis on the top and bottom of the leaf blade. The larvae pass through three instar stages before pupating. Adult flies feed on nectar and plant sap, the females gashing leaves to access the sap and the males sometimes feeding at holes made by the females, being unable to puncture the leaves themselves. Adults of this species are tiny flies, about 2 mm (0.08 in) long, with black and yellow bodies and translucent wings.

Management

Yellow sticky traps are also effectively used in Peru and Guatemala, where farmers will often attach yellow plastic, coated with oil or sticky adhesive, to a frame and walk up and down the rows at dawn and dusk trapping thousands of flies. Application of insecticides such as spinosad and pyrithin kills the leaf miners as they leave the egg and enter the leaf. Be sure that, insecticide should get on the bottom side of the leaf. Spraying Abamectin also reduces the incidence of this pest. Parasitoids include *Chrysochan's puntheus*, *Gronotoma micromorpha, Diglyphus isaca* etc. and predators such as lacewings, lady bird beetle, spiders, red ants etc. are found on leaf miners.

Worldwide a total of at least 106 species within the families Braconidae (5 genera), Diapriidae (1 species), Eulophidae (16 genera), Pteromalidae (8 genera), Tetracampidae (2 genera), and Figitidae (8 genera) have been recorded.

Golden potato cyst nematode: *Globodera rostochiensis* (Wollenweber, 1923)

Common Name	:	Golden potato cyst nematode; Potato cyst nematode; Golden nematode of potato
Scientific Name	:	*Globodera rostochiensis* (Wollenweber, 1923)
Family	:	Heteroderidae
Order	:	Tylenchida

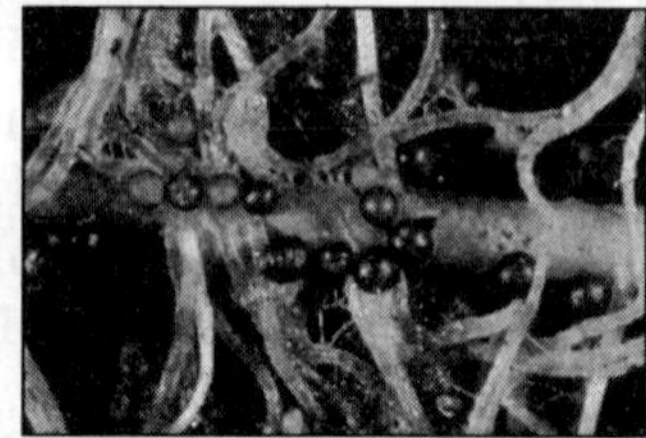

Source:*https://cropscience.bayer.co.uk/threats/pest-and-slugs/potato-cyst-nematode/*

Distribution and Host Range

Wollenweber first identified *Globodera rostochiensis* as *Heterodera rostochiensis* in 1923. According to Krall and Krall (1978), *G. rostochiensis* was brought into Europe by contaminated soil adhering to potato tubers from the Andes mountains in South America. *G. rostochiensis* is a pest of temperate regions all over the world, including temperate countries and temperate regions of tropical countries, like the Nigiris region of India. It is believed that the potato cyst nematode originated in the Andes of South America, from where it travelled to Europe with potatoes. The major hosts of *G. rostochiensis* are restricted to the Solanaceae, in particular potato, tomato and aubergine, A number of weeds in the Solanaceae are also hosts.

Nature and Symptoms of Damage

Like other cyst nematodes, potato cyst nematodes do not produce distinct signs of infestation. Crops will initially show poor growth patches, and plants in these patches may exhibit chlorosis and wilting.

Life History and Description

No egg sacs are produced and the eggs of *G. rostochiensis* are always retained inside the cyst body. The eggshell's surface is smooth and devoid of microvilli. Approximately one month to six weeks after the second-stage juveniles' invasion, the females emerge from the root cortex. Initially pure white, they eventually turn golden yellow as they mature. Without a cone, mature females have a circumference of roughly 500 m. Female cuticles occasionally have a thin sub crystalline layer. Cysts are created from the female's hardened dead cuticle and hold the eggs, the next generation's offspring. The male has a short tail, a vermiform shape, and no bursa. On fixation, the body assumes a curved shape with the posterior region twisted at a 90-degree angle to the remainder of the body. The second-stage juvenile hatches from the egg, the first moult taking place within the egg.

Management

Crop rotation: The population densities of the potato cyst nematodes *G. rostochiensis* and *G. pallida* are frequently lowered through rotation. Nematode densities can rise to extremely high levels when these crops are grown in monoculture for several seasons in infested soil, making crop yields unprofitable. Between host crops, non-host crops like barley are grown to lower nematode population densities.

Trap cropping: Trap cropping has been used successfully for the reduction of cyst nematode populations. Potatoes are grown in order to cause the second stage juveniles to hatch.

Soil solarization: Two layers of polyethylene are layered over the ground, allowing the soil below to heat up quickly. The majority of studies conducted in the late 1990s focused on the fungi *Pochonia*, *Hirsutella*, and *Arthrobotrys* as well as the bacterium *Pasteuria* as potential fungal control agents. Another fungal biocontrol agent on the market is *Paecilomyces chlamydosporia*. Soil fumigants can kill large numbers of nematodes, especially in moist sandy soils under polythene sheeting. The nematicide 1, 3-Dichloropropene is available mixed in various quantities with other compounds, such as C3-chlorinated hydrocarbons and 1, 2-dichloropropane; Telone II consists of 94% 1, 3-D whereas D-D contains around 50%. Other types of fumigants release methyl isothiocyanate (MITC), e.g., dazomet, which is effective against potato cyst nematode.

Resistant Varieties	
World	**India**
Defender: This potato variety is resistant to Colorado potato beetle, which is a common pest in many potato-growing regions. **Viking:** Viking is resistant to both Colorado potato beetle and potato tuber moth, which is a major pest of stored potatoes. **Taura:** Taura is a variety that is resistant to aphids, which can transmit viruses that cause significant yield losses. **Ranger Russet:** This variety is resistant to both Colorado potato beetle and potato tuber moth. **Atlantic:** Atlantic is a popular potato variety that is known for its resistance to both Colorado potato beetle and potato virus Y, which can cause significant yield losses. **Elba:** Elba is resistant to potato virus X, which can also cause significant yield losses.	**Kufri Surya:** Developed by the Central Potato Research Institute (CPRI), Kufri Surya is a high-yielding variety that is resistant to potato tuber moth and potato virus Y. **Kufri Bahar:** Another CPRI-developed variety, Kufri Bahar is resistant to potato tuber moth and has good storage quality. **Kufri Ashoka:** Developed by the Indian Agricultural Research Institute (IARI), Kufri Ashoka is resistant to potato tuber moth and has good yield potential. **Kufri Lauvkar:** This variety is resistant to both potato tuber moth and leafhopper, which can cause significant damage to potato plants. **Kufri Megha:** Developed by the CPRI, Kufri Megha is resistant to potato virus Y and has good yield potential.

Pests of Tomato

Scientific Name	*Solanum lycopersicon*
Family	Solanaceae
Origin	Western South America, Mexico, and Central America
Chromosome Number	2n = 24

The tomato is the edible berry of the plant Solanum lycopersicum, commonly known as the tomato plant. The species originated in western South America, Mexico, and Central America. The Mexican Nahuatl word **tomatl** gave rise to the Spanish word **tomate**, from which the English word tomato derived. It is a rich source of vitamins C and K, potassium, and dietary fiber, and is also low in calories. Tomatoes come in a variety of **colors**, including red, yellow, and green, and can be eaten raw or cooked in a variety of dishes, such as salads, sauces, and soups. The tomato plant is a member of the nightshade family, along with other plants such as eggplants, peppers, and potatoes.

In India, tomato is one of the most important vegetable crops, with a large share in the country's horticulture production. According to the Ministry of Agriculture and Farmers Welfare, the area under tomato cultivation in India was around 632 thousand hectares during the year 2020-21, with a total production of approximately 20.6 million tonnes. The productivity of tomatoes in India during the same period was around 32.6 tonnes per hectare.

Tomatoes are susceptible to a variety of insect pests, which can cause significant yield losses if not controlled. Here are some of the common insect pests of tomatoes and their potential yield losses:

❑ Fruit borer: *Helicoverpa armigera* [Hübner, (1808)]

Common Name	:	Fruit borer; Cotton bollworm; Corn earworm; Old World bollworm.
Scientific Name	:	*Helicoverpa armigera* (Hübner, [1808])
Family	:	Noctuidae
Order	:	Lepidoptera

Source: *https://www.cabidigitallibrary.org/doi/10.1079/cabicompendium.26757*

Distribution and Host Range

The gram pod borer is a polyphagous and highly mobile insect and it is a pest of economic importance on many agricultural and horticultural crops. It is a major pest on a number of crops, including cotton, tobacco, corn, sorghum, sunflower, soybean, lucerne and pepper. It has been recorded on 180 cultivated and wild plant species in at least 45 families. Occasionally it causes significant yield losses in mungbean, vegetable soybean, chickpea and pigeon pea.

Nature and Symptoms of Damage

The neonate larvae feed on the surfaces of leaves or floral buds. However, the grown-up larvae prefer to feed on the contents of reproductive parts such as floral buds, flowers and young fruits. The larvae make the holes on these reproductive parts and feed inside by thrusting their head inside; hence the holes are circular and often surrounded by faecal pellets. Later, the larva feeds on most of the inner contents of the pod and hollows the pod out. Severely damaged pods rot and fall; partially damaged pods may become deformed.

Life History and Description

Egg: The adults lay eggs singly and scattered, usually on or near the leaflets, floral buds or young pods. The eggs are spherical, about 0.5 mm in diameter, creamy white when laid, but later turn to brown and black just before hatching. The egg period is about 4 to 5 days depending on the temperature.

Larva: Upon hatching, the neonate larvae are creamy white with dark brown or black coloured heads and prominent spines on the body. The grown-up larvae vary in color from pale green to brown or even black with lateral stripes on the body. Mature larvae can grow to about 4 cm in length. The larval period is about 15 to 25 days. The larva passes through six instars.

Pupa: Pupation takes place in soil, but sometimes also on plants. Pupae are dark brown. The pupal period varies from 6 to 33 days depending on the temperature. On average, it is about 10 days to two weeks.

Adult: Adults are stout-bodied moths with a wingspan of about 3.5-4 cm, adult males are usually pale yellow in color with olive green or grey; adult females are reddish brown. The male forewings are pale yellow and olive green with light brown obscure transverse lines; female forewings are reddish brown with distinct brownish black transverse lines. The hind wings are white with a brown border.

Management

Avoid growing legumes in the vicinity of other alternate host plants, because the *H. armigera* adults can easily migrate to the newly planted legume crop. It may be too difficult to avoid this situation in countries where the land is highly fragmented. Erecting suitable physical barriers such as nylon nets or planting barrier crops that are non-host plants around the plots can reduce *H. armigera* damage on vegetable legumes. However, these measures cannot prevent the complete entry of the insects, as they are strong flyers. Crop rotation should strictly be followed. If the growers plant vegetable legume (e.g., mungbean) after mungbean or other alternate host plants such as tomato, chickpea, corn, cotton, etc, the damage will be higher from the emerging insects that already pupated in the soil during the previous crop cycle. This is more serious in locations where *H. armigera* diapause occurs during winter. Rotate the legume crop with a non-host cereal crop, cucurbit or cruciferous vegetable. *H. armigera* sex pheromone traps can be used to monitor, mass-trap or disrupt the mating activities of male moths.

Monitoring: Sex pheromone traps baited with *H. armigera* pheromone lures can trap adult male moths to predict the population build-up in the field.

Mass-trapping: Sex pheromone traps baited with *H. armigera* pheromone lures can be used for trapping as many males as possible to reduce chances of females mating and producing viable eggs in the field. However, this has limited effect for polyphagous insects like *H. armigera*, since its population is always higher due to the availability of multiple host plants in crop production systems in the tropics.

Mating disruption: High concentration of full blends or, at times, only one component of the multi-component pheromone is placed in the field to permeate the area with the synthetic chemical. The high concentration of pheromone in the air overwhelms the male, making it impossible to locate a receptive female. Failure to mate results in failure to produce eggs or the production of only nonviable eggs, which reduces the build-up of insect populations. Placing a high concentration of sex pheromone in a slow-release formulation on a 5 and 10 m grid in the field will result in a drastic reduction in male moths being attracted to virgin females, which adversely affects mating in *H. armigera*. Planting of African marigold (*Tagetes erecta* L.) as a trap crop reduces the incidence of *H. armigera*. *H. armigera* adults preferred marigold at flowering stage for oviposition. It is important to synchronize sowing/transplanting of both crops so that their flowering coincides to attract *H. armigera* female adults. Inundatively release *T. pretiosum* @ 40,000/acre 4-5 times from flower initiation stage at weekly intervals. Conserve parasitoids such as *Tetrastichus* spp. (egg), *Telenomus* spp. (egg), *Campoletis chlorideae* (larval) etc. Conserve predators such as *Chrysoperla carnea*, coccinellids, King crow, common mynah, wasp, dragonfly, spider, robber fly, reduviid bug, praying mantis, fire ants, big eyed bugs (*Geocoris* sp), pentatomid bug, earwigs, ground beetles, rove beetles etc. Spray azadirachtin 1% (10000 ppm) neem-based EC @ 400-600 ml in 200 l of water/acre or azadirachtin 5% W/W neem extract concentrate @ 80 g in 160 l of water/acre. Spray Ha NPV 0.43% AS @ 600 ml in 160- 240 l of water/acre or Ha NPV 2% AS @ 100-200 ml in 200 l of water/acre in combination with jaggery @ 1 kg in the evening hours at 10-15 days interval on observing the eggs or early instar larvae. Spray *Bacillus thuringiensis* var *gallariae* @ 400-600 g in 200 l of water/acre. Apply entomopathogenic nematodes (EPNs) @ 20-120 crore infective juveniles of *Steinernema feltiae*/acre. Most insecticide applications are targeted at the larval stages, but as these are only really effective when larvae are small, the need to scout for eggs and spray soon afterward is paramount. Young larvae are difficult to find, and older larvae soon burrow into the floral organs where they become less accessible to contact insecticides, require higher doses to kill and cause direct economic loss. Moreover, resistant larvae were still susceptible while less than 4 days old, so that targeting of neonates is essential in areas where resistant populations are present.

Provide poison bait with carbaryl 50 WP 1.25 kg, rice bran 12.5 kg, jaggery 1.25 kg and water 7.5 lit/ha. Organochlorides, pyrethroids, carbamates and organophosphates were formerly in use, but the pest has developed considerable resistance to them. One approach is to rotate these chemicals every few weeks during the season. Preparations of *B. thuringiensis* are effective during the early part of the season. Spinosad is still effective. A novel method is to apply "**Noctovi**", a product that attracts bollworms from up to 50 meters, integrated with a pesticide, to kill the pests.

Spray with indoxacarb 14.5% SC @ 160- 200 ml in 120-240 l of water/acre or flubendiamide 20% WG @ 40 g in 150-200 l of water/acre or flubendiamide 39.35% M/M SC @ 40 ml in 150-200 l of water/acre or novaluron 10 % EC @ 300 ml in 200-400 l of water/acre or carbaryl 50% WP @ 800 g in 200-400 l of water/acre or chlorantranilioprole 18.5% SC @ 60 ml in 200 l of water/acre or lambda-cyhalothrin 4.9% CS @ 120 ml in 200 l of water/acre or lambda-cyhalothrin 5% EC @ 120 ml in 160- 200 l of water/acre or methomyl 40% SP @ 300-450 ml in 200-400 l of water/acre or phosalone 35% EC @ 514 ml in 200-400 l of water/acre or quinalphos 20% AF @ 600- 700 ml in 300-400 l of water/acre or quinalohos 25% EC @ 400 ml in 200-400 l of water/acre.

❑ Serpentine leaf miner: *Liriomyza trifolii* (Burgess, 1880)

Common Name	:	Serpentine leaf miner
Scientific Name	:	*Liriomyza trifolii* (Burgess, 1880)
Family	:	Agromyzidae
Order	:	Diptera

Source: *https://www.cabidigitallibrary.org/doi/10.1079/cabicompendium.30965*

Distribution and Host Range

L. trifolii is one of the truly polyphagous agromyzids and has been recorded in 25 families. It was first described as *Oscinis trifolii* in the family Chloropidae from flies attacking the leaves of *Trifolium repens* (white clover) in Indiana, USA. Later, it was transferred to the family Agromyzidae in the genus *Agromyza* by Coquillet (1898), then to *Liriomyza* by de Meijere (1925). It is a major pest of a wide variety of ornamental or vegetable crops grown under glass. The host range of *L. trifolii* includes over 400 species of plants in 28 families including both ornamental crops and vegetables.

Nature and Symptoms of Damage

L. trifolii feeding punctures appear as white speckles. Oviposition punctures are usually smaller and are more uniformly round. *L. trifolii* leaf mines can vary in form with the host plant, but when adequate leaf area is available, they are usually long, linear, narrow and not greatly widening towards the end. They are usually greenish white. The frass is distinctive in being deposited in black strips alternately at either side of the mine, but becomes more granular towards the end of the mine.

Life History and Description

L. trifolii eggs are white and slightly translucent. This is a legless maggot with no separate head capsule, transparent when newly hatched but colouring up to a yellow-orange in later instars and is up to 3 mm long. *L. trifolii* larvae and puparia have a pair of posterior spiracles terminating in three cone-like appendages. This is oval and slightly flattened ventrally, with variable colour, pale yellow-orange, darkening to golden-brown. Pupariation occurs outside the leaf, in the soil beneath the plant. *L. trifolii* adult is very small with yellowish head, mesonotum is grey-black with a yellow blotch at the hind-corners.

Management

It is important to destroy and bury the remains of broadleaf weeds and senescent cultures as they can harbor reproductive leaf miners. The use of glue traps can be effective for assessing the presence of adult *L. trifolii*, gauging the best time to apply control measures on a population, and as a direct method of pest suppression. Yellow sticky traps (YSTs) attracted significantly more adult *L. trifolii* than blue, purple or white traps.

Foliar applications of the entomophagous nematode *Steinernema carpocapsae* significantly reduced adult development of *L. trifolii*.

Parasitoids: *Tetrastichus ovularum* (egg), *Gronotoma micromorpha* (larval and pupal), *Diglyphus* sp. (larval), *Opius* sp. (pupal) *Chrysocharis* sp., *Neochrysocharis formosa* (larval) etc.

Predators: Lacewings, lady beetle, spiders, fire ants, dragonfly, robber fly, praying mantis etc. Spray cyantraniliprole 10.26 OD 1.8 ml/lit. For the control of *L. trifolii,* effective insecticides with different modes of action (and with different site of action) should be rotated during the growing season (IRAC, 2014).

❑ Tobacco caterpillar: *Spodoptera litura* (Fabricius, 1775)

Common Name	:	Tobacco caterpillar; Tobacco cutworm; Cotton leafworm; Leaf eating caterpillar
Scientific Name	:	*Spodoptera litura* (Fabricius, 1775)
Family	:	Noctuidae
Order	:	Lepidoptera

Source:*https://apps.lucidcentral.org/pppw*

Distribution and Host Range	Nature and Symptoms of Damage	Life History and Description
	As Described in Potato	

Management

Field sanitation. Install pheromone traps spodolure or litlure @ 4-5/acre or monitoring adult moths' activity. Replace the lures with fresh lures after every 2-3 weeks Setting up of light trap @ 1/acre Ecological engineering of tomato with growing of ovipositional trap crops such as castor. Erecting of bird perches @ 20/acre for encouraging predatory birds such as king crow, mynah etc.

Release egg parasitoid, *Trichogramma pretiosum* @ 20,000/acre/week four times. Spray NSKE 5% against eggs and first instar larva or azadirachtin 5% W/W neem extract concentrate @ 80 g in 160 l of water/acre. Conserve parasitoids such as *Trichogramma chilonis* (egg), *Tetrastichus* spp. (egg), *Telenomus* spp. (egg), *Chelonus blackburni* (egg-larval), *Carcelia* spp. (larval-pupal), *Campoletis chlorideae* (larval), *Eriborus argentiopilosus* (larval), *Microplitis* sp pentatomid bug (*Eocanthecona furcellata*) etc. Apply entomopathogenic nematodes (EPNs) @ 2,50,000 infective juveniles of *Steinernema feltiae*/sq mt area.

Apply trichlorfon 5% GR @ 300 g/acre or trichlorfon 5% dust @ 300 g/acre or spray indoxacarb 14.5% SC @ 160-200 ml in 120-240 l of water/acre or flubendiamide 20% WG @ 40 g in 150-200 l of water/acre or flubendiamide 39.35% M/M SC @ 40 ml in 150-200 l of water/acre or carbaryl 50% WP @ 800 g in 200-400 l of water/acre or chlorantranilioprole 18.5% SC @ 60 ml in 200 l of water/acre or lambda-cyhalothrin 4.9% CS @ 120 ml in 200 l of water/acre or lambda-cyhalothrin 5% EC @ 120 ml in 160- 200 l of water/acre or methomyl 40% SP @ 300-450 ml in 200-400 l of water/acre or novaluron 10 % EC @ 300 ml in 200-400 l of water/acre or phosalone 35% EC @ 514 ml in 200-400 l of water/acre or quinalphos 20% AF @ 600-700 ml in 300-400 l of water/acre or quinalohos 25% EC @ 400 ml in 200-400 l of water/acre or novaluron 5.25% + indoxacarb 4.5% SC @ 330-350 ml in 200 l of water/acre.

Tomato pinworm: *Tuta absoluta* (Meyrick, 1917)

Common Name	:	South American tomato pinworm; Tomato leaf miner; Tomato pinworm; South American tomato moth
Scientific Name	:	*Tuta absoluta* (Meyrick, 1917)
Family	:	Gelechiidae
Order	:	Lepidoptera

Source: *https://agriculture.gov.tt/publications/advisories/tuta-absoluta-tomato-leaf-miner/*

Naming History

T. absoluta was originally described in 1917 by Edward Meyrick as *Phthorimaea absoluta*, based on individuals collected from Huancayo (Peru). Later, the pest was reported as *Gnorimoschema absoluta*, *Scrobipalpula absoluta* (Povolný), or *Scrobipalpuloides absoluta* (Povolný), but was finally described under the genus *Tuta* as *T. absoluta* by **Povolný** in 1994.

Distribution and Host Range

It is well known as a serious pest of tomato crops in Europe, Africa, western Asia and South and Central America, with larvae causing up to 100% loss if not effectively controlled. Reached India and the Himalayans, unconfirmed but possibly also Pakistan and Tajikistan, by 2017. In **India, Maharashtra** state tomato cultivation more affect in November 2016.Tomato is the main host plant, but *T. absoluta* also attacks other crop plants of the nightshade family, including potato, eggplant, pepino, pepper and tobacco. It is known from many solanaceous weeds, including *Datura stramonium*, *Lycium chilense*, and *Solanum nigrum*. Also known from non-Solanaceae hosts in the Amaranthaceae, Convolvulaceae, Fabaceae, and Malvaceae. Laboratory rearing is abnormally difficult because *T. absoluta* requires maternal leaf contact with a suitable host plant for oviposition.

Nature and Symptoms of Damage

The larva feeds voraciously upon tomato plants, producing large galleries in leaves, burrowing in stalks, and consuming apical buds and green and ripe fruits. It is capable of causing a yield loss of 100%. Mining of leaves, stem and pinholes on fruits are peculiar damage characteristics.

Life History and Description

Adults usually lay yellow eggs on the underside of leaves or stems, and to a lesser extent on fruits. After hatching, young larvae penetrate leaves, aerial fruits or stems, on which they feed and develop. Pupae are cylindrical in shape and greenish when just formed becoming darker in color as they are near adult emergence. Adults are 6-7 millimetres in length and present filiform antennae and silver to grey scales. Black spots are present on anterior wings, and the females are wider and more voluminous than the males. The adult moth has a wingspan around 1 centimetre. In favourable weather conditions eight to ten generations can occur in a single year. The pest mainly presents nocturnal habits, and adults usually remain hidden during the day, showing greater morning-crepuscular activity with adults dispersing among crops by flying.

Management

Collect and destroy the pinworm affected plants and fruits. Avoid solanaceous crops after tomato. Use healthy seedlings for transplanting. Keep pheromone traps @ 16 nos./ac to attract and kill the adult moths. Removal of alternative hosts, particularly weeds from the genera *Solanum*, *Datura*, and *Nicotiana*. Pheromone-baited sticky traps can be used to monitor all stage of tomato production and across the production chain in nurseries, farms, greenhouses, and packaging and processing facilities. Light traps and water traps can also be used to capture both sexes. Male annihilation by mass trapping of adults with pheromone traps (delta traps), which are usually efficient against newly introduced pest when population density is low. For mass trapping, it is recommended to use 20-40 traps/ha. A threshold of 3-4 moths per trap per week need to be reached before the beginning of mass trapping.

Augmentative biocontrol for *T. absoluta* is commercially available in South America using the parasitoid *Trichogramma pretiosum*, particularly in Brazil, Chile, Colombia, Ecuador, and Peru. The use of endogenous natural enemies for biocontrol of TPW is one of the key points of conservative strategies. The *Macrolophus basicornis* (Stal) and *M. pygmaeus* (Hemiptera: Miridae) are potential biocontrol agents against (egg predators) TLM. The nymphal stage of the former can consume an average of 331 eggs per day, while the adult can feed upon as many as 100 eggs per day. The parasitoids *Necremnus tutae* and *N. cosmopterix* (Hymenoptera: Eulophidae) are potential biocontrol agents against TLM. The predator *Nesidiocoris tenuis* (Hemiptera: Miridae) can be used for the management of other tomato pests including the whiteflies, thrips, leafminers, and aphids. The generalist egg parasitoid, *Trichogramma achaeae*, is a potential agent for biological control of *T. absoluta*.

Chemical control of the invasive TLM is difficult; however, its arrival to new invaded areas has been linked to an excessive application of broad-spectrum insecticides, in attempts to curb the outbreaks of the pest and to reduce yield losses in tomato crop. Currently, insecticides application seems to be the most commonly used strategy against *T. absoluta* worldwide in open fields of tomato. Spray chlorantraniliprole 18.5% SC @ 60 ml or cyantraniliprole 10% OD @ 60 ml or flubendiamide 20% WG @ 60 ml or indoxacarb 14.5% SC @ 100 ml or neem formulation (azadirachtin 1% or 5%) @ 400-600 ml/ac.

❑ Silverleaf whitefly: *Bemisia tabaci* (Gennadius, 1889)

Common Name	:	Whitefly; Silverleaf whitefly; Sweet potato whitefly
Scientific Name	:	*Bemisia tabaci* (Gennadius, 1889)
Family	:	Aleyrodidae
Order	:	Hemiptera

Source:*https://en.wikipedia.org/wiki/Silverleaf_whitefly*

As Described in Potato

Management: Tomato leaf curl virus tolerant/resistant varieties: Arka Ananya, Kashi Vishesh, Kashi Amrit, COTH 2, TNAU Tomato Hybrid Co3.

❑ Onion thrips: *Thrips tabaci* Lindeman, 1889

Common Name	:	Onion thrips, Potato thrips, Tobacco thrips, Cotton seedling thrips, Western Flower Thrips (WFT)
Scientific Name	:	*Thrips tabaci* Lindeman, 1889
Family	:	Thripidae
Order	:	Thysanoptera

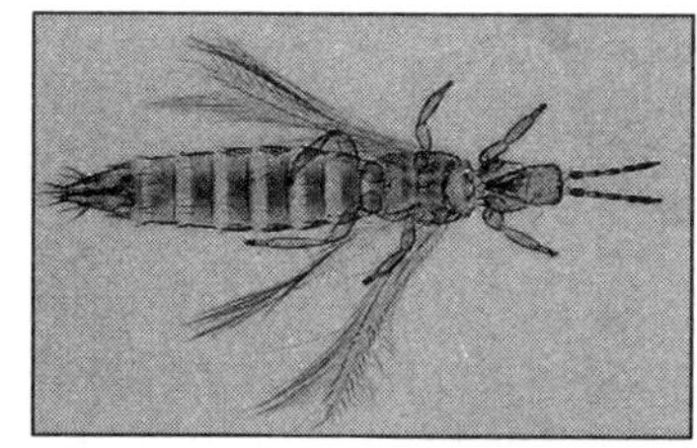

Source:https://keys.lucidcentral.org/keys

Distribution and Host Range

The onion thrips is thought to have originated in the Mediterranean region but is now found on all continents except Antarctica. This thrips was **first found in Hawaii in 1915** and is now present on all islands. It infests a wide range of host plants that include onion, leek and garlic, brassicaceous plants such as cabbage, cauliflower and broccoli, asparagus, sugar beet, melon, pumpkin, marrow and cucumber, strawberry, potato, tobacco, cotton and many fruiting and ornamental plants. Onion thrips was the first vector identified for tomato spotted wilt virus, being reported in 1927.

Nature and Symptoms of Damage

The thrips rasp and pierce the surface of the plant with their mouthparts, mostly choosing young plant growth. They then add digestive juices and suck up the fluids that seep from the wounds. As the plant part grows, so do the damaged regions, leaving **silvery streaks**. The more thrips that are present, the greater the area of plant damaged, reducing the area of foliage available for photosynthesis. At the same time, more water is transpired and pathogens can find a way to gain entry.

The onion thrips is a vector of certain plant viruses, including **iris yellow spot tospovirus**, **strawberry necrotic shock virus**, **tobacco streak virus** and **tomato spotted wilt virus** (only nymphs). It is also a vector of ***Alternaria porri***, which causes the fungal disease known as **purple blotch**.

Life History and Description

The female inserts her saw-like ovipositor into plant tissues and lays her eggs under the epidermis. The eggs are white at first, turning orange later, and hatch in four to five days. The larvae are white or yellowish and suck sap from the plant tissues. Two larval stages lasting about nine days in total are followed by the non-feeding prepupal and pupal stages which last four to seven days in total. Both sexes fully winged with fringed wings. Female colour varying from yellow to brown, depending largely on temperatures during development; Antennae 7-segmented.

Management

Cultural control practices can help reduce onion thrips infestations. Destruction of piles of cull onions between crops reduces the abundance of this pest along with other sanitation techniques such as removing weeds in the field and outlying areas. These practices help eliminate alternative hosts on the onion thrips between crops. Crop rotations to prevent the successive plantings of several onion crops and interplanting with non-host crops can also be effective in deterring large populations. Use yellow sticky traps @ 15/ha.

Release compodaei form grubs of *Chrysoperla cornea* @10,000/ha. Several natural enemies have been introduced to Hawaii in an attempt to help control this pest. However, only the parasite, ***Ceranisus menes***, has become established. Unfortunately, the impact of this parasite is not considered great. They are preyed upon by the mirid *D. tamaninii*. Other potential biocontrol agents of these pests include the phytoseiid predatory mites, *Amblyseius swirskii* Athias-Henriot and *Neoseiulus cucumeris* (Oudemans). Entomopathogenic fungi such as *Beauveria bassiana* (Balsamo-Crivelli) Vuillemin, *M. anisopliae, Lecanicillium lecanii* (Zimmerman) Zare and Gams, and *Metarhizium flavoviride* Gams and Rozsypal var *minus* are potential biocontrol agents of tomato thrips, *Thrips tabaci* Lindeman.

While the onion thrips can be readily killed by many insecticides, they are often difficult to control because of their small size and cryptic habits. Another important aspect of insecticidal control is spraying intervals. In order to control high population densities of this pest during warm, dry periods, repeated applications at 7-10 day intervals are required. Spray, cyantraniliprole 10.26 OD 1.8 ml/lit. Mechanically uproot the diseased plants and destroy them.

❑ Two tailed mealy bugs: *Ferrisia virgata* Cockerell, 1893

Common Name	:	Striped mealybug; Two tailed mealy bug
Scientific Name	:	*Ferrisia virgata* Cockerell, 1893
Family	:	Pseudococcidae
Order	:	Hemiptera

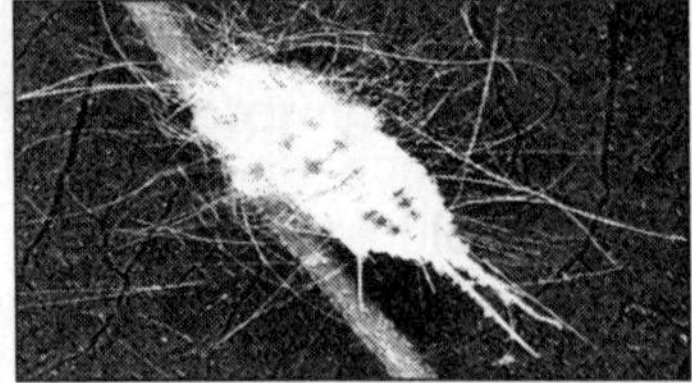

Source:*https://www.cabidigitallibrary.org/doi/10.1079/cabicompendium.30965*

Distribution and Host Range

Ferrisia is a New World genus native to the Americas. As a polyphagous species, the striped mealybug can be found on numerous hosts. Common hosts in Florida are copperleaf, croton, hibiscus, seagrape and citrus as well as popular home garden vegetables such as tomato, eggplant, and pepper.

Nature and Symptoms of Damage

Mealybugs are sap-feeding insects that tap into the phloem via a piercing, straw-like mouthpart known as a stylet. Severe infestations of mealybugs can be fatal to a plant. Large populations of mealybugs appear as accumulations of white, cottony-looking wax on the plant. This wax is produced by special glands and gives the insects the "**mealy**" appearance from which the name "mealybug" is derived. Mealybugs often produce a substance that is sticky and high in carbohydrates known as honeydew. Honeydew is an excellent medium for the growth of sooty mold, a fungus that forms a dark film on the leaf surface and impairs photosynthesis. Large aggregations of mealybugs on plants appear as unsightly white, sticky masses of wax and individuals, which can render plants unmarketable. Leaf discoloration and leaf and fruit drop are also symptoms of mealybug infestations; however, symptoms will vary depending on plant species and plant health status.

The striped mealybug is known to vector plant pathogens, a trait uncommon in mealybugs. It has been reported to transmit *Cocoa swollen shoot virus*, *Citrus tristeza virus*, and *Piper yellow mottle virus*.

Life History and Description

The striped mealybug has three nymphal instars. At the end of the third instar the female moults into the sexually mature adult form. Males begin constructing a cocoon at the onset of the second instar and continue feeding and maturing while inside. The third instar in males is a prepupa stage after which a puparium is formed. The male reaches sexual maturity upon the moult from puparia to the winged adult stage. Reproduction of the striped mealybug occurs sexually. Females do not produce ovisacs but construct "**pads**" made of waxy filaments. Eggs are deposited on the pad and the first instar nymphs hatch within a few hours. There are three to five generations per year.

The striped mealybug is named for the two dark, dorsal stripes that run longitudinally down its body. Additional identifying features of the striped mealybug are the two posterior waxy tails or tassels with a length half that of the mealybug body, the presence of crystalline, hair-like rods extending laterally from the body, and the **absence of an ovisac (egg sac)**. First and second instar nymphs are light yellow with six antennal segments. Adult males are heavily sclerotized, dark gray in color, winged, and have ten antennal segments. Adult females are greenish-yellow in color with two dorsal, dark gray stripes, wingless and antennae with eight segments.

Management

Early detection provides the best chance at managing mealybugs due to the vulnerability of the immature stages. Carefully inspect purchased plants to avoid spreading mealybugs. Scout susceptible plants for mealybugs or masses of cottony wax. Mealybugs can be difficult to see with the naked eye and they often reside in cryptic or hidden locations such as the crooks of branches and undersides of leaves, which may appear distorted. If mealybugs are not apparent but an infestation is suspected, sooty mold and ant activity may also be clues to a mealybug or other honeydew-producing insect problem. Infested plants should be isolated or removed and disposed of immediately to prevent spread. In many commercial greenhouses, highly infested plants are destroyed because such infestations are very difficult to control.

For greenhouses, commercially available insects such as the mealybug destroyer (*Cryptolaemus montrouzieri*), green lacewings, and brown lacewings can be purchased to prevent mealybug outbreaks. Outdoors, these and other naturally present mealybug enemies can be conserved through avoidance of foliarly applied, broad-spectrum insecticides. Another consideration when using biological control agents for mealybug management is the presence of ants. Honeydew is very attractive to ants as a source of food. Some species of ants will defend mealybugs from predation and parasitism to protect their access to the honeydew. If it is suspected that ants are contributing to a mealybug infestation it is recommended to use insecticide baits, traps, or granules combined with barriers like sticky tapes to prevent ants from hindering predation or other mealybug control efforts.

Due to their waxy hydrophobic covering, managing mealybugs with pesticide sprays can be difficult. Contact insecticides are most effective when the younger stages are targeted. This is because first and second instar mealybugs are not protected by the dense waxy covering that develops in the later instars. Insect growth regulators (IGRs), insecticidal soaps, and horticultural oils are suggested for treating early instar mealybugs and can be applied directly to the plant and mealybugs. Systemic insecticides, which are applied to the soil and taken up into the plant by the roots, have also been shown to be effective. However, because mealybugs have overlapping generations, repeated, frequent applications are often necessary and this may hasten the development of insecticide resistance. Frequent pesticide use can also negatively impact beneficial insects. Spray FORS 25 g/lit or neem oil 0.5% along with teepol 1 ml/lit. Spray any following insecticides: Phosphomidon 40 SL 2 ml/lit; Imidacloprid 80.5 SC 0.6 ml/lit; Chlorpriphos 20 EC 2 ml/lit; Thiamethoxam 25 WSG 0.6 mg/lit; Profenophos 2 ml/lit.

❑ Two-spotted spider mite: *Tetranychus urticae* C.L. Koch, 1836

Common Name	:	Red spider mite; Two-spotted spider mite
Scientific Name	:	*Tetranychus urticae* C.L. Koch, 1836
Family	:	Tetranychidae
Order	:	Trombidiformes

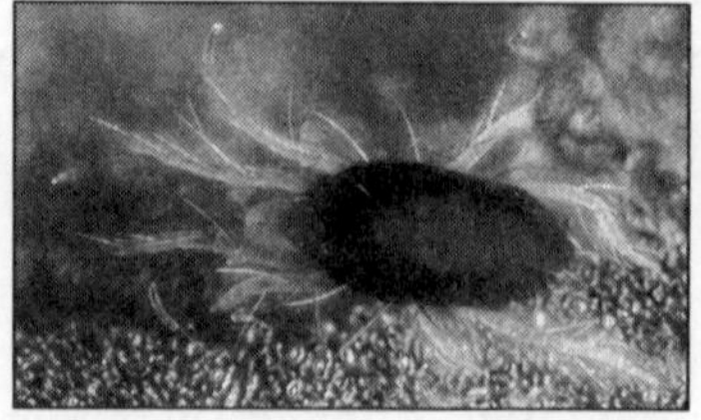

Source: *https://www.cabidigitallibrary.org/doi/10.1079/cabicompendium.30965*

Distribution and Host Range

T. urticae was originally native only to Eurasia, but has acquired a cosmopolitan distribution. It is the most widely known member of the family Tetranychidae or spider mites. Its genome was fully sequenced in 2011, and was the first genome sequence from any chelicerate. This spider mite is extremely polyphagous; it can feed on hundreds of plants, including most vegetables and food crops such as peppers, tomatoes, potatoes, pepinos, beans, maize, and strawberries, and ornamental plants such as roses. It is the most prevalent pest of *Withania somnifera* in India.

Nature and Symptoms of Damage

It lays its eggs on the leaves, and it poses a threat to host plants by sucking cell contents from the leaves cell by cell, leaving tiny pale spots or scars where the green epidermal cells have been destroyed. Although the individual lesions are very small, attack by hundreds or thousands of spider mites can cause thousands of lesions, thus can significantly reduce the photosynthetic capability of plants. They feed on single cells which are pierced with a stylet-like mouthpart and the cell contents are removed, they do damage to the spongy mesophyll, palisade parenchyma, and chloroplasts.

Life History and Description

The egg of *T. urticae* is translucent and pearl-like. It hatches into a larva, and two nymph stages follow: a protonymph, and then a deutonymph, which may display quiescent stages. The adults are typically pale green for most of the year, but later generations are red; mated females survive the winter in diapause. *T. urticae* reproduces through arrhenotoky, a form of parthenogenesis in which unfertilized eggs develop into males. **Inbreeding avoidance:** Inbreeding is detrimental for fitness in *T. urticae*. Inbred progeny matures more slowly than outbred progeny, and inbred female progeny have lower reproductive output. *T. urticae* females apparently are capable of kin recognition and have the ability to avoid inbreeding through mate choice.

Management

Field sanitation, rouging of affected plants. Plant tall border crops such as maize, sorghum etc. Conserve predators such as predatory mites (*Phytoseiulus* spp., *Amblyseius* spp.), staphylinids (*Oligota* spp.), lady bird beetles, lacewings, predatory thrips, anthocorid bugs (*Orius* spp.), mirid bugs, predatory flies (syrphid/hover flies) etc. The mite's natural predator, *Phytoseiulus persimilis*, commonly used as a biological control method, is one of many predatory mites which prey mainly or exclusively on spider mites. Apply fenzaquin 10% EC @ 500 ml in 200 l of water/acre or spiromesifen 22.9% SC @ 250 ml in 200 l of water/acre. Spray wettable sulphur 50 WP 2 g/lit or dicofol 18.5 EC 2.5 ml/lit neem oil may provide control, when combined with a suitable surfactant and diluted with water.

Root-knot nematode: *Meloidogyne* spp. Goldi

Common Name	:	Root-knot nematode
Scientific Name	:	*Meloidogyne* spp. Goldi
Family	:	Heteroderidae
Order	:	Tylenchida

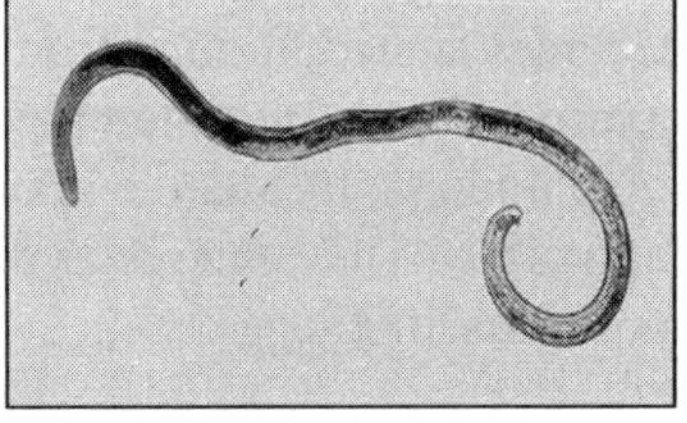

Source: *https://content.ces.ncsu.edu/management-of-root-knot-nematodes-in-bedding-plants*

Distribution and Host Range

Root-knot nematodes were first reported in 1855 by Berkeley, who observed them causing damage on greenhouse cucumbers. Until Chitwood's work in 1949, which defined 4 species and one subspecies (*M. incognita acrita*) within the genus *Meloidogyne*, the root-knot nematodes were all considered the same species, *Heterodera radicola*. The name *Meloidogyne* is of Greek origin, meaning "apple-shaped female." Approximately 100 species of *Meloidogyne* have been described. The most widespread and economically important species are *M. incognita*, *M. javanica*, *M. arenaria*, *M. hapla*, *M. chitwoodi* and *M. graminicola*. Root-knot nematodes are primarily tropical to sub-tropical organisms, however *M. hapla* and *M. chitwoodi* are well adapted to temperate climates. RKN have been found in all agricultural regions of the world and any crop is likely to suffer damage from these parasites.

Nature and Symptoms of Damage

Infected plants in patches in the field. Formation of galls on host root system is the primary symptom. Roots branch profusely starting from the gall tissue causing a "**beard root**" symptom. Infected roots become knobby and knotty. In severely infected plants the root system is reduced and the rootlets are almost completely absent. The roots are seriously hampered in their function of uptake and transport of water and nutrients. Plants wilt during the hot part of day, especially under dry conditions and are often stunted. Seedlings infected in nursery do not normally survive transplanting and those surviving have reduced flowering and fruit production. Nematode infection predisposes plants to fungal and bacterial root pathogens.

Aboveground symptoms of nematode feeding are similar to those resulting from other causes of root injury. Infection by the root-knot nematode causes gall formation, or **"knots"** on roots. Root-knot nematodes are sedentary endoparasites, so they will remain inside the root for the duration of their life once they establish a feeding site near the centre of the root. Galls result from the growth of plant tissues that develop around the feeding nematodes. The nematodes secrete a plant growth hormone that stimulates cell growth, resulting in gall formation. Gall tissue is firm and solid. The galls are part of the root tissue, so removing the root-knot gall from the root is not a viable management option.

Life History and Description

All nematodes pass through an embryonic stage, four juvenile stages **(J1-J4)** and an adult stage. Juvenile *Meloidogynes* parasites hatch from eggs as vermiform, second-stage juveniles (J2), the first moult having occurred within the egg. Newly hatched juveniles have a short free-living stage in the soil, in the rhizosphere of the host plants. They may reinvade the host plants of their parent or migrate through the soil to find a new host root. **J2 larvae** do not feed during the free-living stage, but use lipids stored in the gut. Root-knot nematode females lay eggs into a gelatinous matrix produced by **six rectal glands** and secreted before and during egg laying. As the gelatinous matrix ages, it becomes tanned, turning from a sticky, colourless jelly to an orange-brown substance which appears layered. Root-knot nematodes exhibit a range of reproductive modes, including sexuality (amphimixis), facultative sexuality, meiotic parthenogenesis (automixis) and mitotic parthenogenesis (apomixis). They emerge as adults from the J4 cuticle. A single female nematode can produce 500 to more than 1000 eggs.

Management

Soil solarization is a nonchemical way to reduce soil pest populations, but it requires the affected area to be left bare for six to eight weeks during the hottest part of the year (summer) to be effective. Dense planting with certain marigold varieties for an entire season can help reduce populations of some root-knot nematode species. Root knot nematode tolerant/resistant varieties: Pusa-120, Pusa Hybrid-2, Pusa Hybrid-4, Arka Vardan, Hisar Lalit, TNAU Tomato Hybrid Co3.

Control measures employing organisms antagonistic to root-knot nematodes have been attempted by many researchers. The most commonly used biological control agents are fungi and bacteria. There are many kinds of nematophagous (nematode-feeding) fungi. Some fungi use mycelial traps or sticky spores to capture nematodes, for example, *Arthrobotrys* spp. and *Monacrosporium* spp. Other fungi parasitize eggs and root-knot nematode females, e.g., *Pochonia chlamydosporia* and *Paecilomyces lilacinus*. The major bacterial antagonists are *Pasteuria penetrans* and species of *Bacillus*. Endospores of *P. penetrans* attach to the cuticle of a juvenile nematode, produce penetration structures that enter the nematode, and slowly consume it.

Fumigants (such as 1, 3-dichloropropene, methyl bromide and dazomet) are commonly applied as pre-plant treatments to reduce nematode numbers, but they must thoroughly penetrate large soil volumes to be effective. Some fumigants volatilize very quickly, so treated soil must have a cover or trap to maintain the fumigant in the soil long enough to be effective. The phasing out of methyl bromide (an efficient fumigant) has intensified the search for alternatives that can be used by farmers. In addition to broad-spectrum fumigants, nervous system toxins (including oxamyl and fenamiphos) have been shown to be extremely effective for controlling root-knot nematodes.

Resistant Varieties	
World	**India**
Mountain Magic: This tomato variety is resistant to early blight, late blight, and tomato yellow leaf curl virus, which are all common insect-transmitted diseases. **Defiant:** Defiant is a variety that is resistant to both early and late blight, as well as tomato spotted wilt virus. **Tiren:** Developed in Israel, Tiren is resistant to whiteflies, which are a common pest of tomato plants. **Matina:** Matina is a variety that is resistant to aphids, which can transmit viruses that cause significant yield losses. **Sun Gold:** Sun Gold is a popular variety that is known for its resistance to tomato yellow leaf curl virus, as well as other diseases like early blight.	**Pusa Early Dwarf:** This tomato variety is resistant to tomato leaf curl virus and has good yield potential. **Arka Vikas:** Developed by the Indian Institute of Horticultural Research, Arka Vikas is resistant to both early and late blight, as well as tomato yellow leaf curl virus. **Vaishali:** Vaishali is a variety that is resistant to tomato leaf curl virus and has good yield potential. **Arka Rakshak:** Developed by the Indian Agricultural Research Institute, Arka Rakshak is resistant to both early and late blight, as well as other diseases like bacterial wilt.

3 Pests of Brinjal

Scientific Name	*Solanum melongena*
Family	Solanaceae
Origin	India
Chromosome Number	$2n = 24$
Common names	Eggplant (US, Canada), aubergine (UK, Ireland) or brinjal (Indian subcontinent, Singapore, Malaysia, South Africa)

Eggplant (US, Canada, Australia, New Zealand, Philippines), **aubergine** (UK, Ireland) or **brinjal** (Indian subcontinent, Singapore, Malaysia, South Africa) is a plant species in the nightshade family Solanaceae. ***Solanum melongena*** is grown worldwide for its edible fruit. The eggplant is a delicate, tropical perennial plant often cultivated as a tender or half-hardy annual in temperate climates.

In India, brinjal is an important vegetable crop, with a significant share in the country's horticulture production. According to the Ministry of Agriculture and Farmers Welfare, the area under brinjal cultivation in India was around 528 thousand hectares during the year 2020-21, with a total production of approximately 11.5 million tonnes. The productivity of brinjal in India during the same period was around 21.8 tonnes per hectare. On a global scale, brinjal is one of the most widely cultivated vegetables.

Brinjal is susceptible to several insect pests, which can cause significant yield losses if not managed properly. Here are some of the common insect pests of brinjal and their potential yield losses:

❑ Brinjal fruit and shoot borer: *Leucinodes orbonalis* Guenée, 1854

Common Name	:	Brinjal fruit and shoot borer
Scientific Name	:	*Leucinodes orbonalis* Guenée, 1854
Family	:	Crambidae
Order	:	Lepidoptera

Source: *https://idtools.org/tools/1035/index.cfm?packageID=1101&entityID=2854*

Distribution and Host Range

L. orbonalis, the eggplant fruit and shoot borer or brinjal fruit and shoot borer, is a moth species in the genus *Leucinodes* described by Achille Guenée in 1854. Its native distribution is in the tropical and subtropical parts of Australia and Asia, where it is recorded from Pakistan, Nepal, India, including the Andaman Islands, Sri Lanka, Bangladesh, Myanmar, Laos, Cambodia, Vietnam, Thailand, China, Taiwan, Japan, Malaysia, Singapore, Brunei, the Philippines, and Indonesia (Java).

The primary larval hostplant is eggplant or brinjal, *Solanum melongena*, where most of the economic impact of this species is reported. Secondary hostplants comprise tomato, potato, nightshade, Sodom apple, Ethiopian nightshade, potato tree, nipple fruit, black nightshade, turkey berry, tropical soda apple, *Solanum anguivi*, *Solanum xanthocarpum*, cape gooseberry and *Physalis minima*.

Nature and Symptoms of Damage

Eggs are laid during the night on the lower surface of the young leaves, green stems, flower buds, or calyces of the fruits. Within an hour of hatching, the caterpillar (larva) bores into the nearest tender shoot, flower, or fruit. Soon after boring into shoots or fruits, they plug the entrance hole with excreta. In young plants, caterpillars are reported to bore inside petioles and midribs of large leaves. As a result, the affected leaves may drop off. Larval feeding inside shoots results in wilting of the young shoot. The damaged shoots ultimately drop off, disturbing plant growth and reducing fruit number and size. New shoots may grow but this delays crop maturity. Larval feeding inside the fruit results in the destruction of fruit tissue, making even slightly damaged fruit unfit for marketing. It is a major and regular pest of brinjal causing damage to even 30 -50% of fruits or more.

Life History and Description

Egg: 3-4 days. About 150-350 creamy white eggs laid singly on leaves, tender shoots, flowers and developing fruits. Larva is stout, pink coloured with sparsely distributed hairs on warts on the body and brownish head. Larval period: 15 days – 5 instars.

Pupa: 6-8 days in tough greyish cocoon on plant itself, boat shaped cocoon. Medium sized adult with white wings, flashed with triangular brown and red markings on forewing. Total life cycle: 17-50 days. Larvae grow to 2 cm in length. The forewing ground colour is white, with a light- to dark-brown basal area, delimited by a dark-brown to grey antemedial line. The hindwing ground colour is white.

Management

Intercropping can be used to reduce infestation of *L. orbonalis*. Partners of plant wise have recommended using maize as a barrier crop and intercropping with non-host crops including cowpea, coriander, black gram and green gram. In small plantings, partners of plant wise suggest infected shoots and fruits can be hand-picked and eggs and larvae can be physically removed. They also recommend introducing light traps into fields to attract moths at night. Install pheromone trap @12/ha. A genetically modified brinjal, called *Bt* brinjal, has been developed to fight against *L. orbonalis*. Grow resistance varieties like Annamalai, Pusa purple round, Arka Kusumakar, Doli – 5. Chaklasi Doli, Pusa purple Long, Pusa Purple Round, SM 67, SM 68, Pant Samrat. Encourage the activity of larval parasitoids: *Pristomerus testaceus, Cremastus flavoorbitalis*. Release egg parasitoids: *Trichogramma chilonis* @1.0 lakh/ha. Spray *Bt* formulations of *B. thuringiensis* var.

kurstaki such as **Dipel** @ 1.5 to 2 ml/L of water. Avoid use of synthetic pyrethroids. Avoid using insecticides at the time of fruit maturation and harvest. Neem seed kernel extract (NSKE) 5 % or spray neem seed kernel extract 5 % or any one of the following chemicals starting from one month after planting at 15 days interval.

Insecticides	Dose	Insecticides	Dose
Azadirachtin 1.0% EC (10000 ppm)	3.0 ml/lit.	Phosalone 35 % EC	1.5 ml/lit.
Azadirachtin 0.03 % WSP (300 ppm)	5.0 g/lit.	Quinalphos 20 % EC	1.7 ml/lit.
Dimethoate 30 % EC	7.0 ml/10 lit.	Quinalphos 25 % EC	1.5 ml/lit.
Emamectin benzoate 5 % SG	4 g/10 lit.	Thiodicarb 75 % WP	2.0 g/lit.
Flubendiamide 20 WDG	7.5 g/10 lit.		

Source: *https://agritech.tnau.ac.in/crop_protection/brinjal/brinjal_1.html*

❑ Brinjal lace-wing bug: *Urentius sentis* Distant; *Urentius hystricellus* (Richter, 1869)

Common Name	:	Brinjal lace-wing bug; Tirgid bug
Scientific Name	:	*Urentius sentis* Distant; *Urentius hystricellus* (Richter, 1869)
Family	:	Tingidae
Order	:	Hemiptera

Source: *https://www.researchgate.net/figure/Urentius-hystricellus-20 mm_fig17_270898426*

Distribution and Host Range

The brinjal lace-wing bug is mainly found in South Asia, including countries like India, Bangladesh, Sri Lanka and Pakistan. However, its possible that its rang extends to other neighbouring regions as well.

The brinjal lace-wing primarily targets brinjal (egg plant) plants. It infests the fruits and shoots. Their specific host may vary depending on the species and location, but they are often found on tees, shrubs and herbaceous plants.

Nature and Symptoms of Damage

Lace bugs are usually host-specific and can be very destructive to plants. Most feed on the undersides of leaves by piercing the epidermis and sucking the sap. The then empty cells give the leaves a bronzed or **silvery appearance**.

Life History and Description

Each individual usually completes its entire lifecycle on the same plant, if not the same part of the plant. Most species have one to two generations per year, but some species have multiple generations. Most overwinter as adults, but some species overwinter as eggs or nymphs. This group has incomplete metamorphosis in that the immature stages resemble the adults, except that the immatures are smaller and do not have wings. However, wing pads appear in the second and third instars and increase in size as the nymph matures. Depending on the species, lace bugs have four or five instars.

Egg: White nibble shaped eggs.

Nymph: yellowish white with prominent spines.

Adult: Dorsal side -straw coloured. Ventral side—black coloured. Pronotum and forewings reticulated.

Management

Spray dimethoate 30 EC @ 1 lit/ha or methyl demeton 25 EC @ 1 lit/ha. Implanting crop rotation and maintaining clean farming practices. Encouraging natural enemies like ladybird beetles and parasitic wasps.

❑ Epilachna beetle: *Henosepilachna dodecastigma* (Wiedemann); *H. vigintioctopunctata* (Fabricius, 1775)

Common Name	:	Hadda/spotted beetle; Epilachna beetles
Scientific Name	:	*Henosepilachna dodecastigma* (7-14 spots on each elytra); *H. vigintioctopunctata* (28 spotted beetle)
Family	:	Coccinellidae
Order	:	Coleoptera

Source:*https://en.wikipedia.org/wiki/Henosepilachna_vigintioctopunctata*

As Described in Potato

❑ Brinjal stem borer: *Euzophera perticella* Ragonot, 1888

Common Name	:	Brinjal stem borer
Scientific Name	:	*Euzophera perticella* Ragonot, 1888
Family	:	Phycitidae
Order	:	Lepidoptera

Source: *http://insecta.pro/taxonomy/9735*

Distribution and Host Range

This species is known from India and Sri Lanka. Host range includes Chilli, tomato, brinjal and potato. The first infestation of this pest in eggplant was reported from **Hyderabad** by Rizvi and Sanyal (1977). It feeds mainly on brinjal but sometimes on other solanaceous plants, *viz.* tomato, potato and chilli. It is generally considered as a minor pest of eggplant.

Nature and Symptoms of Damage

Larva bores into main stem of young and old plants and move downwards. Top shoots of young plants crump and wither. Older plants become stunted. Fruit bearing capacity is adversely affected. There is a distinct thickening of stem at the entry point.

Life History and Description

Egg period: 10 days. Creamy and scale-like, laid singly/in batches on young leaves, petioles and branches.

Larva: 26-58 days. Fully grown larva is creamy white with few bristle-like hairs, 20 mm.

Pupa: Pupates within cocoon inside larval tunnel, 9-16 days.

Adult: Greyish brown, forewings with transverse line and white hindwings. Life cycle is completed in 35-76 days.

Management

Collect and destroy the damaged and dead plants. Use light traps @ 1/ha to attract and kill the moths. Conserve larval parasitoids *Pristomerus testaceus, P. euzopherae*. Spray any one of the insecticides starting from one month after planting at 15 days interval. Carbaryl 50 WP 2 kg + wettable sulphur 50 WP 2 kg, endosulfan 35 EC 1.5 L + neem oil 1.5 L, quinalphos 25 EC 1.5 L + neem oil 1.0 L, NSKE 5%, azadirachtin 1.0% 1.0-1.5 L or fenpropathrin 30 EC 250-340 ml or thiodicarb 75 WP 625-1000 g. Avoid using synthetic pyrethroids as they cause resurgence of sucking pests.

❑ Ash weevil: *Myllocerus subfasciatus* Guerin, 1843

Common Name	:	Ash weevils
Scientific Name	:	*Myllocerus subfasciatus* Guerin, 1843, *M. discolour* Schoenherr, 1826, *M. viridanus* Fabricius, 1775, *M. maculosus* Desbrochers des Loges, 1899
Family	:	Curculionidae
Order	:	Coleoptera

Source:https://www.cabidigitallibrary.org/doi/10.1079/cabicompendium.30965

Distribution and Host Range

Myllocerus subfasciatus, is a species of weevil found in India, and Sri Lanka. The Sri Lankan population was earlier identified as a separate species, *Myllocerus spurcatus*. Crop plants include potato, sweet potato, tomato, pepper, beans, peas, cucurbits, cotton and maize etc. where as ornamental plants include roses, marigold, petunia, dahlia, gerbera and chrysanthemum under host range. The distribution and host range for other species is scanty and not clear.

Nature and Symptoms of Damage

Adults are known to attack brinjal. Common symptom is notching of leaf margins. Grubs generally feed on roots causing wilting. Notching of leaf margins by adults. Grubs' feeds on roots resulting in wilting and death of plants.

Life History and Description

Adult weevil light greyish to white with four black spots on the elytral covers. Eggs are light yellow and are laid deep in the soil. Eggs take 3 to 11 to hatch. Grub is small, apodous fleshy, and yellow in colour. Grub period is about 3 to 42. The final instar pupates in soil in earthen cocoons. The pupation period is 5 to 7 days. 500 eggs in soil, 6-7 days. Grub: 30-45 days.

Pupa: Pupates in soil in earthern cocoons. **Adult:** 10-12 days. *M. subfasciatus*: Brown; *M. discolor*: Brown and white spots *M. viridanus*: Small light green weevil.

Management

Collect and destroy adult weevil. In endemic areas apply carbofuran 3G @ 15 kg/ha, 15 days after planting. Spray carbaryl 50 WP 2 kg + wettable sulphur 2 kg or malathion 50 EC 1.5 L carry to pearl millet.

❑ Brinjal Brown leafhopper: *Cestius phycitis* (Distant)

Common Name	:	Brinjal Brown leafhopper; Brinjal hopper
Scientific Name	:	*Cestius phycitis* (Distant)
Family	:	Cicadellidae
Order	:	Hemiptera

Source:*https://agritech.tnau.ac.in/crop_protection*

Distribution and Host Range

It is the most destructive pest in South Asia especially in Summer on brinjal which is next to shoot and fruit borer. High humidity favours the multiplication of leaf hopper. In India it is found in most of the states such as Andhra Pradesh, Assam, Bihar, Delhi, Gujarat, Haryana, Himachal Pradesh, Jammu & Kashmir, Karnataka, Kerala, Maharashtra, Meghalaya, Punjab, Tamil Nadu, Uttarakhand, Uttar Pradesh, West Bengal etc. It has a wide host range with brinjal as the major host.

Nature and Symptoms of Damage

It is a **vector of little leaf of brinjal**. Nymphs and adults suck cell sap from ventral side of leaf and inject toxins into the plant tissues and cause reduction in size of leaves, shortened petioles, excessive growth of branches general stunting of plants, conversion of floral parts into leafy structures and give the plants a bushy appearance. Initially the damage is noticed on old leaves with a yellowish green mosaic symptom followed by brown necrosis and curling along the leaf margin. When the incidence is severe, the necrotic spots coalesce forming brown patches.

Life History and Description

Female hopper lays about 15-20 eggs on ventral surface of leaf into the midrib or veins. On hatching, nymphs move along the veins and midrib. Eggs hatch in 4-11 days. The nymphal period occupies 7-21 days, adult lives for 7 days. Life cycle varies from 2 to 4 weeks. Adults are small, wedge shaped, light brown with a pair of black spots on vertex and on each of the forewings measuring around 3 mm long. Nymphs are pale greenish, almost translucent and walk diagonally. They are found between the veins of leaves on the under surface.

Management

Rogue out infested plants as soon as they appear in the field and completely destroy them. Before transplantation dip the seedlings in 0.2% carbosulfan 25 DS solution to control the insect vectors.

Spray 3-4 times at 10 days interval with methyl parathion 750 ml or dimethoate 500 ml or monocrotophos 500 ml or endosulfan 1.0 L or imidacloprid 125 ml in 500 -750 L of water/ha.

❑ Silvery leaf white fly: *Bemisia tabaci* (Gennadius, 1889)

Common Name	:	White fly; sweet potato white fly; Silvery leaf white fly
Scientific Name	:	*Bemisia tabaci* (Gennadius, 1889)
Family	:	**Aleyrodidae**
Order	:	Hemiptera

Source:https://www.eurekalert.org/multimedia/650418

As Described in Potato

❑ Two-spotted spider mite: *Tetranychus urticae* C.L. Koch, 1836

Common Name	:	Red spider mite; Two-spotted spider mite
Scientific Name	:	*Tetranychus urticae* C.L. Koch, 1836; *Tetranychus cinnabarinus* Boisduval
Family	:	Tetranychidae
Order	:	Trombidiformes

Source:https://www.cabidigitallibrary.org/doi/10.1079/cabicompendium.30965

As Described in Tomato

Resistant Varieties	
World	**India**
Florida Market: This brinjal variety is resistant to root-knot nematodes, which can cause significant damage to the roots of the plant. **Black Beauty:** Black Beauty is a popular variety that is known for its resistance to flea beetles, which can cause significant leaf damage and reduce plant growth. **Machi:** Developed in Bangladesh, Machi is resistant to shoot and fruit borer, which can cause significant damage to the fruit of the plant.	**Pusa Kranti:** Developed by the Indian Agricultural Research Institute, Pusa Kranti is resistant to shoot and fruit borer, as well as other pests like whitefly and aphids. **Arka Keshav:** Developed by the Indian Institute of Horticultural Research, Arka Keshav is resistant to both shoot and fruit borer and spider mites. **Pusa Purple Cluster:** This brinjal variety is resistant to shoot and fruit borer, as well as other pests like aphids and whitefly. **Arka Nidhi:** Developed by the Indian Institute of Horticultural Research, Arka Nidhi is resistant to shoot and fruit borer and has good yield potential. **Vaishali:** Vaishali is a variety that is resistant to shoot and fruit borer, as well as other pests like whitefly and aphids.

Pests of Okra

Scientific Name	*Abelmoschus esculentus* (L.)
Family	Malvaceae
Origin	West African, Ethiopian, Southeast Asian, and South Asian
Chromosome Number	2n = 130

Okra or **okro**, *Abelmoschus esculentus*, known in some English-speaking countries as **lady's fingers**, is a flowering plant in the mallow family. It has edible green seed pods. *Abelmoschus esculentus* is cultivated throughout the tropical and warm temperate regions of the world for its fibrous fruits or pods containing round, white seeds. It is among the most heat- and drought-tolerant vegetable species in the world and will tolerate soils with heavy clay and intermittent moisture, but frost can damage the pods.

In India, okra is an important vegetable crop, with a significant share in the country's horticulture production. According to the Ministry of Agriculture and Farmers Welfare, the area under okra cultivation in India was around 565 thousand hectares during the year 2020-21, with a total production of approximately 10.8 million tonnes. The productivity of okra in India during the same period was around 19.1 tonnes per hectare. On a global scale, okra is widely cultivated in tropical and subtropical regions. Okra is susceptible to several insect pests that can cause significant yield losses if not managed properly. Here are some of the common insect pests that attack okra.

❑ Shoot and fruit borer: *Earias vitella* Fabricius, 1794; *E. insulana* (Boisduval, 1833)

Common Name	:	Shoot and fruit borer
Scientific Name	:	*Earias vitella* Fabricius, 1794; *E. insulana* (Boisduval, 1833)
Family	:	Noctuidae
Order	:	Lepidoptera

Source: https://en.wikipedia.org/wiki/Earias_insulana

Distribution and Host Range

They are distributed across Pakistan, India, Sri Lanka, Bangladesh, Myanmar, Indonesia, New Guinea and Fiji. More abundant in South India than North India. They are oligophagus pests. They tend to be feeding on cotton, bhendi, hibiscus, holly hock and other malvaceous vegetables. ***Earias vittella***, an Asian "spotted bollworm", is a moth species in the family noctuidae. The species was first described by **Johan Christian Fabricius** in 1794. ***Earias insulana***, the Egyptian stemborer, Egyptian bollworm, spiny bollworm or cotton spotted bollworm, is a moth of the family noctuidae. The species was first described by **Jean Baptiste Boisduval** in 1833.

Nature and Symptoms of Damage

Larva bores into tender terminal shoots in the vegetative stage and flower buds, flowers and young fruits in the fruit formation stage. The damaged shoots droop, wither and dry up. The infested fruits present a deformed appearance and become unfit for consumption. Bore holes – plugged with excreta. Initially, the larva tunnels into the buds of their host plant. Later, the larva feeds on the bolls, which become brown and fall off. Secondary invasion by fungi and bacteria sometimes occurs.

Life History and Description

Egg period: 3-5 days. 385-400 eggs/female. Spherical, light bluish, green, crown shaped, laid singly on shoot tips, buds, flowers and fruits.

Larva: 10-17 days. Six instars.

Pupa: 6-10 days. Pupates in an inverted boat shaped cocoon. Pupation takes place in a felt-like cocoon, which is attached to dry leaves of the food plant or to plant debris on the ground. Typically, the pupal stage takes 9-15 days, but may extend to up to two months if development is delayed by low temperatures. The wingspan is 20-22 mm. Adults show strong seasonal polymorphism, depending on the temperature. Two distinct forms are present in some areas: a bright green summer form and a brownish-yellow autumn form.

	E. vitella	*E. insulana*
Larva	Brown, with longitudinal white stripes on dorsal side	Cream coloured body with orange dots on prothorax
Adult	Medium sized, head and thorax ochreous white	Adults are smaller than *E. vitella.* Head and thorax pea green in colour
	Forewings are pale white with a broad wedge shaped horizontal green patch in the middle. (or) 'V' shaped patch.	Forewings uniformly pale yellowish green.

Management

Grow resistant cultivars like AE 57, PMS 8, Parkins Long green, PKX 9275, Karnual Special. Collect and destroy infested shoots, buds, flowers and fruits. Remove the alternate hosts like *Hibiscus cannabinus*, *H. abelmoschus* and *Abutilon indicum* in the cropped area. Set up light traps to monitor the moths and their egg laying @ 12/ha. Set up pheromone traps @ 5/ha. Release egg parasitoid *T. chilonis* and larval parasitoid *Chelonus blackburnii*. Release first instar larvae of *Chrysoperla carnea* @ 1 lakh/ha. Spray *Bt* formulation such as dipel @ 2 g/lit. Spray carbaryl 50% WP 1 kg or endosulfan 35 EC or monocrotophos 36 WSC 1.0 L or NSKE 5% or azadirachtin 5% 400 ml or fenpropathrin 30 EC 250-340 ml or pyridalyl 10 EC 500-750 ml with 500 L-700 L water/ha.

Stem weevil: *Pempherulus affinis* Faust

Common Name	:	Stem weevil
Scientific Name	:	*Pempherulus affinis* Faust
Family	:	Curculionidae
Order	:	Coleoptera

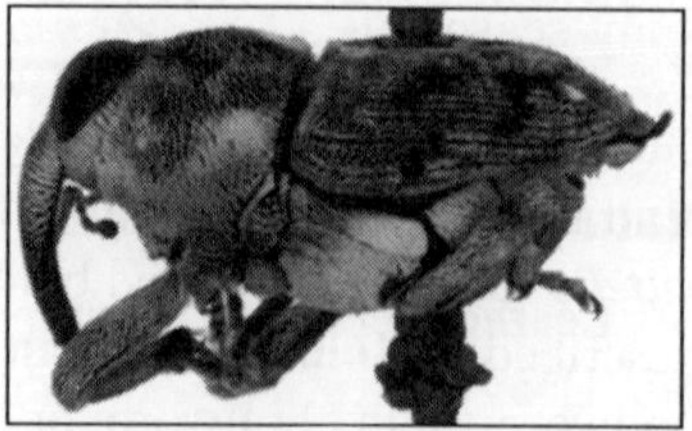

Source:https://agritech.tnau.ac.in/crop_protection/bendi/bendi_4.html

Distribution and Host Range

Distributed across India, Burma, Thailand and Philippines. It is of minor importance but assumes a key pest status in South India. Cotton, bhendi, jute, Indian abutilon, Chinese hibiscus, Kenaf and other malvaceous and tiliaceous plants.Cotton is the most preferred host.

Nature and Symptoms of Damage

This is an important pest of cotton, so the symptoms of damage are well studied in cotton. The damage to cotton starts when plants are young and are about three weeks old. The grubs bite into the region between the bark and the main stem, resulting in swellings on the stem just above the ground level. Young plants are invariably killed on account of the attack of the pest and the older plants that survive, lack vigour and strength, and when strong winds blow, these plants break at the nodes. In okra grubs bore into stem causing gall-like swellings in the stem, near the base.

Life History and Description

Adult is very small weevil measuring 1/8 of inch; dark in colour with two small white patches on the elytra. It lays globular or oval shaped eggs singly in the cavities scrapped out by the weevil at the nodal region of the plants. A female weevil lays an average of 50 eggs with a maximum of 121 eggs. The egg period is 6-10 days. Grub: white, apodous. The grub feeds on stem tissues internally. The larval period lasts 35-37 days. It pupates in pupal chamber. The adult may live for 25-30 days.

Management

Remove the infested plants and destroy as the hibernating adults acts as pests for next crop. Use resistant variety MCU 3 (cotton variety) in endemic areas. Apply carbofuran 3G at 10 kg/ha on 20 days after sowing and earthing-up. Apply farm yard manure at 25 t or 250 kg of neem cake/ha.

Leaf hopper: *Amrasca biguttula biguttula* (Ishida, 1912)

Common Name	:	Jassids/Leaf hopper
Scientific Name	:	*Amrasca biguttula biguttula* (Ishida, 1912)
Family	:	Cicadellidae
Order	:	Hemiptera

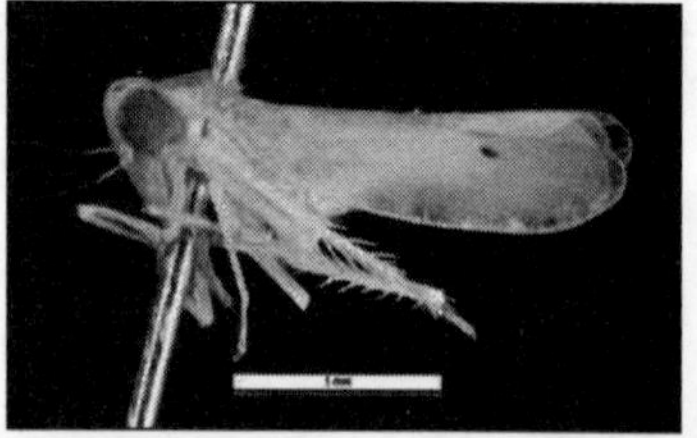

Source:https://www.invasive.org/browse/subthumb.cfm?sub=21559&country=155

Distribution and Host Range

In India, this jassid feeds on sap from a wide range of plants including cotton, okra, eggplant, Chinese hibiscus, and sunflower throughout the year, and on pigeon pea and cowpea during the monsoon season. In Burkina Faso, this jassid attacks cotton, okra, eggplant and hibiscus during the rainy season. It also occurs on various grasses, including lawns of Bermuda grass. It is a pest of cotton, okra, and other crops in Southern Asia and West Africa.

Nature and Symptoms of Damage

Leafhoppers have mouthparts designed for piercing and sucking, enabling them to feed on plant sap. Heavy infestations on cotton, okra, and sunflower make the leaves turn yellow, curl up and fall off. The insects also secrete honeydew, and sooty mould often grows on this, restricting the amount of light reaching the plant's photosynthetic surfaces and reducing the yield. In many areas, this pest regularly occurs on cotton in epidemic numbers.

Life History and Description

On okra, eggs are mainly oviposited inside the tissue of leaf blades, but may also be laid in leaf stalks or in soft twigs. The eggs hatch in six or seven days. There are five nymphal instars, developing over a period of about seven days. Nymphs are wingless. Total lifespan is about one month, with females living a little longer than males. The fecundity of females is about fifteen eggs. Adults are attracted to light, females more than males. The adult cotton jassid is a long and slender insect about 2.6 mm (0.1 in) in length. It is yellowish-green, with a conspicuous black spot on either side of the head and another near the tip of the fore wing. The head is pale green and the membranous wings transparent and iridescent. On leaf surfaces, the insect tends to move about diagonally, and when disturbed it immediately jumps and flies away.

Management

On cotton, it has been found that growing a cultivar with hairs on the undersides of the leaves reduces infestation, and that long hairs are better at deterring the insect from laying than are short hairs; this seems to be due to the hairs preventing the insect from getting close enough to the leaf surface to deposit its eggs. A number of natural enemies help to control populations including ladybirds, predatory lygaeid bugs, and several species of mantis. Entomophthoraceae fungus *Batkoa amrascae* is known to infect the cotton leafhopper, *Amrasca biguttula* in the Philippines. Neem oil can be used as a biopesticide. Treat 100 kg seeds with imidacloprid 48 FS 500-900 ml or imidacloprid 70 WS 500-1000 g or thiamethoxam 70 WS 285 g. Spray imidacloprid 70 WG 30-35 g or midacloprid 17.8 SL 100 ml or thiamethoxam 25 WG 100 g or azadirachtin 5% 400 ml or lambda cyhalothrin 5 EC 300 ml in 500 L water/ha.

❑ Cotton leaf roller: *Sylepta derogate; Haritalodes derogate* (Fabricius, 1775)

Common Name	:	Cotton leaf roller/Okra leaf roller
Scientific Name	:	*Sylepta derogate; Haritalodes derogate* (Fabricius, 1775)
Family	:	Crambidae
Order	:	Lepidoptera

Source:*https://agritech.tnau.ac.in/crop_protection/cotton/crop_prot_crop_insectpest%20_cotton_7.html*

Distribution and Host Range

Distribution is throughout South East Asia and it is considered as minor pest of okra. It is sometimes encountered in Europe, due to accidental import. Host plants includes cotton, okra, Indian abutilon and other malvaceous plants. The larvae feed on *Hibiscus* (including *H. cannabinus*, *H. esculentus*, *H. columnaris* and *H. rosa-sinensis*), *Pavonia*, *Gossypium*, *Anacardium occidentale*, *Sida*, *Glycine max*, *Zizyphus mauritiana* and *Zizyphus jujuba*. It was described by **Johan Christian Fabricius** in 1775.

Nature and Symptoms of Damage

Young larvae feed on epidermis on the under surface for two days later rolls the leaf in the form of trumpets and remains inside (**They roll the leaves of their host plant**). More than one larva can be seen inside the roll. It is fastened by silken threads on marginal portion. In severe cases, defoliation occurs.

Life History and Description

Egg: 2-4 days, green round. 250-300 eggs/female laid on the ventral surface of the leaves.

Larva: 2-3 weeks, glistening green with dark head.

Pupa: 6-12 days. Pupates within the roll or ground or fallen leaf. Adult is a medium sized cream coloured moth with wavy markings. The larvae are green with a dark brown head in early instars, but later becoming dark pink. Full-grown larvae reach a length of about 15 mm. Pupation takes place in the rolled leaf. Adults are pale brown with complex dark brown sinuous lines over each wing as shown in above image. The wingspan is 28-40 mm.

Management

Collect and destroy the rolled leaves as they contain the larval stages. Hand picking and destruction of grown-up caterpillars. Spray carbaryl 50 WP 2 Kg or phasolone 2.5 L in 1000 L of water/ha. Spray any one of the following insecticides: chlorpyriphos 20 EC 2.0 l/ha and dichlorvos 76 WSC 1.0 l/ha.

❑ Dusky cotton bug: *Oxycarenus hyalinipennis* (A. Costa, 1843)

Common Name	:	Dusky cotton bug/Cotton seed bug
Scientific Name	:	*Oxycarenus hyalinipennis* (A. Costa, 1843)
Family	:	Lygaeidae
Order	:	Hemiptera

Source:*https://www.inaturalist.org/photos/41641474*

Distribution and Host Range

This widespread species can be found in the Middle East, Africa, Asia, Europe, Central and South America. It is a polyphagous insect, and it has been documented as a prominent pest upon the following genera withinfamily Malvaceae: *Abutilon*, *Cola*, *Eriodendron*, *Gossypium*, *Malva*, *Sphaeralcea*, *Hibiscus*, *Pavonia*, *Sida*, *Dombeya*, *Sterculia* and *Triumfetta*. Of these, *Gossypium* appears to be the preferred host, but significant pest presence on okra has also been reported.

Nature and Symptoms of Damage

Adults as well as nymphs cause damage by sucking oil from mature seeds, and stored cotton may also be attacked. Additional damage may accrue during processing due to the lint becoming stained by crushed bugs. The pest may damage fruit trees by inducing greasy spots, which is due to sucking and excreting toxic saliva, and by disfiguring fruits with its faeces. In addition, the bugs congregate on walls of buildings without feeding, aggregations that emit an unpleasant odour and could be an urban nuisance.

Life History and Description

This species may have three to four generations per year. Females of these bugs lay about twenty eggs. This species goes through five nymphal stages. A generation lasts about twenty days. Each female lays 20-25 eggs, singly or in small groups on open or damaged cotton bolls and the emerging nymphs, which tend to aggregate, feed on the seeds and mate thereon. *Oxycarenus hyalinipennis* can reach a length of about 3.8 mm in males, of 4.3 mm in females. Therefore, males are slightly smaller than females. Body of these bugs is black with translucent wings. Head is black, with brownish-black antennae. The second antennal segment usually is partially pale yellow. Pronotum is blackish-brown. Corium is usually yellowish-whitish and hyaline. Femora are black, while tibiae are brown with a yellow-white band. Nymphs have pink to red abdomen.

Management

Inspection and removal of wild plants that grow around crops. UV light traps are placed for monitoring in areas where preferred host plants, like cotton or okra, are grown. Entomopathogenic fungi, like *Beauveria bassiana* and *Metarhizium anisopliae* have shown some promise. In Africa astigmatic mites were found on the bugs, which became sluggish and soon died; spiders were also reported to attack this pest. As the pest usually infests the boll or the leaf litter beneath the plant, effective pesticide applications are problematic. During outbreaks, control may be obtained with chemicals, like some organophosphates that have contact and systemic properties, applied early in the morning while the insects are less active.

❑ Red cotton stainer: *Dysdercus koenigii* (Fabricius, 1775); *D. cingulatus* (Fabricius, 1775)

Common Name	:	Red cotton stainer/Red cotton bug
Scientific Name	:	*Dysdercus koenigii* (Fabricius, 1775); *D. cingulatus* (Fabricius, 1775)
Family	:	Pyrrhocoridae
Order	:	Hemiptera

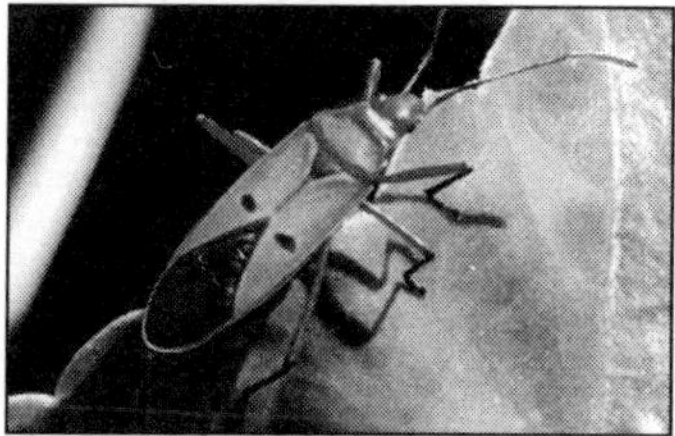

Source:https://inaturalist.nz/taxa/416652-Dysdercus-koenigii

Distribution and Host Range

D. cingulatus occurs in Nepal, Sri Lanka, North-eastern India, Bangladesh, Thailand, Philippines, Sumatra, Borneo, Papua New Guinea, Argentina, and Northern Australia. *Dysdercus koenigii* is commonly found in India, Pakistan and south-eastern Asia. As well as cotton, *D. cingulatus* feeds on a number of other crop plants including okra, muskmallow, hibiscus, white jute, citrus and maize. It also attacks trees including silk cotton tree, kapok, teak and the portia tree.

Nature and Symptoms of Damage

The adults and later stage instars feed on immature cotton bolls and on the developing and ripening seed. By their presence in the bolls, they admit fungi such as *Eremothecium gossypii* which indelibly stains the lint. Like other true bugs, *Dysdercus cingulatus* sucks fluids from its host plants. The only part of the cotton plant affected by this pest is the flower and the seed capsule or boll. As this develops, the insect thrusts its rostrum between the carpels and sucks fluids from the still soft seeds inside. Micro-organisms are admitted in the process and may make the boll contents rot or the lint become discoloured. Meanwhile, the seeds wither, the fibres may fail to expand and the boll may abort. When the seeds of a host plant ripen and it becomes unsuitable, the adult insects migrate to new host plants of the same or different species.

Life History and Description

The female *D. koenigii* usually lays three batches of seventy or eighty eggs in damp soil, under plant litter or in crevices. The eggs are oval and creamy-yellow, and take about six days to hatch. The nymphs pass through five instar stages and become winged adults after fifty to sixty days. The adults survive for a few weeks and there are several generations throughout the year. The adults and later stage instars feed on immature cotton bolls and on the developing and ripening seed. The nymphs moult five times as they grow. The first and second instar nymphs are orange/red, and the third instar has emerging wing pads and is orange at first, deepening in colour by the second day. The fourth instar is crimson and cylindrical with larger, darker wing pads and the fifth instar is similar, with prominent dark wing pads, black antennae and legs. The adult insect is also crimson, with a pair of black spots on the forewings. The membranous hind wings are concealed under the forewings when the insect is at rest. Males are about 14 mm (0.6 in) in length and females are a little larger.

D. cingulatus grows to a length of 12 to 18 mm (0.47 to 0.71 in). It is mainly red but has a white collar and three black spots. It is closely related and very similar to *D. koenigii* but *D. cingulatus* is slightly larger and the femora have varying amounts of black while *D. koenigii* has completely red femora.

Management

Remove debris and ratoon cotton. Avoid planting crops near other possible host plants. Planting cotton annually, if crops are maintained all year round, it increases the chance for cotton stainer populations to persist. Predatory bugs such as *Harpactor costalis* also found to be predating over red cotton bugs. Application of imidacloprid 6% + lambda Cyhalothrin 4% SL (Inovexia) @ 500 ml/ha at fortnightly interval. Spray insecticides like profenophos 50 EC @ 2 ml/l or chloropyriphos 20 EC @ 2 ml/l or acephate 1 g/l. Spray phosphamidon 40 SL @ 600 ml/ha.

❑ Okra Capsule Borer: *Helicoverpa armigera* (Hübner, [1808])

Common Name	:	Fruit borer, Cotton bollworm, Corn earworm, Old World bollworm, Capsule borer (or) Bhendi fruit borer
Scientific Name	:	*Helicoverpa armigera* (Hübner, [1808])
Family	:	Noctuidae
Order	:	Lepidoptera

Source:*https://www.cabidigitallibrary.org/doi/10.1079/cabicompendium.26757*

As Described in Tomato

Silvery leaf white fly: *Bemisia tabaci* (Gennadius, 1889)

Common Name	:	White fly, sweet potato white fly or Silvery leaf white fly
Scientific Name	:	*Bemisia tabaci* (Gennadius, 1889)
Family	:	**Aleyrodidae**
Order	:	Hemiptera

Source: *https://www.eurekalert.org/multimedia/650418*

As Described in Potato

Two-spotted spider mite: *Tetranychus urticae* C.L. Koch, 1836; *Tetranychus cinnabarinus* Boisduval

Common Name	:	Red spider mite; Two-spotted spider mite
Scientific Name	:	*Tetranychus urticae* C.L. Koch, 1836; *Tetranychus cinnabarinus* Boisduval
Family	:	Tetranychidae
Order	:	Trombidiformes

Source: *https://www.cabidigitallibrary.org/doi/10.1079/cabicompendium.30965*

As Described in Tomato

Resistant Varieties	
World	**India**
Clemson Spineless: This okra variety is known for its resistance to root-knot nematodes, which can cause significant damage to the roots of the plant. **Louisiana Green Velvet:** Developed in Louisiana, this okra variety is resistant to several pests, including root-knot nematodes, aphids, and stink bugs. **Emerald**: Emerald is a popular variety that is known for its resistance to flea beetles, which can cause significant leaf damage and reduce plant growth.	**Parbhani Kranti:** Developed by the Vasantrao Naik Marathwada Agricultural University, Parbhani Kranti is resistant to pests like shoot and fruit borer and aphids. **Varsha Uphar:** Developed by the Indian Agricultural Research Institute, Varsha Uphar is resistant to pests like shoot and fruit borer, aphids, and whitefly. **Arka Anamika:** Developed by the Indian Institute of Horticultural Research, Arka Anamika is resistant to pests like shoot and fruit borer, spider mites, and whitefly.

5 Pests of Chilli

Scientific Name	*Capsicum annuum*
Family	Solanaceae
Origin	Modern-day Bolivia; East-central Mexico
Chromosome Number	2n = 24

Chili peppers from Nahuatl *chīlli* are varieties of the berry-fruit of plants from the genus *Capsicum*, which are members of the nightshade family Solanaceae, cultivated for their pungency. Chili peppers are widely used in many cuisines as a spice to add "heat" to dishes. Capsaicin and related compounds known as capsaicinoids are the substances giving chili peppers their intensity when ingested or applied topically. *Capsicum* plants originated in modern-day Bolivia and have been a part of human diets since about 7,500 BC. Chili peppers spread to Asia through their introduction by Portuguese traders, who—aware of their trade value and resemblance to the spiciness of black pepper—promoted their commerce in the Asian spice trade routes. They were introduced in India by the Portuguese towards the end of the 16th century.

In India, chili is one of the most important spice crops and is widely cultivated in several states. According to the Ministry of Agriculture and Farmers Welfare, the area under chili cultivation in India was around 824 thousand hectares during the year 2020-21, with a total production of approximately 3.4 million tonnes. The productivity of chili in India during the same period was around 4.2 tonnes per hectare. On a global scale, chili is widely cultivated in several countries, with the largest producers being China, Mexico, and Peru. Chilli is susceptible to several insect pests that can cause significant yield losses if not managed properly. Here are some of the common insect pests of chilli and their potential yield losses:

❑ Chilli thrips: *Scirtothrips dorsalis* Hood, 1919

Common Name	:	Chilli thrips; Yellow tea thrips
Scientific Name	:	*Scirtothrips dorsalis* Hood,1919
Family	:	Thripidae
Order	:	Thysanoptera

Source: *https://en.wikipedia.org/wiki/Scirtothrips_dorsalis#/media/File:Sd_adult_spread.jpg*

Distribution and Host Range

It is an extremely successful invasive species of pest-thrips. In India, it has been described as a pest of castor, pepper, cotton, tea, mango, and peanut. Outside of India, it has been reported as pest in China on tea and fruits like litchi, in Taiwan on citrus and vegetable, on citrus and tea in Japan, many vegetable and fruit crops in Thailand, peppers and mango in Vietnam, and even seasonally on the Korean peninsula.

Nature and Symptoms of Damage

The characteristic feeding damage of *S. dorsalis* was recognized as **"Murda disease"** on chili long before the thrips was associated with and then determined to be the cause of the blight. Prolonged feeding by thrips curls tender leaves and buds, and will turn fruits and flowers from bronze to black in color, rendering the plant material unmarketable. Even slightly damaged or scarred vegetables or inflorescences are often viewed as unmarketable, and these damaged commodities will fetch a lower price, reducing a grower's return on their investment. Insects feeding in new growth limits and stunts overall plant growth, and may induce abortion of fruit. When thrips feed in high enough densities, or in sufficiently dry climates, this process results in the eventual desiccation and death of their host plant. Even low densities of thrips can contribute to the decline in fruit production and plant health, especially during times of drought. *S. dorsalis* has been implicated in the transmission of several separate **tospoviruses**, but recent experiments have cast some doubt on the efficiency at which *S. dorsalis* actually transmits the virus to its hosts. It may be a member of a class described in a near relative, *Thrips palmi* : an infected non-transmitter with detectable levels of virus.

Life History and Description

S. dorsalis undergoes two nymphal stages followed by two "false" pupal stages, and under optimal conditions, this thrips may reach adulthood in approximately two weeks. Nymphs cntering the metamorphic process drop off of the plant during the first of two pre-pupal stages, and then complete their development in loose soil or leaf litter at the base of their host – but have been observed to pupate in any dark and humid crevice low on the plant, including bark and the folds of tightly packed lower leaves or flowers. The pupal process can range from two days to a full week. Post-emergence, females have a pre-oviposition period of one to two days. Using their ovipositor, females lay single eggs within the plant tissue, and may lay an average of forty eggs during their lifetime. Females of *S. dorsalis* prefer to lay their eggs inside of young leaves and buds at the apical meristem of plants, but as populations increase, they will lay their eggs under the surface of mature leaves.

Management

Grow resistant varieties like G5, K2, X235. Inter crop with a green manure crop *Sesbania grandiflora* to provide shade which regulate the thrips population. Do not grow chilli after sorghum – more susceptible to thrips. Do not follow chilli and onion mixed crop as both the crops are attacked by thrips. Sprinkle water over the seedlings to check the multiplication of thrips.

Entomopathogenic fungi are an emerging control method being used against a variety of insects, including chilli thrips. *Beauveria bassiana* and *Metarhizium* pp. have both attracted research for this use. Multiple such products are available for use in Asian countries. Only one *Beauveria bassiana* product is registered as an insecticide in the United States. Encourage the activity of **predaceous thrips**: *Scolothrips indicus* and *Franklinothrips megalops* in the field. Conserve predators such as predatory mite (*Amblyseius swirskii*), insidious flower bugs (*Orius insidiosus*) etc. Apply neem cake to the beds @ 100 kg/acre in two split doses at the time of planting and 30 days after transplanting.

Only the insecticides spinosyn and abamectin are known to be effective against this pest. Neem based products are considered effective synergists. Systemic neonicotinoids such as imidacloprid were once considered to be sparing of beneficial insects and natural predators, and recommended for integrated pest management of chilli thrips, especially when used as a soil soak or drip irrigation product. The past decade has revealed that neonicotinoids can seriously impact beneficial insects, especially bees, through effects that are not immediately apparent – even at trace concentrations

❑ Yellow mite: *Polyphagotarsonemus latus* (Banks, 1904)

Common Name	:	Muranai mite/Broad mite/yellow mite
Scientific Name	:	*Polyphagotarsonemus latus* (Banks, 1904)
Family	:	Tarsonemidae
Order	:	Acarina

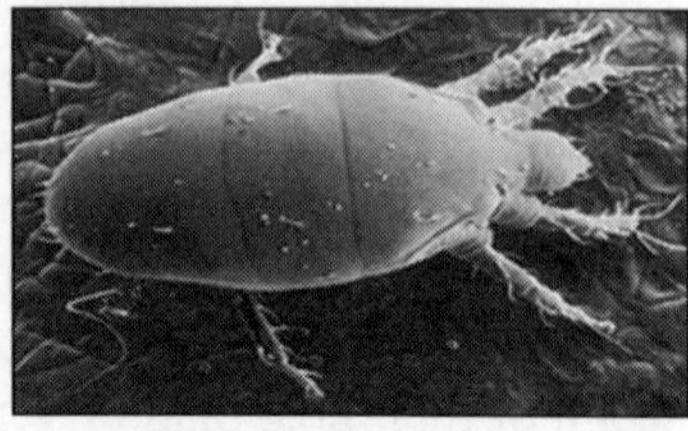

Source:https://en.wikipedia.org/wiki/Polyphagotarsonemus_latus*

Distribution and Host Range

The **broad mite**, *Polyphagotarsonemus latus*, is a microscopic species of mite found on many species of plants, including important agricultural species such as grapes, apples, and other fruits. Broad mites are also currently affecting cannabis plants, as the industry matures with legalization. The mites are found in many areas throughout the world and are major pests in greenhouses.

Nature and Symptoms of Damage

P. latus infestation can cause stunting and twisting of the leaves and flowers, and blackening and death of new growth. The damage resembles that caused by herbicides. The mites prefer areas of high humidity and low temperature. Sudden curling and crinkling of leaves followed by blister patches are initial symptoms of severely attacked plants. Petiole in a few cases becomes elongated and it is referred to **"rat tail"** symptom. Later they stop growing and die.

Life History and Description

The eggs are minute and oval in shape and are laid on the ventral surface of young leaves or on leaf buds. Larva has 3 pairs of legs move sluggishly. The adults measure 0.1 mm in length and bear 4 pairs of the legs. They are yellowish green in colour and translucent in nature. The egg, larval or nymphal and adult period occupies 1.5-2, 1-5 and 8-10 days, respectively.

Management

Chilli crop bordered by two rows of maize at every 0.5-acre area (31.2 × 60 sqm). Broad mite infestations can be controlled through the introduction of predatory mites, such as *Typhlodromips swirskii*, *Neoseiulus californicus*, or *N cucumeris*. Conserve the predators such as predatory mite (***Amblyseius ovalis***), predatory bug (***Orius* spp.**), spiders etc. If the incidence of mites is low, spray neem seed powder extract 4% at 10 days interval

They can be controlled by removing and destroying infested plants, and spraying with an acaricide. Spray dimethoate 30% EC @ 396 ml in 200-400 l of water/acre or emamectin benzoate 5%

SG @ 80 g in 200 l of water/acre or fenazaquin 10% EC @ 500 ml in 160-240 l of water/acre or fenpropathrin 30% EC @ 100-136 ml in 300-400 l of water/acre or fenpyroximate 5% EC @ 120-240 ml in 120-200 l of water/acre or milbemectin 1% EC @ 130 ml in 200 l of water/acre or propargite 57% EC @ 600 ml in 200-250 l of water/acre or spiromesifen 22.9% SC@ 160 ml in 200- 300 l of water/acre or chlorfenapyr 10% SC @ 300-400 ml in 200 l of water/acre or diafenthiuron 50% WP @ 240 g in 200-300 l of water/acre or ethion 50% EC @ 600- 800 ml in 200-400 l of water/acre or hexythiazox 5.45% W/W EC @ 120-200 ml in 250 l of water/acre or lambda-cyhalothrin 5% EC @ 120 ml in 160-240 l of water/acre or or oxydemeton-methy 25% EC @ 800 ml in 200-400 l of water/acre or phorate 10% CG @ 4000 g/acre or phosalone 35% EC @ 514 ml in 200-400 l of water/acre or quinalphos 25% EC @ 600 ml in 200-400 l of water/acre.

❑ Cotton aphid: *Aphis gossypii* Glover, 1877

Common Name	:	Chilli aphid; Cotton aphid; Melon aphid; Melon and cotton aphid
Scientific Name	:	*Aphis gossypii* Glover, 1877
Family	:	Aphididae
Order	:	Hemiptera

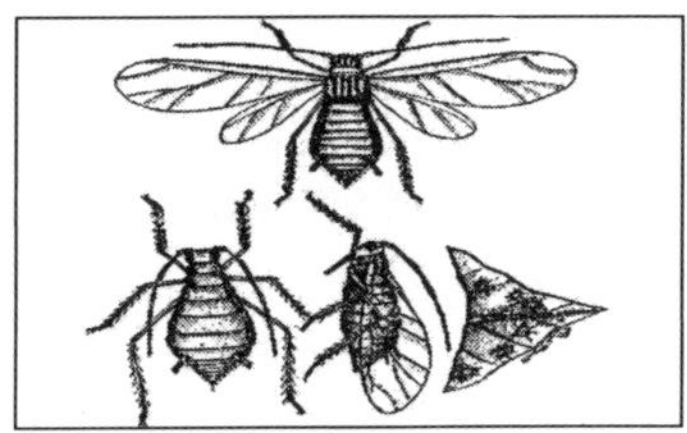

Source:*https://etc.usf.edu/clipart/30300/30359/aphis2_30359.htm*

Distribution and Host Range

It is not known where this species originated, but it is now found in tropical and temperate regions throughout the world except extreme Northern areas. It is common in North and South America, Central Asia, Africa, Australia, Brazil, East Indies, Mexico and Hawaii and in most of Europe. It is cosmopolitan in habitat. It is a widely distributed pest of a variety of agricultural crops in the families cucurbitaceae, rutaceae and malvaceae. The cotton aphid has a very wide host range with at least 60 host plants being known in Florida and perhaps 700 worldwide. Among cucurbit vegetables, it can seriously affect watermelons, cucumbers, cantaloupes, squash and pumpkin. Other vegetable crops attacked include **pepper**, eggplant, okra and asparagus. It also affects citrus, cotton and hibiscus.

Nature and Symptoms of Damage

The adults and nymphs of the cotton aphid feed on the underside of leaves or on the growing tips of shoots, sucking juices from the plant. The foliage may become chlorotic and die prematurely. There is often a great deal of leaf curling and distortion which hinders efficient photosynthesis. Honeydew is excreted by the aphids and this allows sooty moulds to grow, resulting in a decrease in the quantity and quality of the produce. The aphids are a vector of crinkle, mosaic, rosette, CTV and other virus diseases.

Life History and Description

Both winged and wingless forms breed parthenogenetically. The nymphal period lasts for 7-9 days. Adults live for 2-3 weeks and produce 8-22 nymphs per day. Entire life cycle takes 7-9 days. It has 12-14 generations per year. Adult are small succulent, pear-shaped soft bodied insects with prominent reddish eyes and cornicles at dorsal surface of the abdomen that vary in color from yellow to green to black. There are two forms; winged sexual forms (black patch on the back of the abdomen) and wingless forms. Nymphs are light yellowish green, or greenish black or brownish.

The wingless female cotton aphid has an ovoid body about two millimetres long in varying shades of green. The legs are yellow, as are the antennae which are three quarters of the length of the body. The apices of the femora, tibia and tarsi are black. The cylindrical black siphunculi are wide at the base and one fifth of the body length. The winged female has a fusiform body. Its head and thorax are black, the abdomen yellowish-green with black lateral spots and the antennae are longer than those of the apterous female. The nymphs vary in colour, being shades of green, tan and grey. They often have a dark head, thorax and wing pads and the distal portion of the abdomen is usually dark green. The body appears dull because it is dusted with wax secretions. The oval eggs are yellow when first laid but soon turn glossy black.

Management

Conserve parasitoids such as *Aphidius colemani*, *Diaeretiella* spp. *Aphelinus spp*. etc. Conserve predators such as anthocorid bugs/pirate bugs (*Orius* spp.), mirid bugs, syrphid/hover flies, green lacewings (*Mallada basalis* and *Chrysoperla carnea*), predatory coccinellids (*Stethorus punctillum*), staphylinid beetle (*Oligota* spp.), predatory cecidomyiid fly (*Aphidoletis aphidimyza*) and predatory gall midge, (*Feltiella minuta*), earwigs, ground beetles, rove beetles, spiders, wasps etc. Seed treatment with imidacloprid 70% WS @ 400-600 g/100 kg seed. Apply fipronil 5% SC @ 320-400 ml in 200 l of water/acre or oxydemeton methyl 25% EC @ 640 ml in 200-400 l of water/acre or carbofuran 3% CG @ 13320 g/acre or carbosulfan 25% EC @ 320-400 ml in 200- 400 l of water/acre or phorate 10% CG @ 4000 g/acre or phosalone 35% EC @ 800 ml in 200-400 l of water/acre or quinalphos 25% GEL @ 400 g in 200-400 l of water/acre or quinalphos 25% EC @ 400 ml in 200-400 l of water/acre or quinalphos 1.5% DP @ 8000 g/acre. Alternate chemicals at 10 days interval till the end of aphid population

❑ Cotton bollworm: *Helicoverpa armigera* (Hübner, [1808])

Common Name	:	Fruit borer, Cotton bollworm, Corn earworm, Old World bollworm.
Scientific Name	:	*Helicoverpa armigera* (Hübner, [1808])
Family	:	Noctuidae
Order	:	Lepidoptera

Source: *https://www.cabidigitallibrary.org/doi/10.1079/cabicompendium.26757*

As Described in Tomato

❑ Tobacco caterpillar: *Spodoptera litura* (Fabricius, 1775)

Common Name	:	Tobacco caterpillar, Tobacco cutworm; Cotton leafworm; Leaf eating caterpillar
Scientific Name	:	*Spodoptera litura* (Fabricius, 1775)
Family	:	Noctuidae
Order	:	Lepidoptera

Source: *https://apps.lucidcentral.org/pppw*

As Described in Potato

❑ Root-knot nematode: *Meloidogyne* spp. Goldi

Common Name	:	Root-knot nematode
Scientific Name	:	*Meloidogyne* spp. Goldi
Family	:	Heteroderidae
Order	:	Tylenchida

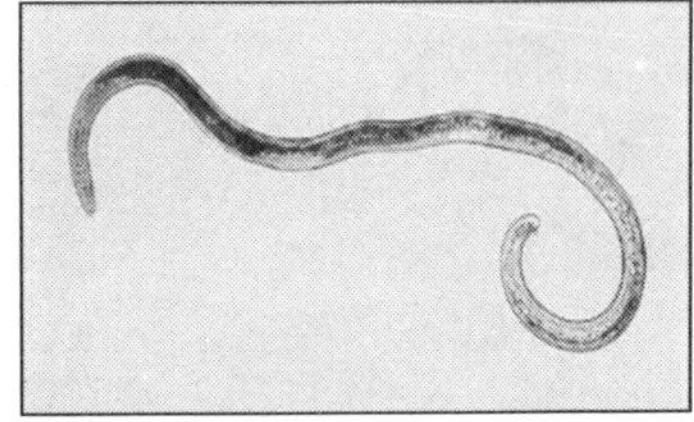

Source: *https://content.ces.ncsu.edu/management-of-root-knot-nematodes-in-bedding-plants*

As Described in Tomato

❑ Two-spotted spider mite: *Tetranychus urticae* C. L. Koch, 1836; *T. cinnabarinus* Boisduval

Common Name	:	Red spider mite; Two-spotted spider mite
Scientific Name	:	*Tetranychus urticae* C. L. Koch, 1836; *Tetranychus cinnabarinus* Boisduval
Family	:	Tetranychidae
Order	:	Trombidiformes

Source: *https://www.cabidigitallibrary.org/doi/10.1079/cabicompendium.30965*

As Described in Tomato

Resistant Varieties	
World	**India**
Ancho 211: This chilli pepper variety is known for its resistance to the tobacco thrips, which can cause significant damage to the plant.	**Pusa Sadabahar:** Developed by the Indian Agricultural Research Institute, Pusa Sadabahar is resistant to pests like the chili thrips and the fruit borer.
Serrano del Sol: Developed in Mexico, this chilli pepper variety is resistant to several pests, including aphids, spider mites, and thrips.	**Punjab Lal:** Developed by the Punjab Agricultural University, Punjab Lal is resistant to pests like the fruit borer and the leaf curl virus.
CM-334: Developed in Thailand, this chilli pepper variety is resistant to pests like the chili fruit borer, which can cause significant damage to the fruit.	**Manikya:** Developed by the Indian Institute of Horticultural Research, Manikya is resistant to pests like the chili thrips and the fruit borer.

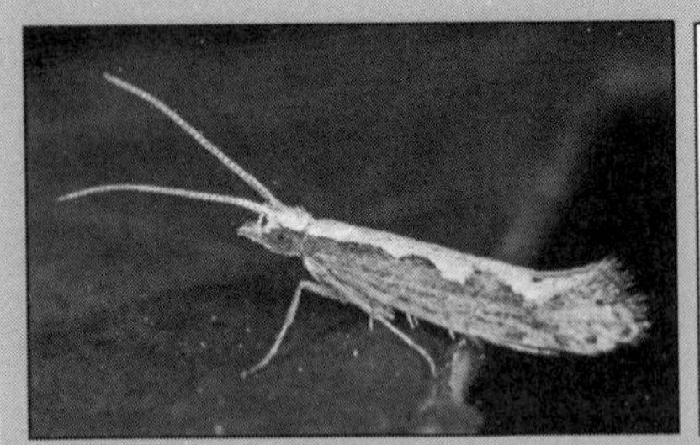

Pests of Cole Crops

Scientific Name	Cauliflower: *Brassica oleracea* var. *botrytis*; Cabbage: *Brassica oleracea* var. *capitata*; Broccoli: *Brassica oleracea* var. *Italica*; Brussels Sprouts: *Brassica oleracea* var. *Gemmifera*; Kale: *Brassica oleracea* var. *Acephala;* Kohlrabi: *Brassica oleracea* var. *Gongylodes*
Family	Cruciferae
Origin	Cabbage and kales originated in Western Europe; cauliflower and broccoli came from the Mediterranean region
Chromosome No.	2n = 18

Cole crops, also known as Brassica vegetables, are a group of vegetables that belong to the family Brassicaceae. They are characterized by their large, leafy heads and include several popular vegetables such as cabbage, broccoli, cauliflower, kale, and Brussels sprouts. These vegetables are known for their nutritional benefits, being rich in vitamins, minerals, and dietary fiber. They also contain compounds such as glucosinolates, which have been shown to have anti-inflammatory and anti-cancer properties. Cole crops are cool-season crops and are typically grown in the fall or spring when temperatures are mild. They are also able to tolerate frost and can be grown in colder regions. Many of these vegetables are also biennial, meaning they require two growing seasons to complete their life cycle, although they are typically harvested in their first year of growth.

Here's an overview of the area, production, and productivity of some common Cole crops in India and worldwide:

Cabbage: In India, cabbage is mostly grown in the northern states such as Punjab, Haryana, and Uttar Pradesh. According to the Ministry of Agriculture and Farmers Welfare, the area under cabbage cultivation in India was around 63.7 thousand hectares during the year 2020-21, with a total production of approximately 1.9 million tonnes. The productivity of cabbage in India during the same period was around 30 tonnes per hectare.

Broccoli: In India, broccoli is mostly grown in the hilly regions of Himachal Pradesh and Uttarakhand. The area under broccoli cultivation in India is relatively small compared to other cole crops. According to the Ministry of Agriculture and Farmers Welfare, the area under broccoli cultivation in India was around 0.3 thousand hectares during the year 2020-21, with a total production of approximately 0.9 thousand tonnes. The productivity of broccoli in India during the same period was around 3 tonnes per hectare.

Cauliflower: In India, cauliflower is widely cultivated in several states, with the largest producer being Maharashtra. According to the Ministry of Agriculture and Farmers Welfare, the area under cauliflower cultivation in India was around 3.6 hundred thousand hectares during the year 2020-21, with a total production of approximately 10.7 million tonnes. The productivity of cauliflower in India during the same period was around 29.7 tonnes per hectare. On a global scale, China is the largest producer of cauliflower, followed by India.

Brussels sprouts: In India, Brussels sprouts are not commonly grown commercially. Data on the area, production, and productivity of Brussels sprouts in India is not readily available. On a global scale, the largest producers of Brussels sprouts are the United States and Belgium.

Cole crops are susceptible to several insect pests that can cause significant yield losses if not managed properly. Here are some of the common insect pests of Cole crops:

❑ Diamond back moth: *Plutella xylostella* (Linnaeus, 1758)

Common Name	:	Diamond back moth; Cabbage moth
Scientific Name	:	*Plutella xylostella* (Linnaeus, 1758)
Family	:	Plutellidae
Order	:	Lepidoptera

Source: *https://a-z-animals.com/animals/diamondback-moth/*

Distribution and Host Range

The species may have originated in Europe, South Africa, or the Mediterranean region, but it has now spread worldwide. Diamondback moths are considered pests as they feed on the leaves of cruciferous crops and plants that produce glucosinolates. The diamondback moth lays its eggs only on plants in the family Brassicaceae. Nearly all cruciferous vegetable crops are attacked, but some are favored over others. Larvae are attracted to the major component of this species-specific pheromone, which is **(Z)11-hexadecenal**.

Nature and Symptoms of Damage

DBM is the worst pest of *Brassicas* in the world, and an increasing problem in canola. Larvae damage leaves, buds, flowers, and seed buds of cultivated cruciferous plants. Although the larvae are small, they can be very numerous and cause complete removal of foliar tissue except for the leaf veins. This is damaging to young seedlings and may disrupt head formation in cabbage, broccoli, and cauliflower. The presence of larvae in florets can result in complete rejection of the produce. The feeding habit of the first instar is leaf mining, although they are so small, the mines are difficult to detect. The larvae emerge from these mines to moult and subsequently feed on the lower surface of the leaf. Their chewing results in irregular patches of damage, though the upper leaf epidermis is often left intact. These irregular patches are called **window panes**.

Life History and Description

Eggs: The eggs are oval and flattened, measuring 0.44 mm long and 0.26 mm wide. They are yellow or pale green at first, but darken later. They are laid singly or in groups of two to eight eggs in depressions on the surface of leaves. Females may deposit up to 300 eggs in total, but average production is probably half that amount. The larvae emerge from the eggs in about six to seven days. Larvae: The larvae have four instars, each with an average development time of about four days. The larval body form tapers at both ends. The larvae have a few short black hairs and are colourless in the first instar, but pale or emerald green with black heads in later instars. Of the five pairs of prolegs, one protrudes from the posterior end, forming a distinctive "V". The larvae are quite active, and when disturbed, may wriggle violently, move backward, and spin a strand of silk from which to dangle.

Pupa: The yellowish pupae are about 8 mm long and are wrapped in a loose silk cocoon. They are usually found on the lower or outer leaves of the food plant, but on cauliflower and broccoli, pupation may occur in the florets. It is possible for a pupa to fall off of its host plant. The pupal stage lasts on average for about eight days, but ranges from five to fifteen days. Before emergence occurs, pupa will turn from a yellowish color to a brown color.

Adult: The lifespan averages three to four weeks for females, but less for males. Diamondback moths overwinter as adults among field debris of cruciferous crops, and active adults may be seen during warm periods at any time during the winter in temperate areas. Moths are active usually at twilight and at night, feeding on flowers of cruciferous plants, but they also fly in the afternoon during mass outbreaks.

Management

Remove and destroy all debris and stubbles after harvest of crop. Grow mustard as trap crop at 2:1 ratio (cabbage: mustard) to attract DBM for oviposition at least 10 days ahead of planting of main crop. Pheromone traps @12/ha. Crop rotation with cucurbits, beans, peas, tomato and melon. Blue-light traps can catch a lot of adult diamondback worms. Larval parasitoid: *Diadegma semiclausm* @1,00000/ha (Hills–below 25-27°C) *Cotesia plutellae* (plains) at 20000/ha release from 20 days after planting. *Bacillus thuringiensis var kurstaki* 2 g/lit. Common enemies of the moth include the parasitoids *Trichogramma chilonis* and *Cotesia plutella* and the predator *Chrysoperla carnea*, a lacewing. Lacewings feed on eggs and young larvae, while the parasitoids attack the eggs. These organisms can recognize diamondback sex pheromones, larval frass odors, and green leaf volatiles emitted from cabbage. Spray mustard crop with dichlorvos 76 WSC 0.076% to avoid dispersal of the larvae. Neem seed kernel extract 5%. Cartap hydrochloride 0.5% at 10, 20 and 30 DAS (nursery) and primordial stage. The diamondback moth was the first insect found to have become resistant to biological control by the *Bt* toxin (from *Bacillus thuringiensis*) in the field.

❑ Cabbage head borer: *Hellula undalis* (Fabricius, 1794)

Common Name	:	Cabbage head borer; cabbage webworm; Old World webworm
Scientific Name	:	*Hellula undalis* (Fabricius, 1794); *H. rogatalis* (Hulst, 1886)
Family	:	Crambidae
Order	:	Lepidoptera

Source: *https://plantwiseplusknowledgebank.org/doi/10.1079/PWKB.Species.27375*

Distribution and Host Range

It is a widespread species which is found from Europe across Asia to the Pacific. It was first described from Italy. The larvae feed on a wide range of plants, mainly of the family Brassicaceae. Recorded food plants include broccoli, crucifers, head cabbage, Chinese cabbage, spoon cabbage, daikon radish, horseradish, mustard, radish and turnip.

Nature and Symptoms of Damage

It is considered a serious agricultural pest. The larvae initially bore into the stem of growing shoots, later instars mine the leaves and leaf stems. It makes a web of silk around the feeding area which accumulates frass. The larva webs the leaves and bore into the stem, stalks or leaf veins.

Life History and Description

The caterpillar is 12-15 mm long and is whitish with pinkish-brown longitudinal stripes. The wingspan is about 18 mm. and adult moths have fawn forewings, each with sinuous pale lines and a kidney-shaped mark. The hindwings are a uniform grey darkening at the margins. Pupation occurs within this silken shelter. The pupa is formed in a loose cocoon of webbed-together particles of soil or other matter and is about 8 mm long, shining pale brown with a dark stripe on the back.

Management

Collect and destroy mechanically caterpillars in the early stages of attack. Regular examinations of young plants in nurseries and after transplanting, looking for the larvae, their webs, frass and any damage symptoms. Male activity can be determined in the field by using a sticky trap baited with two laboratory-reared one-day old virgin females. Uprooting and burning of any cabbage and other related plant debris, and crop rotation. Protecting seedling beds and greenhouses with close mesh nets or screens. Parasitoids of the families Braconidae and Ichneumonidae attacked the pest in Malaysia, as well as the ant *Solenopsis geminate* (F.). Infection with a microsporidium caused 80% mortality in the laboratory. Carbamates and organophosphates controlled the moth when applied at first pest appearance on plants. The moth was highly sensitive to various *Bacillus thuringiensis* formulations. *B. thuringiensis* @ 2 g/lit at primordial stage. Cartap hydrochloride @ 500 g/ha or malathion 50 EC @500 ml/ha

❑ Leaf Webber: *Crocidolomia binotalis* Zeller, 1852

Common Name	:	Leaf Webber
Scientific Name	:	*Crocidolomia binotalis* Zeller, 1852; *Crocidolomia pavonana* (Fabricius, 1794)
Family	:	Crambidae
Order	:	Lepidoptera

Source: *https://en.wikipedia.org/wiki/Crocidolomia_pavonana*

Distribution and Host Range

This pest is widely distributed in Burma, Sri Lanka and India. In India it is distributed throughout the country. It is a serious pest of cabbage in India. It also infests radish, mustard, turnip and other crucifers. The species was first described by **Johan Christian Fabricius** in 1794.

Nature and Symptoms of Damage

Damage is caused mainly by the caterpillars. The caterpillars form silken web around the leaves. They feed upon the leaves making them completely skeletonised. They also feed on flower buds and bore into pods. They make the vegetable inconsumable by failing with excreta. If the apical meristem is damaged, multiple heads may be produced or the plant may die. The larvae from a single egg cluster can destroy a whole cabbage or cauliflower plant.

Life History and Description

After copulation the female moth laid eggs on the lower surface of the leaves. The eggs are laid in masses of 40-100. Larvae hatch out from the eggs in 5-15 days, depending upon the season. The larvae are gregarious in nature and feed on leave surface. Larval period lasts for 24-27 days in summer and 50-52 days in winter. The larva is green in colour when fully grown measures about 2 cms in length. It pupates inside the soil by making an earthen cocoon around itself. The adult moth bears pale yellow-coloured fore wings with ferruginous (iron rust) markings and tuft of hairs. The larva is green coloured with median and lateral white strips. The prothoracic shield of larva is black. It has also been found to pupate by making cocoon within the webbed-up leaves and flowers of the host plant. The pupal period lasts for 14-40 days depending upon season. During summer the development occurs rapidly.

Management

The adult moth can be killed through light traps. Remove and destroy the webbed leaves with caterpillars within. The larvae are parasitized by hyperparasites like *Diplazon orientalis* (cam.), *Apanteles crocidolomia* (Ahmed.), *Microbracon melleus* (Pam.) *Plexorista solennis* (Walk.) etc. Encourage the activity of parasitoid: *Cotesia crocidolomiae*. Several parasitoids are known to attack the larvae of this moth in different parts of its range. These include braconid wasps and tachinid flies, and in India the larvae are preyed on by a predatory bug in the family Pentatomidae. Application of non-residual insecticides like malathion, monocrotophos and quinalphos is preferred.

❑ Cabbage looper: *Trichoplusia ni* (Hübner, 1800–1803)

Common Name	:	Cabbage looper
Scientific Name	:	*Trichoplusia ni* (Hübner, 1800-1803)
Family	:	Noctuidae
Order	:	Lepidoptera

Source: *https://entnemdept.ufl.edu/creatures/veg/leaf/cabbage_looper.htm*

Distribution and Host Range

The cabbage looper can be found across North America and Eurasia, as far South as Florida and as far North as British Columbia. The cabbage looper can be found from England to South-eastern Europe. The cabbage looper is a generalist insect that can reside and feed on over 160 host plants. The cabbage looper's preferred hosts are crucifers such as cabbage and broccoli, because it grows faster on these plants, possibly due to nutritional or chemical differences. Tobacco can also be a host for the cabbage looper. However, it is not preferred because gummosis, a gummy substance produced by some plants, and trichomes, hair-like appendages, harm early larvae survival. Older larvae are more resistant to these defences. The cabbage looper is a member of the family noctuidae, **one of the largest families in Lepidoptera**. It is related to other vegetable pests, like the cutworm and armyworms.

Nature and Symptoms of Damage

Similar to the diamondback moth, the cabbage looper is one of the most problematic cabbage pests. The larvae eat large holes in the underside of leaves and consume developing cabbage heads. In addition, they leave behind sticky frass, contaminating the plants. They also consume the leaves of myriad host plants beyond cabbages. Although it is a damaging pest, the cabbage looper can be tolerated. For example, plant seedlings can endure the cabbage looper. However, the cabbage looper becomes more problematic once the plant begins heading.

Life History and Description

Egg: The cabbage looper eggs are generally yellow-white in color, dome-shaped, and patterned with ridges. They are 0.6 mm in diameter and 0.4 mm in height, and they are usually laid singly on the underside of leaves. In one day, 40-50 females can lay 1000-2000 viable eggs. Viable eggs hatch after about three days, while unviable eggs fail to develop and collapse within that period. Eggs are mostly found on leaves that are both larger and higher on the plant. It is not clear why eggs are preferentially laid on these leaves.

Larva: Cabbage looper larvae are a type of cabbage worm, green in colour with a white stripe on the side. After hatching, they are green and slightly hairy, but eventually turn green and lose the hair, leaving only a few bristles. They are identified by their looping behaviour, in which they arch their body in a loop when they crawl. Larvae are generally 3-4 cm long, and can have four to seven instars within 9-14 days. Larvae initially do not consume much food but increase their consumption during their lifetime until they are consuming three times their weight daily.

Pupa: When they pupate, they attach to the undersides of leaves and form a silky cocoon. This stage can last 4-13 days, depending on the temperature of the environment. Male pupae are slightly larger than female.

Adult: The adult form is a moth with gray-brown front wings and light brown back wings. It is about 2.5 cm long and has a wingspan of 3.8 cm. Because they are nocturnal, adults spend their days protected by their host plants and begin activity 30 minutes before sunset. Males can be distinguished from females by light brown hairs that lie flat against their abdomen. Mating occurs 3 or 4 days after metamorphosis, during which 300-1400 eggs are oviposited. From egg to adulthood, the cabbage looper's life cycle is generally 24-33 days long.

Management

The synthetic female pheromone has been used with black light traps to study cabbage looper populations in various regions of the US. Synthetic male pheromone has also been developed and was found to be effective in attracting and trapping both male and female cabbage loopers. The blend of male pheromones helped to trap females seeking mates and individuals seeking food. Hand pick and destroy the caterpillars. Set up light trap @1/ha. General predators like spiders, ants, and lady beetles' prey on cabbage looper eggs and larvae, removing 50% of the eggs and 25% of the larvae within three days. Lady beetles consume at the highest rate. Other common predators of cabbage looper larva include *Orius tristicolor, Nabis americoferus,* and *Geocoris pallens*. While the cabbage looper frequently encounters parasites, its most common parasite is the tachinid fly. Spray insecticides like malathion 50EC @ 0.1% ha. The moth is susceptible to viral diseases including *nucleopolyhedrovirus* (NPV). *Trichoplusia ni* is the only other insect to have developed resistance to *Bt* toxin in agricultural systems, specifically in greenhouses.

❑ Cabbage butterfly: *Pieris brassicae* (Linnaeus, 1758), *P. rapae* (Linnaeus, 1758)

Common Name	:	Cabbage butterfly; Cabbage white, Cabbage moth; Large cabbage white
Scientific Name	:	*Pieris brassicae, P. rapae* (Linnaeus, 1758)
Family	:	Pieridae
Order	:	Lepidoptera

Source: *https://stock.adobe.com/in/search?k=%22pieris+brassicae%22*

Distribution and Host Range

The large white is common throughout Europe, North Africa, and Asia to the Himalayas often in agricultural areas, meadows and parkland. The large white butterfly's habitat consists of large, open spaces, as well as farms and vegetable gardens, because of the availability of its food source. Some favoured locations include walls, fences, tree trunks, and often their food plant. They primarily hover around these locations, which should contain both wild and cultivated crucifer, as well as oil-seed rape, cabbages, and brussels sprouts.

Nature and Symptoms of Damage

The crops most susceptible to *P. brassicae* damage in areas in Europe are those in the genus *Brassica* (cabbage, mustard, and their allies), particularly brussels sprouts, cabbage, cauliflower, kohlrabi, rape, swede, and turnip. The attacks to crops are rather localized and can lead to 100% crop loss in a certain area. In addition, because of its strong inclination to migrate, adults may infest new areas that were previously free from attack. Because many of the host plants of *P. brassicae* are sold for consumption, damage by these butterflies can cause a great reduction of crop value. Larvae may also bore into the vegetable heads of cabbage and cauliflower and cause damage.

Life History and Description

Egg: The large white ova are pale yellow, turning darker yellow within twenty-four hours of being oviposited. A few hours prior to hatching, they become black, the shell more transparent, and the larvae visible within.

Larvae: Large white larvae experience four moultings and **five instars**. The first instar follows hatching of the egg into large white larvae. The larvae are a light yellow in colour with distinctive brown heads and have soft bodies. The larvae appear as if they are very hairy. Following a moulting, the larvae enter the second instar. They have **tubercles** covered with black hair. In the third instar, large white larvae display more activity. This instar is when the larvae are observed to eat voraciously, and cause significant amounts of damage to their host plant. At this point, they are observed to be more yellow in colour, studded with black dots. Following the third instar, the larvae go through the fourth instar, with similar appearances as the larvae of the third instar, but with more aggrandized size and feeding behaviour. The large white larvae are observed to be cylindrical, robust, and elongated by the fifth instar, yellow in colour and with bright colouration on their abdomen and thorax. They are also observed to have a grey and black head. This instar requires maximum food quality and quantity in order to aid in full development, otherwise the larva dies before becoming an adult butterfly.

Adults: For both males and females, the wings are white with black tips on the forewings. The female also has two black spots on each forewing. The underside of each wing is a pale greenish and serves as excellent camouflage when at rest. The black markings are generally darker in the summer brood. The large white butterfly's wingspan reaches 5 to 6.5 cm on average.

 Male	 Female
The upper side of the male is creamy white. The forewing is irrorated (sprinkled) with black scales at the base and along costa for a short distance. The apex and termen above vein 2 are more or less broadly black with the Inner margin of the black area containing a regular even curve.	The upper side of the female is similar to that of the male, but the irroration of black scales at the bases of the wings is more extended. The black area on apex and termen of forewing is broader, its inner margin less evenly curved. A conspicuous large, black spot also exists in the outer half of interspace 1 near the base of interspace 3.

Management

Collect and destroy caterpillars in the early stage of attack from field. Conserve parasitoids like *Cotesia glomeratus*. Biological control includes the introduction of *Apanteles glomerates*, which parasitises the larva of cabbage butterfly. Spray insecticides like quinalphos 25 EC @1000 ml. Crop spray with malathion (0.05%) or diazinon (0.02%) three weeks before harvesting can reduce the infestation of this pest.

❑ Cabbage aphid: *Brevicoryne brassicae* (Linnaeus, 1758)

Common Name	:	Cabbage aphid; Cabbage aphis; Mealy cabbage aphid
Scientific Name	:	*Brevicoryne brassicae* (Linnaeus, 1758)
Family	:	Aphididae
Order	:	Hemiptera

Source: *https://www.armuro.com/en/cabbage-aphid-pest-management/*

Distribution and Host Range

Brevicoryne brassicae, commonly known as the **cabbage aphid** or **cabbage aphis**, is a destructive aphid (plant louse) native to Europe that is now found in many other areas of the world.

The aphids feed on many varieties of produce, including cabbage, broccoli (especially), brussels sprouts, cauliflower and many other members of the genus *Brassica*, but do not feed on plants outside of the family Brassicaceae. The insects entirely avoid plants other than those of Brassicaceae.

Nature and Symptoms of Damage

Aphids feed by sucking sap from their host plants. They produce a sugary waste product called honeydew, which is fed on by ants. In turn, the ants provide the aphids with protection from natural enemies. Continued feeding by aphids causes yellowing, wilting and stunting of plants. Severely infested plants become covered with a mass of small sticky aphids, which can eventually lead to leaf death and decay. Cabbage aphids feed on the underside of the leaves and on the center of the cabbage head. They prefer feeding on young leaves and flowers and often go deep into the heads of brussels sprouts and cabbage.

Life History and Description

The egg stage is the overwintering stage of aphids. Generations are overlapping, with up to 15 generations during the crop season. The total life cycle duration ranges between 16 to 50 days depending on temperature. The life cycle is shorter at higher temperatures. In instances where eggs are not produced, the female gives birth to nymphs. Nymphs differ from adults in having less developed caudae and siphunculi. Adult cabbage aphids can take on two forms: winged and wingless. Wingless adults are 1/10 inches long, oval-shaped and appear grayish-green or grayish-white due to their waxy covering. On the upper abdominal surface, eight dark brown or black spots are located beneath the waxy coating.

The cabbage aphid is difficult to distinguish from the turnip aphid (*Lipaphis erysimi*). The cabbage aphid is 2.0 to 2.5 mm long and covered with a grayish waxy covering, but the turnip aphid is 1.6 to 2.2 mm long and has no such covering. Moreover, the cabbage aphid and green peach aphid can be confused when they are both found feeding on cabbage plants. However, they have distinguishing morphological characteristics. For instance, the cabbage aphid is waxy with short cornicles. On the other hand, the green peach aphid lacks a waxy covering, and has long cornicles. Apart from these, green peach aphids mainly attack cabbage before heading begins, but cabbage aphids may attack the crop at any stage.

Management

The field should be ploughed immediately after harvest to prevent the spread of aphids to other crops. It is important to rid the field and surrounding areas of any alternate host plants like mustards or other cruciferous weeds. Destruction of plant debris at the end of the season can help kill overwintering aphid eggs in temperate climates. Different varieties of cultivars have varying resistance to *B. brassicae*. For example, the cauliflower cultivar **'Smilla'** could be a good choice because it affects adult reproductive parameters. Install yellow sticky trap @12 no/ha to monitor "macropterous" adults (winged adult).

Diaeretiella rapae is a common wasp parasitoid of cabbage aphids. The parasitic wasp *D. rapae* lays eggs within half-grown nymphs and mummifies them, forming a light brown, hard shell around the aphid. Although *D. rapae* is a very common parasite it is not always effective in controlling aphids. Other controlling insects include ladybird beetles, syrphid fly larvae, and lacewing larvae.

Some insecticidal soaps may be effective in treating aphid infestations. Seed extract of the Chinaberry tree, leaf extract of peppermint, and seeds and leaf extract of flowering lantana have showed promising results against cabbage aphid. Spray any one of the following insecticides; azadirachtin 0.03% WSP (300 ppm) @ 5.0 g/lit, dimethoate 30% EC @ 6.0 ml/10 lit., malathion 50% EC @ 1.5 ml/lit, phosalone 35% EC @ 1.5 ml/lit. and quinalphos 25% EC @ 1.0 ml/lit.

❑ Mustard aphid: *Lipaphis erysimi* (Kaltenbach, 1843)

Common Name	:	Mustard aphid; Turnip aphid
Scientific Name	:	*Lipaphis erysimi* (Kaltenbach, 1843)
Family	:	Aphididae
Order	:	Hemiptera

Source: *https://www.cabidigitallibrary.org/doi/10.1079/cabicompendium.30965*

Distribution and Host Range

Originally a European species, the turnip aphid is now found in most parts of the world in tropical and temperate locations. Host plants include cabbage, cauliflower, broccoli, brussels sprouts, kale, kohlrabi, radish and turnip, as well as shepherd's purse, wild mustard and other cruciferous weeds. This aphid is found on older leaves of brassica plants and on the roots. It is one of several species of aphid to feed on brassicas; the cabbage aphid (*Brevicoryne brassicae*) feeds only on these plants, while the green peach aphid is found on many crops and plants including brassicas.

Nature and Symptoms of Damage

Clusters of nymph and adults may be seen on the tender leaves, flower, stocks and pods, both nymph and adults suck the sap from leaves, buds and pods. Sucking the cell sap and giving out honeydew. Plants remain stunted and sooty molds grow on the honeydew excreted by the insects. The infested leaves turn on yellowish pale and acquire a curly appearance and ultimately the flowers fail to form pods. Curling of infested leaves and at advanced stage plants may wither and die. The species can be a **vector** of at least ten plant viruses including cabbage black ringspot virus, radish mosaic virus, cauliflower mosaic virus and turnip mosaic virus.

Life History and Description

The turnip aphid is almost entirely viviparous, although eggs have occasionally been seen. The wingless females produce up to six offspring per day over a period of twenty to forty days, a total of eighty to one hundred young. Winged females are able to disperse to other plants, but produce fewer offspring. The wingless female is pale green or whitish green with two rows of dark bands on the thorax and abdomen which unite into a single band near the tip of the abdomen. The antennae are dark, the legs are pale with dark joints and the cornicles are pale with dark tips. The body is **faintly dusted with a white powder**. The winged female is a similar size and has a black head and thorax and a pale green abdomen with black bands near the tip and black patches on the sides. The antennae and legs are dark, and the cornicles are black at the base and yellowish towards the tips. Wingless males have occasionally been seen; these are smaller than the females and olive-green to brownish in colour.

Management

Set up yellow sticky trap to monitor aphid population. Destroy the affected parts along with the aphid population in the initial stage. Predatory bird *Motacilla cospica* will actively feed over aphids in February-March. Ladybird beetles *viz*., *Cocciniella septempunctata*, *Hippodamia variegata* and *Cheilomones vicina* are most effcient pradators of the mustard aphid. Adult beetle may feed an average of 10 to 15 adults/day. Several species of syrphid fly *i.e*., *Sphaerophoria* spp., *Eristallis* spp., *Metasyrphis* spp., *Xanthogramma* spp and *Syrphus* spp. are predating on aphids. The lacewing, *Chrysoperla carnea* predates on the mustard aphid colony. Spray the crop with one of the following in the flowering stage; oxydemeton methyl, dimethoate @ 625 1000 ml per ha. Spray the crop with one of the following insecticides in the aphid appearance; Imidacloprid 17.8% @ 0.25 ml/l, thiamethoxam 25 WG @ o.2 g/l, dimethoate 30EC @ 1 ml/l of water.

❑ Cabbage fly: *Delia radicum* (Linnaeus, 1758)

Common Name	:	Cabbage fly; Cabbage root fly; Root fly; Turnip fly; Cabbage maggot; Root maggot
Scientific Name	:	*Delia radicum* (Linnaeus, 1758)
Family	:	Anthomyiidae
Order	:	Diptera

Source: *https://www.flickr.com/photos/ajblake/12401635763*

Distribution and Host Range

The flies can be found all over Europe. After overwintering as pupae in the soil, the flies emerge in spring, feed on nectar, and lay eggs close to plants of the genus *Brassica*. This species is univoltine in Northern Europe and bi- or trivoltine in Central Europe.

Nature and Symptoms of Damage

Larvae feed on roots and can completely destroy the root system. The first sign of a problem is wilting of the plant on sunny days and yellowing or purpling of outer leaves. Later, plants collapse, wilt down, and die. On inspection of the root area, you may find the legless white maggots feeding, the small brown, oblong pupae, or tunnels from maggot feeding. In brassica root crops such as turnips, radishes, and rutabaga, maggot feeding tunnels on or in the root render it unmarketable.

Life History and Description

Cabbage root maggot (CRM) overwinters as small brown pupae in the soil near roots of fall brassica crops where the larvae fed. Adults emerge in spring and can travel up to a mile in search of host plants. Eggs are laid in the soil at the base of the stem of host crops. Cool, moist soil conditions favor survival of the eggs, and soil temperatures that exceed 95°F in the top 2-3 inches will kill them. Larvae feed on roots and pupate in the soil. A late summer flight may damage fall root crops. There are 3-4 generations per year in central New England. Cabbage root maggot (CRM) flies are delicate, hump-backed gray-brown flies, about 5-7 mm long. Onion, seedcorn and cabbage maggot flies are difficult to distinguish with the naked eye, but each will only be found on and near their appropriate crop family. Small, white, bullet-shaped eggs are laid in soil. Maggots are white and legless and can be found in and around roots.

Management

Rotate crops to keep maggot populations low; greater distances are more effective. Rotate spring crops to fields that were not planted with fall brassicas. Delay planting until after first flight is done and soil temperatures are high enough to kill eggs (95°F). Planting in late-May into June is generally safer than in the first half of May. Cover recently seeded or transplanted crops with floating row covers as a barrier against cabbage root maggot flies. Place the cover as soon as the transplants are set. Do not use where brassicas were grown last year, as pupae left in the soil could emerge under the cover. Place cover over the crop at the time of seeding or transplanting and seal the edges with soil. Replace cover after weeding operations. As soil temperatures rise, first flight ends, and crops grow large, covers can be safely removed. Till under fall crop residue to expose and help reduce populations of overwintering pupae.

Soil-dwelling beetles, including ground beetles (carabids) and staphylinid beetles, feed on cabbage maggot eggs, larvae, and pupae and can cause high levels of mortality. One staphylinid species, *Aleochara bilineata*, also parasitizes maggot larvae and has been shown to respond to chemicals given off by plants that suffer maggot damage. Soil application of the **entomopathogenic nematode *Steinernema feltiae*** has shown efficacy against cabbage maggot in trials even at low soil temperatures 50°F/10°C. Apply by suspending infective juvenile nematodes in water and treating transplants prior to setting in the field, or in transplant water used in the water wheel transplanter, as a drench after transplanting, or a combination of pre-plant and post-plant applications. Post-plant treatments are likely to be needed if maggot flight begins >1 week after transplanting. Rates of 100,000 to 125,000 infective juveniles per transplant have been shown to be needed to achieve reduction in damage.

Direct application of insecticides to the root zone is considered the most effective means for controlling maggot damage. Insecticides should be applied as a narrow band with enough water to penetrate the root zone. For direct seeded crops, apply insecticides over the row. For transplanted crops, spray should be directed to the base of the plant. A wider spray band reduces the concentration of the insecticide over the row and therefore decreases its effectiveness. Some materials may be applied as a transplant tray drench or in transplant water, or in-furrow before or during seeding or transplanting. Be sure to read the label of any material you choose to use to determine which methods it is labelled for.

❑ Cabbage painted bug: *Bagrada hilaris* (Burmeister, 1835)

Common Name	:	Cabbage painted bug; Bagrada bug; Painted bug
Scientific Name	:	*Bagrada hilaris* (Burmeister, 1835)
Family	:	Pentatomidae
Order	:	Hemiptera

Source: *https://www.cabidigitallibrary.org/doi/10.1079/cabicompendium.8302*

Distribution and Host Range

It is native to South-eastern Africa. The Bagrada bug is an invasive pest species, native to Africa, which has spread to India, Pakistan, parts of Southeast Asia, and Italy. In the United States, it was first found in Los Angeles County in 2008. It is a major pest insect of *Brassica oleracea* crops (including cabbage, kale, cauliflower, Brussels sprouts, and broccoli), and related crucifers such as turnips, rape, and mustard. Besides crucifers, the bugs are known on papaya, sorghum, maize, potato, cotton, caper, pearl millet, and some legumes.

Nature and Symptoms of Damage

Adults and nymphs of the bagrada bug feed on leaves, stems, flowers, and seeds. They insert their needle-like mouthparts into plant tissues, inject digestive enzymes, and suck the juices. On leaves and stems, starburst-shaped lesions form. Leaves eventually have large stippled areas and may wilt and die. Ultimately damage may result in "**scorched**" leaves, stunting, blind terminals, and forked or multiple heads on cauliflower, broccoli, and cabbage. Bagrada bugs are particularly damaging to small plants and may kill seedlings.

Life History and Description

All life stages may be present together on plants, especially when pest densities increase, generations overlap, and food sources decrease. Even though bagrada bugs prefer cool-season cole crops, their development is favored by warmer temperatures. Adults tend to fly when temperatures are above 85°F. Adult bugs are black with orange and white markings; the shield-shaped body is about 1/4 inch (5-7 mm) long and about half as wide at the broadest part. Adults may be confused with harlequin bugs, *Murgantia histrionica*, but are smaller at about 1/3-1/5 the size. Eggs are barrel-shaped and deposited singly or in small clusters of about six. Eggs are initially white but turn orange or red prior to hatching. Females lay eggs in the soil beneath host plants but may also oviposit on leaves or on hairy stems of non-host plants. In addition, eggs are often laid on plant protective coverings such as mesh screens or floating row covers. Female bug can lay up to 150 eggs within two to three weeks. Eggs can hatch in as little as four days. The nymph passes through five instars. Newly moulted nymphs of all stages are orange-red but legs, head, and thorax darken quickly to black. The brightly coloured nymphs may be confused with lady beetles but lack their shiny, hardened wings. Older nymphs develop dark wing pads and white spots on the abdomen prior to becoming adults.

Management

Remove weed hosts in and near planting areas. Bagrada bug adults, eggs, and nymphs in the soil or container media can be controlled by steam or chemical treatment before planting. Removal of plant residue after harvest can reduce carryover between crops. Picking the bugs off plants by hand is only feasible if pest populations are very low. **Pyramid traps** baited with crushed sweet alyssum, inside polypropylene bags, can also be used to catch and destroy bugs, particularly when numbers are high. *Idris elba* a potential control agent for *B. hilaris*, benefit the broccoli crops. Insecticide controls for worms may also control this pest.

❑ Crucifer flea beetle: *Phyllotreta cruciferae* (Goeze, 1777)

Common Name	:	Crucifer flea beetle; Canola flea beetle; Rape flea beetle
Scientific Name	:	*Phyllotreta Cruciferae* (Goeze, 1777)
Family	:	Chrysomelidae
Order	:	Coleoptera

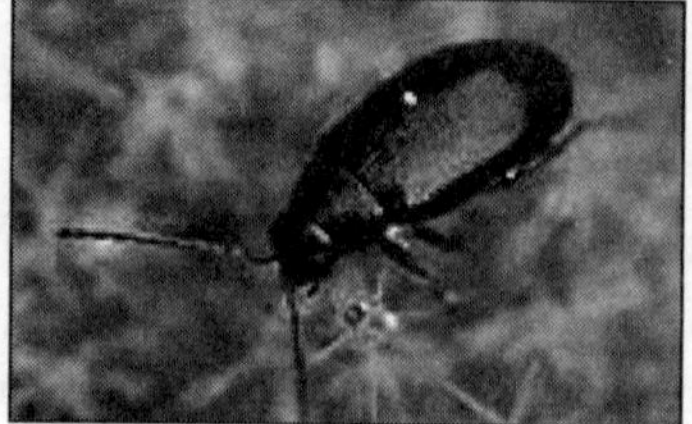

Source: *https://en.wikipedia.org/wiki/Phyllotreta_cruciferae*

Distribution and Host Range

It is found in Europe and Northern Asia (excluding China) and North America. These flea beetles only feed on brassica crops; those found on corn or solanaceous crops are different species.

Nature and Symptoms of Damage

Adults feed on leaves leaving small round holes which can become enlarged as the leaves grow. Heavy feeding can kill seedlings outright or delay maturity, reduce yield, or make crops unmarketable.

Life History and Description

Adults overwinter outside the field in woods or hedgerows and move into the field. Adults mate and lay eggs singly or in groups of 3-4 in soil at base of plant. Eggs hatch in 11-13 days (at 77°F). Larvae emerge and feed on root hairs for 25-30 days, then pupate for 10-15 days before re-emerging as adult beetles. There are at least two generations per year, with the second-generation adults emerging, but they overlap considerably such that crops are almost always at risk whenever they are planted. In mid-September, adult beetles leave fields to overwinter in areas with leaf litter or crop residues. The crucifer flea beetle is uniformly black and shiny, about 2 mm in length, while the striped flea beetle has two yellow stripes on its back.

Management

Crop rotation: break the cycle. Plant spring crops as far as possible from last season's fall brassica crops. Delay planting until July to break the reproductive cycle. Use row covers or insect netting. Covers provide excellent protection if well secured around all edges immediatcly after seeding or transplanting. Remove and replace the same day for cultivation, as needed. Trap cropping: take advantage of flea beetles' preferences for certain crops and use more attractive types to lure FB to one area where you can kill them more effectively. Plant the trap earlier than main crop and be prepared to spray it regularly, or beetles will move into your main crop. Destroy crop residue (above and below ground) promptly to starve adults, they will move to a new field. Discing may kill eggs and larvae of beetles in soil. Provide adequate water and nutrients for crop growth; avoid soil compaction. Intercropping can limit damage, as beetles will have a harder time finding host plants and will move out of the field. **Mulches:** Plastic, straw, or living mulches can hamper flea beetles' ability to find host plants, can prevent egg-laying in the field, encourage ground-dwelling beneficial insects like ground beetles that feed on larval or adult flea beetles.

A native parasitoid wasp, *Microctonus vittatae*, is found throughout North America and can kill adult flea beetles, although the rate of parasitization is low. Generalist predators such as lacewing larvae (*Chrysoperla* spp.), big eyed bugs (*Geocoris* spp.), and damsel bugs (*Nabis* spp.) have also been known to feed on adult stages of flea beetles. Flowering plants such as anise, dill, chamomile, marigold, or clover can be grown around the host plants to enhance floral resources and encourage the native parasitic wasp and other generalist predators. **Entomopathogenic nematodes** in the families *Steinernematidae* and *Heterorhabditidae* can attack the larval stage of flea beetles, thereby reducing the size of the population within a field over time. Spinosad and a carbamate provided most consistent damage reductions. Seed treatments with a neonicotinoid also gave good control.

❑ Tobacco caterpillar: *Spodoptera litura* (Fabricius, 1775)

Common Name	:	Tobacco caterpillar; Tobacco cutworm; Cotton leafworm; Leaf eating caterpillar
Scientific Name	:	*Spodoptera litura* (Fabricius, 1775)
Family	:	Noctuidae
Order	:	Lepidoptera

Source:*https://apps.lucidcentral.org/pppw*

As Described in Potato

Resistant Varieties	
World	**India**
Cruiser: This cabbage variety is resistant to the diamondback moth, a major pest of cole crops. **Blue Vantage:** Developed by the University of Florida, this broccoli variety is resistant to aphids, which can cause significant damage to the plant. **Green Duke:** This kale variety is resistant to the cabbage looper, a pest that can cause significant damage to the plant.	**Pusa Mukta:** This cabbage variety is resistant to the diamondback moth and the cabbage butterfly, two major pests of cole crops. **Pusa Meghna:** This cauliflower variety is resistant to aphids and the cabbage butterfly. **Pusa Komal:** This broccoli variety is resistant to aphids and the diamondback moth.

Pests of Root Crops

Common Name	Scientific Name	Family	Origin	Chromosome Number
Sweet potato	*Ipomea batatas* (L.)	Convolvulaceae	America	2n=90
Carrot	*Daucus carota* subsp. *sativus*	Apiaceae	Persia	2n=18
Radish	*Raphanus raphanistrum* subsp. *sativus*	Brassicaceae	Southeast Asia	2n=18
Beetroot	*Beta vulgaris* subsp. *vulgaris*	Amaranthaceae	Middle East	2n=18
Turnip	*Brassica rapa* subsp. *rapa*	Brassicaceae	Mediterranean region	2n=20
Cassava	*Manihot esculenta*	Euphorbiaceae	South America	2n=36
Elephant Foot Yam	*Amorphophallus paeoniifolius*	Araceae	Island Southeast Asia	2n=26

Root crops are plants that are grown for their edible roots, tubers, or rhizomes. These crops are an important source of food and nutrition in many parts of the world. Here are some examples of root crops that are commonly grown in India along with their botany, area, and production:

Potato: Potatoes (*Solanum tuberosum*) belong to the family Solanaceae. They are a staple food in many parts of the world, and are rich in carbohydrates, vitamins, and minerals. India is one of the largest producers of potatoes in the world. According to the National Horticulture Board, the total area under potato cultivation in India was 0.48 million hectares in 2020-21, with a total production of 53.31 million tonnes. The pests of potato are already discussed in chapter 1.

Sweet Potato: Sweet potatoes (*Ipomoea batatas*) belong to the family Convolvulaceae. They are a good source of carbohydrates, vitamins, and minerals. Sweet potatoes are widely grown in India, especially in the southern states. According to the National Horticulture Board, the total area under sweet potato cultivation in India was 0.15 million hectares in 2020-21, with a total production of 6.61 million tonnes.

Carrot: Carrots (*Daucus carota*) belong to the family Apiaceae. They are a good source of vitamin A and other nutrients. Carrots are widely grown in India, especially in the northern states.

According to the National Horticulture Board, the total area under carrot cultivation in India was 0.06 million hectares in 2020-21, with a total production of 1.22 million tonnes.

Beetroot: Beetroot (*Beta vulgaris*) belongs to the family Amaranthaceae. It is a good source of fiber, vitamins, and minerals. Beetroot is widely grown in India, especially in the northern states. According to the National Horticulture Board, the total area under beetroot cultivation in India was 0.02 million hectares in 2020-21, with a total production of 0.46 million tonnes.

Tapioca: Tapioca (*Manihot esculenta*) belongs to the family Euphorbiaceae. It is a starchy root that is widely used in cooking. Tapioca is mostly grown in the southern states of India. According to the National Horticulture Board, the total area under tapioca cultivation in India was 0.08 million hectares in 2020-21, with a total production of 10.35 million tonnes.

These are just a few examples of the many different types of root crops that are grown in India.

Sweet potato weevil: *Cylas formicarius* (Fabricius, 1798)

Common Name	:	Sweet potato weevil
Scientific Name	:	*Cylas formicarius* (Fabricius, 1798)
Family	:	Apionidae; Brentidae
Order	:	Coleoptera

Source: *https://www.cabidigitallibrary.org/doi/10.1079/cabicompendium.17408*

Distribution and Host Range

Sweet potato weevil was first noted in the United States in Louisiana in 1875, and then in Florida in 1878 and Texas in 1890, probably entering by way of Cuba. It is found in Africa, Australia, Caribbean, Europe, Northern Asia (excluding China), Central America, North America, Oceania, South America, Southern Asia, Pacific Ocean, and temperate Asia. This weevil feeds on plants in the plant family convolvulaceae. Although it has been found associated with several genera, its primary hosts are in the genus *Ipomoea*. Among vegetable crops only sweet potato, *Ipomoea batatas*, is a suitable host. Native plants can be important hosts of sweet potato weevil. Railroad vine, bayhops, and morning glory, wild potato vine, are among the suitable wild hosts.

Nature and Symptoms of Damage

A symptom of infestation by sweet potato weevil is yellowing of the vines, but a heavy infestation is usually necessary before this is apparent. Thus, incipient problems are easily overlooked, and damage not apparent until tubers are harvested. The principal form of damage to sweet potato is mining of the tubers by larvae. The infested tuber is often riddled with cavities, spongy in appearance, and dark in color. In addition to damage caused directly by tunnelling, larvae cause damage indirectly by facilitating entry of soil-borne pathogens. Even low levels of feeding induce a chemical reaction that imparts a bitter taste and terpene odour to the tubers. Larvae also mine the vine of the plant, causing it to darken, crack, or collapse. The adult may feed on the tubers, creating numerous small holes that measure about the length of its head. The adult generally has limited access to the tubers, however, so damage by this stage is less severe than by larvae. Adult feeding on the foliage seldom is of consequence.

Life History and Description

A complete life cycle requires one to two months, with 35 to 40 days being common during the summer months. Adults do not undergo a period of diapause in the winter, but seek shelter and remain inactive until the weather is favourable. All stages can be found throughout the year if suitable host material is available.

Egg: Eggs are deposited in small cavities created by the female with her mouthparts in the sweet potato root or stem. The female deposits a single egg at a time, and seals the egg within the oviposition cavity with a plug of faecal material, making it difficult to observe the egg. Most eggs tend to be deposited near the juncture of the stem and root (tuber) or in the soil or in stem tissue. The egg is oval in shape and creamy white in color, 0.7 mm in length and 0.5 mm in width. Duration of the egg stage varies from about five to six days during the summer to about 11 to 12 days during colder weather. Females apparently produce two to four eggs per day, or 75 to 90 eggs during their life span of about 30 days. **Larva:** When egg hatches the larva usually burrows directly into the tuber or stem of the plant. The larva is legless, white in color, and displays three instars. The mean head capsule widths of the instars are 0.29 to 0.32 mm, 0.43 to 0.49 mm, and 0.75 to 0.78 mm for instars 1 to 3, respectively. The larva creates winding tunnels packed with faecal material as it feeds and grows.

Pupa: The mature larva creates a small pupal chamber in the tuber or stem. The pupa is similar to the adult in appearance, although the head and elytra are bent ventrally. The pupa measures about 6.5 mm in length. Initially the pupa is white, but with time this stage becomes grayish in color with darker eyes and legs. Duration of the pupal stage averages 7 to 10 days, but in cool weather it may be extended to up to 28 days.

Adult: Normally the adult emerges from the pupation site by chewing a hole through the exterior of the plant tissue, but sometimes it remains for a considerable period and feeds within the tuber. The adult is striking in form and color. The body, legs, and head are long and thin, giving it an ant-like appearance. The head is black, the antennae, thorax and legs orange to reddish brown, and the abdomen and elytra are metallic blue. The snout is slightly curved and about as long as the thorax; the antennae are attached at about the mid-point on the snout. The beetle appears smooth and shiny, but close examination shows a layer of short hairs. The adult measures 5.5 to 8.0 mm in length. Under laboratory conditions at 15°C, adults can live over 200 days if provided with food and about 30 days if starved. In contrast, their longevity decreases to about three months if held at 30°C with food, and eight days without food. Adults are secretive, often feeding on the lower surface of leaves, and are not readily noticed. The adult is quick to feign death if disturbed. Adults can fly, but seem to do so rarely and in short, low flights. However, because they are active mostly at night, their dispersive abilities are probably underestimated. Females feed for a day or more before becoming sexually active, but commence oviposition shortly after mating; the average preoviposition period is seven days.

Management

Remove previous sweet potato crop residues and alternate host, *Ipomoea* sp. and destroy them. Discourage growing sweet potato in the same field year after year. Use pest free planting materials mulch with leaves of *Chromolaena doormats, Clerodendron infortunatum* at 3 tonnes/ha at 30 days after planting (DAP). Use cut sweet potato tubers (100 g) as trap during 50-80 DAP at 10 days intervals. Set the traps at 5 m apart at 4 pm and collect and destroy adult weevils at 6 am next day. Dip planting materials in monocrotophos 36 WSC 15 ml per L of water. Rake up soil and earth up at 50 days after planting.

❑ Sweet Potato Blue Pansy: *Junonia orithya* (Linnaeus, 1758)

Common Name	:	Sweet Potato Blue Pansy
Scientific Name	:	*Junonia orithya* (Linnaeus, 1758)
Family	:	Nymphalidae
Order	:	Lepidoptera

Source: *https://en.wikipedia.org/wiki/Junonia_orithya*

Distribution and Host Range

Junonia orithya is a nymphalid butterfly with many subspecies occurring from Africa, through Southern and South-eastern Asia, Cambodia and in Australia. In India, its common English name is the **blue pansy**, but in Southern Africa it is known as the **eyed pansy** as the name *blue pansy* refers to *Junonia oenone*. In Australia, this butterfly is known as the **blue argus**, but this name also is used for the *Aricia anteros* in Europe.

Host range: sweet potato, weed striga

Nature and Symptoms of Damage

Major symptoms are **defoliation** of plant leaves. It is actually a beneficial insect as it feeds on *Striga*, a weed parasite on sugarcane roots.

Life History and Description

Moths are medium-sized with only two pairs of functional legs. More than half of fore wings are velvety black. Hind wings are blue shaped with velvety black towards the base; thus, wing pattern resembles the pansy flower. Incubation, larval, pupal periods, adult longevity and life cycle last for 3, 14 to 16, 4 to 8, 3 to 7 and 27 to 29 days respectively.

Larvae: Head and body of a very dark shining black shading into brown head on a short neck, latter of an orange colour for a short distance; caudal extremity also tipped with orange. Body covered with perpendicular spines armed with strong radial hairs. Head bifurcated, reddish spot in centre of face, a small spinous process in the angle of each eye.

Pupae: The pupa is "suspended by tail, naked; wing-covers of a muddy yellow; rest of body of a purplish colour variegated by lines of a dull creamy white. Slight projections of an angular nature along abdomen."

Adults: The adults occur in open areas, often sitting on bare ground. This species has a stiff flap and glide style of flight and maintains a territory, driving away other butterflies that enter it.

Management

After harvesting, give deep ploughing and flood infested fields to kill pupae and to prevent carry-over of pests. Collect and destroy egg clusters and leaves bearing caterpillars to prevent population build-up. Spray dichlorvos 660 ml to control widespread infestation.

Tortoise beetles: *Aspidomorpha miliaris* (Fabricius, 1775); *Cassida circumdata* Herbst, 1799; *Chirida bipunctata* (Linnaeus, 1767)

Common Name	:	Tortoise beetles; Leaf-mining beetles
Scientific Name	:	*Aspidomorpha miliaris* (Fabricius, 1775); *Cassida circumdata* Herbst, 1799; *Chirida bipunctata* (Linnaeus, 1767)
Family	:	Cassididae; Chrysomelidae
Order	:	Coleoptera

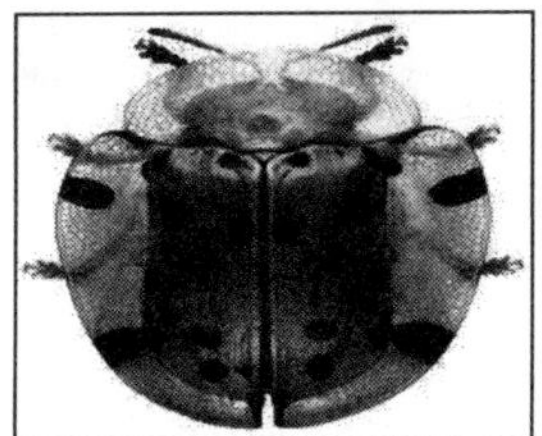

Source: *https://en.wikipedia.org/wiki/Aspidimorpha_miliaris*

Aspidomorpha miliaris

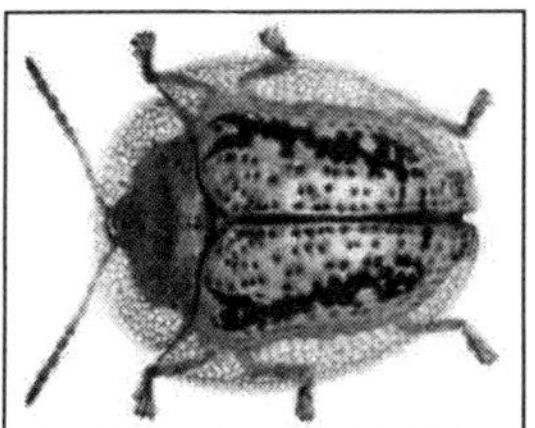

Source: *https://en.wikipedia.org/wiki/Cassida_circumdata*

Cassida circumdata

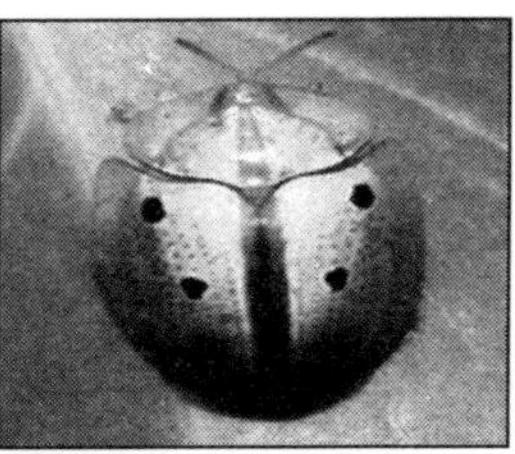

Source: *https://indiabiodiversity.org*

Chirida bipunctata

Distribution and Host Range

Throughout Africa, Southern China, Southeast Asia becomes serious occasionally. Sweet potato, Ipomoea morning glory, coffee, beet, potato and various flowers. There are many *Cassida* and *Aspidimorpha* species in Pacific island countries, almost all feeding on convolvulaceae. The following have been recorded on sweetpotato: *Cassida compuncta* (Fiji); *C. diomma* (Fiji and Samoa); *C. papuana* (Papua New Guinea and Solomon Islands), and *Cassida* species on *Merremia peltata* (Solomon Islands). Sweetpotato, kangkong (*Ipomoea aquatica*), and related *Ipomoea* species. Possibly, the beetles feed on crops and weeds in other families.

Nature and Symptoms of Damage

Skeletonization of leaves by grubs. Later grubs and adults gnaw holes in leaf lamina. Grubs are green, flat with anal projection always carry debris on its back. Pupation takes place in ventral surface of leaves. Adults feed on leaves, making small to medium-size holes. The larvae at first eat the leaf surface; later, they eat their way through the leaf.

Life History and Description

The "**cassidoids**" have a rounded outline with the edges of the pronotum and elytra expanded, spreading out to cover the legs and head. They are often colourful and metallic, with ornate sculpturing; a few species have the ability to change the colour due to water movements within the translucent cuticle. All members of the subfamily have the mouthparts reduced into a cavity in the head capsule, the legs have four segmented tarsi. The hispoids have larvae that are leaf miners, while the cassidoids feed on the plant surfaces, sometimes covering their bodies with faecal shields. Although faecal shields are thought to provide defense, no evidence exists for such a role. These metallic coloured beetles are active during monsoon. Eggs are laid on ventral leaf surface. Grubs are nocturnal in habit.

Species	Adult	Grub	Egg	Life cycle
Aspidomorpha miliaris	Broad oval shaped, brownish-red in colour with black dots	Flattened with spiny processes covering their body. Dried excreta are seen on the anal process	Laid in 5 to 10 rows	Egg, grub and pupal stages last for 9 to 11, 15 to 20 and 4 to 6 days respectively. Life cycle is completed in 28 to 36 days.
Cassida circumdata	Broad oval shaped, greenish-yellow in colour with green crescent mark in middle	Pale greenish in colour	Laid singly. Fastened on leaf surface by filaments	Egg, grub and pupal stages last for 3 to 5, 10 to 15 and 6 to 8 days respectively. Life cycle is completed in 30 days.
Chirida bipunctata	Small metallic green in colour with six black spots on elytra	Pale greenish in colour	Laid singly	Egg, grub and pupal stages last for 4 to 6, 12 to 14 and 5 to 8 days respectively. Life cycle is completed in 30 days.

Management

Removal of convolvulaceous weeds in the surrounding area may reduce their numbers. Harvest the infested crop, collect the vines and destroy them, and then plant a new crop. Tortoise beetles are attacked by (chalcid) wasps in other countries, parasitic flies, and lady beetle larvae. It is likely that these parasites and predators attack tortoise beetles in Pacific Island countries. Conserve or encourage larval parasitoids *Tetrastichus* sp, predator *Stalilia* sp., (Mantidae). Chemical control of this pest is seldom necessary.

❑ Willow-carrot Aphid: *Cavariella aegopodii*

Common Name	:	Willow-Carrot Aphid
Scientific Name	:	*Cavariella aegopodii*
Family	:	Aphididae
Order	:	Hemiptera

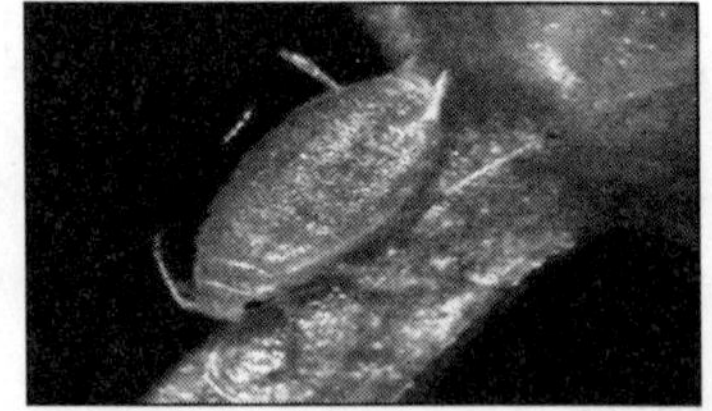

Source: *https://influentialpoints.com/Gallery/Cavariella_aegopodii_Willow-carrot_aphid.htm*

Distribution and Host Range

The willow-carrot aphid host alternates from willows (*Salix* spp) to umbellifers (Apiaceae). The preferred primary hosts are crack willow (*Salix fragilis*) and white willow *Salix alba*, although some willow species seem only to be colonized in spring, by winged forms from populations which have overwintered parthenogenetically. Preferred secondary hosts are cultivated umbellifers such as carrots (*Daucus carota*) and fennel (*Foeniculum vulgare*) and several wild umbellifers. *Cavariella aegopodii* is widespread throughout temperate and warm temperate parts of the world.

Nature and Symptoms of Damage

Aphids feed on carrot foliage, but they are a key pest because they can transmit diseases such as motley dwarf virus. If aphid infestation is heavy, it may cause leaves yellow, necrotic spots on leaves and stunted shoots; aphids secrete a sticky, sugary substance called honeydew, which encourages the growth of sooty mold on the plants. Willow carrot aphid is primarily of concern because of its efficiency in vectoring a number of serious virus diseases. It transmits carrot motley dwarf, carrot red leaf, and parsnip yellow fleck. It is also a vector of *Celery mosaic virus, Sugar beet mosaic virus,* and *Cauliflower mosaic virus*. It seldom reaches numbers that trigger the need for chemical intervention.

Life History and Description

Most species of aphids have similar life cycles. Aphid females give birth to live offspring all year without mating. When vegetable crops are not available, aphids live on a wide variety of weed hosts. In summer and fall, aphids may produce winged females and later winged males. They mate and produce eggs for overwintering, especially in colder climates. Otherwise, the adult aphids overwinter on crops, weeds or trees. There may be as few as two generations or as many as 16 generations each year, depending on the species and climate. Willow carrot aphid is the main aphid pest of carrot crops. Distinguishing features include the presence of cornicles, which project backwards from the body of the aphid and will generally not move very quickly when disturbed; willow carrot aphid will also attack turnip, parsley and celery. The green peach aphid is slender, dark green to yellow, and has no waxy bloom. The wingless form of the green peach aphid is pale green. The winged form has a black head and thorax. It is primarily an early year pest and transmits virus diseases.

Management

Use tolerant varieties, sanitation for curbing the spread of the viruses, ploughing all crop residues under as soon as harvest, use of reflective mulches such as silver coloured plastic can deter aphids from feeding. Little is known regarding the parasites of willow carrot aphid. The presence of bloated mummies indicates parasite activity. Predators such as green lacewing larvae, lady beetles, and syrphid fly larvae prey on this aphid as well as on other aphid species. Use of insecticidal soaps or oils such as neem or canola oil etc. are followed to control the aphids.

❑ Carrot rust fly: *Chamaepsila rosae* (Fabricius, 1794)

Common Name	:	Carrot rust fly
Scientific Name	:	*Chamaepsila rosae* (Fabricius, 1794)
Family	:	Psilidae
Order	:	Diptera

Source:*https://www.trueleafmarket.com/pages/carrot-rust-fly-pest-guide*

Distribution and Host Range

Carrot Fly is widely distributed around the world anywhere *Apium* grows and **Host Plants include** *Apium* crops such as carrot, parsnip, celeriac, hemlock, celery.

Nature and Symptoms of Damage

The larva is the damaging stage, and feeds on umbelliferous species, mainly carrots, but also targets celery, celeriac, chervil, parsnips, and parsley. Newly hatched larvae enter through the root surface and mine the lower portion of the carrot roots (upper portion in parsnips) which causes scarring on older plants or kills younger plants. The tunnels created in carrots turn a red rusty color and may become colonized by fungi or bacteria. Above-ground symptoms include wilting and plant stunting

Life History and Description

Carrot rust flies overwinter as pupae in the soil near the host plant, or sometimes as larvae within carrot roots. Adults emerge during May and June in favourable cool, moist conditions. Females lay up to 40 eggs on the soil surface, near the base of plants in clusters of 1 to 3 eggs. When hatched, the larvae feed on the roots for a few weeks, and eventually pupate in the soil for approximately 25 days. The carrot rust fly has 1 to 3 generations per year in Utah, with the second generation emerging in August. Not all generations may be damaging, because the marketable hosts may not be present in the field at the time.

Adult: 1/5 inch long, slender, black abdomen and thorax, orange-coloured head, and yellow legs. Wings are a dark transparent color and $\frac{1}{2}$ inch wide in full span. The abdominal tip for females is pointed, and rounded on males.

Egg: White, 0.6-0.9 mm long and 0.15 mm wide.

Nymph: Yellow-brown and 1/5 inch in length.

Management

Timely harvest: Harvest all carrots in blocks as soon as they are ready. This will prevent larvae from spreading from plant to plant within the soil.

Delay planting: Planting carrots after mid-June will avoid the peak egg-laying period. **Avoid planting near other host plants and weeds**. Carrot rust flies attack both umbelliferous crop and weed species such as wild carrot (*Daucus carota*) and water hemlock (*Conium maculatum*).

Crop Rotation: Rotating to non-susceptible hosts every year will break the carrot rust fly life cycle and prevent the population from building.

Remove crop residue: Remove all carrots and related host crops from the ground at the end of the growing season to prevent overwintering populations. **Use floating row covers**, where practical to prevent flies from landing near host plants and laying eggs. Natural enemies of carrot rust flies include the parasitoids *Chorebus gracilis*, *Eutrias tritoma*, and *Aleochara sparsa* which target the early larval and pupa stages of the carrot rust fly. Granular insecticides are usually best when incorporated into the furrow at planting to prevent larval attack on the roots.

❑ Mustard saw fly: *Athalia lugens* (Klug, 1813)

Common Name	:	Mustard saw fly
Scientific Name	:	*Athalia lugens* (Klug, 1813)
Family	:	Tenthredinidae
Order	:	Hymenoptera

Source: *https://inaturalist.ca/taxa/504973-Athalia-lugens*

Distribution and Host Range

It is a serious pest of radish. The pest attack is observed in the vegetative and flowering stage of the crop. This pest is widely distributed in Indonesia, Formosa, Myanmar and the Indian Sub-continent. Host range includes **Mustard**, toria, rapeseed, cabbage, cauliflower, knol-khol, turnip, radish, etc.,

Nature and Symptoms of Damage

The grubs alone are destructive. They bite holes into leaves preferring the young growth and skeletonize the leaves completely. Sometimes, even the epidermis of the shoot is eaten up. Although the seedlings succumb; the older plants, when attacked, do not bear seed.

Life History and Description

Dark green larvae have 8 pairs of abdominal prolegs. There are five black stripes on the back, and the body has a wrinkled appearance. A full-grown larva measures 16-18 mm in length. The adults are small orange yellow insects with black markings on the body and have smoky wings with black veins. The mustard sawfly breeds from October to March and undergoes pupal diapause during summer. The adults emerge from these cocoons early in October. They live for 2-8 days and lay 30-35 eggs singly, in slits made with saw like ovipositors along the underside of the leaf margins. Egg period is 4-8 days and the larvae feed exposed in groups of 3-6 on the leaves during morning and evening. They remain hidden during the day time and, when disturbed, fall to the ground and feign death. There are 7 instars with a larval period of 16-35 days. Pupation is in water proof oval cocoons in soil and the pupal period is 11-31 clays. Lifecycle is completed in 31-34 days. It completes 2-3 generations from October to March.

Management

Hand picking of larvae when the area involved is small. Conserve larval parasitoid *Perilissus cingulator* and bacterium, *Serratia marcescens*. Spraying with malathion 50 EC (1 ml/litre of water) twice at an interval of 10 days is recommended.

❑ Beet cyst nematode: *Heterodera schachtii* (A. Schmidt, 1871)

Common Name	:	Beet cyst nematode; Beet cyst eelworm; Sugar beet nematode
Scientific Name	:	*Heterodera schachtii* (A. Schmidt, 1871)
Family	:	Heteroderidae
Order	:	Tylenchida

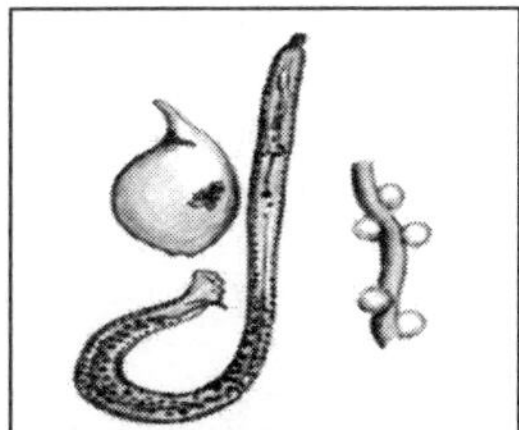

Source: *https://scandposters.com/shop/heterodera-schachtii-11608p.html*

Discovery

In the early 1800s, "beet fatigue" was used to describe the decreased sugar beet yields which occurred after repeated planting on the same field. At first, this decrease was believed to be the result of nutrient depletion, but in 1859 the botanist H. Schacht discovered nematode cysts on the roots of affected plants and hypothesized that they were responsible for the disease. It wasn't until 1871 that another researcher, Schmidt, created the genus *Heterodera*, and named the nematode *H. schachtii* in honor of its discoverer.

Distribution and Host Range

It infects more than 200 different plants including economically important crops such as sugar beets, cabbage, broccoli, and radish. *H. schachtii* is found worldwide.

Nature and Symptoms of Damage

Stunted growth and yellowing are early signs of the disease. Infection can be confirmed by the presence of maturing cysts on plants' roots. Affected plants are marked by stunted growth, wilting, yellowing, decreased yields, and death. While there are many methods of control, crop rotation with non-susceptible plants is preferred.

Life History and Description

The cycle begins with eggs deposited either in a gelatinous mass or inside a cyst formed from the body of the female. The eggs become embryonated, then molt, forming the first and second larval stages. These can exist within the cyst for several years; however, some will exit the cyst every year. Hatching can be stimulated by the presence of the host plant. The J2 (stage two, infective larvae) penetrate the root until they reach the vascular tissue. If the plant is suitable, the larva will release chemicals from the stylet to form a pocket of lysed cells called a syncytium. This will be the larva's food source for the rest of its life. The juveniles then go through a second, third, and fourth (final) moult. The stage 4, and later adult, female is swollen and becomes flask shaped. The male releases from the syncytium, fertilizes the attached female, and leaves the root. The females produce a gelatinous mass in which they lay some of the eggs. The rest of the eggs remain inside the female. As the feeding stops, the female dies, and her body toughens, the cuticle becoming a protective envelope for the eggs.

Management

By growing non-susceptible plants for 2 or 3 years between sugar beet planting, nematode levels can be dramatically reduced. This is the primary method of control used commercially. *Heterodera schachtii* is susceptible to infection by *Verticillium suchlasporium* and other fungi. Ethylene dibromide and metham-sodium are effective at controlling the nematode, but economic and environmental concerns generally prevent the use of fumigants as a form of control.

❑ Cassava green mite: *Mononychellus tanajoa* (Bondar, 1938)

Common Name	:	Cassava green mite
Scientific Name	:	*Mononychellus tanajoa* (Bondar, 1938)
Family	:	Tetranychidae
Order	:	Trombidiformes

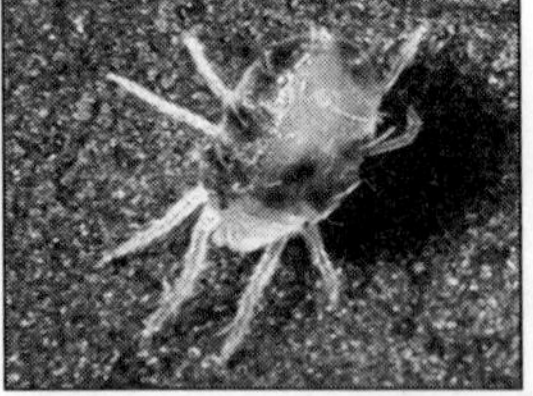

Source: *https://apps.lucidcentral.org/ppp/text/web_full/entities/cassava_green_mite_438.htm*

Distribution and Host Range

Restricted to Africa, North (Mexico) and South America, the Caribbean (Dominican Republic, Trinidad and Tobago). It is not recorded in Oceania. The mite is native to the tropical parts of Central and South America. The distribution of the mite is still to be resolved due to confusion with other similar species. Hosts include cassava, and other *Manihot* species.

Nature and Symptoms of Damage

The mite pierces and sucks juices from the leaves, most commonly from the underside; this causes yellowing, mottling, death and leaf fall. Stems show a 'candle stick' effect with the loss of terminal shoots.

Life History and Description

There are four stages, a larva with six legs, two nymphs and the adult. From egg to adult takes about 12 days at 27°C. Adults are green at first; later, they become yellowish-green. The adult female lives for about 12 days and lays about 60 eggs. They grow to 0.8 mm, slightly larger than males. Populations are greatest during dry seasons: rainfall tends to wash the mites from the leaves.

Spread occurs by mites walking from plant to plant, and when they are blown in the wind or carried in water. Long distance spread is by human beings moving planting material, nursery plants, and marketing leaves as a vegetable. Spread also occurs on farm vehicles and other machinery. Survival is on leaves and stems for up to 60 days.

Management

Cultural control is limited in its effectiveness, although selection of planting material from healthy plants, early planting in the rainy season and intercropping with pigeon pea have been suggested. Varieties with tolerance to the green cassava mite have been bred at IITA, Ibadan, Nigeria. Mites of the family **Phytoseiidae** are the most important predators of cassava green mite because they are effective even when there are low numbers of mites to eat, and they are also easy to rear. Introductions began with *Amblyseius* species from South America to Africa in the mid-1980s. However, more success was obtained with *Typhlodromalus aripo* introduced in 1993; it is now considered the key predator of green cassava mite in the African cassava belt. Good effect occurs when it is present with another introduced species, *Typhlodromalus manihoti*.

Chemical control is not a recommended method of control because it is too expensive when cassava is produced only for household use; also, there is the possibility that extensive use will select resistant populations of mites. Most importantly, pesticides will interrupt the biological control of predatory mites. However, although abamectin has been found effective.

❑ Greater and lesser yam beetle: *Heteroligus meles* (Billberg, 1815) and *Heteroligus appius* (Burmeister, 1847)

Common Name	:	Greater and lesser yam beetle; Green vegetable bug; Shield bug
Scientific Name	:	*Heteroligus meles* (Billberg, 1815) and *Heteroligus appius* (Burmeister, 1847)
Family	:	Dynastidae
Order	:	Coleoptera

Source: *https://www.insecte.org/forum/viewtopic.php?t=120298*

Distribution and Host Range

Heteroligus meles is widespread in tropical Africa. *Heteroligus appius* is native to Australia and is widely distributed across the eastern and south-eastern parts of the country. It is also found in some regions of new Zealand, particularly in the North Island, and its distribution might be limited to these areas.

The green vegetable bug is known to have a diverse host range, and it feeds on various plants, including crops and wild plants. Some of the host plants attached by the *H. appius* are: Beans, peas, soybeans, lentils, legumes and fabaceae members.

Nature and Symptoms of Damage

It attacks the tubers. Adult beetles eat the planting setts and plants may wilt and die. The holes in tubers reduce market value.

Life History and Description

Adult beetles are 23-33 mm long, dark brown to black, with 2 prominent knobs on the head. The beetles lay eggs in the soil close to river banks and these hatch to produce creamy-white to grey larvae, which feed on grass roots and other organic matter. From egg to adult takes 22-24 weeks and emergence coincides with the beginning of the rains and the planting of yams. Further attack occurs just before harvest when the beetles again feed voraciously and then migrate to the breeding sites.

Management

Yam beetles can be controlled by planting as late as possible in the season.

Green peach aphid: *Myzus persicae* (Sulzer, 1776)

Common Name	:	Green peach aphid, green fly or Peach-potato aphid
Scientific Name	:	*Myzus persicae* (Sulzer, 1776)
Family	:	Aphididae
Order	:	Hemiptera

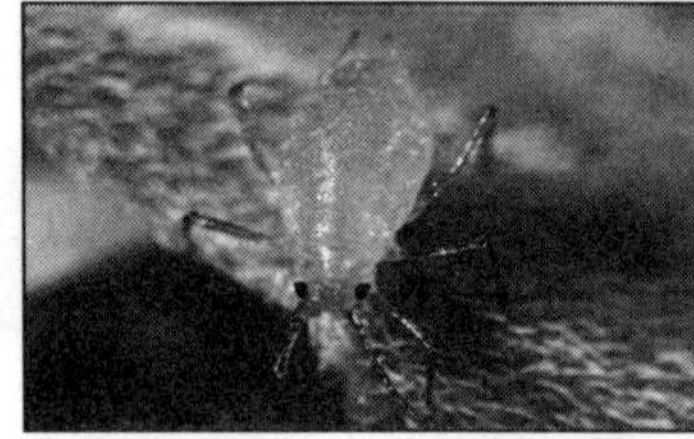

Source:*https://inpn.mnhn.fr/espece/cd_nom/52046/tab/taxo*

As described in Potato

Resistant Varieties	
World	**India**
Yellowstone: This carrot variety, developed by the USDA, is resistant to the carrot rust fly, a major pest of carrots. **Detroit Dark Red Supreme:** This beet variety is resistant to the beet leaf miner, a pest that can cause significant damage to the plant. **Purple Top White Globe:** This turnip variety is resistant to the turnip aphid, a pest that can cause significant damage to the plant.	**Pusa Rudhira:** This beet variety is resistant to the beet webworm, a pest that can cause significant damage to the plant. **Pusa Meghna:** This carrot variety is resistant to the carrot fly, a major pest of carrots. **Pusa Swarnima:** This turnip variety is resistant to the turnip aphid.

8

Pests of Bulb Crops

Common Name	Scientific Name	Family	Origin	Chromosome Number
Onion	*Allium cepa* L.	Amaryllidaceae	Iran, western Pakistan and Central Asia	2n=16
Garlic	*Allium sativum*	Amaryllidaceae	South Asia, Central Asia and North-eastern Iran	2n=16
Leek	*A. ampelopresum* var. *Porrum*	Amaryllidaceae	Mediterranean region	2n-32
Fennel	*Foenicum vulgare*	Apiaceae/ Unbelliferae	Mediterranean region; Southern Europe; Middle East and North Africa	2n=22

Bulb crops are plants that produce edible bulbs that are harvested for food. These bulbs are swollen underground plant structures that store nutrients and provide energy for the plant. Here are some examples of bulb crops that are commonly grown in India along with their botany, area, and production:

Onion

Onions (*Allium cepa*) belong to the family Amaryllidaceae. They are biennial plants that are usually grown as annuals. The bulbs are used in a wide variety of dishes, and India is one of the largest producers of onions in the world. According to the National Horticulture Board, the total area under onion cultivation in India was 1.14 million hectares in 2020-21, with a total production of 26.90 million tonnes.

Garlic

Garlic (*Allium sativum*) belongs to the family Amaryllidaceae. It is a perennial plant that is usually grown as an annual. The bulbs are used for both culinary and medicinal purposes, and India is one of the largest producers of garlic in the world. According to the National Horticulture Board, the total area under garlic cultivation in India was 0.29 million hectares in 2020-21, with a total production of 1.19 million tonnes.

Leek

Leeks (*Allium ampeloprasum var. porrum*) are a member of the onion family. They are biennial plants that are usually grown as annuals. Leeks are often used in soups and stews. They are not widely grown in India, but are imported from other countries.

Fennel

Fennel (*Foeniculum vulgare*) belongs to the family Apiaceae. It is a perennial herb that is grown for both its bulb and its seeds. Fennel bulbs are used in a variety of dishes, and fennel seeds are used as a spice. Fennel is commonly grown in India, especially in the northern states.

These are just a few examples of the many different types of bulb crops that are grown in India.

❑ Onion thrips: *Thrips tabaci* Lindeman, 1889

Common Name	:	Onion thrips
Scientific Name	:	*Thrips tabaci* Lindeman, 1889
Family	:	Thripidae
Order	:	Thysanoptera

Source: *https://academic.oup.com/jipm/article/6/1/6/2936974*

As described in Tomato

❑ Onion fly: *Delia antiqua* (Meigen, 1826)

Common Name	:	Onion fly, Onion maggot
Scientific Name	:	*Delia antiqua* (Meigen, 1826)
Family	:	Anthomyiidae
Order	:	Diptera

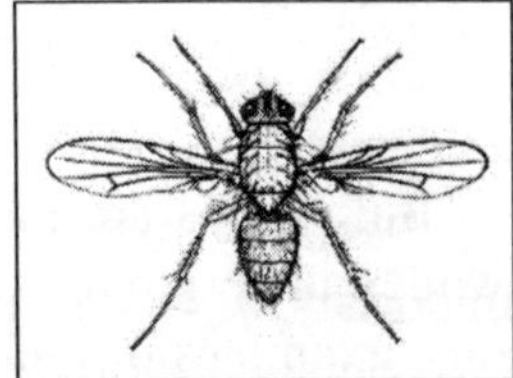

Source: *https://www.cabidigitallibrary.org/doi/10.1079/cabicompendium.28162*

Distribution and Host Range

The onion fly is found in North America, Western Europe, Russia, Central Asia, China, Japan, and Korea, but is absent from deserts. In the far North of its range, it has one generation per year, but further South, two, three, or four generations may occur in one year. Major hosts include onion, garlic, leek and carrot.

Nature and Symptoms of Damage

Onion maggot larvae attack germinating seedlings, feeding on the developing roots and epicotyl, and can continue to feed on the expanding bulbs during later stages of growth. This results in increased rot in bulbs held in storage. When eggs hatch, larvae feed on roots and can cause complete destruction of the root system. In onions, newly hatched larvae crawl behind the leaf sheath and enter the bulb, and feed on the roots, stem, and developing bulb. Feeding damage also encourages entry of soft rot pathogens.

Life History and Description

Three overlapping generations of onion maggot occur each year. Onion maggot overwinters as a pupa in the soil, although some adults may survive in protected areas. Emergence occurs in the spring and typically extends from April to June. Second or summer generation flies are active from late June to early August. A third flight can take place from early August to October. The adults spend little time within the fields during the day, preferring to rest at field margins in taller and denser vegetation. The flies are most active in onion fields during dusk and dawn or on overcast days. Onion maggot damage is greatest after consecutive years of wet springs. Onion maggot eggs are white, elongated, and about 0.04 inch long and are laid on the soil near the stem and occasionally on the young leaves and neck of the onion plant. The legless maggots are tapered, creamy white, and reach a length of about 0.031 inch. The pupa is chestnut brown and about 0.031 inch long. Adult onion flies are slightly smaller than houseflies. They have longer legs, are slenderer, and overlap their wings when at rest.

Management

Avoid planting in soils that are high in undecomposed organic matter, such as fields just coming out of pasture or very weedy situations. Use herbicides to kill cover crop strips 3 to 4 weeks before seeding. In soils amended with animal manures, allow adequate time for the manure to break down before planting. Avoid planting successive rotations of onion crops. Early spring-planted crops are more likely to be damaged when the soil is too cool for rapid germination and emergence. If serious infestations are expected, wait until the soil warms up in spring, or, if feasible, plant in fall while the soil is still warm. When planting, use a chain drag or similar implement behind the drill to cover the seed row. Consider planting into a "stale" seedbed. Use an appropriate insecticide in the seed box at planting if problems are expected.

Fungi: Naturally-occurring fungal diseases occasionally will reduce onion maggot numbers significantly, particularly when flies are abundant and relative humidity is high. During a fungal epidemic dead, diseased flies can be seen clinging to the highest parts of plants along field edges.

Beetles: Predaceous ground beetles which eat onion maggot eggs, larvae and pupae can also be important in reducing maggot numbers. Because these soil-inhabiting beetles are susceptible to insecticides, broadcast soil insecticide treatments should be avoided whenever possible.

Nematodes: Soil application of the entomopathogenic nematode *Steinernema feltiae* has shown efficacy against cabbage maggot in trials even at low soil temperatures. Apply by suspending infective juvenile nematodes in water and treating transplants prior to setting in the field, or in transplant water used in the water wheel transplanter, as a drench after transplanting, or a combination of pre-plant and post-plant applications. Post-plant treatments are likely to be needed if maggot flight begins >1 week after transplanting. Rates of 100,000 to 125,000 infective juveniles per transplant have been shown to be needed to achieve reduction in damage. Nematodes need a moist soil environment to survive.

Direct application of insecticides to the root zone is considered the most effective means for controlling maggot damage. Insecticides should be applied as a narrow band with enough water to penetrate the root zone. For direct seeded crops, apply insecticides over the row. For transplanted crops, spray should be directed to the base of the plant.

Soil application products labelled for use against onion maggot: Check labels for specific crops allowed and other restrictions, including options for soil drench in direct-seeded and transplanted crops and transplant drench. Target the seed furrow or the base of the plants after transplanting, and use at least 100-200 gallons of water per acre to help the insecticide penetrate to the root zone. chlorpyrifos; diazinon; cyromazine (insect growth regulator).

❑ Onion Bulb Mite: *Rhizoglyphus echinopus* (Fumouze & Robin, 1868)

Common Name	:	Onion Bulb Mite
Scientific Name	:	*Rhizoglyphus echinopus* (Fumouze and Robin, 1868)
Family	:	Acaridae
Order	:	Sarcoptiformes

Source:*https://ipm.ucanr.edu/agriculture/onion-and-garlic/bulb-mites*

Distribution and Host Range

From their original discovery in Europe, bulb mites have now been found throughout the United States, Canada, Japan, and Bermuda Islands. These mites are easily transported in shipments of infested bulbs. Bulb mites have been recorded feeding on forced iris, lily, narcissus, orchid, hyacinth and tulip bulbs, dahlia tubers, and freesia and gladiolus corms. These mites also infest vegetable bulbs.

Nature and Symptoms of Damage

Bulbs infested with bulb mites may rot and fail to produce new growth, or new growth may be off color, stunted, and distorted. Although bulb mite is not considered a primary pest of bulbs, it is often responsible for serious losses; slightest injury to a bulb will allow bulb mites to enter and become established. Once mites are inside the bulb, they rapidly turn the bulbs into rotten pulp. Infestations of the bulb mite generally indicate that the bulbs have already been injured. This damage could have been caused by other pests, such as the bulb scale mite or bulb flies, mechanical injury, or improper storage. The root primordia of freesia and gladiolus may be bruised at planting. Apparently, bulb mites can attack healthy new roots and corms, especially in greenhouses. The mites may penetrate into lily stems which become brittle. Infested lilies are often dwarfed, distorted, and the stem roots are suppressed. Bulb mites attack the young root tips of *Hippeastrum* and *Eucharis*. When bulb mites attack *Gloriosa*, the new tubers get numerous small cavities and tunnels and become distorted. Bulb mites may enter prematurely opened tulip buds (due to high storage temperatures or ethylene generated by diseased bulbs in storage) and cause bud necrosis.

Life History and Description

Bulb mites are rarely noticed as isolated individuals, but rather as large colonies. All stages of the mite can be found throughout the year. Development may occur in five or six stages. In those forms with six stages, life cycle proceeds from egg to larva to protonymph to hypopus to tritonymph to adult. Females lay up to 700 eggs each depending on the host. The eggs mature in 5.1 to 27 days. The total life cycle from egg to adult could be as short as 12.2 days (at 25°C).

Adult: Mature bulb mites vary from 0.5 to 0.9 mm long and have four pairs of legs. Their bodies are shiny, white, somewhat transparent, and smooth with reddish brown appendages.

Egg: The egg is white and translucent, 0.12 mm long, and ellipsoidal.

Larva: Shortly after hatching, the larva is 0.15 to 0.2 mm long and when well-developed is 0.25 mm long. White and oval, larvae have only three pairs of legs and lack genital suckers.

Protonymph: The protonymph has four pairs of legs; it is oval and approximately 0.4 mm long. This stage can be distinguished from the tritonymph by having two genital suckers, whereas the tritonymph has three or four suckers.

Deutonymph or Hypopus: This quiescent stage is oval, convex on top, flattened below, brown, and 0.2 to 0.3 mm long. The mouthpans are absent. On the back lower side is a conspicuous sucker plate.

Tritonymph: The tritonymph is about 0.5 mm in length and has not yet developed a distinct genital aperture.

Management

It is very important to avoid rough handling of bulbs to prevent injury that might afford an entry point for fungi and bulb mites. Bulb mites cannot withstand drought and dry bulbs in storage are usually not attacked. A predaceous mite, *Cosmolaelaps claviger*, feeds readily on *R. echinopus* and other soil organisms. *R. robini* has an alarm pheromone, citral, which although not toxic to the mites, was definitely repellent.

Bulb mites are very tolerant of a number of synthetic pesticides apparently due to active oxidases, esterases, and transferases that detoxify such chemicals. Soaking bulbs in a miticide before planting has been shown to prevent bulb mite injury. Steam sterilization and methyl bromide at low concentrations eliminated the mites from soil.

❑ Two-spotted spider mite: *Tetranychus urticae* C.L. Koch, 1836; *T. cinnabarinus* (Boisduval)

Common Name	:	Red spider mite; Two-spotted spider mite
Scientific Name	:	*Tetranychus urticae* Koch; *Tetranychus cinnabarinus* (Boisduval)
Family	:	Tetranychidae
Order	:	Trombidiformes

Source:*https://www.cabidigitallibrary.org/doi/10.1079/cabicompendium.30965*

As Described in Tomato

List of pests that are associated to onion, garlic, leek and fennel crops which are of miner importance :

Common name	Scientific name	Family	Order	Specific management
		Pests of Onion		
Cut worms	Various species	Noctuidae	Lepidoptera	hand picking, Row covers
Army worms	Various species	Noctuidae	Lepidoptera	hand picking, Row covers
		Pests of Garlic		
Garlic root maggot	*Bradysia* sp.	Sciaridae	Diptera	Crop rotation, soil treatment, EPN.
Garlic leaf miner	*Acrolepiopsis assetella*	Acrolepiidae	Lepidoptera	Pruning of affected leaves, Biological control

Common name	Scientific name	Family	Order	Specific management
Pests of leek				
Leek moth	*Acrolepiopsis assectella*	Acrolepiidae	Lepidoptera	Pruning of affected leaves
Allium leaf miner	*Phytomyza glymnostoma*	Agromyzidae	Diptera	Pruning of affected leaves
Pests of Fennel				
Fennel weevil	*Ceutorhynchus pleurostigma*	Curcutionidae	Coleoptera	Crop rotation, insecticidal sprays targeted at adult stages

Resistant Varieties	
World	**India**
Redwing: This onion variety, developed by the USDA, is resistant to thrips, a major pest of onions.	**Agrifound Red:** This onion variety is resistant to the onion thrips.
Sivan: This garlic variety is resistant to the onion thrips, a pest that can cause significant damage to the plant.	**Agrifound Light Red:** This onion variety is resistant to the onion maggot, a pest that can cause significant damage to the plant.
Pikant: This shallot variety is resistant to the onion fly, a pest that can cause significant damage to the plant.	**Bhima Shubhra:** This garlic variety is resistant to the garlic shoot borer, a pest that can cause significant damage to the plant.

9 Pests of Cucurbits

Crop	Scientific Name	Family	Origin	Chromosome No.
Watermelon	*Citrullus lanatus*	Cucurbitaceae	Africa	2n = 22
Muskmelon	*Cucumis melo*	Cucurbitaceae	South Africa and Africa	2n = 24
Cucumber	*Cucumis sativus*	Cucurbitaceae	India	2n = 14
Bottle gourd	*Lagenaria siceraria*	Cucurbitaceae	Africa	2n = 22
Pumpkin	*Cucurbita pepo*	Cucurbitaceae	Central & North America	2n = 20
Bitter gourd	*Momordica charantia*	Cucurbitaceae	Tropical regions	2n = 22
Ridge gourd	*Luffa acutangula*	Cucurbitaceae	South-east Asia	2n = 26
Snake gourd	*Trichosanthes cucumenna*	Cucurbitaceae	Tropical Asia	2n = 22
Ash gourd	*Benincasa hispida*	Cucurbitaceae	South Asia	2n = 24

Cucurbits are a family of plants that includes many different types of fruits, including pumpkins, melons, and gourds. Here are some examples of cucurbit crops that are commonly grown in India along with their botany, area, and production:

Watermelon

Watermelon (*Citrullus lanatus*) belongs to the family Cucurbitaceae. It is a large, juicy fruit that is high in water content and rich in vitamins and minerals. Watermelons are widely grown in India, especially in the northern and western states. According to the National Horticulture Board, the total area under watermelon cultivation in India was 0.20 million hectares in 2020-21, with a total production of 6.16 million tonnes.

Muskmelon

Muskmelon (*Cucumis melo*) belongs to the family Cucurbitaceae. It is a sweet, juicy fruit that is rich in vitamins and minerals. Muskmelons are widely grown in India, especially in the northern and western states. According to the National Horticulture Board, the total area under muskmelon cultivation in India was 0.17 million hectares in 2020-21, with a total production of 4.96 million tonnes.

Cucumber

Cucumber (*Cucumis sativus*) belongs to the family Cucurbitaceae. It is a crunchy, refreshing fruit that is rich in vitamins and minerals. Cucumbers are widely grown in India, especially in the northern and western states. According to the National Horticulture Board, the total area under cucumber cultivation in India was 0.07 million hectares in 2020-21, with a total production of 2.59 million tonnes.

Bottle Gourd

Bottle gourd (*Lagenaria siceraria*) belongs to the family Cucurbitaceae. It is a long, cylindrical fruit that is often used in cooking. Bottle gourds are widely grown in India, especially in the northern and western states. According to the National Horticulture Board, the total area under bottle gourd cultivation in India was 0.17 million hectares in 2020-21, with a total production of 2.98 million tonnes.

Pumpkin

Pumpkin (*Cucurbita* spp.) belongs to the family Cucurbitaceae. It is a large, round fruit that is often used in cooking and decoration. Pumpkins are widely grown in India, especially in the northern and western states. According to the National Horticulture Board, the total area under pumpkin cultivation in India was 0.14 million hectares in 2020-21, with a total production of 1.59 million tonnes.

These are just a few examples of the many different types of cucurbit crops that are grown in India.

❑ Melon fly: *Bactrocera cucurbitae* (Coquillett, 1849)

Common Name	:	Melon fly
Scientific Name	:	*Bactrocera cucurbitae* (Coquillett, 1849)
Family	:	Tephritidae
Order	:	Diptera

Source: *https://link.springer.com/referenceworkentry/10.1007/978-1-4020-6359-6_4542*

Distribution and Host Range

The melon fly is well distributed over most of India, which is considered its native home, and throughout most of South-eastern Asia. It was introduced into the Hawaiian Islands from Japan about 1895. By 1897, when it was first observed, it was already a serious pest. More than 125 species of plants, including cucurbits, tomatoes, and many other vegetables, have been recorded as hosts of the melon fly. Occasional hosts include: eggplant, fig, mango, orange, papaya and peach. Wild hosts include: balsam apple; Chinese cucumber, *Momordica* spp.; colocynth; two genera of cucurbits—*Sicyos* sp.; Field Pumpkin; striped cucumber; and passion-flower, *Passiflora* spp.

Nature and Symptoms of Damage

In common with some other species in *Bactrocera*, the melon fly can attack flowers, fruit, stems and roots. In Hawaii, pumpkin and squash have been heavily attacked even before the fruit had set, with eggs laid into unopened male and female flowers, with larvae successfully developing in the taproots, stems and leaf stalks.

Life History and Description

Development from egg to adult under summer conditions requires from 12 to 28 days, according to the individual and to host and weather conditions. The developmental periods may be extended considerably by cool weather. The length of the stages in the Philippine Islands, at an average temperature of 86°F, was 1.73 days for eggs, 4 to 9 days for larvae, and 7 to 11 days for pupae. In Philippines, the preoviposition period lasted 7 to 26 days and the oviposition period 39 to 95 days.

Egg: The egg is pure white, about 2 mm long, elliptical, nearly flat on the ventral surface, more convex on the dorsal. Eggs often are somewhat curved.

Larva: The larva has three instars. The larva is white, except when its appearance is altered by the color of the food within the alimentary canal. The larva has a typical fruit fly larval shape – cylindrical-maggot shape, elongate, anterior end narrowed and somewhat curved ventrally, with anterior mouth hooks, ventral fusiform areas and flattened caudal end. The last instar larva ranges from 7.5 to 11.8 mm in length. The larva of the melon fly is particularly distinctive in having a dark sclerotized horizontal line below the spiracular region on the caudal end, with a curved ridge on each side of it. No other known fruit fly larva has this combination of characters, plus other features of the anterior spiracles and cephalo-pharyngeal skeleton.

Pupa: The puparium is about 5 to 6 mm in length and varies in color from dull red or brownish yellow to dull white, depending on the host.

Adult: The adult fly is 6 to 8 mm in length. Distinctive characteristics of the adult are the wing pattern, long third antennal segment, dorsum of the thorax reddish yellow with light yellow markings and without black markings, and head yellowish with black spots.

Management

The most effective cultural management technique to destroy the infested fruit that is not marketable, and then to dispose of the crop residues as soon as harvest is complete. There are two common mechanical methods of control. One is to use a protective covering to wrap the fruit while it develops. The other is to use baited traps. The latter is less cost effective and also best way to control them without affecting environment. Braconid parasitoids, *Fopius arisanus* or *Pysttalia fletcheri* attacked both melon fly eggs and larvae. Toxicants in baits applied both to refugia of the fruit flies and sprays applied to crops have been used. Proteinaceous liquid attractants in insecticide sprays are an effective method of controlling melon fly populations. This bait insecticide is sprayed on broad leaf plants that serve as refugia for melon flies. These baits encourage the adults to feed on the spray residue.

❑ Red pumpkin beetle: *Aulacophora foveicollis* (Lucas, 1849)

Common Name	:	Red pumpkin beetle
Scientific Name	:	*Aulacophora foveicollis* (Lucas, 1849)
Family	:	Chrysomelidae
Order	:	Coleoptera

Source:*https://apps.lucidcentral.org/pppw_v10/text/web_full/entities/pumpkin_beetle_040.htm*

Distribution and Host Range

A. foveicollis has a wide distribution across southern Europe, Asia, Australia and Africa. It is a serious pest of cucurbit crops in North-western India. Cucurbits are hosts; common cucurbits are cucumber, melon, pumpkin, watermelon and gourds. Similar species are pests of these plants in Papua New Guinea, Indonesia, the Philippines, Japan, India, and Australia. *A. foveicollis* favours pumpkin over other cucurbit crops, but will also feed on squash, muskmelon, cucumber, watermelon and the sponge gourd.

Nature and Symptoms of Damage

They feed on the leaves, buds and flowers and can defoliate the plants; the grubs bore into the roots and damage the stems and fruits that lie on the soil. Interestingly, adult beetles cut discs from the leaves. It is possible they do this to stop the flow of sap into these discs before feeding on them. There may be substances in the sap which are toxic to the beetle. Often, several beetles are found feeding together on the same leaf while others are untouched.

Life History and Description

In Northern India, the beetles hibernate over winter. After mating the female lays batches of about eight eggs in the soil. The eggs are orange and oval and hatch in one to two weeks. The grubs at first feed on leaf debris, roots and parts of the host plant in contact with the soil. They pass through four moults as they grow, and pupate in earthen chambers just below the surface of the soil. After a further week to two and a half weeks, adult beetles emerge, climb the host plant and start feeding. The females start laying eggs within a week or so. There may be five generations over the course of the summer. The adult *Aulacophora foveicollis* measures 5 to 8 mm (0.2 to 0.3 in) in length and about 3.5 mm (0.14 in) in breadth. The colour of the elytra varies from pale orange-yellow to bright orange-red to medium brown, and the abdomen is black with soft white hairs. The grubs are found in the soil and are slender and creamy-yellow, with pale brown heads and prothorax.

Management

Avoid planting new crops next to those already infested with the beetles. Fast growing varieties are more likely to outgrow the damage caused by the beetles. The beetles contain chemicals that visual predators do not like, and are avoided by them. The bright colours of this beetle warn predators that they are distasteful. Use wood ash. Add ½ cup of wood ash and ½ cup of lime in 4 L water; leave to stand for some hours and then strain; test on a few infested plants first to make adjustment to the strength before going into large-scale spraying. Use plant-derived products, such as neem, derris or pyrethrum (with the addition of soap). Note, a variety of *Derris*, brought many years ago to Solomon Islands from Papua New Guinea, is effective as a spray. It contains rotenone, an insecticide, so it should be used with caution. There may be varieties of *Derris* (fish poisons) that can be tried. Alternatively, synthetic pyrethroids are likely to be effective, but will also kill natural enemies.

❑ Cucumber moth: *Diaphania indica* (Saunders, 1851)

Common Name	:	Cucumber moth; Cotton caterpillar; Snake gourd semi looper
Scientific Name	:	*Diaphania indica* (Saunders, 1851)
Family	:	Crambidae
Order	:	Lepidoptera

Source: *https://www.inaturalist.org/taxa/51922-Diaphania-indica*

Distribution and Host Range

Diaphania indica is not restricted to the Americas, and is also found across the tropical and sub-tropical regions of Africa, Asia and Oceania. The moth is also present in Madeira (Portugal), but is not recorded in the rest of Europe. *D. indica* primarily feed on plants within the Cucurbitaceae family, including economically important crops such as cucumber, melon, pumpkin and watermelon.

Nature and Symptoms of Damage

Diaphania indica is considered a serious pest in Africa and Asia, and greatly reduces fruit yield on some hosts in some years. Leaf feeding often results in skeletonization, and in serious outbreaks, leads to much of the foliage on plants being destroyed. However, more serious damage tends to occur on flowers and in fruit. Damage to the inner portions of flowers can prevent fruit developing. While entry of larvae into soft fruit and feeding on the rind of hard fruit often leaves the fruit unmarketable, particularly after suffering from secondary infection by pathogens.

Life History and Description

Eggs are white or whitish in colour they also turn yellow as they develop. They are small, usually laid in very small clumps of around 2-6 eggs, and are roughly 0.7-0.95 mm long and 0.3- 0.6 mm wide. It has five larval instars, with mature larvae growing up to 25 mm. Upon maturity, two white dorsal stripes can be seen to run the length of their bodies and they may have 4 very small black spots in a square just behind the head. Pupae are 12-20 mm long and around 3-4 mm wide, and are often found in a loose cocoon formed by spinning leaves together with silk. The pupae turn from white to brown as develop. Adults are about 13-16 mm long, with a wingspan of 24-33 mm. Their wings have a white and that is banded by brown, and exhibit a purple iridescence.

Management

By planting early, before the moths have arrived; By placing row covers and mulches over plants, which can either be removed after flowering or can be kept on only during the night when the moths are active, but allowing for activity by daytime pollinators; and by planting trap crops, such as summer squash, which are preferred and deter moths from feeding on more valuable crops. Once moths have established within the crop, destruction of infested plants is the best means of eradication. This can be followed by a crop rotation or crop break, and removal of debris and wild hosts, to prevent the potential build-up of the moths.

The biological pesticide, *Bacillus thuringiensis* var. *kurstaki*, has also given some success. Many natural enemies, including predators and parasitoids, have been identified. However, only a few have shown any promise as effective biological control agents. One of these is the entomopathogenic nematode, *Steinernema carpocapsae*, which is available for use.

❑ Squash bug: *Anasa tristis* (De Geer),1773

Common Name	:	Squash bug
Scientific Name	:	*Anasa tristis* (De Geer), 1773
Family	:	Coreidae
Order	:	Hemiptera

Source: *https://www.marylandbiodiversity.com/view/11015*

Distribution and Host Range

Anasa tristis is a species of bug in the family Coreidae. It is a major pest of squash and pumpkins, found throughout North America, and is a vector of the cucurbit yellow vine disease bacterium. These bugs can emit an unpleasant odour when disturbed. *Anasa tristis* can be found on various members of the gourd family Cucurbitaceae, but most often occurs on pumpkins and squashes. Some varieties and cultivars are more susceptible to attack than others.

Nature and Symptoms of Damage

Anasa tristis is a true bug that feeds by sucking sap, mainly from the leaves, but sometimes also the fruit. The heavier the infestation, the greater the damage to the plant. Sometimes one plant or part of a plant can be heavily attacked while surrounding plants are untouched. Besides the direct damage their feeding causes to the plant, these insects can act as vectors for cucurbit yellow vine disease caused by the bacterium *Serratia marcescens*. This disease can kill the plants.

Life History and Description

In the Southern part of its range, the adult female *Anasa tristis* lays two or three batches of about eighteen eggs, but in the Northern part of the range it just lays a single batch. The eggs are oval, somewhat flattened and bronze in colour, and are deposited on the underside of the leaves of the host plant. They may be clustered close together or more widely dispersed but are often regularly arranged. The eggs hatch after seven to nine days into nymphs which have five instar stages. The first instar nymphs are green and about 2.5 mm (0.1 in) in length. Each successive instar is larger and less hairy and grey. The fifth instar is grey, with developing wing pads and about 10 mm (0.4 in) in length. The complete nymphal stage lasts about 33 days. The adult *Anasa tristis* is a greyish-brown, somewhat flattened insect reaching a length of about 1.5 cm (0.6 in) and a width of 0.75 cm (0.3 in). There is often a row of alternate brown and gold spots along the margin of the abdomen. Adults survive for three or four months.

Management

The best method for control is prevention through sanitation. Remove old cucurbit plants after harvest. Keep the garden free from rubbish and debris that can provide overwintering sites for squash bugs. At the end of the gardening season, compost all vegetation or thoroughly till it under. Handpick or vacuum any bugs found under wooden boards. During the growing season, pick off and destroy egg masses as soon as you see them. Use protective covers such as plant cages or row covers in gardens where squash bugs have been a problem in the past and remove covers at bloom to allow for pollination. Trellising: Using a trellis for vining types of squash and melons can make them less vulnerable to squash bug infestation. Resistant varieties: Some squash varieties, including butternut, royal acorn, and sweet cheese, are more resistant to squash bugs. The parasitic tachinid flies *Trichopoda pennipes,* which lays its eggs on squash bugs, has been introduced into California and may be found in some gardens. Look for the eggs of this parasite on the undersides of squash bugs.

Squash bugs are difficult to kill using insecticides because egg masses, nymphs, and bugs are often hidden near the crown of the plant and difficult to reach with sprays. Several insecticides are available that are less toxic to the environment including products containing soaps and oils such as neem oil, horticultural oil, and canola oil. These soaps and oils are most effective on the smallest nymphs, but good penetration throughout the canopy is essential so that nymphs under the leaves and deep within plants will be covered. Other more toxic pesticides are also registered for use on squash bugs; however, these materials should be used with caution because of negative impacts on bees and beneficial insects such as predators and parasites that help to keep other pest insects and mites in check. In addition, they are not likely to give better control than handpicking combined with softer chemicals.

❑ Serpentine leaf miner: *Liriomyza trifolii* (Burgess, 1880)

Common Name	:	Serpentine leaf miner
Scientific Name	:	*Liriomyza trifolii* (Burgess, 1880)
Family	:	Agromyzidae
Order	:	Diptera

Source: *https://www.cabidigitallibrary.org/doi/10.1079/cabicompendium.30965*

As Described in Tomato

❑ Epilachna beetle: *Henosepilachna dodecastigma* (Wiedemann); *H. vigintioctopunctata* (Fabricius, 1775)

Common Name	:	Hadda/spotted beetle; Epilachna beetles
Scientific Name	:	*Henosepilachna dodecastigma* (7-14 spots on each elytra); *H. vigintioctopunctata* (28 spotted beetle)
Family	:	Coccinellidae
Order	:	Coleoptera

Source: *https://en.wikipedia.org/wiki/Henosepilachna_vigintioctopunctata*

As Described in Potato

❑ Green peach aphid: *Myzus persicae* (Sulzer, 1776)

Common Name	:	Green peach aphid, green fly or Peach-potato aphid
Scientific Name	:	*Myzus persicae* (Sulzer, 1776)
Family	:	Aphididae
Order	:	Hemiptera

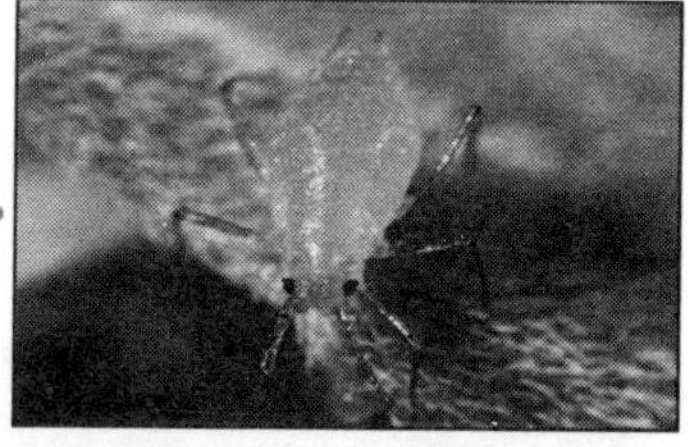

Source: *https://inpn.mnhn.fr/espece/cd_nom/52046/tab/taxo*

As Described in Potato

Some other Pests of Cucurbits

Common Name	Scientific Name	Family	Order
Cucumber beetle	*Acalymma vittatun*	Chrysonelidae	Coleoptera
Cucumber vine bore	*Melittia cucurbitae*	sesiidae	Lepidoptera
Squash vine bore	*Melittia satyriniformis*	Sesiidae	Lepidoptera

Resistant Varieties	
World	**India**
Diva: This cucumber variety, developed by the USDA, is resistant to the cucumber beetle, a pest that can cause significant damage to the plant.	**Arka Samrat:** This cucumber variety is resistant to the cucumber beetle.
Super Melon: This melon variety is resistant to the melon fly, a pest that can cause significant damage to the plant.	**Arka Harit:** This melon variety is resistant to the melon fly.
Payzawat: This pumpkin variety is resistant to the squash bug, a pest that can cause significant damage to the plant.	**Arka Bahar:** This squash variety is resistant to the squash bug.
Diplomat: A squash variety that is resistant to the squash vine borer.	**Pusa Sheetal:** A cucumber variety that is resistant to the cucumber beetle.
Honeydew Green Flesh: A melon variety that is resistant to the melon aphid.	**Pusa Sadabahar:** A pumpkin variety that is resistant to the fruit fly.
Athena: A cucumber variety that is resistant to the cucumber beetle.	**CO-1:** A bottle gourd variety that is resistant to the fruit fly.
Butternut Elite: A squash variety that is resistant to the squash bug.	**Pusa Ujjwal:** A sponge gourd variety that is resistant to the fruit fly.
Magnum: A watermelon variety that is resistant to the watermelon mosaic virus and the watermelon fruit fly.	**Arka Anamika:** A bitter gourd variety that is resistant to the fruit fly.

Pests of Legumes

Crop	Scientific Name	Family	Origin	Chromosome No.
Chickpea	*Cicer arietium*	Leguminaceae	South-west Asia	2n = 16
Pigeon pea	*Cajanus cajan*	Leguminaceae	India, South-east Asia	2n = 22
Black gram	*Vigna mungo*	Leguminaceae	South Asia	2n = 22
Green gram	*Vigna radiata*	Leguminaceae	South Asia	2n = 22
Soybean	*Glycine max*	Leguminaceae	East Asia	2n = 40
Pea	*Pisum sativum*	Leguminaceae	Mediterranean region	2n = 14
Broad bean	*Vicia faba*	Leguminaceac	Mediterranean region	2n = 12, 14, 16
Lima bean	*Phaseolus lunatus*	Leguminaceae	South America	2n = 24, 28
Winged bean	*Psophocarpus tetragonolobus*	Leguminaceae	South-east Asia	2n = 22
Lentil	*Lens culinaris*	Leguminaceae	South-west Asia	2n = 14
Cowpea	*Vigna unguiculata*	Leguminaceae	Africa	2n = 22, 24

Legumes are a family of plants that includes many different types of crops, including beans, lentils, peas, and chickpeas. Here are some examples of legume crops that are commonly grown in India along with their botany, area, and production:

Chickpea

Chickpea (*Cicer arietinum*) belongs to the family Fabaceae. It is a highly nutritious legume that is rich in protein, fiber, and other essential nutrients. Chickpeas are widely grown in India, especially in the northern and central states. According to the Ministry of Agriculture and Farmers' Welfare, the total area under chickpea cultivation in India was 7.58 million hectares in 2020-21, with a total production of 11.24 million tonnes.

Pigeon Pea

Pigeon pea (*Cajanus cajan*) belongs to the family Fabaceae. It is a drought-resistant legume that is widely grown in India, especially in the southern and central states. Pigeon peas are a rich source of protein, fiber, and other essential nutrients. According to the Ministry of Agriculture and Farmers'

Welfare, the total area under pigeon pea cultivation in India was 5.21 million hectares in 2020-21, with a total production of 4.91 million tonnes.

Black Gram

Black gram (*Vigna mungo*) belongs to the family Fabaceae. It is a highly nutritious legume that is rich in protein, fiber, and other essential nutrients. Black gram is widely grown in India, especially in the southern states. According to the Ministry of Agriculture and Farmers' Welfare, the total area under black gram cultivation in India was 3.23 million hectares in 2020-21, with a total production of 2.13 million tonnes.

Green Gram

Green gram (*Vigna radiata*) belongs to the family Fabaceae. It is a highly nutritious legume that is rich in protein, fiber, and other essential nutrients. Green gram is widely grown in India, especially in the southern and central states. According to the Ministry of Agriculture and Farmers' Welfare, the total area under green gram cultivation in India was 4.10 million hectares in 2020-21, with a total production of 2.78 million tonnes.

Soybean

Soybean (*Glycine max*) belongs to the family Fabaceae. It is a highly nutritious legume that is rich in protein, fiber, and other essential nutrients. Soybeans are widely grown in India, especially in the central and western states. According to the Ministry of Agriculture and Farmers' Welfare, the total area under soybean cultivation in India was 11.58 million hectares in 2020-21, with a total production of 13.80 million tonnes.

These are just a few examples of the many different types of legume crops that are grown in India.

Legume pod borer: *Maruca vitrata* (Fabricius, 1787)

Common Name	:	Legume pod borer
Scientific Name	:	*Maruca vitrata* (Fabricius, 1787)
Family	:	Crambidae
Order	:	Lepidoptera

Source:*https://uk.inaturalist.org/taxa/122668-Maruca-vitrata*

Distribution and Host Range

M. vitrata is considered the most serious pest of food legumes in tropical Asia, sub-Saharan Africa, South America, North America, Australia and Pacific. *M. vitrata* most likely can feed on at least 45 different host plant species, including two non-leguminous hosts (*Sesamum* sp. and *Hibiscus* sp.) in tropical Asia and Sub-saharan Africa. It is a major pest on at least nine cultivated legume species (*Vigna unguiculata* subsp. *sesquipedalis*, *V. radiata*, *V. mungo*, *Cajanus cajan*, *Lablab purpureus*, *Phaseolus angularis*, *P. vulgaris*, *Sesbania cannabina* and *S. grandiflora*) year-round.

Nature and Symptoms of Damage

Infestation starts in the terminal shoots but later spreads to the reproductive structures. The larvae move from one flower to the other, and each may consume about four to six flowers before completing the larval stage. Infestation is highest on flowers, followed by floral buds, pods, and leaves. The mature larvae, especially from the third instar, are capable of damaging pods, and occasionally the peduncle and stems. First instar larvae prefer to feed on flowers rather than pods or leaves. The larvae feed on floral buds, flowers, and pods by webbing. Often the damaged pods and inflorescence show frass.

Life History and Description

Egg: The females lay eggs singly or in smaller groups of 2-16 on the floral buds, flowers and pods. Occasionally they are also laid on the leaves, leaf axils, terminal shoots and stem. Eggs are oval in shape and pale yellow in color. The egg period is about 2 to 4 days.

Larva: The larva is whitish to pale brown in color, with irregular but prominent brownish black spots on the dorsal side. The head capsule is light to dark brown. The larva has five instars and the larval period varies from 2 to 3 weeks depending on the temperature.

Pupa: Pupation occurs inside the silken cocoon, either in the soil or under plant debris. Sometimes pupation also takes place within the feeding web in the host plants. The pupal stage lasts for 5 to 10 days.

Adult: The adult moths of *M. vitrata* have light brown forewings with white patches, and white hind wings with an irregular brown border. Wings are 20-25 mm long. It often rests with the wings outspread. Adults live from 1 to 3 weeks.

Management

Early sown crops may escape from *M. vitrata* damage, because the pod borer population tends to increase over the season. Mixed cropping and intercropping can reduce the incidence of *M. vitrata*. For instance, intercropping of common bean with maize significantly minimizes pod borer damage on beans. Grow Sun hemp as a trap crop against *M. vitrata*. The plant is highly attractive to the egg laying female moths, but highly unsuitable for the developing larvae of *M. vitrata*, and thus can be used as a 'dead-end' trap crop. Sex pheromone lures of *M. vitrata* are commercially available and can be used for monitoring. *Maruca vitrata* multiple nucleopolyhedrovirus (MaviMNPV) recently has been developed as a biopesticide in Taiwan and Benin, and can be used to replace chemical pesticides. SlNPV is effective either alone or in combination with neem. In addition, *Bacillus thuringiensis* formulations. Several parasitoid species have been reported for *M. vitrata* in tropical Asia and Africa. AVRDC – The World Vegetable Center identified three relatively specific parasitoids *viz.*, an egg-larval parasitoid, *Phanerotoma syleptae*, and two larval parasitoids, *Therophilus javanus* and *T. marucae* of *M. vitrata*. Chemical pesticides may highly be effective against early larval stages, before the larvae entering into the reproductive parts of the plants. Avoid using the same pesticide group or compounds having the same mode of action, since *M. vitrata* is able to develop resistance quickly.

❑ Lima bean pod borer: *Etiella zinckenella* (Treitschke, 1832)

Common Name	:	Lima bean pod borer
Scientific Name	:	*Etiella zinckenella* (Treitschke, 1832)
Family	:	Pyralidae
Order	:	Lepidoptera

Source: *http://www.agroatlas.ru/en/content/pests/Etiella_zinckenella/index.html*

Distribution and Host Range

E. zinckenella widely occurs in Asia, sub-Saharan Africa, South America, North America, Australia, Europe and Caribbean. Although it has been reported on several legume crops, it causes significant yield losses in lentil, peas and soybean.

Nature and Symptoms of Damage

Infestation of *E. zinckenella* usually starts late in the season. The larvae feed on floral buds, flowers, and pods by making rough and irregular incisions. The pods may have several entry holes. They feed on the seeds inside the pods. Often the damaged pods and inflorescence show light coloured frass and loosely spun webs.

Life History and Description

Egg: The females lay eggs singly or in smaller groups of 2-12 on immature pods and around the calyx. Eggs are shiny white. The egg period is about 4 to 5 days, although it could be as high as three weeks under low temperature.

Larva: The upper surface of the larva is reddish-pink, whereas the sides and the lower surface of the body are pale green in color. The larval period varies from 3 to 6 weeks depending on the temperature. In parts of Russia and neighbouring countries, it overwinters as larva. Toward pupation, the larva moves down to the soil surface for pupation either in the soil or under plant debris.

Pupa: Pupa is light green when newly formed, and later it turns to light brown. The pupal stage lasts for 1 to 3 weeks.

Adult: The adult is a greyish brown snout moth. The forewings have a distinct pale-white band along the costal margin. Hind wings are partially transparent with a dark marginal line. Wings are about 20 mm long. Adults live 2 to 3 weeks.

Management

Choose tolerant or resistant cultivars available in the region. For instance, the soybean accession PI 227687 is consistently resistant to *E. zinckenella*. Several parasitoid species have been reported for *E. zinckenella* in tropical Asia, Europe and North America. For instance, *Apanteles hanoii*, *A. taragamae*, *Bracon* sp., *Trathala flavoorbitalis* and *Tropobracon luteus* have been recorded from *E. zinckenella* in Vietnam. Biopesticides such as *B. thuringiensis* and neem are highly effective against *E. zinckenella*. Do not spray broad-spectrum chemical pesticides. If necessary, spray a systemic pesticide after consulting with local extension staff.

❑ Blue Butterfly: *Lampides boeticus* (Linnaeus, 1767)

Common Name	:	Blue butterfly
Scientific Name	:	*Lampides boeticus* (Linnaeus, 1767)
Family	:	Lycaenidae
Order	:	Lepidoptera

Source: https://in.pinterest.com/pin/517210338431953686/

Distribution and Host Range

Blue butterflies occasionally cause serious yield losses in food legumes in Asia, sub-Saharan Africa, Europe, Australia and the Pacific. They mainly feed on legumes.

Nature and Symptoms of Damage

The larva bores into the floral buds, flowers and green pods soon after emergence from eggs, and feeds on the inner contents. Damage on the pods is characterized by round holes.

Life History and Description

Egg: The spherical shaped eggs are laid singly on floral buds, flowers and immature pods. Sometimes they are also laid on growing shoots and leaves. Eggs are pale blue or greenish white in color. The egg period is about 4 to 7 days.

Larva: The larva is relatively sedentary and it is yellowish green in color. The entire body of the larva has small and sparse setae. In general, the larva looks like a slug. The larval period varies from 2 to 4 weeks depending on the temperature.

Pupa: Pupation occurs on the leaves, twigs and pods, and to some extent in the soil or under plant debris. Pupa is reddish brown lasts for a week.

Adult: The adult is a medium-sized butterfly. The wings are metallic blue to dusky blue in color. The tail of hind wings is black and tipped with white about 3 cm long.

Management

Blue butterfly larvac occur infrequently in vegetable legumes. In addition, they are attacked by several parasitoids such as *Trichogramma chilotraeae*, *T. bactrae* and *Cotesia specularis*. If necessary, spray the most effective biopesticides based on *Paecilomyces lilacinus*, *Vetricillium lecani* and neem. These are superior to *B. thuringiensis* and other entomopathogenic fungi.

❑ Bean fly: *Ophiomyia phaseoli* (Tryon. 1895); *Melanagromyza obtusa* Malloch

Common Name	:	Bean fly
Scientific Name	:	*Ophiomyia phaseoli* (Tryon. 1895), *Melanagromyza obtusa* Malloch
Family	:	Agromyzidae
Order	:	Diptera

Source: *http://krishimala.com/catalogue/stem-fly-bean-fly*

Ophiomyia phaseoli

Source: *http://krishimala.com/catalogue/red-gram-pod-fly*

Melanagromyza obtusa

Distribution and Host Range

Bean flies are one of the most destructive pests of food legumes, especially during the crops' seedling stage. They occur in Asia, Africa, Australia and Oceania. Larvae of these insects feed on legumes as internal feeders and leaf miners. *O. phaseoli* has the widest distribution and host range, and causes the maximum damage. The young larvae of *M. obtusa* attach themselves to the soft seeds inside the pods, and initially feed on the seed surface. They subsequently mine into the seeds, and the mines are often filled with faecal matter. Older larvae feed deep into the seeds, at times eating the embryo. Usually, a larva completes its development in one seed. The fully grown larvae come out of the seed, leaving behind a clear exit hole. Thus, the damaged pod is poorly filled.

Nature and Symptoms of Damage

The most serious damage by *O. phaseoli* adults starts at the unifoliate leaf stage. The unifoliate leaves show several feeding and oviposition punctures on the upper surface with corresponding light-yellow spots, especially in the basal portion of the leaf. These feeding and oviposition wounds could predispose the plant for the entry of pathogens. The larvae start feeding in the leaf tissue, leaf lamina and then the petiole and stem. The larvae feed voraciously in the cortex, and continue downwards into the tap root. Because of the severe disturbances in the transport of water and nutrients, the plants, especially in the seedling stage, wilt and die.

Life History and Description

Ophiomyia phaseoli

Egg: The adult females of *O. phaseoli* lay eggs in unifoliate or early defoliate leaves. They usually lay the eggs on the upper leaf surfaces, often near the midrib close to the petiole. The eggs are inserted between the epidermis and spongy parenchyma. The egg is oval shaped, milky white in color and opaque or translucent. Each female lays about 300 eggs throughout its life. The egg period is 2 to 4 days depending on the temperature.

Maggot: The larva of *O. phaseoli* has three instars. The newly hatched pale larvae remain motionless beneath the leaf epidermis in a cavity made by its mother during egg laying. One to two hours after emergence, it starts feeding inside a mine directed toward the vein of the leaf. On reaching the midrib, the larva constructs a tunnel in it and moults into the second instar. The yellowish white second instar larva moves its head constantly from side to side within the relatively straight mine built in the leaf vein. The light yellow-coloured third instar larva actively feeds in the petiole or stem. In younger plants, the larva continues feeding inside the stem until or slightly below the soil level. However, it feeds only in the junction of petiole and stem until its pupation in older plants. The larval period is about 8 to 9 days.

Pupa: The larva of *O. phaseoli* pupates on young plants beneath the epidermis of the stem near the soil surface. Under high larval density, pupation may also take place inside the stem pith. In mature plants, pupation takes place at the junction of the leaf lamina and petiole. The pupa is yellow with a brownish tinge and is barrel shaped. The color of the puparium becomes dark brown shortly before adult emergence.

Adult: The adult *O. phaseoli* flies are metallic black in color, with light brown eyes and hyaline wings having a distinct notch in the coastal region. The longevity of adults could be as high as 1.5 months, with an average of 3 weeks. However, the copulating male usually lives for about 10 days, and the egg laying female lives for 1 to 3 weeks.

Melanagromyza obtusa Malloch

Egg: *M. obtusa* lays eggs singly on the green pods. The freshly laid eggs are white and broad. The egg period is 3 to 10 days depending on the temperature.

Maggot: The freshly hatched larva of *M. obtusa* is white with dark brown or black mouth parts. The fully grown larva is sub-cylindrical, creamy white with dark black mouth parts. The body acquires a yellow tinge just before pupation. The larval period varies from 6 to 19 days depending on the temperature.

Pupa: The larva of *M. obtusa* briefly enters into a pre-pupal stage. The pupa is enclosed in a hard chitinous puparium that is attached to the inner side of the pod wall. The newly formed pupa is yellowish white and gradually turns to creamy yellow, reddish brown and darker. The pupal period varies from 1 to 3 weeks.

Adults: The newly emerged adult of *M. obtusa* is dull white and changes to black in an hour. The life span is only 7 to 12 days.

Management

Choose resistant or moderately resistant cultivars available in the region. Earth up the plants three days after the appearance of the cotyledons above ground, so that most of the plants can overcome bean fly infestation. Although intercropping is not highly useful in reducing bean fly incidence, intercropping jute with mungbean simultaneously in alternate rows could reduce the bean fly infestation. Growing pearl millet and mungbean as intercrops with pigeon pea reduce the damage of *M. obtusa*. Cultivation of onion as an intercrop with common bean lowers bean fly infestation. Parasitoids such as *Opius phaseoli* against *O. phaseoli* and *Eucoilidea* sp. against *O. spencerella* and *O. centrosematis* are efficient parasitoids. Protect the population of these parasitoids by avoiding the use of broad-spectrum pesticides. Effective seed-dressing insecticides have been identified.

❑ Cowpea aphid: *Aphis craccivora* C.L. Koch, 1854

Common Name	:	Cowpea aphid; Groundnut aphid; Black legume aphid,
Scientific Name	:	*Aphis craccivora* C.L. Koch, 1854[
Family	:	Aphididae
Order	:	Hemiptera

Source: *https://uk.inaturalist.org/taxa/145414-Aphis-craccivora*

Distribution and Host Range

Infests cowpea in India, Philippines, Thailand, Southern United States, tropical Africa, and Latin America. This is a serious pest on cowpea, yard-long bean, hyacinth bean and peanut starting from the seedling stage to pod-producing stage. It acts as a direct pest and also transmits virus diseases.

Nature and Symptoms of Damage

A. craccivora prefers to feed on legume crops; it is commonly known as "**cowpea aphid**." Both the nymphs and adults possess piercing and sucking mouthparts. They occur in large numbers on the tender shoots, lower leaf surfaces, petioles, flowers and pods, and suck the plant sap. Slightly infested leaves exhibit yellowing. Severe aphid infestations cause stunting, crinkling and curling of leaves, delayed flowering, shrivelling of pods, resulting in yield reduction. Young plants may be killed due to heavy infestation. *A. craccivora* also transmits bean common mosaic virus and cucumber mosaic virus in a non-persistent manner. Large populations of the pest secrete substantial quantities of honeydew, which favours the growth of sooty mold on leaves and reduces the photosynthetic efficiency of the plants.

Life History and Description

Adult: Unlike many insects, most aphids reproduce asexually in the tropics. They usually reproduce through parthenogenesis and are viviparous. The early instar nymphs are grey in color, whereas the late instar nymphs and adult are black. Both wingless and winged forms occur. Winged forms are produced when population density is high, when host plants are of inferior quality, etc. The wingless forms are more common. Aphids mostly are found in groups. The nymphal period is about 5 to 8 days, and the total lifecycle is 11 to 14 days.

Management

Avoid monoculture and follow crop rotation. The selected field should be located away from other legume crops. Use entomopathogenic fungi (EPF) such as *Beauveria bassiana*, *Metarhizium anisopliae*, *Verticillium lecanii* and *Hirsutella thompsonii* at a concentration of 1×10^8 conidia ml^{-1}. Use neem oil, either alone or in combination with the EPF biopesticides. The ladybird beetles (*Menochilus sexmaculatus, Brumus suturalis, Harmonia dimidiate, Brumus suturalis* and *Coccinella septempunctata*) and green lacewings (*Chrysoperla carnea*) are efficient predators of aphids. Protect the population of these predators by avoiding the use of broad-spectrum pesticides. *A. craccivora* can develop resistance to pesticides. Use only those pesticides that have been recommended by local extension staff. Do not use the same compound or pesticide group continuously to avoid the development of pesticide resistance in insects.

❑ Beet army worm: *Spodoptera exigua* (Hübner, 1808)

Common Name	:	Beet army worm
Scientific Name	:	*Spodoptera exigua* (Hübner, 1808)
Family	:	Noctuidae
Order	:	Lepidoptera

Source: *https://entnemdept.ufl.edu/creatures/veg/leaf/beet_armyworm.htm*

Distribution and Host Range

Like *S. litura*, *S. exigua* is also a polyphagous and nocturnal insect that mainly feeds on vegetable soybean, besides other vegetables such as tomato, eggplant, hot and sweet pepper, onion, etc.

Nature and Symptoms of Damage

The larvae cause defoliation. Sometimes, the larvae may also cut the seedlings or young plants at soil level. Occasionally the larvae may feed on the pods.

Life History and Description

Egg: The eggs are laid in groups of 100-150 and covered with brown hairs from the body of the mother, similar to *S. litura*. The egg period is about 3 to 5 days.

Larva: The grown-up larvae are brownish green dorsally and pale-yellow coloured ventrally with a lateral white or yellow stripe. Larval period is about 2 to 3 weeks. The larva passes through five instars.

Pupa: Pupation takes place in earthen cocoons in soil. Pupae are light brown. The pupal period varies from 7 to 11 days.

Adult: Adults of *S. exigua* are medium-sized moths with a wing span of about 30 mm. The adults are usually brown coloured; the forewings are mottled brown in color. The hind wings are grey with a brown line along the border. The adult period is about 10 days, and on average a single female lays about 500-600 eggs.

Management

Similar to *S. litura*.

❑ Bean foliage beetles: *Ootheca* spp.

Common Name	:	Bean foliage beetles
Scientific Name	:	*Ootheca* spp.
Family	:	Chrysomelidae
Order	:	Coleoptera

Source: *https://plantwiseplusknowledgebank.org/doi/10.1079/pwkb.20147800119*

Distribution and Host Range

Ootheca mutabilis (Schönherr) and *O. bennigseni* Weise are important foliage feeders on food legumes such as cowpea and common bean in Eastern and Southern African countries, especially Burundi, Kenya, Rwanda, Tanzania and Zambia. They attack the foliage soon after germination, causing yield losses of 27- 100%.

Nature and Symptoms of Damage

The adult beetles start feeding on leaves of newly planted legume crops, especially cowpea and beans. They feed on the foliage between the veins, and cause extensive defoliation. Damage to the growing shoots of young seedlings and heavy infestation completely destroy a crop. The adults occasionally feed on the floral parts. Additionally, larvae feeding on lateral roots cause wilting and premature senescence in bean plants. Apart from direct feeding, the beetles also vector Cowpea yellow mosaic virus.

Life History and Description

Egg: The females lay eggs in clusters of about 60 eggs per cluster in soil close to the legume plants. Each female lays up to eight egg clusters. The eggs are elliptical and yellow in color. The egg period is about 2 to 3 weeks.

Larva: The larva of *Ootheca* spp. develops through three instars, followed by a pre-pupal stage. The larval period varies from 5 to 11 weeks depending on the temperature.

Pupa: The larva pupates in an earthen cell within the soil. The pupal stage lasts for about 16 days. Soil temperature plays an important role in its development.

Adult: The adults of *Ootheca* spp. undergo an obligatory diapause until the onset of the rainy season. The adult beetles are shiny, oval shaped and about 6 mm long. The adults vary in color ranging from orange to brown, and at times blackish.

Management

Choose tolerant or resistant cultivars available in the region. For instance, several bean lines are reported to be moderately resistant to *O. bennigseni* in Tanzania. Consult the local extension agency for the availability of tolerant or resistant varieties. Biopesticides such as neem are highly effective against *Ootheca* spp. Use biopesticides if they are available and recommended in the region. Locally prepared botanical extracts such as aqueous extract from vernonia (*Vernonia lasiopus* var. *iodocalyx*) leaves are proven effective in reducing the infestation of *Ootheca* spp. Do not control the *Ootheca* infestation with broad spectrum chemical pesticides. If necessary, spray a recommended pesticide after consulting with local extension staff.

Thrips: *Megalurothrips distalis* (Karny); *M. usitatus* (Bagnall); *M. sjostedti* (Tribom)

Common Name	:	Thrips
Scientific Name	:	*Megalurothrips distalis* (Karny); *M. usitatus* (Bagnall); *M. sjostedti* (Tribom)
Family	:	Thripidae
Order	:	Thysanoptera

Source: *https://keys.lucidcentral.org/keys/v3/thysanoptera*

Distribution and Host Range

M. distalis and *M. usitatus* are widely distributed in South and Southeast Asia and Oceania; *M. sjostedti* predominantly occurs in Africa. They mainly feed on the flowers of legumes, and can cause 100% yield losses if left uncontrolled.

Nature and Symptoms of Damage

Thrips remain hidden inside the flower buds and flowers. Both the larvae and adults feed on the tender leaves in the beginning. However, they prefer to feed mostly on flowers. Slightly infested leaves exhibit silvery feeding scars. In severe infestations on the flowers, the open flowers are discoloured and distorted showing elongated brownish streaks; they dry out, and fall prematurely without forming pods. Infested pods are scarred and deformed.

Life History and Description

Egg: The females lay eggs within the leaf tissues, especially in the terminal leaflets. The egg may not be visible to the naked eye. The egg period is about 2 to 3 days.

Larva: The larva of *M. distalis* is whitish translucent. *M. usitatus* larva is pale yellow in color, and turns to yellowish to orange-red, whereas the larva of *M. sjostedti* is whitish in the beginning and later turns to yellow to orange. The larval period varies from 1 to 2 weeks depending on the temperature. As pupation nears, the larva stops feeding and moves down to the soil surface either in the soil or under plant debris.

Pupa: The pupal stage lasts for five days to one week. Moisture plays an important role, because dryness in the soil could lead to the desiccation and death of the pupae.

Adult: The adults of *M. distalis* are brownish in color, whereas the adults of *M. usitatus* are dark brown. The adults of *M. sjostedti* are black in color. The adults of *Megalurothrips* are about 1.5-1.65 mm long.

Management

Choose tolerant or resistant cultivars available in the region. Grow vegetable legume (yard-long bean and common bean) seedlings in insect-proof (50-64 mesh) net houses, net tunnels, greenhouses, or plastic houses to avoid early infestation, especially in the dry season. Predators such as *Orius albidipennis* and *Paederus sabaeus* feed on *M. sjostedti* in West Africa. Parasitoids such as *Ceranisus menes* and *C. femoratus* are effective candidates against *M. sjostedti* and *M. usitatus*. However, they are unable to provide complete control. Use blue sticky traps to monitor thrips at regular intervals and determine when other pest management controls are required. Entomopathogenic fungi could play a vital role in managing bean flower thrips, because of the moisture and humidity within the flower buds. For instance, 100% mortality of the adults of *M. sjostedti* was recorded at the highest concentration (1×10^8 conidia ml^{-1}) of *Metarhizium anisopliae* at 8 days post-inoculation. At the same concentration, daily pollen consumption was significantly reduced at 2 days after treatment in infected adults. Do not control the thrips infestation with broad-spectrum chemical pesticides, as a resurgence of thrips will likely occur.

❑ Pod bugs: *Clavigralla gibbosa* Spinola, 1837, *C. scutellaris* (Westwood, 1842), *C. tomentosicollis* (Stal.)

Common Name	:	Pod bugs
Scientific Name	:	*Clavigralla gibbosa* Spinola, 1837, *C. scutellaris* (Westwood), *C. tomentosicollis* (Stal.)
Family	:	Coreidae
Order	:	Hemiptera

Source: *https://indiabiodiversity.org/species/show/276126*

Distribution and Host Range

C. gibbosa and *C. scutellaris* are distributed in the tropics and sub-tropics, whereas *C. tomentosicollis* is predominantly present in Africa. They mainly feed on vegetable and grain legumes. These bugs comprise a serious group of pests causing damage to food legumes. They can cause yield loss of 20-100% in different parts of Asia and Africa.

Nature and Symptoms of Damage

The nymphs and adults have piercing and sucking mouthparts. They penetrate the pod walls and suck the sap from developing seeds inside. Occasionally they also feed on stems, leaves and flower buds. Feeding on the pods causes yellow blotches. Severe infestations lead to shrivelled pods and seeds. The damage is serious during prolonged dry weather conditions.

Life History and Description

Egg: The females lay eggs mostly on the leaves and pods. On average, each *C. gibbosa* and *C. scutellaris* female lays about 60-200 eggs, whereas *C. tomentosicollis* lays about 120 eggs. The egg is brown in color. *C. scutellaris* eggs are smooth and shiny, and the eggs of *C. gibbosa* are roughly sculptured. Eggs are laid in clusters of 2-60. *C. gibbosa* generally lays clusters of 3-15 eggs, whereas *C. scutellaris* lays clusters of 18-20. The egg period varies from 2 to 5 days. However, it may be prolonged up to three weeks under low temperature conditions.

Nymph: The newly hatched nymphs of *Clavigralla* are reddish in color and later turn brown. Nymphs are gregarious. The nymphal period is about 1 to 3 weeks, depending on the temperature.

Adult: The *Clavigralla* bugs are brown-gray in color. In the field, *C. gibbosa* and *C. scuttellaris* are often mistaken for each other. However, *C. scutellaris* is more robust than *C. gibbosa* and *C. tomentosicollis*. The adult longevity is more than three months for the *Clavigralla* bugs. Although the males and females are similar, the female is slightly larger with a rounded abdomen.

Management

Inter-cropping of legumes with millets such as sorghum could delay the infestation of pod bugs. Parasitoids such as *Gryon fulviventris* against *C. tomentosicollis* in Africa, an unidentified *Gryon* sp. against *C. gibbosa*, and *Gryon clavigrallae* Mineo against *C. gibbosa* and *C. scutellaris* in Asia are found to be effective candidates for biological control. If the parasitoids are present in the field, avoid using broad spectrum chemical pesticides that would be lethal to these natural enemies. Do not spray broad-spectrum chemical pesticides.

❑ Bean bugs: *Riptortus pedestris* (Fabricius, 1775); *R. clavatus* (Thunberg, 1783)

Common Name	:	Bean bugs
Scientific Name	:	*Riptortus pedestris* (Fabricius, 1775), *R. clavatus* (Thunberg, 1783)
Family	:	Alydidae
Order	:	Hemiptera

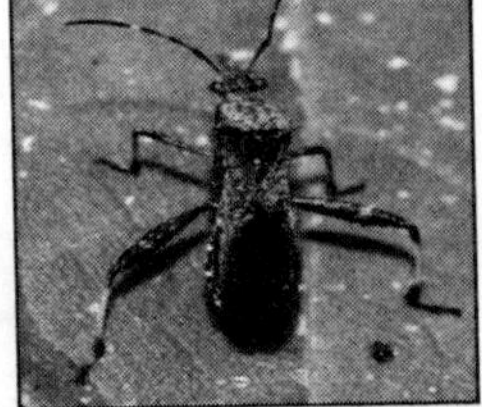

Source:https://www.flickr.com/photos

Distribution and Host Range

Bean bugs are serious pests of food legumes and they feed mainly on soybean. They occur in South and Southeast Asia including Japan, Korea and Taiwan. They can cause significant reduction in pod and grain yields and quality.

Nature and Symptoms of Damage

The damage symptoms are similar to *Clavigralla* bugs.

Life History and Description

Egg: The females lay single eggs mostly on the bases of younger flowers and pods. On average, each female lays about 115 eggs. The egg period is 3 to 5 days.

Nymph: The nymphs are brownish black and hemispherical, resembling brown ants. The nymphal period is 2 to 3 weeks, and the nymphal stage is made up of five instars.

Adult: The *Riptortus* bugs are slender and longer (about 18 mm) than *Clavigralla* bugs, and brown in color.

Management

Delayed sowing from normal planting season of legumes helps avoid damage from bean bugs due to lower pest densities. Inter-cropping of legumes (*e.g.*, soybean) with trap crops (e.g., sesame and corn) can enhance the performance of parasitoids such as *G. japonicum* and *O. nezarae* and thus reduce the infestation of *Riptortus* bugs. Entomopathogenic fungi such as *B. bassiana* could be used to manage *Riptortus* bugs. Do not spray broad-spectrum chemical pesticides. Spray systemic insecticides.

❑ Southern green stink bug: *Nezara viridula* (Linnaeus, 1758)

Common Name	:	Southern green stink bug
Scientific Name	:	*Nezara viridula* (Linnaeus, 1758)
Family	:	Pentatomidae
Order	:	Hemiptera

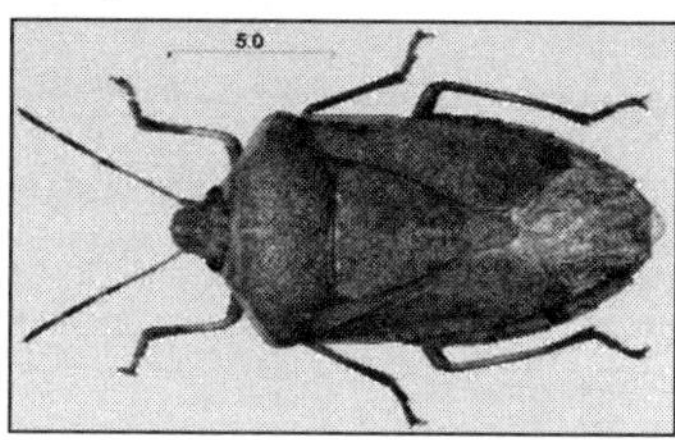

Source: *https://www.researchgate.net/figure/Nezara-viridula*

Distribution and Host Range

N. viridula is a cosmopolitan and highly polyphagous pest species feeding on 30 plant families. Although it causes economic damage to many crop species, it mainly feeds on legumes.

Nature and Symptoms of Damage

The damage symptoms are similar to other pod bugs, causing drying of shoots, shrivelled pods and seeds. In addition, the bugs may carry the spores of fungal pathogens from plant to plant, and mechanically transmit plant pathogens while feeding.

Life History and Description

Egg: The barrel-shaped eggs are laid in clusters of 80-100 on the lower leaf surfaces and pods, in the upper regions of the crop. The eggs turn to deep yellow and finally reddish a few days before hatching. The egg period varies from 5 to 10 days.

Nymph: The newly hatched nymphs remain in groups near the egg-shells for a day or two and they do not feed. Although the second instar nymphs start feeding, they remain in groups until the third instar. The brightly coloured nymphs develop through five instars and the larval period is about 3 to 7 weeks, depending on the temperature.

Adult: Although the nymphs are brightly coloured with multiple color patterns, the adult is green. Adults live up to three weeks in hot summer weather, but they live longer over winter. In regions with a cold winter, the autumn generation will overwinter or diapause. Most diapausing adults turn to a reddish-brown color. The adult is about 15 mm long.

Management

Early maturing legume crops could be used as a trap crop for *N. viridula*. However, adults of *N. viridula* will quickly move from the trap crop to the main crop if they are at more attractive stages. Hence, chemical control of early instar *N. viridula* in trap crops is necessary to prevent movement into the main crop. Egg parasitoids such as *Ooencyrtus malayensis*, *Trissolcus basalis*, *T. rudus*, *T. mitsukurii*, *T. nakagawai*, *Telenomus cyrus*, *T. pacificus* and *T. comperei* are found in different countries in South and Southeast Asia. The Reduviid predator, *Sycanus collaris* also keeps this pest under control. Avoid using broad-spectrum chemical pesticides if these natural enemies are present in the field. If necessary, especially under exceedingly high populations of *N. viridula*, spray a systemic pesticide.

❑ Cotton bollworm: *Helicoverpa armigera* (Hübner, [1808])

Common Name	:	Fruit borer, Cotton bollworm, Corn earworm, Old World bollworm, Gram pod borer
Scientific Name	:	*Helicoverpa armigera* (Hübner, [1808])
Family	:	Noctuidae
Order	:	Lepidoptera

Source: *https://www.cabidigitallibrary.org/doi/10.1079/cabicompendium.26757*

As Described in Tomato

❑ Silvery leaf white fly: *Bemisia tabaci* (Gennadius, 1889)

Common Name	:	White fly, Sweet potato white fly or Silvery leaf white fly
Scientific Name	:	*Bemisia tabaci* (Gennadius, 1889)
Family	:	**Aleyrodidae**
Order	:	Hemiptera

Source: *https://www.eurekalert.org/multimedia/650418*

As Described in Potato

❑ Green leaf hopper: *Empoasca kerri* Pruthi, *E. facialis* Jacobi, *E. fabae* (Harris, 1841)

Common Name	:	Green leaf hopper
Scientific Name	:	*Empoasca kerri* Pruthi, *E. facialis* Jacobi, *E. fabae* (Harris, 1841)
Family	:	Cicadellidae
Order	:	Hemiptera

Source: *https://plantwiseplusknowledgebank.org*

As Described in Potato

Tobacco caterpillar: *Spodoptera litura* (Fabricius, 1775)

Common Name	:	Tobacco caterpillar; Tobacco cutworm; Cotton leafworm; Leaf eating caterpillar
Scientific Name	:	*Spodoptera litura* (Fabricius, 1775)
Family	:	Noctuidae
Order	:	Lepidoptera

Source: *https://apps.lucidcentral.org/pppw*

As Described in Potato

Two-spotted spider mite: *Tetranychus urticae* C.L. Koch, 1836; *T. cinnabarinus* Boisduval

Common Name	:	Red spider mite; Two-spotted spider mite
Scientific Name	:	*Tetranychus urticae* C.L. Koch, 1836; *Tetranychus cinnabarinus* Boisduval
Family	:	Tetranychidae
Order	:	Trombidiformes

Source: *https://www.cabidigitallibrary.org/doi/10.1079/cabicompendium.30965*

As Described in Tomato

Resistant Varieties	
World	**India**
Ancona: A bush bean variety that is resistant to the bean beetle.	**Pusa Arhar 16:** A pigeon pea variety that is resistant to pod borer.
Calima: A pea variety that is resistant to the pea aphid.	**Pusa Bhairav:** A mung bean variety that is resistant to the bean aphid.
Jaguar: A lima bean variety that is resistant to the leafhopper.	**TARM-1:** A soybean variety that is resistant to the stem fly.
Labrador: A pole bean variety that is resistant to the bean beetle.	**Pusa-105:** A chickpea variety that is resistant to pod borer.
Robust: A fava bean variety that is resistant to the black bean aphid.	**PKM 1:** A cowpea variety that is resistant to the cowpea pod borer.

Pests of Leafy Vegetables

Common Name	Scientific Name	Family	Origin	Chromosome Number
Amaranthus	*Amaranthus viridis* L.	Amaranthaceae	Central and South America	2n = 32
Spinach	*Spinacia oleracea* L.	Amaranthaceae/ Chenopodiaceae	Central Asia, Persia	2n = 12
Fenugreek	*Trigonella foenum-graecum*	Fabaceae	Iran to the North of India	2n = 16
Coriander	*Coriandrum sativum*	Apiaceae	Mediterranean region, South-west Asia	2n = 22

Leafy vegetables are a type of vegetables that are mainly grown for their green leaves and are widely consumed in various cuisines around the world. Some examples of leafy vegetables along with their botany, area, and production in India are:

Spinach

Spinach (*Spinacia oleracea*) is an annual plant that belongs to the family Amaranthaceae. It is grown in almost all states of India. The total area under spinach cultivation in India is around 64,000 hectares, and the total production is around 660,000 metric tonnes.

Fenugreek

Fenugreek (*Trigonella foenum-graecum*) belongs to the family Fabaceae. It is mainly grown in the states of Rajasthan, Gujarat, and Uttar Pradesh. The total area under fenugreek cultivation in India is around 237,000 hectares, and the total production is around 315,000 metric tonnes.

Amaranth

Amaranth (*Amaranthus* spp.) belongs to the family Amaranthaceae. It is mainly grown in the states of Uttar Pradesh, Madhya Pradesh, and Rajasthan. The total area under amaranth cultivation in India is around 20,000 hectares, and the total production is around 25,000 metric tonnes.

Coriander

Coriander (*Coriandrum sativum*) belongs to the family Apiaceae. It is mainly grown in the states of Rajasthan, Gujarat, and Andhra Pradesh. The total area under coriander cultivation in India is around 190,000 hectares, and the total production is around 520,000 metric tonnes.

Some of the pests of leafy vegetabels are described here under:

❑ Amaranthus stem weevil: *Hypolixus truncatulus*

Common Name	:	Amaranthus stem weevil
Scientific Name	:	*Hypolixus truncatulus*
Family	:	Curculionidae
Order	:	Coleoptera

Source: *https://guatemala.inaturalist.org/observations/57105105*

Distribution and Host Range

Specific major pest. Widely distributed in India and neighbouring countries. It attacks Amaranthus (both wild and cultivated) and leafy vegetables with large leaves.

Nature and Symptoms of Damage

Adult females bite circular holes in the stems, lay eggs singly in each hole and cover the hole with black coloured secretion. Newly emerged grubs bite into stems, feed on pith region making irregular zigzag tunnels and fill with excreta. Stems split longitudinally. Plants dry completely. Adult feeds on tender leaves, makes circular holes in stems, branches and mid-ribs. Attack causes stunting of plants, twisting and swelling of branches and stem and suppression of shoot and leaf production.

Life History and Description

Egg: Females lay eggs singly in each hole and cover holes with secretion. A female lay 30-34 smooth, oval and pale-yellow eggs, egg period 4 to 10 days.

Grub: A single stem contains 17-20 grubs in it. Grubs are stout, curved, apodous and white in colour and about 13-17 mm long. Grub stage lasts for 12-24 days.

Pupa: Full-fed grubs form a greyish-brown hard compact gall like chamber and pupate therein. On emergence, they remain inside the stem for 5 to 6 days, then cut epidermal membrane and emerge out.

Adult: Adults are ash-grey in colour, 10-15 mm long with elbowed antennae and brown elytra.

Management

Destroy all wild amaranthus plants in the vicinity. As soon as infestation is observed, remove and destroy promptly all the affected plants with grubs inside. Spraying with malathion @ 0.05% or dichlorvos @ 0.05% is also effective. After spraying the crop with insecticides observe a waiting period of 7-10 days.

❑ Amaranthus leaf caterpillar: *Spoladea recurvalis* (Fabricius, 1775)

Common Name	:	Amaranthus leaf caterpillar; Beet webworm moth; Hawaiian beet webworm moth; Spinach moth
Scientific Name	:	*Spoladea recurvalis* (Fabricius, 1775)
Family	:	Crambidae
Order	:	Lepidoptera

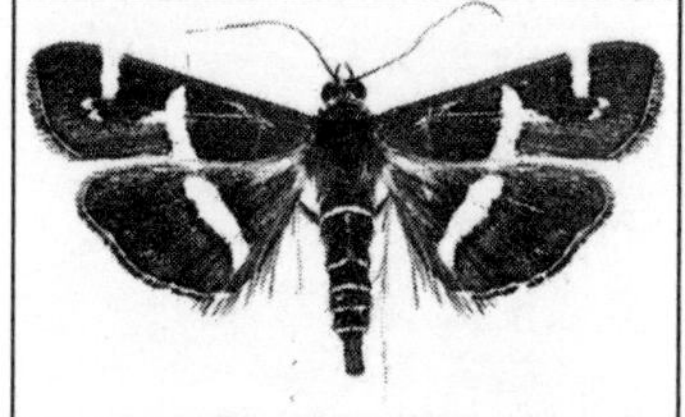

Source: *https://www.cabidigitallibrary.org/doi/10.1079/cabicompendium.28245*

Distribution and Host Range

They are distributed across tropical and sub-tropical regions of Africa, Asia, Australia and Hawaii Islands. The larvae feed on spinach, beet, cotton, maize and soybean. They feed on the underside of the leaves protected by a slight web.

Nature and Symptoms of Damage

Damage is caused by caterpillars by feeding initially on epidermis and palisade tissues of leaves, later they web the leaves together with silvery silken threads secreted by them and feed within. Gradually these webbed leaves become completely devoid of chlorophyll and dry up.

Life History and Description

Eggs: Eggs are spherical in shape and snow white in colour. Eggs hatch in about 3-4 days.

Larvae: Caterpillars are greenish in colour with white lines and black crescents on thorax below the lateral line. Full grown larva measures 17-20 mm in length. Larval period is 12-16 days.

Pupae: Pupae are 10-14 mm long and brownish in colour. The pupa is formed within a slight cocoon in a folded piece of leaf. It is very pale brown. The pupal period lasts about 12 days.

Adults: Adults are black coloured, slender bodied moths about 10 mm long and having thin long filiform antennae. Both pairs of wings are dark fuscous in colour having broad white fuscia in the middle and outer margins are fringed with short hairs. Wing expanse is 15-20 mm. Total life cycle is completed in 3-4 weeks.

Management

Collect and destroy affected plant parts with caterpillars. Set up light trap @ 1/ha to attract and kill the adults. Spray malathion 50 EC 500 ml or dichlorvos 375 ml in 500 L of water per ha after the harvest of leaves and stems.

Some other Pests			
Common Name	**Scientific Name**	**Family**	**Order**
Spinach blue beetle	*Altica caerulescens* (Baly)	Alticidae	Coleoptera
Locusts	Desert locust: *Schistocerca gregaria* Forsskål, 1775 Bombay locust: *Patanga succinct* (Johannson, 1763) Migratory locust: *Locusta migratoria* (Linnaeus, 1758)	Acrididae	Orthoptera
Hairy caterpillar	*Olepa ricini* (Fabricius, 1775)	Arctiidae	Lepidioptera
Stem fly	*Ophiomyia* spp.	Agromyzidae	Diptera
Cowpea aphid	*Aphis craccivora* C.L. Koch, 1854	Aphididae	Hemiptera
Serpentine leaf miner	*Liriomyza trifolii* (Burgess, 1880)	Agromyzidae	Diptera
Lucerne weevil	*Hypera postica* (Gyllenhal, 1813)	Curculionidae	Coleoptera
Spotted pod borer	*Maruca testulalis* (Fabricius, 1787)	Crambidae	Lepidoptera

Resistant Varieties	
World	**India**
Bloomsdale Long Standing Spinach: This spinach variety is known for its resistance to the spinach leaf miner, a common pest that damages the leaves of spinach plants. **Bright Lights Swiss Chard:** This colorful chard variety has shown resistance to both leaf miners and aphids. **Black Seeded Simpson Lettuce:** This popular lettuce variety has shown resistance to aphids and leaf miners. **Rainbow Chard:** This chard variety has demonstrated resistance to leaf miners. **Redbor Kale:** This kale variety has shown resistance to cabbage worms, which are known to eat holes in the leaves of kale plants. **Fordhook Giant Swiss Chard:** This chard variety has shown resistance to leaf miners and other pests. **Tyee Spinach:** This variety of spinach is resistant to both the spinach leaf miner and aphids. **Southern Giant Curled Mustard Greens:** This mustard greens variety has shown resistance to aphids and cabbage worms. **Vates Blue Curled Kale:** This kale variety has shown resistance to cabbage worms and aphids. **Arugula:** This leafy green has demonstrated resistance to flea beetles, which are known to eat small holes in the leaves of many vegetables.	**Palak 2 Spinach:** This variety of spinach is resistant to the leaf miner, a pest that can cause significant damage to the leaves of spinach plants. **Arka Nishant Coriander:** This coriander variety has shown resistance to aphids and whiteflies. **Pusa Himani Lettuce:** This lettuce variety has demonstrated resistance to aphids. **Arka Anamika Beet Greens:** This beet greens variety has shown resistance to leaf miners. **Arka Kesar Amaranth:** This variety of amaranth is resistant to the leaf webber, a pest that can cause significant damage to the leaves of amaranth plants. **Arka Komal Indian Spinach:** This variety of Indian spinach is resistant to the leaf miner. **Arka Anupama Mustard Greens:** This mustard greens variety has shown resistance to aphids and cabbage worms. **Arka Kiran Leafy Radish:** This leafy radish variety has shown resistance to aphids and whiteflies. **Arka Sanjivani Coriander:** This coriander variety has demonstrated resistance to aphids. **Arka Arunima Amaranth:** This variety of amaranth is resistant to the leaf webber.

PART B

PESTS OF FRUIT CROPS

G. Yashaswini
(Ph.D. Scholar)
Department of Entomology
Professor Jayashankar Telangana State Agricultural University
Rajendranagar, Hyderabad, Telangana-500030

Pests of Mango

Scientific name	*Mangifera indica*
Family	Anacardiaceae
Origin	Southern Asia
Chromosome number	2n=40

Mango (*Mangifera indica*) is a tropical fruit tree that belongs to the family Anacardiaceae. It is one of the most important fruit crops in India and is widely cultivated throughout the country. The fruit is usually harvested when it is ripe, and it has a sweet, juicy flesh that is rich in vitamins A and C. Mango is an important fruit crop in India for both domestic consumption and export. It is widely consumed as a fresh fruit, as well as in processed forms such as pulp, juice, and pickles. Mango also has significant medicinal properties and is used in traditional Ayurvedic medicine to treat a variety of ailments.

India is the largest producer of mangoes in the world, accounting for around 40% of the total global production. The major mango-producing states in India are Uttar Pradesh, Andhra Pradesh, Maharashtra, Karnataka, and Bihar. In 2020-2021, the total area under mango cultivation in India was around 2.28 million hectares, and the total production was around 25.8 million metric tonnes.

Insect pest incidence in mango can have a significant economic impact on the crop, both in terms of yield losses and increased production costs. Some of the common insect pests of mango are given under:

❑ Mango leafhopper: *Idioscopus clypealis* (Lethierry, 1889), *I. nitidulus* (Walker, 1870) and *Amritodus atkinsoni* (Lethierry, 1889)

Common Name	:	Mango leafhopper
Scientific Name	:	*Idioscopus clypealis* (Lethierry, 1889); *I. nitidulus* (Walker, 1870) *Amritodus atkinsoni* (Lethierry, 1889)
Family	:	Cicadellidae
Order	:	Hemiptera

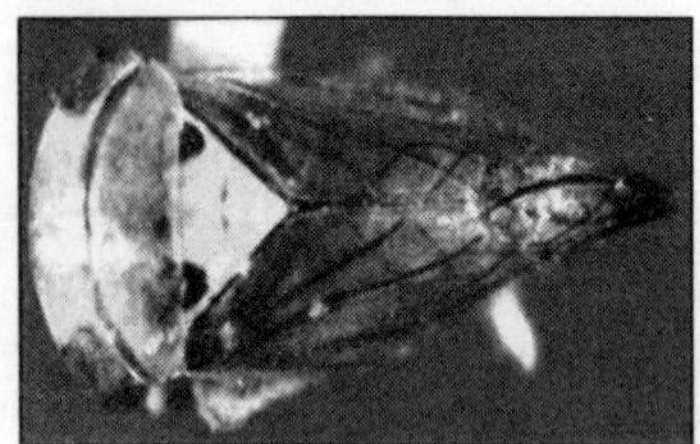
Idioscopus clypealis
Source:
https://www.nbair.res.in/databases

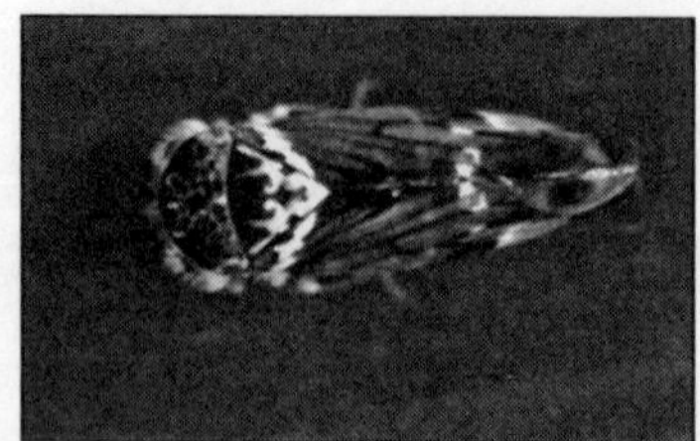
I. nitidulus
Source:
https://www.nbair.res.in/databases

Amritodus atkinsoni
Source:
https://www.nbair.res.in/databases

Distribution and Host Range

Leafhoppers are the major sucking pests of mango. Asia is home to 15 species of mango, three of which, *Amritodus atkinsoni*, *Idioscopus nitidulus*, and *I. clypealis* are of economic importance. They are distributed across mango growing regions of the country; however, the geographical distribution of the various species is not constant. For instance, *A. atkinsoni* and *I. clypealis* are more severe in Northern states while *I. nitidulus* and *I. nagpurensis* are predominant in the Southern part of India.

Nature and Symptoms of Damage

Both nymphs and adults suck the sap from tender shoots and inflorescence resulting in withering and shedding of flower buds and also wilting and drying of shoots and leaves. The flower stalks and leaves in infested trees become sticky due to the deposition of honey-dew secreted by the hoppers that encourages the growth of black sooty mould on foliage and other parts. At the times when there are no flowers, the hoppers hide in the cracks and crevices of the bark.

Life History and Description

Eggs are laid in single into the tissues of the young leaves, shoots, flower stalk and unopened flowers. Incubation period: 4-7 days. Nymphal period: 8-13 days, 5 instars. Life cycles last two to three weeks. Eggs are cigar-shaped, creamy-yellow in colour. Size: 0.9-1 mm in length. Nymphs are highly active, pale yellow, and hide under lower shoots or in the crevices in the bark of trees. *I. niveosparsus*—Three spots on scutellum and white band across the wing; *I. clypealis*- Two spots on scutellum and dark spot on the vertex; *A. atkinsoni*- Two spots on scutellum.

Management

Avoid dense planting, maintain clean orchards. Prune overlapping branches and infested shoots. Protect and encourage biocontrol agents like predators, *Mallada boninensis*, *Chrysopa lacciperda*, egg parasitoid, *Polynema* spp. *Gonatocerus* sp. *Tetrastichus* sp. and fungus, *Verticillium lecanii*. Apply bio-agents, *Metarhizium anisopliae* @ 1 × 108 cfu/ml or *Beauveria bassiana* @ 108 cfu/ml on tree trunk once during off season and twice at 7 days interval during flowering season. Three to five sprays depending on pest intensity, first spray before flowering with cypermethrin 25% 3 ml or fenvelerate 20% 5 ml or deltamethrin 2.8% 9 ml or profenophos 40% + cypermethrin 4% 15 ml or chlorpyriphos 50% + cypermethrin 5% 10 ml per 10 lit. of water. Second at panicle initiation stage with quinalphos 25% 20 ml or profenophos 50% 10 ml per 10 lit. of water. Subsequent sprays with imidachloprid 17.8% 3 ml or clothianidin 50% (WDG) 1.2 gm or thiamethoxam 25% (WDG) 1 gm or triazophos 40% 10 ml or phenthoate 50% 20 ml or dimethoate 30% 10 ml or deltamethrin 1% + triazophos 35% 10 ml or lambda cyhalothrin 5% 6 ml per 10 lit. of water.

Mango nut weevil: *Sternochetus mangiferae* (Fabricius, 1775)

Common Name	:	Mango seed weevil, mango stone weevil, mango nut weevil
Scientific Name	:	*Sternochetus mangiferae* (Fabricius, 1775)
Family	:	Curculionidae
Order	:	Coleoptera

Source: *http://databases.nbair.res.in/insectpests/index.php*

Distribution and Host Range

S. mangiferae has not been reported to complete development in any host except mango (*Mangifera indica*) in almost all major mango producing areas of the world: Oceania, Asia, Africa, North America, Caribbean and South America.

Nature and Symptoms of Damage

The grub tunnels in a zig-zag manner through the pulp endocarp, seed coat and finally reaches the cotyledons and destroys them. As the fruit develops the tunnel gets closed. The adults that emerge from the pupae also feed on the developing seed and hasten the maturity of infested fruit.

Life History and Description

Eggs are elliptical, about 0.8 mm long and 0.3 mm wide and are creamy-white in colour when freshly laid. They are laid singly in small cavities made by the female in the skin of young fruits or inflorescences. The female then covers each egg with a brown exudate and cuts a very small crescent-shaped area (0.3 mm) in the fruit, near the back end of the egg. The wound creates a sap flow, which hardens and covers the egg with a protective coating. Several eggs may be laid in each fruit. Incubation period: 5 to 7 days.

Larvae are white grubs. Newly hatched larvae are extremely slender and elongated and about 1 mm long. Mature larvae are about 17 mm long. The development of the larva is usually completed within the maturing seed, but also very occasionally within the flesh. Pupae are whitish when newly formed, but change to a very pale red colour just before the adult emerges. They are about 8 mm long and 7 mm wide. Pupation takes place in the seed within the stone of the fruit.

Adults are weevils with a compact body, about 8 mm long. They are usually active at dusk. Adults can fly and pretend to be dead when touched or disturbed. Females start egg laying 3 to 4 days after mating, when the fruit is about marble-size. They can live for two years.

Management

Under-sized fruits left on the tree should be picked and destroyed. Undertake general cleanliness and destruction of the weevils on the bark. Spray application of malathion 50 EC 1 ml/L; carbaryl 3-4 kg (4 g/L of water) or quinalphos 3- 4 L (2 ml/L of water) in 1500-2000 L water per ha in Sept-Oct on the tree first at marble stage of the fruit and second at 15 days interval. During non-flowering season direct spray towards the base of the trunk. The infested bark should be washed with kerosene emulsion. Spray deltamethrin 1.5-2.0 L (1 ml/L of water) in 1500-2000 L water per ha after six weeks of fruit set.

Mealybug: *Drosicha mangiferae* Stebbins, 1903

Common Name	:	Mealybug, Giant scales or Monophlebids
Scientific Name	:	*Drosicha mangiferae* Stebbins, 1903
Family	:	Monophlebidae
Order	:	Hemiptera

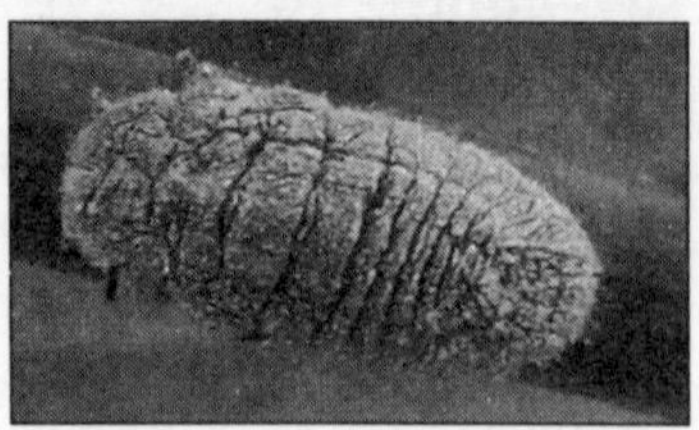

Source: *https://www.nbair.res.in/databases*

Distribution and Host Range

In India, it is widely distributed along the Indo-gangetic plains and found in Punjab, Uttar Pradesh, Bihar and Delhi causing severe damage to mango crop. It attacks mostly apple, apricot, ber, cherry, citrus sp., fig, grape vine, guava, jack, jamun, litchi, mulberry, and pomegranate in addition to mango.

Nature and Symptoms of Damage

The nymphs and female bugs suck sap from tender leaves, shoots and fruit peduncles. As a result, the affected parts are shrivelled and get dried. Severe infestation affects the fruit set and causes fruit drop. They secrete honey dew, over which sooty mould develops. Due to the growth of sooty mould on the leaves, photosynthetic activity is affected.

Life History and Description

D. mangiferae single female lays upto 400-500 eggs as a mass in the soil. The total duration of females ranged from 77 to 135 days and for males 67 to 119 days. Females lay their eggs directly on the host in a fluted ovisac that is attached to the body of the adult female. Inseminated eggs produce hermaphrodites and uninseminated eggs produce males. The first instar nymphs are also called as crawlers, which are mobile. They settle on the plants, start sucking the sap and form the colonies. Females actually are hermaphrodites that frequently inseminate themselves.

Management

Proper orchard maintenance by removal of weeds, *Clerodendrum inflortunatum* that harbor mealy bugs. Flood orchard with water and raking of soil around tree trunk exposes the eggs to sun and natural enemies thereby destroying them. Banding of tree trunk with polythene sheets (400 gauge) 30 cm above ground level and just below the junction of branching to obstruct the ascent of the nymphs. Application of *Beauveria bassiana* (2 g/L) or 5% NSKE around the tree trunk. Release predators, *Menochilus sexmaculatus*, *Rodolia fumida*, *Sumnius renardi* and Australian ladybird beetle, *Cryptolaemus montrouzieri* @ 10-15 no./tree. Application of methyl parathion dust 2% @ 250 g per tree in the soil around the trunk.

Leaf webber: *Orthaga euadrusalis* Walker, 1858

Common Name	:	Leaf webber
Scientific Name	:	*Orthaga euadrusalis* Walker, 1858
Family		Pyralidae
Order		Lepidoptera

Source: *https://en.wikipedia.org/wiki/Orthaga_euadrusalis*

Distribution and Host Range

Mango leaf webber is the prominent pest of mango in tropics of mango growing regions. It had become a serious pest of mango in Northern India especially in old, crowded orchards where there is excessive shade and also in mango orchards of Nepal, Sri Lanka, Indonesia and Japan.

Nature and Symptoms of Damage

Infestations of leaf webber may begin as early as seedling stage and persist even during flowering and fruiting. Webbing of terminal leaves and tender shoots with several caterpillars found inside. Caterpillars initially scrap and feed on the terminal leaves within the web and give burnt appearance to leaves.

Life History and Description

The life cycle completes in 3-4 weeks. Dull green eggs are laid in clusters of about ten on buds and young leaves, which hatches in a week. Larva is pale greenish with brown head and prothoracic shield which undergo 6 moulting with 7 instars. The larvae transform into pupa in about 6 weeks. Pupation takes place inside the webs in silken cocoons. The pupal stage is 16 -18 days longer in the soil. The adult is usually of medium size greyish color, with deep brown forewings with dirty white hind wings. Females are usually larger than male.

Management

Neelum- resistant variety. Webbed leaves should be removed mechanically along with larva and pupa and destroyed. Pruning of overcrowded branches and proper orchard maintenance. Encourage the activity of predators, carabid beetle *Panera lacticincta*, reduvid *Occama* sp. Spray quinalphos @ 0.05% when initial infestation is observed.

❑ Thrips: *Caliothrips indicus* (Bagnall, 1913); *Rhipiphorothrips cruentatus* Hood, 1919; *Scirtothrips dorsalis* Hood, 1919

Common Name	:	Thrips
Scientific Name	:	*Caliothrips indicus* (Bagnall, 1913)
		Rhipiphorothrips cruentatus Hood, 1919
		Scirtothrips dorsalis Hood, 1919
Family	:	Thripidae
Order	:	Thysanoptera

Source:
https://thrips.info/w/media/thumb/b/b5/RhipCruFull.jpg/450px-RhipCruFull.jpg

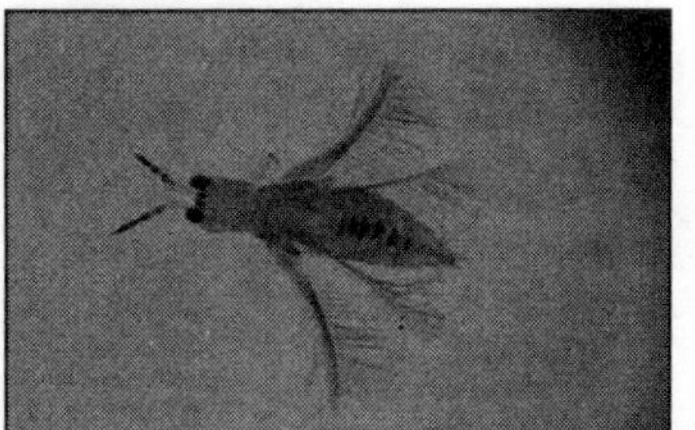

Source:
https://upload.wikimedia.org/wikipedia/commons/thumb/f/f2/Sd_adult_spread.jpg/330px-Sd_adult_spread.jpg

Distribution and Host Range

Thrips are emerging as one of serious pests of mango in India. Several species of thrips are reported to infest mango in India and other countries. Species which are encountered frequently are *Caliothrips indicus*, *Rhipiphorothrips cruentatus*, *Scirtothrips dorsalis*, *Thrips palmi*. The former two species feed mainly on foliage while the latter two colonize on leaves, buds, inflorescence and fruits.

Nature and Symptoms of Damage

Laceration of leaf tissues as a result of sucking of the cell sap by nymphs and adults. Silvery sheen on affected leaves bearing small spots of faecal matter. *C. indicus* and *R. cruentatus* feed on leaves and causes stippling on leaves. *S. dorsalis* mainly feed on inflorescens and fruits which show discolored tissues that subsequently turn brown.

Life History and Description

C. indicus – Larvae are tiny, wingless and pale. Adults are blackish brown with brown and white banded forewings. The eggs are oval and duration of egg instar is slightly longer *i.e.* 7-10 days. Males are shorter than females.

S. dorsalis – Completes life cycle in 14-20 days and is capable of reproducing both sexually and parthenogenetically. It typically has 4-8 generations per year. Female lays eggs within leaves, flowers or fruits. The larva emerges from eggs deposited on the host plant and feeds during its first two larval stages which then enter a pre-pupal stage and later a pupal stage during which it does not feed.

R. cruentatus – Dark brown body, antennae, legs and fore wing pale with the veins and all basically being yellow. Head with complex irregular sculpture, with a transverse ridge near posterior and basal reticulate collar; cheeks sharply incut behind eyes and constricted to basal neck. A female lay about 45-55 eggs, nymph, adult period are 2-3 weeks and five days respectively.

Management

Monitor for thrip infestation by placing sticky traps at regular intervals. Promoting natural enemies that include predatory thrips, predatory mites (*Amblyseius* sp.) anthocorid bugs or minute pirate bugs (*Orius* sp.), ground beetles, lacewings, hoverflies, and spiders. If the infestation is severe, spray with either dimethoate (0.05%) or spinosad (0.0112%) or thiamethoxam (0.05%).

❑ Stem borer: *Batocera rufomaculata* (De Geer, 1775)

Common Name	:	Stem borer, Red-spotted longhorn beetle, mango tree borer, tropical fig borer, bark borer
Scientific Name	:	*Batocera rufomaculata* (De Geer, 1775)
Family	:	Cerambycidae
Order	:	Coleoptera

Source: *https://en.wikipedia.org/wiki/Batocera_rufomaculata*

Distribution and Host Range

This pest is widely distributed in India and *B. rufomaculata* is polyphagous and about 50 host plant species (of 18 different plant families) are known. Major host plants are mango, rubber, jack-fruit, fig, papaya, apple, eucalyptus and mulberry, moringa and silk cotton.

Nature and Symptoms of Damage

Grubs feed inside the stem, boring upward making irregular tunnels which results in interruption of nutrient and water transport in the tissue. Drying of terminal shoot in early stages and severe symptoms causes wilting of branches or entire tree.

Life History and Description

The female cuts the tree bark and lays eggs singly into these cuts, laying a total of up to 200 eggs. Egg is a brownish-white cylinder, 6.2 mm, with narrowly rounded ends. On hatching the larvae start to tunnel into the sapwood of the trunk or branches. Larval development takes about 2 years. As a very large species, the larval tunnel measures 2 or 3 centimeters in width that is correspondingly large and very damaging to the tree. The adult beetle emerges by a short tunnel running to the exterior and ending in a circular exit-hole. The maximum life recorded for the adult is eight months.

Management

Remove and destroy dead and severely affected branches of tree. Remove alternative host like mango, moringa, silk cotton in the near vicinity. Grow tolerant mango varieties *viz.,* Neelam, Humayudin. Avoid injury at the base of trunk while pruning. Keep the orchard healthy following good agricultural practices. Kill the stem borer larvae by inserting a flexible wire inside the hole and plug the hole with the cotton wick soaked in petrol or chloroform or kerosene and seal it with mud. Prune and burn all attacked shoot and branches during winter. Exclude alternative host trees, such as silk cotton, fig tree and remove the infested branches from the garden to prevent the spread of the pest.

❑ Shoot borer: *Chlumetia transversa* (Walker)

Common Name	:	Shoot borer
Scientific Name	:	*Chlumetia transversa* (Walker)
Family		Noctuidae
Order		Lepidoptera

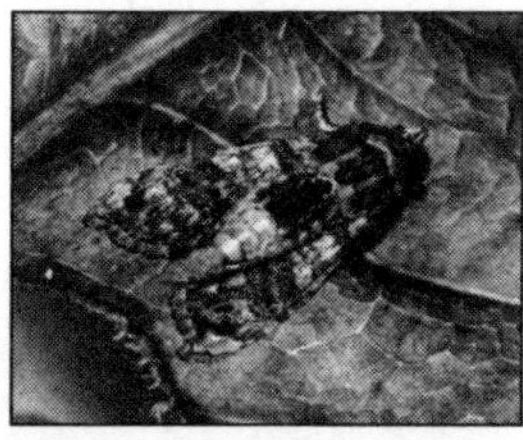

Source: *http://databases.nbair.res.in/insectpests/index.php*

Distribution and Host Range

This pest can be found throughout India and is serious in seedlings and young trees (mango and litchi).

Nature and Symptoms of Damage

Tunneling from top-down wards of the tender terminal shoots. Stunting of seedlings with terminal bunchy appearance. Larvae of this moth bore into the young shoot resulting in dropping of leaves and wilting. Terminal shoot damage. Similar symptoms also noticed on panicles.

Life History and Description

Female moths lay eggs on tender leaves. Young larvae after hatching enter the midrib of leaves and then enter into young shoots through the growing points by tunnelling downwards. Four overlapping generations of the pest are found in a year and it overwinters in pupal stage. Young caterpillars are yellowish orange with dark brown pro-thoracic shield. Full grown caterpillars (20-24 mm) are dark pink with dirty spots. Adult moths are stout grayish brown in color with wings having wavy lines and measure about 17.5 mm at expanded wings. Hind wings are light in color.

Management

Attacked shoots should be clipped off and destroyed. Effective control of the pest can be attained by spraying quinalphos (0.05%) at fortnightly intervals from the commencement of new flush.

❑ Scale insect: *Aspidiotus destructor* Signoret, 1869

Common Name	:	Scale insect, Coconut scale, transparent scale, bourbon scale
Scientific Name	:	*Aspidiotus destructor* Signoret, 1869
Family	:	Coccidae, Diaspididae
Order	:	Hemiptera

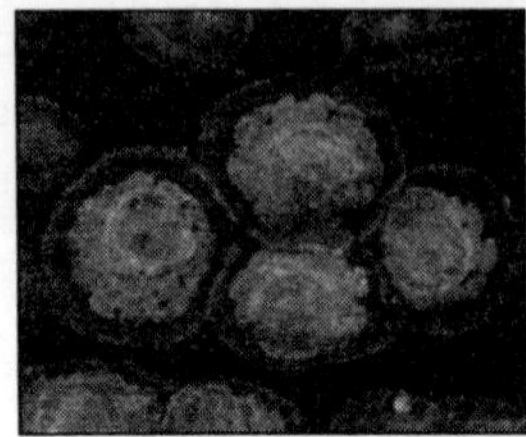

Source: *http://databases.nbair.res.in/insectpests/index.php*

Distribution and Host Range

It has been recorded worldwide in tropical and subtropical areas, including China, Southeast Asia, India, Pakistan, Russia, Brazil, Central America and Caribbean, Pacific Islands, Africa and North America. Host range: It is a polyphagous species and recorded from hosts belonging to more than 60 plant families. Common hosts are banana, coconut, guava, mango, palm, papaya, breadfruit, ginger, bird of paradise, sugarcane, ficus, apple, plumeria, avocado, citrus and grape.

Nature and Symptoms of Damage

It occurs more in summer. A severe infestation, scale forms a continuous crust over flower spikes, young nuts and lower surface of leaves. On leaves, *A. destructor* causes scales with yellow spots developing where the crawlers have settled and grown into adults. Nymphs reside and develop in leaf by sucking the sap. Entire leaves may turn yellow to brown and fall. Sooty mould may develop. In extreme cases, the leaves dry out, entire fronds drop off and the crown dies. Heavy infestation results in stunting of new leaves, reduction of crop yield or complete crop failure. Infested coconut fronds exhibit yellow areas on the upper surface, formed by numerous yellow spots each marking the position of the coconut scale on the under surface.

Life History and Description

Egg: Hatching the young scales on the undersides of the leaves.

Nymph: Covered with circular waxy secretion.

Adult: The scale is bright yellow and round or reddish (female) and oval (male) covered with semi-transparent greyish white flat scale. Females are always wingless and remain under their scale their entire life. Adult males have one pair of membranous wings, move about actively in search of females and do not feed during adult stage.

Management

Pruning and training of fruit trees and proper disposal of infested leaves, branches and twigs will help control scale insects on nursery plants and trees. Excessive use of plant fertilizers contributes to scale outbreaks. Release of predatory coccinellids, *Chilocorus nigritius* is found to be effective. Over 40 species of parasitoids and predators, and several fungal pathogens, are known to attack coconut scale. In the absence of these natural enemies, population explosions of this pest can occur. *Aphytis melinus* and *A. lingnanensis* are the most common parasitoid species controlling the coconut scale populations in Fiji and the *A. melinus* and/or another parasitoid, *Comperiella bifasciata* were introduced into Hawaii, California, Argentina and other regions for the control of coconut scale. Spray Fish Oil Rosin Soap (FORS) 2.5% or spray malathion. A second round is given after 20 days.

❑ Termites: *Odontotermes* obesus (Rambur)

Common Name	:	Termites
Scientific Name	:	*Odontotermes obesus* (Rambur)
Family	:	Termitidae
Order	:	Isoptera

Source: https://www.forbes.com/home-improvement/pest-control/types-of-termites/

Distribution and Host Range

Odontotermes obesus (Rambur) is a widespread termite species in South Asia causing significant losses annually. It is a widespread species in Pakistan, Bangladesh and India. It feeds on wood, surface debris such as twigs, bark fragments, dry leaves, grasses, and dried vegetable matter. It is a common wood eater, damaging firewood, floor timber, wooden boxes, baskets, and railway sleepers.

Nature and Symptoms of Damage

The worker termites feed on roots, shoots and trunks of the mango tree moving upward making the tunnels. Mud galleries on tree trunk which when nudged shows the damage caused due to feeding of tissues inside.

Life History and Description

These are social insects, live in termitaria, in distinct castes, workers, kings and queen. The queen of a colony can lay up to 1000 eggs per day on plants and in the soil. Workers are small (4 mm) and have a soft, white body and a brown head. The larvae hatched from the eggs turn into nymphs that develop into one of three adult phases: reproductive adults, workers or soldiers. Termites are white in colour, prefer darkness and remain underground.

Management

Orchards should be kept clean and free of all refuse vegetation all the dead and decaying wood should be regularly removed. Knock down the mud galleries on trunk and dust with 2% methyl parathion dust or spray the trunk with malathion (1.5 ml/l). Application of finely ground mahua cake, followed by irrigation, helps to drive away the termites. For the control of termites, dusting with 2% methyl parathion at 22 to 27 kg/ha in soil around the infested plants, and raking it into the soil has proved effective. Drench the soil with chlorpyriphos (1 ml/l) at the base of the tree.

Shoot gall psylla: *Apsylla cistellata* (Buckton, 1896)

Common Name	:	Shoot gall psylla
Scientific Name	:	*Apsylla cistellata* (Buckton, 1896)
Family	:	Psyllidae
Order	:	Homoptera

Source: *https://www.agric.wa.gov.au/sites/gateway/*

Distribution and Host Range

Mango shoot gall psylla, *Apsylla cistellata* is a monophagous pest of mango. It was first recorded from Dehradun, India and is distributed in plains of Northern India, Nepal and Bangladesh and in Northeastern States. It is reported from Uttar Pradesh, Bihar and Tarai regions of North India.

Nature and Symptoms of Damage

Psyllid feeding makes the buds develop into hard conical green galls which are usually seen during September-October. Generally terminal shoots are affected. Green conical galls are formed in leaf axis in response to egg-laying by adult insects or feeding by nymphs. In due course of time, infested twigs dry and show die-back symptoms.

Life History and Description

Shoot gall psylla is active from August onwards. It is a univoltine pest with one generation per year. Adult females lay eggs into the midrib of leaves in March-April and they hatch in the last week of August. There are five to six nymphal instars and the freshly hatched nymphs are yellowish in colour, but colour changes with the age. Nymphal period lasts for 140 days. Nymphs emerge during August-September and crawl to the adjacent buds to suck the sap. Second instar nymphs migrate to the already formed gall. Adults may live up to 30-72 h.

Management

New mango orchard in humid region needs to be discouraged. Galls with nymphs should be collected and destroyed. Spray thiomithoxam (0.05%) or quinalphos (0.05%) at fortnightly interval starting from the middle of August.

Midge: *Erosomyia indica* Felt., *Dasineura amraramanjarae* Grover, 1965, *Procystiphora mangiferae* (Felt, 1927) and *Procontarinia matteiana* Kieffer & Cecconi, 1906

Common Name	:	Midge
Scientific Name	:	*Erosomyia indica* Felt., *Dasineura amraramanjarae* Grover, 1965, *Procystiphora mangiferae* (Felt, 1927), *Procontarinia matteiana* Kieffer and Cecconi, 1906
Family	:	Cecidomyiidae
Order	:	Diptera

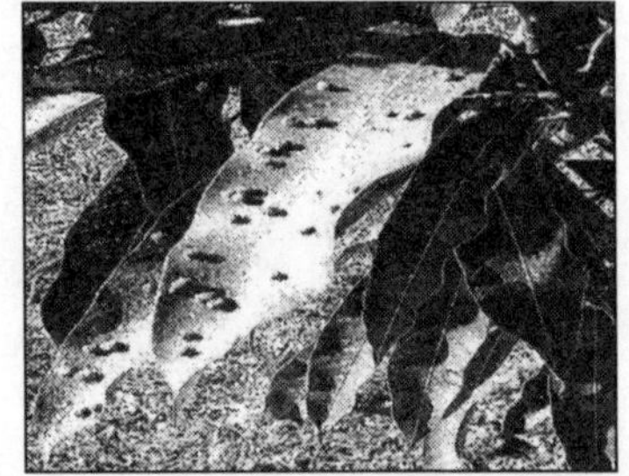

Source: *https://agritech.tnau.ac.in/crop_protection/crop_prot_crop_insectpest%20_Mango.html*

Distribution and Host Range

Midges are important sucking pests of mango across the world. Thirteen midge species have been found associated with 16 types of gall makers. Major species are inflorescence midge, *Dasineura amaramanjarae*, mango blossom gall midge, *Procontarinia mangiferae* and mango leaf gall midge, *P. matteiana*. Mango midge, *Erosomya indica* has gained much attention in recent past as it has become major pest in all mango growing areas of the world.

Nature and Symptoms of Damage

Inflorescence midge (*Erosomyia indica*): Attacks at flower bud burst stage and fruit set stage during January and May. Appearance of black spots on the inflorescence. Leaf gall midge (*Procontarinia matteiana*): Wart-like galls produced on leaves that reduce photosynthetic activity leading to leaf drop and lowered fruit production. Infested plant material and wind currents are responsible for its spread.

Life History and Description

Midge flies are very small 1-2 mm in length. Female lay eggs into the tissue of young leaves leaving a small reddish spot. The leaf tissue under the red spot becomes swollen and soft. Within seven days, gall formation begins and reaches a maximum diameter of 3-4 mm. From underside of the leaf adults usually emerge leaving the pupal skin sticking out from the emergence hole. Full grown pinkish larva drops on soil for pupation. A maggot light yellowish in colour larva moults three times. Adult yellowish fly: *Erosomyia indica*; light orange fly: *Procystiphora mangiferae*; orange red fly: *Dasineura amaramanjarae*.

Management

Deep ploughing of orchard exposing pupae and diapausing larvae to sun's heat kills them. Monitor larval population and follow effective control measures based on population. Spray thiamethoxam (0.05%) or dimethoate (0.05%) at bud burst stage.

❑ Bark-eating caterpillar: *Indarbela quadrinotata* (Walker, 1856)

Common Name	:	Bark-eating caterpillar
Scientific Name	:	*Indarbela quadrinotata* (Walker, 1856)
Family	:	Cossidae
Order	:	Lepidoptera

Source: *https://agritech.tnau.ac.in/crop_protection/guava/guava_5.html*

Distribution and Host Range

This pest is found damaging varieties of trees all over India. Three species of this pest have been recorded in India, *viz., Indarbela quadrinotata*, *I. tetraonis* and *I. quadrinotata* is found in Uttar Pradesh, Maharashtra and Madhya Pradesh.

Nature and Symptoms of Damage

Caterpillars feed on the bark and bore at stem joints. Larva remains hidden inside the tunnel during day time and becomes active in the night. Several caterpillars may attack the same tree at different locations which can cause serious injury to the bark and the death of small branches. The holes left on the trunk may lead to infestation by other insects or plant pathogens. Affected branches break at the points of attack. A severe infestation may arrest the growth of the tree and die within 2-3 years if untreated.

Life History and Description

Female lays egg below the bark or in between cracks. Eggs hatch in about 8-10 days and the larvae bore into the tree feeding on the bark for 9-11 months. When full-grown, they make a hole into the wood and pupate inside. The pupal stage lasts 3-4 weeks. The moths emerge with the onset of monsoon and are short lived. There is only one generation per year. The full-grown caterpillar is dirty brown in colour and is about 35-45 mm in length. The moth is light grey in colour with dark brown dots and measures about 35-40 mm with expanded wings.

Management

Maintain a healthy orchard by clearing the affected branches of the fross and faeces. Scrape the loose bark to prevent oviposition by adult beetles. If infestations are severe then apply the copper oxychloride paste on the trunk of the tree. Hook out the grub from the bore hole. Inject 5-10 ml of dichlorvos 76 EC @ 4 ml/l into the tunnel and cover with cotton swab is quite effective due to its contact and fumigant action.

❑ Fruit fly: *Bactrocera dorsalis* (Hendel, 1912)

Common Name	:	Oriental fruit fly, mango fruit fly
Scientific Name	:	*Bactrocera dorsalis* (Hendel, 1912)
Family	:	Tephritidae
Order	:	Diptera

Source: *http://databases.nbair.res.in/insectpests/index.php*

Distribution and Host Range

In India, eight species of genus *Bactrocera* are identified among quarantine pests with the oriental fruit fly *B. dorsalis* being the most destructive fruit fly of mango, followed by Peach fruit fly *B. zonata* and Guava fruit fly *B. correcta*. The flies attack fruits at different stages of maturity but damage is more obvious at harvest period.

Nature and Symptoms of Damage

The damage to trees caused by fruit flies results from oviposition in fruit and soft tissues of vegetative parts of certain plants, feeding by the larvae, and decomposition of plant tissue by invading secondary microorganisms. Larval feeding in fruits is the most damaging. Damage usually consists of breakdown of tissues and internal rotting associated with maggot infestation, but this varies with the type of fruit attacked. Infested young fruit becomes distorted, hardened and usually drop; mature attacked fruits develop a water-soaked appearance. The larval tunnels provide entry points for bacteria and fungi that cause the fruit to rot. When only a few larvae develop, damage consists of an unsightly appearance and reduced marketability because of the egg laying punctures or tissue break down due to the decay.

Life History and Description

The white, elongate and elliptical egg measures about 1.17 × 0.21 mm and has a chorion without sculpturing. The third-instar, which has a typical maggot appearance, is about 10 mm in length and creamy white. The mature larva emerges from the fruit, drops to the ground, and forms a tan to dark brown puparium about 4.9 mm in length. The adult, which is noticeably larger than a house fly, has a body length of about 8.0 mm; the wing is about 7.3 mm in length and is mostly hyaline. The color of the fly is very variable, prominant yellow and dark brown to black markings on the thorax. Generally, the abdomen has two horizontal black stripes and a longitudinal median stripe extending from the base of the third segment to the apex of the abdomen. These markings form a T-shaped pattern, but the pattern varies considerably. The ovipositor is very slender and sharply pointed.

Management

Sanitation of orchards. Removal and destruction of fallen fruits. Affected fruits should be collected and destroyed. Install fruit fly traps @ 4 Rakshak traps/ha or 10 bottle traps/ha from March to June. Release of parasitoids such as *Opius longicaudatus*, *O. vandenboschi*, *O. oophilus* and *Bracon* sp. Rake up the soil below the tree and drench with chlorpyriphos 20 EC@ 2.5 ml/l. Setting up of methyl eugenol traps to lure the males in the orchard @ 10/ha. Spraying malathion @ 2 ml + Jaggery@ 10 g/l at ripening stage.

Resistant Varieties

World			India		
Tommy Atkins	Haden	Keitt	Dashehari	Langra	Chausa
Kent	Alphonso	Ataulfo	Neelam	Alphonso	Kesar
Valencia Pride	Glenn		Himsagar	Totapuri.	

Alphonso: This variety of mango is considered to be one of the best in the world, and is popular in India as well as in other countries. It is resistant to several types of insect pests, including mango hopper and fruit fly.

Tommy Atkins: This is a popular commercial variety of mango that is grown in many parts of the world. It is known to be resistant to several pests, including the Caribbean fruit fly and the mango seed weevil.

Kesar: This variety of mango is primarily grown in India, and is known for its sweet, aromatic flavor. It is resistant to several pests, including the fruit fly and the mango shoot borer.

Palmer: This variety of mango is grown in Florida and is known for its large size and juicy texture. It is resistant to several pests, including the Caribbean fruit fly and the Mediterranean fruit fly.

Kensington Pride: This variety of mango is popular in Australia and is known for its sweet, tangy flavor. It is resistant to several pests, including the mango seed weevil and the fruit fly.

Haden: This is a popular variety of mango that was originally developed in Florida. It is resistant to several pests, including the Caribbean fruit fly and the mango seed weevil.

Amrapali: This is a relatively new variety of mango that was developed in India. It is known for its sweet, aromatic flavor and is resistant to several pests, including the mango shoot borer and the fruit fly.

Kent: This variety of mango is grown in many parts of the world and is known for its large size and sweet flavor. It is resistant to several pests, including the mango seed weevil and the Caribbean fruit fly.

Keitt: This is a popular variety of mango that is grown in the United States and is known for its sweet, juicy flavor. It is resistant to several pests, including the Caribbean fruit fly and the mango seed weevil.

Banganapalli: This is a popular variety of mango that is grown in India and is known for its sweet, tangy flavor. It is resistant to several pests, including the mango shoot borer and the fruit fly.

Pests of Banana

Scientific name	*Musa acuminata*
Family	Musaceae
Origin	Southeast Asia
Chromosome number	2n = 22 (Diploid)

Banana belongs to the Musaceae family and is a perennial herb. Banana is an important fruit crop in India, both for domestic consumption and export. The fruit is a berry and is typically elongated and curved, with a fleshy pulp and numerous seeds. India is the largest producer of bananas in the world, accounting for more than 25% of the global banana production. The major banana-producing states in India are Maharashtra, Gujarat, Tamil Nadu, Karnataka, and Andhra Pradesh. The total area under banana cultivation in India is around 0.8 million hectares, with an annual production of around 30 million tons.

The economic impact of insect pest incidence in banana is significant and can result in reduced yield and increased production costs. Insect pests can cause significant damage to banana crops, leading to yield losses and increased production costs. Some of the common insect pests of banana are given here under:

❑ Banana leaf eating caterpillar: *Spodoptera litura* (Fabricius, 1775)

Common Name	:	Banana leaf eating caterpillar, tobacco cutworm, cotton leafworm
Scientific Name	:	*Spodoptera litura* (Fabricius, 1775)
Family		Noctuidae
Order		Lepidoptera

Source: *http://databases.nbair.res.in/insectpests/index.php*

As Described in Potato

Rust thrips: *Chaetanaphothrips signipennis* (Bagnall, 1914)

Common Name	:	Thrips
Scientific Name	:	*Chaetanaphothrips signipennis* (Bagnall, 1914)
Family		Thripidae
Order		Thysanoptera

Source: *https://agritech.tnau.ac.in/ta/crop_protection/images/banana/Thrips_Adult.jpg*

Distribution and Host Range

Rust thrips occur in coastal areas of Queensland and Northern New South Wales. This pest has been found in citrus and in some native plants but the main host is bananas.

Nature and Symptoms of Damage

Distinctive reddish brown oval stains on the finger, can extend the entire length. In severe cases peel splits and the exposed flesh quickly discolors.

Life History and Description

Adult banana rust thrips reproduce sexually. After mating, females lay eggs in plant tissues where the thrips feed and hatch in 6-9 days. The newly hatched yellow nymphs feed for a few days before moulting and after 8-10 days, mature nymphs move off the host plant into the soil and undergo pupation with the adult emerging in 6-10 days. The entire life cycle is completed in approximately 28 days. Kidney shaped eggs are invisible to naked eye, laid just below the fruit or inside the pseudostem. Larva are wingless creamy white, smaller but have the same shape as the adult. Pupae are white like the larvae, can crawl, 1 mm in length. Adult are slender, creamy yellow to golden brown with delicate feathery wings and 1.5 mm long. Their wings have dark, eye-like spots at the base and are fringed; when the wings are folded, the adult appears to have a black line down its back.

Management

Use healthy and pest free suckers for planting. Destroy all volunteer plants and old neglected plantations. Use blue pan water sticky trap @ 4-5/acre. Hot water treatment of suckers prior to planting. Collect and destroy the damaged leaves, flowers and fruits along with life stages. At the time of shooting, cover the bunch firmly with 100-gauge thickness polythene sleeve having 6 to 10% holes or polypropylene bunch leaves. When the bud is in upright position, bud injection with imidacloprid 17.8EC @ 2 ml per bud using disposable syringe. Spray the bunch with chlorpyriphos @ 2.5 ml/litre of water/acetamiprid 20 SP (0.0025 %) *i.e.,* 1.25 g/10 liter of water along with sticking agent (@ 0.5 ml/litre of water, two times *i.e.,* one at the time of opening of hands and second spray after all the hands opened.

Aphids: *Pentalonia nigronervosa* (Coquerel, 1859)

Common Name	:	Aphids
Scientific Name	:	*Pentalonia nigronervosa* (Coquerel, 1859)
Family	:	Aphididae
Order	:	Hemiptera

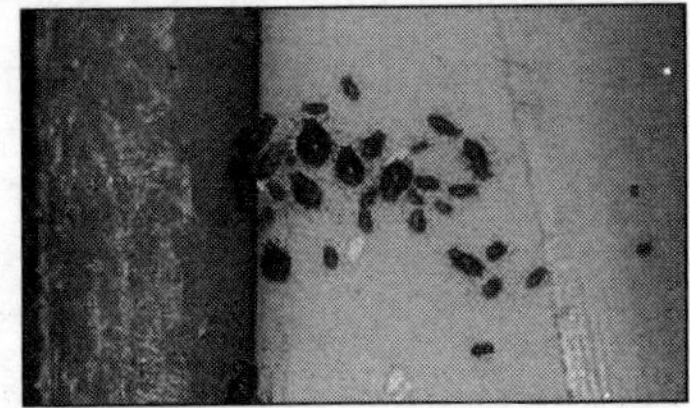

Source: *https://upload.wikimedia.org/wikipedia/commons/thum b/e/e6/Pentalonia_nigronervosa*

Distribution and Host Range

It is widely distributed in India, Sri Lanka and Australia. It is an important pest of banana, small and large cardamom, *Colocasia* sp. and *Allocasia* sp.

Nature and Symptoms of Damage

Banana leaves are bunched into a rosette appearance with leaf margins becoming wavy and upward rolling thereby reducing the growth and vigor of plant. Severely infected plants do not produce bunches and act as a vector of bunchy top disease. Noticed in colonies on leaf axils and pseudostem.

Life History and Description

It is a phloem feeder that uses its long stylet to pierce plant tissues to suck the sap directly from the vessels. Reproduction is entirely parthenogenetic. Females give birth directly to live young female. The life cycle from nymph to adult is completed in 9 to 16 days. Egg stage not present and young ones are born live. Nymphs are oval or slightly elongated, reddish brown with six segmented antennae. Reddish to dark brown adult almost black, shiny, small to medium sized.

Management

Adopt clean cultivation using healthy and pest free suckers. Remove the affected plants and do not take up ratoon and inter crops. Use of braconid wasps, *Lysiphlebius testaceipes* as parasitoid. Release predators such as lady bird beetles and lace wings @ 5 insects/plant. Apply bio control agent *Beauveria bassiana* (2 ml in 100 ml water) between the leaf sheath at the base. Drench the petioles, furled leaves, whorls or young suckers with soapy water or insecticidal soap. Spray dimethoate (75 ml/100 lit) or acephate (1.3 g/lit) on infested plants and suckers.

❑ Rhizome/Corm weevil: *Cosmopolites sordidus* (Germar)

Common Name	:	Banana weevil, banana root borer
Scientific Name	:	*Cosmopolites sordidus* (Germar)
Family	:	Curculionidae
Order	:	Coleoptera

Source: *http://databases.nbair.res.in/insectpests/index.php*

Distribution and Host Range

The rhizome weevil is distributed in India, South East Asia, Australia, Hawaii Islands, Tropical South Africa and Tropical America. It is found to be a major pest on banana and cocoa.

Nature and Symptoms of Damage

The young grub tunnels into the base of suckers, roots and rhizome/corm. Presence of larval tunnels on the entire length of corm rhizome. Yellowing and withering of leaves, reduced plant vigour, root destruction, reduced fruit production and are easily blown over by the wind.

Life History and Description

Females lay eggs singly in small cavities at the base of pseudostem, in the upper part of the corm, in roots near the soil surface and at the end of stumps. They hatch after 6 to 8 days and pupation takes place in holes bored by the grubs and adults emerge from the pupae in 5 to 7 days after pupation. White coloured eggs, elongate to oval, about 2 to 3 mm long and present on upper surface and crevices of rhizome. Legless grubs, creamy white with red head having strong mouthparts, stout and distinctly curved. Pupa are white and found inside the rhizome tunnels. Adult weevils newly emerged are reddish brown which turns almost black after a few days, hard-shelled having a long-curved snout and about 10 to 16 mm long. They are active at night, may live up to two years but are very sensitive to dehydration and will die within 48 hours if kept in a dry substrate.

Management

Practice clean cultivation with the suckers pruned periodically and infested clumps are removed and destroyed. Crop rotation with non-host crops like paddy and sugarcane. Ensure proper fertilization and weed removal. Use of pheromone trap @ 16 traps/ha. Disc-on-stump traps can be used for trapping weevils. Application of bio control agents, *Beauveria bassiana* and *Metarhizium anisopliae* @ 3 ml in 100 ml of water causes more than 90% mortality of the weevils. Application of carbofuran 3G @ 40 g or rugby 10G @ 10 g/plant neem cake @ 500 g/plant at planting and then at three months after planting. Sucker dipping in triazophos solution (2.5 ml in 1 lit water) for about 20 minutes kills the eggs and grubs. Remove the entire plants after harvest and treat the pit with carbaryl (1 g/lit) after or chlorpyriphos (2.5 ml/lit of water).

❑ Stem weevil/pseudostem borer: *Odoiporus longicollis* G. A. K. Marshall, 1930

Common Name	:	Banana stem weevil, rhizome weevil, pseudostem borer
Scientific Name	:	*Odoiporus longicollis* G. A.K. Marshall, 1930
Family		Rhynchophoridae
Order		Coleoptera

Source: *http://databases.nbair.res.in/insectpests/index.php*

Distribution and Host Range

It is widely distributed throughout Bhutan, Cambodia, China, Hong Kong, India, Andaman and Nicobar Islands, Indonesia, Japan, Laos, Malaysia, Myanmar, Nepal, Pakistan, Philippines, Singapore, Sri Lanka, Taiwan, Thailand and Vietnam. It is a major pest of banana.

Nature and Symptoms of Damage

Presence of small pinhead-sized holes on the stem. Jelly exudation on the stem is the initial symptom of damage. Due to secondary infection of pathogens, rotting occurs and a foul odour is emitted. After flowering, when tunnelling occurs in the true stem and peduncle, the fruits do not develop properly.

Life History and Description

Gravid females lay eggs at random on cut ends of pseudostem. The incubation period ranges from 3 to 8 days. The larvae pass through five instars with the fifth instar larvae entering a non-feeding pre-pupal stage and after 15 days of pupation, adult emerges. The total life cycle completes about in 55-60 days. Eggs are creamy, cylindrical with rounded ends. Grubs are fleshy, yellowish white dark brown head and apodous. Pupate in fibrous cocoon, pale yellow colour and is exarate. Brownish black adult measures 23-39 mm.

Management

After harvesting the bunch, remove pseudostem from ground level and destroy them in order to avoid it serving as a breeding site for the pest. Uproot and destroy infested plants. Use longitudinal pseudostem traps @ 100/ha for trapping weevils. Swabbing with chlorpyripos 2.5 ml/l + adjuvant 1 ml/l on the stem prevents infestation of stem weevil. When jelly exudation is noticed, inject 2 ml triazophos solution. Two injections per plant at 2 and 4 feet above the ground level till flowering. The injection needle should enter only two or three leaf sheaths and should not touch the central core.

❑ Tingid or Lace wing bug: *Stephanitis typicus* Distant

Common Name	:	Tingid, coconut lace wing bug, banana lace bug
Scientific Name	:	*Stephanitis typicus* Distant
Family		Tingidae
Order		Heteroptera

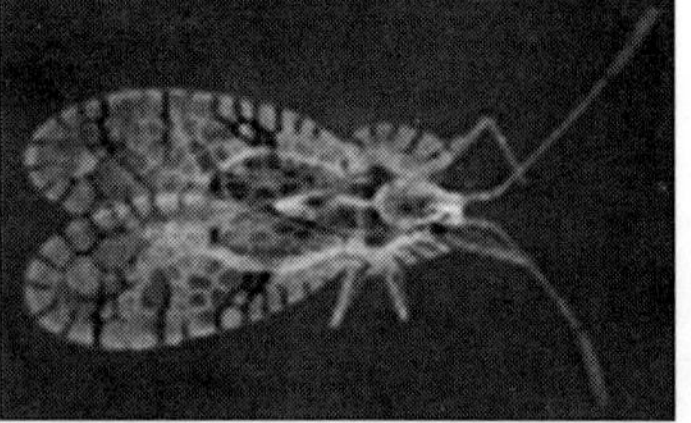

Source: *http://databases.nbair.res.in/insectpests/index.php*

Distribution and Host Range

It is distributed in India, Sri Lanka, South-East Asia and the tropical west Pacific region. It is a major pest of banana, ginger, turmeric, cardamom and jasmine.

Nature and Symptoms of Damage

Both nymphs and adults feed in colonies on undersurface of leaves and cause discoloration. Grubs bore into the rhizome and cause death of the plant. Presence of dark-coloured tunnels in the rhizomes. Death of unopened pipe, withering of outer leaves.

Life History and Description

Yellow colour nymphs found on the under surface and yellow colour adult with minute fringed wings, seen under surface of leaves.

Management

Collect and destroy the damaged leaves, flowers and fruits along with life stages. Use yellow sticky trap at 15/ha. Spraying dimethoate 30 EC 850 ml/ha, methyl demeton 25 EC 2 ml/lit, carbendazim 3 g/litre of water.

Hard scale: *Aspidiotus destructor* Signoret

Common Name	:	Hard scale, coconut scale, transparent scale, bourbon scale
Scientific Name	:	*Aspidiotus destructor* Signoret
Family	:	Diaspididae
Order	:	Hemiptera

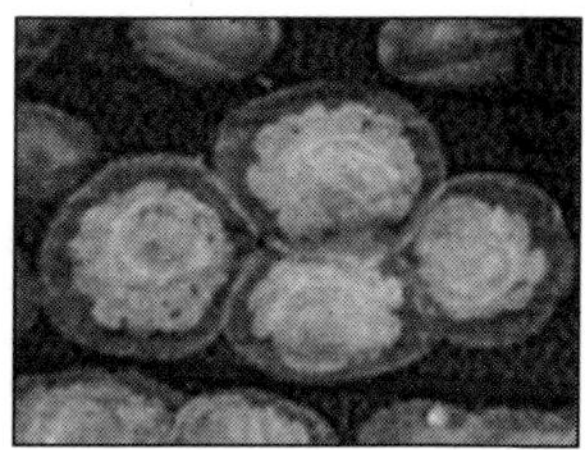

Source: *http://databases.nbair.res.in/insectpests/index.php*

As Described in Mango

Banana scab moth: *Nacoleia octasema* (Meyrick, 1886)

Common Name	:	Banana scab moth
Scientific Name	:	*Nacoleia octasema* (Meyrick, 1886)
Family		Crambidae
Order		Lepidoptera

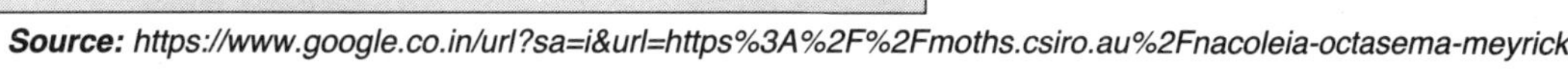

Source: *https://www.google.co.in/url?sa=i&url=https%3A%2F%2Fmoths.csiro.au%2Fnacoleia-octasema-meyrick-*

Distribution and Host Range

Banana scab moth, *Nacoleia octasema*, is a serious pest of bananas and it may also attack *Heliconia* sp. and *Pandanus* sp.

Nature and Symptoms of Damage

Banana scab moth females lay eggs on the outside of the banana flower bracts or on nearby leaves as the flower first emerges. Upon hatching, the larvae enter the flower and feed on the developing fruits within. Feeding results in irregular dark brown to black corky blotches on the fruit skin. Light damage may be superficial and confined to the upper end and outer side of the curved fingers. Heavier infestations can scar the entire fruit, cause deformed fingers, or penetrate into the flesh of the fruit.

Life History and Description

Eggs are laid singly or in small, flattened, almost transparent clusters of a few to over 20 eggs. The eggs hatch in 3-4 days and the larvae enter the banana flower where they feed and grow for another 11-19 days before forming pupae inside a loose silken cocoon. Pupation may occur between the banana fingers, in folds of the dead leaves still attached to the pseudostem, or in litter near the base of the plant. Adult moths emerge from the pupae in 8-10 days and are short-lived, dying after about 3-10 days. Females lay approximately 80-120 eggs during their lifetime. The moths are rarely seen, because they hide among dead leaves and vegetation during the day and are active only during the early night.

Management

Careful selection of suckers of equal size will ensure a concentrated bunching cycle that streamlines control. A range of spiders and other general predators exert a measure of natural control.

Parasitoid, *Chelonus* sp., lays its egg inside the egg of the scab moth. Use biological insecticides: Spinosad, *Beauvaria bassiana*, *Metarhizium anisopliae* or *Bacillus thuringiensis*.

❑ Burrowing nematode: *Radopholus similis* (Cobb, 1893) Thorne, 1949

Common Name	:	Burrowing nematode
Scientific Name	:	*Radopholus similis* (Cobb, 1893) Thorne, 1949
Family	:	Pratylenchidae
Order	:	Tylenchida

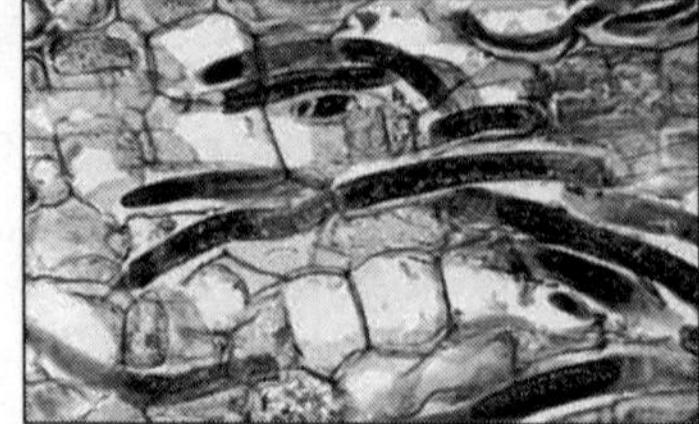

Source:*https://upload.wikimedia.org/wikipedia/commons/thumb/f/f6/Radopholus_similis.jpg/330px-Radopholus_similis.jpg*

Distribution and Host Range

R. similis (Nematoda, Tylenchida, Pratylenchidae) was first observed by **Nathan A. Cobb** in necrotic banana roots from Fiji in 1891. *R. similis* is found in tropical environments and is therefore common in Africa, Asia, Australia, South and Central America, and Southern areas of North America. *R. similis* parasites can be found in tropical climates, and therefore infect a lot of plants native to tropical areas. Common hosts that are economically important include: banana, coconut, coffee, ginger, sugarcane, ornamentals, and tea.

Nature and Symptoms of Damage

Toppling of plants often occurs during windy conditions when bunches are present, hence the general name of **'Toppling Disease'**. Other symptoms caused by decreased water and nutrient uptake are slow plant growth, flower drop, and vine dieback. Symptoms are more pronounced during dry periods, but if moisture becomes available early in the disease (e.g., tropical monsoon rains) leaves are replaced. Burrowing nematode attacks both young and old plants. Thin, white feeder roots have purplish lesions and are quickly destroyed. Lesions are harder to see on older, brown roots, which are slower to rot.

Life History and Description

The burrowing nematode is an obligate parasite and needs a living host to survive, though its various stages can move from root to soil and vice versa. It is classified as a migratory endoparasite, completing its life cycle as it tunnels through the root cortex. Females and juvenile stages are infective but males with their weak stylets do not feed. *R. similis* usually penetrates roots near the tip, but can invade along the entire length of the root. They move between cells of the root cortex, feeding on them until the cells collapse and form necrotic passages. In most hosts, *R. similis* does not damage the central cylinder, though the citrus race reportedly feeds on the phloem, girdling and destroying the stele. Migration and egg-laying are stimulated by nutritional factors: females need healthy tissue to feed on, but eggs are laid in root tissue that quickly decomposes. Females usually reproduce sexually, but can also reproduce without males. This phenomenon was once considered parthenogenesis, but recent studies suggest it might be hermaphrodism. Females lay 4 to 5 eggs per day (2 per day in citrus) for several weeks as they move through the root cortex.

All nematode stages are vermiform (wormlike), colourless and less than 1 mm in length. Adult males and females are different in appearance (sexual dimorphism), the males having poorly developed stylets and a knob-like head caused by an elevated, constricted lip region. Both males and females have long, tapered tails with rounded or indented ends. The male has a sharp, curved spicule, enclosed in a bursa, or sac. Females are between 550 and 880 μm in length and about 24 μm in diameter, with well-developed stylets 16 to 21 μm long. Males are smaller than females, 500 to 600 μm in length. Juveniles are often present in both root and soil samples and average between 315 to 400 μm in length with stylets 13 to 14 μm long.

Management

Cultural practices that maintain plant health and vigor may improve yield by allowing plants to rapidly replace roots damaged by *R. similis*. Incorporating organic material into the soil provides nutrients and improves its cation-exchange and water-holding capacity, which may also increase the number of beneficial microorganisms and nematode antagonists in the root zone. Some cover crops, like sunnhemp (*Crotalaria*) or marigold (*Tagetes*), produce chemicals that are toxic to nematodes (allelopathy) and may reduce burrowing nematode populations in the soil. Biological controls of plant-parasitic nematodes target different stages of nematode development using unique modes of action. The fungi *Paecilomyces lilacinus* and *Trichoderma atroviride* destroy nematode eggs, while toxic metabolites from non-pathogenic strains of *Fusarium oxysporum* inhibit or kill juveniles. Mycorrhizal fungi appear to compete with plant-parasitic nematodes for nutrients, such as phosphorus. The bacterium *Pseudomonas* kills juveniles and adults by producing lethal hydrogen cyanide. Conversely, *Pasteuria* sp. are bacterial hyperparasites that kill nematodes after attaching endospores to their outer cuticle. Despite their potential, the use of biological controls for plant-parasitic nematodes is quite limited at present. Soil fumigation with methyl bromide, 1,3 dichloropropene, or chloropicrin can provide good control of burrowing nematodes but these fumigants must be applied pre-plant. Non fumigant nematicides such as aldicarb and phenamiphos can be used post-plant and usually give systemic plant protection and reasonable control of burrowing nematodes. Use preplant nematicides and nematicides at planting (1,3-D at 300 l/hectare). Post plant application of nematicides (DBCP at 25 l/hectare). Clean or pare infected tissue from rhizome. In India, **"paring and pralinage"** is a common practice. Infested tissue is pared from the corm and it is then to coated with a layer of clay containing a granular nematicide such as carbofuran (Furadan).

❑ Root-lesion nematode: *Pratylenchus coffeae* Goodey, 1951

Common Name	:	Root-lesion nematode
Scientific Name	:	*Pratylenchus coffeae* Goodey, 1951
Family	:	Pratylenchidae
Order	:	Tylenchidae

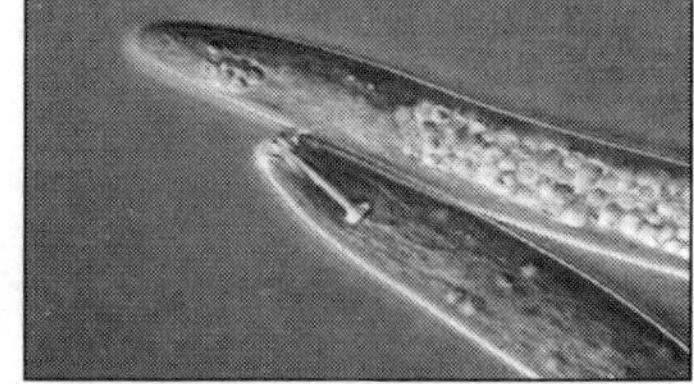

Source: *https://upload.wikimedia.org/wikipedia/commons/thumPratylenchus_coffeae.jpg/330px-Pratylenchus_coffeae.jpg*

Distribution and Host Range

Pratylenchus coffeae is a plant-pathogenic nematode infecting several hosts including potato, banana, sweet potato, strawberry, Persian violet, peanut and citrus.

Nature and Symptoms of Damage

The symptoms of damage caused by *P. coffeae* are very similar to those caused by *R. similis*. They include stunting of the plants, slowing of the vegetative phase, reduction in the number of leaves, lower bunch mass and reduced lifespan of plantations.

Life History and Description

Lesion nematodes are migratory endoparasites. The stylet is a hollow spear-shaped structure used to puncture plant cells for entry, to inject saliva that begins digestion, and then to withdraw cell contents for ingestion. Some species have males and females that mate, other species have only females and reproduce by parthenogenesis without mating. Lesion nematodes typically lay eggs inside of host plant tissue or in the soil nearby. Upon feeding, the nematode undergoes three more molts into a third and fourth stage juvenile, and then into an adult. Lesion nematode may exit the host root and later enter the same or a different root. The various juvenile life stages of lesion nematodes look very similar to adults, differing only in body size and lack of a developed reproductive system. The adult female can be easily recognized by having a vulva and functional reproductive system; males have a bursa and spicules.

Management

Fallowing for a period of six months or longer. Crop rotation with non-host crops. Use of disease-free planting material. Storage of large corms in the sun for two weeks prior to planting. Use of cover crop *calapogonium*. Removal of infested portions of corm before planting. Hotwater treatment at 55°C for 15-25 min. Paring and pralinage. Carbofuran 3 g @40 g/plant at 90 days after planting. Application of neem cake.

❑ Spiral nematode: *Helicotylenchus multicinctus* (Cobb, 1893) Golden, 1956

Common Name	:	Spiral nematode
Scientific Name	:	*Helicotylenchus multicinctus* (Cobb, 1893) Golden, 1956
Family	:	Hoplolaimidae
Order	:	Tylenchida

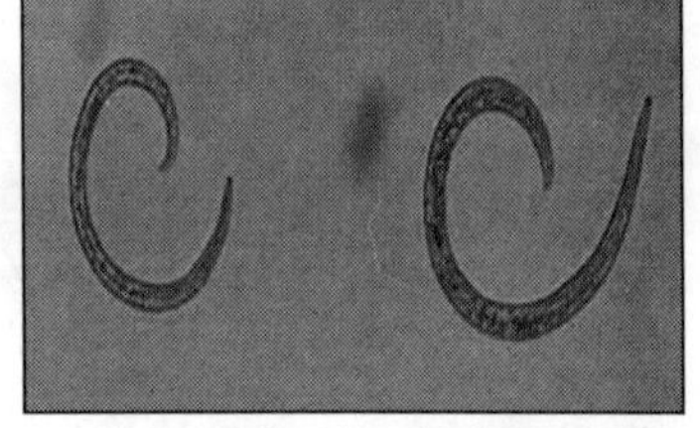

Source: *https://www.researchgate.net/publication/*

Distribution and Host Range

Found in most banana and plantain growing regions of the world including tropical and temperate regions of Asia, Africa, North America, Central America, South America and the Pacific Islands.

Nature and Symptoms of Damage

Helicotylenchus multicinctus causes small necrotic lesions on roots, and with heavy infestation these lesions coalesce, leading to root necrosis and die-back of roots. Plant stunting and reduction in yield can result.

Management

Nematodes are spread through the soil and through infested banana plantlets. The best option is to ensure that banana corms are free of any nematodes prior to planting. Researchers in Hawaii found that a hot-water treatment at 50°C for 10 minutes was enough to kill all nematodes in a corm 2-6 inches thick. Soil solarization, or heating and insulating of the soil, can cause nematode death although heat may not penetrate deep enough to kill all nematodes. Cover crops such as sunn hemp and some species of marigold may reduce the number of spiral nematodes in the soil prior to banana establishment. Nematicides are also an option. In Africa, nematicides applied with drip irrigation have showed to decrease cost and increase effectiveness.

❑ Root knot nematode: *Meloidogyne incognita* (Kofoid & White, 1919)

Common Name	:	Southern root-nematode, cotton root-knot nematode
Scientific Name	:	*Meloidogyne incognita* (Kofoid & White, 1919)
Family	:	Heteroderidae
Order	:	Tylenchida

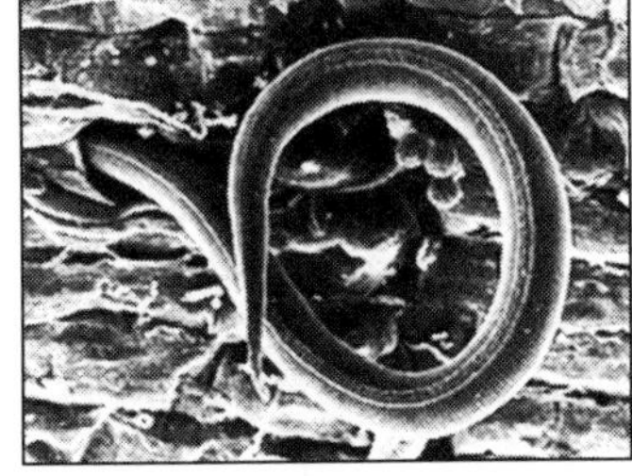

Source: *https://upload.wikimedia.org/wikipedia/commons/thumb/e/e6/A_juvenile_rootknot_nematode_%28Meloidogyne_incognita*

As Described in Tomato

Resistant Varieties	
World	**India**
Gros Michel – This variety is resistant to the banana weevil borer in some areas. **FHIA-18** – This variety has shown resistance to black sigatoka and has some tolerance to Panama disease. **Pisang Awak** – This variety has shown resistance to the banana weevil borer and nematodes. **Lady Finger** – This variety has shown resistance to the banana weevil borer and nematodes in some areas.	**Robusta** – This variety is known to be resistant to Panama disease. **Nendran** – This variety is known to be resistant to nematodes and has some tolerance to sigatoka leaf spot. **Poovan** – This variety has shown some resistance to nematodes and has some tolerance to sigatoka leaf spot. **Red Banana** – This variety has shown some resistance to nematodes and has some tolerance to sigatoka leaf spot.

Pests of Papaya

Scientific name	*Carica papaya* L.
Family	Caricaceae
Origin	Mesoamerica
Chromosome number	2n = 18

Papaya, also known as *Carica papaya*, is a tropical fruit tree that belongs to the Caricaceae family. It is a fast-growing tree that can reach up to 10 meters in height. The fruit is a large, pear-shaped berry with a thin, smooth skin that turns from green to yellow as it ripens. The flesh inside is a bright orange color and contains numerous black seeds in the centre. The fruit is rich in vitamins A, C, and E, and is also a good source of dietary fiber.

Papaya is widely grown in India and is an important fruit crop in the country. According to the Ministry of Agriculture and Farmers Welfare, the total area under papaya cultivation in India was 128,600 hectares in 2020-21, with a total production of 3.1 million metric tons.

Like many other fruit crops, papaya is susceptible to a range of insect pests that can cause significant economic damage. The most common insect pests of papaya include papaya fruit fly, papaya mealybug, and papaya whitefly. These pests can cause damage to the fruit, leaves, and stems of the plant, leading to reduced fruit quality and yield losses. In severe cases, infestations can result in complete crop losses.

❑ White fly: *Bemisia tabaci* (Gennadius, 1889)

Common name	:	Tobacco whitefly, sweetpotato whitefly, cotton whitefly
Scientific name	:	*Bemisia tabaci* (Gennadius, 1889)
Family	:	Aleyrodidae
Order	:	Hemiptera

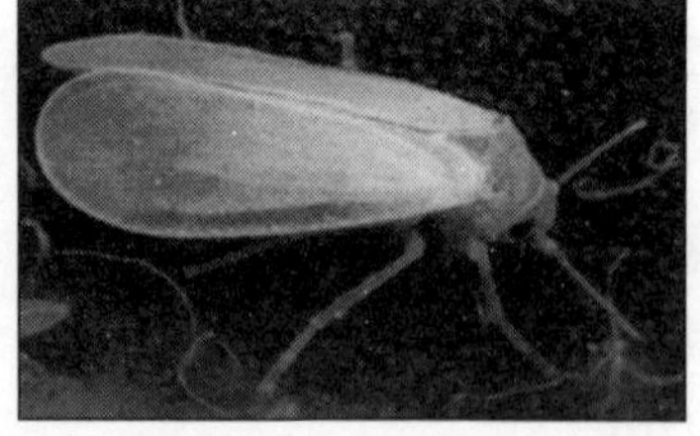

Source: *http://databases.nbair.res.in/insectpests/index.php*

As Described in Potato

❑ Fruit fly: *Bactrocera dorsalis* (Hendel, 1912)

Common name	:	Oriental fruit fly, mango fruit fly
Scientific name	:	*Bactrocera dorsalis* (Hendel, 1912)
Family	:	Tephritidae

Source: *http://databases.nbair.res.in/insectpests/index.php*

As Described in Mango

❑ Ash weevils: *Myllocerus viridanus* Fabricius, 1775

Common name	:	Ash weevils, sweet potato beetle, pod borer, green weevil
Scientific name	:	*Myllocerus viridanus* Fabricius, 1775
Family	:	Curculionidae
Order	:	Coleoptera

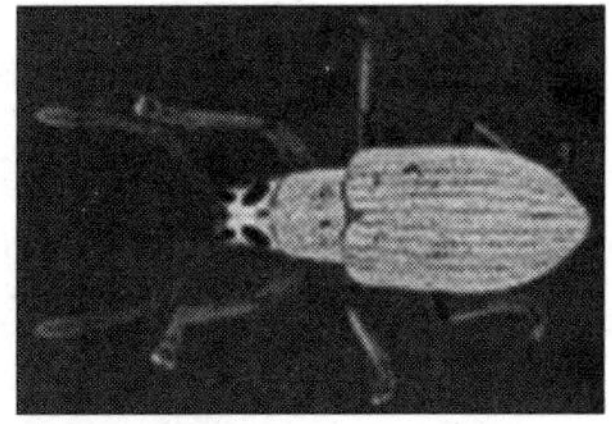

Source: *http://databases.nbair.res.in/insectpests/index.php*

Distribution and Host Range

Myllocerus viridanus, often known as sweet potato beetle, pod borer or ash weevil is a species of weevil native to India and Sri Lanka. It attacks mostly bajra, maize, sorghum, pulses, groundnut, cotton, guava.

Nature and Symptoms of Damage

Grubs feed on the roots which results in wilting of young saplings. Adult beetle feeds on leaves and makes notching of leaf margin.

Life History and Description

The female lays 150 to 350 eggs superficially in the soil over a period of 20-90 days and the grubs hatch out in 4-8 days. Grubs pass through 4 instars in a period of about 40-75 days and pupate in soil. Adult weevils are greenish white in color measuring 5 mm to 15 mm. They complete 3-5 generations in a year.

Management

Collect and destroy the adults. Apply Neem cake @ 500 kg/ha at the time of last ploughing. In endemic areas, apply carbofuran 3 G @15 kg/ha on 15 days after planting. Spray carbaryl 50 WP @3 g + wettable sulphur 2 g/litre.

❑ Green peach aphid: *Myzus persicae* (Sulzer, 1776)

Common Name	:	Green peach aphid; Green fly; Peach-potato aphid
Scientific Name	:	*Myzus persicae* (Sulzer, 1776)
Family	:	Aphididae
Order	:	Hemiptera

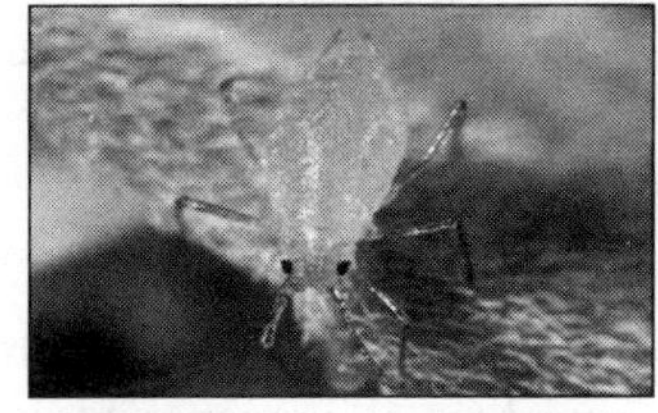

Source: *https://inpn.mnhn.fr/espece/cd_nom/52046/tab/taxo*

As Described in Potato

Papaya mealybug: *Paracoccus marginatus* Williams & Granara de Willink, 1992

Common Name	:	Papaya mealybug
Scientific Name	:	*Paracoccus marginatus* Williams & Granara de Willink, 1992
Family	:	Pseudococcidae
Order	:	Hemiptera

Source: *https://alchetron.com/Paracoccus-marginatus*

Distribution and Host Range

Papaya mealybug is a polyphagous pest attacking on economically important tropical fruits, vegetables, cotton and ornamental plants. It has caused havoc in agriculture and horticultural crops ever since its first report from Coimbatore in 2007. Now it had spread in Tamil Nadu, Andhra Pradesh and Maharashtra. The papaya mealybug is believed to be native of Mexico and/or Central America. It is polyphagous pest infesting papaya, guava, cotton, red gram, mulberry, tapioca, tomato, brinjal, teak and weeds.

Nature and Symptoms of Damage

Both nymphs and adults suck the sap from leaves, fruits and stem. While feeding it injects a toxic substance into the leaves, resulting in chlorosis, plant stunting, leaf deformation or crinkling, early leaf and fruit drop and death of plants. Besides these bugs secrete honeydew resulting in formation of back sooty mould which affects the photosynthesis of plants. The quality of fruits is deteriorated and fruits may fail to develop normally.

Life History and Description

Females usually lay 100-600 eggs in an ovisac that is three to four times the body length and entirely covered with white wax. Egg laying usually continues for one to two weeks. Eggs hatch in about 10 days and nymphs or crawlers begin to actively search for feeding sites. Females have three instars whereas males have four instars. Males have longer development time (27-30 Days) than females (24-26 days).

Eggs are greenish yellow in colour and are laid in ovisacs. Nymphs are greenish-yellow in colour with yellowish body fluid. Males are pink, especially during prepupal and pupal stages. The adult female is yellow, approximately 3 mm long and 1.4 mm wide and is covered with a white waxy coating. Adult males are approximately 1.0 mm long, with an elongate oval body. Adult males have 10 segmented antennae and well-developed wings.

Management

Pruning of infested branches and burning them. Removal and destruction of crop residues, weeds or alternate hosts. Avoid the movement of planting material from infested areas to other areas. Control ant movement and do not use infested plant material as mulch. Application of sticky bands or alkathene sheet or a band of insecticide on arms or on main stem to prevent movement of crawlers.

Parasitoids: *Anagyrus loecki*, *Apoanagyrus californicus*, *Acerophagus*, sp. *Pseudophycus* sp. In India, papaya mealybug was successfully managed by the hymenopteran parasitoid *Acerophagous papaya* that was imported and introduced from Mexico in 2010-11 by NBAIR, Bangalore. Predators: Australian ladybird beetle *Cryptolaemus montrouzieri*, indigenous *Scymnus* sp., cecidomyiidae *Diadiplosis coccidarum*, chrysopid larva and adults and syrphid fly larvae. Locate ant colonies and destroy them with drenching of chlorpyriphos 20 EC @ 2.0 ml/litre of water. Apply recommended chemical insecticides such as profenophos 50 EC (2 ml/litre), chlorpyriphos 20 EC (2 ml/litre), buprofezin 25 EC (2 ml/litre), dimethoate 30 EC (2 ml/litre), thiomethoxam 25 WG (0.6 g/litre), imidacloprid 17.8 SL (0.6 ml/litre).

❑ Red Spider mite: *Tetranychus urticae* C.L. Koch, 1836

Common Name	:	Red Spider mite
Scientific Name	:	*Tetranychus urticae* C.L. Koch, 1836
Family	:	Tetranychidae
Order	:	Trombidiformes

Source: *https://upload.wikimedia.org/wikipedia/commons/thumb/5/52/Tetranychus_urticae_%284883560779%29.jpg/330px-Tetranychus_urticae_%284883560779%29.jpg*

As Described in Tomato

❑ Fruit fly: *Bactrocera diversus* (Coquillett), *B. cucurbitae* (Coquillett)

Common Name	:	Three-striped fruit fly, guava fruit fly; Melon fruit fly, melon fly
Scientific Name	:	*Bactrocera diversus* (Coquillett); *B. cucurbitae* (Coquillett)
Family	:	Tephritidae
Order	:	Diptera

Source: *http://databases.nbair.res.in/insectpests/index.php*

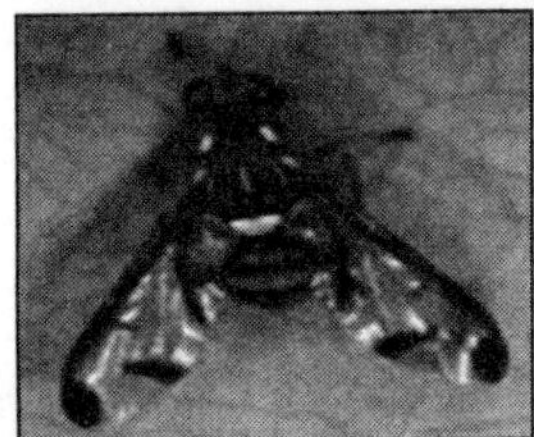

Source: *http://databases.nbair.res.in/insectpests/index.php*

Distribution and Host Range

It is distributed throughout all the guava orchards in the country. Besides guava it also infests tomato and other commercial fruits.

Nature and Symptoms of Damage

The female punctures outer wall of mature fruits with the help of its pointed ovipositor and insert eggs in small clusters inside mesocarp of mature fruits. On hatching, the maggots feed on fruit pulp and the infested fruits start rotting due to further secondary infection.

Life History and Description

Female flies insert eggs under the skin of fruit in clusters of 10 to 50 about 1/25 to 1/8 inch below the fruit surface. The eggs measure about 1/25 by 1/250 inch and are white, elongate, and elliptical. They hatch in 1-1/2 days. The white larva is legless, and resembles an elongated cone. There are 3 larval stages, or instars. The third instar is about 2/5 inch long. The entire larval stage lasts for 11-15 days. When mature, larvae drop to the ground and pupate in the soil. The puparium is yellowish-brown and seed-like. Adults emerge in about 10 days. Generally, the abdomen has two horizontal black stripes and a longitudinal median stripe extending from the base of the third segment to the apex of the abdomen. These markings may form a "T" shaped pattern, but the pattern varies considerably. Females begin to lay eggs about 8 days after emergence from the puparium. Under optimum conditions, a female can lay more than 3,000 eggs during her lifetime.

Management

Collect and destroy the adult flies. Prior to harvest, collect and dispose off infested and fallen fruits to prevent further, multiplication and carry-over of population. Ploughing of orchard during November-December to expose pupae to sun's heat which kills them. If infestation is heavy, bait splash (mix 100 g of jaggery in one litre of water and add 1 ml of deltamethrin) on the trunk only, once or twice at weekly interval is recommended. Hot water treatment of fruit at 48 ± 1 ºC for 45 min. Male annihilation technique: Set up fly trap using methyl eugenol. Prepare methyl eugenol 1 ml/L of water + 1 ml of malathion solution. Take 10 ml of this mixture per trap and keep them at 25 different places in one ha between 6 and 8 am.

❑ Grasshopper: *Poekilocerus pictus* (Fabricius, 1775)

Common name	:	Grasshopper
Scientific name	:	*Poekilocerus pictus* (Fabricius, 1775)
Family	:	Pyrgomorphidae
Order	:	Orthoptera

Source: *https://upload.wikimedia.org/wikipedia/commons/thumb/7/70/Poekilocerus_pictus.jpg/330px-Poekilocerus_pictus.jpg*

Distribution and Host Range

It is distributed throughout Mangochi, Republic of Malawi, Ethiopia, West Africa, East Africa, South Africa, Egypt, Nigeria, India, Pakistan and Yemen. *P. pictus* is feeder of alfalfa, betal creepers, brinjal, cassava, castor, citrus, corn, cowpea, forest trees, maize, mango orchards, okra, papaya etc.

Nature and Symptoms of Damage

Both nymphs and adults suck the sap from the lower leaf surfaces through their piercing and sucking mouthparts. While sucking the plant sap, they also inject toxic saliva into the plant tissues, which leads to yellowing. When several insects suck the sap from the same leaf, yellow spots appear on the leaves, followed by crinkling, curling, bronzing, and drying, or "hopper burn".

Life History and Description

Adult females lay eggs along the midrib and lateral veins of the leaves. The egg period is 4 to 11 days. The nymphs resemble the adults, but lack wings and are pale green in color. They tend to move sideways when disturbed. The nymphal period varies from one to four weeks depending on the temperature. The adults are wedge-shaped, pale green insects. They have fully developed wings with a prominent black spot on each forewing. The adults may live for one to two months.

Management

Parasitoids: *Lymaenon empoascae* (egg), *Anagrus flaveolus*, *Stethynium triclavatum*. Predators: Birds, praying mantis, blister beetle, ground beetle, spider, hoverfly etc.

❑ Reniform nematode: *Rotylenchulus reniformis* Linford and Oliveira, 1940

Common name	:	Reniform nematode
Scientific name	:	*Rotylenchulus reniformis* Linford and Oliveira, 1940
Family	:	Hoplolaimidae
Order	:	Tylenchida

Source:https://upload.wikimedia.org/wikipedia/commons/thumb/0/04/

Distribution and Host Range

R. reniformis has been reported from thousands of localities in the Americas, Africa, Europe, Asia, and Australia. It has a wide host range that includes fruit trees, lentil, cotton, pigeon pea, tea, tobacco, soybean, pineapplc, banana, okra, coconut, cabbage, sweet potato, alfalfa, corn, asparagus, palm, cucumber, tomato, squash, cassava, radish, eggplant, guava, melon, and ginger.

Nature and Symptoms of Damage

The above-ground symptoms appear as moderate to severe leaf chlorosis and plant stunting. Some wilting may occur during periods of peak transpirational stress on the plant. Reniform nematode presence on the roots may be observed with the aid of a 10x hand lens. The small sand-like bodies which remain attached, after the root system is carefully washed, are egg masses of the nematode. Fruits produced are smaller than normal and may be slightly insipid.

Life History and Description

The predominant reniform species found on papayas in most of the world is *R. reniformis*. Many commonly cultivated crops as well as weeds are hosts of the reniform nematodes. Because of their small size, they do not travel distances of more than a few inches in their lifetime. Juveniles that hatch from eggs are less than 500 μm long. After undergoing several molts, female juveniles become young adults and penetrate the root cortext and become sedentary. The portion of the body that remains outside the root enlarges and becomes kidney-shaped, hence the name "reniform." After maturation the female secrets a gelatinous substance around her body into which she lays about 100 eggs. A complete life cycle is possible in about 25 days. The reniform nematode feeds near the phloem in papaya roots inducing the formation of giant cells. These are centers of high metabolic activity that compete with other parts of the plant for food and nutrients. The nematode also may feed in the root cortex and cause mechanical breakdown of the cortical cells, thus providing suitable sites for attack by fungi.

Management

Use resistant/tolerant varieties. Sowing should be completed within recommended periods. Intercropping with sunnhemp or marigold or daincha. Use mahua, castor, neem and karanj cakes, biogas sludge applied at 1.0 t/acre during pit preparation. Apply 2 tons of FYM enriched with *Pochonia chlamydosporia* and *Paecilomyces lilacinus*/acre before sowing, along with 100-200 kg of neem or pongamia cake. Apply neem-based products (Neemagon, Bioneem, Neemraj etc.) for controlling this pest.

Resistant Varieties	
World	**India**
Red Lady: This is a popular papaya variety from Thailand that is resistant to papaya ring spot virus and papaya mealybug. **Maradol:** This is a large papaya variety that is grown in Mexico and has resistance to papaya ring spot virus and spider mites. **Sunrise Solo:** This papaya variety from Hawaii is resistant to papaya ringspot virus and is also known to have some resistance to the papaya fruit fly. **Tainung No. 1:** This is a Taiwanese variety that is resistant to papaya ringspot virus, as well as papaya leaf distortion mosaic virus.	**CO-7:** This is a variety of papaya developed by the Indian Council of Agricultural Research (ICAR) that is resistant to papaya ringspot virus and papaya leaf curl virus. **Pusa Dwarf:** This is another ICAR-developed papaya variety that is resistant to papaya ringspot virus, as well as mealybugs and whiteflies. **Surya:** This papaya variety from Kerala is known to have some level of resistance to papaya ringspot virus and spider mites.

15 Pests of Guava

Scientific name	*Psidium guajava*
Family	Myrtaceae
Origin	Tropical America
Chromosome number	2n = 22

Guava is a tropical fruit crop that belongs to the family Myrtaceae and is botanically known as *Psidium guajava*. It is believed to have originated in Central America but is now grown in many tropical and subtropical regions of the world including India. Guava fruits are highly nutritious and are a rich source of vitamins A and C, fiber, and antioxidants.

Guava is an important fruit crop in India and is grown in several states across the country. The major guava-growing states in India are Uttar Pradesh, Maharashtra, Andhra Pradesh, Bihar, and Tamil Nadu. In recent years, the production of guava in India has increased significantly, and India is now the leading producer of guava in the world.

However, like all other crops, guava is susceptible to attack by a range of insect pests, which can cause significant economic losses if not managed properly. Some of the common insect pests of guava include fruit flies, scale insects, mealybugs, and whiteflies. These pests can cause direct damage to the fruit and foliage, leading to reduced yields and poor fruit quality. Additionally, they can also transmit plant diseases, further impacting the productivity of the crop. Effective pest management practices, including the use of integrated pest management (IPM) strategies, can help to minimize the impact of insect pests on guava production. This can include the use of biological control agents, cultural practices, and chemical pesticides, used judiciously and according to recommended guidelines, to ensure optimal control of pest populations.

❑ Tea mosquito bug: *Helopeltis antonii* V. Signoret, 1858

Common name	:	Tea mosquito bug
Scientific name	:	*Helopeltis antonii* V. Signoret, 1858
Family	:	Miridae
Order	:	Hemiptera

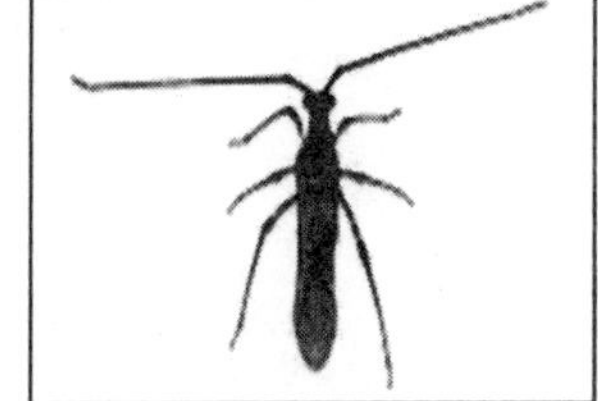

Source: *http://databases.nbair.res.in/insectpests/index.php*

Distribution and Host Range

Helopeltis antonii are found in a region known as the old-world tropics which encompasses places such as India, Northern Australia, Guinea, Vietnam, Tanzania, Nigeria, and Indonesia. It is polyphagous pest; its incidence has been reported on many fruit crops including guava.

Nature and Symptoms of Damage

Nymphs and adults feed on tender leaves, shoots and fruits. In case of severe incidence of this pest, brown patches can be seen on the new leaves. Brown to black dots appear on the infested flower buds, and scales appear on fruits. Severe infestation of this pest leads to heavy flower drop.

Life History and Description

Adult bugs are small, active and have elongated body (7-9 mm) with long legs and antennae. Young nymphs are hairy amber coloured and identical to ants. It completes its life cycle within 26-35 days. The adult lays elongated and sausage-shaped eggs that possess two filamentous long processes, which remain cutting out from the tender plant tissue in which the eggs are bedded by the female. Incubation period varies between 5 and 27 days. The newly hatched nymphs resemble spider in general appearance with elongated appendages. They undergo five moults and complete one generation in 2 weeks or more in cold weather.

Management

Removal of alternative or weed host serves as effective practice in reducing this pest incidence. In case of severe incidence of this pest, spraying of insecticides like malathion (0.1%) or neem oil (2%) at 15-day intervals on young fruits reduced its infestation significantly.

❑ Fruit borers: *Conogethes punctiferalis* (Guenée, 1854)

Common name	:	Fruit borers
Scientific name	:	*Conogethes punctiferalis* (Guenée, 1854)
Family	:	Crambidae
Order	:	Lepidoptera

Source: *https://upload.wikimedia.org/wikipedia/commons/thumb/b/b6/Conogethes_punctiferalis.jpg/330px-Conogethes_punctiferalis.jpg*

Distribution and Host Range

Conogethes punctiferalis, the **durian fruit borer** or **yellow peach moth**, is a moth of the family Crambidae. It is found from India and Pakistan through South-east Asia to Australia. It has been reported from various parts of the world, mainly because larvae are imported alongside fruit. Records include Hawaii, Great Britain and the Netherlands. Larvae of this pest feed on variety of host plants, including spices, vegetables and fruit crops. Among the fruit crops, this pest occurrence was reported from temperate, tropical and subtropical fruits, like banana, citrus, sapota, pomegranate, mango, guava, grape, apple and peach.

Nature and Symptoms of Damage

Fruits become malformed at the larval entry point. Infestation of this pest can be seen as larval faecal matter exuding out of the borer hole at the basal end of the fruit. Such fruit becomes weak, rots and falls down.

Life History and Description

Eggs: Eggs are round and light yellow in color, and 0.63 × 0.41 mm in size. After incubation of 6-7 days, the eggs turn dark brown with a dark head.

Larvae: The larva of the moth has a black head and a pale greenish body with a pinkish suffusion dorsally. Coloration can vary by type of food. Fully grown larvae are 16 to 26 mm and are rather stout, pale, or reddish-brown with numerous flattened horny warts that have short bristly hairs. The prothoracic shield is large and the head is reddish-brown.

Pupae: The pupa measures 15 mm long and is brown in color. The pupa is enclosed by a white silken cocoon.

Adults: Adults are pale straw yellow with numerous small black spots and a wing span of 18 to 24 mm.

Management

Collect and destroy damaged fruits. Clean cultivation as weed plants serve as alternate hosts. Use light trap @ 1/ha to monitor the activity of adults. Malathion 50 EC 0.1% two rounds, one at flower formation and next at fruit set.

❑ Fruit borer: *Deudorix isocrates* (Fabricius, 1793)

Common name	:	Fruit borers, Anar butterfly, common guava blue
Scientific name	:	*Deudorix isocrates* (Fabricius, 1793)
Family	:	Lycaenidae
Order	:	Lepidoptera

Source: *http://databases.nbair.res.in/insectpests/index.php*

Distribution and Host Range

D. isocrates, affects wide range of host plants, including, aonla, apple, ber, beal, citrus, guava, litchi, loquat, mulberry, peach, pear, plum, pomegranate, sapota and tamarind. It is geographically distributed all over India. Its incidence was found in very severe form during the fruiting stage in guava. This pest infests all stages of fruit development.

Nature and Symptoms of Damage

The female lays eggs singly on calyx of flowers or small fruits. On hatching, the caterpillars bore inside the developing fruits. Caterpillar feeds on pulp and seeds just beneath the rind; then the infested fruits suffer from secondary infection of bacteria and fungi which subsequently leads to fruit rot. The striking features of damage are identified by unpleasant odour and excreta of the caterpillars coming out of entry point; the excreta are found stuck around the holes. Occasionally the holes may also be seen plugged with the anal end of a caterpillar.

Life History and Description

The adult butterfly is bluish brown in colour and bears an orange spot on each of the forewings and black spots on the hindwings. The eggs are laid singly on flowers and tender fruits. Eggs are shiny white in colour and oval in shape. The egg hatches out within 7-10 days. The caterpillar measures 16-20 mm long, is dirty brown and has short hairs on its body. Larval period varies from 14 to 45 days. Just before pupation, the caterpillars come out of the fruits and tie the stalk of fruit with the main branch of the tree with fine silken strands to ensure that the fruit does not fall down and then re-enter the fruit and pupate therein or on fruit stalk. Pupal period varies from a week to more than a month. The total life cycle completes in 1-2 months. It competes four generation in a year. On guava fruit borer, life cycle completes in 34-42 days.

Management

Cultivation of pomegranate should be discouraged close to guava as this is the most preferred host of this pest. Regular collection of infested fruits and their destruction to check the further spread and carryover the population. To prevent the infestation of pest, spray carbaryl (0.2%) or ethophenprox (0.05%) at the beginning of fruiting season and before ripening of fruits. At least 15 days waiting period should be observed before beginning of harvest. The spray may be repeated at fortnightly intervals depending on severity of attack.

❑ Guava fruit fly: *Bactrocera diversa* (Coquillett, 1904)

Common name	:	Guava fruit fly, Three-striped fruit fly
Scientific name	:	*Bactrocera diversa* (Coquillett, 1904)
Family	:	Tephritidae
Order	:	Diptera

Source: *http://databases.nbair.res.in/insectpests/index.php*

Distribution and Host Range

Fruit flies are the major constraint in tropical and subtropical fruit crop production. This species of fruit fly is generally referred as "oriental fruit fly". This species is polyphagous; quite severe incidence has been reported on mango. Its incidence has been also reported on guava along with *B. zonata*. Its occasional occurrence has been reported on jamun.

Nature and Symptoms of Damage

The infestation begins when the female fruit fly pierces the fruit with its elongated and thorny ovipositor for egg laying. The fruit skin is injured, secondary infection starts on the fruit, and ultimately fruit starts to decay. The maggot that emerges from the egg feed on the decaying fruit tissue, on which yeasts and bacteria multiply. During the process of egg laying, small depressions are seen on the fruits. The damaged part of the fruit becomes soft at the place of larval feeding and later on leads to putrification, and subsequently fruit drop occurs.

Life History and Description

Female fruit flies lay eggs under the skin of host fruits. The egg development completes in 2 days, but depending on the prevailing temperature, it may vary. Maggots that emerge from the eggs make tunnel and feed on the pulp; maggots undergo two moulting, drop from the fruit and enter into the soil for pupation. The pupal period completes in 7-18 days. The adult females sexually mature in 16-38 days. Fruit flies complete many generations in a year.

Management

Collect and destroy fallen and infested fruits. Summer ploughing to expose pupa. Use methyl eugenol lure trap (25/ha) to monitor and kill adults of fruit flies. Prepare methyl eugenol and malathion 50 EC mixture at 1:1 ratio (take 10 ml mixture/trap). Inseciticides: malathion 50 EC 0.05%. Bait spray combining molasses or jaggery 10 g/l and one of the insecticides, malathion 50 EC

2 ml/l dimethoate 30 EC 1 ml/lit, two rounds at fortnight interval before ripening of fruits. Field release of parasitoids such as *Opius compensates*, *Spalangia philippinensis*, parasitoid wasp, *Diachasmimorpha kraussi*.

Aphid: *Aphis punicae* Passerini, 1863

Common name	:	Aphid
Scientific name	:	*Aphis punicae* Passerini, 1863
Family	:	Aphididae
Order	:	Hemiptera

Source: *https://www.google.co.in/imgres?imgurl=https%3A%2F%2Fars.els-cdn.com%2Fcontent%2Fimage%*

Distribution and Host Range

Aphis punicae is native to the Mediterranean area, but is now also found in the Middle East, Ethiopia, India, Pakistan, Japan, and Korea. It is also recorded from pomegranate, pigeon berry and common lantana, crossvine and trumpet vine, and cape leadwort.

Life History and Description

Eggs are very small white to dull white in cloured. Both winged and wingless forms breed parthenogenetically. The nymphal period lasts for 7-9 days. Adults live for 2-3 weeks and produce 8-22 nymphs per day. Entire life cycle takes 22-25 days. It has 12-14 generations per year. The body of the apterous female is light green, including the cauda and siphunculi, length of the female body is 1.0-2.0 mm. The head and thorax of alate females are dark, as are the siphunculi, whereas the abdomen and cauda are greenish and body length is 1.4-1.9 mm.

Nature and Symptoms of Damage

Nymphs and adults suck the sap from leaves, shoots and fruits. Yellowing of leaves and wilting of terminal shoots.

Management

Collect and destroy the infested plant parts. Maintain adequate aeration by proper training and pruning. Conserve predators such as ladybird beetles *i.e., Scymnus*, *Chilomenus sexmaculatus*, preying mantids, green lacewings, etc. Release first instar larva of *Chrysoperla carnea* @ 15/flowering branch (four times) at 10 days interval from the time of flower initiation.

Whitefly: *Aleurodicus dispersus* Russell, 1965

Common name	:	Spiraling whitefly
Scientific name	:	*Aleurodicus dispersus* Russell, 1965
Family	:	Aleyrodidae
Order	:	Hemiptera

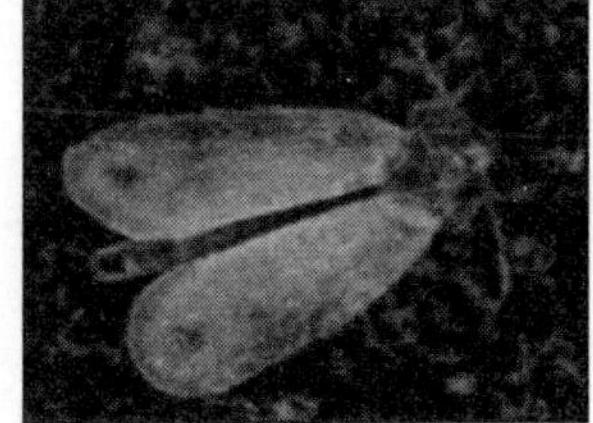

Source: *http://databases.nbair.res.in/insectpests/index.php*

Distribution and Host Range

It is reported in Central and South America, the Caribbean and Southern Florida, USA, India, Sri Lanka, Africa, Indonesia, Thailand, Taiwan and Northern Australia. It is found on plants like guava, cassava, cotton, chillies, tomato, brinjal, bhendi, papaya, crotons and weeds such as *Euphorbia, Corchorus, Eclipta, Vernonia, Vicoa, Acalypha, Alternanthra, Amaranthus, Convolvulus, Abutilon* etc.

Nature and Symptoms of Damage

Chlorotic spots, yellowing, downward curling and drying of leaves. Vector of potato leaf curl disease.

Life History and Description

The female white flies lay eggs singly on the underside of the leaves. Eggs are smooth, sub elliptical, stalked at broader basal end. Its colour is light yellow, when freshly laid, turn dark brown later on. The eggs hatch in 5-17 days. It is louse like, sluggish creature having pale-yellow body. The nymphal stage lasts 14 to 81 days. Convex in shape and possesses deep yellow patches on the abdomen. In 2-8 days, the pupae change into white flies. Adult fly is small winged insect having light yellow body of 1.0-1.5 mm length dusted with a white waxy powder. Wings are pure white and have prominent long legs. The life cycle is completed in 14-122 days. Eleven generations of this pest are completed in a year.

Management

Remove and destroy damaged leaves along with life stages. Remove and destroy weed plants like *Abutilon*, *Acalypha*, *Euphorbia*, etc., in the nearby vicinity as these plants are alternate hosts. Use yellow sticky traps at 15/ha to attract and kill the adults. Release *Chrysoperla carnea* predators at 10000/ha to kill all life stages. Encourage the activity of predators such as *Encarsia* and Coccinellids, *Chilocorus nigrita*, *Chilomenus sexmaculatus*, etc. Spray fish oil rosin soap 25 g/L or NSKE 5% or neem oil 0.03% 1 ml/l or phosalone 35 EC 3 L or triazophos 40 EC 3 L or acephate 75 SP 1.5 kg in 1500-2000 L per ha., two to three times based on the incidence. Avoid using synthetic pyrethroids and extending crop growth. Conserve spiraling whitefly parasitoids, *Encarsia haitiensis* and *E. guadeloupae*.

☐ Scarlet Mite: *Brevipalpus phoenicus* (Geijskes, 1936)

Common name	:	Scarlet mite, false spider mite, red and black flat mite
Scientific name	:	*Brevipalpus phoenicus* (Geijskes, 1936)
Family	:	Tenupalpidae
Order	:	Trombidiformes

Source: *https://upload.wikimedia.org/wikipedia/commons/thumb/6/67/Flat_mite%2C_Brevipalpus_phoenicis.jpg/330px-Flat_mite%2C_Brevipalpus_phoenicis.jpg*

Distribution and Host Range

This species occurs globally, and is a serious pest to such crops as citrus, tea, papaya, guava and coffee, and can heavily damage numerous other crops.

Nature and Symptoms of Damage

Both nymphs and adults suck the cell sap from fruits which results in browning of nodal regions and appearance of brown patches on calyx and surface of fruits. In severe infestation, these symptoms cover the entire surface of fruits leading to splitting of fruits.

Life History and Description

Brevipalpus phoenicis lays approximately 50 to 60 eggs during adulthood. The eggs hatch 8 to 16 days after being laid singly on stalks of fruits, calyx and leaves. One day before the eggs hatch, they turn opaque white and the red eyes of the larvae within become visible. Adult specimens can grow to 280 μm (0.011 in) long (including the rostrum) and 150 μm (0.0059 in) wide. They are flat, oval, and have a dark green to red-orange colour.

Management

Collect and destroy the damaged plant parts. Spray wettable sulphur 3 kg or dicofol 2 L in 1500 to 2000 L of water per ha.

❑ Bark eating caterpillars: *Indarbella quadrinotata* (Walker, 1856)

Common name	:	Bark-eating caterpillar
Scientific name	:	*Indarbela quadrinotata* (Walker, 1856)
Family	:	Cossidae
Order	:	Lepidoptera

Source: *https://agritech.tnau.ac.in/crop_protection/guava/guava_5.html*

As Described in Mango

Resistant Varieties	
World	**India**
Hong Kong Pink: This variety is known for its pink flesh and high resistance to pests like fruit flies, mealybugs, and scale insects. **Detwiler:** This variety is grown in Florida and is highly resistant to nematodes and fruit flies. **Supreme:** This variety is grown in California and is resistant to root-knot nematodes. **Mexican Cream:** This variety is known for its creamy texture and is resistant to several pests including fruit flies and mealybugs. **Ruby Supreme:** This variety is grown in California and is known for its sweet flavor and resistance to root-knot nematodes. **Beaumont:** This variety is grown in Texas and is resistant to several pests including fruit flies and scale insects. **Chinese White:** This variety is grown in China and is resistant to several pests including fruit flies and thrips. **Red Malaysian:** This variety is grown in Malaysia and is resistant to several pests including fruit flies and scale insects. **Taiwan Guava:** This variety is grown in Taiwan and is resistant to several pests including fruit flies and spider mites. **Apple Guava:** This variety is grown in Hawaii and is resistant to several pests including root-knot nematodes and fruit flies.	**Allahabad Safeda:** This is a popular variety of guava that is grown in many parts of India. It is known for its sweet and juicy flesh and is resistant to several insect pests, including fruit flies. **Lalit:** This variety is grown in the Northern parts of India and is known for its high yield and resistance to several pests, including mealybugs and whiteflies. **Arka Mridula:** This variety was developed by the Indian Institute of Horticultural Research and is resistant to several pests, including scale insects and fruit borers. **Apple Guava:** This variety is resistant to several pests, including the guava fruit fly and scale insects. It is grown in many parts of India and is known for its sweet and juicy flesh. **Harijha:** This variety is grown in the Northeastern parts of India and is resistant to several pests, including the guava fruit fly and scale insects. It is known for its high yield and sweet flavor.

16

Pests of Sapota

Scientific name	*Manilkara zapota*
Family	Sapotaceae
Origin	South Mexico
Chromosome number	2n = 26

Sapota, also known as chikoo, is a tropical fruit crop that is grown mainly in India, as well as in other tropical and subtropical regions of the world. The botanical name of sapota is *Manilkara zapota*, and it belongs to the family Sapotaceae.

Sapota is an important fruit crop in India, especially in the states of Maharashtra, Gujarat, Andhra Pradesh, and Karnataka. It is also grown in other tropical and subtropical countries such as Mexico, Brazil, Thailand, and the Philippines. The economic importance of sapota lies in its high nutritional value, as it is a rich source of dietary fiber, vitamins (A and C), minerals (potassium, calcium, and iron), and antioxidants. The fruit is consumed fresh, as well as processed into pulp, juice, and other value-added products such as jam, jelly, and ice cream.

Insects that can cause damage to sapota crops include mealybugs, scale insects, and fruit flies. Mealybugs and scale insects feed on the sap of the tree, causing stunted growth, yellowing of leaves, and reduced fruit production. Fruit flies can cause significant damage by laying eggs inside the fruit, leading to fruit decay and spoilage. Proper pest management strategies, including the use of insecticides and biological control agents, can help minimize the economic impact of these pests on sapota crops.

Bud borer: *Eustalodes achrasella* (Bradley, 1981)

Common name	:	Bud borer
Scientific name	:	*Eustalodes achrasella* (Bradley, 1981)
Family	:	Gelechiidae
Order	:	Lepidoptera

Source: *https://agritech.tnau.ac.in/crop_protection/sapota/budworm.png*

Distribution and Host Range

It is a common pest of sapota throughout the year in India. It is recorded that the damage ranged from 2-15 %.

Nature and Symptoms of Damage

The insect bores into the flower buds through petal and causes considerable bud and flower drops. One larva could damage 26-35 buds before reaching pupation resulting in shedding of buds and flowers.

Life History and Description

Eggs of *A. achrasella* are laid on flower buds or developing fruits singly and turn brown at time of hatching. The larvae pass through four instars on sapota buds. The pupation take place either inside or outside the flower buds. The duration of the pupa varied from 5-9 days. Life cycle completed in 27-33 days. The newly formed adults are flimsy and soft. The ovipositional period varies from 3-8 days. Female lays on an average 56-57 eggs and survive for 4-8 days. Female lay eggs singly which are oval and white in colour. The caterpillar is light yellow in colour and pinkish brown with black head at maturity. A newly formed pupa is obtect type, brick red in colour and changed to dark brown before adult emergence. Grey moth with black patches on wings.

Management

Erect blue light trap for monitoring population of bud borer. Spray of azadirachtin 0.15 EC at the rate of 40 ml/10 liters of water. Application of polytrin C44 (profenphos and cypermethrin) @1 ml/l or emamectin benzoate 5 SG @ 0.45 gm/lit. or deltamethrin 2.8 EC @ 1 ml/lit. or lambda cyhalothrin 5 EC @ 1 ml/lit. or profenofos 40 EC @ 1 ml/lit of water at the initiation of damage and subsequent two sprays at an interval of one month. The precaution should be taken to avoid immediate repetition of any insecticide in the subsequent spray.

❑ Sapota seed borer: *Trymalitis margarias* Meyrick, 1905

Common name	:	Sapota seed borer, Sapodilla seed borer
Scientific name	:	*Trymalitis margaritas* Meyrick, 1905
Family	:	Tortricidae
Order	:	Lepidoptera

Source: *http://v3.boldsystems.org/index.php/Taxbrowser_Taxonpage?taxid=970444*

Distribution and Host Range

Monophagous pest, feeds only on sapota. The sapota seed borer is an exotic pest that has been introduced into India a decade back and established over a period of time. This pest has spread to major sapota growing belts in Gujarat, Karnataka and Tamil Nadu.

Nature and Symptoms of Damage

Newly hatched larva enters into the seed through the pulp and feeds exclusively on endosperm of the seed. Its entry into the seed is seen as streak and later it disappears as the seed hardens. Black larval head capsule is seen in the hole on the cotyledons. Full grown larvae prepare a tunnel to come out from the fruit. Through this exit hole the fungus as well as ants enters inside the fruits and the fruit becomes unfit for consumption.

Life History and Description

A female moth lays eggs on fruits of marble/lime size when the seed coat is soft. Incubation period is 10-12 days. Neonate larva bores into the fruit and finally enters the seed. The larvae feeds on the endosperm of the seed, completes its larval period inside the seed. The larval period lasts for 10 to 13 days. For pupation, mature larva comes out of the seed by tunneling out the pulp. Pupation takes place on leaves by folding leaf margins and pupal period lasts for 12-13 days. The longevity of adults is 3-5 days. The total life cycle completes in 32-38 days.

The first instar larvae are very minute, white in colour with pinkish tinge possess segmented body without hair. Fully developed larva is pinkish in colour, 12 to 13 mm in length and come out of the seed for pupation. The pupae are obtect type, brown in colour and entangled in white silken material. Adults are small (7 to 11 mm long) with whitish forewings having grayish spots, hind wing creamy in colour with thick hairs at the margins. Moth looks to possess bell shaped wings and resembles bird droppings.

Management

Sanitation of the orchard eliminate the sources of seed borer infestation. Collection and destruction of the off-season stray. Domestic quarantine is the best way to limit its spread. Erect blue light traps in the orchard during cropping season that attracts adult moths that minimize the incidence. First spray intervention should be made when the fruits are of small lime size and thereafter the sprayings should be repeated at fortnightly interval during main cropping season. Alternate the sprays of deltamethrin 2.8 EC @ 1 ml/lit or profenophos 40 EC @1 ml/lit or lambda cyhalothrin or profenofos 50 EC at the rate of 1.5 ml/lit or indoxacarb 14.5SC at the rate of 0.5 ml/lit or novaluron 10 EC at the rate of 0.5 ml/lit or *Bt* @ 1 ml/lit at monthly interval may bring down the seed borer infestation.

❑ Sapota leaf webber: *Nephopteryx eugraphella* Ragonot 1888

Common name	:	Sapota leaf webber, Chichoo moth
Scientific name	:	*Nephopteryx eugraphella* Ragonot 1888
Family	:	Pyralidae
Order	:	Lepidoptera

Source: *https://agritech.tnau.ac.in/crop_protection/sapota/Sapota-Nephopteryx%20eugraphella.jpg*

Distribution and Host Range

It is a major pest of sapota, occurs widely in India. Host range includes sapota and bakul.

Nature and Symptoms of Damage

The larvae fold the leaves together and feed on green matter of leaves, often on buds and flowers and sometimes on tender fruits as well. The larvae bore into the buds, which wither and move on to other buds thus, damaging many of them. The infestation of this pest can be easily spotted by the presence of webbed shoots, appearance of dark brown patches on leaves and clusters of dead leaves.

Larval feeding causes serious damage to young terminals and buds which reduces flowering and fruiting.

Life History and Description

The pest is found throughout the year but the activity increases with the appearance of new shoots and buds. With the onset of spring season, the female moths start laying pale-yellow, oval shaped eggs singly or in batches of 2 or 3, on leaves and buds of young shoots. A female may lay as many as 374 eggs in 7 days. The eggs hatch in 3-5 days. The larvae feed for 17-32 days and complete development. They undergo pupation in the soil for 7-11 days. The life-cycle is completed in 32-45 days. There are 7-9 generations of this pest in a year.

Eggs are laid singly or in batches of 2-3 on tender leaves, petioles, branches or buds. Neonate larva is pink in colour that turns yellow and finally green at maturity. Hairs are present on the dorsal side of the body. Head is pale yellow. Fully grown larva is of 19 mm in size with 3 longitudinal pinkish brown strips on each side of the body. Pupation takes place in soil in earthen cell with exit hole. The newly formed pupa is green in colour that turns reddish within 24 hours and dark brown on maturity. It measures 10 mm × 2.5 mm. It is broad at the posterior end and narrow at the anterior end. The moth is small, gray coloured, slender bodied insect having black forewings with yellow spots on the basal half and black transverse lines on the remaining half. Both the wings are fringed at the outer margin. Wing span is 20 mm.

Management

Removal and destruction of infested leaves and affected fruits by sapota moth. Spray quinolphos 25EC @2 ml/lit of water.

❑ Sapota fruitfly: *Bactrocera dorsalis* (Hendel, 1912)

Common name	:	Oriental fruit fly, mango fruit fly
Scientific name	:	*Bactrocera dorsalis* (Hendel, 1912)
Family	:	Tephritidae

Source: *http://databases.nbair.res.in/insectpests/index.php*

As Described in Mango

❑ Leaf miner: *Acrocercops gemoniella* Stainton, 1863

Common name	:	Leaf miner
Scientific name	:	*Acrocercops gemoniella* Stainton, 1863
Family	:	Gracillariidae
Order	:	Lepidoptera

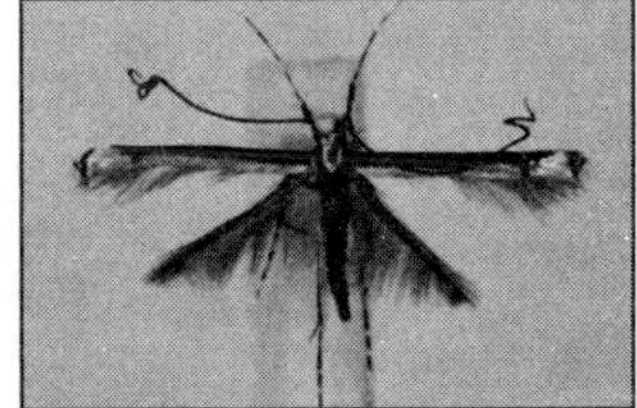

Source: *https://artsandculture.google.com/asset/acrocercops-gemoniella-stainton-1863/3QG2Ze2EnzdLHA*

Nature and Symptoms of Damage

The maggots feed inside the leaves by leaving characteristic mines. The upper portion of the affected leaves turns white in colour and dry in case of severe damage.

Life History and Description

Leaf miner larvae are dull white and turn pinkish before pupation. After full development, the larvae fall off to the soil where they pupate and emerge after 7-9 days. The adult is a silvery grey moth, lays eggs on tender leaves. The total life cycle was 20 to 40 days.

Management

Spraying of systemic insecticides like methyl demeton @1 ml/l of water helps to reduce pest density effectively.

❑ Mealy bug: *Rastrococcus iceryoides* (Green, 1908)

Common name	:	Mealy bug
Scientific name	:	*Rastrococcus iceryoides* (Green, 1908)
Family	:	Pseudococcidae
Order	:	Hemiptera

Source:*https://idtools.org/tools/1044/index.cfm?packageID=1113&entityID=3476*

Distribution and Host Range

It is distributed throughout the Indian region and Malaysia and has extended its range to East Africa, where it was probably introduced at the beginning of the twentieth century.

Nature and Symptoms of Damage

Pink colour nymphs and adults of the mealy bug are present in colonies on the lower surface of the leaves, inflorescence, branches, fruits and near the fruit stalk. Nymphs and adults suck the cell sap from the leaves and fruits weakening the fruit bearing branches. In case of severe infestation, the affected leaves turn yellowish and fruiting is reduced. During feeding, bugs secrete honey dew on which sooty mould develop producing characteristic black coloring on the affected part of the tree.

Life History and Description

The insects are oval in shape with seventeen pairs of waxy pin like marginal tussels found around their bodies. There are three nymphal instars for females and male moults to fourth instar also. Mealy bug reproduced sexually and one female lay 168-298 eggs within 5-6 days. The incubation period is 5-7 days. The nymphal period of male and female is 16-22 and 18-24 days, respectively. Total life span of the female is 45-57 days and that of males is 1-3 days. Insects are oval in shape with pinkish waxy particle on their bodies. All three instars of female and the second instar male possessed a pair of short waxy anal projection.

Management

Proper orchard maintenance by removal of weeds that harbor mealy bugs. Banding of tree trunk with polythene sheet (400 gauge) 30 cm above ground level and just below the junction of branching to obstract the migration of the nymphs. Application of *Beauveria bassiana* (2 g/l) or 5.00 per cent NSKE around the tree trunk. Release of predators, *Menochilus sexmaculatus*, *Rodolia fumida*, *Sumnius renardi* and Australian lady bird beetle, *Cryptolaemus montrouzieri* @ 10-15 No./tree are effective in controlling the nymphs of the mealy bug. 2-3 sprayings of malathion 50 EC (0.05%) or buprofezin 25 SC @ 1.25 ml/lit (0.03%) at an interval of 15 days controls the pest effectively.

☐ Green Scale: *Coccus viridis* (Green, 1889)

Common name	:	Green Scale
Scientific name	:	*Coccus viridis* (Green, 1889)
Family	:	Coccidae
Order	:	Hemiptera

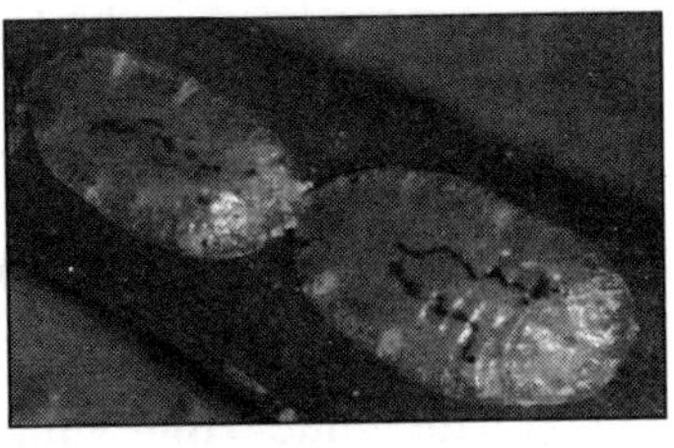

Source: *http://databases.nbair.res.in/insectpests/index.php*

Distribution and Host Range

Occurs in the tropical regions of the world. The host range includes vegetable, fruit and ornamental crops as well as many native plants.

Nature and Symptoms of Damage

Scales damage plants by sucking out plant sap as a result leaves 'turn' to yellow and wilt.

Life History and Description

Eggs are whitish green and elongate-oval laid singly and hatch beneath the female where they are protected. Eggs hatch from a few minutes to several hours after being laid. Nymphs, or immature green scales are oval, flat and yellowish green in color, and have six short legs. There are three nymphal stages before becoming an adult, each stage being larger and more convex than previous stage. The adult female is shiny pale green with a conspicuous black, irregular U-shaped internal marking that is dorsally visible to the naked eye. Adult scales are 2.5-3.25 mm.

Management

Prune and destroy the infested shoots at initial stage of infestation. After two weeks release 20 predator beetles viz., *C. montrouzieri* beetle per tree. Encourage parasitoids *viz., Aneristis* sp, *Coccophgagus cowperi*, *C. bogoriensis*. Spray the affected patches quinolphos 25 EC @ 120 ml using a gator sprayer in 200 l of water and add 200 ml of any agricultural wetting agent in 200 l of the spray solution.

☐ Hairy caterpillar: *Metanastria hytaca* Cramer, 1782

Common name	:	Bud worm
Scientific name	:	*Metanastria hytaca* Cramer, 1782
Family	:	Lasiocampidae
Order	:	Lepidoptera

Source: *http://databases.nbair.res.in/insectpests/index.php*

Distribution and Host Range

Host range includes ashew, badam, moringa, sapota, jamun, guava, babul, sal tree, needlewood tree, Spanish cherry etc.

Nature and Symptoms of Damage

Early instars are gregarious feeders of tender foliage and full-grown caterpillars feed voraciously on mature leaves as well. During day time they congregate in large numbers on the ground under dry leaves near the base of the tree, in crevices of bark or lower parts of well shaded branches and feed voraciously on foliage during night. These hairy caterpillars scrape the green tissues when young and start defoliating the leaves and inflorescence branches.

Life History and Description

Adults have grayish head and thorax and whitish abdomen. Forewings are reddish brown spot ringed with white. Hind wings are white. Larva is yellowish brown with black spots and long lateral tufts of hairs.

Management

Field sanitation by maintaining free from weeds and debris. Collect and destroy the egg mass. Burn the groups of larvae found on tree trunks with torches. Spray chlorpyriphos 20EC @ 20 ml/10 lit. water. Field release of chalcidid wasp, *Brachymeria* sp.

❑ Stem borer: *Plocaederus ferrugineus* Linnaeus

Common name	:	Stem borer
Scientific name	:	*Plocaederus ferrugineus* Linnaeus
Family	:	Cerambycidae
Order	:	Coleoptera

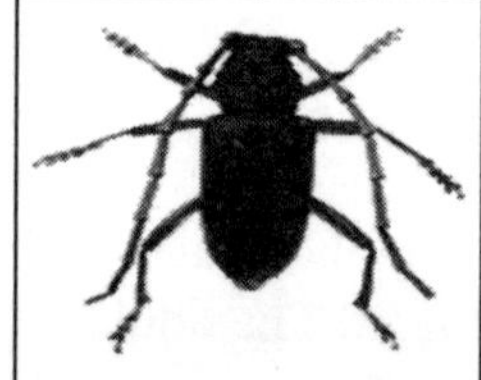

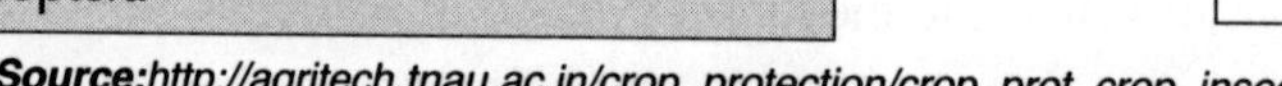

Source:*http://agritech.tnau.ac.in/crop_protection/crop_prot_crop_insectpest%20_sapota%20-%20Copy_clip_image002_0000.jpg*

Distribution and Host Range

It is a major pest distributed throughout South India and Maharashtra. Host range includes cashew, moringa, silk cotton and citrus trees.

Nature and Symptoms of Damage

Presence of small holes at the collar region. Gummosis. Extrusion of frass through the bore holes at the collar region. Yellowing and shedding of leaves. Drying up of twigs and gradual death of the tree.

Life History and Description

Adult is medium sized reddish-brown beetle. Head and thorax are dark brown or almost black.

Management

Collect and destroy the damaged plants. Field sanitation. Swab coal tar + kerosene @ 1:2 or carbaryl 50 WP 20 g/l on the basal portion of the trunk (3 feet height). After scraping the loose bark to prevent oviposition by adult beetles. If infestations are severe then apply the copper oxychloride paste on the trunk of the tree. One celphos tablet (3 g aluminum phosphide) per hole. Apply carbofuran 3G 5 g per hole and plug with mud.

Resistant Varieties	
World	**India**
Prolific: This variety of sapota is popular in India and is resistant to fruit flies, which can cause significant damage to the crop. **Tikal:** This variety of sapota is grown in Central and South America and is resistant to pests such as mealybugs and scales. **Tainung No. 1:** This variety of sapota is grown in Taiwan and is resistant to pests such as thrips and whiteflies. **Russel:** This variety of sapota is grown in Florida and is resistant to pests such as scale insects and mealybugs. **Makok:** This variety of sapota is grown in Thailand and is resistant to pests such as fruit flies and mealybugs.	**Cricket Ball:** This variety is known for its resistance to fruit borer and mealybug, two common insect pests that affect Sapota. **Kirtibartiya:** This variety is resistant to scale insects, which are a common pest in Sapota orchards. **Pala:** This variety is known for its resistance to fruit borer and mealybug, as well as other insect pests such as whiteflies and thrips. **Prolific:** This variety is resistant to fruit borer and other insect pests such as thrips and mites. **Kalipatti:** This variety is resistant to fruit borer and mealybug, and is known for its high yield and good quality fruit.

Pests of Custard Apple

Scientific name	*Annona reticulate* L.
Family	Annnonaceae
Origin	New World tropics
Chromosome number	2n = 14

Custard apple, also known as sugar apple or sweetsop, is a tropical fruit that is grown for its sweet and creamy pulp. The botanical name of custard apple is *Annona squamosa* and it belongs to the family Annonaceae. The tree of custard apple is small to medium-sized, evergreen and has a round canopy. Custard apple is an important fruit crop in tropical and subtropical regions of the world, including India, where it is known as "**Sitaphal**". It is mainly cultivated for its edible fruit, which is a fleshy syncarp consisting of many carpels fused together. The fruit is green in color when unripe and turns brownish-yellow when ripe. The pulp of custard apple is white and contains numerous seeds. The fruit is sweet, fragrant, and has a creamy texture.

In India, custard apple is primarily grown in the states of Maharashtra, Andhra Pradesh, Gujarat, and Karnataka. The total production of custard apple in India is around 410,000 metric tons, with Maharashtra being the largest producer. Apart from India, custard apple is also grown in other tropical countries such as Thailand, Indonesia, and Mexico.

Like other fruit crops, custard apple is also susceptible to a number of insect pests and diseases. Some of the common insect pests of custard apple include fruit fly, mealybugs, scale insects, and aphids. These pests can cause significant damage to the fruit and reduce the yield. To control these pests, farmers often use chemical insecticides, although integrated pest management (IPM) practices are also becoming popular.

❑ Fruit borer: *Anonaepestis bengalella* Ragonot, 1894

Common name	:	Fruit borer, atis borer moth or custard-apple caterpillar
Scientific name	:	*Anonaepestis bengalella* Ragonot, 1894
Family	:	Pyralidae
Order	:	Lepidoptera

Source: *https://norfolkmoths.co.uk/micros.php?bf=14390&photoid=1407558398*

Distribution and Host Range

It is found from India to Java and the Philippines and has also been recorded from Australia and Taiwan. The larvae feed on *Annona squamosa* and *A. reticulata*.

Nature and Symptoms of Damage

Caterpillar makes irregular tunnels and damages the mesocarp by feeding the internal content of the fruits. The presence of excreta of the caterpillars near the entry holes on the affected fruits. The growth of affected fruits is arrested and later fall down.

Life History and Description

Eggs are laid singly on immature fruit. Upon hatching, the caterpillar bore into the fruits where they pupate. Fully developed gray to black coloured caterpillars is about 20 mm long.

Adult: light brown with transparent wing.

Management

Chrysoperla zastrowii, coccinellids, king crow, common mynah, wasp, dragonfly, spider, robber fly, reduviid bug, preying mantid, fire ants, big eyed bugs (*Geocoris* sp), pentatomid bug (*Eucanthecona furcellata*), earwigs, ground beetles, rove beetles etc are predators. Collect and destroy the damaged fruits. Spray malathion 0.1% two times once at flower formation and second at fruit set.

❑ Fruit fly: *Bactrocera zonata* (Saunders)

Common name	:	Fruit fly
Scientific name	:	*Bactrocera zonata* (Saunders)
Family	:	Tephritidae
Order	:	Diptera

Source: *http://databases.nbair.res.in/insectpests/index.php*

Distribution and Host Range

Bactrocera zonata is native to South and Southeast Asia. It was first reported from Bengal (India) and is now widespread in India, Pakistan and present throughout South and Southeast Asia. It is found in more than 20 countries in Asia and Africa. It is a major pest of mango, peach, guava, custard apple, citrus, etc.

Nature and Symptoms of Damage

Maggots bore into the semi ripened fruits and feed on the pulp. Affected fruits become shrivelled, deformed, rot and drop.

Life History and Description

Under optimum conditions, a female can lay more than 3000 eggs during its lifetime. Development from egg to adult under summer conditions requires about 16 days. The mature larva emerges from the fruit, drops to the ground, and forms a tan to dark brown puparium. Pupation occurs in the soil. About nine days are required for attainment of sexual maturity after the adult fly emerges. Adult brown or dark brown with hyaline wings and yellow legs.

Management

Collect fallen infested fruits and dispose them by dumping in a pit and covering with soil. Provide summer ploughing to expose the pupa. Immersion of fruits in hot water (45 to 47°C) for 60 minutes to kill eggs and maggots. Field release of natural enemies *Opius* and parasitoids: *Diachasmimorpha longicaudata*, *D. tryon*, *D. kraussi*, *Fopius arisanus*. Monitor the activity of flies with methyl eugenol sex lure traps. Use bait spray combing any one of the insecticides and molasses or jaggery 10 g/l, fenthion 100EC 1 ml/l, malathion 50EC 2 ml/l, dimethoate 30 EC 1 ml/l, carbaryl 50 WP 4 g/l. two rounds at 2 weeks interval before ripening of fruits. Prepare bait with methyl eugenol 1% solution mixed with malathion 0.1%. Take 10 ml of this mixture per trap and keep them in 25 different places in one hectare. Spray malathion 50 EC at 0.1% or fenthion 100 EC at 1ml/lit.

❑ Tailed mealy bug: *Ferrisia virgata* Cockerell, 1893

Common name	:	Tailed mealy bug, striped mealybug, guava mealybug, grey mealybug
Scientific name	:	*Ferrisa virgata* Cockerell, 1893
Family	:	Pseudococcidae
Order	:	Hemiptera

Source: *https://entnemdept.ufl.edu/creatures/orn/mealybug/ferrisia_virgata.htm*

As Described in Tomato

❑ Florida wax scale: *Ceroplastes floridensis* Comstock, 1881

Common name	:	Florida wax scale
Scientific name	:	*Ceroplastes floridensis* Comstock, 1881
Family	:	Coccidae
Order	:	Hemiptera

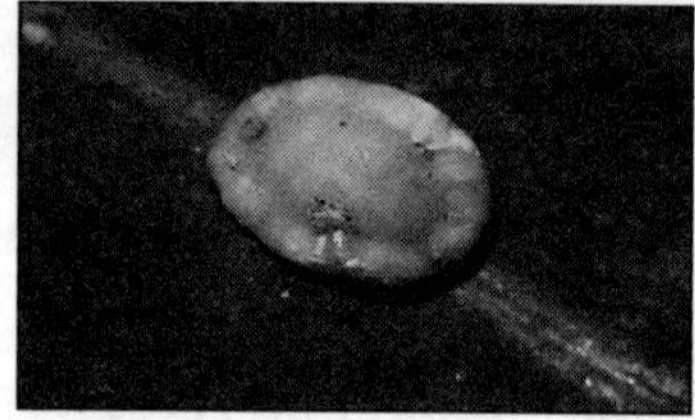

Source: *https://www.biodiversidadvirtual.org/insectarium/Ceroplastes-floridensis-img1276230.html*

Distribution and Host Range

Florida wax scale is thought to have originated from the Northern Neotropical region and now occurs throughout the world. It has been reported infesting a wide range of host plants including citrus, custard apple, almond, quince, apple, fig, Japan plum, myrtle, ferns, oleander, mango, red bay, pomegranate, inkberry, custard apple, andromeda and anthurium.

Nature and Symptoms of Damage

The direct damage is caused by insertion of stylets during feeding by the nymphs, which causes premature leaf drop and drying of twigs. Sooty mould develops on honeydew excreted by these scale insects and incase of severe infestations shoots or branches die and host's death may also occur.

Life History and Description

Females lay about 2000 eggs which are pink to dark red. First stage (instar) nymphs, called crawlers hatch from eggs over a period of 2 to 3 weeks. Immediately after hatching the first instar crawlers come out which are pink in colour. The crawlers undergo three moults and develop into adults. The wax-covering secreted around their body gives them a star-like appearance. Soft scales have 3 or 4 instars in the female and 5 in the male. The adults are elliptical, reddish brown with short anal process. The adult female is reddish which is coated with a thick layer of pinkish-white wax. Adults are mostly found on twigs and branches. The size of the female is about 2 to 4 mm in length and 1 to 3.5 mm in width. Females have 2 to 3 immature stages without any pupa-like instars while males have 4 immature stages with the two pupa-like instars.

Management

Collect and destroy damaged leaves. Apply well rotten sheep manure @ 4 t/acre in two splits or poultry manure in 2 splits. Control ants and dust which can give the scale a competitive advantage. Field release of ladybird beetle. Spray dormant oil in late winter before spring. Spray horticultural oil, if needed, year-round.

Resistant Varieties	
World	**India**
African Pride: This variety is grown in South Africa and is known for its resistance to fruit flies. **Pink's Mammoth:** This variety is grown in Australia and is known for its resistance to fruit flies. **Arka Sahan:** This is an Indian variety that has shown resistance to mealybugs, scale insects, and fruit flies. **Late Gold:** This is a Mexican variety that has shown resistance to fruit flies. **Fino de Jete:** This is a Spanish variety that has shown resistance to fruit flies. **Pierce:** This is a Florida variety that has shown resistance to thrips and mites. **African Gold:** This is a South African variety that has shown resistance to fruit flies. **Hilary White:** This is an Australian variety that has shown resistance to fruit flies. **Lisa:** This is a Florida variety that has shown resistance to thrips and mites.	**Arka Sahan:** This variety is known for its resistance to mealybugs, which are a common pest of custard apple. It is a high-yielding variety that produces sweet and juicy fruits. **Balanagar:** This variety is resistant to fruit fly, which is a major pest of custard apple. The fruits of Balanagar are large and sweet, with a high pulp content. **Arka Anoop:** This variety is resistant to fruit fly and mealybugs. It produces medium-sized fruits with a sweet and juicy pulp. **Red Sitaphal:** This variety is resistant to mealybugs and scales. It produces medium-sized fruits with a reddish skin and a sweet, creamy pulp. **Sharifa:** This variety is resistant to mealybugs and scales. It is a high-yielding variety that produces large, sweet, and aromatic fruits. **Kaveri:** This is an Indian variety that has shown resistance to mealybugs and scale insects.

Pests of Citrus

Scientific name	Citrus sps.
Family	Rutaceae
Origin	Southeast Asia
Chromosome number	2n = 18

Citrus is a genus of flowering trees and shrubs in the Rutaceae family, which includes fruits such as oranges, lemons, limes, grapefruits, and mandarins. Citrus fruits are rich in vitamin C, flavonoids, and other nutrients that provide various health benefits. They are also widely used for making juices, jams, marmalades, and other food products. India is one of the largest citrus fruit producers in the world, with the major citrus growing states being Maharashtra, Andhra Pradesh, Tamil Nadu, and Punjab. The total area under citrus cultivation in India is around 11 lakh hectares, with an annual production of over 1.5 crore tons.

Citrus crops are susceptible to various pests and diseases that can cause significant damage to the plants and reduce yields. Some of the major insect pests that affect citrus crops include aphids, scales, mites, and mealybugs, while diseases like citrus canker, citrus greening, and black spot can also cause significant losses.

Citrus leaf miner: *Phyllocnistis citrella* Stainton, 1856

Common name	:	Citrus leaf miner
Scientific name	:	*Phyllocnistis citrella* Stainton, 1856
Family	:	Gracillariidae
Order	:	Lepidoptera

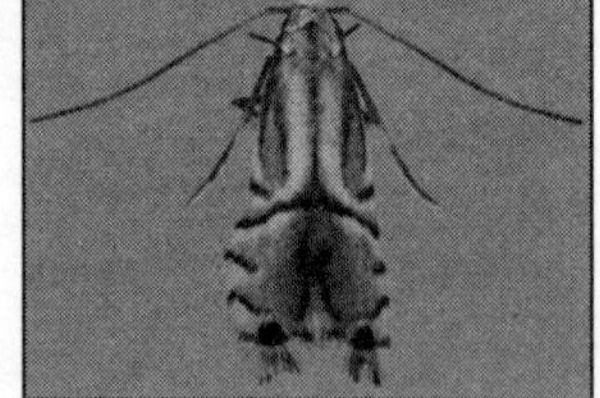

Source: *http://databases.nbair.res.in/insectpests/index.php*

Distribution and Host Range

The citrus leafminer (CLM), *Phyllocnistis citrella,* a widespread asian species, described from Calcutta, India, is a potentially serious pest of citrus and related Rutaceae and some related ornamental plants. CLM is known from East Africa — Sudan to Yemen, and through Southern Asia — Saudi Arabia to India and Indonesia, North to Hong Kong and China, Philippines, Taiwan, and Southern Japan. *Citrus* spp., bael, Nelthare, Arabian Jasmine, Curry leaf tree, orange jasmine, karanja tree, North Indian rosewood, phalsa are attacked by CLM.

Nature of Damage

Silvery serpentine mines are usually on the under surface of the leaf. Mining of the leaves causes them to curl up, distorted and thereby reducing the photosynthetic area of the young foliage. In case of severe infestation, mines can also be seen on the upper side of the leaves as well as on shoot portion of new twigs. Damage by this pest predisposes the acid lime plants for development of canker disease.

Marks of identification

Eggs are laid singly usually on the underside of leaves near the midrib and look like tiny water droplets, hatch within 3-5 days. The young pale-yellow larvae immediately start feeding between epidermal layers of the leaf. The full-grown larva measures 5.1 mm in length and is pale yellow or pale green with light-brown well-developed mandibles. They settle down in galleries near the leaf margin for pupation. The total life cycle is about 2-3 weeks. Adult is a tiny silvery-white moth about 2 mm long with fringed wings. Fore wings have brown stripes and a prominent black spot near the apical margin while hind wings are pure white with a wing spread of 4-5 mm.

Management

Avoid pruning during active growth periods as it may inducc further new flush and thereby allow the pest to have a greater number of generations. If necessary, prune only the infested shoots during winter from the inner canopy. Remove the water shoots from the tree canopy as they are the preferred sites of attack. Conserve the bio-agents (Coccinellids, Chrysopids predators and eulophid parasitoids) by avoiding application of insecticides during late winter to early spring. The spray timings are most important in managing leaf miner because before entering in leaf tissue it is highly susceptible to the toxic effect of pesticides. Foliar application of neem oil 5 ml or imidacloprid17.8 SL @0.5 ml or phosolone 35 EC @1.5 ml or fenvalerate 20 EC @1.0 ml or spinosad 45 SC @ 0.34 ml or novaluron 10 EC @ 0.87 ml/l of water.

❑ Citrus psylla: *Diaphorina citri* Kuwayama, 1908

Common name	:	Citrus psylla, Asian citrus psylla
Scientific name	:	*Diaphorina citri* Kuwayama, 1908
Family	:	Liviidae
Order	:	Hemiptera

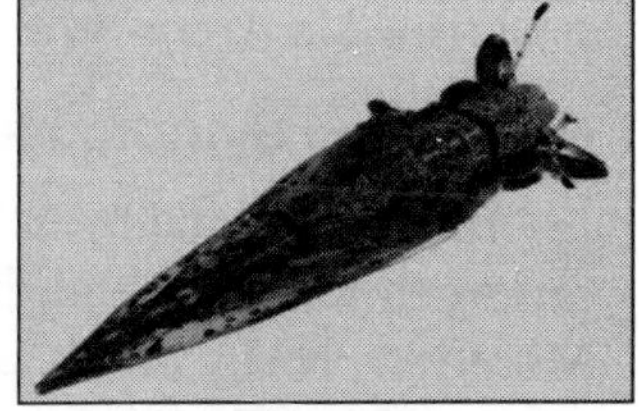

Source: *http://databases.nbair.res.in/insectpests/index.php*

Distribution and Host Range

The Asian citrus psyllid is widely distributed in Southern Asia. It is an important pest of citrus, certain deciduous plants and families of rutaceae in several countries. It is a vector of a serious citrus disease called greening disease or Huanglongbing.

Nature of Damage

Nymphs and adults suck the cell sap from the leaves, tender shoots and flowers causing curling of leaves, defoliation and drying of twigs. Nymphs secrete whitish crystalline honey dew which attracts the growth of fungus, adversely affecting the photosynthesis. Late instar nymphs and adults also transmit the citrus greening disease. In case of severe attack, the leaf buds, flower buds and leaves may wilt and die.

Life History and Description

Females lay more than 800 eggs on tips of growing shoots and between unfurling leaves. The eggs are bright yellow and deposited on unopened leaf buds. Nymphs pass through five instars. Early instar nymphs are green or dull orange and late instar nymphs are bright yellowish orange. Adult is 3-4 mm long, mottled brown in color, with transparent wings. Total life cycle requires 15 to 47 days. Adults may live for several months. There are nine to ten generations a year.

Management

Collateral host like curry leaf plant should not be grown in the vicinity of citrus orchards as it is the most preferred host plant of psylla. Two releases of Chrysopid predator, *Mallada desjardensi* @ 30 larvae/tree in each flushing season reduces the citrus psylla incidence. Foliar application of quinalphos 25 EC @ 1 ml or novaluron 10 EC @ 0.55 ml or thiamethoxam 25 WG @0.32 g/l of water at bud burst stage.

❑ Citrus blackfly: *Aleurocanthus woglumi* Ashby, 1915

Common name	:	Citrus blackfly
Scientific name	:	*Aleurocanthus woglumi* Ashby, 1915
Family	:	Aleyrodidae
Order	:	Hemiptera

Source: *http://databases.nbair.res.in/insectpests/index.php*

Distribution and Host Range

The citrus blackfly is an important whitefly pest in several countries and can infest more than 300 host plants, including cultivated plants, ornamentals and weeds of which citrus is a favoured host. It was first detected in India in 1910, and in 1915 it was reported in other parts of Asia. In India it is established in Amravati, Nagpur and Wardha districts of Maharashtra as a pest of citrus.

Nature and Symptoms of Damage

Both adults and nymphs suck plant sap and results in the curling of leaves and also the premature fall of flower buds and the developing fruits thereby resulting in reducing the vitality of the tree. Moreover, honey dew secretion favours rapid development of black sooty mould that covers entire plant surface. The process of photosynthesis is hampered greatly resulting in stunted growth of plants, low intensity of flowering and scarce fruiting.

Life History and Description

The adults emerge in flushing seasons and the females lay yellowish brown oval shaped eggs which are arranged in a spiral manner on underside of leaves with 15-22 eggs in a cluster. The eggs hatch in 7-14 days and the nymphs on emergence start feeding on cell sap and settle on the lower side of the leaf. The nymphs are scale like, shiny black and spiny with marginal fringes. Oval, black in colour pseudo pupa and its dorsum is arched with long black spines, the margins have rounded black teeth. Adults are ashy coloured with brick red abdomen, smoky wings. There are two distinct broods in a year.

Management

Close planting, water logging should be avoided. Excessive irrigation and nitrogen fertilization should be avoided. Avoid growing collateral hosts of the pest, guava, sapota and pomegranate. Foliar application of imidacloprid 17.8 SL @ 0.5 ml or acephate 75 WP @ 1.25 g or phosalone 35 EC @1.5 ml or dimethoate 30 EC@ 2 ml or novaluron 10 EC @ 0.79 ml/l of water on the lower sides of leaves covering the entire tree canopy at 50% egg hatching stage. Second spray should be given after 15 days with any of the above insecticides or neem oil @10 ml/l of water.

❑ Citrus whitefly: *Dialeurodes citri* (Ashmead)

Common name	:	Citrus whitefly
Scientific name	:	*Dialeurodes citri* (Ashmead)
Family	:	Aleyrodidae
Order	:	Hemiptera

Source: *http://databases.nbair.res.in/insectpests/index.php*

Distribution and Host Range

It is a native of India, America, Guatemala, Bermuda, Chile, Peru, Argentina, Brazil, France, Sri Lanka, China, Taiwan, Vietnam, Japan, Macao, Pakistan and Sikkim. Host range includes citrus, allamanda, banana shrub, chinaberry, coffee, Australian banyan, jasmine, lilac, mock olive, pear, pomegranate, tree of heaven, trumpet vine, umbrella tree, water oak, persimmon, and wild olive.

Nature and Symptoms of Damage

Both nymphs and adults suck the plant sap and secrete honeydew due to which sooty mould develops on the leaves. Severe infestation results in black fungal layer manifestation, covering entire plant parts including fruits due to which photosynthesis is affected.

Life History and Description

The adult female lays about 150 eggs which are oval, pale yellow on the lower surface of leaves which hatches in about 10 days. The nymphs are oval in shape, scale like, blackish with marginal bristle like fringes and are stationary. Nymphal life averages 23 to 30 days. Pseudo-pupa is oval, pale yellow, with an orange or yellow band in the middle of the body. Pseudo pupal development requires 13 to 30 days. Adult is 1.5 mm long with white or greyish wings, pale yellow body and red constricted eyes. The adult lives an average of about 10 days. The entire life cycle requires 41 to 333 days.

Management

As given in blackfly.

Mealy bug: *Planoccus citri* Risso, 1813

Common name	:	Mealy bug
Scientific name	:	*Planoccus citri* Risso, 1813
Family	:	Pseudococcidae
Order	:	Hemiptera

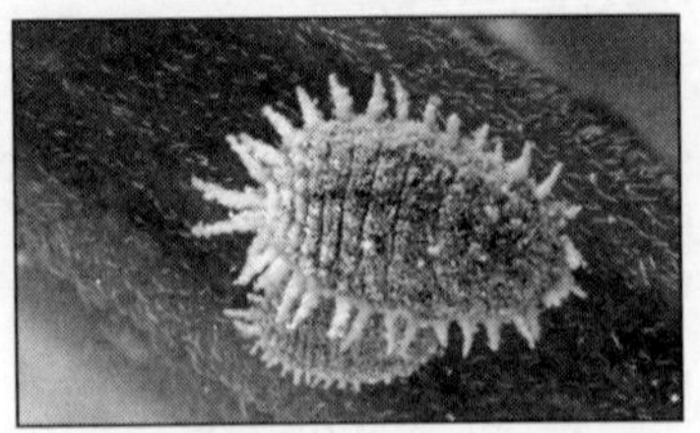

Source: *https://antropocene.it/en/2023/01/29/planococcus-citri-2/*

Distribution and Host Range

The citrus mealybug, *Planococcus citri* has a world-wide distribution and diverse host plants (Citrus spp., mango, grapes, custard apple, coffee, etc). In temperate regions of the world this mealybug poses a problem in greenhouse horticulture, and in the tropics and sub-tropics on outdoor crops. It is a serious pest on *Citrus* spp.

Nature and Symptoms of Damage

Both nymphs and adults suck the sap from the cells of tender branches and fruits. Turn pale colour. Affected plant parts, wilt and dry up. Large amounts of honey dew excrete – sooty mould fungus. Fungus covers the foliage and fruits. In severe infestation the flowers do not form fruits.

Life History and Description

Eggs are laid in clusters, protective cottony mass. Nymphs are amber coloured with white waxy coating with filaments. Adult male is winged, long antenna and without mouth parts, whereas female is wingless, flat body and short, waxy filaments along the margins.

Management

Collect and destroy the damaged leaves, twigs and stems. Debark branches and apply methyl parathion paste. Use sticky trap (5 cm length) on fruit bearing shoots. Field release of Australian lady bird beetle *Cryptoleamus montrouizeri* 10 per tree. Spray dichlorvas 0.2% in combination with fish oil rosin soap 25 g/lit. Single soil application of aldicarb 10 G at 50 g/tree at the time of pruning. Soil treatment with chlorophyriphos apply on the near the tree trunk. Spraying of trees with acephate, methomyl, or chlorpyriphos.

Citrus aphid: *Toxoptera aurantii* (Boyer de Fonscolombe)

Common name	:	Citrus aphid
Scientific name	:	*Toxoptera aurantii* (Boyer de Fonscolombe)
Family	:	Aphididae
Order	:	Hemiptera

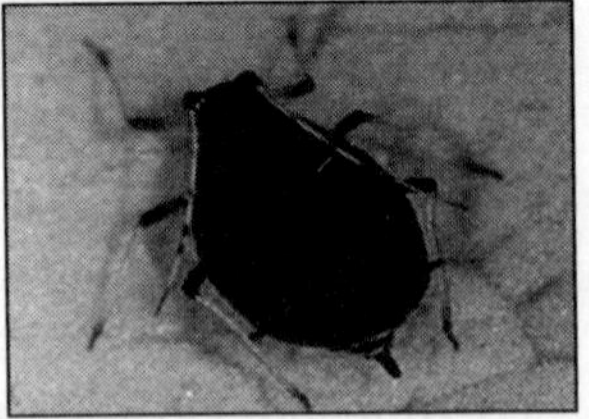

Source: *https://upload.wikimedia.org/wikipedia/commons/thumb/0/0f/Toxoptera_aurantii.jpg/330px-Toxoptera_aurantii.jpg*

Distribution and Host Range

Found in all citrus growing regions as minor pest. It attacks mostly rutaceae and rosaceae families.

Nature and Symptoms of Damage

Nymphs and adults suck sap from tender leaves and shoots during winter to early spring. Affected leaves turn yellow, curled, deformed and dry up. Growth of young shoots is adversely affected. Plant growth is stunted. Sooty mould is produced on honeydew excreted by aphids. Aphids also act as the active vectors of citrus tristeza virus.

Life History and Description

Each aphid produces about 5 young nymphs/day for a period of 1-3 weeks parthenogenetically. The nymphs are dark reddish brown and approximately less than 0.1 mm in length. Adults are soft-bodied, pear-shaped, tiny sucking insects, measuring less than 2 mm in length and are pale yellowish green to black in colour. They have a pair of cornicles arising from 5th abdominal segment. Single life-cycle normally takes 6 to 8 days.

Management

Foliar application of dimethoate 30 EC @ 2 ml or acephate 75 WP @1 g or imidacloprid 17.8 SL @ 0.4 ml/l on identified infested trees during winter season reduces the infestation levels. If needed, second and third sprays should follow at 10 days intervals.

❑ Cottony cushion scale: *Icerya purchase* Maskell, 1878

Common name	:	Cottony cushion scale, fluted scale, citrus fluted scale
Scientific name	:	*Icerya purchase* Maskell, 1878
Family	:	Monophlebidae
Order	:	Hemiptera

Source: *https://www.livescience.com/15292-insect-incest-male-reproduction.html*

Distribution and Host Range

Cottony cushion scale is minor, occasionally serious. It is polyphagous commonly collected on acacia, citrus, guava, pigeonpea, casuarina, etc.

Nature and Symptoms of Damage

Both nymphs and adults suck the sap from leaves. They excrete honey dew and development of sooty mould fungus is seen.

Life History and Description

The mature females have bright orange-red, yellow, or brown bodies covered with yellowish or white wax. The most conspicuous feature is the large fluted egg sac, which will frequently be two to 2.5 times longer than the body. The egg sac contains about 1000 red eggs. The newly hatched nymphs are bright red with dark antennae and thin brown legs. After three molts the adult begins to deposit eggs and secrete the conspicuous egg sac. As the egg sac is formed the scale's abdomen becomes more and more tilted until the scale appears to be standing on its head. Males are rare. They are winged with a dark red body and dark colored antennae. It is interesting that female is always a hermaphrodite with both testes and ovaries. If self-fertilization occurs only hermaphrodites are produced; however, when a hermaphrodite mates with a male, more males and hermaphrodites are produced.

Management

Spray dormant oil in late winter before spring. Spray horticultural oil, if needed, year-round. Apply mixture of manure compost tea, molasses, citrus oil. Garlic-pepper tea also helps. Natural predators usually keep this insect in check. Control ants and dust which can give the scale a competitive advantage. Field release of vedalia and Australian ladybugs.

❑ Fruit sucking moth: *Eudocima materna* Linnaeus, 1767; *Eudocima homaena* (Hübner, 1816)

Common name	:	Fruit sucking moth, Fruit piercing moth
Scientific name	:	*Eudocima materna* Linnaeus, 1767; *Eudocima homaena* (Hübner, 1816)
Family	:	Erebidae
Order	:	Lepidoptera

Source: *http://databases.nbair.res.in/insectpests/index.php*

Source: *http://databases.nbair.res.in/insectpests/index.php*

Distribution and Host Range

These are the most dreary moths found throughout the world. A wide range of cultivated and wild fruits, including banana, citrus, guava, mango, passionfruit, pineapple, capsicum, melon and tomato are attacked by this pest.

Nature and Symptoms of Damage

Adult moths are active during dusk and suck the juice from the ripening yellow colour fruits. The punctures produced during feeding by the adult moths leads to fruit rot due to invasion by secondary pathogens.

Life History and Description

The female moth lays eggs on weeds like *Tinospora cardifolia*, *T. semilacina*, *Cocculus hirsutus*, *Convolvulus arvensis* etc where the caterpillar develops after hatching. Eggs are round, translucent, measuring about 1 mm in diameter and egg period is 8-10 days. The caterpillar is a semilooper, dark brown with yellow and red spots. Full grown caterpillars are 50-60 mm long, stout, velvety-blue with yellow patterns on dorsal and lateral sides. Larval period is 28-35 days. Pupation takes place in a transparent pale whitish silken cover enclosed in leaf fold. Pupal period is 14-18 days. *Eudocima materna*: Adults have three black spots on the fore wings and a circular spot in the hindwing. *E. homaena*: The adults have pale orange brown body with forewings dark greyish and the hind wings orange red with two black curved patches.

Management

Destroy fallen fruits and larval host plants by burrying in the ground. Generation of smoke in the late evening hours in orchards repels the pest. Bagging of fruits is effective but very laborious and expensive. Poison baiting with malathion 50 EC @ 10 ml + 100 g jaggary +100 ml mandarin juice + 900 ml of water (two bottles containing poison bait per 25-30 trees). Foliar application of neem oil 1% or malathion 50 EC @ 2 ml at 10 -15 days interval during fruit maturity till harvest reduces the infestation levels.

❑ Citrus butterfly: *Papilio demolious, P. Polytes, P. helenus* Linnaeus, 1758

Common name	:	Common lime butterfly, lemon butterfly, citrus swallowtail, Common mormon
Scientific name	:	*Papilio demolious, P. Polytes, P. helenus* Linnaeus, 1758
Family	:	Papilionidae
Order	:	Lepidoptera

lemon butterfly

(***Source:*** *http://databases.nbair.res.in/insectpests/index.php*)

Citrus swallowtail

(***Source:*** *http://databases.nbair.res.in/insectpests/index.php*)

Distribution and Host Range

It is distributed all over the world in Africa, greater part of Asia, Thailand and Japan. Host range includes citrus and other rutaceae plants. Eg: *Aegle marmelos*.

Nature and Symptoms of Damage

The young larvae found on the upper surface of leaves, feeding on the leaf lamina from margin to midrib. Grown up larvae feed on matured leaves and cause severe defoliation of the entire plant.

Life History and Description

Yellowish white, round, smooth eggs are laid singly on tender leaves and shoots. Egg hatches in about 3-8 days. Freshly hatched caterpillars are dark brown and soon develop irregular white markings on their body resembling bird's drop. The caterpillars attach themselves to branches with silk, transforming into pupae. They remain in the pupal form for 2-3 weeks before emerging as adults. *P. demoleus* is a big beautiful butterfly with yellow and black markings on all the four wings, having wing expanse of about 50-60 mm. Its hind wings have a brick red oval patch near the anal margin and there is no tail like extension behind though common in Papilionidae. *P. polytes* males are black and females vary in form. *P. helenus* has black wings with three white distal spots.

Management

Hand pick the larvae and destroy. Field release of parasitoids *Trichogramme evanescens* and *Telenomus* sp on eggs. *Brachymeria* sp on larvae and *Pterolus* sp. on pupae. Spray entomogenous fungus, *Bacillus thuringiensis* 1 g/L nematode DD- 136 strain or neem seed extract 3%. Spray quinalphos 25 EC or carbaryl 50 WP 2.0 L in 1500-2000 L of water per ha.

❑ Bark eating caterpillar: *Indarbela quadrinotata* (Walker, 1856)

Common name	:	Bark-eating caterpillar
Scientific name	:	*Indarbela quadrinotata* (Walker, 1856)
Family	:	Cossidae
Order	:	Lepidoptera

Source:https://agritech.tnau.ac.in/crop_protection/guava/guava_5.html

As Described in Mango

❑ Citrus rust mite: *Phyllocoptruta oleivora* (Ashmead, 1879)

Common name	:	Citrus rust mite, Eriophyid mite
Scientific name	:	*Phyllocoptruta oleivora* (Ashmead, 1879)
Family	:	Eriophyidae
Order	:	Acarina

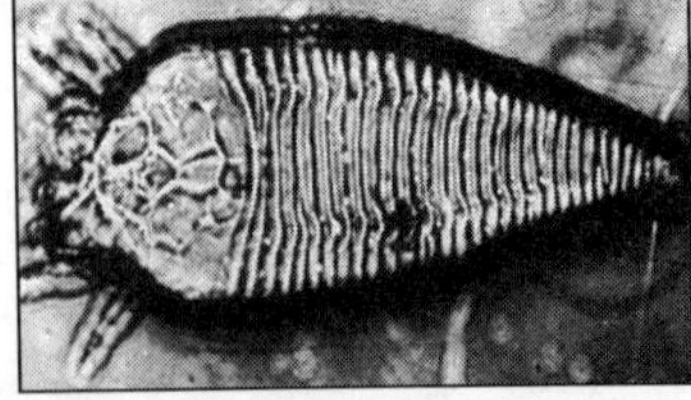

Source:https://www.insectimages.org/browse/subthumb.cfm?sub=7219&order=291

Distribution and Host Range

This species has been reported as a serious pest of citrus in most humid regions of the world and is currently considered the most economic arthropod pest of citrus, causing fruit rind russeting resulting in loss in yield and fruit quality. It infests twigs, leaves, and fruit of all citrus species and varieties (Ex: lemons, grapefruit, oranges, tangerines).

Nature and Symptoms of Damage

Citrus mite attack is known as 'Rusting' on Grapefruit, 'Lalya' on Nagpur mandarin, Mangu on Sathdudi sweet orange and rind disorder in Kinnow. Rust mite infestation produces a multitude of brown–reddish black spots on the fruit surface. The rust mite attacks the berry size fruits of both Ambia and Mrig inflicting undesirable brown irregular patches on them that fetches low market price to the fruits.

Life History and Description

The eggs are smooth, spherical, semi-translucent and are laid in groups in indentations on fruits and on ventral surfaces of leaves. Egg period is 3 days. The newly hatched larva resembles the adult, changing in color from clear to lemon yellow and nymphal development completes in 2-11 days. Adults are very small (150-165 μm), fusiform, dorsally flattened and yellow. The life cycle is completed in 7-10 days in summer and 14 days in winter. A female lays 20 to 30 eggs during a life span of 20 days.

Management

Water stress often aggravates mite problem. Make sure that trees are well irrigated, particularly during the stress in peak summer and winter. Foliar application of wettable sulfur 85 DP @ 3 g or dicofol 18.5 EC @ 2 ml or propargite 57 EC @ 1 ml or ethion 50 EC @ 1 ml/l of water and make all season HMO (2%) immediately after fruit set and during active period of mites checks the pest effectively.

❑ Citrus leaf mite: *Eutetranychus orientalis* (Klein, 1936)

Common name	:	Citrus leaf mite
Scientific name	:	*Eutetranychus orientalis* (Klein, 1936)
Family	:	Tetranychidae
Order	:	Acarina

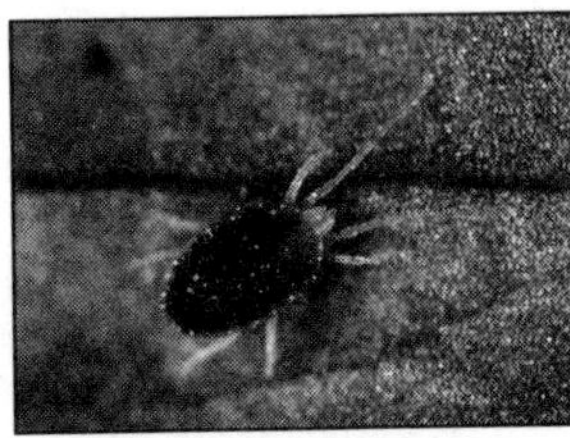

Source: *https://www.safj.co.za/tag/eutetranychus-orientalis/*

Distribution and Host Range

It is distributed throughout Afghanistan, Cyprus, Taiwan, Egypt, India, Iran, Israel, Jordan, Kenya, Lebanon, Mozambique, Pakistan, Sudan, Turkey and Venezuela. Serious pest in lower altitudes and attacks citrus species, golden shower tree, castor, nerium, neem, Indian rosewood, Indian coral tree, papaya, almond, peach, pear and curry leaf.

Nature and Symptoms of Damage

Mites suck the sap of leaves predominantly from the upper surface of leaves; the affected leaves turn chlorotic and finally drop off resulting in poor plant growth. Infestation starts along the midrib of leaves and later spreads along lateral veins, as a result the region on either side of the midrib and veins turns pale-yellow. In case of severe mite infestation, the upper leaf surface turns pale completely. The webbing produced by the mite trap dust particles; hence the infested leaves are covered with fine dust particles. However, the lower surface remains free of mites and their feeding injury, and appears normal green. In some cases, mite infested fruits also appear chlorotic.

Life History and Description

It passes through egg, larva, protonymph, deutonymph and adult stages. The eggs of *E. orientalis* are oval or circular and flattened, coming to a point dorsally. Newly laid, eggs are bright and hyaline, but later they take on a yellow, parchment-like color. Total developmental stage from egg to adult is 12-13 days. The abdomen of female larvae and nymphs is greenish brown, while the abdomen of male larvae is reddish brown. The protonymph is pale-brown to light-green, with legs shorter than the body. The deutonymph is pale-brown to light-green. Adult female is broad, oval and flattened. Adult male are elongate and triangular in shape with long legs. Short setae are found on legs and body of both sexes at all stages.

Management

Prefer relatively resistant citron (*Citrus medica*), lime variety kagzi lime, *C. sinensis*, *C. aurantifolia* and sweet orange. Avoid susceptible sour lemon variety, sweet lime (*C. limmetioides*), Kharna khattai, grape fruit and *Citrus acida*. Select resistant root stock *Citrus aurantiifolia* followed by *Citrus reshini* and *C. amblycarpa*. Remove alternate host plants like castor, echandinii, amaltas, *Melia* sp., in orchards. Irrigate judiciously, particularly during summer to prevent water stress conditions and resultant flare up. Conserve coccinellid beetles *viz., Scymnus gracilis, Stethorus pauperculus* and predatory thrips *viz.,* Scolothrips, predatory mites *viz., Amblyseius cucumeris, A. hibisci, Pronematus* sp. and *Agistemus* sp. Apply aldicarb 10 G 5 g/nursery plant or spray insecticides *viz.,* dicofol 18.5 EC, fenpropathrin 10 EC, monocrotophos 36 SL, methyl demeton 25 EC, wettable sulphur 3 g/L, permethrin 25 EC 1.0 L in 1000 L of water/h.

❑ Lime/orange tree borer: *Cheledonium cinctum* (Guérin-Méneville)

Common name	:	Lime tree borer, Citrus borer, orange borer
Scientific name	:	*Cheledonium cinctum* (Guérin-Méneville)
Family	:	Cerambycidae
Order	:	Coleoptera

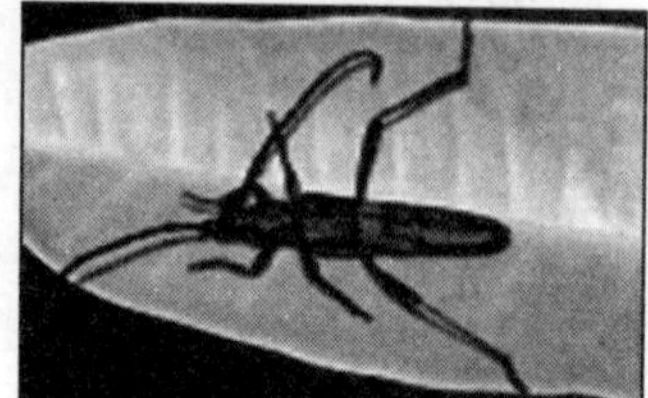

Source: *http://databases.nbair.res.in/insectpests/index.php*

Distribution and Host Range

It is a major pest found in citrus growing regions. It attacks orange.

Nature and Symptoms of Damage

Grub tunnels into the trunk and feeds on the internal content of the trunk resulting in death of the tree. Adult feeds on the leaf tissue along the midrib, keeping margins intact.

Life History and Description

One female lay 35 -85 eggs singly in cracks on bark upto 2 feet height from the ground. Grubs' feeds on sapwood making horizontal galleries before entering into centre of the trunk, larval period is 267-290 days. Pupation takes place inside the gallery pupal period 33-43 days. Adult is sluggish.

Management

Prune the infested branches. Plug the fresh boreholes with absorbent cotton soaked in monocrotophos 5 ml/20 ml water.

❑ Citrus nematode: *Tylenchulus semipenetrans* Cobb, 1913

Common name	:	Citrus nematode, citrus root nematode
Scientific name	:	*Tylenchulus semipenetrans* Cobb, 1913
Family	:	Tylenchulidae
Order	:	Tylenchida

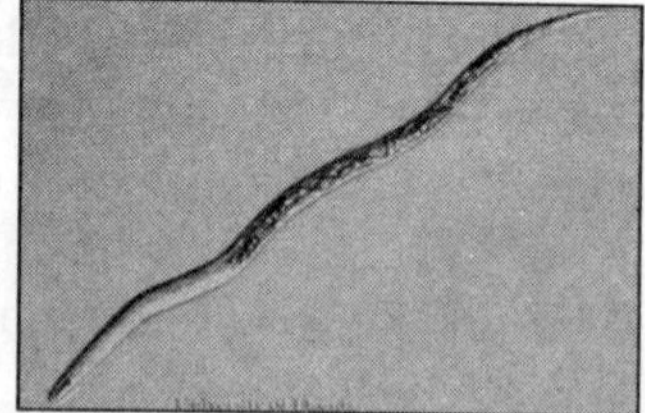

Source:*https://entnemdept.ufl.edu/creatures/nematode/citrus_nematode01.jpg*

Distribution and Host Range

It is a world-wide pest of citrus. In India, it is widely distributed in citrus orchards grown in Andhra Pradesh, Assam, Himachal Pradesh, Haryana, Punjab, Rajasthan, U.P., M.P., Bihar, Gujarat and Maharashtra. It has a narrow host range as 50 species or hybrids of citrus and plants belonging to

Family Rutaceae. Hosts belonging to families other than Rutaceae include grapevine, olive, pear, persimon and loquat. It is the causal organism of slow decline of citrus, citrus decline, citrus dieback.

Nature and Symptoms of Damage

Citrus nematode is a sedentary semi-endoparasite that attacks roots by burrowing its anterior end deep inside the root cortex while the posterior end remains outside in the soil. Feeder roots particularly in the upper soil layer are destroyed as nematode prefers to habitat upper soil layers, resulting in reduced uptake of water and minerals from the soil. While juveniles remain in superficial layers of the young root tissue, young females penetrate deep in the cortical tissue where they form 'feeding site' consisting of 6-10 cortical cells called **'Nurse Cells'**.

Initially symptoms are often unnoticed in the seedlings. General reduction in tree growth and vigour. Yellowing and shedding of leaves. Dieback of twigs and under-sized fruits resembling more or less symptoms of drought and malnutrition. Young trees develop slowly and production is delayed. In heavily infested roots, soil particles usually adhere with root-lets and finally the cortex separates readily from the vascular stele. Heavily infested roots are darker in colour with reduced branch rootlets. Mature trees can tolerate a considerable number of these nematodes before showing lack of vigor and decline symptoms. If, a heavily infested orchard site is replanted with a susceptible rootstock without soil fumigation, the roots of the young trees are heavily parasitized, tree growth is stunted, and fruit production is reduced. This condition is also referred to as the citrus replant problem.

Life History and Description

The first stage juvenile develops within the egg and moult once before hatching as second juvenile. Hatching in soil occurs when environmental conditions including temperature, moisture and aeration are satisfactory. Eggs hatch in 12 to 14 days at about 24°C. The second stage male juveniles develop to maturity within 7 days without feeding and the second stage female juveniles require 14 days to locate the host root, feed and moult. The life cycle from egg to egg is completed in 6 to 8 weeks.

Management

Avoidance of infested planting materials and contaminated farm implements. Provision of adequate light and water drainage. Use of resistant root stock. Pre-plant application of carbofuran 3 G 100 g/tree. Application of *Pseudomonas fluorescens* @ 20 g tree.

❑ Lesion nematode: *Pratylenchus coffeae* Goodey, 1951

Common name	:	Lesion nematode
Scientific name	:	*Pratylenchus coffeae* Goodey, 1951
Family	:	Pratylenchidae
Order	:	Tylenchida

Source:*https://upload.wikimedia.org/wikipedia/commons/thumb/7/78/Pratylenchus_coffeae.jpg/330px-Pratylenchus_coffeae.jpg*

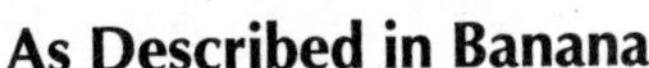

As Described in Banana

Resistant Varieties	
World	**India**
Valencia orange: This is a popular variety of orange that is commonly grown in many citrus-growing regions around the world. Valencia oranges are known to be relatively tolerant to citrus psyllids and citrus leaf miners. **Ponkan mandarin:** This is a type of mandarin orange that is widely grown in China and other parts of Asia. Ponkan mandarins are known to be resistant to citrus red mite and some scale insects. **Navel orange:** This is a popular variety of orange that is commonly grown in many citrus-growing regions around the world. Navel oranges are known to be relatively tolerant to some types of scale insects. **Meyer lemon:** This is a hybrid citrus fruit that is a cross between a lemon and a mandarin orange. Meyer lemons are known to be resistant to some types of scale insects and aphids. **Lisbon lemon:** This is a type of lemon that is commonly grown in many citrus-growing regions around the world. Lisbon lemons are known to be resistant to some types of scale insects and aphids.	**Nagpur Mandarin:** This variety is resistant to the citrus leaf miner and the Asian citrus psyllid, which are common pests of citrus crops in India. **Khasi Mandarin:** This variety is resistant to the citrus tristeza virus, which can cause significant damage to citrus crops. **Kinnow Mandarin:** This hybrid variety of mandarin and sweet orange is resistant to citrus greening disease, a serious pest that can cause significant damage to citrus crops. **Rough Lemon:** This variety is resistant to citrus canker, a bacterial disease that can cause significant damage to citrus crops. **Pummelo:** This variety is resistant to citrus black spot, a fungal disease that can cause significant damage to citrus crops. **Acid Lime:** This variety is resistant to the citrus psyllid, which can transmit the bacteria that causes citrus greening disease.

19

Pests of Grapes

Scientific name	*Vitis vinifera* L.
Family	Vitaceae
Origin	Middle East
Chromosome number	2n = 38

Grapes are one of the oldest and most important cultivated crops in the world. They belong to the family Vitaceac and the genus *Vitis*, which includes more than 60 species. Grapes are grown in many parts of the world, with major producers including Italy, Spain, the United States, and China. In India, grapes are grown primarily in the states of Maharashtra, Karnataka, and Andhra Pradesh. The total area under grape cultivation in India is around 140,000 hectares, with an annual production of over 2 million tons.

Grape crops are susceptible to various pests and diseases that can cause significant damage to the plants and reduce yields. Some of the major insect pests that affect grape crops include grape phylloxera, grape berry moth, and grape leafhopper, while diseases like powdery mildew, downy mildew, and botrytis can also cause significant losses.

❑ Girdle beetle: *Sthenias grisator* (Fabricius, 1787)

Common name	:	Girdle beetle
Scientific name	:	*Sthenias grisator* (Fabricius, 1787)
Family	:	Cerambycidae
Order	:	Coleoptera

Source: *https://www.cerambycoidea.com/forum/topic.asp?TOPIC_ID=21881*

Distribution and Host Range

It is reported in Punjab and Andhra Pradesh. It is only a minor pest on grape, preferring Virginia creeper. Hosts include grape and virginia creeper.

Nature and symptoms of damage

The girdling by the female causes the terminal growth of the new shoots to bend over above the upper girdle and drop to the ground. Later the whole infested shoot dies back to the lower girdle and falls from the vine. Vines 'pruned' by the grape cane girdler have a ragged appearance suggesting serious injury to the plant. Girdling of the terminal growth has little or no effect on the crop unless fruit-producing nodes are close to attacked shoot tips.

Life History and Description

The female hollows out a small cavity in the shoot, places a single egg into it, and fills the egg cavity with frass. Then she proceeds to girdle the cane at two places: just below the egg cavity and several inches above. The egg is 0.7 mm long, and off-white. Egg period is about 10. The fully-grown larva is white with a brown head, legless, and measures 8 mm in length. It burrows in the center of the shoot on either side of the egg cavity, larval development takes over a month. The shoot in which the larva feeds either breaks off at the girdled point or dies back to the first node below the egg cavity and drops to the ground. The pupa is light- colored but becomes darker just prior to emergence. Adult develops in two weeks. The shiny-black adults are small, 3 mm long weevils with a characteristic curved snout. Egg-laying continues for about one month.

Management

Hand picking of the adults at night with the help of torchlight. Eggs are placed under the bark of girdled branches, which quickly dries up. Such dry twigs are collected from vineyards and burned. A piece of cloth is soaked in an insecticide solution like chlorpyrifos and then wrap around the stem. Spraying of chlorpyrifos (0.1%) is also effective. Spray application of following insecticides phosalone 35 EC 0.07%, quinalphos 25 EC 0.05%, carbaryl 50 WP 0.1%, first round immediately after pruning and repeat it 2-3 times.

❑ Flea beetle: *Scelodonta strigicollis* (Motschulsky)

Common name	:	Flea beetle
Scientific name	:	*Scelodonta strigicollis* (Motschulsky)
Family	:	Chrysomelidae
Order	:	Coleoptera

Source: *http://databases.nbair.res.in/insectpests/index.php*

Distribution and Host Range

It is a regular and serious pest in India. Hosts include grape, plum, apple, quince, beech, elm and Virginia creeper.

Nature and Symptoms of Damage

The adult beetles scrap the sprouting buds after each pruning. Damaged buds fail to sprout. The beetles also feed on tender shoots and leaves, and tendrils causing substantial damage. The tender shoots may wither and drop down. The losses are heavy when the sprouting buds are damaged after forward pruning. Damage is caused by adult beetles feeding on primary buds, which prevents them from developing into shoots, thus resulting in a decreased yield. The greatest economic loss occurs when beetles feed on buds from "bud swell" until the "first leaf separates from the shoot tip" stages. Although primary damage is caused by adult flea beetle to the developing buds, larval damage can also occur on the foliage and is typically limited to several leaves and vines.

Life History and Description

Eggs are laid near the buds or loose cane are yellow to orange, cylindrical in shape, rounded on 1 end and 1 mm in length and 0.4 mm in width. Newly hatched larvae is dark brown in colour but late turns light brown, 7-9 mm in length, and whole body is covered with back shiny and rectangular plates of various sizes which gives the spotted appearance of larvae. Pupae bright yellow, 4-6 mm long, and with conspicuous reddish-brown eyes. Adults are oval in shape, metallic shining blue, and 4-5 mm in length.

Management

Remove loose bark of the stem and apply paste of copper oxychloride and carbaryl 50% WP after pruning to expose and kill the beetles. Spray insecticides like carbaryl (0.15%) or quinalphos (0.05%) from the fourth day after pruning at an interval of 3-5 days until the emergence of the leaves is effective in protecting the sprouting bud from the attack.

❑ Grape leaf folder: *Desmia funeralis* (Hübner, 1796)

Common name	:	Grape leaf folder
Scientific name	:	*Desmia funeralis* (Hübner, 1796)
Family	:	Crambidae
Order	:	Lepidoptera

Source: *https://upload.wikimedia.org/wikipedia/commons/thumb/a/ac/Desmia_maculalis.jpg/330px-Desmia_maculalis.jpg*

Distribution and Host Range

It is found across the Southern parts of the United States to California, North to the Northeastern states and Southeastern Canada as a minor pest of grapes.

Nature and Symptoms of Damage

A larva feeds within the protection of the fold, held in place by bands of silk thread skeletonizing the leaf of the upper surface. When the larvae are numerous the injury to the vine becomes conspicuous, even at a considerable distance, because the light color of the under surface of the folded leaves contrasts boldly with the dark green of the upper side normally presented, thus giving the vine a patchy appearance. Larvae roll muscadine leaves, which are thinner than bunch grape leaves.

Life History and Description

Eggs are small (about 1/32 inches long), flat, iridescent, elliptical structures laid singly on the underside of a leaf, often in the angles between a vein and the leaf surface. Larvae (3/4 inch long) are glossy, translucent yellow green on the sides and somewhat darker above, with scattered fine yellow hairs on each segment. Pupae (1/2 inch long) are light brown just after pupation, but soon turn dark. The adult is a very dark brown, almost black, moth with a wingspread of about 1 inch. The front wings each have two white spots and hindwings of the female also have two white spots, while those of the male have only one large white spot. There are two white bands across the abdomen. The male antennae are thickened and distorted in the center; the female antennae are smooth.

Management

Simple method to control the pest population is to collect and burn the infested leaves. Larval parasitoid: *Bracon cushmani*, *Cardiochiles* sp and predators: Lacewing, spider. Effective insecticides include methoxyfenozide, chlorantraniliprole (rynaxypyr), spinosad, and spinetoram.

Thrips: *Rhipiphorothrips cruentatus* Hood

Common name	:	Thrips
Scientific name	:	*Rhipiphorothrips cruentatus* Hood
Family	:	Thripidae
Order	:	Thysanoptera

Source: *https://thrips.info/w/media/thumb/b/b5/RhipCruFull.jpg/450px-RhipCruFull.jpg*

Distribution and Host Range

Thrips pose an increasing threat to grape cultivation in all the grape growing areas in India. Three species namely *Scirtothrips dorsalis*, *Thrips hawaiiensis* and *Rhipphorothrips cruentatus* are found causing damage to grapevine.

Nature and Symptoms of Damage

Damage is caused both by nymphs and adults by rasping the lower surface of the leaf with their stylets and sucking the oozing cell sap. The injured surface is marked by the number of minute spots thereby producing a speckled silvery effect. Curling of the leaves is observed in case of heavy incidence. The thrips also attack blossoms and developing berries. The affected berries develop a corky layer and become brown and fetches low price in the market.

Life History and Description

Hyaline, globular eggs are laid in mass are inserted in the tender tissue on the underside of the leaves. Nymphs tiny, slender, fragile and straw yellow in colour hatch in 8-10 days. After feeding, nymphs move down to the soil and pupate in top 8-18 cm. Nymphs are similar to adults but are without wings. Adults with heavily fringed wings. Total life cycle is completed in about 15 days.

Management

Deep ploughing in summer or exposure/raking of soil in vineyards helps to destroy its pupal stages and minimize the incidence. Weeds and alternate host plants and plant debris from previous crops should be removed. The green lacewing *Chrysoperla carnea* is commonly associated predator with insect pests in the vineyards. Spraying of fungal pathogens namely *Verticillium lecanii* or *Beauveria bassiana* @ 5 ml or 5 g/L helps in reducing thrips population in cold and humid climate especially when temperatures are between 20-25°C and humidity of above 70%. Different neem formulations (EC based) depending upon the strength of botanical *viz.*, 1% @ 2.5 ml and 5% @ 0.5 ml/L can be sprayed per acre. Alternate spraying of insecticides like phosphamidon (0.05%) or monocrotophos (0.1%) or malathion (0.05%) offer a good control over the pest.

❑ Mealy bug: *Ferrisia virgata* Cockerell, 1893

Common Name	:	Striped mealybug; Two tailed mealy bug
Scientific Name	:	*Ferrisia virgata* Cockerell
Family	:	Pseudococcidae
Order	:	Hemiptera

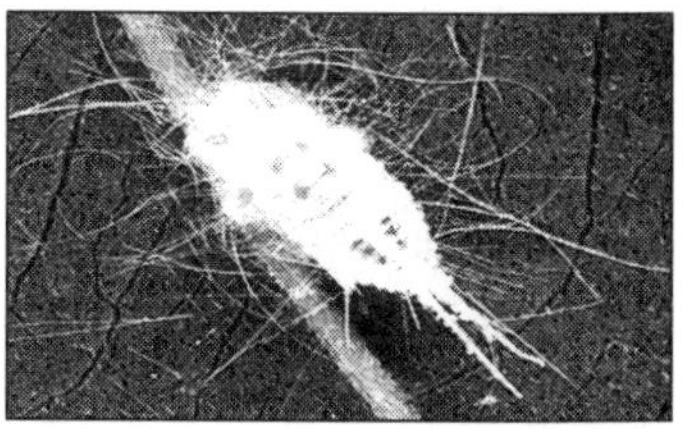

Source: *https://www.cabidigitallibrary.org/doi/10.1079/cabicompendium.30965*

As Described in Tomato

❑ Leaf eating caterpillar: *Spodoptera litura* (Fabricius, 1775)

Common Name	:	Tobacco caterpillar, Tobacco cutworm; Cotton leafworm; Leaf eating caterpillar
Scientific Name	:	*Spodoptera litura* (Fabricius, 1775)
Family	:	Noctuidae
Order	:	Lepidoptera

Source: *https://apps.lucidcentral.org/pppw*

As Described in Potato

❑ Red spider mites: *Tetranychus urticae* C.L. Koch, 1836

Common name	:	Red spider mite
Scientific name	:	*Tetranychus urticae* C. L. Koch, 1836
Family	:	Tetranychidae
Order	:	Trombidiformes

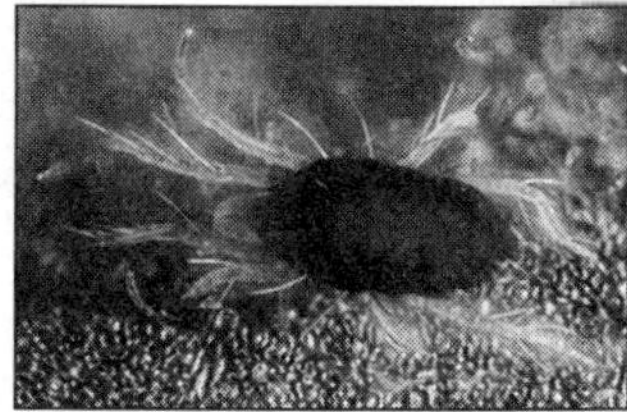

Source: *https://upload.wikimedia.org/wikipedia/commons/thumb/5/52/Tetranychus_urticae_%284883560779%29.jpg/330px-Tetranychus_urticae_%284883560779%29.jpg*

As Described in Tomato

❑ Berry plume moth: *Oxyptilus regulus* Meyrick, 1906

Common name	:	Berry plume moth
Scientific name	:	*Oxyptilus regulus* Meyrick, 1906
Family	:	Pterophoridae
Order	:	Lepidoptera

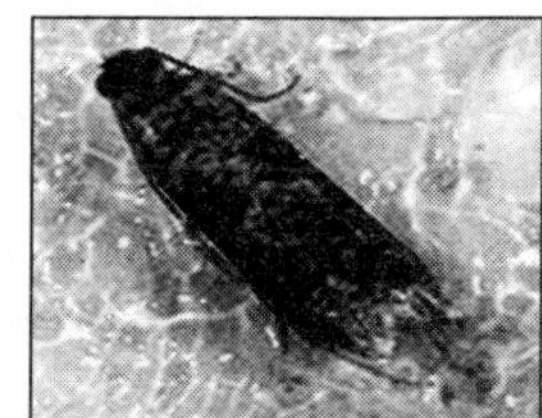

Source: *http://agritech.tnau.ac.in/crop_protection/crop_prot_crop_insectpest%20_grapes%20Copy%20-%20Copy%20-%20Copy_clip_image036.jpg*

Distribution and Host Range

The grape berry moth is the most common and destructive of all grape insect pests. It is found in Australia, but has recently also been recorded from Southern India.

Nature and Symptoms of Damage

Early instar larvae web the flower buds. Matured larvae attack bunch of fruit. Caterpillar bore into green berry fruit and starts tunneling. Feeds on internal content. Affected berries are known as "stung berries".

Life History and Description

Larva is small, pale green or pink with median red line and adult is small moth.

Management

Collect and destroy the infested leaves and bury with soil. Practice summer ploughing to kill the pupae. Use pheromone trap to attract male and kill the adult. Spot application of bubrofezin and acetemprid for effectively manage this pest.

❑ Root knot nematode: *Meloidogyne* spp. Goldi

Common Name	:	Root-knot nematode
Scientific Name	:	*Meloidogyne* spp. Goldi
Family	:	Heteroderidae
Order	:	Tylenchida

Source: *https://content.ces.ncsu.edu/management-of-root-knot-nematodes-in-bedding-plants*

As Described in Tomato

Resistant Varieties	
World	**India**
Chambourcin: This is a hybrid grape variety that is resistant to a range of fungal diseases and pests, including phylloxera. **Marquette:** Another hybrid variety, Marquette is resistant to pests such as Japanese beetles and grape phylloxera. **Norton:** This grape variety is known for its resistance to pests such as powdery mildew and black rot. **Frontenac:** This grape variety is resistant to a range of pests and diseases, including phylloxera, downy mildew, and black rot. **Chancellor:** This is a disease-resistant grape variety that is known for its resistance to phylloxera and black rot. **Muscadine:** This is a native grape variety that is resistant to a range of pests and diseases, including phylloxera, downy mildew, and powdery mildew. **Concord:** This grape variety is resistant to many pests, including Japanese beetles and grape phylloxera. *These grape varieties are grown in various parts of the world, including the United States, France, and Italy, among others.	**Thompson Seedless:** This is a popular seedless grape variety that is resistant to several insect pests, including thrips, mealybugs, and scale insects. **Flame Seedless:** This is another popular seedless grape variety that is resistant to thrips and spider mites. **Red Globe:** This is a popular red grape variety that is resistant to thrips and spider mites. **Sonaka:** This is a recently developed seedless grape variety in India that is resistant to several insect pests, including thrips and mealybugs. **Sharad Seedless:** This is another popular seedless grape variety that is resistant to thrips and mealybugs. **Manik Chaman:** This is a black seeded grape variety that is resistant to several insect pests, including thrips and spider mites. *These grape varieties have been developed by the Indian Council of Agricultural Research (ICAR) and other research institutes in India to combat insect pest problems in grape cultivation.

20

Pests of Pomegranate

Scientific name	*Punica granatum* L.
Family	Lythraceae
Origin	Mediterranean region
Chromosome number	2n = 18

Pomegranate is a fruit-bearing deciduous shrub or small tree, scientifically known as *Punica granatum*, which belongs to the family Lythraceae. It is native to regions of Iran, but is now widely cultivated in many parts of the world, including India, the Middle East, Mediterranean regions, and parts of North and South America. In India, pomegranate is grown in states like Maharashtra, Karnataka, Andhra Pradesh, Rajasthan, Tamil Nadu, and Gujarat, among others. The fruit is generally harvested from September to December, and the crop requires warm, dry weather with low humidity. The major varieties grown in India are Bhagwa, Ganesh, Ruby, and Arakta.

Like other fruit crops, pomegranate can be affected by a variety of insect pests and diseases, which can cause significant economic losses for farmers. Common pests of pomegranate include mealybugs, scales, fruit flies, and thrips, while diseases such as fungal infections and bacterial wilt can also affect the crop. Appropriate pest management practices, such as cultural practices, use of natural enemies, and judicious use of pesticides, can help to minimize yield losses and protect the crop.

❑ Pomegranate fruit borer: *Deudorix isocrates* (Fabricius, 1793)

Common name	:	Pomegranate fruit borer, common guava blue, anar butterfly
Scientific name	:	*Deudorix isocrates* (Fabricius, 1793)
Family	:	Lycaenidae
Order	:	Lepidoptera

Source: *https://indiabiodiversity.org/observation/show/1732392*

As Described in Guava

❑ Thrips: *Scirtothrips dorsalis* Hood, 1919 and *Rhipiphorothrips cruentatus* Hood

Common name	:	Chilli thrips, yellow tea thrips; Grapevine thrips, cashew leaf thrips
Scientific name	:	*Scirtothrips dorsalis* Hood, 1919; *Rhipiphorothrips cruentatus* Hood
Family	:	Thripidae
Order	:	Thysanoptera

Source:
https://upload.wikimedia.org/wikipedia/commons/thumb/f/f2/Sd_adult_spread.jpg/330px-Sd_adult_spread.jpg

Source:
https://thrips.info/w/media/thumb/b/b5/RhipCruFull.jpg/450px-RhipCruFull.jpg

Distribution and Host Range

R. cruentatus is widespread in India and Sri Lanka, and is also recorded from Pakistan, Bangladesh, Afghanistan, Myanmar, Oman, Taiwan and Hainan. Host range includes grapes, rose, crape myrtle, Pomegranate. *S. dorsalis* has been reported from South Africa, the Ivory Coast, West Africa and East Africa. Host range includes banana, bean, cashew, castor, citrus, cocoa, corn, cotton, eggplant, grapes, litchi, longan, mango, melon, peanut, pepper, poplar, rose, strawberry, sweet potato, tea, tobacco, tomato, and wild yams etc.

Nature and Symptoms of Damage

Leaf tips turn brown and get curled due to the feeding of thrips on the underside of the leaves by rasping the surface and sucking the oozing cell- sap leading to drying and shedding of flowers. Scrapping on fruits leads to scab formation, reducing market value.

Life History and Description

Female lays on an average 50 dirty white bean-shaped eggs on the under surface of leaves. Newly hatched nymphs are reddish and turn yellowish brown as they grow. The incubation period is 3-8 days. Pupal period lasts for 2-5 days. Adults: *Rhiphiphorothrips cruentatus* – Minute, slender, soft bodied insects with heavily fringed wings, blackish brown with yellowish wings and measure 1.4 mm long. *Scirtothrips dorsalis* – Straw yellow in color and seen with two black stripes on the body.

Management

Avoid intercultivation of crops like chilli and onion. Remove and destroy affected plant parts. Use of blue sticky traps @ 1 trap/10 plants. Spray acetamiprid 20 SP @ 0.005% to 0.01% *i.e.*, 25 to 50 g/100 l or spinosad 45 SC @ 0.25 ml/l i.e. 25 ml/100 l or NSKE 5% or *Verticillium lecani* (2 × 108 cfu/g) @ 200 g/100 l starting from prior to flowering at the interval of 10 days. Spray chloropyriphos @ 0.02% or imidacloprid @ 0.04% or deltamethrin 0.15 or dichlorovos @ 0.05% as prophylactic or on observing the symptoms. Spray dimethoate 0.06% prior to flowering. In severe conditions, spray methyl oxy- demeton 0.05% and repeat after fruit set.

❑ Stem borer: *Coelosterna spinator* Fletcher

Common name	:	Pomegranate stem borer
Scientific name	:	*Coelosterna spinator* Fletcher
Family	:	Cerambycidae
Order	:	Coleoptera

Source: *http://agropedia.iitk.ac.in/content/pomegranate-stem-borer#:~:text=Coelosterna%20spinator%20(Febricius)%20have%20been,also%20attacks%20the%20living%20branches.*

Distribution and Host Range

It is a polyphagous pest of minor importance boring the stems and trunk of pomegranate trees. It prefers breeding in dead wood but also attacks the living branches. The grubs of stem borer bore into the cambium then girdle the stem or branch causing death of the tree.

Nature and Symptoms of Damage

Grubs feed internally on sapwood while adult beetles are active by the day and feed by gnawing the green bark of shoots. Holes made by grubs are seen on bark of main stems. Similarly, excreta and dry powdered material is seen near the base of plants.

Life History and Description

Egg period is 12 to 15 days, grub stage lasts for 9 to 10 months and pupal period is 16 to18 days. There is only one generation per year and longevity of beetles is 45 to 60 days. Beetles *C. spinator*, have pale yellowish-brown body with light grey elytra and are 30 to 35 mm long.

Management

Prevent plants from becoming weak due to poor nutrition, attack by another insect etc. Hand picking and killing of adults in kerosene water. The grubs of stem borer can be killed by inserting a hooked wire down the hole. Pruning of dead branches during pre-monsoon and before taking bahar. Do not heap dead or uprooted wood within or near orchards. Attract and kill by installing the light traps with 200 watts sodium bulb. Application of paste 10 liters of water + red soil (4 kg) + chlorpyriphos 20 EC (20 ml) + copper oxychloride (25 g) with the help of brush, up to 1-2 feet above from second year crop onwards. Inject the damaged stems holes with dichlorvos 76 EC @ 70-80 ml/liter. Apply dichlorvos solution with the help of squeeze bottle till the bored tunnel is filled and then close with the wet mud.

❑ Bark-eating caterpillar: *Indarbela quadrinotata* (Walker, 1856)

Common name	:	Bark-eating caterpillar
Scientific name	:	*Indarbela quadrinotata* (Walker, 1856)
Family	:	Cossidae
Order	:	Lepidoptera

Source: *https://agritech.tnau.ac.in/crop_protection/guava/guava_5.html*

As Described in Mango

Fruit piercing/sucking moth: *Eudocima materna* Linnaeus, 1767; *Eudocima homaena* (Hübner, 1816)

Common name	:	Fruit sucking moth, Fruit piercing moth
Scientific name	:	*Eudocima materna* Linnaeus, 1767; *Eudocima homaena* (Hübner, 1816)
Family	:	Erebidae
Order	:	Lepidoptera

Source: *http://databases.nbair.res.in/insectpests/index.php*

Source: *http://databases.nbair.res.in/insectpests/index.php*

As Described in Citrus

Ash whitefly: *Siphoninus phillyreae* (Haliday, 1835)

Common name	:	Ash whitefly, pomegranate whitefly
Scientific name	:	*Siphoninus phillyreae* (Haliday, 1835)
Family	:	Aleyrodidae
Order	:	Hemiptera

Source:*https://entnemdept.ufl.edu/creatures/orn/ash_whitefly.htm*

Distribution and Host Range

It is reported in North, Central and South America, Africa, Asia, Europe and Australia. Host range includes pomegranate, citrus, loquat, ornamentals, etc.

Nature and Symptoms of Damage

Nymphs and adults suck the sap from leaves. Honey dew secreted leads to development of sooty mould fungus. Yellowing of leaves. Dropping of affected leaves.

Life History and Description

The adult appears much like a typical whitefly with a light dusting of white wax. Depending on temperature, females live from 30 to 60 days, while males live an average of nine days. Winged females lays eggs laid in a circle on the underside of the leaves. When the nymphs emerge, they rarely move far and feed on the plant sap until pupation. Short glass like rods of wax along the sides of the body seen in nymphs. Whitefly pupal case with two longitudinal tufts of white wax.

Management

Field sanitation, removal of host plants. Maintain adequate aeration by proper training and pruning. Install yellow sticky traps @ 4-10 traps/acre. Release of predators *viz.*, Coccinellid predator,

Cryptolaemus montrouzieri and lacewing and release of parasitoids viz., *Encarsia haitierrsis* and *E. guadeloupae*. Spray neem oil 3% or NSKE 5%.

❑ Shot hole borer: *Xyleborus perforans* (Wollaston, 1857)

Common name	:	Shot hole borer, island pinhole borer
Scientific name	:	*Xyleborus perforans* (Wollaston, 1857)
Family	:	Curculionidae
Order	:	Coleoptera

Source: *https://bugwoodcloud.org/images/1536x1024/5567644.jpg*

Distribution and Host Range

It is distributed throughout Bangladesh, Cambodia, China, Hong Kong, India, Andaman and Nicobar Islands, Laos, Malaysia, Myanmar, Nepal, Pakistan, Philippines, Singapore, Sri Lanka, Taiwan, Thailand, Vietnam, Papua New Guinea and Australia. It attacks hundreds of host plant species in many plant families.

Nature and Symptoms of Damage

Adult females bore into the basal part of the stem and roots. Causes small shot holes on roots, main trunk, wilting and finally leads to death of the tree.

Life History and Description

Eggs are oval or round, shiny and iridescent white. Larvae are white and legless, and can be up to 4 mm long. Adult is about 2-3 mm long, black to reddish-brown, and cigar shaped. They have a short, stubbed head capsule, with chewing mouthparts. Male adults do not fly. Two generations per year.

Management

Avoid water logging and rake the soil. Infested young plants should be uprooted and burnt. Parasitoids: *Trichogramma*, *Tetrastichus* spp., *Telenomus* spp., *Chelonus blackburni*, *Carcelia* spp. *Campoletis chlorideae*, *Bracon* spp. Predators: *Chrysoperla* sp. rove beetles, spiders, parasitic wasp, coccinellids, robber fly, dragonfly, Beduviid bug (*Geocoris* sp.), praying mantis, fire ants, pentatomid bug (*Eocanthecona furcellata*), earwigs, ground beetles, common mynah, king crow. Soil drenching with chlorpyriphos (0.2%) in and around the affected trees is effective as prophylactic spray chlorpyriphos (0.2%) and carbaryl (0.2%).

❑ Tailed mealy bug: *Ferrisia virgata* Cockerell, 1893

Common name	:	Tailed mealy bug, striped mealybug, guava mealybug, grey mealybug
Scientific name	:	*Ferrisa virgata* Cockerell, 1893
Family	:	Pseudococcidae
Order	:	Hemiptera

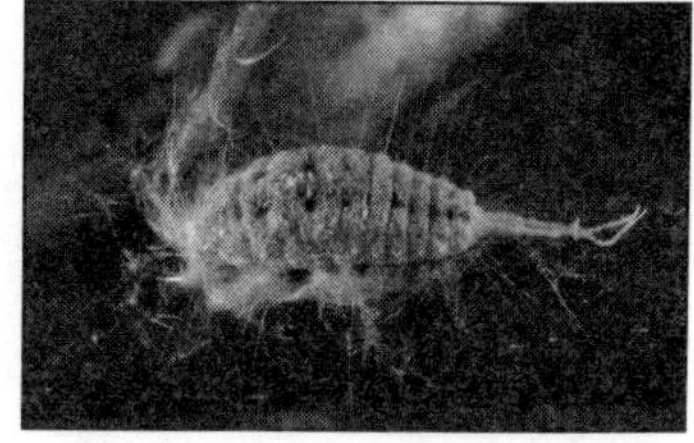

Source: *https://entnemdept.ufl.edu/creatures/orn/mealybug/ferrisia_virgata.htm*

As Described in Tomato

❑ Aphid: *Aphis punicae* Passerini, 1863

Common name	:	Aphid
Scientific name	:	*Aphis punicae* Passerini, 1863
Family	:	Aphididae
Order	:	Hemiptera

Source: *https://www.google.co.in/imgres?imgurl=https%3A%2F%2Fars.els-cdn.com%2Fcontent%2Fimage%*

As Described in Guava

Resistant Varieties	
World	**India**
Wonderful: This is a popular variety of pomegranate that is widely grown in many parts of the world. It is known for its resistance to pests like whiteflies and scales. **Mollar de Elche:** This is a Spanish variety of pomegranate that is also resistant to whiteflies and scales. It is a highly prized variety that is known for its sweet and juicy arils. **Parfianka:** This is a cultivar of pomegranate that is native to Uzbekistan. It is resistant to pests like thrips and scales and is known for its large, sweet, and juicy arils. **Salavatski:** This is a Russian variety of pomegranate that is resistant to pests like scales, mealybugs, and thrips. It is a highly productive variety that produces large and sweet fruits. **Ariana:** This is an Iranian variety of pomegranate that is resistant to pests like scales, mealybugs, and thrips. It is a highly productive variety that is known for its sweet and flavourful arils.	**Ganesh:** This variety is resistant to fruit fly and scales. **Mridula:** Mridula is resistant to mealybug and scales. **Jalore Seedless:** This variety is resistant to fruit fly, scales and thrips. **Jyoti:** Jyoti is resistant to fruit fly, scales and thrips. **Kandhari:** Kandhari is resistant to scales and thrips. **Mridang:** Mridang is resistant to scales and thrips. **Phule Arakta:** This variety is resistant to fruit fly, scales and thrips. **Ruby:** Ruby is resistant to fruit fly, scales and thrips. *These varieties have been developed through selective breeding and genetic research to resist insect pests and reduce the use of chemical pesticides.

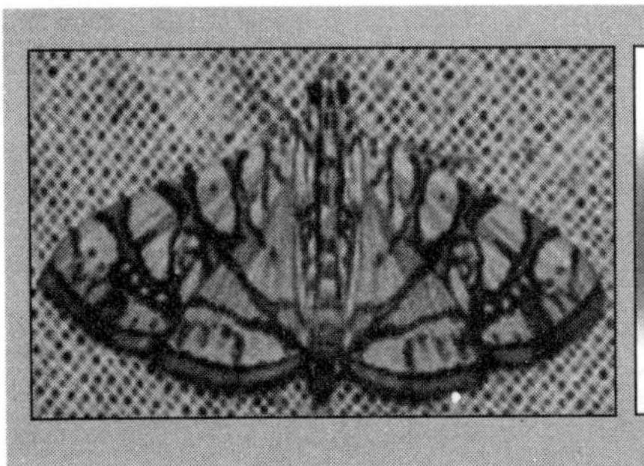

Pests of Jackfruit

Scientific name	*Artocarpus heterophyllus* Lam.
Family	Moraceae
Origin	India
Chromosome number	2n = 56

Jackfruit is a tropical fruit that is popular in many parts of the world, especially in South and Southeast Asia. Jackfruit trees (*Artocarpus heterophyllus*) belong to the Moraceae family and are native to India. They are evergreen trees that can grow up to 80 feet tall and have a broad canopy. India is the largest producer of jackfruit in the world, followed by Bangladesh, Thailand, and Indonesia. Jackfruit is also grown in other tropical regions including parts of Africa, South America, and Southeast Asia.

Jackfruit crops can be affected by a number of insect pests, including fruit flies, mealybugs, and scale insects. These pests can cause damage to the fruit, reducing its quality and marketability. In addition, infestations can lead to increased management costs and reduced yields. It is important for farmers to use integrated pest management strategies to control these pests and minimize their impact on the crop.

❑ Shoot and Fruit Borer: *Glyphodes caesalis* Walker, 1859

Common name	:	Shoot and Fruit Borer, Jack fruit borer
Scientific name	:	*Glyphodes caesalis* Walker, 1859
Family	:	Crambidae
Order	:	Lepidoptera

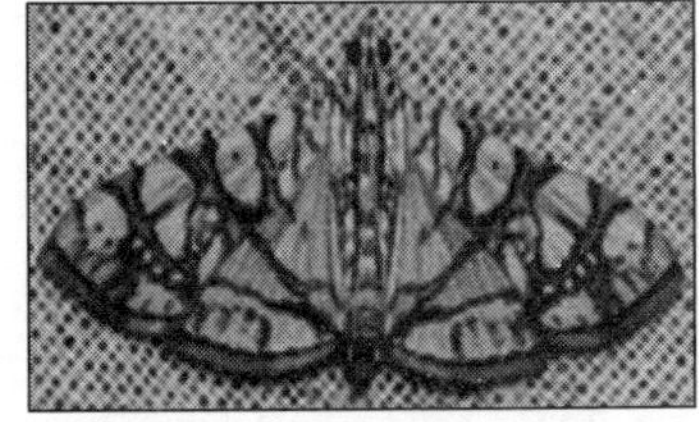

Source: *http://databases.nbair.res.in/insectpests/index.php*

Distribution and Host Range

Shoot and fruit borer is one of the major pests of jackfruit in India and other jackfruit grown countries (East Pakistan, Bangladesh etc). It causes varying degree of damage between 3-28%

depending upon the climatic conditions. The humid tropics are most favourable for the growth and development of *Diaphania* spp.

Life History and Description

The life cycle is completed in around 26-36 days depending on the season. The adult lays eggs on flower buds and young shoots. Incubation period varies from 3 to 5 days. First instar is very tiny, full-grown caterpillar is pinkish and head and prothoracic shield is yellow. Single short bristly hairs arise from the black flattened horny warts on each body segment. The larval period varies from 11 to 13 days and comprises of five instars and a prepupal stage. Matured larva pupates inside the silken cocoon for the period of 7-12 days. Pupa is reddish brown. Adult moth is whitish brown and half an inch long. Wings have black specks on margin bands and greyish elliptical pattern on wings. Wings span 25-30 mm. Female is larger than male.

Nature and Symptoms of Damage

Adult moth lays eggs on apical buds or tender shoot on both the male and female spikes. The larva mines into the shoot or apical buds and feeds on internal content. A mass of excreta can be seen outside of the entry hole. It is also found to feed on leaves and flower buds. Severe infestation leads to flower or fruit drop. It also attacks nursery plants by boring into the tender apical bud resulting in production of lateral shoots. The early infestation on fruit causes deformation and immature fruit drops off. The rotting occurs on the infested portion as a secondary infection.

Management

Removal and destruction of the affected shoots, flower buds and fruits in the initial stage of attack reduce the infestation of the pest. Covering of fruit with alkathene bags reduces the infestation significantly by preventing oviposition. Application of cypermethrin 10 EC at 1.0 ml or fenitrothion 50 EC at 2.0 ml per litre of water at flowering stage reduces the infestation. A second spray should be done 15-20 days after first spray, if necessary.

❑ Bud Weevils: *Ochyromera artocarpi* Marshall; *Onychocnemis careyae* Mshll, *Teluropus ballardi* Mshll

Common name	:	Bud weevils, Brown weevils
Scientific name	:	*Ochyromera artocarpi* Marshall; *Onychocnemis careyae* Mshll, *Teluropus ballardi* Mshll
Family	:	Curculionidae
Order	:	Coleoptera

Source: *https://www.wikiwand.com/sv/Ochyromera*

Distribution and Host Range

The bud weevil is a precise pest of jackfruit and is reported from Kerala, Karnataka, Tamilnadu etc in India.

Nature and Symptoms of Damage

The grubs and adults feed on leaves, tender buds, shoots and fruits. *O. artocarpi* attacks by boring inside tender buds, shoots and fruits. *O. careyae* and *T. ballardi* feeds on leaves of the jackfruit.

Severe infestation induces premature falling of fruits and bud. Adult weevils are brownish, usually seen feeding on leaves.

Life History and Description

O. artocarpi is a small greyish weevil with stout fore femur and yellow setae over the body. *O. careyae* is a reddish-brown weevil with dark head and shiny short white setae. The elytral suture is blackish brown and a patch extending from the base to beyond the middle. Pronotum coarsely reticulated and legs coarsely punctuated and clothed with curved white setae. The egg is pearly white, smooth and oblong oval measuring. The eggs hatch in 3 to 4 days and the newly hatched legless grub is pale white with a pale brown head. It bores through the tissue in all directions and becomes mature in 12 to 15 days. The full-grown grub is whitish in color and head is light brown but darker at the frontal region and much narrower than thorax and with a conspicuous dark line in frons. The pupal stage lasts for 5 to 6 days. The adult emerges by boring a hole on the outer skin.

Management

Collection and destruction of infested flower buds, fallen fruits checks the further spread of infestation by weevil. Application of carbaryl 50 WP at 2 g/l reduces the weevil population. Remove the infested shoots, flower buds and fruits to check infestation. Pipunculid fly, *Verrallia virginica* caused 50-60% parasitism of adult spittle bugs.

❑ Aphids: *Greenidea artocarpi* (Westwood, 1890); *Toxoptera aurantii* (Boyer de Fonscolombe)

Common name	:	Aphids, Brown Citrus Aphid
Scientific name	:	*Greenidea artocarpi* (Westwood, 1890); *Toxoptera aurantii* (Boyer de Fonscolombe)
Family	:	Aphididae
Order	:	Hemiptera

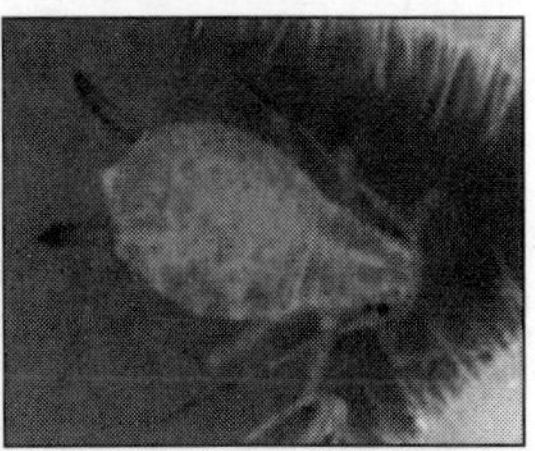

Source: *http://databases.nbair.res.in/insectpests/index.php*

Source: *https://upload.wikimedia.org/wikipedia/commons/thumb/0/0f/Toxoptera_aurantii.jpg/330px-Toxoptera_aurantii.jpg*

Distribution and Host Range

Greenidea artocarpi species is found in Southern India and Sri Lanka and also from South-east Asia. It has been recorded on 3-4 breadfruit and jackfruit species (*Artocarpus altilis*, *A. heterophyllus*, *A. incisa*, *A. integrifolia*). *Toxoptera aurantii* is distributed throughout the tropics and subtropics including the Pacific Islands. It is also found in greenhouses in temperate regions. It has a broad host range, particularly important on citrus, cacao, coffee, and tea, but also attacks other crops such as sugar apple, fig, and mango, and a variety of ornamentals.

Nature and Symptoms of Damage

Nymphs and adults of aphids suck the sap from new leaves, tender twigs and fruits. They feed as a colony and severe de-sapping results in curling and shriveling of affected parts and dries up finally. In some cases, galls may also be formed on the leaves due to the feeding injury.

Life History and Description

G. artocarpi is pale brownish green aphids feeding on lower sides of young leaves, and it is medium-sized, relatively long-bodied. Cornicles are brown-black, very long and slender. In India it is found in Meghalaya, Karnataka and Tamil Nadu. *T. aurantii* adults are oval, shiny black or reddish brown, either with or without wings and having black-and-white band on antennae. The cauda is finger-shaped, blunt and slightly constricted. It has a stridulatory apparatus consisting of ridges on the abdomen and pegs on hind tibia. The life cycle is temperature dependent, and it matures within 6 days at 25°C and 20 days at lower than 15°C.

Management

Collection and destruction of infected plant parts. Application of wood ash or cow dung ash is one of the cultural practices which desiccate them to die. In case of severe infestation, spraying of acephate at 1 g/l reduces the population. Aphids can be controlled through applying the neem oil (1%) or spray dimethoate (0.03%).

❑ Spittle Bug: *Cosmoscarta relata* Distant, 1900

Common name	:	Spittle Bug
Scientific name	:	*Cosmoscarta relata* Distant, 1900
Family	:	Cercopidae
Order	:	Hemiptera

Source: *http://databases.nbair.res.in/insectpests/index.php*

Distribution and Host Range

Spittle Bug, *Cosmoscarta relata* is a serious pest of jackfruit trees, especially in South India.

Nature and Symptoms of Damage

The nymphs and adults suck the sap from tender twigs, shoots and leaves. It results in drying of terminal shoots, yellowing and curling of leaves and the tree becomes weak. The peak infestation is found at flowering stage and it severely affects fruit set.

Life History and Description

The bugs are 15 mm long, with blunt red head and prominent eyes which resemble a frog and known as frog hoppers. The adult lays eggs inside tender shoots. It secretes spit-like frothy mass over the body which protects the bug from enemies. The total life cycle takes about 2 months.

Management

Keep orchard clean. Proper training and pruning of the tree should be done. Collect and destroy frothy mass with brush. Remove and destroy the affected shoots. Application of recommended dose of fertilizers and sufficient irrigation supports tolerance of tree. Spray quinalphos 0.05% or neem oil 0.03% at flowering stage. Adults can be controlled by dusting with carbaryl 1.5D.

Mealy bug: *Drosicha mangiferae* Stebbins, 1903

Common name	:	Mealybug, Giant scales or Monophlebids
Scientific name	:	*Drosicha mangiferae* Stebbins, 1903
Family	:	Monophlebidae
Order	:	Hemiptera

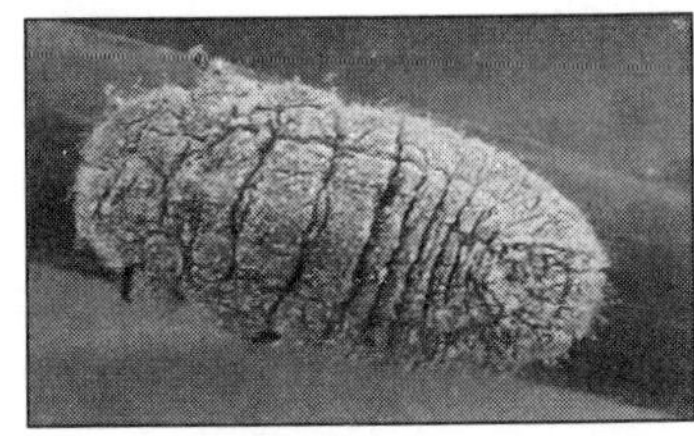

Source: *https://www.nbair.res.in/databases*

As Described in Mango

Mealy bug: *Planococcus lilacinus* (Cockerell, 1905)

Common name	:	Oriental cacao mealy bug
Scientific name	:	*Planococcus lilacinus* (Cockerell, 1905)
Family	:	Pseudococcidae
Order	:	Hemiptera

Source: *https://www.flickr.com/photos/pointnshoot/50079805876*

Distribution and Host Range

It has been reported in the tropical and subtropical regions of the world *viz*., Africa, Australia, Asia, Central and South America, and the Caribbean on over 30 plant families. It is highly polyphagous pest, attacks more than 30 families of tropical and subtropical fruit trees.

Nature and Symptoms of Damage

The scales tend to congregate in huge number and they suck the sap from leaves as well as tender shoots. Severe infestation causes drying and withering of affected parts.

Life History and Description

P. lilacinus is brownish red scale with a rounded body. Mealy bug wax covers the body except the median dorsal area. Wax develops into thick segmental clumps on mature females; legs yellowish brown; 18 pairs of short marginal wax filaments are present. The armoured body significantly varied with host and environment.

Management

Removal and destruction of affected shoots. In case of severe infestation, spraying dimethoate 30% EC at 2 ml/l or buprofezin at 1 ml/l is recommended.

❑ Leaf Webber: *Glyphodes bivitralis* Guenée, 1854

Common name	:	Leaf Webber, Leafroller moth
Scientific name	:	*Glyphodes bivitralis* Guenée, 1854
Family	:	Crambidae
Order	:	Lepidoptera

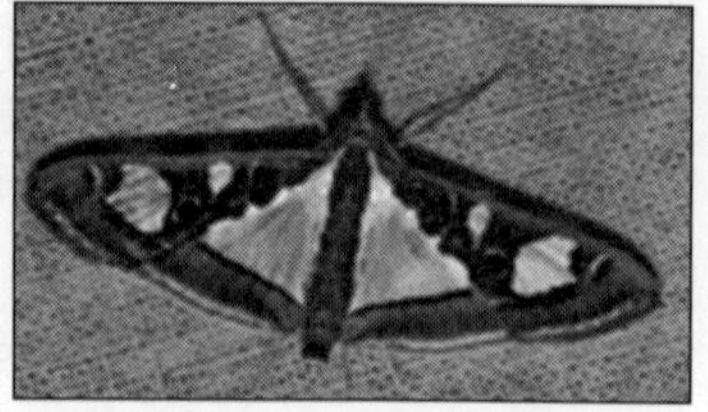

Source: *http://databases.nbair.res.in/insectpests/index.php*

Distribution and Host Range

It is native to South-east Asia, including Hong Kong, India, Japan, Taiwan and Thailand. It is also found in Queensland, Hawaii and Maldives.

Nature and Symptoms of Damage

G. bivitralis larvae feed on leaves by folding the leaf margin with silken thread and remain inside.

Life History and Description

The eggs are minute, spherical to flattened distributed in two to seven per cluster on the buds, flowers, and other actively growing portions of the plant. Their color is white initially, but changes to yellow after about 24 hours. Hatching occurs in about four days. Egg production to be 300-400 eggs per female. There are five instars. Total larval development time averages 14 days. Prior to pupation larvae tend to turn a dark copper color. Pupation usually occurs in a leaf fold; often dead, dry material. The pupa is elongate, light brown to dark brown in color, and tapers to a point at both ends. Pupation usually lasts about eight to nine days. Emerging moths fly during much of the evening hours, but most flight occurs three to five hours after sundown, with peak flight at approximately midnight.

Management

Mechanical clipping and burning of affected shoots. Release of pupal parasitoid, *Tetrastichus howardi* @20,000/ac. Release of egg parasitoid, *Trichogramma chilonis* @ 2cc/ac. Removal and destruction of folded leaves. Spray with neem oil 1500 ppm at 3 ml/l of water along with spreader and sticker.

❑ Tussock Moth: *Perina nuda* Fabricius, 1787

Common name	:	Tussock moth, Banyan tussock moth, clearwing tussock moth
Scientific name	:	*Perina nuda* Fabricius, 1787
Family	:	Erebidae
Order	:	Lepidoptera

Source: *https://commons.wikimedia.org/wiki/Category:Perina_nuda*

Distribution and Host Range

It is found in the Indian subregion, Sri Lanka, to Southern China Hong Kong, Thailand and Sundaland.

Nature and Symptoms of Damage

The larvae fold or web leaves together and feed inside the folds. In severe case, it causes extensive defoliation.

Life History and Description

The male moth's wings are predominantly scaleless, hence the "clearwing" alternative common name. The female moth lays 50-400 light pink eggs in clusters or in rows on the leaves and the eggs turn red later on. Larvae undergo six moults within 16-20 days. Larvae pupate on the upper surface of leaves. Adult emerges after 5-9 days of pupation, and the entire life cycle completes within 27-39 days.

Management

Collection and destruction of infected leaves with larvae. Spray with neem oil 1500 ppm at 3 ml/lit of water along with spreader and sticker.

❑ Bark-eating Caterpillars: *Indarbela quadrinotata* (Walker, 1856)

Common name	:	Bark-eating caterpillar
Scientific name	:	*Indarbela quadrinotata* (Walker, 1856)
Family	:	Cossidae
Order	:	Lepidoptera

Source: *https://agritech.tnau.ac.in/crop_protection/guava/guava_5.html*

As Described in Mango

❑ Trunk borer: *Aprioma germari* Hope, 1831

Common name	:	Trunk borer, mulberry longhorn beetle, brown mulberry longhorn, longhorn stem borer, jackfruit longhorn beetle, mulberry longicorn beetle.
Scientific name	:	*Aprioma germari* Hope, 1831
Family	:	Cerambycidae
Order	:	Coleoptera

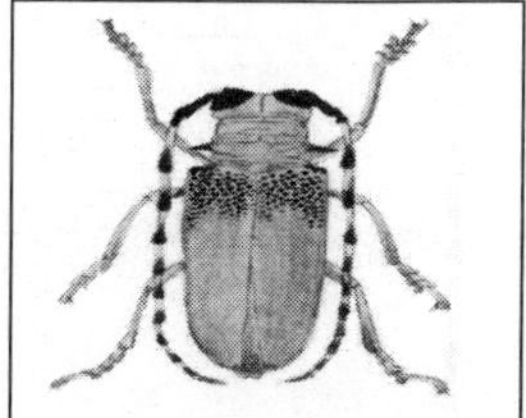

Source: *https://en.wikipedia.org/wiki/Apriona*

Distribution and Host Range

The main hosts of *A. germari* include plants from nineteen families and thirty-six genera of plants such as Salicaceae, Moraceae, Ulmaceae and Rosaceae. It is distributed throughout Cambodia, China,

Tibet, India, Korean Republic, Laos, Malaysia, Myanmar, Nepal, Pakistan, Taiwan, Thailand, Vietnam.

Nature and Symptoms of Damage

The adults of *A. germari* eat tender tree bark for maturation feeding and leave irregular scars on the tree. This usually leads to serious damage to twigs. Larvae of are the most damaging lifestage for the hosts. Resin bleeds can be observed from oviposition holes and larval tunnels in the bark and boring down along the heartwood of trunk, they have to bore transverse tunnels for frass ejection leaving a row of frass expulsion holes outside the trunk. Usually, these round holes are on the same side of the trunk and both the diameters of holes and the distances between two adjacent holes gradually increases from the top to the bottom of the tree. Frass accumulates at the base of the tree.

Life History and Description

Females mate and lay eggs 10-15 days after emergence. Eggs are laid under the bark, in oviposition slits chewed out by the female. Larvae feed first in the sapwood and then bore into the heartwood, with small frass expulsion holes made through the bark. Several larvae may be present in the same tree. The overwintering stage is the egg or larva. The pupal stage of *A. germari* occurs between the middle of June and the middle of August.

Management

Pruning of affected stem/branches and fumigation on main stem. Removal and destruction of affected branches, killing the grubs with a stiff wire or closing hole with mud. Place aluminium phosphide inside the hole and seal hole with bordeaux paste reduces the infestation.

❑ Fruit flies: *Bactrocera dorsalis* (Hendel, 1912)

Common name	:	Oriental fruit fly, mango fruit fly
Scientific name	:	*Bactrocera dorsalis* (Hendel, 1912)
Family	:	Tephritidae

Source:http://databases.nbair.res.in/insectpests/index.php

As Described in Mango

❑ Castor capsule borer: *Conogethes punctiferalis* (Guenée, 1854)

Common name	:	Castor capsule borer
Scientific name	:	*Conogethes punctiferalis* (Guenée, 1854)
Family	:	Crambidae
Order	:	Lepidoptera

Source:https://upload.wikimedia.org/wikipedia/commons/thumb/b/b6/Conogethes_punctiferalis.jpg/330px-Conogethes_punctiferalis.jpg

As Described in Guava

Resistant Varieties	
World	**India**
Black Gold: This variety of jackfruit was developed in the Philippines and is resistant to fruit flies and other pests. It is known for its sweet, juicy fruit and is popular in Southeast Asia. **NS-1:** NS-1 is a jackfruit variety developed in India that is resistant to both fruit flies and shoot borers. It produces large, sweet fruit that is popular in South India. **Gold Nugget:** This variety of jackfruit was developed in Florida, USA, and is resistant to a range of pests, including fruit flies and leaf-eating caterpillars. Its fruit is small and sweet, and it is often used in cooking. **J31:** J31 is a hybrid jackfruit variety developed in Malaysia that is resistant to a range of pests, including fruit flies and mealybugs. Its fruit is known for its sweet, juicy flavor and is popular in Southeast Asia. **Thongsomboon:** Thongsomboon is a Thai variety of jackfruit that is resistant to both fruit flies and shoot borers. Its fruit is known for its sweet, aromatic flavor and is often used in desserts and other sweet dishes.	**J-31:** This variety is known for its resistance to the jackfruit borer. It is a popular commercial variety in India and is also resistant to fruit fly. **Koozha:** This variety is resistant to the jackfruit borer as well as the stem borer. It is a popular variety in Kerala. **Varikka:** This variety is resistant to the jackfruit borer and is also known for its large fruit size. It is a popular variety in Kerala. **Idiyan:** This variety is resistant to the jackfruit borer and is known for its high yield. It is a popular variety in Kerala and Tamil Nadu. **Koozha chakka:** This variety is resistant to the jackfruit borer and is known for its small fruit size. It is a popular variety in Kerala. **Thondan:** This variety is resistant to the jackfruit borer and is also known for its high yield. It is a popular variety in Tamil Nadu. **Ayyalur local:** This variety is resistant to the jackfruit borer and is known for its early bearing and sweet fruit. It is a popular variety in Tamil Nadu.

Pests of Fig

Scientific name	*Ficus carica*
Family	Moraceae
Origin	Mediterranean region
Chromosome number	2n=26

The fig is a fruiting tree or shrub belonging to the genus *Ficus*, which is a member of the Moraceae family. It is an ancient crop that has been cultivated for thousands of years in the Mediterranean and Middle Eastern regions. Botanically, the fig fruit is a type of inverted flower with a soft, fleshy, pear-shaped body, containing tiny seeds on the inside. The fig tree has a unique pollination system in which tiny wasps enter the fruit through a tiny opening called the ostiole.

India is one of the major producers of figs in the world, with most of the production centered in the northern states of Uttar Pradesh, Jammu and Kashmir, and Himachal Pradesh. In recent years, the production of figs in India has been increasing due to their high demand in both domestic and international markets.

❑ Mealybug: *Drosicha stebbengii* (Stebbing, 1902)

Common name	:	Mealybug
Scientific name	:	*Drosicha stebbengii* (Stebbing, 1902)
Family	:	Monophlebidae
Order	:	Hemiptera

Source: *https://static.vikaspedia.in/media/images_en/agriculture/crop production/integrated-pest-managment*

Distribution and Host Range

D. stebbingi feeds on 62 host plants under 51 genera and 28 families including fruits crops, forest trees, ornamental plants and weeds.

Nature and Symptoms of Damage

Attacks primarily older, well-shaded groves planted on heavy soils. They will feed on the roots, bark, foliage, and fruit. The mealybug injects toxic salvia while extracting plant sap resulting in defoliation, fruit discoloration, fruit splitting, and fruit drop. Mealy bugs usually gather in large numbers, causing premature leaf drop and twig dieback when they feed. Like psyllids, they secrete honeydew, which attracts black sooty mold.

Life History and Description

The life cycle of *D. stebbingi* starts with purple-colored egg laying in loose soil around infected trees. The nymphs emerge with the rise in temperature and travel up the trees via stem to feed on cell sap, adjacent to the fruiting parts. Therefore, heavy immature fruit falling occurs. The flying males emerge to mate with the flightless mature females while crawling down to the ground for egg laying. Males are winged and short-lived after mating, and do not cause damage to the trees. *D. stebbingi* has a total life cycle of 24-26 days.

Management

Prune affected shoots during winter. Destroy ant colonies. Grow attractant plants bachelor's buttons or cornflower, coriander attract wasps. Collect and destroy the damaged leaves, twigs and stems. Use sticky barrier (5 cm length) on trunk. Coccinellids *R. fumida*, chrysopid *Chrysoperla zastrowii* silemi and drosophilid *Cacoxenus perspicax*, *R. fumida*.

❑ Leaf roller: *Choreutis nemorana* (Hübner, [1799])

Common name	:	Fig-tree skeletonizer moth or tig leaf roller
Scientific name	:	*Choreutis nemorana* (Hübner, [1799])
Family	:	Choreutidae
Order	:	Lepidoptera

Source: *https://upload.wikimedia.org/wikipedia/commons/thumb/4/41/Choreutidae_-_Choreutis_nemorana.J*

Distribution and Host Range

This species is widespread from the Canary Islands and Madeira, through the Mediterranean Region and North Africa to Asia. In 2009, it was first recorded in Belgium. This species is common wherever there are *Ficus carica* trees.

Nature and Symptoms of Damage

Damage is caused by larvae, which at younger ages gnaw the upper parenchymal cells of young leaves, leaving the lower parts of the leaves intact. Older caterpillar feed on both the upper and lower parenchymal cells, leaving the leaf nerves intact, causing the symptom of skeletonized leaves. During feeding, they often fold the top of leaves and feed inside that shelter. As a consequence of damage, the leaves are twisted and discolored, scarring and cracking occur and leaves look shabby or even fall off. Grown larvae pupate in a white silk cocoon on the upper side of fig leaf, under the bent tip of leaf or on the other parts of the plants.

Life History and Description

Adults of the fig-tree skeletonizer moth have a wing span between 16 and 20 mm. The color of the body is brown dorsally and light gray on the ventral side. The forewings are almost trapezoidal in shape with a wavy edge, orange-brown to dark brown in color with wavy silvery-gray transverse stripes, which give a characteristic pattern when the wings are folded. The hind wings are dark brown, with orange parts in the middle. From the ventral side, both pairs of wings are gray-brown. The eggs are spherical, whitish-creamy, 0.5 mm in diameter. The fully grown caterpillar is about 15-20 mm long, light green, shiny, semi-transparent, with a yellowish-brown head. On its dorsal side, there is a light longitudinal stripe in the middle of the body, and numerous black verrucae present on the thoracic and abdominal tergites. The pupa is dark brown, 7-8 mm long.

Management

Deep ploughing and soil solaraisation before planting. Collect and burn all infested leaves. Conserve parasites such as *Apanteles angeleti*, *Trathala flavoorbitalis* and *Cadurcia vanderwulpi*. Conserve predators such as lacewings, assassin bugs, and minute pirate bugs.

❑ Fig moth: *Cadra cautella* (Walker, 1863)

Common name	:	Fig moth, almond moth, tropical warehouse moth
Scientific name	:	*Cadra cautella* (Walker, 1863)
Family	:	Pyralidae
Order	:	Lepidoptera

Source: *https://bugguide.net/node/view/1035098*

Distribution and Host Range

Almond moths are found around the world. Although it thrives best in tropical climates, it has spread to many regions around the globe due to its tendency to infest dry goods that are shipped internationally. It is a serious pest of dried fruits such as currants, raisons, dried apples, dates, berries, figs, almonds, walnuts, tamarind seeds, etc. It has also been recorded on lac, malted milk, dried mango, pulp, garlic bulbs, various cereal grains and grain products.

Nature and Symptoms of Damage

The caterpillars make tunnels in the food materials. The number of silken tube is sometimes extremely high and these clog the mill machinery where the infested grains have been sent for milling.

Life History and Description

The eggs are translucent yellow with a sculptured surface. The larvae range from 1.5-15 mm in length and are light brown with dark brown spots with a sparse covering of hair. Pupae are dark-brown and found within a relatively light pupal case. The adult forewings are greyish-brown with scattered darker patches. The wing span is 11-20 mm and both fore and hind wings have broadly rounded tips and short fringes of hairs.

Management

Sieving, picking out, or winnowing. It is important to destroy any insects found in the by-products or left-overs immediately. Larvae living inside the grain are only inadequately eliminated. Larval parasitoid, *Habrobracon hebetor*; Pupal parasitoid, *Antrocephalus mitys*. Spray neem oil.

Western flower thrips: *Frankliniella occidentalis* Pergande, 1895

Common name	Western flower thrips
Scientific name	*Frankliniella occidentalis* Pergande, 1895
Family	Thripidae
Origin	Thysanoptera

Source: https://www.cabidigitallibrary.org/doi/10.1079/cabicompendium.24426

Distribution and Host Range

It is of American origin and is one of the most destructive pest thrips of the world. It causes direct damage by feeding on a variety of hosts including groundnut, cotton, tobacco, vegetables (cucurbits, cabbage, eggplant, tomato, carrot, peas, beans, capsicum, etc.), fruits (grapes, apple, peach, plum, etc.) and ornamentals (gladiolus, hibiscus, geranium, roses, orchids, etc.). *Frankliniella occidentalis* causes great havoc by transmitting as many as five tospoviruses, including the tomato spotted wilt virus.

Nature and Symptoms of Damage

Western flower thrips prefer to feed on developing plant tissues such as growing tips and flower buds. When these tissues develop further, leaves and flowers can appear grossly deformed. Severely infested flower buds may not open at all.

Life History and Description

The eggs are microscopic, kidney-shaped and creamy white in color. The eggs hatch between two to seven days, depending upon temperature. Larvae and adults tend to gather near the mid-vein or borders of the host leaf. The two larval stages are completed in eight to ten days and the pupal stage lasts for 2.6- 3.3 days. Pupae are generally found on leaves, leaf litter or on the axils of leaves, in curled leaves or under the calyces of flowers and fruits.

Management

Monitor the tree regularly. Adult thrips can be monitored by mass trapping with coloured (blue, yellow or white) sticky traps or water traps in the nursery or orchard. Ploughing and harrowing, and solarisation can kill pupae in the soil from previously infested trees. Inter-cropping with tomatoes reduces the populations of thrips. Various biological control agents, including minute pirate bugs, *Orius* spp. and entomopathogenic nematodes, *Thripinema* sp.

Scale: *Lepidosaphes conchiformis* (Gmelin, 1790)

Common name	:	Fig scale
Scientific name	:	*Lepidosaphes conchiformis* (Gmelin, 1790
Family	:	Diaspididae
Order	:	Hemiptera

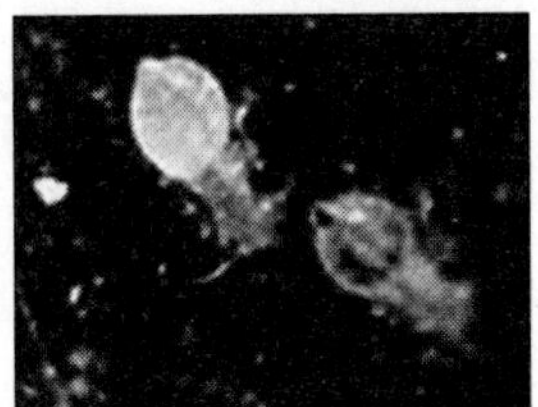

Source: https://www.google.co.in/url?sa=i&url=http%3A%2F%2Fwww.insectsofiran.com%2Fothers

Distribution and Host Range

L. conchiformis is polyphagous and is recorded from North Africa, Europe, South America, Near and Middle East, and Australia. It is reported on over sixty plant species from eighteen different families.

Nature and Symptoms of Damage

The direct damage is caused by insertion of stylets during feeding by nymphs, which can cause premature leaf drop and twig dieback. High populations can cause host death. Severe infestations may result in shoot or branch dieback. When large populations of scale occur, sooty mold may become a problem due to the mold's growth on the large quantities of honeydew excreted by these scales.

Life History and Description

Eggs laid by female scale are pale orange, they turn pink before hatching. Red eyespots are visible within the eggs before they hatch. Crawlers can be dispersed by wind and workers, or on farm machinery. Once settled crawlers shed their skin (moult). Adult- ridges of letter 'H' are distinct and are characteristic of black scale. The female dies 38 after laying eggs, though the scale covering remains on the leaves or twigs.

Management

Collect the egg carrying female in mounds before spreading to hibernation places. Parasites: *Aphytis maculicornis* and *Coccophagoides utilis*. Parasitoids: *Encarsia perniciosi* and *A. diaspidis*. Predators: *Chilocorus infernalis*, *C. rubidus*, *Pharoscymnus flexibilis*.

❑ Coccid: *Planococcus lilacinus* (Cockerell, 1905)

Common name	:	Oriental cacao mealy bug
Scientific name	:	*Planococcus lilacinus* (Cockerell, 1905)
Family	:	Pseudococcidae
Order	:	Hemiptera

Source: *https://www.flickr.com/photos/pointnshoot/50079805876*

As Described in Jackfruit

❑ Stem borer: *Batocera rufomaculata* (De Geer, 1775)

Common name	:	Stem borer, Red-spotted longhorn beetle, mango tree borer, tropical fig borer, bark borer
Scientific name	:	*Batocera rufomaculata* (De Geer, 1775)
Family	:	Cerambycidae
Order	:	Coleoptera

Source: *https://en.wikipedia.org/wiki/Batocera_rufomaculata*

As Described in Mango

❑ Fruitflies: *Bactrocera dorsalis* (Hendel, 1912)

Common name	:	Oriental fruit fly, mango fruit fly
Scientific name	:	*Bactrocera dorsalis* (Hendel, 1912)
Family	:	Tephritidae

Source: *http://databases.nbair.res.in/insectpests/index.php*

As Described in Mango

Resistant Varieties	
World	**India**
Brown Turkey: This is a popular variety of fig that is grown in many parts of the world. It is resistant to several insect pests, including fig rust mite and fig fruit fly. **Black Mission:** This is another popular variety of fig that is resistant to many insect pests, including the fig beetle and the fig fruit fly. **Kadota:** This variety of fig is resistant to several insect pests, including the fig fruit fly, mealybug, and spider mites. **Desert King:** This is a newer variety of fig that is resistant to several insect pests, including the fig beetle and the fig fruit fly. **Excel:** This variety of fig is resistant to several insect pests, including the fig fruit fly, spider mites, and scale insects.	**Anjeer:** Anjeer is a popular fig variety in India and is cultivated in many regions of the country. It is a deciduous tree that grows up to 10-12 meters in height. Anjeer figs are rich in vitamins and minerals and are often consumed as a dried fruit. **Gular:** Gular is another important fig variety in India, also known as Cluster Fig or Indian Fig. It is a medium-sized tree that grows up to 20 meters in height. Gular figs are eaten fresh or dried and are used in various cuisines. **Umran:** Umran is a fig variety that is grown mainly in the North-western region of India. It is a deciduous tree that grows up to 10 meters in height. Umran figs are juicy and sweet and are commonly used to make jams, jellies, and other preserves.

23 Pests of Ber

Scientific name	*Ziziphus mauritiana*
Family	Rhamnaceae
Origin	India
Chromosome number	2n=48

Ber, also known as Indian jujube or Chinese date, is a deciduous tree belonging to the family Rhamnaceae. It is widely grown in arid and semi-arid regions of India, Pakistan, Bangladesh, and other parts of Southeast Asia. The scientific name of Ber is *Ziziphus mauritiana*.

In India, Ber is grown on approximately 140,000 hectares of land, with an annual production of around 1.5 million tonnes. The major producing states are Uttar Pradesh, Rajasthan, and Maharashtra. Ber is an important crop for small and marginal farmers as it provides a source of income and nutrition. However, the crop is vulnerable to insect pests, such as fruit flies, thrips, and mites, which can cause significant yield losses if not managed properly.

❑ Ber fruit fly: *Carpomyia vesuviana* Costa

Common name	:	Ber fruit fly
Scientific name	:	*Carpomya vesuviana* Costa
Family	:	Tephritidae
Order	:	Diptera

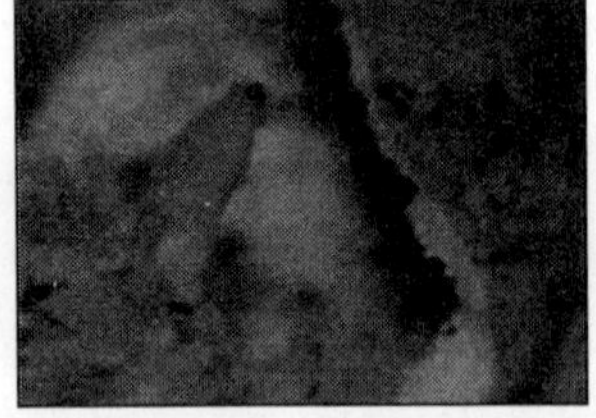

Source: *http://databases.nbair.res.in/insectpests/index.php*

Distribution and Host Range

This fruit fly is the most destructive pest of ber and is monophagous pest that infests only on *Zizyphus* species growing under arid and semi arid region in India and also in Oriental Asia, Middle East, Temperate Asia, China and South Europe. It contributes towards low yield and poor quality of fruits and causes yield loss upto 80% under severe infestation.

Nature and Symptoms of Damage

The maggots start infestation with the onset of fruit setting. The newly hatched maggot's start feeding on the pulp and make galleries with accumulated excreta and result in rotting of fruits. The larva burrows the flesh round the centre leaving excreta that give fruits a bitter taste.

Life History and Description

The fruit fly is easily distinguished in having distinctive pattern of black marks on the scutum and scutellum, and distinct yellow and brown bands on the wings. Two to three generations are completed. Eggs are laid in cavities made on the fruit with the ovipositor. The punctures appear as black spots in depression later on. Maggots bore into the pulp forming reddish brown galleries. The full-grown maggot falls to ground to pupate in soil 5 to 7.5 cm deep for periods varying from 14 to 300 days depending upon the climate.

Management

Clean cultivation surrounding the orchard through destruction of pruned parts of cultivated as well as the wild bushes. Deep and through racking up of soil during hot summer to expose the residual pupa to hot summer. Use of resistance varieties like Tikadi, Katha and Illaichi for fruit fly management. The braconid: *Biostres vandenboschi*, *Bracon fletcheri* and *Omphalia* sp. The wasp parasitoid: *Fopius carpomyia* was found at larval stage of fruitfly and the ovipositor is very suitable to parasitize the hidden host in fruits. The extract of azadiractin 1% and *Ocimum sanctum* 1% were effective upto 10 days after spraying. Application of neem powder and tobacco leaf extracts would significantly reduce *C. vesuviana* damage. Bait spray combining molasses or jaggery 10 g/L and one of insecticides, malathion 50 EC 2 ml/L, dimethoate 30 EC 2 ml/L of two rounds at fortnight interval before ripening of the fruits.

❑ Ber stone weevil: *Aubeus himalayanus* Voss

Common name	:	Ber stone weevil
Scientific name	:	*Aubeus himalayanus* Voss
Family	:	Curculionidae
Order	:	Coleoptera

Source: *https://niphm.gov.in/IPMPackages/Ber.pdf*

Distribution and Host Range

Ber stone weevil, *Aubeus himalayanus* is an emerging pest of ber in arid and semi-arid region of India.

Nature and Symptoms of Damage

When damaged fruits are cut open, developing seed is completely eaten away by the pest. In the hollowed area, each of these fruits have a grub, a pupa or an adult which is identified as ber seed weevil. The infested fruits are round in shape and varied in size ranging from pea to pebble. The fruits do not attain maturity and never increase in size more than pebble.

Life History and Description

Black colour egg laid with marking in the stylar end of fruits. Mouth parts are converted into snout. The grubs are white in color. The adult is blackish color with abdomen rounded.

Management

Infested dropped fruits should be collected and burned to break the generation cycle. Deep and through racking up of soil during hot summer to expose the residual adult to hot summer. The varieties of ber like Kali, Katha, Illaichi and Tikadi were found resistant to stone weevil. Collection and destruction of adult weevil immediately after detection can also reduce the population. NSKE 5% and azadirachtin were also found to be superior in minimizing weevil incidence. Application of spinosad 2.5 SC and indoxacarb 14.5 EC or dimethoate 30 EC just before the fruit setting and repeat the sprays at three weeks interval.

❑ Ber butterfly: *Tarucus Theophrastus* (Fabricius, 1793)

Common name	:	Ber butterfly, Common tiger blue, Pointed Pierrot, African Pierrot
Scientific name	:	*Tarucus Theophrastus* (Fabricius, 1793)
Family	:	Lycaenidae
Order	:	Lepidoptera

Source: *https://upload.wikimedia.org/wikipedia/commons/thumb/d/d9/Moors_*

Distribution and Host Range

It is found in Northern and Western Africa, Arabia, Persia, Baluchistan, North Western Himalayas, Assam, Punjab, Western, Central and Southern India, Srilanka and Upper Burma.

Nature and Symptoms of Damage

The newly sprouting tender shoots and leaves are attacked by ber butterfly. Due to its attack, leaves dry up and tender shoots do not grow properly. Larvae feed on sprouting tender shoots, leaves and flower buds. Infested leaves give whitish look due to feeding of chlorophyll and finally the leaves remain with long streaks.

Life History and Description

Female upper side: dark brown; bases of the wings suffused with bluish scales. Fore wing: the transverse disco cellular spot continues posteriorly by a black spot in interspace to coalescent with a similar spot. The larva just half an inch in length when full grown, is much flattened, the head is pale ochreous and completely hidden under the second segment. Colour pale green, the whole upper surface is covered with a shagreening of small white tubercles.

Management

Spray of dimethoate 0.05%, deltamethrin 0.0014% and fenvalerate 0.0005% would be most effective against 3rd to 6th instar larvae. Quinalphos (0.05%) and triazophos (0.1%) were also effective against larval population and leaves damage.

Ber fruit borer: *Meridarchis scyrodes* Meyrick

Common name	:	Ber fruit borer
Scientific name	:	*Meridarchis scyrodes* Meyrick
Family	:	Carposinidae
Order	:	Lepidoptera

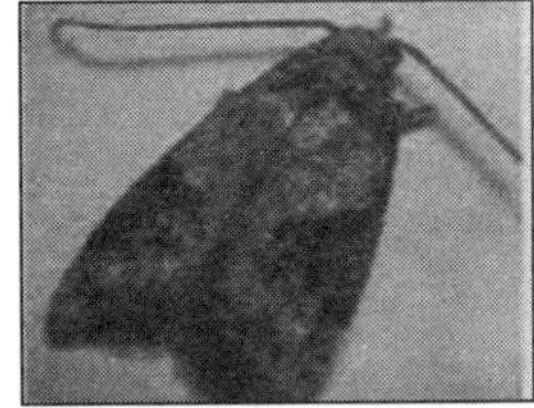

Source: *https://www.google.co.in/url?sa=i&url=https%3A%2F%2Fwww.thepharmajournal.com%*

Distribution and Host Range

It is distributed all over the country. It is not a major pest of Bikaner area but it is major in Sirohi, Jalore, Barmer districts of Rajasthan and Gujarat. It is a polyphagous pest and feeds on crops like ber, aonla etc.

Nature and Symptoms of Damage

The larva bores into the fruit feeding on the pulp and accumulates faecal frass within.

Life History and Description

Adult is a small dark brown moth. Eggs are laid on young fruits. Early instar larva is light yellowish and full-grown larva is red in colour. Pupation takes place in the soil. Adult emerges from the soil.

Management

Remove wild ber trees around the ber orchard. Rack the soil under tree or near trees to destroy the maggots and residual pupae present in the soil. Collection and proper destruction of infested fallen fruits. Harvest of fruits at immediate after maturity (green stage) and growing of resistant cultivars like Safeda, Illaichi and Tikadi found to have less incidence of fruit borer. The Neem Seed Kernel Extract (NSKE) at 5% found as effective as like synthetic chemicals. Methanol extracts of *Annona reticulata*, *Azadirachta indica* and *Ocimum sanctum* at 1% concentration recorded 60-70 % mortality after 48h after spray. Sprays of dimethoate 30 EC + jaggery solution (1.0%) at marble stage and one spray at maturation stage result in minimum infestation. Control schedule comprises of malathion at 2 ml or fenvalerate at 1 ml/lit of water first spray at marble stage, second spray at 15 days later and third spray at fruit ripening stage by alternate use of insecticides would be effective against the fruit borer.

Bark eating caterpillar: *Indarbela quadrinotata* (Walker, 1856)

Common name	:	Bark-eating caterpillar
Scientific name	:	*Indarbela quadrinotata* (Walker, 1856)
Family	:	Cossidae
Order	:	Lepidoptera

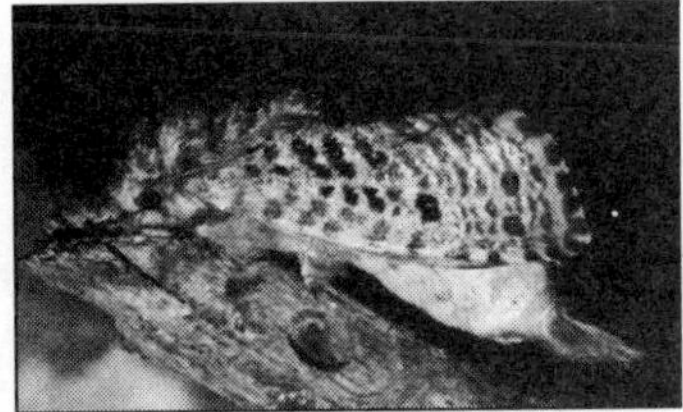

Source: *https://agritech.tnau.ac.in/crop_protection/guava/guava_5.html*

As Described in Mango

Termite: *Odontotermes obesus* (Rambur 1842)

Common name	:	Termite
Scientific name	:	*Odontotermes obesus* (Rambur 1842)
Family	:	Termitidae
Order	:	Blattodea

Source: *https://www.jaytaylorexterminating.com/blog/post/wilmington-s-complete-guide-to-termite-prevention*

As Described in Mango

Hairy Caterpillars: *Olene mendosa* Hübner, 1823; *Euproctis fraterna* Moore, 1883

Common name	:	Hairy Caterpillars
Scientific name	:	*Olene mendosa* Hübner, 1823; *Euproctis fraterna* Moore, 1883
Family	:	Erebidae
Order	:	Lepidoptera

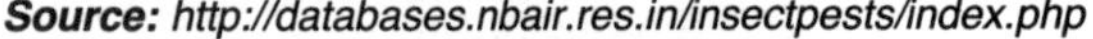

Source: *http://databases.nbair.res.in/insectpests/index.php*

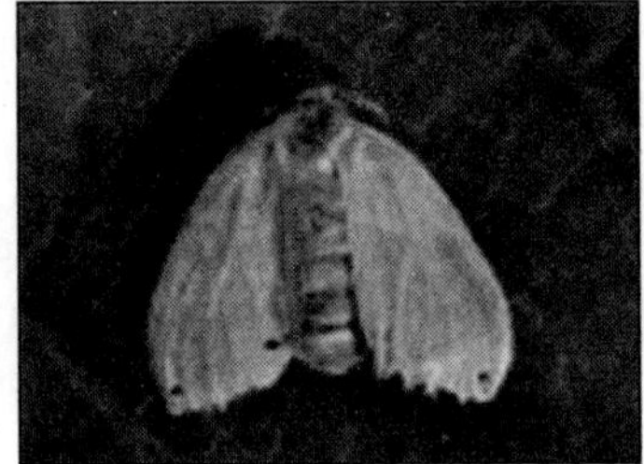

Source: *http://databases.nbair.res.in/insectpests/index.php*

Distribution and Host Range

It is found in India, Bangladesh, Sri Lanka, Indonesia, Taiwan, Thailand and Australia. Host range includes castor, linseed, groundnut pigeonpea, grapevine, cotton, pomegranate, mango, coffee, pear and rose.

Nature and Symptoms of Damage

Hairy caterpillars feed on the young leaves and fruits. The older caterpillars spread in all directions and devour leaves and fruits and sometimes even tender shoots. They start eating new foliage as it grows after pruning and this is continued by overlapping generations.

Life History and Description

The full-grown larva of *E. fraterna* is reddish brown with a dark brown head. The larva pupates on the plant in a yellowish, hairy cocoon from which a yellowish moth with pale transverse lines on the forewings emerges. It then lays flat, circular yellowish eggs in masses on the lower surface of the leaves. The females lay 92-241 eggs, which hatch in 9-14 days. As many as six generations each of 44-84 days duration have been observed in a year.

Management

BHC 10% can be dusted to control caterpillars in the young stages. All the instars were controlled by treatment with trichlorphon or 0.05% methyl parathion. Effective control of 3rd to 6th instar larvae by 0.005% cypermethrin, 0.0014% deltamethrin, 0.0075% fluvalinate and 0.0005% fenvalerate. A spray of 0.05% monocrotophos was found effective in controlling the pest.

Resistant Varieties

Umran: Umran is a high-yielding variety of ber that is resistant to fruit flies, scale insects, and mealybugs. It is a popular variety in the state of Rajasthan.

Gola: Gola is a popular variety of ber that is resistant to fruit flies. It is known for its sweet and juicy fruits and is grown extensively in the states of Maharashtra, Karnataka, and Andhra Pradesh.

Banarasi Karaka: Banarasi Karaka is a variety of ber that is resistant to fruit flies, mealybugs, and scale insects. It is a high-yielding variety and is grown in the Northern parts of India, particularly in Uttar Pradesh.

Kaithli: Kaithli is a variety of ber that is resistant to fruit flies and scale insects. It is a high-yielding variety and is grown in the states of Uttar Pradesh and Bihar.

Chhuhara: Chhuhara is a variety of ber that is resistant to fruit flies and scale insects. It is a popular variety in the state of Punjab.

Sanaur 1: This variety of Ber is resistant to the fruit fly pest and is also tolerant to drought. The fruit of this variety is small, sweet, and has a thick flesh.

Mundia: This variety of Ber is resistant to the fruit fly pest and is also tolerant to high humidity. The fruit of this variety is small, sweet, and has a good shelf life.

*These are just a few examples of Ber varieties that are resistant to insect pests, and there may be other varieties as well that have similar resistance.

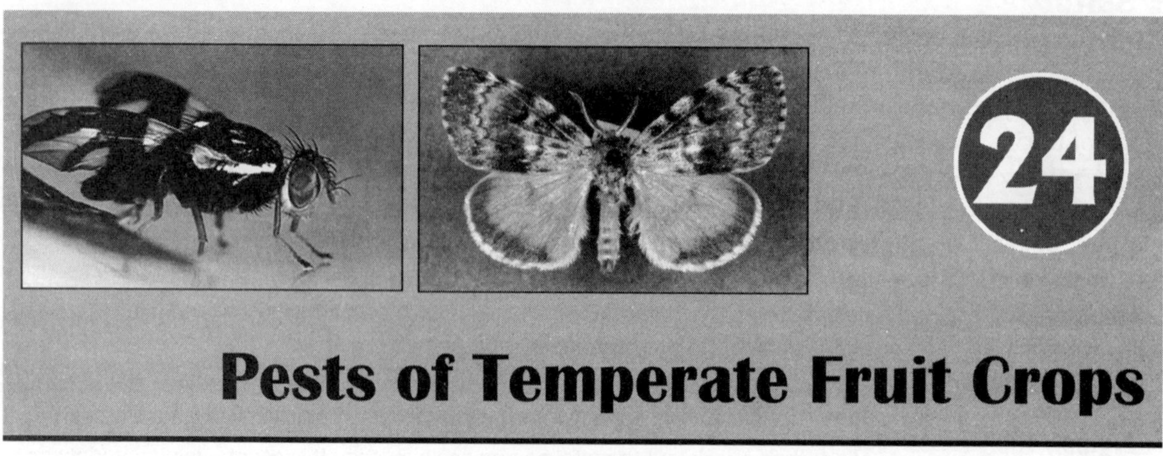

Pests of Temperate Fruit Crops

Temperate fruits are usually classified by their growth habit as tree fruits (apple, pear, peach), vine fruits (grape, kiwifruit), or small fruits (strawberry, raspberry, currant, and blueberry).

PESTS OF APPLE, PEAR, PEACH

Common name	Apple	Pear	Peach
Scientific name	*Malus domestica*	*Pyrus communis* L.	*Prunus persica*
Family	Rosaceae	Rosaceae	Rosaceae
Origin	Central Asia	China and Asia Minor	Eastern China
Chromosome number	2n = 34	2n = 16	2n = 16

Temperate fruit crops are those that grow in temperate regions with moderate to cool temperatures, including deciduous fruit trees such as apples, pears, plums, cherries, peaches, and apricots, as well as small fruits such as grapes, strawberries, raspberries, and blueberries. These crops are mainly grown in the temperate regions of the world, including Europe, North America, and parts of Asia, but are also grown in some parts of India where the climate is suitable.

In India, temperate fruits are grown in the states of Jammu and Kashmir, Himachal Pradesh, and Uttarakhand. The major temperate fruit crops grown in India are apples, pears, peaches, apricots, cherries, and plums. The total area under cultivation of these crops is around 245,000 hectares, and the total production is around 2.4 million tonnes.

Temperate fruit crops are susceptible to a variety of insect pests and diseases, which can significantly reduce yields and quality. Some of the major insect pests of temperate fruit crops include aphids, mites, leafhoppers, fruit flies, codling moths, and borers cause significant losses in fruit yield and quality. Integrated pest management practices, including the use of resistant varieties, cultural practices, and chemical control measures, are used to manage these pests and diseases in temperate fruit crops.

❑ San Jose scale: *Quadraspidiotus perniciosus* Comstock, 1881

Common name	:	San Jose scale
Scientific name	:	*Quadraspidiotus perniciosus* Comstock, 1881
Family	:	Diaspididae
Order	:	Hemiptera

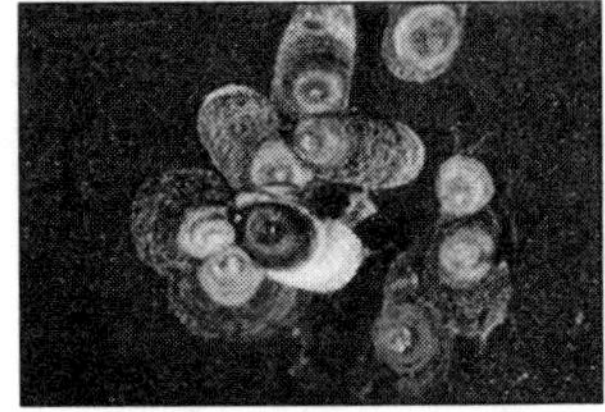

Source: *https://treefruit.wsu.edu/wp content/uploads/2017/03/OPM_SJSF5.jpg*

Distribution and Host Range

Q. perniciosus originated in Siberia, North East China and the Northern part of the Korean peninsula. It has spread to every continent except Antarctica and is a major pest of fruit trees.

Nature and Symptoms of Damage

Nymph and female scales attack all above ground parts. Feeding site turns into a characteristic purplish red colour. Initially growth of plant is checked but as scale increases in number, plant may die. Fruits will have distinct "measles" spots on the surface.

Life History and Description

Female scales give birth to 200-400 nymphs that emerge from under the edge of the scale covering. These tiny yellow crawlers upon settling, insert their mouthparts into host plant and begin feeding and secrete a white waxy material; eventually the waxy covering turns black and is known as the black cap stage. The male scale covering begins to elongate, while the females remain circular. Males molt a total of four times. Following the final molt, adult male scales emerge from the scale covering as tiny, yellow winged insects. They mate with the females who remain under the scale covering. Female insect is yellow lemon covered with grey scales. Female scales are very prolific and over a 6-week period can produce approximately 400 young. It takes 25 days for males to mature and 31 days for females. Five to six generations in a year.

Management

Select nursery stock free scale infestation. Pruning of infested branches and twigs. Collection and destruction of pruned infested material. Grow attractant flowers for natural enemies *viz.*, sunflower family, carrot family plants, buckwheat. Parasitoids such as *Encarsia perniciosi* and *Aphytis diaspidis* and coccinellid predators such as *Chilocorus infernalis*, *C. rubidus*, *Pharoscymnus flexibilis*. Spray malathion 50% EC @ 600-800 ml in 600-800 l of water/acre or oxydemetom-methyl 25% EC @ 1680-2240 ml in 600-800 l of water/acre or lime sulphur 22% SC @ 800-2000 ml/acre (use 2% pre-blossom and 1% post-blossom in conventional sprayers). Fumigate nursery stock with HCN gas or methyl bromide. Summer spray with phosalone 50 EC 0.05% or fenitrothion 50 EC 0.05%. Winter spray with diesel oil emulsion at 8-12 l/tree (diesel oil 4.5 l, soap 1 kg, water 54 -72 l).

❑ Woolly aphid: *Eriosoma lanigerum* (Hausmann)

Common name	:	Apple wooly aphid, wooly apple aphid
Scientific name	:	*Eriosoma lanigerum* (Hausmann)
Family	:	Aphididae
Order	:	Hemiptera

Source: *https://a-z-animals.com/animals/woolly-aphids/*

Distribution and Host Range

E. lanigerum is native to North America but it is now found in all of the regions of the world where apples are grown. It was first recorded from Great Britain in 1787.

Nature and Symptoms of Damage

Nymphs and adults suck cell sap from bark of twigs and from underground parts. Underground feeding produces large knots on roots. Heavily infested plants have a short fibrous root system and yellowish foliage which can be easily uprooted.

Life History and Description

The female laid a single, long, oval, cinnamon-colored egg in the crevices of bark. Eggs hatched in the spring into wingless, parthenogenetic, viviparous stem mothers. Nymphs hibernate underground on the roots of the tree. When elms are prevalent, eggs are usually laid in fall in the cracks or crevices of bark. These fed on elm buds and leaves for two generations during May and June, causing the elm leaves to curl into a rosette. They then produce a winged third generation that migrate to apple. After establishing new colonies the migrants produce repeated generations during the summer. Adult and nymphs are reddish brown in colour. Covered with waxy filaments, they feed in wounds on the trunk and branches of the tree. In fall, winged aphids develop in both aerial and root colonies. They flew back to elm, where they give birth to males and females. Both males and females are wingless. Each female produces 116 young ones. 13 generations are produced in a year.

Management

Use resistant root stocks M 778, M 779, MM 14, MM 110, MM 112. Conserve parasitoids such as *Aphelinus mali* and predators such as *Coccinella septumpunctata*, *Chrysoperla zastrowi sillemi*, *Menochilus sexmaculatus*, *Syrphus confrator*. Apply carbofuran 3% CG @ 166 g/tree or phorate 10% CG 100-150 g/tree or spray chlorpyrifos 20% EC @ 1500-2000 ml in 600-800 l of water/acre or malathion 50% EC @ 600-800 ml in 600-800 l of water/acre or oxydemetommethyl 25% EC @ 600-800 ml in 600-800 l of water/acre or quinalphos 25% EC @ 1200-1600 ml in 200-400 l of water/acre. Spray dimethoate 30 EC 0.06% or methyl demeton 25 EC 0.025%.

❑ Codling moth: *Cydia pomonella* (Linnaeus, 1758)

Common name	:	Codling moth
Scientific name	:	*Cydia pomonella* (Linnaeus, 1758)
Family	:	Tortricidae
Order	:	Lepidoptera

Source: *https://upload.wikimedia.org/wikipedia/commons/thumb/8/85/Cydia_pomonella_*

Distribution and Host Range

The origin of the codling moth is thought to be Eurasia, where both apples and walnuts originated. It spread along with its cultivated hosts throughout Europe and later to the Americas. Now it is common in most areas where apples, pears or walnuts are grown.

Nature and Symptoms of Damage

On apples, larvae penetrate into the fruit and tunnel to the core, leaving holes in the fruit that are filled with reddish-brown, crumbly droppings called frass. If left uncontrolled, larvae can cause substantial damage, often infesting 20 to 90% of the fruit, depending on the variety and location. Late maturing varieties are more likely to suffer severe damage than early varieties.

Life History and Description

Eggs are deposited singly on apples and leaves. Each egg is about the size of a pin head and is translucent, gradually darkening as the egg nears hatching. The number of eggs laid per female ranges from 30 to 70 and hatch in six to 14 days. The larvae burrow into the fruit. The first instar larvae have a pink body with a black head. Codling moth overwinters as full-grown larvae within thick, silken cocoons under loose scales of bark and in soil or debris around the base of the tree. Larvae appear to be cannibalistic. Full grown larva pinkish or creamy white with brown head and pupates in the soil litter. After completing development, they leave the fruit and drop from the trees to search out pupation sites and continue the life cycle in the soil or on debris under the tree; some crawl back up the tree to pupate in bark crevices. The moths are active only a few hours before and after sunset, and they mate when sunset temperatures exceed 62°F. Adults are about 1/2 to 3/4 inch long with mottled gray wings that they hold tent like over their bodies. Adult forewings are dark grayish with waxy lines with a copper-colored eye like circle toward margin.

Management

Field sanitation. Collect and destroy the infested fruits and cocoons. Banding – corrugated cardboard bands should be applied to tree trunks. Use sex pheromone trap. Mass trap males with codling moth lure traps. Release egg parasitoids, *Trichogramma embryophagum* at 2000/tree. Apply Virosoft CP4 Granulovirus. Spray DDVP 0.04%. Apply diazinon, acetamiprid during egg laying stage.

❑ Apple root borer: *Dorysthenes hugelii* (Redtenbacher, 1848)

Common name	:	Apple root borer
Scientific name	:	*Dorysthenes hugelii* (Redtenbacher, 1848)
Family	:	Cerambycidae
Order	:	Coleoptera

Source: *https://www.inaturalist.org/taxa/708055-Dorysthenes-huegelii/browse_photos*

Distribution and Host Range

The apple root borer, *Dorysthenes hugelii* is confined to foot hills of Himalayan range and is a serious pest of apple in Kumaon hills. The main host of this borer is living and dead roots of apple trees.

Nature and Symptoms of Damage

The grubs feed on the roots and internal tissues and girdle them, as a result the main roots are severely damaged from the base and the trees, if young, die away while the older ones become weak and fall down with strong winds.

Life History and Description

Female lays eggs singly or in small clusters in soil are 1.3 mm in size. Newly laid eggs are white with a tinge of yellow and become dark brown before hatching. Grubs are eruciform, yellowish-white in colour and have 8-9 instars feed on the root have longevity of 3.5 years. 10 larval stages develop over 20-21 months, with mature larvae almost reaching 80 mm in length and 12 mm in width. The pupae are about 48 mm long and usually found about 20-30 cm deep in the soil. Pupation takes place inside earthen cell in the soil. The adult beetle is chestnut red in color and bears long serrated antennae. Full grown grub is creamy white, 7.5-10 cm long.

Management

Avoid dry sandy soils for planting apple orchards. Inter culturing in the orchard helps in killing of grubs. Use well-rotted FYM and mix thoroughly with soil around the tree. Once infestation has occurred, it is important to treat the tree basins with phorate granules (10G) @ 100 grams per tree or carbofuran 3G @ 32.5 kg/ha in the soil.

❑ Stem borer: *Apriona cinera* Chevrolat, 1852

Common name	:	Poplar stem borer, apple stem borer
Scientific name	:	*Apriona cinera* Chevrolat, 1852
Family	:	Cerambycidae
Order	:	Coleoptera

Source:https://upload.wikimedia.org/wikipedia/commons/thumb/2/25/Apriona_cinerea_-_Female_

Distribution and Host Range

A. cinerea is native to the western ranges of the Himalayas and in the areas adjoining India and Pakistan. In India, they are found in North-western states, including Jammu and Kashmir, Himachal Pradesh, Uttarakhand, Uttar Pradesh, Haryana and Punjab.

Nature and Symptoms of Damage

Damage is caused by both grub and adult. Grub is more destructive and makes a tunnel and reaches close to trunk of tree. Vitality and productivity of plant is greatly impaired.

Life History and Description

Female lays egg inside cavity on a shoot or on the trunk of the tree. Larvae are dirty white with a reddish-brown head and thoracic shield. Grub emerges in 7-8 days and start feeding by boring inside the stem. Grub longevity 2 years. Grub remains quiescent during winter. Pupae are small, yellow-brown and observed as pupal cases partially protruding from the adult exit holes in the trunk. Pupation takes place inside a tunnel made in the woody tissue. Adult clearwing moths possess transparent wings with striking dark markings along the margins. Adult beetles are 35-50 mm long and grey in colour having long antennae.

Management

Keep the orchard healthy following good agricultural practices. Prune and burn all attacked shoot and branches during winter. Kill the stem borer larvae by inserting a flexible wire inside the hole and plug the hole with the cotton wick soaked in petrol and seal it with mud. Spray dimethoate 30% EC

@ 594-792 ml in 600-800 l of water/acre. Inject 10 ml of monocrotophos 36 WSC and plug with wet clay to kill the grub.

Indian gypsy moth: *Lymantria obfuscate* Walker, 1865

Common name	:	Indian gypsy moth
Scientific name	:	*Lymantria obfuscate* Walker, 1865
Family	:	Lymantriidae
Order	:	Lepidoptera

Source: *https://www.cabidigitallibrary.org/doi/10.1079/cabicompendium.31813*

Distribution and Host Range

L. obfuscate is found in the montane and sub-montane regions of South Western Himalayas, West and USA and Canada. It is a major pest of apple and apricot in Kashmir and Himachal Pradesh feeding on apple foliage. Besides apple it also causes serious damage to apricot, walnut, willow and poplar.

Nature and Symptoms of Damage

Caterpillars are gregarious but voracious feeder. They eat voraciously on leaves at night time. Under heavy infestation entire leaf is eaten sparing only hard vein. Defoliation of host completely results in failure of fruit formation.

Life History and Description

The egg mass is approximately 1.5 inches long and 0.75 inches wide. Eggs, 500 to 1000 are laid in sheltered areas such as underneath the bark of trees. Caterpillars have five pairs of blue dots followed by six pairs of red dots lining the back. Young caterpillars primarily feed during the day whereas the older caterpillars feed at night. Older caterpillars are approximately 1.5 to 2.0 inches long. Larval period 66-100 days. The pupae are dark brown, shell-like cases approximately two inches long and covered with hairs located in tree bark crevices or leaf litter. Adult emerge from the pupae in 10 to 14 days. Females have white to cream-colored wings, tan body, and two-inch wingspan. Both adult female and male can be identified by the inverted V-shape that points to a dot on the wings. Gypsy moth has only one generation per year.

Management

Egg mass covered with yellowish hair which is easily visible should be hunted and destroyed. Put a burlap at the base of tree trunk to provide shelter for larvae during day time and examine frequently to destroy the larvae underneath the burlap.

Blossom thrips: *Thrips carthami* Shumsher

Common name	:	Blossom thrips
Scientific name	:	*Thrips carthami* Shumsher
Family	:	Thripidae
Order	:	Thysanoptera

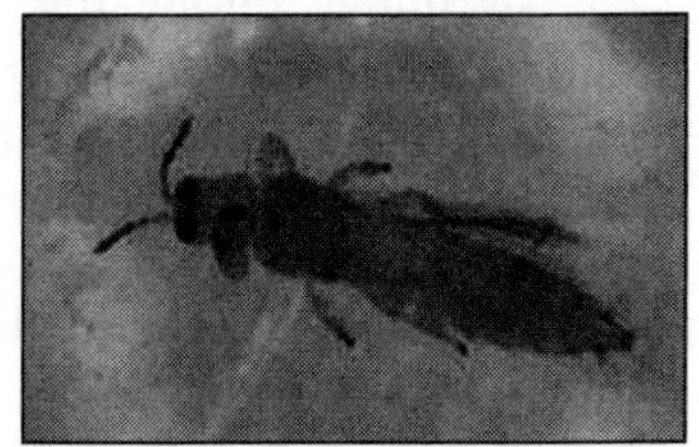

Source: *http://v3.boldsystems.org/pics/GMPPO/BIOUG70295-E11%2B1624979788.jpg*

Distribution and Host Range

Described from Kashmir, India and is recorded across Northern India to Southern China. Host range includes apples, cherries, pears, and plums etc.

Nature and Symptoms of Damage

The surface of the leaf develops a crinkled silvery appearance as a result of damage to cells below the surface. Lightly-infested plants show silvery feeding scars on the under surface of leaves, especially alongside the midrib and veins. Heavily-infested plants show silvering and browning of leaves, stunting of young leaves and terminal growth, with fruit scarred and deformed. Developing leaves become distorted in the growing tips.

Life History and Description

The eggs of thrips are deposited within plant tissues singly. Larvae have two stages, which feed on plant tissues. The second instar larvae, when mature, fall to ground, where they molt to prepupae and pupae in the soil. After emergence, the adults move to the growing parts of the plants such as young leaves, flowers, or young fruits, where they feed and lay 200 eggs. Adults are usually found on young leaves, while larvae are found on lower or older leaves. At 25°C, the life cycle is completed in approximately 17 days. Adults are winged sucking rasping insects ranging from 5-14 mm in length. Their slender bodies are shiny pale or black with silver stripes. Life cycle completed in 11-43 days.

Management

Spray thiacloprid 21.7% SC @ 0.4-0.5 ml/l of water.

❑ Tent caterpillar: *Malacosoma californicum* Packard, 1864

Common name	:	Tent caterpillar
Scientific name	:	*Malacosoma californicum* Packard, 1864
Family	:	Lasiocampidae
Order	:	Lepidoptera

Source: *https://www.butterfliesandmoths.org/species/Malacosoma-californicum*

Distribution and Host Range

Important pest of apple, in North Western India. Besides apple it also attacks poplar, alder, aspen, willow, oak, maple, mahogany, nine-bark, sumac, wild currant, serviceberry and wild rose.

Nature and Symptoms of Damage

Caterpillars during the night rest at their nest and the day they feed on leaves. In severe infestation, the entire plant may be defoliated and subsequently the caterpillar may feed on bark of twigs. When severe infestation 40 -50 per cent plants in orchard may be defoliated producing a poor harvest.

Life History and Description

In late spring or early summer, female moth's deposit egg mass (200 to 400) encircling small twigs or on tree trunks. The adult moth uses a sticky, frothy substance called spumaline as an adhesive to attach eggs to bark or twigs. Caterpillars hatch from eggs in early spring about the time host plants leaf out. The tent caterpillar feed on new leaves, forming small webs within a few days after hatching and enlarging the webs as they grow. Cocoons are formed in the web, under bark, in dead plant material on the ground, or inside a rolled leaf. Adult tent caterpillars are brown and yellowish moths with two diagonal markings on the front wings. The moths live for only a few days, during which they mate and lay eggs. There is only one generation of tent caterpillars per year. Male are short lived and female may survive for 2 to 5 days.

Management

Remove egg masses from twigs or other sites. Cut out infested twigs and dip in a bucket of soapy water. Tent caterpillars have many natural enemies. Some birds eat the caterpillars, and small mammals consume the pupae. The larvae of a tachinid fly parasitize the caterpillars.

❑ Apple maggot: *Rhagoletis pomonella* (Walsh, 1867)

Common name	:	Apple maggot
Scientific name	:	*Rhagoletis pomonella* (Walsh, 1867)
Family	:	Tephritidae
Order	:	Diptera

Source: *https://upload.wikimedia.org/wikipedia/commons/thumb/8/8f/Rhagoletis_pomonella.jpg/330px-Rhagoletis_pomonella.jpg*

Distribution and Host Range

It is a pest of apple across Eastern North America from Eastern North Dakota and Southern Manitoba to Nova Scotia, Southward to Eastern Texas to Central Florida, occurring over the entire middle and Eastern region of the United States.

Nature and Symptoms of Damage

Damage caused by maggots. Maggots are called “railroad” because they leave brown winding trail just under fruit skin. Burrowing of maggot sometime reduce apple to a brown rotten mass. Premature fall of infested fruits.

Life History and Description

Females lay about 300 eggs over a 30-day life span. Female flies lay their eggs singly in apples and other fruits. Apple maggot eggs hatch in 3 to 7 days as small, cylindrical, cream-coloured larvae known as maggots. Maggots are carrot shaped, white and legless. The apple maggot has one generation per year. Infested fruit fall to the ground; larvae leave the fruit, burrow into the soil, and molt into a fourth instar and then into a pupal stage to overwinter in the soil under the infested tree. In early summer, apple maggot flies emerge from the soil and forage in the host tree canopy. An apple maggot flies measures 1/4 inch long has a black body, dark red eyes, black and creamy-white striped abdomen and a white spot on the thorax between the pair of transparent wings.

Management

The systematic destruction of infested apples and the elimination of hawthorn and abandoned apple trees in the vicinity of orchards. Apple maggots in fruits may be killed by placing the fruit in cold storage at 32°F for a period of 40 days. Sticky traps, including yellow rectangles and red spheres, are used to monitor adults and time treatments. Hymenopterous larval parasites: *Rhagoletis pomonella* are braconid wasp, *Opius melleus*, and egg parasite: tiny mymarid wasp, *Patasson conotracheli*. Spray acetamiprid or beta-cyfluthrin or chlorantraniliprole.

❑ Root knot nematode: *Meloidogyne* spp. Goldi

Common Name	:	Root-knot nematode
Scientific Name	:	*Meloidogyne* spp. Goldi
Family	:	Heteroderidae
Order	:	Tylenchida

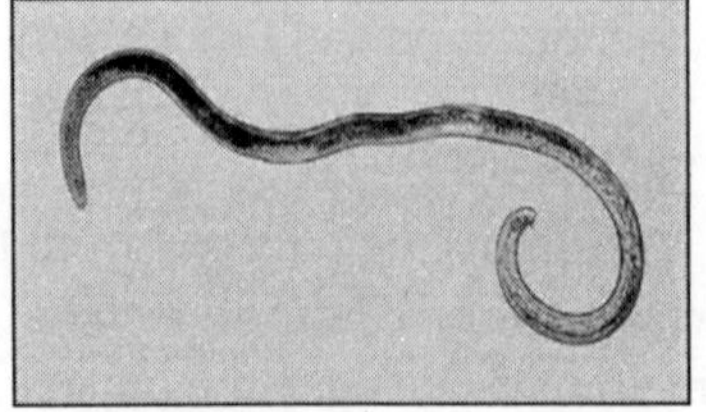

Source: *https://content.ces.ncsu.edu/management-of-root-knot-nematodes-in-bedding-plants*

As Described in Tomato

25 Pests of Kiwi Fruit

Scientific name	*Actinidia deliciosa* (A. Chev.) C.F. Liang & A.R. Ferguson
Family	Actinidiaceae
Origin	China
Chromosome number	2n = 174

Brown headed leaf roller: *Ctenopseustis obliquana* (Walker, 1863)

Common name	:	Brown headed leaf roller
Scientific name	:	*Ctenopseustis obliquana* (Walker, 1863)
Family	:	Tortricidae
Order	:	Lepidoptera

Source:https://upload.wikimedia.org/wikipedia/commons/thumb/a/a1/Ctenopseustis_obliquana_female.jpg/330px-Ctenopseustis_obliquana_female.jpg

Distribution and Host Range

Ctenopseustis obliquana is a native of New Zealand. The larvae feed on a wide range of plants, including various broadleaved and coniferous trees and ferns, *Eucalyptus*, *Quercus*, *Acacia*, *Larix*, *Picea*, *Pinus* and *Pseudotsuga* species.

Nature and Symptoms of Damage

Early instar larvae web together leaf edges or leaves and fruit to form a shelter to live in often rolling the leaves into a tube. Later instars feed on leaves, buds, and fruit of the host plant.

Life History and Description

Females lay eggs in smooth masses composed of up to 150 individual eggs. Larvae exhibited 5 or 6 instars. Pupation occurs in the larval nest. The larval head is dark brown to reddish brown and marked with faint red mottling. Adults are brown to brownish gray with a variable wing pattern. Most individuals have several dark markings along the costa, including a remnant of the median fascia. Hind wings are mottled in both males and females. It completes 4-6 overlapping generations per year.

Management

Provide irrigation at critical stages of the plant and avoid water logging. Collection and destruction of eggs and early-stage larvae and crop debris. Conserve natural enemies through ecological engineering. Augmentative release of natural enemies. Predators: Predatory mite, Predatory Wasp. Larval parasitoids: *Trigonospila brevifacies*, Braconid wasp, *Dolichogenidea tasmanica*, *Goniozus jacintae*.

❑ Green headed leaf roller: *Planotortrix excessana* (Walker, 1863)

Common name	:	Green headed leaf roller
Scientific name	:	*Planotortrix excessana* (Walker, 1863)
Family	:	Tortricidae
Oder	:	Lepidoptera

Source: *https://idtools.org/id/leps/tortai/Planotortrix_excessana.htm*

Distribution and Host Range

P. excessana native to New Zealand feed on many forest, orchard and garden shrubs and trees. It prefers trees with broad leaves or needles, *Eucalyptus* species, *Sequoia sempervirens*, *Pinus* species, *Pseudotsuga menziesii*, *Dicksonia squarrosa*, *Metrosideros diffusa* and *Peraxilla tetrapetala*.

Nature and Symptoms of Damage

They web together leaf edges or leaves and fruit to form a shelter to live in often rolling the leaves into a tube. The caterpillars eat leaves and fruit.

Life History and Description

Females lay eggs in masses that have an opaque coating. Egg development- 11 days. Last instar larval head is transparent light brown to green and may have faint brown mottling. The prothoracic shield is pale green with no lateral shading. Pupation takes place within the webbed foliage. Forewings are pale orange brown to dark reddish brown. Males are generally darker than females. Most individuals lack prominent wing markings except for a dark spot in the distal one-third of the forewing. Some individuals have a series of faint dark spots covering the wing and/or a white or pale spot in the basal one-third of the wing. Males have a forewing costal fold.

Management

Destroy crop debris, eggs and early-stage larvae. Provide irrigation at critical stages of the plant and avoid water logging. Conserve natural enemies through ecological engineering. Augmentative release of natural enemies. Predators: Predatory mite, Predatory Wasp. Larval parasitoids: *Trigonospila brevifacies*, Braconid wasp, *Dolichogenidea tasmanica*, *Goniozus jacintae*.

❑ Greedy scale: *Hemiberlasia rapax* (Comstock, 1881)

Common name	:	Greedy scale
Scientific name	:	*Hemiberlasia rapax* (Comstock, 1881)
Family	:	Diaspididae
Order	:	Hemiptera

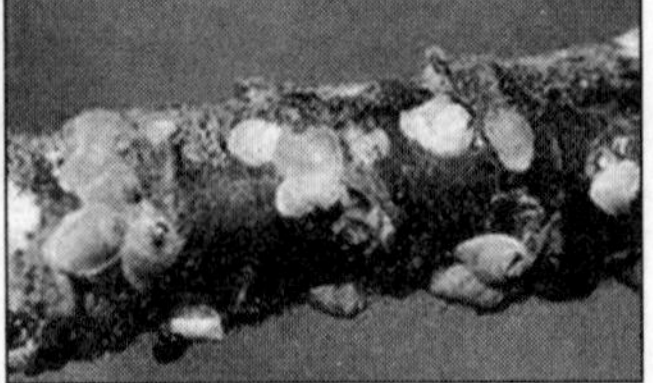

Source: *https://www.biodiversidadvirtual.org/insectarium/data/media/9244/Hemiberlesia-rapax-414336.jpg*

Distribution and Host Range

Greedy scale is found in all tropical regions of the world. Hosts of the greedy scale include acacia koa, apple, avocado, azalea, bamboo, chinaberry, citrus, coconut palm, *Ficus* sp., geranium, guava, peach, pear, persimmon, plumeria, rose.

Nature and Symptoms of Damage

Scale insects attack the bark and fruit of kiwi. Infestations are spread by mobile, young scale nymphs or 'crawlers' while older nymphs and adults are sedentary. Heavy infestations affect the vigor of the plant and result in the presence of scales on fruit, causing it to be off grade.

Life History and Description

Eggs are laid under armor of the female where they develop and hatch. The crawler stage is short, and do not feed. Newly settled nymphs insert their piercing, sucking mouthparts into plant tissue and start feeding on plant juices. Female nymphs shed their skin twice as they grow and develop. Males have a 5-stage development and do not feed during the last two stages. The cast skins, called exuviae, are incorporated into the armor forming a dot near the center. Female greedy scales appear larvae-like remain under armor in one place throughout their lives to feed and reproduce. Males are tiny, winged creatures with eyes and legs. They do not feed, living only a few hours to mate.

Management

Provide irrigation at critical stages of the plantand avoid water logging. Collection and destruction of eggs and early-stage larvae and crop debris. Conserve natural enemies through ecological engineering. Augmentative release of natural enemies. Parasitoids: *Aphytis* wasps, *Encarsia* sp. Predators: Green lacewings, Minute pirate bugs, and Ladybird beetle, *Chilocorus bipustulatus*, *C. infernalis*, *C. cacti*.

❑ Passion vine hopper: *Scolypopa australis* (Walker, 1851)

Common name	:	Passion vine Hopper
Scientific name	:	*Scolypopa australis* (Walker, 1851)
Family	:	Ricaniidae
Order	:	Hemiptera

Source: *https://www.citscihub.nz/Phil_Bendle_Collection:Hopper_%28Passionvine%29_Scolypopa_australis*

Nature and Symptoms of Damage

They suck sap from succulent shoots and the result is distortion of fruit and leaves. Plants will get stunted, wilted and dieback overall. Because of the copious production of honeydew, the likelihood of sooty mould is very high.

Life History and Description

Passion vine hopper overwinters as an egg, with this stage lasting about six months. The eggs are inserted in plant stems, with relatively soft, dead or dying stems. The nymph stage lasts about three months are greenish with a fluffy tail. The adult stage lasts about 3-5 months look for light brown small moths.

Management

Collection and destruction of eggs and early-stage larvae and crop debris. Provide irrigation at critical stages of the plant and avoid water logging. Conserve natural enemies through ecological engineering. Augmentative release of natural enemies. Egg parasitoids: *Scolypopa australis*. Predators: Spider, birds.

❑ Thrips: *Heliothrips haemorrhoidalis* (Bouché, 1833)

Common name	:	Greenhouse thrips, glasshouse thrips, black tea thrips
Scientific name	:	*Heliothrips haemorrhoidalis* (Bouché, 1833)
Family	:	Thripidae
Order	:	Thysanoptera

Source:https://thrips.info/wiki/Heliothrips_haemorrhoidalis

Distribution and Host Range

H. haemorrhoidalis is widely distributed in tropic and subtropic regions. Greenhouse thrips are found on wild and cultivated plants. This thrips is found on crotons, ardisia, avocado, azalea, dahlias, dogwood, ferns, Chinese banyan, guavas, hibiscus, natal plum, magnolia, mangoes, maple, orchids, palms, philodendron, phlox, pinks, viburnum and many other ornamentals.

Nature and Symptoms of Damage

Thrips uses its mouth-parts to rasp the leaf surface, rupture the epidermal cells, and feed on exuding cell contents. Feeding spots turn yellow then brown, and the surrounds become silvery where air enters the emptied cells.

Life History and Description

Female insert microscopic eggs inside plant tissues above the soil surface. Whitish larval stage with red eyes; turn yellowish in color with maturity but retain red eyes. Pre-pupa and pupa are whitish to slightly yellow. The larval abdomen is up-turned and has a dot of excrement on it. Adults have blackish-brown body with lighter posterior abdominal segments and white legs. Four translucent wings with numerous fringes surrounding each wing, folded back over the thorax and abdomen when at rest.

Management

Sprinkle water over the seedlings to check the multiplication of thrips. Release or augment the biological control agents like larval parasitoids- *Thripobius semiluteus* and predators like Predatory mite, predatory thrips, hover fly, mirid bug etc. Spray malathion.

❑ Red spider mite: *Tetranychus urticae* C. L. Koch, 1836

Common Name	:	Red spider mite; Two-spotted spider mite
Scientific Name	:	*Tetranychus urticae* Koch; *Tetranychus cinnabarinus* Boisduval
Family	:	Tetranychidae
Order	:	Trombidiformes

Source: *https://www.cabidigitallibrary.org/doi/10.1079/cabicompendium.30965*

As Described in Tomato

26 Pests of Strawberry

Scientific name	*Fragaria ananassa*
Family	Rosaceae
Origin	Europe
Chromosome number	2n = 56

Leaf roller: *Ancylis comptana* (Frölich, 1828)

Common name	:	Strawberry leaf-roller, Comptan's ancylis moth
Scientific name	:	*Ancylis comptana* (Frölich, 1828)
Family	:	Tortricidae
Order	:	Lepidoptera

Source: *https://upload.wikimedia.org/wikipedia/commons/thumb/a/a0/Ancylis_comptana*

Distribution and Host Range

Strawberry leafroller is found from the United Kingdom and Scandinavia to Northern Spain and Turkey, Asia Minor, Kazakhstan, Uzbekistan, Russia, China, Mongolia, Korea and Japan. The larvae feed on strawberry, raspberry, salad burnet, white dryas, and Thymus.

Nature and Symptoms of Damage

It ties one or more strawberry leaves together with white webbing to create shelters. Larvae can also create shelters by binding leaves or the sepals of the calyx to fruit and may feed from these sheltered areas on the surface or internal tissues of fruit.

Life History and Description

Adult moths have a wingspan of 10 to 13 mm. Forewings are light to dark reddish brown, with lighter tan and white areas streaked with darker brown, particularly on distal ends. Hindwings are gray. The eggs are oval and attached to the leaf surface. The larvae progress through five instars. The pupae change from yellowish to dark brown over time. For early instars, the head is brown and the body is pale green, but in later instars the head is a yellowish brown and the body is gray-brown, with a gray underside. Eggs are laid singly on the undersides of leaves; a female lays 20-120 eggs in her lifetime. After an incubation period of 5-17 days, first instars feed on leaf tissue and spin a silky covering near the base of the leaf between two prominent veins. Larvae migrate to the tops of leaves and begin to fold and roll them together. Pupae are formed within the leaf roll.

Management

Remove accumulated dead plant material where larvae may overwinter, and remove leaves that show signs of damage. Parasitoid species, *Itoplectis conquisitor*, *Pediobus facialis*, *Macrocentrus ancilovorous* and *Cremastes cookie* and predators on larvae include the bugs *Nabis americoferus* and *Podisus maculiventris*.

❑ White grub: *Phyllophaga* spp. (Harris)

Common name	:	White grub, May beetles, June bugs, July beetles
Scientific name	:	*Phyllophaga* spp. (Harris)
Family	:	Scarabaeidae
Order	:	Coleoptera

Source: *https://upload.wikimedia.org/wikipedia/commons/thumb/0/09/Phyllophaga_*

Distribution and Host Range

Phyllophaga spp. and related insects are distributed throughout the United States and Canada. However, the distribution of individual species usually is more restricted.

Nature and Symptoms of Damage

Plants affected by this insect can show early signs of wilting, remain small, weak, and both yield and fruit quality is affected. Soil disclosure at the bottom, the larva is seen gathering on the roots. If large numbers of insects are present, plants may die.

Life History and Description

Small masses of 15 to 20 eggs occur in cells in the soil hatch in 3 to 4 weeks. A dull pearly white when first deposited, the oval to spherical egg turns dark just before hatching. Newly hatched grubs feed on plant roots throughout the summer and complete 1/3 of their development before fall. These grubs burrow below the frostline (to a depth of 1.5 meters) and hibernate. The young grub is creamy white and the C-shaped grub has a distinct brown head; a shiny, smooth body; and three pairs of legs just behind the head. Grubs dig cells in the soil and pupate. Approximately the same size as the adult, the pupa may be creamy white, pale yellow, or dark brown. White grubs complete one generation every 3 years.

Management

Collection and destruction of adult beetles in soapy water. Good cultivation before planting will injure grubs and expose them to birds and the sun. Installation of light trap. Leave one or two rows of strawberry plants to serve as a trap before plowing infested plantings under shortly after harvest. Rotate strawberry sites yearly with lettuce or cole crops. Soil solarization.

Western flower thrips: *Frankliniella occidentalis* Pergande, 1895

Common name	:	Western flower thrips
Scientific name	:	*Frankliniella occidentalis* Pergande, 1895
Family	:	Thripidae
Order	:	Thysanoptera

Source:*http://databases.nbair.res.in/insectpests/index.php*

Distribution and Host Range

The western flower thrips is an invasive pest insect in agriculture. This species of thrips is native to the Southwestern United States but has spread to other continents, including Europe, Australia, and South America via transport of infested plant material. Western flower thrips is a polyphagous species with host plants as alfalfa, apricots, artichoke, carnations, chrysanthemum, corn, cotton, cucumber, eggplant, gerbera, gladiolus, grapefruit, grapes, impatiens, melons, nectarines, peaches, peanut, peas, pepper, plums, Spanish needle, strawberry, tomato, watermelon, and wild radish.

Nature and Symptoms of Damage

Both nymphs and adult thrips can injure the plant by rasping the plant bud, flower, leaf tissues and then suck the exuding sap. Thrips feed on strawberry blossoms cause the stigmas and anthers to turn brown and wither prematurely, but not before fertilization. With high populations, surface of the berry may become cracked and discolored. Fruit damage includes surface russeting around planting materials from late green to ripe fruit. Larvae and adult thrips will be sucking on the fruits and brown scaly sucking patches round the planting materials.

Life History and Description

Eggs are laid in plant tissue, both in flower bottoms and in leaves. In the pre-pupating stage, the greater part of the thrips drops on the ground and looks for some dirt or creep under plastic to pupate. The adult thrips will move to plants again and after a number of days they will start laying eggs. Adult thrips wings are fringed with setae, small hairs.

Management

Monitor with sticky traps. Crop rotation should be adopted to avoid the pest infestation, especially with legumes and cow pea. Destroy refuse from the old orchards after harvest to reduce pest infestation. In hill system, renew the beds after harvesting of first fruiting season if pest population is there. If no problem is there maintaining the orchard for 4-6 years old depending on profitability of crop.

Red Spider mite: *Tetranychus urticae* C. L. Koch, 1836

Common Name	:	Red spider mite; Two-spotted spider mite
Scientific Name	:	*Tetranychus urticae* Koch; *Tetranychus cinnabarinus* Boisduval
Family	:	Tetranychidae
Order	:	Trombidiformes

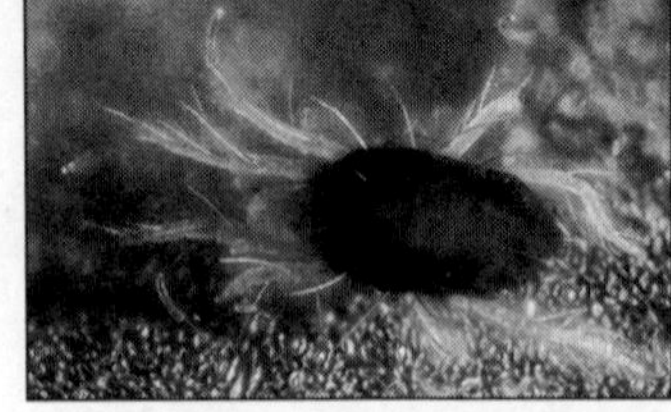

Source: *https://www.cabidigitallibrary.org/doi/10.1079/cabicompendium.30965*

As Described in Tomato

Pests of Raspberry

Scientific name	*Rubus idaeus* L.
Family	Rosaceae
Origin	Asia Minor and North America
Chromosome number	2n = 14

❑ Epilachna beetle/Hadda beetle/Spotted leaf beetle: *Henosepilachna vigintioctopunctata* (Fabricius, 1775)

Common name	:	Epilachna beetle, Hadda beetle, Spotted leaf beetle, 28-spotted potato ladybird
Scientific name	:	*Henosepilachna vigintioctopunctata* (Fabricius, 1775)
Family	:	Coccinellidae
Order	:	Coleoptera

Source: *https://upload.wikimedia.org/wikipedia/commons/9/99/Henosepilachna_vigintioctopunctata.jpg*

As Described in Potato

❑ Raspberry fruit borer: *Oberea bimaculata* Olivier, 1795

Common name	:	Raspberry cane borer
Scientific name	:	*Oberea bimaculata* Olivier, 1795
Family	:	Cerambycidae
Order	:	Coleoptera

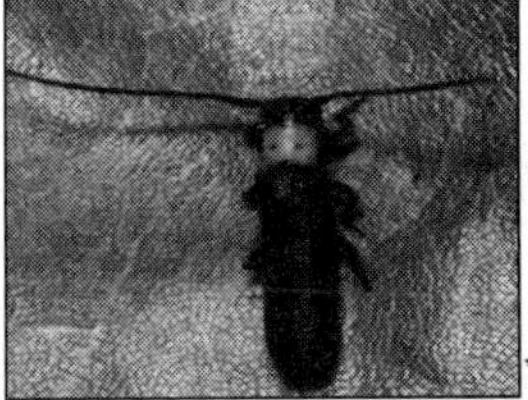

Source: *https://ag.umass.edu/fruit/fact-sheets/raspberry-ipm-raspberry-cane*

Distribution and Host Range

Raspberry cane borers have a wide distribution and are found all over the Southeastern United States. The main host plants are species of raspberries and blackberries. These raspberry cane borers are known to damage roses as well.

Nature and Symptoms of Damage

The damage caused by raspberry cane borers is very distinctive. The two rings of holes made by female borers are often visible to the naked eye. The plant tissue between the rings eventually dies and the shoots above this point will wilt. The growing tips of canes dying back, look for the two rings of holes just below the wilted parts. They are roughly 1 inch apart, and the cane often breaks easily at this point.

Life History and Description

Eggs are spherical, dome-shaped with a flat base, yellowish and turn brownish as the embryo develops. They are laid singly on tender leaves and take 2-4 days for hatching. Full grown larva are green, pale yellow, pale brown or greyish but always with a dark stripe on the lateral sides of the body. Body also bears inconspicuous tubercles and scattered small hairs. There are 6 larval instars and the entire larval development takes 20-25 days. Pupation takes place in the soil. Pupal period is 10-15 days. Adult moths are medium sized, with a wing span of 3-4 cm. They are extremely variable in colour from buff to light brownish to greyish-brown, marked with dark greyish irregular lines on the fore wing and a broad blackish band near the outer margin. Hind wing is dull whitish in colour, with outer margin broadly black.

Management

Scout raspberries at least once a week in June and July for signs of cane borers. Look for the two rings of holes below any wilted tips. Pruning and destroying symptomatic canes several inches below the lower ring is the most effective way of managing this pest. Infested canes should be burned or disposed of far from the growing site. Eliminate wild *Rubus* species from the vicinity of the planting as thoroughly as possible.

❑ Spotted cutworm: *Xestia c-nigrum* (Linnaeus, 1758)

Common name	:	Spotted cutworm
Scientific name	:	*Xestia c-nigrum* (Linnaeus, 1758)
Family	:	Noctuidae
Order	:	Lepidoptera

Source: *https://upload.wikimedia.org/wikipedia/commons/thumb/d/de/Xestia.c-nigrum.7381.jpg/330px-Xestia.c-nigrum.7381.jpg*

Distribution and Host Range

It is a common species throughout Europe and North Asia and Central Asia, South Asia, China, Japan and Korea. It is also found in North America, from coast to coast across Canada and the Northern United States to Western Alaska. Host plants include arrot, celery, cotton, crucifers, flax, grape vine, legumes, tobacco, tomato.

Nature and Symptoms of Damage

Larvae feed on leaves, sever seedlings and eat roots.

Life History and Description

Adult forewing is purplish grey or purplish fuscous with a leaden gloss; costal area at middle ochreous, merged with the bluntly triangular orbicular stigma: cell, a submedian basal blotch, and costal spot before apex purplish black; claviform stigma minute; reniform large, the lower lobe purplish; hindwing ochreous whitish, in female with the termen broadly fuscous. Larva pink with a broad dark brown subdorsal band. A lateral yellow band with a brown spot on it. Head reddish brown in color.

Management

Control weeds, grasses, and debris that provide cover. Capture spotted cutworm moths in blacklight traps. Encourage natural enemies of cutworms like birds and spiders. Lacewing, lady beetle, spider, fire ant, dragon flies, robber fly, reduviid bug, praying mantis, black drongo, wasp, common mynah (King crow), big-eyed bug, earwig, ground beetle, pentatomid bug.

❑ Aphids: *Amphorophora idaei* (Börner, 1939)

Common name	:	Aphids
Scientific name	:	*Amphorophora idaei* (Börner, 1939)
Family	:	Aphididae
Order	:	Hemiptera

Source: *https://www.google.co.in/url?sa=i&url=https%3A%2F%2Finfluentialpoints.com%2FGallery%*

Distribution and Host Range

Raspberry can be colonised by the large raspberry aphid in Northern and Western Europe.

Nature and Symptoms of Damage

This aphid rarely produces any visible damage to leaves and stems. The most obvious evidence of attack is the presence of sticky honeydew on leaves, laterals, flowers and fruits positioned immediately below aphid colonies. The aphids can become so numerous that they colonise the main stems of primocanes. Dense colonies are usually very restless and aphids are easily detached from plants during harvest. They can then readily contaminate the harvested fruit.

Life History and Description

Eggs laid the previous autumn hatch in March/April and develop into asexual female aphids which feed on the tips of developing buds and laterals, often those located on the tops of the fruiting canes. As the summer progresses the spring adults give rise to several generations of wingless aphids, initially feeding on the fruiting cane. Just prior to harvest, winged aphids appear and migrate onto primocanes under the fruiting cane and to other feeding sites within the existing and other nearby plantations. In late summer/autumn males and females are produced and, after mating, eggs are laid close to the base of the current season's primocanes.

Management

Remove and destroy all the infected leaves, twigs and fruits to prevent further spread of pests. Deep summer ploughing to expose soil inhabiting or resting stage of various stages of insect pests. In summer, keep the vines open, avoid crowding and excessive shading of vines. Plant the crop in well prepared, fertile land, but do avoid applying nitrogenous fertilizer, as this will promote new growth, which makes the plants juicy and attractive to aphids. Collect and destroy different developmental stages of insect pests. Conserve predators such as ladybird beetle, syrphids, coccinellids, chrysopids, wasp, surface bugs, spiders, different species of parasitic wasps and predatory mites through ecological engineering.

☐ Red spider mite: *Tetranychus urticae* C. L. Koch, 1836

Common Name	:	Red spider mite; Two-spotted spider mite
Scientific Name	:	*Tetranychus urticae* Koch; *Tetranychus cinnabarinus* Boisduval
Family	:	Tetranychidae
Order	:	Trombidiformes

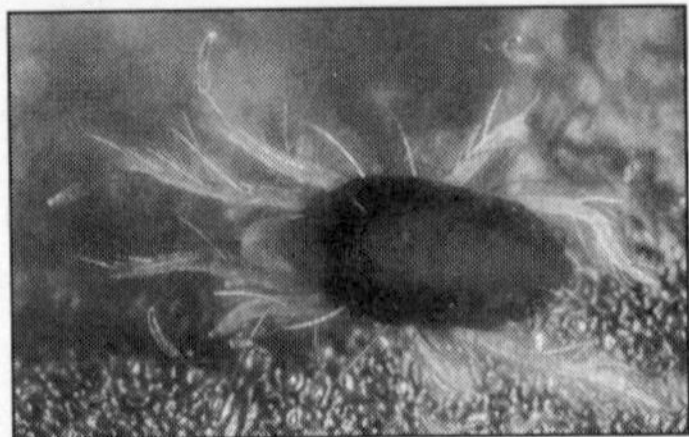

Source: *https://www.cabidigitallibrary.org/doi/10.1079/cabicompendium.30965*

As Described in Tomato

Resistant Varieties	
World	**India**
Honeycrisp apple: This apple variety is known to be resistant to apple scab, a fungal disease that can cause significant damage to apple crops. **Liberty apple:** Another apple variety that is resistant to apple scab, as well as powdery mildew and cedar apple rust. **Aurora pear:** This pear variety is resistant to fire blight, a bacterial disease that can cause significant damage to pear trees. **Montmorency cherry:** This cherry variety is resistant to fruit flies, which can damage the fruit. **Stanley plum:** This plum variety is resistant to brown rot, a fungal disease that can damage fruit. **Harcot apricot:** This apricot variety is resistant to bacterial canker, a disease that can cause significant damage to apricot trees. **Redhaven peach:** This peach variety is resistant to peach leaf curl, a fungal disease that can cause significant damage to peach trees.	**Apples:** Some of the apple varieties that are resistant to insect pests in India include Red Delicious, Golden Delicious, Granny Smith, Gala, and Rome Beauty. These varieties are less susceptible to common pests like apple maggot, codling moth, and apple scab. **Pears:** Some of the pear varieties that are resistant to insect pests in India include Bartlett, Anjou, Bosc, and Comice. These varieties are less susceptible to pests like pear psylla, mites, and leafrollers. **Plums:** Some of the plum varieties that are resistant to insect pests in India include Santa Rosa, Stanley, Methley, and Shiro. These varieties are less susceptible to pests like plum curculio and Japanese beetle. **Cherries:** Some of the cherry varieties that are resistant to insect pests in India include Bing, Rainier, Lambert, and Montmorency. These varieties are less susceptible to pests like cherry fruit fly and plum curculio. **Peaches:** Some of the peach varieties that are resistant to insect pests in India include Red Haven, Elberta, Cresthaven, and Julyprince. These varieties are less susceptible to pests like oriental fruit moth and peachtree borer. **Apricots:** Some of the apricot varieties that are resistant to insect pests in India include Goldcot, Moorpark, and Perfection. These varieties are less susceptible to pests like plum curculio and borers.

PART C

PESTS OF PLANTATION CROPS

U. Mahesh
(Ph.D. Scholar)
Department of Plantation, Spices, Medicinal and Aromatic Crops
Dr. YSR Horticultural University, Thadepalligudem
West Godavari, Andhra Pradesh

Pests of Coconut

Scientific Name	*Cocos nucifera*
Family	Arecaceae
Origin	South East Asia
Chromosome Number	2n = 32

Coconut (*Cocos nucifera*) is a tropical fruit tree that belongs to the family Arecaceae. It is widely grown in tropical and subtropical regions, including India, the Philippines, Indonesia, and Thailand. In India, coconut is grown in several states, including Kerala, Tamil Nadu, Andhra Pradesh, Karnataka, and Maharashtra. According to the Ministry of Agriculture and Farmers' Welfare, the total area under coconut cultivation in India is around 2.16 million hectares, and the total production is around 21.88 billion coconuts. India is the third-largest producer of coconut in the world, after Indonesia and the Philippines.

The major pests and diseases that affect coconut production are the red palm weevil, Rhinoceros beetle, coconut mite, black-headed caterpillar, and leaf-eating caterpillar. These pests can cause significant damage to the coconut tree, resulting in reduced yield and quality of coconut. To control these pests, various management strategies are employed, including the use of chemical pesticides, biocontrol agents, and cultural practices.

❑ Rhinoceros beetle: *Oryctes rhinoceros* (Linnaeus, 1758)

Common Name	:	Elephant beetle; Hercules beetle; Atlas beetle
Scientific Name	:	*Oryctes rhinoceros* (Linnaeus, 1758)
Family	:	Scarabaeidae
Order	:	Coleoptera

Source: *https://upload.wikimedia.org/*

Distribution and Host Range

Oryctes rhinoceros is one of the most damaging insects to palms in Asia and the Pacific Islands. Adults eat the leaves and burrow into the crown, stunting plant development. It is one of the most damaging insects to coconut palm and African oil palm in South and Southeast Asia and the Western Pacific Islands. In India, the infestation in oil palm was more prevalent in mature plantations (10-15 years old) compared to immature or younger plantings. It has a wide distribution in Asia, Australia and Pacific Islands and is reported from all regions where coconut is grown. It attacks coconut, oil palm, date palm, sugarcane, banana, sisal, pineapple, papaya etc.

Nature and Symptoms of Damage

Adult beetles cause severe damage to young as well as old trees. The beetles live in crevices between the leaf sheaths near the crown and burrow into the softer portion feeding on the unopened fronds and inflorescence. The beetles chew the internal tissues and after injecting the juicy part throws out the fibrous part which comes out of holes is an indication for the presence of beetle in the crown. The infested fully opened fronds showing the characteristic 'v' shaped cuts on leaf lets. The young seedlings are often killed when the growing points are damaged. The repeated attack in old trees causes stunting of growth and present sickly appearance to the trees. Bore holes with chewed fibre sticking out at the base of central spindle is the typical symptom of attack.

Life History and Description

The adult beetle is black, stout measures 5 cm long and has a long horn projecting dorsally from the head. The horn is longer in male and shorter in female beetle. The female lays globular eggs singly in decaying organic matter such as manure pits, dead tree trunks compost heaps. The fecundity of the insect is 140-150 eggs per female. The egg period is 8-18 days. The newly hatched grub feeds on decaying organic matter. The grown-up grub is stout, white, 'C shaped, sluggish and has a pale brown head. The larval period is 100-180 days. It pupates in earthen cells at a depth of 30-90 cm or more. The pupal stage lasts for 10-25 days. The adults make their way out and fly to the trees and live for more than 200 days.

Management

Remove and burn all dead coconut trees in the garden to maintain good sanitation. Collect and destroy the various bio-stages of the beetle from the manure pits whenever manure is lifted from the pits. Application of green muscardine fungus, *Metarrhizium anisopliae* @ 5×10^{11} spores/m^3 – spray 250 ml *Metarrizhium* culture + 750 ml water in manure pits to check the perpetuation of the pest. Field release of Baculovirus oryctes inoculated adult rhinoceros beetle @ 15 beetles/ha reduces the leaf and crown damage caused by this beetle. Soak castor cake at 1 kg in 5 liter of water in small mud pots and keep them in the coconut gardens to attract and kill the adults. Apply mixture of either neem seed powder + sand (1:2) @150 g per palm or neem seed kernel powder + sand (1:2) @150 g per palm in the base of the 3 inner most leaves in the crown. During peak period of population build up, the adult beetle may be extracted from the palm crown using **GI hooks**. Set up light traps following the first rains in summer and monsoon period to attract and kill the adult beetles. The topmost three leaf axils around the spindle may be filled with any of the following mixtures as a prophylactic measure: Sevidol 8G 25 g + fine sand 200 g, which is to be done thrice in a year in April-May, September-October and December-January. For seedlings, apply naphthalene balls 10.5 g covered with fine sand, once in 45 days. Place phorate 10 G 5 g in perforated sachets in two inner most leaf axils for 2 times at 6 months intervals. Treat manure pits and other possible breeding sites with 0.01% carbaryl (50 % WP) on w/w basis. Treatment will have to be repeated every six months.

Trap method: Set up rhino lure pheromone trap @ 5 traps/ha to trap and kill the beetles. The dispenser may be hanged in a plastic bucket having 2 liter of insecticide solution once in a week. Trapped beetles can be disposed off.

❑ Red palm weevil: *Rhynchophorus ferrugineus* (Olivier, 1790)

Common Name	:	Red palm weevil
Scientific Name	:	*Rhynchophorus ferrugineus* (Olivier, 1790)
Family	:	Curculionidae
Order	:	Coleoptera

Source: *https://www.biobestgroup.com/*

Distribution and Host Range

It is distributed in Pakistan, India, Sri Lanka, South East Asia to China, Taiwan and Solomon Islands. In India it occurs in all coconut growing tracts. It also infests oil palm, date, sago and other species of Palmae.

Nature and Symptoms of Damage

The hole can be seen on the stem with chewed up fibres protruding out. Many times, reddish brown liquid can be seen oozing out from the hole. The grubs cause damage inside the stem or crown by feeding on soft tissues and often cause severe damage especially when a large number of them bore into the soft, growing parts. In case of severe infestation, the inside portion of trunk is completely eaten and become full of rotting fibres. In case of young palms, the top withers while in older palms the top portion of trunk bends and ultimately breaks at the bend. Sometimes the gnawing sound produced by the feeding grubs inside will also be audible. In the advanced stage of infestation yellowing of the inner whorl of leaves occur. The crowns fall down or dry up later when palm is dead.

Life History and Description

The weevil is reddish brown with 6 dark spots on the thorax a conspicuous snout with tuft of hairs. The female weevil lays eggs in small holes scooped out by her on the soft regions of young palms up to 7 years of age. In the grown-up trees the eggs are laid in the cuts or wounds present on the trunk or leaf stalk. The plant sap oozing out of wounds and cut attract the weevil for oviposition. The eggs are creamy white in colour. The eggs hatch out in 2-3 days' time into soft white grub. The grub is apodous which tunnel into the trunk and feeds on the internal succulent tissues. The larval period ranges between 45 and 75 days. The full-grown grub is stout, fleshy, and apodous with a conical body bulged in middle and tapering towards the ends. It pupates in a fibrous cocoon made out of fibrous strands. The pupal period last for 2-3 weeks. The total life cycle is completed in about 4 months. The adult weevils are reddish brown with long curved, pointed snout. The male weevil can be distinguished from the female by the presence of tuft of hairs along the dorsal aspect of snout.

Management

Remove and burn all wilting or damaged palms in coconut gardens to prevent further perpetuation of the pest. Avoid the cutting of green leaves. If needed, they should be cut about 120 cm away from the stem in order to prevent successful inward movement of the grubs through the cut end. In attacked palms, observe for the bore- holes and seal them except the top most one. Through the top most hole, pour 1% carbaryl (20 gm/lt) or 0.2% trichlorphon @ one litre per palm using a funnel. Then plug this hole also. If needed repeat after one week. When the pest infestation is through the crown, clean the crown and slowly pour the insecticidal suspension. In case of entry of weevil through the trunk, the hole in trunk may be plugged with cement/tar. A slanting hole is made with the aid of an auger and the insecticide solution is poured with funnel. Fill the crown and the axils of top most three leaves with a mixture of fine sand and neem seed powder or neem seed kernel powder (2:1) once in three months to prevent the attack of rhinoceros beetle damage in which the red palm weevil lays eggs.

Trap method

Coconut log traps: Setting up of attractant traps (mud pots) containing sugarcane molasses 2½ kg or toddy 2½ litres (or pineapple or sugarcane activated with yeast or molasses) + acetic acid 5 ml + yeast 5 g + longitudinally split tender coconut stem/logs of green petiole of leaves of 30 numbers in one acre to trap adult red palm weevils in large numbers. Incorporate any of the insecticide to each trap to kill the weevils trapped.

Pheromone trap

Install pheromone trap @ one trap per ha

Step 1: Specialized buckets with 3 of 4 holes are made, the bucket is wound with coconut fibre/jute sack, so that the pests can enter.

Step 2: The lure (Ferrolure) is suspended inside the bucket and one lit of water is added along with 100 g pineapple/sugarcane, 2 g yeast and 2 g carbaryl in the bucket.

Step 3: The bait buckets are placed at sites in the farm, where infestation is seen most.

Step 4: After a week the water is checked for the catch and re filled to prevent mosquitoes from breeding.

❑ Black headed caterpillar: *Opisina arenosella* (Walker, 1864)

Common Name	:	Leaf Eating Caterpillar; Black headed caterpillar
Scientific Name	:	*Opisina arenosella* (Walker, 1864)
Family	:	Oecophoridae
Order	:	Lepidoptera

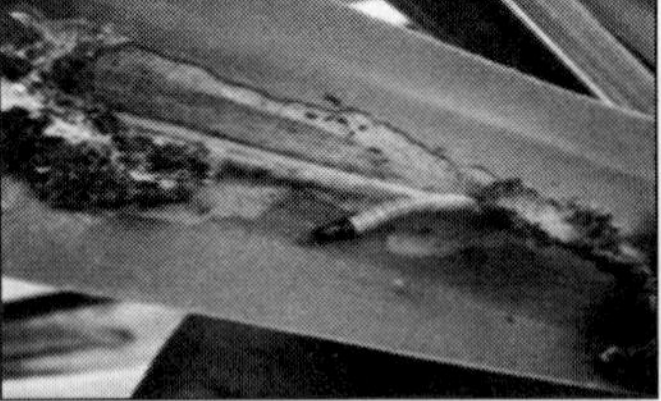

Source: *https://agritech.tnau.ac.in/*

Distribution and Host Range

This insect pest is considered a serious defoliating pest of coconut. It is present in India, Sri Lanka, Bangladesh, Myanmar, Thailand and Indonesia. In India, it occurs more commonly along the West and East coast regions. It infests on coconut, *Palmyra* (Borassus), *Corypha*, *Hyphaene*, *Phoenix*, *Roystonia* and banana.

Nature and Symptoms of Damage

The larva infests the under surface of leaves and it construct small galleries with silk frass and excreta and remain inside throughout. It feeds on the green parenchymatous tissues of leaflets from under surface leaving a thin parchment like upper epidermis undamaged. The infested leaflets slowly turn grey to brown and dry up in patches along the area where each larva has been feeding. When a large number of leaves are affected, the crown presents a scorched appearance from a distance. The damage by the caterpillar is severe during summer month.

Life History and Description

The adult moth is small and greyish white. It lays eggs near the tip of the leaflets of the older leaves. The eggs are very small and hatch out in five days. The fecundity of the insect is 60-250 eggs/female. The newly hatched out larva construct silken tunnel or galleries. On the under surface of leaves where they live and feed. The larva is light green with a dark brown head measures 15 mm in length. The larval period is about 45 days. It pupates inside the galleries for 12 days. The total life cycle is completed in about two months.

Larva: Caterpillar is greenish brown with dark brown head and prothorax, and a reddish mesothorax. It has brown stripes on the body.

Pupa: It pupates inside the web itself in a thin silken cocoon

Adult moth: greyish white in colour.

Female: Long antenna and three faint spots on the forewings.

Male: Fringed hairs in hind wings in apical and anal margin.

Management

As a prophylactic measure, the first affected leaves may be cut and burnt during the beginning of the summer season. Among the larval parasitoids, Bethylid, *Goniozus nephantidis*, is the most effective in controlling the pest. The optimum level of release is 1:8 of host-parasitoid ratio. The parasitoid should be released @ 3000/ha under the coconut trees when the pest is in the 2nd or 3rd instar larval stage. Parasitoid release trap may be used to release the parasitoid at the site of feeding. Parasitoids should not be released in the crown region since they will be killed by predators like spiders and reduviid bugs. This should be released only three weeks after chemical spray. Release the larval (Bethylid, Braconid and Ichneumonid) and pupal (Eulophid) on (chalcid) parasitoids and predators periodically from January, to check the build-up of the pest during summer. When infestation is very severe in young palms and if the biocontrol is not likely to be effective, spray the undersurface of the fronds with dichlorvos 0.02%, malathion 50 EC 0.05% (1 ml/lt), quinalphos 0.05%, phosalone 0.05%.

❑ White grub: *Leucopholis coneophora* Burm.

Common Name	:	White Grub; Cockchafer beetle
Scientific Name	:	*Leucopholis coneophora* Burm.
Family	:	Melolonthidae
Order	:	Coleoptera

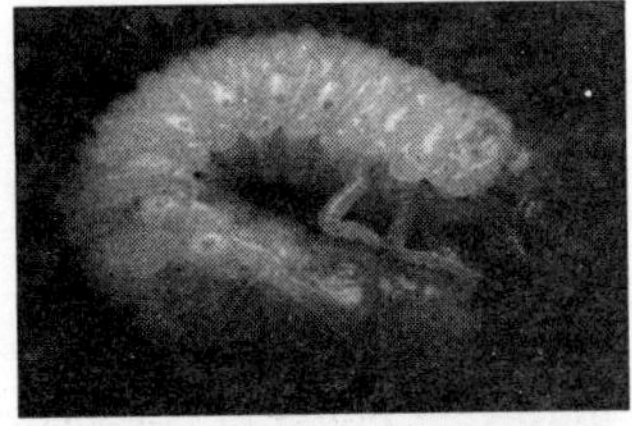

Source: http://1.bp.blogspot.com/

Distribution and Host Range

White grubs are common throughout North America, although species distribution varies greatly. White grubs feed on the roots of coconut, corn, timothy, Kentucky bluegrass, sorghum, soybean, strawberry, potato, barley, oat, wheat, rye, bean, turnip, and to a lesser degree, other cultivated crops. They are predominantly noticed in sandy as well as sandy clay soils in coastal districts, feeding on the roots of coconut seedlings.

Nature and Symptoms of Damage

In nursery the grubs' feet the tender roots and tunnel into the hole of the collar region resulting in drying and yellowing. In older plantations infestations results in yellowing of leaves, premature nut shedding, delayed flowering, retardation in growth and yield decline. White grubs are exposed when base of tree dug. Tuber crops grown as intercrops are also affected.

Life History and Description

The adult is cheshunt coloured beetle. It lays eggs in soil a depth of 7.5-15 cm and they hatch in 20 days. The younger stage of grub feeds on grass roots and organic matter, later stages feeding on coconut roots. The grub is white, fleshy, stout and 'C shaped. It pupates in the soil for about 25 days. The insect has an annual life cycle.

Egg: Oval in shape and creamy white in color when freshly laid. Prior to hatching they turn to dirty white.

Grub: Curved, fleshy and wrinkled. They are creamy white in color with brown head.

Adult: Brown coloured beetle with striated wings not covering the abdomen fully.

Management

Repeated ploughing once a week for 4 to 5 times after first rains in summer reduce the pest population by exposing the pest to predation by birds and other animals. Plant neem twigs with leaves in coconut gardens after rain to attract and kill adult beetles. Plough or dig the infested soil synchronizing with pre-monsoon showers. Set up light trap @ 1/ha or bonfire. Collect and destroy the adult beetles attracted to trees like neem, *Ailanthus* and *Acacia* on the receipt of monsoon showers. Soil application – malathion 5 D 25 kg/ha at the time of planting.

❑ Coconut eriophyid: *Aceria guerreronis* Keifer, 1965

Common Name	:	Coconut eriophyid; Perianth mite
Scientific Name	:	*Aceria guerreronis* Keifer, 1965
Family	:	Eriophyidae
Order	:	Acarina

Source: *https://agritech.tnau.ac.in/*

Distribution and Host Range

It is one of the most serious arthropod pests of coconut. It was first described in 1965 from specimens from Guerrero State, Mexico. In India it was first reported in Ernakulam district of Kerala in 1998 at Ambalour panchayat. Presently it is present all the coastal states of India mainly Kerala, Tamil Nadu, Andhra Pradesh, Odisha, West Bengal and Maharastra. It may reduce 7.5-60% yield losses of coconut. It is present in the Americas, Africa and in South-East Asia. Although coconut palm appears to be the only host of coconut mite, but it also attacks *Lytocaryum weddellianmum*,

Borassus flabellifer and *Syagrus romanzoffiana*. Pest population occurs round the year but population maximum during June-September coinciding with the onset of monsoon.

Nature and Symptoms of Damage

The mite infests and develops on the meristematic tissues of the growing nuts under the perianth by desapping the soft tissues of the buttons. In the damaged buttons/nuts, an initial symptom will be exhibited in the form of triangular pale white or yellow patches close to each perianth. Different stages of mite live in white, tender portion covered by the inner tracts of the perianth and suck the sap continuously when the feeding activity is enhanced due to the increased population build-up it results in physical damage to newly formed tissues which become necrotic. Intensive damage leads to the formation of brown coloured patches later on. In addition, as the nut grows in size, longitudinal fissures and splits occur on the outer surface of the husk. Occasionally brownish gummy exudates are seen oozing out from the affected surface. Severe infestation results in poor growth reduced size and copra content and malformed nuts with cracks and hardened husk

Life History and Description

It is found under the tracts of fertilized female flowers. It is very minute in size measuring 200-250 micron in length and 36-52 micron in width with two pairs of legs. It is pale in colour with elongate body and worm like in appearance. The life cycle of this mite consists of egg, two larval instars and one adult stage is completed in 10-12 days.

Management

Collect and destroy all the fallen buttons of the affected palm. Grow intercrop (sun hemp, four crops/year) and shelter belt with casuarina all-round the coconut garden to check further entry. Providing adequate irrigation. Apply urea 1.3 kg, super phosphate 2.0 kg and muriate of potash @ 3.5 kg/palm/year. Increased quantity is recommended to increase the plant resistance to the mite. Soil application of micro nutrients like, borax 50 g + gypsum 1.0 kg + manganese sulphate 0.5 kg/palm/year TNAU micronutrient solution 200 ml/tree. Entomofungal pathogen *Hirsutella thompsonii* and *Verticillium lecanii* are reported to be promising in managing the mites. Both the pathogens are mass multiplied by a commercial firm and sold in the market.

Spot application of eco-friendly botanicals

Azadirachtin 1% (5 ml in one lit. of water). Neem oil + Teepol (30 ml in one lit. of water). Triazophos 40 EC 5 ml/lit or monocrotophos 36 WSC @ 2 ml/lit or carbosulfan 25 EC 2 ml/lit in alternation with neem azal 1% 5 ml/lit as spot application. Neem cake application @ 5 kg per palm per year. Preparation of neem oil + garlic emulsion (2%).

❑ Coconut scale: *Aspidiotus destructor* Signoret, 1869

Common Name	:	Coconut scale
Scientific Name	:	*Aspidiotus destructor* Signoret, 1869
Family	:	Diaspididae
Order	:	Hemiptera

As Described in Mango

Termites – *Odontotermes obesus* (Rambur 1842)

Common Name	:	Termites
Scientific Name	:	*Odontotermes obesus* (Rambur 1842)
Family	:	Termitidae
Order	:	Isoptera

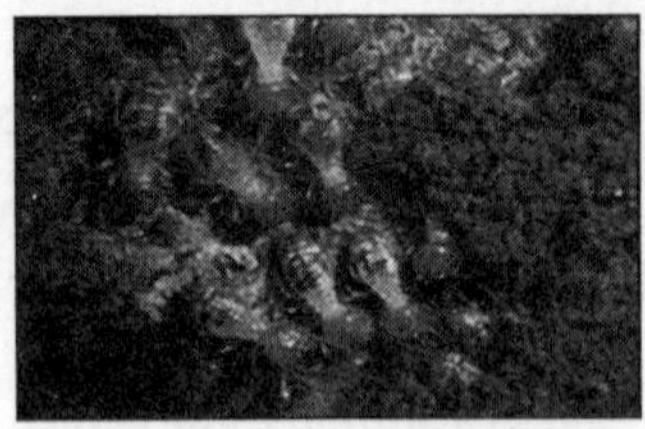

Source: *http://1.bp.blogspot.com/*

As Described in Mango

Mealy bugs: *Pseudococcus longispinus* (Targioni Tozzetti, 1867)

Common Name	:	Mealy bugs
Scientific Name	:	*Pseudococcus longispinus* (Targioni Tozzetti, 1867)
Family	:	Pseudococcidae
Order	:	Hemiptera

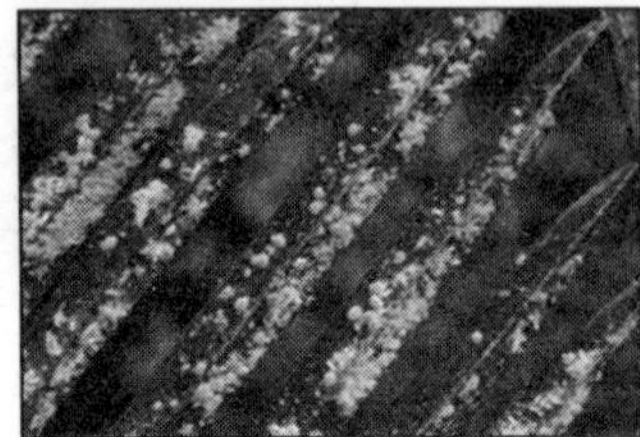

Source: *https://agritech.tnau.ac.in/*

Distribution and Host Range

Mealy bugs are seen in crowd in the young shoots, stems, and leaves. Dark green leaves will be flattened and crinkled. Due to the segregation of honey-like compounds, the leaves hampered with proper photosynthesis. It also encourages the growth of black sooty mould. The growth of apical regions of the shoots are slow down. Host plants includes marigolds, hibiscus, mango, apple, apricot and many other fruit and vegetable crops.

Nature and Symptoms of Damage

It occurs more in summer. Scale insects' effects on leaves and nuts of coconut palms. A severe infestation, scale forms a continuous crust over flower spikes, young nuts and lower surface of leaves. On leaves, *A. destructor* causes scales with yellow spots developing where the crawlers have settled and grown into adults. Nymphs reside and develop in leaf by sucking the sap. Entire leaves may turn yellow to brown and fall. Sooty mould may develop. The bright yellow colour of affected coconut palms is clearly visible from a great distance. In extreme cases, the leaves dry out, entire fronds drop off and the crown dies. Heavy infestation results in stunting of new leaves, reduction of crop yield or complete crop failure. Infested coconut fronds exhibit yellow areas on the upper surface, formed by numerous yellow spots each marking the position of the coconut scale on the under surface.

Life History and Description

It is circular hard scale occurs as persistent pest of coconut. A female lays up to 90 eggs under its shield like scale. The crawlers move out and distribute themselves to healthy leaflets. The life cycle is 32 days for male and 35 days for female.

Egg: Hatching the young scales on the undersides of the leaves.

Nymph: Covered with circular waxy secretion.

Adult: The scale is bright yellow and round or reddish (female) and oval (male) covered with a semi-transparent greyish-white flat scale. Females are always wingless and remain under their scale their entire life. Adult males have one pair of membranous wings, move about actively in search of females and do not feed during adult stage.

Management

Due to the vulnerable nature of the juvenile stages, early detection provides the best chance of managing mealybugs. In order to avoid the spread of mealybugs, carefully inspect purchased plants. Look for mealybugs or clusters of cottony wax on sensitive plants. Hand picking and scrap-out with a tooth brush is followed at low level of infections. Release of predatory coccinellids, *Chilocorus nigritius* is found to be effective. Spray Fish Oil Rosin Soap (FORS) 2.5% or spray malathion. A second round is given after 20 days.

❑ Slug caterpillar: *Conthyla rotunda* H.

Common Name	:	Slug caterpillar
Scientific Name	:	*Conthyla rotunda; Macroplectra nararia; Latoia (Parasa) lepida*
Family	:	Limacodidae
Order	:	Lepidoptera

Source: *https://agritech.tnau.ac.in/*

Distribution and Host Range

It is a sporadic pest. *C. rotunda* is common in West coast, while *M. nararia* is common in Godavari district in India. *L. lepida* mainly found in South East Asian region including India, Sri Lanka, Vietnam, Malaysia, Indonesia and Japan. Although slug caterpillars are minor pest but sometimes, in congenial weather they become major pest. Beside coconut, these infest mango, castor, cashew and pomegranate.

Nature and Symptoms of Damage

Initially, caterpillar feeds the under surface of coconut leaflets by scrapping the surface tissues which gives a glistening appearance on the feeding area. Leaf spot-like black halo marking develops on the feeding areas which later coalesce and form bigger lesions. During severe infestation caterpillars feed on the entire leaflet sparing only the midrib. They also feed on buds, flower shoots and developing fruits.

Life History and Identification

In the male insect's head is greenish, with red brown at the sides and the thorax is green with a brown stripe on the vertex. Hindwing is yellowish at base and reddish brown towards margin. In the female, the reddish-brown stripe on the thorax is much wider and nearly the whole of the hindwing is reddish brown. Larva has greenish body with white lines and four rows of spiny scoli tipped red or black, which cause irritation and pain and slug like, hence also called "nettle grub". Adult female lays flat shiny eggs on the under surface of leaves in batches of 20-30, egg period is 6-7 days. Larval period is about 42 days. It pupates in a compact elliptical chocolate brown shell-like cocoon, which is convex above and flat below. Cocoons are covered with irritating spines and hairs; pupal period is 21 days. C. *rotunda* larva is dorsally and dorso-laterally black or grey in colour. Adult is a small greyish brown moth. Forewings are slight dark in colour with series of black points; hind wings slightly darker.

Management

Set up light traps to trap and collect adult moths. About 5 light traps may be installed per hectare. Encourage the population of braconid parasitoid, *Apanteles parasae* and the tachinid parasitoid, *Chaetexorista javana*, both of which attacked the older larvae. Collect and destroy the immature stages of the insects by conducting study (or neem campaign) wherever possible and spray carbaryl 50 WP 2 gm/lit. Spray carbaryl 50 WP 2 g/l. Spray dichlorvos 76 WSC 2 ml/lit.

❑ Tingid or Lace wing bug: *Stephanitis typicus* Distant

Common name	:	Tingid, coconut lace wing bug, banana lace bug
Scientific name	:	*Stephanitis typicus* Distant
Family	:	Tingidae
Order	:	Heteroptera

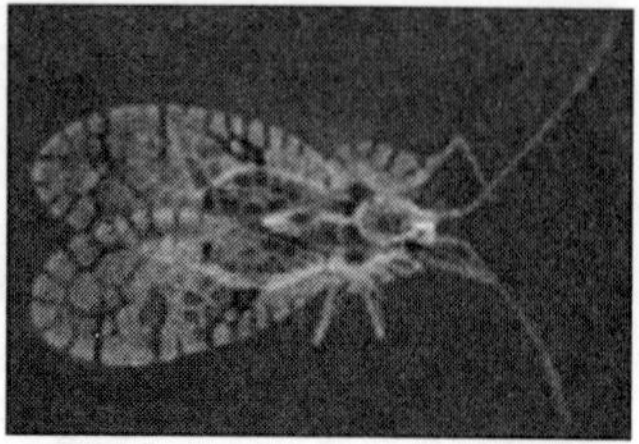

Source: *http://databases.nbair.res.in/insectpests/index.php*

As Described in Banana

Resistant Varieties	
World	**India**
Makapuno Coconut: Makapuno is a dwarf mutant of the coconut that is resistant to the coconut mite (*Aceria guerreronis*). This variety is popular in the Philippines, where it is grown for its soft, jelly-like flesh. **Vanuatu Tall Coconut:** This variety is tolerant to the rhinoceros beetle and is grown extensively in Vanuatu, an island nation in the South Pacific. **Fiji Dwarf Coconut:** Fiji Dwarf is resistant to the rhinoceros beetle and is widely cultivated in Fiji and other Pacific islands. **Tagnanan Tall Coconut:** This variety is tolerant to the coconut scale insect (*Aspidiotus destructor*) and is grown in the Philippines. **Malayan Yellow Dwarf Coconut:** This variety is resistant to the rhinoceros beetle and is grown in Malaysia and other Southeast Asian countries.	**West Coast Tall:** This variety of coconut is widely cultivated in India, particularly in the Southern states of Kerala, Tamil Nadu, and Karnataka. It is known for its high yield and resistance to pests and diseases. **Chowghat Orange Dwarf:** This variety is a hybrid of the West Coast Tall and the Malayan Dwarf, and is known for its high yield and resistance to pests and diseases. **Lakshadweep Ordinary Tall:** This variety is native to the Lakshadweep Islands and is known for its tolerance to pests and diseases, as well as its ability to grow in saline conditions. **Kalparaksha:** This variety is native to the state of Kerala and is known for its resistance to the rhinoceros' beetle. **Malayan Dwarf:** This variety is a dwarf type of coconut and is known for its resistance to the coconut mite.

29 Pests of Arecanut

Scientific Name	*Areca catechu*
Family	Arecaceae
Origin	Malayan Archipelago/Indonesia/Philippines
Chromosome Number	2n = 32

Arecanut, also known as betel nut, is the fruit of the areca palm (*Areca catechu*). It is widely grown in tropical regions of the world, including India, Sri Lanka, Indonesia, Malaysia, and the Philippines. The fruit of the areca palm is a drupe, which contains a single seed surrounded by a fibrous outer layer. The seed, or nut, is chewed for its stimulant properties in many parts of the world, especially in Asia. The active ingredient in arecanut is arecoline, which produces a mild stimulating effect similar to caffeine.

Arecanut is an important cash crop in India, particularly in the Southern states of Karnataka, Kerala, and Tamil Nadu. It is also grown in parts of Assam, West Bengal, Odisha, and Andhra Pradesh. In India, arecanut is mainly grown as a plantation crop and is often intercropped with coconut and other trees. In terms of production, India is the largest producer of arecanut in the world, with an estimated production of over 4 lakh metric tonnes. Karnataka is the largest producer in India, followed by Kerala and Assam. Other major producers of arecanut in the world include Indonesia, the Philippines, and Papua New Guinea.

Arecanut is susceptible to a range of pests and diseases, including stem bleeding, leaf rot, and bud rot. Insect pests that can cause damage to the crop include the arecanut leaf beetle, arecanut leafhopper, and arecanut defoliator. These pests can cause significant yield losses if not managed properly.

❑ Spindle bug: *Carvalhoia arecae*

Common Name	:	Spindle bug
Scientific Name	:	*Carvalhoia arecae*
Family	:	Miridae
Order	:	Hemiptera

Source: https://tse1.mm.bing.net/

Distribution and Host Range

The spindle bug, *Carvalhoia arecae*, infests the leaf axils, and its highest population is found from August to September. It is mostly seen in the regions of Middle East and South East Asia affecting the arecanut plantations at large scale.

Nature and Symptoms of Damage

Nymphs and adult suck sap, which results in linear black necrotic streaks on the central shoot, stunted and twisted growth. Affected central shoots do not open fully and leaves become dry and shed off. Sap sucking bug – damage the unopened spindle leaf. Inhabit the inner most leaf axils, usually below the spindle. Suck the sap from tender leaflets and spindle. Severe infestation – blackish brown linear lesions on the spindle leaf. Stunted growth and twisted. Leaves become dried and shed.

Life History and Identification

Eggs are laid within tender spindle. Egg and nymphal periods last for 9 to 10 and 15 to 20 days respectively. Nymphs are deep greenish to violet brown in colour with thorax and border of abdomen light violet brown and head is light yellow with red eyes. Adult bug is hairy dark violet brown with black tipped abdomen.

Management

Filling the inner most leaf axils. Introduction of predators like king crow, ground beetles, wasps and spider. Spray the spindles with lindane 20 EC 2 ml/1 or carbaryl 50% WP 2.5 g/l. Spray application of dimethoate 0.05% or Phorate 10% G (10 g/palm).

❑ Inflorescene caterpillar: *Tirathaba mundella* Walker, 1864

Common Name	:	Inflorescence caterpillar
Scientific Name	:	*Tirathaba mundella* Walker, 1864
Family	:	Pyraustidae
Order	:	Lepidoptera

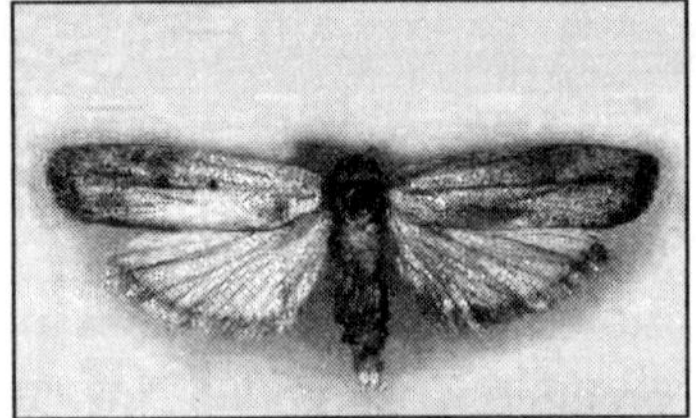

Source: *https://agritech.tnau.ac.in/*

Distribution and Host Range

Tirathaba mundella causes considerable economic loss to the crop by directly damaging economic parts of the palms *i.e.*, inflorescence and developing buttons. *T. mudella* is widely distributed in India and South East Asian countries like Thailand, Indonesia and Solomon Island. The attack is severe in certain pockets of Karnataka and Kerala.

Nature and Symptoms of Damage

Tender branches of inflorescence are webbed together with silken threads of caterpillar. Wet mass of excreta protrudes out of the web. Bore holes are seen at the base of unopened spathes and buttons, which are plugged with excreta. Caterpillars feed on the inflorescences and rachillae. Webbing and feeding the inflorescence. Spathe opening is delayed. Yellowing of spadices. Presence of small holes with frass and drying on the spathe.

Life History and Identification

Larva is dirty yellow or white with brown head. Adult moth is small with ashy wings. Eggs are laid on tender spathes. Egg, larval and pupal periods last for 5, 25 and 10 days respectively. Pupation occurs within galleries.

Management

The biocontrol agents *viz*. B. *nephantidis* and E. *punctulatus* could efficiently be utilized for suppressing *T. mundella* and shall further strengthen the biocontrol research in arecanut pest management. Infected spadices may be forced open and sprayed with malathion 0.05%.

❑ Root grub: *Leucopholis lepidophora* Blanchard, 1850

Common Name	:	Root grub
Scientific Name	:	*Leucopholis lepidophora* Blanchard, 1850
Family	:	Scarabaeidae
Order	:	Coleoptera

Source: *https://plantwiseplusknowledgebank.org/*

Distribution and Host Range

L. burmeisteri is considered as a major species distributed in coastal and hilly regions of Karnataka and Kerala.

Nature and Symptoms of Damage

Grubs feed on growing roots of the tree. Infested palms show a sickly appearance and yellowing of leaves. Tapering of stem and reduction in yield was observed.

Life History and Description

Adult beetle is chestnut brown in colour. There is less literature related to life history and description.

Management

Collection and destruction of adult beetles on emergence from soil is an effective management practice. Digging and forking of the soil. Addition of organic amendments and anti-feedants (neem, pongamia and oilcake). Soil application of phorate around the plant twice a year *i.e.*, before onset of southeast monsoon (May) and after the monsoon (September-October). In severely infected gardens, the soil should be drenched with eco-friendly insecticides.

❑ Black headed caterpillar: *Opisina arenosella* (Walker, 1864)

Common Name	:	Leaf Eating Caterpillar; black headed caterpillar
Scientific Name	:	*Opisina arenosella* (Walker, 1864)
Family	:	Oecophoridae
Order	:	Lepidoptera

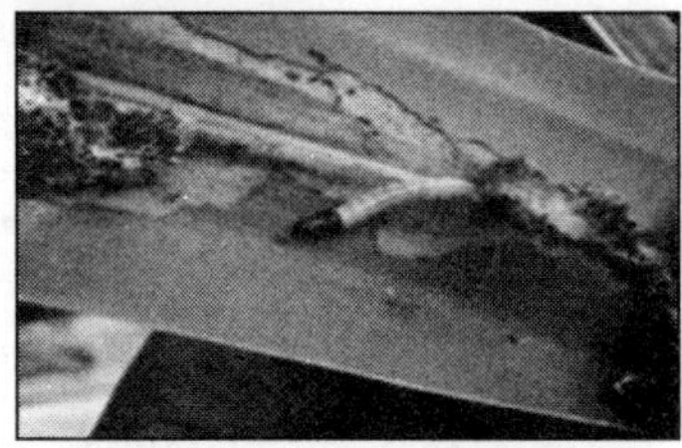

Source: *https://agritech.tnau.ac.in/*

As Described in Coconut

Cholam or white mite: *Oligonychus indicus* (Hirst, 1923)

Common Name	:	Cholam or white mite
Scientific Name	:	*Oligonychus indicus* (Hirst, 1923)
Family	:	*Tetranychidae*
Order	:	*Trombidiformes*

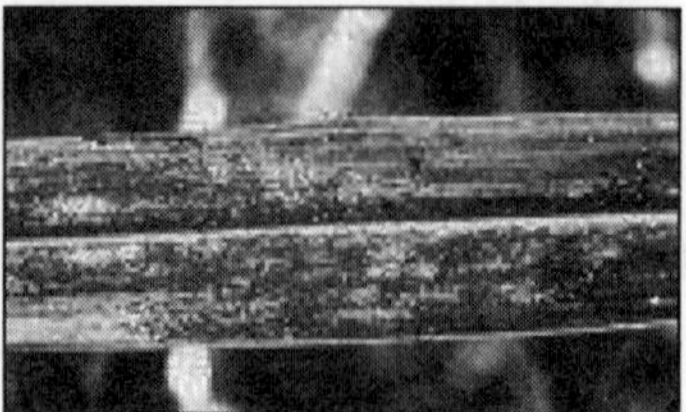

Source: *https://agritech.tnau.ac.in/*

Distribution and Host Range

Oligonychus is a genus of mites in the family Tetranychidae, the spider mites. Many members of this genus are familiar pests of plants. There are about 200 described species. *Oligonychus indicus*, a polyphagous pest, is serious on banana during summer and the rainy season and also seen in arecanut plantations at large scale. This species is widely distributed in India. The attack of this mite on sugarcane is more in North India and less in South India and causes 20-30% damage to the crop.

Nature and Symptoms of Damage

Adults and nymphs' presence on the lower surface of leaves. The colony is found under white webs. Feed on lower surface of arecanut leaves. Feeding of this mite causes the appearance of reddish spots which increase with the severity of attack. These spots later coalesce to form large red patches and spread on the leaf surface to turn the colour of the leaf red.

Life History and Description

It is grayish green mite with black blotches scattered over dorsum. There are 30 overlapping generation in a year; all stages occur together living in a delicate web of silk and breeding is continuous. The mite spreads by wind and also by crawling from plant to plant, when leaves touch each other. Adult males feed very little and the main damage is caused by the females and immature stages. Soft leaf varieties of sugarcane are more susceptible to attack than those having hard leaves.

Management

Removal of heavily infested and dried leaves and burning. Spraying under surfaces of leaves and crown with Dicofol (2 ml/litre) or Rogor (1.5 ml/litre). Repeat spraying at an interval of 15-20 days.

Pentatomid bug (*Halyomorpha mannoreal* F.)

Common name	:	Brown marmorated stink bug
Scientific name	:	*Halyomorpha mannoreal*
Family	:	Pentatomidae
Order	:	Hemiptera

Source: *https://upload.wikimedia.org//Pentatomidae//*

Distribution and Host range

This pest causes tender nut drop in arecanut. The incidence is generally occurring during April-July.

Nature and Symptoms of Damage

The bug pierces tender nuts and suck kernel sap. The typical symptom of attack is premature shedding of nuts with pin- prick like black puncture marks. The infestation also led to blackish discolouration to kernel.

Management

Spray Dimethoate (Rogor 30 EC) @1.5 ml/liter of water to the developing bunches. Spray Neem oil @ 5 ml/liter of water is also effective.

❑ Arecanut scale: *Aonidiella orientalis* (Newstead, 1894)

Common name	:	Oriental yellow scale
Scientific name	:	*Aonidiella orientalis* (Newstead, 1894)
Family	:	Diaspididae
Order	:	Hemiptera

Source: *https://upload.wikimedia.org/wikipedia/commons/thumb/c/c1/Aonidiella_orientalis.jpg/330px-Aonidiella_orientalis.jpg*

Distribution and Host Range

This species is likely native to Asia. It can be found nearly worldwide today because it has been introduced to many areas with shipments of plants and then began a slow spread. It is common in many tropical and subtropical areas, and it can survive in greenhouses in cooler regions. It is not known from Europe. Some ports check for this and other scales in quarantined plant shipments.

Nature and Symptoms of Damage

These sucking insects colonize on leaves, spathe, leaf sheaths and bunch and eventually suck plant sap from the infested tissues. Though, the insect is found throughout the year, but copious population is noticed between October and February. The insect damages the plant by sucking sap, weakening it. The physical damage includes discoloration and deformation of leaves. Flowers and fruits fail to develop. When the insects feed on the fruits they are discoloured and warped, reducing their value on the market. Infestations can kill plants, even established trees. The scale insect sucks sap from leaves, rachillae and nuts. The feeding leads to yellowing of nuts and severe infestation leads to withering and shedding of nuts.

Life History and Description

It is an agricultural pest on a wide variety of crop plants. This is a scale insect, a tiny insect which is most easily identified by the female, which attaches itself to a host plant, loses its legs, and remains stationary covered by a somewhat rounded scale-like shield of wax. In this species, the female forms a flat, circular scale which is white, brown, or yellow in colour. It is up to 2.6 millimetres long. The insect within is no more than 1.4 millimetres long. The winged male of this species also produces a scale.

Management

Infested twigs, branches, and shoots can be removed from trees, slowing the spread of the scale. Pesticides have been used, but are less popular now as attention turns to biological pest control. There are many natural enemies of the scale which can be reared and released in infested orchards, reducing scale populations. Regulate shade in the garden. Spray Neem oil @ 5 ml/liter of water. Ladybird beetles, *Chilocorus nigrita* and C. *circumdatus* are effective against scale insect.

Resistant Varieties	
World	**India**
Currently, there are no known arecanut varieties that are completely resistant to insect pests. However, there are certain varieties that have shown some level of resistance or tolerance to pests. For example, the "**Suma**" variety is known to be less susceptible to the Rhinoceros beetle and the "**Mangala**" variety has shown some resistance to the coconut hispine beetle.	There are several varieties of arecanut that have been reported to be resistant to these pests. Some of the varieties that have been found to be resistant to the coconut mite include **Sumatra** and **Mohitnagar**. Varieties such as **Sreeranga**, **Bhaskara** and **Kallara** have shown resistance to the red palm weevil.

30 Pests of Cocoa

Scientific Name	*Theobroma cocoa*
Family	Malvaceae
Origin	Amazon valley of South America
Chromosome Number	2n = 20

Cocoa, also known as cacao, is a tropical crop primarily grown for its beans, which are used to make chocolate and other cocoa-based products. The botanical name of cocoa is *Theobroma cacao* and it belongs to the family Malvaceae. Cocoa is an important crop for many countries in Africa, Asia, and the Americas, including Ghana, Côte d'Ivoire, Indonesia, Nigeria, and Brazil. In India, cocoa is mainly grown in the southern states of Kerala, Tamil Nadu, and Karnataka. The area under cocoa cultivation in India is relatively small, with an estimated production of around 20,000 tonnes per year.

Cocoa plants are susceptible to a number of pests and diseases, which can cause significant yield losses if left unchecked. Some of the major pests of cocoa include cocoa pod borer, cocoa mirid bug, and cocoa swollen shoot virus. In addition to pests, cocoa can also be affected by various diseases such as black pod disease, witches' broom, and frosty pod rot.

❑ Cocoa mirids: *Helopeltis clavifer* (Walker)

Common Name	:	Cocoa mirids
Scientific Name	:	*Helopeltis clavifer* (walker)
Family	:	Miridae
Order	:	Hemiptera

Source: *https://plantwiseplusknowledgebank.org/*

Distribution and Host Range

Mirids are the major insects that affect cocoa worldwide. In Ghana, cocoa mirids have been recognized as a serious pest since 1908 due to their devastating effect. The most common species in

Ghana and West African countries are *Distantiella theobroma* and *Sahlbergella singularis*. In South-East Asia the *Helopeltis* spp. is responsible for the damage related to mirids while monalonion species are present in South and Central America. Mirid damage alone, if left unattended for three years, can reduce yields by as much as 75%.

Nature and Symptoms of Damage

Cocoa mirids pierce the surface of cocoa stems, branches and pods, killing the penetrated host cells and producing unsightly necrotic lesions. Mirids feeding on shoots often result in the death of terminal branches and leaves, causing dieback. Mated female mirids lay up to 60 eggs that are embedded in the bark of stems or inside the pod husk. Pests usually occur on trees exposed to sunlight since such trees tend to bear more fresh shoots and pods. Although the insect is attracted to trees exposed to sunlight, after locating their source of food they inhabit shady areas on trees. Some indigenous plants grown with cocoa have been identified as alternative hosts for some species of mirids.

Life History and Identification

Mirids are found throughout the year especially duning August to April. They cause damage to seedling, cherelles and shoots by sucking the sap from their tissues. Mirid bugs are usually oval or elongated in shape with a triangular-shaped segment at the base of their wings. The head is angled downwards from their body and features a long needle-like feeding tube that is used to spear prey and suck their blood. Nymphs (or larvae) are usually similar in appearance to the adults, but without wings.

Management

Shade and canopy management should be designed to achieve a balance between mirid control, flowering and black pod management. Alternative hosts should not be used as shade trees on cocoa farms. The application of Integrated Pest Management (IPM) is a key tool in controlling mirids. The black ant (*Dolichoderus thoracicus*) has been used in some farms as a control measure. Another ant (*Oecophylla smaragdina*) has also been used although this one can be aggressive. The use of organochlorine insecticide has proved to be effective in Ghana. The current recommended insecticides are imidacloprid, actellic/talstar and promecarb. Insecticides are applied as foliar spray four times per year at monthly intervals using motorized mist-blowing machines. An alternative approach is to apply two sprays of persistent or systemic insecticides a year on mature cocoa under closed canopy. Reduced insecticide use also allows populations of natural enemies to increase and provide a more suitable environment for biological control.

❑ Cocoa pod borer: *Conopomorpha cramerella* (Snellen, 1904)

Common Name	:	Cocoa pod borer
Scientific Name	:	*Conopomorpha cramerella* (Snellen, 1904)
Family	:	Gracillariidae
Order	:	Lepidoptera

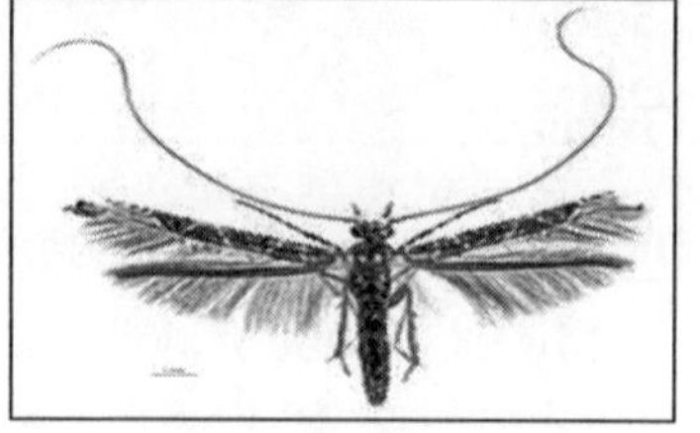

Source: *https://upload.wikimedia.org/*

Distribution and Host Range

The Cocoa pod borer also known as cocoa moth, is caused by the insect *Conopomorpha cramerella*. It was first noted in 1841 as a serious threat, causing vast losses in the cocoa industry during the 1890s and 1900s. CPB now affects almost all cocoa producing provinces in Indonesia. By 2000, CPB had infested 60000 ha, inflicting losses of US$ 40 million per year. The spread of CPB along with the decline in the price of cocoa led to decreases in production of malaysia.

Nature and Symptoms of Damage

CPB attacks both young and mature cocoa pods. A common symptom of infested pods is unevenness and premature ripening. Infestation of young pods results in heavy losses because the quantity and quality of the bean becomes seriously affected.

Life History and Description

CPB moth is 7 mm long and brown in colour with a white strip on the forewings. The female lives for about 5-7 days and lays 100-200 eggs on the surface of the cocoa pod. The larval period is about 14-18 days, then 5-8 days before hatching as a moth.

Management

Sanitation practices involving the complete harvesting of ripe or damaged pods, burying of pod husk, placenta, rotten pods and all harvest remains are recommended. Regular pruning of the cocoa canopy to less than 4 m in height is also good practice. Pod-sleeving with plastic bags also reduces attacks of CPB. Pods should be sleeved when they are about 8-10 cm long and the sleeves should be left throughout the pod maturation period. Ants such as the black ant (*Dolichoderus thoracicus*) and weaver ant (*Oecophylla smaragdina*) are recommended. The fungus *Beauvaria bassiana* has also been found to infect larvae and pupae, causing a 100% death rate. The use of traps with synthetic pheromones or female pod borer moths can control the attack if enough males are caught, thereby interrupting their reproduction cycle. Improved control using relatively small amounts of contact pyrethroid or carbamate insecticides, applied to the undersides of lower branches, keeps the CPB population below economic damage levels. However, this is used as a last resort due to the high cost of pesticides and the low prices of cocoa.

❑ Tea mosquito bug: *Helopeltis antonii* V. Signoret, 1858

Common name	:	Tea mosquito bug
Scientific name	:	*Helopeltis antonii* V. Signoret, 1858
Family	:	Miridae
Order	:	Hemiptera

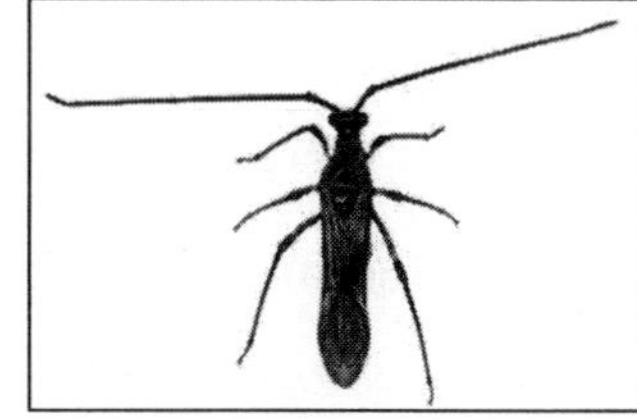

Source: *http://databases.nbair.res.in/insectpests/index.php*

As Described in Guava

❑ Mealy bugs: *Planococcus lilacinus* (Cockerell, 1905); *Planococcus citri* (Risso)

Common Name	:	Mealy bugs
Scientific Name	:	*Planococcus lilacinus* (Cockerell, 1905); *Planococcus citri* (Risso)
Family	:	Pseudococcidae
Order	:	Hemiptera

Source: *https://agritech.tnau.ac.in/*

Distribution and Host Range

Mealy bugs are emerging insect pest of cocoa in India, which is mostly confined during summer season.

Nature and Symptoms of Damage

Feeding on tender apical shoots results in reduced growth and such shoots deformed into a slender hair like processes resembling a brush. Colonization of flower cushions results in cushion abortion and continuous attack results in withering and drying up of flower cushions. Infestation of cherelle's by mealy bug induces cherelle wilt. Feeding on the rind of pods results in irregular cracks and pitting. Usually, beans are not affected by mealy bug colonized on mature pods. Seedlings and young plants colonized by the mealy bugs show retarded growth and excessive branching at undesired height. The population of mealy bug attains peak during April-May.

Life History and Identification

As discussed in coffee.

Management

As discussed in coffee.

❑ Aphids: *Aphis aurantii* Boyer de Fonscolombe, 1841

Common Name	:	Aphids; Brown citrus aphid
Scientific Name	:	*Aphis aurantii* Boyer de Fonscolombe, 1841
Family	:	Aphididae
Order	:	Hemiptera

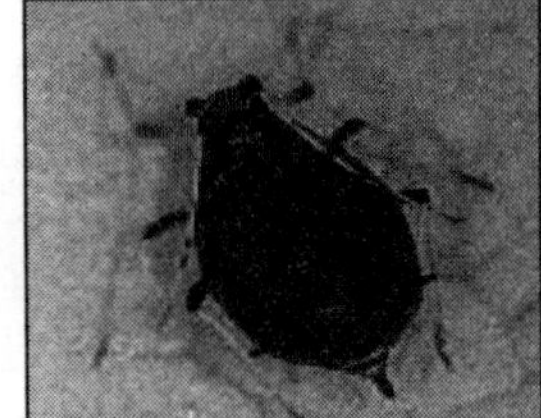

Source:*https://upload.wikimedia.org/*

Distribution and Host Range

The brown citrus aphid is an aphid in the superfamily Aphidoidea in the order Hemiptera. It is a true bug and sucks sap from plants. It is known to hosts in well over 150 plant species. The aphid is present throughout the year, but population is found to be low from February to July, with a peak from August to January.

Nature and Symptoms of Damage

Aphids colonize terminal and growing shoots of cocoa causing leaf deformation during summer. They can also colonize on succulent stem, flower buds and small cherelles, which may cause premature shedding of flowers and curling of leaves. Extensive damage is not reported.

Life History and Description

Adult apterae of *Aphis aurantii* are oval, shiny black, brownish-black or reddish brown with rather short black and white banded antennae. The antennal terminal process is more than 3.5 times the length of the base of the last antennal segment (*Aphis gossypii*, which has the terminal process less than 3.5 times longer than the base of the last antennal segment). The cauda and siphunculi are black, and siphunculi are 1.0-1.5 times the length of the cauda. The cauda usually has less than 20 hairs (*Aphis* (*Toxoptera*) *citricidus*, which usually has more than 20 hairs on the cauda). A stridulatory apparatus is present below and in front of the siphunculi. The body length of *Aphis* (Toxoptera) *aurantii* apterae is about 2 mm long.

Management

Timely pruning of the cocoa trees will reduce the colony build up. A number of natural enemies feed on the aphids and reduce the population. These include coccinelrid beetles (*Coccineila septempunctata, Scymnus cocciuora, Chilocorus nigrita* etc.), syrphids (*Eristalis* spp., *Volucella* spp.) and chrysopids (*Chrysoperla carnea*). In case of several incidence of aphid, management may be directly resorted to application of chemical insecticides like spraying of dimethoate (0.06%) 30 EC 2 rrri/lit. Will reduce the incidence and spread of aphid. If the infestation is recurring, second spray may be given after an interval of 20 to 30 days.

Integrated Pest Management package for Managing Pests of Cocoa

Integrated Pest Management (IPM) is the management of any insect pest by utilizing all available pest management tactics in compatible and sustainable manner, which maintains the pest population at level below the economic injury. It includes cultural, mechanical, physical, chemical and biological control measures and host plant resistance.

Cultural and Mechanical control

Maintain a healthy and balanced ecosystem to preserve natural enemies that kill/manage pest population naturally. Planting/growing of tolerant or resistant varieties which can sustain and produce well under heavy insect pest incidence. Plant a barrier crop that is not attractive to stem borers, such as *Leucaena glauca*, cocoyam, sweet potato or *Pueraria* species. The barrier must be at least 15 m wide and established early for new plantings. Maintain a complete canopy in young plantings, temporary shading is needed, e.g., with bananas and plantains. Alternative hosts of any insect pest of cocoa should not be used as shade trees on cocoa farms. Remove chupons regularly because mirids are attracted to the young and soft shoots which cocoa trees produces throughout the season. Do not prune too heavily as this may stress the trees and cause the growth of new chupons, which increase TMB feeding. Regular and complete harvesting of pods is almost certainly the most effective cultural technique of reducing carry over stages of insects like fruit borer etc. Hand picking and destruction of borer infested pods is important strategy. Removal and destruction of stem borer infested branches can reduce the incidence of this pest. Rat traps and nooses are popular, but of little effective for lowering populations and so a combination of good practices will be successful. These must be implemented over large areas as rodents reproduce and spread quickly. Areawide/community-based management of rodents will always effective than individual farm wise management.

Resistant Varieties	
World	**India**
T x 303: T x 303 is another variety of cocoa that is resistant to cocoa pod borer. This variety was developed by the Cocoa Research Institute of Ghana in collaboration with the International Institute of Tropical Agriculture (IITA). **Sca 6:** Sca 6 is a variety of cocoa that is resistant to both cocoa pod borer and black pod disease. This variety was developed by the Cocoa Research Unit of Trinidad and Tobago. **UF 273:** UF 273 is a variety of cocoa that is resistant to both cocoa pod borer and Phytophthora palmivora, the fungus that causes black pod disease. This variety was developed by the University of Florida. **CCN-51:** This variety was developed in Ecuador and is known for its high productivity and disease resistance, including resistance to cocoa pod borer and black pod disease. **TSH-1188:** This variety was developed in Trinidad and Tobago and is resistant to cocoa pod borer and several other pests. **UF-273:** This variety was developed in Brazil and is resistant to cocoa pod borer and witches' broom disease. **CATIE-R6:** This variety was developed in Central America and is resistant to cocoa pod borer, frosty pod rot, and black pod disease. **SCAVINA-6:** This variety was developed in Costa Rica and is resistant to cocoa pod borer and several other pests.	**DR-2:** DR-2 is a variety of cocoa that is highly resistant to cocoa pod borer. This variety was developed by the Central Plantation Crops Research Institute (CPCRI) in India. **IMC 67:** IMC 67 is a variety of cocoa that is resistant to cocoa pod borer, black pod disease, and witches' broom disease. This variety was developed by the Indian Cocoa Research Institute.

Pests of Oil Palm

Scientific Name	*Elaeis guineensis*
Family	Arecaceae
Origin	West Africa
Chromosome Number	2n = 32

Oil palm is a tropical crop that belongs to the family Arecaceae. The scientific name of oil palm is *Elaeis guineensis*, and it is native to West and Central Africa. Oil palm cultivation requires a warm, humid climate, and it is mainly grown in tropical regions such as Southeast Asia, West Africa, and South America. In India, oil palm is grown mainly in the southern states of Andhra Pradesh, Karnataka, and Tamil Nadu.

Insect pests pose a significant threat to oil palm cultivation, with the most important pests being the rhinoceros beetle, the red palm weevil, and the bagworm. These pests cause damage to the trunk and leaves of the oil palm, which can lead to reduced yields and even the death of the tree if left unchecked. Control measures such as insecticide application and cultural practices are used to manage pest populations and minimize the damage caused by these insects.

❑ Spindle bug: *Carvalhoia arecae*

Common Name	Spindle bug
Scientific Name	*Carvalhoia arecae*
Family	Miridae
Order	Hemiptera

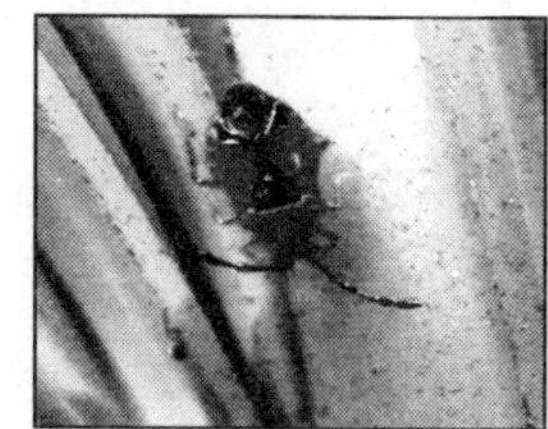

Source: *https://tse1.mm.bing.net/*

As Described in Arecanut

❑ Rhinoceros beetle: *Oryctes rhinoceros* (Linnaeus, 1758)

Common Name	:	Elephant beetle; Hercules beetle; Atlas beetle
Scientific Name	:	*Oryctes rhinoceros* (Linnaeus, 1758)
Family	:	Scarabaeidae
Order	:	Coleoptera

Source: *https://upload.wikimedia.org/*

Distribution and Host Range

As mentioned in Coconut.

Nature and Symptoms of Damage

Adult beetles bore into the palms and chew the tender tissues. Spindle to break and droop. Entry holes – presence of chewed-up tissues. Infested leaves – shortened, broken and distorted. Fruits – the upper portion of the bunch get underdeveloped and dried. Damage to the heart of the palm – way for the entry of fungi and bacteria. Induce rotting in the bud.

Life History and Identification

As mentioned in Coconut.

Management

As mentioned in Coconut.

❑ Red palm weevil: Rhynchophorus ferrugineus (Olivier, 1790)

Common Name	:	Red palm weevil
Scientific Name	:	*Rhynchophorus ferrugineus* (Olivier, 1790)
Family	:	Curculionidae
Order	:	Coleoptera

Source: *https://www.biobestgroup.com/*

Distribution and Host Range

As mentioned in Coconut.

Nature and Symptoms of Damage

Rhinoceros beetle attacked palms are more prone to infestation by red palm weevil. Grubs bore into stem and feed on softer tissues of stem, meristem and mesocarp of fruits. Infested palms gradual wilt and drying of outer whorl of fronds is seen. Rotting of spear occurs in severe cases. Red palm weevil lays eggs on injuries made by rhinoceros beetle on bunches. Larvae feed on the mesocarp of fruits and penetrate into peduncle for pupation. Infestation causes qualitative and quantitative loss of the fruits.

Life History and Identification

As mentioned in Coconut.

Management

As mentioned in Coconut.

❑ Mealy bugs: *Dymicoccus brevipes* (Cockerell, 1893)

Common Name	:	Mealy bugs
Scientific Name	:	*Dymicoccus brevipes* (Cockerell, 1893)
Family	:	Pseudococcidae
Order	:	Hemiptera

Source: *https://agritech.tnau.ac.in/*

Distribution and Host Range

The species is found primarily on pineapple and other species in the genus *Ananas*, but also infests citrus trees, cotton, banana, coffee and other plants. *Dysmicoccus brevipes* can be found in a wide variety of regions. It has been found in Hawaii, the Pacific, Central and South America, Australia and Africa.

Nature and Symptoms of Damage

Mealy bugs infest the spear leaves of oil palm seedlings in the nursery and main field. Yellowing of young leaves and stunted growth of palms. It is also infests the unripe and ripe oil palm fruits. It results in pre anthesis of male and female inflorescences.

Life History and Identification

The species is **ovoviviparous**, and the female gives birth to live young, typically two or three hundred, after which she dies. The first stage larvae are known as "crawlers" and disperse, sometimes being conveyed by the wind to new host plants. The larval stage is variable but lasts for about five weeks. The only larval stages that feed are the first and the beginning of the second instar stage. After the third moult, the larva becomes mature, and the total lifespan averages 95 days.

Management

Collection and destruction of infested plant parts. Collect planting material from unaffected plantation. Release coccinellid beetle, *Cryptolaemus montrouzieri* @ 10/tree. Spraying with dimethoate at 0.03% or methyl demeton at 0.025%.

❑ Burrowing rat: *Tatera indica* (Hardwicke, 1807)

Common Name	:	Burrowing rat; Rodents
Scientific Name	:	*Tatera indica* (Hardwicke, 1807)
Family	:	Muridae
Order	:	Rodentia

Source: *https://encrypted-tbn0.gstatic.com/*

Distribution and Host Range

The Indian gerbil (*Tatera indica*) also known as antelope rat, is a species of rodent in the family Muridae. It is found in southern Asia from Syria to Bangladesh. It is the only species in the genus *Tatera*. Members of the genus *Gerbilliscus* have historically been placed in *Tatera*.

Nature and Symptoms of Damage

The burrowing rats burrow down to the bole of the palms and make cavities into the hole. Feed the sweet inner cabbage portion. No external symptoms are seen. Entire meristematic region is devoured. Suddenly the leaves look wilted or dried and death of the palm.

Life History and Identification

Head and body length is 17-20 cm. Tail is 20-21 cm. Dorsal surface including entire head is light brown or light brown with rusty wash. Underparts are white. Tail fully furred, dark blackish brown with grayish sides and prominent black tuft on tip. Fur on body soft, sparse underneath; tail fur is longer. Eyes are large and prominent. Bounding gait is distinguished when running.

Management

Rodent management envisages a comprehensive programme involving.

Orchard sanitation: Field sanitation, clean cultivation.

Mechanical barrier: At the time of planting – rodent infested areas, can be covered with 22-gauge galvanized iron (chicken) wire mesh around the bole.

Traps: Different traps are available in the market. Cage trap, spring death trap, death fall trap, bamboo noose trap etc. Trap shyness may become a problem after continuous use. Cleaning and washing the traps daily. Changing the places for keeping the traps frequently etc.

Poison baiting: A number of rodenticides are available in the market under acute poisons and chronic poisons. Zinc phosphide is used as acute poison, but induces bait shyness in rodents. Single dose anticoagulant – Bromadiolone (0.005%). It is available in wax cake formulations. Multiple dose anticoagulants – Warfarin, Fumarin. The basins should be placed in the field in the evening and removed in the morning. Dead rats should be buried to avoid secondary poisoning. A large number of predators used to regulate the rodent population in nature. Introduction of predators – Snakes, vultures, mongoose, cats and dogs.

Management of Oil Palm pests in General

Remove dead palm trunks and empty bunch heaps from the field and maintain good field sanitation. Hand picks the adults of rhinoceros beetle using iron hook. Collect and destroy all the various bio stages of the rhinoceros beetle from the manure pits. Set up light trap following the first rains in summer and monsoon period to attract the rhinoceros beetle and red palm weevil. Soak castor cake at 1 kg in 5 litres of water in small mud pots and keep them in the oil palm garden to attract and kill the adults of rhinoceros' beetle. Keep the mud pots containing toddy, acetic acid, oil palm petioles and yeast to attract and kill the adult red palm weevil. Do not cut the green leaves of oil palm and cut them at 120 cm away from the base if it is needed. Avoid cuts and injuries on oil palm. Release exotic predator reduvid bug, *Platymeris laevicollis* at 6 bugs per palm at regular intervals to reduce the population of rhinoceros' beetle. Apply entomopathogenic fungus *Metarrhiziwn anisopliae* @ 5 × 10 spores 3/m at the breeding site of the rhinocerous beetle. Release *Oryctes baculovirus* inoculated beetles in the oil palm plantation to minimize the pest incidence. Place 3-4 naphthalene balls in the youngest spear axils at weekly intervals to deter the rhinoceros' beetle. Fill the crown and top most three-leaf axils with a mixture of carbaryl 10 D and fine sand (1:2 by volume) once in 3 months. Drench the manure pit with carbaryl 0.1 % solution once in three months. Follow root feeding of monocrotophos at 10 ml + 10 ml water for 3 times at 3 weeks interval of time to control red palm weevil. Place 1-2 phorate sachets (0.2 g ai) in the axils of the new leaves to minimize the infestation of spindle bug.

Resistant Varieties	
World	**India**
Elaeis guineensis: This is the most widely cultivated oil palm species, and there are several varieties that have been developed or identified as resistant to different insect pests. For example, the Dura × Pisifera hybrid variety is resistant to the African oil palm weevil (*Elaeidobius kamerunicus*), while the Tenera variety is resistant to the same pest as well as to the rhinoceros beetle (*Oryctes rhinoceros*). **Elaeis oleifera:** This species is native to South America and is less widely cultivated than *Elaeis guineensis*. However, it has been found to be more resistant to certain insect pests, such as the red palm mite (*Raoiella indica*) and the coconut hispine beetle (*Brontispa longissima*), than *Elaeis guineensis.* **Hybrids:** There are also several hybrid varieties of oil palm that have been developed for their resistance or tolerance to insect pests. For example, the DxP (Dura × Pisifera) hybrid is resistant to the African oil palm weevil and the rhinoceros beetle, while the DxT (Dura × Tenera) hybrid is resistant to the rhinoceros beetle and tolerant to the bagworm (*Metisa plana*). **Other varieties:** Some other oil palm varieties that have been identified as resistant or tolerant to certain insect pests include the Deli × La Mé hybrid, which is resistant to the rhinoceros beetle and the bagworm, and the Malayan Dwarf variety, which is tolerant to the coconut hispine beetle.	**Tenera:** It is a hybrid variety of oil palm obtained by crossing the Dura and Pisifera varieties. Tenera is highly resistant to rhinoceros beetle and red palm weevil. **Ganesh:** It is a variety of oil palm developed by the Oil Palm Breeding Programme of the Central Plantation Crops Research Institute (CPCRI), Kasaragod, Kerala. Ganesh is resistant to rhinoceros beetle, red palm weevil, and bagworm. **Co 86032:** It is a variety of oil palm developed by the Tamil Nadu Agricultural University, Coimbatore. Co 86032 is resistant to rhinoceros beetle and red palm weevil. **Dura:** It is a traditional variety of oil palm that is resistant to scale insects and bagworm. However, it is susceptible to rhinoceros beetle and red palm weevil. **Yangambi:** It is a variety of oil palm developed by the Institut National pour l'Etude Agronomique du Congo (INEAC), Congo. Yangambi is resistant to rhinoceros beetle, but susceptible to red palm weevil.

Pests of Palmyrah Palm

Scientific Name	*Borassus flabellifer*
Family	Arecaceae
Origin	Tropical Africa
Chromosome Number	2n = 36

Palmyrah palm, also known as *Borassus flabellifer*, is a tropical tree species belonging to the family Arecaceae. It is an important multi-purpose crop grown for its fruit, sap, fiber, and timber in various parts of South Asia, Southeast Asia, and Africa. Palmyrah palm is an important crop in Sri Lanka and India, particularly in the states of Tamil Nadu, Kerala, Andhra Pradesh, and Karnataka. In India, the total area under palmyrah cultivation is about 92,000 hectares, and the total production of fruits is around 210,000 tons per year. The fruits are consumed fresh or processed into various products such as jaggery, syrup, toddy, vinegar, and alcoholic beverages.

Like many crops, palmyrah palm is also affected by various pests and diseases, which can reduce its yield and quality. Some of the common pests of palmyrah palm include rhinoceros beetle, red palm weevil, and shoot borer. These pests can cause significant damage to the tree and reduce the yield of fruits and sap. Proper management practices such as regular monitoring, sanitation, and timely application of pesticides can help control these pests and minimize their damage.

❑ Rhinoceros beetle: *Oryctes rhinoceros* (Linnaeus, 1758)

Common Name	:	Rhinoceros beetle; Elephant beetle; Hercules beetle; Atlas beetle
Scientific Name	:	*Oryctes rhinoceros* (Linnaeus, 1758)
Family	:	Scarabaeidae
Order	:	Coleoptera

Source: *https://upload.wikimedia.org/*

As Described in Coconut

❑ Red palm weevil: *Rhynchophorus ferrugineus* (Olivier, 1790)

Common Name	:	Red palm weevil
Scientific Name	:	*Rhynchophorus ferrugineus* (Olivier, 1790)
Family	:	Curculionidae
Order	:	Coleoptera

Source: *https://www.biobestgroup.com/*

As Described in Coconut

❑ Black headed caterpillar: *Opisina arenosella* Walker

Common Name	:	Leaf Eating Caterpillar; Black headed caterpillar
Scientific Name	:	*Opisina arenosella* Walker
Family	:	Oecophoridae
Order	:	Lepidoptera

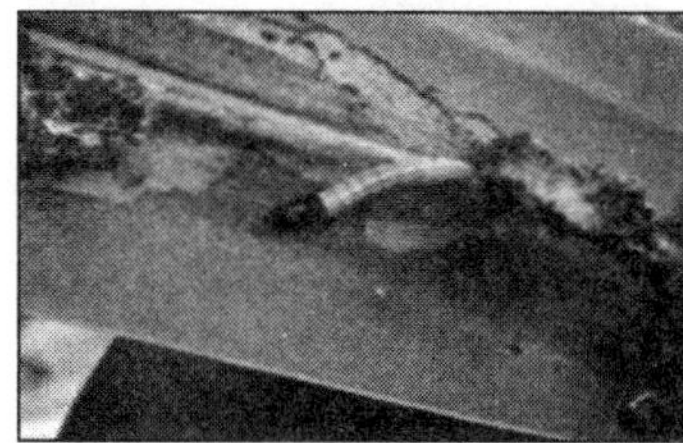

Source: *https://agritech.tnau.ac.in/*

As Described in Coconut

Resistant Varieties

Palmyra palm (*Borassus flabellifer*) is an important multipurpose tree found in various parts of India. There are no varieties of Palmyra palm that are resistant to insect pests. However, some integrated pest management strategies such as regular cleaning of the tree, removal of old fronds, and use of insecticides can help to control pest infestations.

Pests of Betel Vine

Scientific Name	*Piper betle*
Family	Piperaceae
Origin	Eastern Malaysia
Chromosome Number	2n=26,32

Betel vine, also known as Paan, is a perennial, evergreen climber plant belonging to the family Piperaceae. The plant is native to Southeast Asia, where it has been cultivated and used for thousands of years for its medicinal and cultural significance. Betel vine is primarily cultivated in India, Bangladesh, and Sri Lanka. In India, the major states producing betel vine are West Bengal, Assam, Bihar, and Andhra Pradesh. The crop requires a warm and humid climate, and well-drained soil. The crop is generally propagated through stem cuttings, and trained to grow on support structures such as trellises.

Like other crops, betel vine is susceptible to insect pests and diseases, which can cause significant yield losses. Some of the common insect pests of betel vine include leaf eating caterpillars, mites, and thrips. In addition, diseases such as leaf spot and stem rot can also affect the crop. To manage these pests and diseases, farmers often use a combination of cultural, biological, and chemical control methods.

❑ Aphids: *Aphis gossypii Glover*, 1877

Common Name	:	Cotton aphid; Melon aphid
Scientific Name	:	*Aphis gossypii* Glover, 1877
Family	:	Aphididae
Order	:	Hemiptera

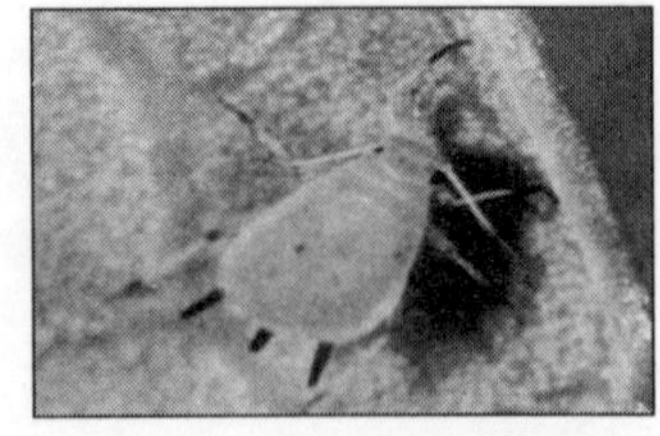

Source:https://entomologytoday.org/

As Described in Chilli

❑ Scale insect: *Lepidosaphes cornutus* Ramk

Common Name	:	Scale insect
Scientific Name	:	*Lepidosaphes cornutus* Ramk.
Family	:	Diaspididae
Order	:	Hemiptera

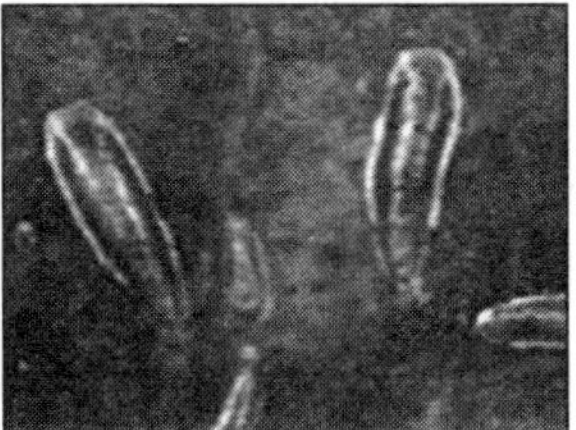

Source: *https://static.vikaspedia.in*

Distribution and Host Range

Information is very scanty.

Nature and Symptoms of Damage

Both nymph and adults infest the leaves, petioles and main veins. The scale infested leaves lose their colour, exhibit warty appearance, crinkle and dry up ultimately. The affected vines present a sticky appearance and wilt in due course.

Life History and Identification

Scales have unusual life cycles. The eggs are laid underneath the waxy covering and hatch over a period of one to three weeks. The newly hatched scales move about over the plant until they locate succulent new growth. They insert their piercing-sucking mouthparts into the plant and begin feeding. Female scales lose their legs and antennae during the first moult. They moult a second time before reaching maturity and do not pupate. The cast skins (exuviae) are incorporated in the scale cover. Male scales go through two additional moults and pupate underneath the wax. Adult males are tiny two-winged, gnat-like insects without mouthparts. *Lepidosaphes* is small, dark, boat shaped.

Management

Select scale free seed vines. Spray NSKE 5 % @ 50 g/L or chlorpyriphos 20 EC 2 ml/L or malathion 50 EC 1 ml/L of water.

❑ White fly: *Aleurocanthus nubilans* (Buckton) and *Dialeurodes pallida*

Common Name	:	White fly
Scientific Name	:	*Aleurocanthus nubilans* (Buckton); *Dialeurodes pallida*
Family	:	Aleurodidae
Order	:	Hemiptera

Source: *http://antropocene.it/g*

As Described in Potato

❑ Mealy bug: *Geococcus citrinus* Kuwana

Common Name	:	Mealy bug
Scientific Name	:	*Geococcus citrinus* Kuwana
Family	:	Pseudococcidae
Order	:	Hemiptera

Source:*https://www.yates.co.nz/*

Distribution and Host Range

Information related to this pest is scanty.

Nature and Symptoms of Damage

Both nymph and adults found on the root regions and de-sap the root portions.

Life History and Description

Information related to this pest is scanty.

Management

Spray chlorpyriphos 20 EC 2 ml/L or dimethoate 2 ml/L. Concentrate the spray towards the collar region.

Resistant Varieties	
World	**India**
Bangla: This variety is also known as Bangla desi and is widely cultivated in Bangladesh. It is resistant to thrips and mites. **Sri Lankan:** This variety is native to Sri Lanka and is resistant to thrips and mites. **Thailand**: This variety is cultivated in Thailand and is resistant to pests such as thrips and mites.	**Mitha Paan:** From west Bengal reported that, had lower infestation of mites and thrips compared to other cultivars. **Vrindavani and Gauhar:** From Karnataka, India reported that, they were less susceptible to thrips and mites compared to other cultivars. **Karpooravalli:** This variety of betel vine is native to India and is known to be resistant to pests such as thrips, mites, and leafhoppers. **Sanchi:** This variety is grown in the central region of India and is resistant to pests such as thrips and leafhoppers.

34 Pests of Cashew

Scientific Name	*Anacardium occidentale* L.
Family	Anacardiaceae
Origin	Brazil
Chromosome Number	2n = 42

The cashew nut tree (*Anacardium occidentale*) is a tropical evergreen tree that belongs to the family Anacardiaceae. It is native to Northeastern Brazil but is now widely cultivated in tropical regions of the world. India is one of the major producers and exporters of cashew nuts in the world. The major cashew nut-producing states in India are Kerala, Karnataka, Goa, Maharashtra, Andhra Pradesh, and Tamil Nadu. According to the Ministry of Agriculture and Farmers Welfare, the area under cashew cultivation in India was around 9.4 lakh hectares in 2020-21, and the total production was around 6.2 lakh metric tonnes.

Cashew nut cultivation is affected by several insect pests, including stem and root borers, shoot and fruit borers, leaf and bark eating caterpillars, scales, and mites. These pests cause significant yield losses and reduce the quality of the nuts. The most damaging pest is the tea mosquito bug, which feeds on the tender parts of the cashew plant and reduces the yield. The stem and root borers cause damage to the stem and roots, leading to stunted growth and death of the plant. Several integrated pest management strategies, including biological control, chemical control, and cultural practices, are used to control insect pests in cashew nut cultivation.

❑ Tea mosquito bug: *Helopeltis antonii* V. Signoret, 1858

Common Name	:	Tea Mosquito bug
Scientific Name	:	*Helopeltis antonii* V. Signoret, 1858
Family	:	Miridae
Order	:	Hemiptera

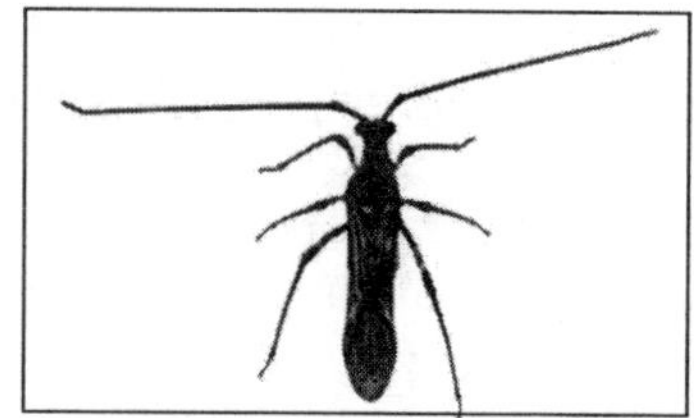

Source: https://rizosfir.files.wordpress.com/

As Described in Guava

❑ Cashew stem and root borer: *Plocaederus ferrugineus* Linn.

Common Name	:	Cashew stem and root borer
Scientific Name	:	*Plocaederus ferrugineus* Linn.
Family	:	Cerambycidae
Order	:	Coleoptera

Source: *https://plantwiseplusknowledgebank.org/*

As Described in Potato

❑ Apple and Nut borer: *Thylocoptila paurosema* Meyrick, 1888

Common Name	:	Apple and Nut borer
Scientific Name	:	*Thylocoptila paurosema* Meyrick, 1888
Family	:	Pyralidae
Order	:	Lepidoptera

Source: *https://v3.boldsystems.org/*

Distribution and Host Range

It causes 10% yield loss during years of severe infestation in certain cashew growing areas. It is present throughout the cashew growing regions of Kerala, Karnataka, Tamil Nadu and Maharashtra. Other species like *Nephopteryx* sp. present on mango, *T. panrosema* on *Cassia fistula*.

Nature and Symptoms of Damage

The caterpillars attack the fruits at all the stages and cause shrivelling and premature fall of nuts. In the early stages, the young larvae move to the joints of nut and apple, scrape the epidermis and then bore into them. In later stages, they bore into tender apples and nuts and feed on them. The borer affected nuts do not develop, become shrivelled and dried up resulting in pre mature fall of nuts and apples. The borer tunnel near the junction of apples and nuts, and the entry holes are plugged with excreta. Only a single caterpillar is generally seen either in the apple or nut, but there are reports of up to five larvae occurring in apples and three in nuts. The caterpillar bore through the apple from one end to the other.

Life History and Description

The adult is a medium sized moth with dark fore-wings and pale dark hind wings. There are 5 larval instars lasting for 15- 33 days. The fully grown larvae drop to the ground and pupate in earthen cocoons. The pupal period lasts for about 8-10 days.

Management

Removal and destruction of dead and dried inflorescence during the pre-flowering season is an effective cultural method for controlling pest population. Spray flubendiamide @ 2 ml/10 lit at the time of fruit setting. Spraying dichlorovas @ 2 ml/L of water during the off-season. Three larval parasitoids *viz., Panerotoma* sp., *Trathala flavorbitalis* and one unidentified tiny dipteran fly occur on apple and nut borer larvae and a maximum of 46.2 to 50 % parasitism.

Thrips: *Rhynchothrips raoensis* Hood, 1912; *Selenothrips rubrocinctus* (Giard, 1901)

Common Name	:	Flower thrips, Foliage thrips
Scientific Name	:	*Rhynchothrips raoensis* Hood, 1912; *Selenothrips rubrocinctus* (Giard, 1901)
Family	:	Thripidae
Order	:	Thysanoptera

Source: *https://tse3.mm.bing.net/*

Distribution and Host Range

It is distributed throughout cashew growing regions. Among the flower thrips, *S. dorsalis* and *R. raoensis* are prevalent in the East coast regions of India, whereas in West coast regions, *H. ceylonicus* and *F. schultzei* are prevalent. Many agricultural and horticultural crops are hosts for these pests. *S. rubrocinctus* hosts include arecanut, avocado, guava, pear, mango, rose and *R. cruentatus* hosts include arecanut, cocoa, almond, custard apple, grapevine, pomegranate, mango, rose, castor, cardamom, jatropha.

Nature and Symptoms of Damage

Adults and nymphs are seen in colonies on the lower surface of leaves and suck the sap from leaves, inflorescence and apples and nuts. As a result of their rasping and sucking activity the leaves become pale brown, scab on floral branches, apples and nuts, forms corky layers on the affected parts. In severe cases there will be shedding of leaves and stunting of growth of trees.

Life History and Description

They are minute, slender, fragile, soft bodied, fast-moving insects and adults have fringed wings. The nymphs emerge in about 10 days. The nymphs of red-banded thrips *S. rubrocinctus* can be distinguished by their greenish yellow colour and red bands across the first and last abdominal Segments.

Management

Spray dimethoate 30 EC or 1.5 ml in 1L of water or lambda-cyhalothrin (0.6 ml/lit) or quinolphos (2 ml/lit) or carbaryl (1 g/lit) is effective for managing thrips. Several predators like various syrphids (*Paragus* sp.), coccinellids (*Pseudospidemerus circumflexa*, *Menochilus sexmaculata*, *Coccinella transversalis*, *Scymnus* sp., *Illeis cincta*), lace wing bugs etc helps to manage this pest.

Mealy bug: *Ferrisia virgata* Cockerell, 1893

Common Name	:	Mealy bug
Scientific Name	:	*Ferrisia virgata* Cockerell, 1893
Family	:	Pseudococcidae
Order	:	Hemiptera

Source: *https://cashew.icar.gov.in/*

As Described in Tomato

❑ Leaf miner: *Acrocercops syngramma* (Meyrick 1914)

Common Name	:	Leaf miner
Scientific Name	:	*Acrocercops syngramma* (Meyrick 1914)
Family	:	Gracillariidae
Order	:	Lepidoptera

Source: *https://cashew.icar.gov.in/*

Distribution and Host Range

Infestation by this pest is common in the post monsoon flushes and young plantations all over the country. Other hosts include Mango and jamun.

Nature and Symptoms of damage

Adult start mining the epidermal layer on the upper surface of the tender cashew leaves. As a result of feeding, the affected areas form blistered patches of greyish white in colour. As the infested leaves mature the damage is manifested as big holes. Nursery seedlings and young plantations are more prone to the infestation of this pest than the older ones.

Management

Spray dimethoate 30 EC 0.03% (@ 1.5 ml/lit) during the month of October-November at new flush emergence stage. Neem oil spray are also effective. But under severe incidence in nursery and young plants, spraying is required. Two larval parasitoids *viz., Chelonus* sp. and *Sympiesis* sp. have been recorded on leaf miners in Kerala and Goa. Three larval parasitoids namely, *Chyrsocharis* sp., *Aprostocetus* sp. and *Closterocerus* sp. (Eulophidae) are found to manage this pest even up to 50%.

❑ Leaf and blossom webber: *Lamida moncusalis* Walker, [1859]

Common Name	:	Leaf and blossom webber
Scientific Name	:	*Lamida moncusalis* Walker, [1859]
Family	:	Pyralidae
Order	:	Lepidoptera

Source: *https://i.ytimg.com/*

Distribution and Host Range

It is distributed across all cashew growing areas especially East coast tracts of India. Hosts include Mango, jamun, Indian marking nut tree.

Nature and Symptoms of Damage

Presence of webs on the terminal portions of new shoots and blossom is the initial symptoms of infestation. The caterpillars remain inside web and feed on them. The incidence is found severe mostly on young trees.

Life History and Description

The eggs are laid singly or in small groups of 3-5 on the leaves. Freshly laid eggs are yellowish green in colour. The caterpillar is dark green in colour with yellow longitudinal bands and pinkish dorsal lines. There are five larval instars. Pupation takes place in cocoons in the leaf webs or in the soil. The life cycle is completed in 37 days.

Management

Spray of flubendiamide (@ 2 ml/10 lit) at flushing period will effectively control this pest. Braconids (*Apanteles* spp.), elasmid (*Elasmus* sp., *Elasmus johnstonii* F.), *Apanteles* sp. and and a tachinid fly (*Blepharella lateralis*) occur as parasitoid on leaf and blossom webber. The green lace wing, *Chrysoperla* sp. also predates on this pest.

❑ Nut Bug: *Paradasynus rostratus* (Distant)

Common Name	:	Nut bug
Scientific Name	:	*Paradasynus rostratus* (Distant)
Family	:	Coreidae
Order	:	Hemiptera

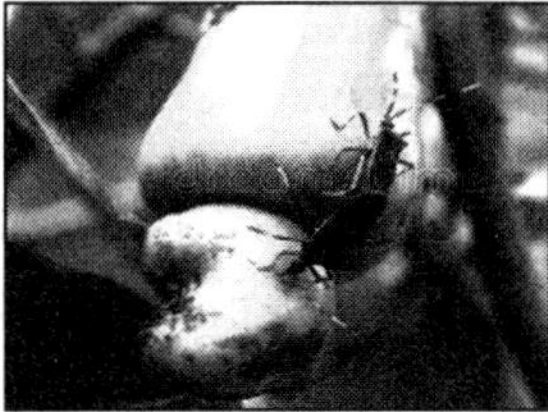

Source: *https://tse1.explicit.bing.net/*

Distribution and Host Range

The genus *Paradasynus* China (1934) comprises of seven species restricted to the Oriental Region (Coreoidea SF Team, 2019). *Paradasynus rostratus* occurring in the Western Ghats and Deccan Plateau and the adjacent areas is endemic to South India. Distant (1908) originally described it in *Pendulinus* Thunberg.

Nature and Symptoms of Damage

Suck sap from the tender nuts that result in shrivelling and drying of nuts. Adults mostly feed on the pedicel of the flowers and peduncles of developing fruits. In the case of newly formed and partially mature fruits, they also feed on the fruit surface near the calyx. Yellow gummy exudates ooze out of the feeding punctures. When disturbed, adults fly away with ejection of a jet of watery fluid. Infested flower peduncles developed small purple lesions and further feeding resulted in complete drying up of the flowers, causing direct economic loss. Since the nut crinkle feeds on the developing fruits and flowers, the damage and economic loss is significant.

Life History and Description

Yellow boat shaped eggs are laid on leaf surface in groups of 52. Incubation for 8-11 days followed by 5 nymphal instars which last for 4 weeks.

Management

Same as other hemipteran pests. The alternate hosts are major determinants of its survival and extent of damage on coconut. Hence, this observation is relevant in the management of the pest where the collateral hosts coexist with coconut.

❑ Bud worm/shoot borer: *Anarsia epotias* Meyrick, 1916

Common Name	:	Bud worm/shoot borer
Scientific Name	:	*Anarsia epotias* Meyrick, 1916
Family	:	Gelechiidae
Order	:	Lepidoptera

Source: *https://tse2.mm.bing.net/*

Distribution and Host Range

Anarsia epotias is a moth in the family Gelechiidae. It was described by Edward Meyrick in 1916. It is found in Bengal, Tamil Nadu, Kerala and Karnataka.

Nature and Symptoms of Damage

Webbed flowers and buds. Shedding of buds and flowers. Bore holes and excreta seen on attacked flowers.

Life History and Description

Larva is small, slender, pinkish brown with black head. Adult is a grey moth with black patch on wings. Eggs deposited on axils of terminal leaves singly or in batches of 10-20 @ 60 eggs per female. Incubation for 3 days followed by 5 larval instars which lasts for 14-16 days. 4th instar larva makes tunnelling's in which pupation occurs for 7-10 days.

Management

Same as other lepidopteran pests.

❑ Slug caterpillar: *Parasa lepida* (Cramer, 1799)

Common Name	:	Nettle caterpillar, blue-striped nettle grub, castor slug caterpillar
Scientific Name	:	*Parasa lepida* (Cramer, 1799)
Family	:	Limacodidae

Source: *https://metastudio.org/*

Distribution and Host Range

It is a minor pest native to Indo-Malayan region, including India, Indonesia, Bangladesh, Vietnam, Burma, Sri Lanka, Malaysia and Thailand, China, Nepal, Hongkong, Japan, Laos, Kampuchea, and Pakistan. Coconut, castor, oil palm, cacao, coffee, mulberry, pineapple, mango, pomegranate, and tea are all targets to this slug caterpillar. It is seen mostly to attack at vegetative and flowering stage and parts affected are leaves and fruits.

Nature and Symptoms of Damage

Larva stages are the infective stage of the insect to the plants. The caterpillar feeds on the leaves gregariously in the beginning, subsequently they disperse resulting in severe defoliation. This ultimately affects the growth and yield of the crop.

Life History and Description

Parasa lepida life history consists of egg, larva, pupa and adult stages. The duration of the egg stage was six days, the larval stage was forty days and the pupal stage was twenty-two days. This may fluctuate based on climate changes also. The infective stage is the larva and this stage lasts for about more than a month which is a great disadvantage to the crop growers.

The female adult lay the eggs which are flat and they overlap each other. These eggs are covered by a thin transparent layer of cement type material. In a week, the hatched-out larvae are seen in pale green, white or brilliant yellowish green coloured on the dorsal side. There are 3 green stripes running through the body of the caterpillar. A sub-dorsal and sub-lateral series of short spinous tubercles with red-tipped spines on the anterior and posterior tubercles. A series of red tipped short spined tubercles are seen along the sub lateral and sub dorsal sides of the posterior and anterior tubercles. This larva feed voraciously on leaves and enter pupal stages which are purple brown in color. Then the adult comes out of the pupa after 3 weeks. The male has a greenish head with red brown color on the sides. The thorax is in green shade with a brown band on the vertex with brown abdomen. The forewings are pale green in color, which is similar to that of a pea plant. The costa has a red-brown basal area. The outer area is reddish brown and it is widest at the inner boundary. Hindwing is yellowish at the base and reddish brown near the border. Leg joints have whitish tips. The female has reddish-brown line on the thorax which is significantly larger compared to the male and the entire hindwing is nearly reddish brown in color.

Management

Set up light traps to monitor and kill the adult moths. Spray the crown with carbaryl 0.1 % (or) dichlorovos 0.02 per cent or malathion 0.05 per cent solution. In severe cases, root feeding of monocrotophos may be taken up with safety precautions. Collect all the stages of pests *viz*. eggs on tree trunks, leaves, larvae during migration stage, pupae in soil and leaf sheath and adult moth during emergence and destruction. Organise mass collection campaign involving farmers, school children and college students. Spray dichlorovos @ 2 ml/litre using specially designed tractor mounted tall tree sprayer. Dust methyl parathion or endosulfan dust @ 1 kg/tree using power operated bellowed crane duster to reach tall trees. Encourage the predatory birds to pick up the larval stages.

Resistant Varieties

BPP-1: This variety is resistant to stem and root borer, and also has good yield potential.

BPP-2: This is a high-yielding cashew variety that is resistant to several insect pests such as stem and root borers, leaf miners, and scales. It is widely grown in India and other parts of the world. This variety is resistant to tea mosquito and stem and root borer, and is also known for its high yield potential.

BPP-3: This variety is resistant to stem and root borer, and also has good yield potential.

BPP-5: This variety is resistant to stem and root borer, and has good yield potential.

EAT-1: This is another high-yielding variety that is resistant to several insect pests including stem and root borers, tea mosquito, and scales. It is widely grown in India and other parts of the world.

Goa-1: This variety is resistant to leaf and blossom webber, and is also drought tolerant.

Goan-1: This is a cashew variety that is resistant to stem and root borers, scales, and leaf miners. It is grown in India and other parts of the world.

Kalamkati: This variety is resistant to several insect pests such as tea mosquito, stem and root borers, scales, and leaf miners. It is grown in India and other parts of the world.

Priyanka: This variety is resistant to stem and root borer, and has good yield potential.

Ullal-1: This variety is resistant to tea mosquito, stem and root borers, and leaf miners. It is a high-yielding variety and is grown in India.

Vengurla-3: This variety is resistant to stem and root borer, and also has good yield potential.

Vengurla-4: This variety is known for its resistance to stem and root borer, and also has high yield potential.

Vridhachalam-1: This variety is resistant to tea mosquito, stem and root borer, and also has good yield potential.

35 Pests of Coffee

Scientific Name	*Coffea arabica, C. canephora, C. liberica*
Family	Rubiaceae
Origin	Ethiopia
Chromosome Number	2n = 44 (C. arabica), 2n = 22 (*C. canephora, C. liberica*)

Coffee is a widely cultivated crop and one of the most popular beverages in the world. The coffee plant belongs to the family Rubiaceae and is native to tropical regions of Africa, specifically Ethiopia and Sudan. There are two main species of coffee grown commercially: *Coffea arabica* and *Coffea robusta*. Arabica coffee is considered to be of higher quality and is grown at higher elevations, while robusta coffee is hardier and is grown at lower elevations.

Coffee is an important crop in many countries and is a major source of income for farmers. In India, coffee is mainly grown in the states of Karnataka, Kerala, and Tamil Nadu. According to the Ministry of Agriculture and Farmers' Welfare, the area under coffee cultivation in India was around 4.54 lakh hectares, with a production of 3.16 lakh MT during 2019-20.

Coffee is susceptible to several pests and diseases that can cause significant yield losses. The most common pests that affect coffee are coffee berry borer, leaf miner, white stem borer, and mealybugs. Diseases such as coffee rust and leaf spot can also cause considerable damage to coffee crops. Here are some important pests described in detail:

❑ Coffee white stem borer: *Xylotrechus quadripes* Chevrolat, 1863

Common Name	:	Coffee white stem borer
Scientific Name	:	*Xylotrechus quadripes* Chevrolat, 1863
Family	:	Cerambycidae
Order	:	Coleoptera

Source: *https://tse2.mm.bing.net/*

Distribution and Host Range

Serious pest of arabica coffee in India. Alternate host plants include Robusta coffee, teak, etc.

Nature and Symptoms of Damage

Grub bores into the hardwood and make the tunnels may extend even into the roots. Tunnels tightly filed with the excreta of the grubs. Infested plants show visible ridges around the stem. Yellowing and wilting and drying of leaves. Young plants (7 to 8 years old) attacked by the borer may die in a year. Older plants withstand the attack for a few seasons. However, such plants are less productive.

Life History and Description

Grub white or yellowish with anterior end broader and tapering towards tail end and lasts for 10 days. Adult slender, long beetle (2.5 cm), males are generally smaller than females. In males, head shows distinctly raised black ridges and the hind femur extends beyond the apex of the elytra. In female, black ridges on the head are not much conspicuous and the hind femur does not extend beyond the apex of the elytra. Characteristic white markings are seen on the elytra. Pupation takes place for 10 days and adult 30 days. The entire life cycle is completed in a year.

Management

Maintain optimum shade on the estates. Tracing, uprooting the infested plants and burn prior to flight periods (*i.e,* during March and September). If the uprooted stem is intended for fuel purpose, it should be immersed under water for atleast 10 days. Look for ridges on the main stem and thick primaries every year. Remove the loose scaly bark of the main stem and thick primaries using coir glove or coconut husk to remove cracks and crevices on which eggs are normally deposited. Scrubbing during flight periods kills the eggs and grubs present in the bark region. Deep scrubbing should be avoided as the sharp implement may injure the green wood and eventually kill the plant. Field release of predators *Apenesia* sp. for effective control of white stem borer. When 2.5% field infection reported, spray of white muscardine fungus *Beaveria bassiana* @ 20 g/litre can be taken up. Spraying the main stem and thick primaries with neem seed kernel extract 5% can be applied frequently to get control of the pest. Spraying of chlorpyriphos 20 EC at 600 ml in 200 litres of water along with 200 ml wetting agent on the main stem and thick primaries during early part of flight period; April and October.

❑ Coffee berry borer: *Hypothenemus hampei* (Ferrari, 1867)

Common Name	:	Coffee berry borer
Scientific Name	:	*Hypothenemus hampei* (Ferrari, 1867)
Family	:	Scolytidae
Order	:	Coleoptera

Source: *https://tse3.mm.bing.net/*

Distribution and Host Range

The Coffee Berry Borer (CBB) is the most serious pest of all coffee cultivars in the world. In India, the pest was first noticed on a few plantations in the Nilgiris during early 1990.

Nature and Symptoms of Damage

Female beetle bores into the berries through the navel region. Pinhole at the tip of the berries indicate the presence of the pest. Under Severe infestation, two or more holes may be seen. Powdery substance found pushed out through the holes. They attack both young and ripe berries and make tunnels in the bean and lay eggs. Larvae feed on the beans and make small tunnels. On severe infestation, 30-80% berry loss can be seen.

Life History and Description

Adult berry borer is a small black beetle with a sub cylindrical body covered with thick hairs. Mating takes place inside the berries. Female lays about 15 eggs in the tunnel. Eggs hatch in about 10 days. Larvae feed on the beans and make small tunnels. Larval and pupal periods last for 20 and 7 days respectively. Development from egg to adult takes 30 days. The short life cycle enables the pest to complete several generations in a year.

Management

Maintain optimum shade, good drainage and proper training of the plant. Timely and clean harvest using picking mat and phytosanitary measures like removal of left over berries on plant and gleanings (berries fallen on ground) are the most effective measures to manage CBB. Dry the berries to the following moisture level parchment – 10%, Arabica cherry – 10.5%, robusta cherry – 11.0%. Transportation of infested coffee to uninfected areas is the main reason for spread. Crop bags should be fumigated before delivery to estates to avoid cross infestation. Dipping infested berries in boiling water for 2-3 minutes kills all the stages inside. Install broca traps @ 60 nos. per ha for mass trapping. Install multiple funnel trap and pitfall trap to collect and kill the adults. Pesticide should be applied at extreme caution and only if no other options is available. Spray white muscardine fungus *Beauveria bassiana* @ 20 g/l. Release of parasitoids *Cephalonomia stephendarix* and *Phymastichus coffea* effectively controls this pest. For spot sprays, chlorpyriphos 20 EC at 600 ml in 200 litres of water along with 200 ml of wetting agent may be used at right time *i.e.*, 120-150 days after blossom (Aug-Sept for Arabica and Sept- Oct for Robusta) can control pest.

❑ Shot hole borer: *Xylosandrus compactus* (Eichhoff, 1875)

Common Name	Shot hole borer
Scientific Name	*Xylosandrus compactus* (Eichhoff, 1875)
Family	Scolytidae
Order	Coleoptera

Source: *https://tse1.mm.bing.net/*

Distribution and Host Range

Host range includes, Avocado, clerodendron, cocoa, crotalaria, croton, dadap, dendrobium, mahogany, mango, neem etc.

Nature and Symptoms of damage

It is a major pest in robusta coffee affecting the secondary and tertiary branches. Small shot holes can be seen on the branches. Damage by extensive tunnelling within the branches, which limits the flow of sap. Affected branches dry up and drooping of leaves can be seen. Withered or dried branches with shot-holes indicate the presence of the pest. Leaves above the point of attack fall prematurely. Withering is faster in young branches and delayed in older twigs. Severe infestation results in the loss of productive branches.

Life History and Description

Adult beetle is brown to black with a short, sub cylindrical body. Females are darker and larger, whereas males are dull and small. Body is covered with fine hairs. Female beetle bores into the bark of tertiary branches and lays up to 50 eggs. Egg period 7 days, grub period 20 days. Grubs feed on ambrosia, a fungal growth developed on the beetle excreta. Grubs pupate near the exit in cocoons. Pupal period 10 days. Total lifecycle is completed in 35-45 days. Adult – brown to black with a short, sub cylindrical body and covered with fine hairs.

Management

Pest prefers to breed in the suckers during dry period. So, remove and destroy all the unwanted/infested suckers during summer. Maintain thin shade and drainage. Prune the affected twigs 5-8 cm beyond the shot hole and burn. This operation should commence from september onwards, as soon as the first symptom of attack like drooping of leaves is noticed and continued as a routine measure at regular intervals. Spray chlorpyriphos 20 EC.

Green scale: *Coccus viridis* (Green, 1889)

Common Name	:	Coffee green scale
Scientific Name	:	*Coccus viridis* (Green, 1889)
Family	:	Coccidae
Order	:	Hemiptera

Source: *https://alchetron.com*

Distribution and Host Range

The green scale is a serious sucking pest of coffee, particularly arabica. Host range: Citrus, mango, loquat, guava, sapota and a number of weeds.

Nature and Symptoms of Damage

Nymphs and adults suck sap from under surface of the leaves close to the midrib and veins, green shoots, spikes and berries. Upward curling of leaves and tender twigs drop. Heavy loss of the sap causes debility or even death of the plant. Honeydew excreted by the scale forms a layer on the leaves and acts as a medium for the growth of the "sooty mould".

Life History and Description

Adults flat, oval, light green with an irregular, distinct intestinal loop of blackish spots visible through the dorsum. It is sedentary and leads its whole life usually in one place. Reproduction is by parthenogenesis. Nymphs are pale yellow. Three nymphal instars with a total duration of 4 to 6 weeks. Nymphs are disseminated on their own, or through wind. Green scale is a summer pest.

Management

Control ants as in the case of mealy bugs. Remove and burn weeds which harbour the scale. Spray white halo fungus *Verticillum/Lecanicillium lecanii* @ 20 g/litre. Spray the affected patches with quinalphos 25 EC @ 2 ml/litre or dimethoate 30 EC @ 1.5 ml/l.

❑ Brown scale: *Saissetia coffeae* (Walker, 1852)

Common Name	:	Coffee brown scale
Scientific Name	:	*Saissetia coffeae* (Walker, 1852)
Family	:	Coccidae
Order	:	Hemiptera

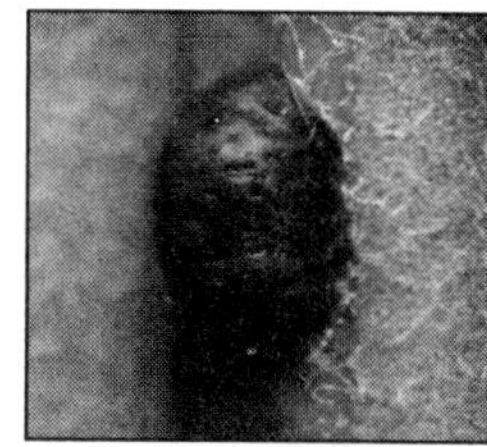

Source: *https://live.staticflickr.com/*

Distribution and Host Range

Saissetia coffeae is present in West, Central and East Africa, Madagascar, tropical and subtropical Asia, North, Central and South America and the Caribbean region. In Hawaii this scale attacks several ornamental plants including Crytomiun and other ferns, *Clermontia parviflora,* Pipturus, *Solanum santiwongsei* (Zimmerman, 1948), Dendrobium orchids, and proteas. Bittermelon is also a known host of the hemispherical scale. In other parts of the world, its main host is coffee, and alternative hosts include tea, Citrus, guava, mango, and many other cultivated and wild plants.

Nature and Symptoms of Damage

Nymphs and adults suck sap from under surface of the leaves. Honeydew excretes favours development of sooty mould fungus. Hemispherical scales feed on plant juices and cause a loss of vigor, spots on the foliage due to toxins in the scale saliva, deformation of infested plant parts, loss of leaves, retarded plant growth, and even death of the plant (Dekle, 1965; Reinert, 1974; Beardsley and Gonsalves, 1975; Valand *et al.*, 1989). In India, these scales have been responsible for causing premature death of pointed gourd vines (Valand *et al.*, 1989). Hemispherical scales are found clustered on the shoots, leaves, and young fruit of plants. They are often arranged in an irregular line near the edge of the leaf blade (Hill, 1983).

Life History and Description

Nymphs are yellow, greenish-brown or dark pink, flat and oval. **'H'** shaped yellow mark (Half grown scales). Adult female is hemispherical, body is covered by a brown hard shield. About 500 eggs are laid under the body of the female, so they are protected. After hatching, the first immature stage, the crawlers, walk about to find a place to feed. Crawlers can also spread on the wind, as well as planting materials, and even on animals, including human beings. There are two other immature stages before the adult stage. The body of the adult expands into a shell-like structure, and the scale remains in place feeding and producing large numbers of eggs and nymphs. The adults live for about 8 days. The scale is said to prefer hot, dry conditions.

Management

Control ants as in the case of mealy bugs. Remove and burn weeds which harbour the scale. Several parasites known to attack this scale in Hawaii are *Encyrtus infelix* (Embleton), *Encyrtus barbatus* Timberlake, *Tomocera californica* Howard, and the wasps *Microterys flavus* (Howard), *Scutellista cyanea* Motschulsky and *Aneristus ceroplastae* Howard. Spray the affected patches quinalphos 25 EC @ 120 ml using a gator sprayer in 200 l of water and add 200 ml of any agricultural wetting agent in 200 l of the spray solution.

❑ Mealy bugs: *Planococcus lilacinus* (Cockerell, 1905); *P. citri* Risso, 1813; *Ferrisia virgata* Cockerell, 1893

Common Name	:	Oriental cacao mealybug; Lilac mealybug
Scientific Name	:	*Planococcus lilacinus* (Cockerell, 1905), *Planococcus citri* Risso, 1813, *Ferrisia virgata* Cockerell, 1893
Family	:	Pseudococcidae
Order	:	Hemiptera

Source: *https://tse2.explicit.bing.net/*

Distribution and Host Range

Mealy bugs are the most important sucking pests of coffee. *P. citri* and *P. lilacinus* are the most common species infesting coffee. Coffee mealybug has been reported in the tropical and subtropical regions of the world. It has been found in Africa, Australia, Asia, Central and South America, and the Caribbean. *P. lilacinus* attacks cocoa, guavas, coffee and other tropical and sub-tropical fruits and shade trees.

Nature and Symptoms of Damage

Mealy bugs infest tender branches, nodes, leaves, spikes, berries and roots in large numbers. Both nymphs and adults suck the sap. Young plants succumb to heavy infestation. Leaves become chlorotic, flower buds abort and berries become small if severely infested. A black fungus (sooty mould, *Capnodium* sp.) develops on the honeydew excreted by the bugs. Consequently, the leaves of infested plants become black, affecting photosynthesis.

Life History and Description

Males are smaller and winged whereas, females are wingless with oval body. Mealybugs are a diverse group of sap-sucking insects that feed on plants. The female Cacao mealybug is is oval in shape, up to 5 mm long, and is covered in powdery white wax secretions. Combined with the underlying body colour the overall appearance may be pale mauve (a light purple-pink). There is usually a slightly darker line down the centre of the back, and 18 waxy filaments (clumps) protruding from each side. The winged adult male and wingless female are very different in appearance. The sexes are less distinct in the immature stages. Adult females and the mostly immobile nymphs form dense colonies on a wide range of host plant species. Adults are 1-3 mm in size. Round, soft-bodied insects that are brownish red or tan in colour, with clumped segments of pink/purple wax covering their bodies. They can have an indistinct black stripe on their back. Adult males have wings whereas adult females are wingless. The newly hatched nymphs are light yellow, then become pale maroon in colour.

Management

Maintain adequate shade. Destroy nests of red ant and cocktailed ant. Control ants by dusting quinalphos 1.5% or malathion 5% around the base of coffee and shade trees. Spray the affected patches with quinalphos 25 EC 300 ml. Infested roots – drench the soil near the root zone with any one of the above insecticides at the same dosage. In the case of young plants (2-4-year-old) drenching with dimethoate 30 EC @ 3 ml per litre of water effective in root and shoot mealy bugs. Field release of two introduced natural enemies *viz.*, predatory lady bird beetle *Cryptolaemus montrouzieri* and the parasitoid *Leptomastix dactylopii*.

❑ Red borer: *Polyphagozerra coffeae* Nietner, 1861

Common Name	:	Red borer
Scientific Name	:	*Polyphagozerra coffeae* Nietner, 1861
Family	:	Cossidae
Order	:	Lepidoptera

Source: *https://tse4.mm.bing.net/*

Distribution and Host Range

Host range: Tea, cinnamon, sandal, cotton, orange, teak and many forest trees. *Polyphagozerra coffeae*, the red coffee borer or coffee carpenter, is a moth of the family Cossidae. It was described by John Nietner in 1861 and is found in Asia. Records from the Moluccas and New Guinea refer to *Polyphagozerra reticulata*, which was previously considered to be a synonym of *P. coffeae*. It is a widespread pest that attacks many plants.

Nature and Symptoms of Damage

Larva causes damage in Arabica and Robusta coffee by boring into young stem, primary and secondary branches to feed on the wood. In early stages of attack, young plants or branches show signs of wilting. Infested part bears one or two holes through which, pellet like excrement of the larva hangs out and accumulate at the base of the plant. In advanced cases, the branch or the whole plant dries up.

Life History and Description

Eggs are laid on the barks. Egg period is 8 to 12 days. Red larva enters through the junction of leaf stalk and twig, constructs a tunnel that extends even up to the roots. Larval and pupal stage together last for about 12 to 24 months. After moth emergence, pupal skin protrudes outside through exit hole. Adult is a orange coloured, medium sized moth with spotted wings.

Management

Cut and burn red borer infested plant or twigs. Same as white stem borer management. Field release of white muscardine fungus *B. bassiana* and braconid parasite *Amyosoma zeuzerae* for control of the red borer. Cultural methods of control include hand picking of adults and larva immediately after an infestation is spotted or planting barrier crops such as taro, sweet potato, *Leucaena glauca* or *Pueraria*. Many parasitoids and predators are used for biological control. To control larva, *Bracon zeuzerae*, larva of *Eulophonotus myrmeleon*, and *Pantorhytes* species are used. Woodpeckers are also effective.

Root lesion nematode: *Pratylenchus coffeae Goodey,* 1951

Common name	:	Root lesion nematode
Scientific name	:	*Pratylenchus coffeae Goodey,* 1951
Family	:	Pratylenchidae
Order	:	Tylenchida

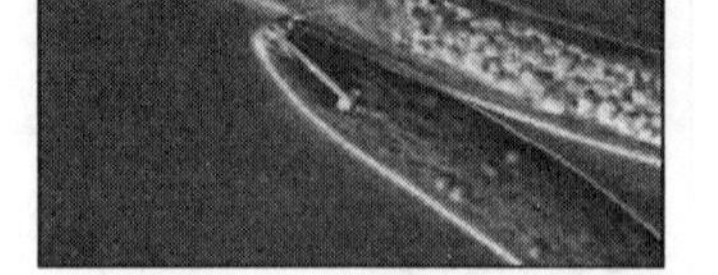

Source: *https://upload.wikimedia.org/wikipedia/commons/thumb/7/78/Pratylenchus_coffeae.jpg/330px-Pratylenchus_coffeae.jpg*

Distribution and Host Range

The host range for lesion nematodes is very extensive, over 160 hosts, and includes both grasses and broadleaf plants including crops and weeds. Due to the wide host range, crop rotation is not generally effective as a means of control. Corn and other grain crops, and alfalfa are favorite hosts.

Nature and Symptoms of Damage

Nematodes feed and destroy the tap root, secondary roots and feeder roots. Affected plants put forth adventitious roots at the collar region during rainy season. Such plants have loose anchorage and could be easily dislodged. Affected old plants lack secondary and tertiary roots. Affected young plants become unhealthy with lean and lanky stem. Older leaves become yellow and drop, leaving very few undersized, chlorite and crinkled leaves at the tip of the main stem giving a tufted appearance. Affected bearing plants show thinner main stem and have inadequate foliage to support the crop. Fresh leaves produced during pre-monsoon period are smaller, crinkled, chlorotic and leathery, but the leaves produced during monsoon are normal and healthy. Death of leaves will continue till December, leaving one or two pairs of leaves at the tip during next summer or producing a goose-neck after the receipt of rains.

Life History and Description

The nematode lays eggs in the root-lesions. Development from egg to adult takes about a month. All stages of the nematodes are attracted to the young and vigorously growing roots but only the second stage juveniles enter the roots at the piliferous zone. Robusta exhibits tolerance to the nematodes at all stages, and the nematode takes more time to complete its life cycle in robusta than in Arabica. The nematode spreads to other areas through estate implements, rain water, plants taken from the infested nurseries and soils taken from infested blocks. The pest is persistent in the soil and roots all-round the year. Higher population is noticed during the months of July, August and September when there is heavy rainfall and increased root activity. The population declines from December to March.

Management

Nursery: Dig up the nursery site and expose the soil to the sun during summer. Sieve and dry jungle soil and farmyard manure thoroughly before use. Avoid obtaining nursery plants from infested areas.

Field: Uproot and burn the affected plants. Dig up pits and expose the soil to the sun for at least one summer. Take care to keep the pits free from weeds. Plant the area with Robusta (if suitable) or Arabica – Robusta grafted plants (Arabica scion grafted on to Robusta root stock at topee stage).

Resistant Varieties	
World	**India**
BRS 189: Developed by the Brazilian Agricultural Research Corporation, this variety of cashew nut is resistant to pests such as the cashew stem and root borer and the cashew leafminer. **BRS 226:** Another variety developed by the Brazilian Agricultural Research Corporation, BRS 226 is resistant to the cashew leafminer and other pests such as fruit flies and mites. **BRS 275:** This variety, also developed by the Brazilian Agricultural Research Corporation, is resistant to the cashew leafminer and has a high yield potential. **KUL 2:** Developed by the Kerala Agricultural University in India, KUL 2 is resistant to the cashew stem and root borer and has a high yield potential. **Vengurla 4:** Developed by the Central Plantation Crops Research Institute in India, Vengurla 4 is resistant to the cashew leaf miner and has a good yield potential. **Goa 1:** Another variety developed by the Central Plantation Crops Research Institute in India, Goa 1 is resistant to the cashew leaf miner and has a high yield potential. **Kolhapur 5:** Developed by the Dr. Balasaheb Sawant Konkan Krishi Vidyapeeth in India, Kolhapur 5 is resistant to the cashew stem and root borer and has a good yield potential.	**Sln.9:** This is a variety of Coffea arabica that is resistant to coffee berry disease, which is caused by the fungus *Colletotrichum kahawae*. This variety is widely grown in India and has good yields. **S.795:** This is a hybrid variety of Coffea arabica and *Coffea canephora* that is resistant to coffee leaf rust, which is caused by the fungus *Hemileia vastatrix*. This variety is popular in India and is known for its good quality beans. **Cauvery:** This is a variety of Coffea arabica that is resistant to both coffee berry disease and coffee leaf rust. It was developed by the Coffee Research Institute in India and is a popular choice for growers. **Selection 5:** This is a variety of *Coffea robusta* that is tolerant to white stem borer, which is a common pest in coffee plantations. This variety has good yields and is resistant to other diseases as well. **Selection 9:** This is another variety of *Coffea robusta* that is resistant to white stem borer. It has good yields and is known for its high caffeine content. **Selection 6:** This is a variety of *Coffea arabica* that is resistant to leaf miner, which is a common pest in coffee plantations. It is also resistant to coffee berry disease and has good yields.

36 Pests of Tea

Scientific Name	*Camellia sinensis*
Family	Theaceae
Origin	East Asia (China)
Chromosome Number	2n = 30

Tea (*Camellia sinensis*) is a perennial evergreen crop and is one of the most important plantation crops in the world. It is primarily grown for the production of tea leaves, which are processed and used to make various types of tea. Tea is native to China and has been cultivated for thousands of years. Today, tea is grown in many countries, including India, China, Sri Lanka, Kenya, and others.

In India, tea is mainly grown in the North-eastern states of Assam, West Bengal, and Tripura, as well as in the Southern states of Tamil Nadu and Kerala. India is one of the largest tea producers in the world, with an annual production of around 1,300 million kg. Tea is an important cash crop in India, providing employment to millions of people, and earning valuable foreign exchange for the country.

Tea is susceptible to a number of insect pests, including tea mosquito bug, tea red spider mite, and tea thrips. These pests can cause significant yield losses and reduce the quality of the tea leaves. Here are some important pests described in detail:

❑ Red spider mite: *Oligonychus coffeae* (Nietner)

Common Name	:	Red spider mite
Scientific Name	:	*Oligonychus coffeae* (Nietner)
Family	:	Tetranychidae
Order	:	Acari

Source: *https://centralpestcontrol.ie/wp/*

Distribution and Host Range

It is the most widely distributed and probably also the most serious pest of tea in North-Eastern

India, and also occurs on tea in other parts of India and in other countries. Tea red spider mite also infests cotton, castor, jute, mulberry, shade tree (*Grevillea robusta*) and some other plants.

Nature and Symptoms of Damage

This mite prefers the middle zone of the bush (30 cm below the plucking surface). Nymphs and adults' lacerate cells, producing minute characteristic reddish brown marks on the upper surface of mature leaves, which turn red in severe cases, resulting in crop losses from 17 to 46 per cent. *Oligonychus coffeae* normally attack the upper surface of the mature leaves in which the sap is not flowing freely. In a severe infestation, particularly under conditions of dry weather, lower surface and the young leaves are almost equally attacked. The affected leaves turn brown, then bronze, and may eventually dry up and fall off. High temperature, dry conditions, and absence of shade are conducive to outbreak of this pest.

Life History and Description

The adult female is elliptical in shape bright crimson anteriorly and dark purplish brown posteriorly. While eggs are round, dark red and shiny. The life cycle is completed in 10-14 days. Immature stages include egg, larva, protonymph, deutonymph. Egg stage lasts for 4-6 days and nymphal stage lasts for 6-8 days.

Management

Predators: Predatory mite, Predatory thrips, *Oligota* spp., *Orius* sp (pirate bug), Hover flies, Mirid bug.

❑ Scarlet mite: *Brevipalpus californicus* (Banks); *B. phoenicis* (Geijskes, 1936)

Common Name	:	Scarlet mite
Scientific Name	:	*Brevipalpus californicus* (Banks); *B. phoenicis* (Geijskes, 1936)
Family	:	Tenuipalpidae
Order	:	Acari

Source: *https://www.agro.basf.co.za/*

Distribution and Host Range

It occurs in almost all the tea growing Asian and African countries. It causes crop losses of 8 to 17% in South India.

Nature and Symptoms of Damage

Mites congregate on the under surface of mature leaves. Both nymphs, and adults suck the cell contents from the under surface of leaves, mainly along the midribs and base of the petiole. Infested leaves have brown scurf followed by splitting of petiole and defoliation.

Life History and Description

Adult is scarlet red in colour and ovate in shape. Eggs are bright red colour and elliptical in shape and laid on the leaf petiole, at the base of the leaf hair, or inside cracks and crevices of the stem.

Immature stages include egg, larva, protonymph, deutonymphs. Egg stage lasts for 7-10 days and nymphal stage lasts for 23-26 days. The life cycle is completed in 30 to 60 days.

The female is 228 microns long. Immature specimens are reddish and adults are rufous amber. The body shape from above is ovate-sagittate with the width approximately 2/3 that of the length. The dorsal cuticular surface of the body is conspicuously reticulated.

Management

In the past, sulfur was used as a control method for *Brevipalpus* spp. in Florida. The use of sulfur in today's management programs should be minimized given its toxic effects on beneficial arthropods.

❑ Purple mite: *Calacarus carinatus* (Green)

Common Name	:	Purple mite
Scientific Name	:	*Calacarus carinatus* (Green)
Family	:	Eriophyidae
Order	:	Acari

Source: *https://www.researchgate.net/*

Distribution and Host Range

This is a major pest in South India. Assam type of tea is more susceptible to purple mite.

Nature and Symptoms of Damage

High mite infestation is found on the leaves at the middle level of the tea bushes Adults and nymphs suck the sap from under surface of mature leaves. Damaged leaves show coppery brown discolouration.

Life History and Description

Adult is very small, spindle shaped and dark purple in colour with five longitudinal white waxy ridges on the dorsal side. Immature stages include egg, larva, protonymph, deutonymphs. Egg stage lasts for 3-5 days and nymphal stage lasts for 3-6 days. Development period lasts from 6 to 11 days.

Management

Spray any one of the following Insecticides: Dicofol 18.5 EC 1250 ml/ha; Ethion 50 EC 500 ml/ha; Fenazaquin 10 EC 1000 ml/ha; Fenpyroximate 5 EC 300-600 ml/ha; Flumite 20 SC or Flufenzine 20SC 400-500 ml/ha; Phosalone 35 EC 1028 ml/ha; Propargite 57 EC 750-1250 ml/ha.

❑ Pink (or) orange mite: *Acaphylla theae* (Watt, 1898)

Common Name	:	Pink mite/orange mite
Scientific Name	:	*Acaphylla theae* (Watt, 1898)
Family	:	Eriophyidae
Order	:	Acari

Source: *http://agritech.tnau.ac.in/*

Distribution and Host Range

It is an important mite in India. Assam type of tea is susceptible to this mite.

Nature and Symptoms of Damage

Damage is restricted to top 10-15 cm of tender leaves. Affected leaves turn pale and show upward curling. In severe infestation, leaves become leathery and brownish.

Life History and Description

Adult is very minute, orange coloured and carrot shaped. Adults and nymphs found on the under surface (abaxial) of young leaves. Immature stages include egg, larva, protonymph, deutonymphs. Egg stage lasts for 2-3 days and nymphal stage lasts for 4-6 days.

Management

Spray any one of the following insecticides: Ethion 2 ml/lit of water; Azadirachtin 5 EC 200 ml/ha; Dicofol 18.5 EC 1250 ml/ha; Fenazaquin 10 EC 1000 ml/ha; Fenpyroximate 5 EC 300-600 ml/ha; Flumite 20 SC/Flufenzine 20SC 400-500 ml/ha; Phosalone 35 EC 1028 ml/ha; Propargite 57 EC 750-1250 ml/ha; Spary wettable sulphur 2 gram/lit of water.

❑ Tea totrix: *Homona coffearia* (Nietner, 1861)

Common Name	:	Tea totrix
Scientific Name	:	*Homona coffearia* (Nietner, 1861)
Family	:	Totricidae
Order	:	Lepidoptera

Source: https://alchetron.com

Distribution and Host Range

This pest is widely distributed all over the country but is considered as serious pest of tea in Southern parts of India. The larvae feed on *Acacia auriculiformis*, *Arachis hypogaea*, *Bauhinia*, *Cajanus indicus*, *Calophyllum inophyllum*, *Camellia sinensis*, *Cinnamomum*, *Citrus*, *Coffea*, *Crotalaria*, *Derris*, *Eucalyptus alba*, *Eugenia polyantha*, *Glochidion*, *Gossypium*, *Linum*, *Melochia indica*, *Nephelium*, *Pluchea indica* and *Pyrus*.

Nature and Symptoms of Damage

Newly hatched larvae mostly move upwards to the growing points of their host plant and begin feeding. From the second to the fifth and final instar, caterpillars make leaf nests by webbing the leaves using silken threads and feed from inside. Young larvae prefer tender leaves while the older larvae prefer matured leaves.

Life History and Description

The tea tortrix has a life cycle which takes about 35 to 49 days to complete. Brown coloured adult moth is bell shaped in outline while at rest. Immediately after copulation, adult females lay 100 to

150 clusters of egg on the surface of the leaves of host plant. Eggs are scaly and minute with overlapping appearance. After 6 to 8 days of laying, larvae hatch from the eggs. Larvae complete five instars and become fully grown after 3 to 4 weeks. Fully grown caterpillar is about 22 mm in length. Pupation occurs in the folds of the leaves. After 9-15 days of pupal life, adult emerges.

Management

Adults can be mechanically removed by hand and light traps. Parasite *Macrocentrus homonae* used successfully in tea estates of Sri Lanka and India. New Guinea effectively used *Theronia simillima* and *Camptotypus clotho* to control the caterpillars and adults. Several chemical pesticides such as aminocarb, fenitrothion and formothion are effective, but they also destroy natural enemies of the moth.

❑ Sapling borer: *Sahyadrassus malabaricus* Moore

Common Name	:	Stem borer
Scientific Name	:	*Sahyadrassus malabaricus* Moore
Family	:	Hepialidae
Order	:	Lepidoptera

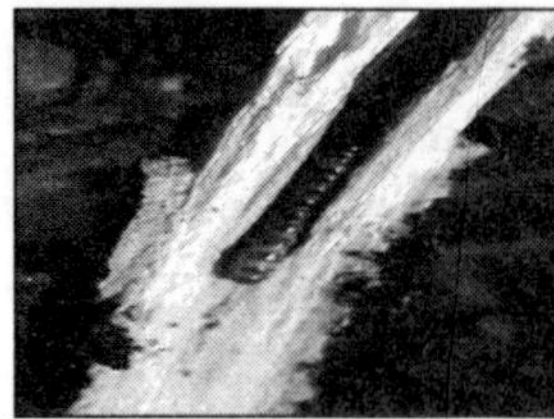

Source: *https://agritech.tnau.ac.in/crop_protection/clove/clove_1.html*

Distribution and Host Range

The stem borer is the most serious pest of clove in India and is generally seen in clove plantations grown near forest clearings. The pest has a wide host range and has been recorded on more than 40 species of woody plants and trees.

Nature and Symptoms of Damage

The larva of the stem borer girdles the stem of young clove trees at the basal region and bores downward into the root zone. The girdled region and the bore-hole are covered with frass consisting of coarse wood particles that are formed as a mat-like structure. The infested trees wilt and defoliate and succumb to the pest attack subsequently.

Life History and Description

Egg: The eggs are laid on the weeds around the basins of clove trees.

Larva: Early instar larvae feed on the weed plants and the later instars migrate to the clove trees and bore into the stem. The larvae are creamy white with a black head and fully grown larvae measure about 90 mm in length. The dorsal sclerites of the thoracic and abdominal segments are brown.

Pupa: Pupation occurs within the larval tunnel.

Adult: The adult is a large sized moth with a wing span of about 110 mm with greyish-brown mottled forewings.

Management

The base of clove trees is to be inspected regularly for symptoms of pest infestation. In case the pest infestation is noticed on the stem, the mat-like frass has to be removed and quinalphos 0.1%

sprayed around and injected into the bore hole. Swabbing the basal region of the main stem of young clove trees with carbaryl paste and keeping the basins of clove trees free of weeds are prophylactic measures for preventing the pest infestation.

Thrips: *Scirtothrips bispinosus*

Common Name	:	Thrips
Scientific Name	:	*Scirtothrips bispinosus*
Family	:	Thripidae
Order	:	Thysanoptera

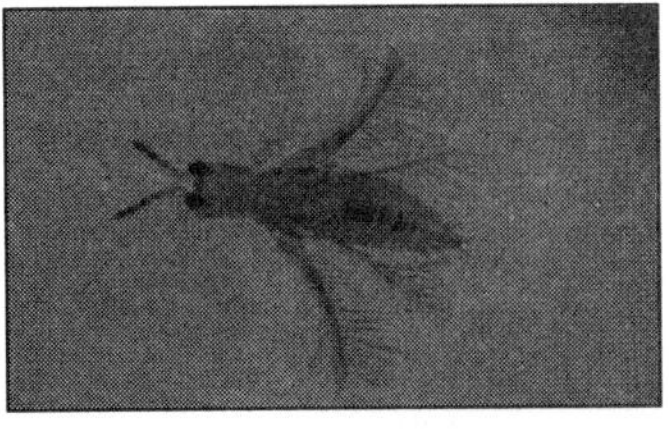

Source: *https://agritech.tnau.ac.in/crop_protection/tea/thrips.png I*

Distribution and Host Range

It is an extremely successful invasive species of pest-thrips. In India, it has been described as a pest of castor, pepper, cotton, tea, mango, and peanut. Outside of India, it has been reported as pest in China on tea and fruits like litchi, in Taiwan on citrus and vegetable, on citrus and tea in Japan, many vegetable and fruit crops in Thailand, peppers and mango in Vietnam, and even seasonally on the Korean peninsula.

Nature and Symptoms of Damage

Thrips prefer young leaves and buds. Leaf surface becomes uneven, curled and matty. Feeding marks on the unopened buds – parallel brown lines on the leaves. Thrips lacerate leaf tissues and suck oozing sap. Lacerations appear as brownish irregular streaks or silvery patches on the leaf surface. Infested leaves become distorted, crinkled or mottled. Damage is more pronounced in exposed areas during dry weather.

Life History and Description

Adults are minute with brownish abdomen. Wings are characteristically fringed with fine hairs. Thrips insert eggs singly into the leaf tissues. Eggs hatch in 9 days. There are two nymphal instars followed by prepupal and pupal stages. The pupae remain on the leaf, or drop to the ground. Immature stages last for 3 weeks. Under favourable conditions, there could be 12 generations in a year.

Management

Maintain optimum overhead shade, Spary any one of the insecticides like Dimethoate 30 EC 2 ml/lit, Chlorpyriphos 20 EC 2 ml/lit, Deltamethrin 2.8 EC 120-150 ml/ha, Azadirachtin 5 W/W 200 ml/ha, Quinalphos 25 EC 760 ml/ha.

Natural enemies: Predators: *Anthocoris* and *Orius* spp., predatory thrips (*Aeolothrips intermedius*, *Mymarothrips garuda*), *Chrysoperla carnea*, *Mallada* spp., praying mantids, ladybird beetles, syrphid flies, spiders etc.

Pathogens: *Steinernema* spp., *Verticillium lecanii*, *Beauveria bassiana*, *Metarhizium anisopliae*, *Paecilomyces fumerosus*.

❑ Tea aphid: *Toxoptera aurantii* (Boyer de Fonscolombe)

Common name	:	Tea aphid
Scientific name	:	*Toxoptera aurantii* (Boyer de Fonscolombe)
Family	:	Aphididae
Order	:	Hemiptera

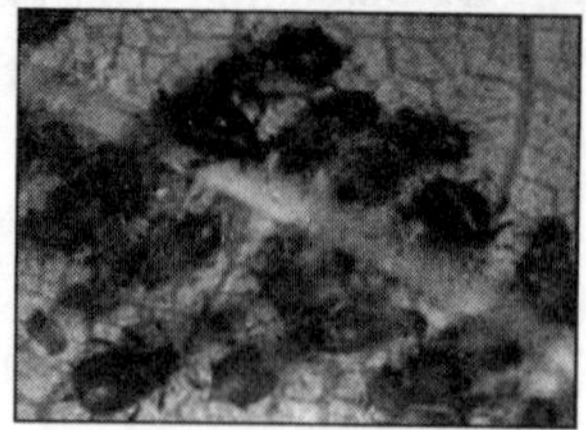

Source: *http://eagri.org/eagri50/ENTO331/lecture29/tea/016_clip*

As Described in Citrus

Management

Natural enemies: Parasitoids: *Aphidius colemani, Aphelinus* sp and *Diaeretiella* sp.

Predators: Fire ant, Robber fly, Big-eyed bug (*Geocoris* sp), Earwig, Ground beetle, Cecidomyiid fly, Lacewing, Ladybird beetle, Spider, Praying Mantis, Reduviid, Dragon fly, hoverfly.

❑ Tea leaf roller: *Caloptilia theivora* (Walsingham, 1891)

Common Name	:	Tea leaf roller
Scientific Name	:	*Caloptilia theivora* (Walsingham, 1891)
Family	:	Gracillariidae
Order	:	Lepidoptera

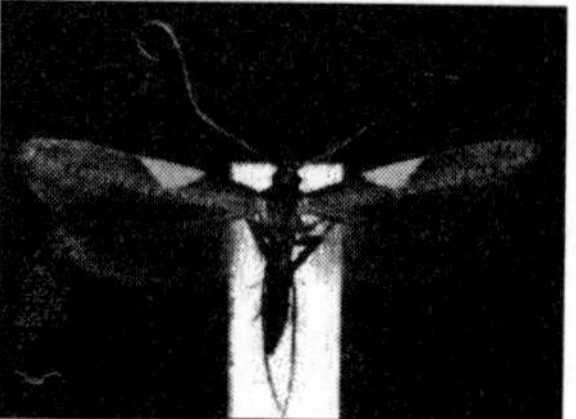

Source: *data:image/jpeg;base64,*

Nature and Symptoms of Damage

Second instar larvae mine the tender leaf and reaches leaf margin. Fourth instar larva rolls the leaves from tip downwards. Larva yellowish. Adult is a microlepidopteran with long antenna, golden iridescent patches in forewing and abdomen.

Management

Spray NSKE 5 % or endosulfan 35 EC, phosalone 35 EC, chlorpyriphos 20 EC, dimethoate 30 EC, malathion 50 EC, phenthoate 50 EC 1000 ml with water 500 L per ha.

❑ Tobacco caterpillar: *Spodoptera litura* (Fabricius, 1775)

Common Name	:	Tobacco caterpillar; Tobacco cutworm; Cotton leafworm; Leaf eating caterpillar
Scientific Name	:	*Spodoptera litura* (Fabricius, 1775)
Family	:	Noctuidae
Order	:	Lepidoptera

Source: *https://en.wikipedia.org/wiki/File:Spodoptera_litura.jpg*

As Described in Potato

❑ Broad (or) Yellow mite: *Polyphagotarsonemus latus* (Banks, 1904)

Common Name	:	Broad/Yellow mite
Scientific Name	:	*Polyphagotarsonemus latus* (Banks, 1904)
Family	:	Tarsonemidae
Order	:	Acari

Source: *http://agritech.tnau.ac.in/*

As Described in Chilli

❑ Tea mosquito bug: *Helopeltis antonii* V. Signoret, 1858

Common Name	:	Tea Mosquito bug
Scientific Name	:	*Helopeltis antonii* V. Signoret, 1858
Family	:	Miridae
Order	:	Hemiptera

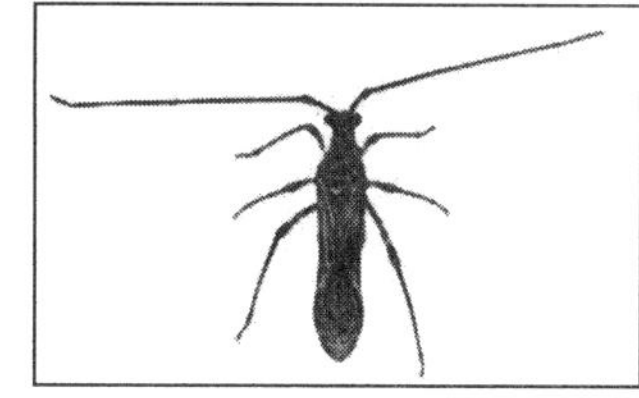

Source: *https://rizosfir.files.wordpress.com*

As Described in Guava

Natural enemies associated with tea mosquito bug

Parasitoids: Mymarid, *Erythmelus helopeltidis*.

Predators: *Chrysoperla zastrowii* sillemi, *Mallada* sp, *Oxyopes* sp. (Spider), Reduviid bug Praying Mantids.

Pathogens: Nematodes (*Hexamermis* sp.) *Beauveria bassiana*.

❑ Shot hole borer: *Euwallacea fornicates* (Eichhoff, 1868)

Common Name	Shot hole borer
Scientific Name	*Euwallacea fornicatus* (Eichhoff, 1868)
Family	Scolytidae
Order	Coleoptera

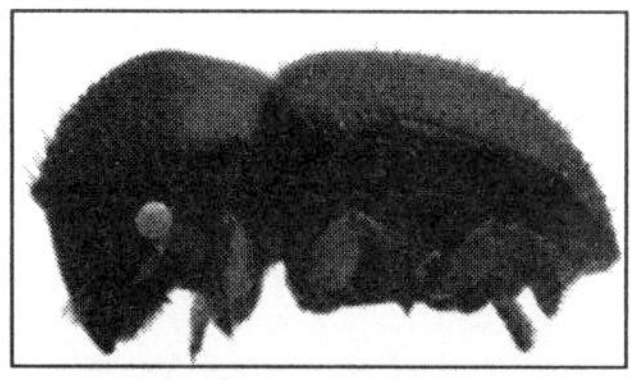

Source: *https://agritech.tnau.ac.in/*

As Described in Coffee

❑ Red borer: *Polyphagozerra coffeae* Nietner, 1861

Common Name	:	Red borer
Scientific Name	:	*Polyphagozerra coffeae* Nietner, 1861
Family	:	Cossidae
Order	:	Lepidoptera

Source: *https://tse4.mm.bing.net/*

As Described in Coffee

Resistant Varieties

Assam: Assam tea is grown in the North-eastern part of India, and it is resistant to pests such as tea mosquito and thrips.

Darjeeling: Darjeeling tea is a high-quality tea that is grown in the Darjeeling district of West Bengal, India. It is resistant to pests such as red spider mites and tea mosquitoes.

Kenya tea: Kenya is one of the largest producers of tea in the world, and its tea varieties are known for their resistance to pests such as tea mosquito and thrips.

Ceylon tea: Ceylon tea is grown in Sri Lanka, and it is resistant to pests such as tea mosquito and red spider mites.

China tea: China is one of the oldest tea-producing countries, and its tea varieties are resistant to pests such as tea leafhopper and scale insects.

Japanese tea: Japanese tea varieties are resistant to pests such as tea scale insects and tea leafhoppers.

TV1: This is a hybrid variety of tea that is resistant to pests like red spider mite and mosquito bug.

UPASI-9: Developed by the UPASI Tea Research Foundation, this variety is resistant to pests like tea mosquito bug, thrips, and red spider mite.

UPASI-15: Another variety developed by the UPASI Tea Research Foundation, UPASI-15 is resistant to tea mosquito bug, thrips, and red spider mite.

Tocklai Selection-9: Developed by the Tocklai Tea Research Institute in Assam, this variety is resistant to pests like tea mosquito bug, thrips, and red spider mite.

PH-1: Developed by the Tea Research Association in India, PH-1 is resistant to pests like red spider mite, mosquito bug, and helopeltis.

BV-1: This is a variety of tea that is resistant to pests like tea mosquito bug and red spider mite.

37 Pests of Rubber

Scientific Name	*Hevea brasiliensis*
Family	Euphorbiaceae
Origin	Brazil
Chromosome Number	2n=36

Rubber is an important commercial crop that is widely cultivated in tropical and subtropical regions around the world. Botanically, rubber is known as *Hevea brasiliensis* and belongs to the Euphorbiaceae family. It is a tall, fast-growing tree that can reach up to 30 meters in height. The tree has a straight trunk with smooth, grayish bark, and large, glossy green leaves.

Rubber cultivation requires a warm and humid climate with an annual rainfall of around 2000-3000 mm. The crop is mostly grown in Southeast Asia, India, Sri Lanka, Africa, and Latin America. In India, Kerala, Tamil Nadu, and Karnataka are the major rubber-producing states.

Rubber is susceptible to a number of pests and diseases that can cause significant damage to the crop. Some of the major pests include the rubber plant bug, mealybugs, spider mites, and bark-eating caterpillars. These pests can cause yield losses by feeding on the leaves, bark, or latex of the tree.

Scale insect: *Parasaissetia nigra* (Nietner, 1861)

Common Name	Scale insect
Scientific Name	*Parasaissetia nigra* (Nietner, 1861)
Family	Coccidae
Order	Hemiptera

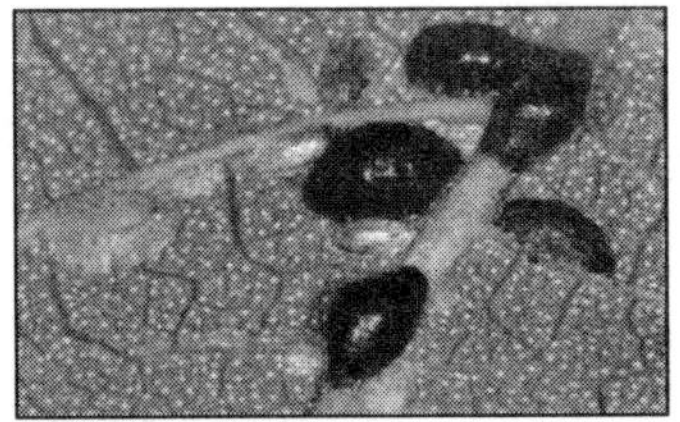

Source: https://tse1.mm.bing.net

Distribution and Host Range

Native to Africa, this scale has a cosmopolitan distribution throughout the world. Present in Hawaii since 1895, the scale is present on all major islands except Lanai. Hosts of the nigra scale include Anthurium, bamboo, coffee, cotton, croton, eggplant, fig, edible ginger, guava, macadamia, ornamentals, and pineapple.

Nature and Symptoms of Damage

Occur on leaflets petioles and tender shoot portions and suck the sap, severely affected portions dry up and die. The scale feeds from the phloem of the host plant and may be found on leaves or twigs containing chlorophyll. Damage due to feeding of an individual scale is small. However, when large populations are present, yellowing, defoliation, reduction in fruit set, and a loss in plant vigour may result.

Life History and Description

This scale is believed to reproduce parthenogenetically, or non-sexually. Females are able to lay viable eggs without fertilization by males. Males have not been found in this species, and populations are believed to be comprised solely by females. Under laboratory conditions, generations of this scale were continuous when raised on potato sprouts at 75°F. One generation (egg to reproducing female) was completed in 45 to 60 days. Laboratory rearing on Annona and Citrus gave similar results.

Management

Removal of affected leaves and branches will prevent the spread. Natural biological control is usually sufficient to keep populations of this scale at bay. Single tree or branch infestations may be cut and left on the ground for parasites to emerge from. Several natural enemies of the nigra scale are present in Hawaii. Parasites include *Microterys flavus*, *Encyrtus kotinskyi*, *Encyrtus infelix*, *E. barbatus*, *Tomocera californica*, *Scutellista cyanea*, *Coccophagus hawaiiensis*, *Aneristus ceroplastae*, and *Quaylea whittieri*. Several general predators attack this scale, they include some beetles, butterflies and moths, flies, thrips, and mites. The nigra scale is also attacked by a fungus, probably *Entomophthora pseudococci*. If natural control is insufficient in widespread attacks, trees may be banded to keep off attendant ants. Banding involves either painting or spraying a 1% dieldrin on to the plant stem. Oil spraying using 10 pints of white oil in 40 gallons of water has also proven satisfactory. When severe infestation is noted, spray malathion at 0.05%.

❑ Cockchafer grub: *Holotrichia serrata* (Fabricius, 1781)

Common Name	:	Sugarcane white grub or Cockchafer grub
Scientific Name	:	*Holotrichia serrata* (Fabricius, 1781)
Family	:	Scarabaeidae
Order	:	Coleoptera

Source: *https://tse3.mm.bing.net/*

As Described in Potato

❑ Bark feeding caterpillar: *Aetherastis circulata* Meyr.; *Ptochoryctis rosaria* Meyr

Common Name	:	Bark feeding caterpillar
Scientific Name	:	*Aetherastis circulata* Meyr. *Ptochoryctis rosaria* Meyr
Family	:	Yponomeutidae
Order	:	Lepidoptera

Source: *https://tse1.mm.bing.net*

Nature and Symptoms of Damage

The caterpillars build galleries with faecal matter and silk all over the trunk region and branches of trees. They generally feed on dead bark and occasionally on live bark causing exudation of latex. Deep scar is found at the regions of feeding.

Management

When the infestation is severe, apply sevin 5% at the rate of 10 kg per ha or ekalux 1.5% or fenval 0.4% dust at the rate of 7 kg per ha (provisional recommendation) with a power duster.

Termites: *Odontotermes* obesus (Rambur)

Common name	:	Termites
Scientific name	:	*Odontotermes obesus* (Rambur)
Family	:	Termitidae
Order	:	Isoptera

Source: *https://www.forbes.com/home-improvement/pest-control/types-of-termites/*

As Described in Mango

Wood borers

Wood borers attack partially dried bark of rubber and make tunnels into wood. The opening of tunnels is easily noticeable by the wood dust ejected from them. Such trees may break and fall. The bark of affected region should be scraped lightly and painted with a combination of carbaryl 0.5 per cent (Sevin 50 WP, 10 g/l) + Quinalphos 0.25 per cent (Ekalux 25 EC, 10 ml/l) thrice at weekly intervals for control of the borer beetles.

Invertebrate pests like slugs, snails, mites and nematodes as well as vertebrate pests like rats, porcupines, etc., cause damage to rubber plants.

Two tailed mealy bugs: *Ferrisia virgata* Cockerell, 1893

Common Name	:	Striped mealybug; Two tailed mealy bug
Scientific Name	:	*Ferrisia virgata* Cockerell, 1893
Family	:	Pseudococcidae
Order	:	Hemiptera

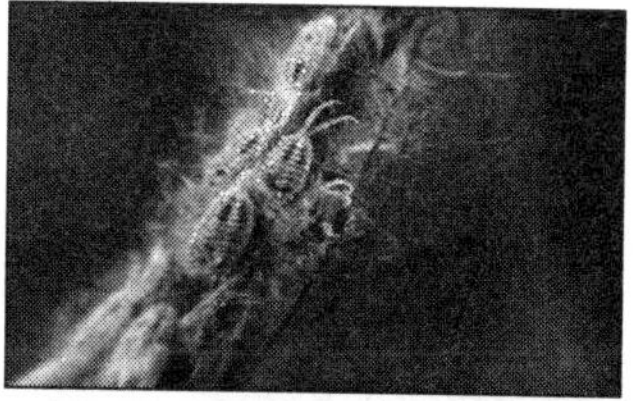

Source: *https://tse4.mm.bing.net/*

As Described in Tomato

Slugs and Snails

Common Name	:	Brown slug
Scientific Name	:	*Mariaella dussumieri* Gray, 1855
Family	:	Ariophantidae
Order	:	Stylommatophora

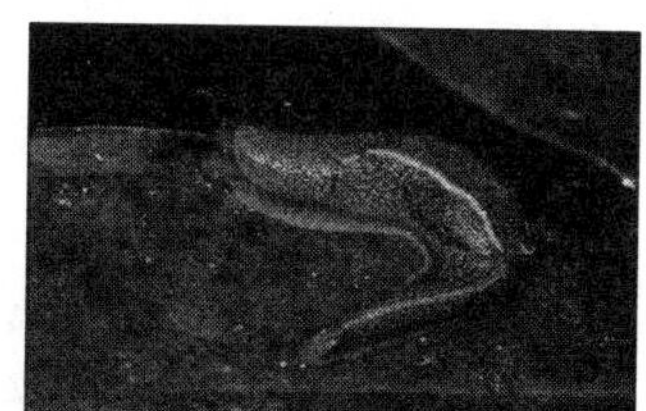

Source:*https://encryptedtbn0.gstatic.com/*

Common Name	:	Snail
Scientific Name	:	*Crypotazona bistrialis*
Family	:	Ariophantidae
Order	:	Stylommatophora

Source: *https%3A%2F%2Flandsnails.org%*

The slugs *Mariaella dussumieri* and snails *Crypotazona bistrialis* damage young rubber. They climb on the stems and feed on the terminal and auxiliary buds arresting growth of young plants. Shoots become compact cluster with club shaped appearance. Occasionally they climb on mature trees and drink latex from the tapping cut and collection cups. They usually feed during night and remain concealed during the day time under mulch or other materials lying on the ground. Their presence can be detected by the spring like excreta and glistening lines of dried slimy secretion. The slugs and snails can be controlled by application of metaldehyde either as a bait or as a paint at the base of young plants. Mataldehyde baits (Metabait 2.5 per cent, 5 g per plant or Snail kill are recommended 20 g/plant). Bordeaux pastes 10 per cent painted as a band at the base of the stem repels the slugs and snails for over a month.

Rats

The Indian mole rat *Bandicota bengalensis*, the large bandicoot rat *Bandicota indica* and field rat *Rallus meltada* destroy the nursery plants and young plants in the field by eating the tap root. For control of rat's baits containing zinc phosphide (80 w/w) is used. This poison can be placed inside a food material like tapioca and used as bait. Prebaiting (without the poison) will be necessary. Bromodiolone 0.005 per cent (Roban) bait is as effective single dose anticoagulant bait.

Porcupine

Porcupine gnaw away the bark from the base of rubber trees and ring bark them. Such trees dry up. They also pull-out young plants and feed on their tap root. The common species found in India is *Hystrix indica*. Zinc phosphide bait in salt meats or applied as a slurry with wheat flour at the base of plants is effective for control. Phorate (Thimet 10 G) 10-15 g/plant applied at the base repels porcupine.

Nematodes

Root knot nematodes *Meloidogyne incognita* attack the roots of rubber seedlings in the nursery. The infected lateral roots show swellings. Plants become stunted and discoloured and the leaves shed. Systemic insecticides like Carbofuran 3 per cent (Furadan 3G, 15 kg/ha) is effective for control of nematodes.

Mites

Yellow mites *Hemitarsonemus latus* suck sap from the tender leaves. In the nursery plants this may cause defoliation. Mites can be controlled by spraying wettable sulphur 0.2 per cent (Sulfex 80 WP, 2.5 g/l) or dicofol 0.05 per cent (Kelthane 18 EC, 3 ml/l).

Wild animals

Other wild animals like rabbit, wild boar, elephant, etc., also may cause damage to rubber plants. These are serious problems in plantations nearer to forests. They can be kept away by installing an electric fence.

Resistant Varieties

GT 1: This is a variety of rubber tree that was developed in India. It is resistant to the Pink Mealybug and also shows good resistance to the South American Leaf Blight disease.

PB 235: This is another high-yielding rubber tree variety that was developed in Malaysia. It is resistant to the South American Leaf Blight disease and also shows good resistance to the Corynespora Leaf Fall disease, which is caused by the fungus *Corynespora cassiicola.*

PR 107: This is a variety of rubber tree that was developed in Thailand. It is resistant to several insect pests, including the Red Spider Mite (*Oligonychus coffeae*) and the Pink Mealybug (*Maconellicoccus hirsutus*).

RRII 105: This variety of rubber, developed by the Rubber Research Institute of India (RRII), is resistant to the South American leaf blight disease caused by *Microcyclus ulei.* This disease is a major threat to rubber plantations in India.

RRII 203: This variety of rubber is resistant to the white root disease caused by the fungus *Rigidoporus microporus.* This disease is a major threat to rubber plantations in India, but the RRII 203 variety has been developed to be resistant. This is a variety of rubber tree that was developed by the Rubber Research Institute of India. It is resistant to several insect pests, including the Red Spider Mite, the Pink Mealybug, and the Shot Hole Borer (*Xyleborus fornicatus*).

RRII 414: This variety of rubber is resistant to the spiralling whitefly, which is a major pest of rubber plantations in India. The RRII 414 variety has been developed to be resistant to this pest.

RRIM 600: This variety of rubber is resistant to the pink disease caused by the fungus *Corticium salmonicolor.* This disease can cause significant damage to rubber trees, but the RRIM 600 variety has been developed to be resistant.

RRIM 600: This is a high-yielding rubber tree variety developed by the Rubber Research Institute of Malaysia. It has shown good resistance to the South American Leaf Blight disease, which is caused by the fungus *Microcyclus ulei.*

PART D

PESTS OF SPICE CROPS

D. Saicharan
(Ph.D. Scholar)
Department of Entomology
Professor Jayashankar Telangana State Agricultural University
Rajendranagar, Hyderabad, Telangana

38 Pests of Pepper

Scientific Name	*Piper nigrum*
Family	Piperaceae
Origin	Malabar Coast of India
Chromosome Number	2n = 52

Pepper is a perennial flowering vine that belongs to the family Piperaceae. Its scientific name is *Piper nigrum*. India is one of the major producers of pepper in the world. Pepper is mainly grown in the southern states of Kerala, Karnataka, Tamil Nadu, and Andhra Pradesh. According to the latest statistics from the Ministry of Agriculture and Farmers Welfare, the total area under pepper cultivation in India is around 3,63,000 hectares, and the total production is around 66,500 metric tonnes.

Insect pests are one of the major constraints to pepper production in India, as they can cause significant yield losses and reduce the quality of the harvested produce. Insect pest infestations on pepper crops can cause significant economic damage ranging from 10-30% of the total yield, with thrips causing 20-30%, mealybugs causing 15-20%, spider mites causing 10-20%, and fruit flies causing 25-30% of the total yield loss. Some of the insect pests that affect pepper in India and their economic importance are as follows:

❑ Pollu beetle: *Longitarsus nigripennis* (Motschulsky)

Common Name	:	Pepper Pollu Beetle
Scientific Name	:	*Longitarsus nigripennis* (Motschulsky)
Family	:	Chrysomelidae
Order	:	Coleoptera

Source: *https://www.researchgate.net/figure*

Distribution and Host Range

India (West Coast area) and host plants include only Pepper (No alternate host reported so far).

Nature and Symptoms of Damage

The grubs bore into the berries of pepper.The infested berries dry up and turn dark in colour. Berries are hollow and crumble when pressed. Such hollow berries are called "POLLU" (Empty). Grub may also eat the spike causing the entire region beyond it to dry up. When contents of one berry is exhausted, the grub move to next and feed continuously. The grubs bore into the berries of pepper.The infested berries dry up and turn dark in colour. Berries are hollow and crumble when pressed. Such hollow berries are called "POLLU" (Empty). Grub may also eat the spike causing the entire region beyond it to dry up. When contents of one berry is exhausted, the grub move to next and feed continuously. The grubs bore into the berries of pepper.The infested berries dry up and turn dark in colour. Berries are hollow and crumble when pressed. Such hollow berries are called "POLLU" (Empty). Grub may also eat the spike causing the entire region beyond it to dry up. When contents of one berry is exhausted, the grub move to next and feed continuously.

The grubs bore into the berries of pepper. The infested berries dry up and turn dark in colour. Berries are hollow and crumble when pressed. Such hollow berries are called "**POLLU**" (Empty). Grub may also eat the spike causing the entire region beyond it to dry up. When contents of one berry is exhausted, the grub move to next and feed continuously.

Life History and Description

Adult is a bluish yellow shining flea beetle. Eggs are laid on the berries and lay 1-2 eggs in each hole, egg period 5-8 days, larval period 30-32 days. Pupation occurs in soil in a depth of 5.0-7.5 cm. Pupal period 6-7 days. Life cycle completed in 40-50 days. Four overlapping generations in a year.

Management

Regulation of shade in the plantation reduces the population of the pest in the field. Tilling the soil at the base of the vines at regular intervals. Rake the soil and incorporate quinalphos 1.5 D, carbaryl 5 D, Endosulfan 4 D @ 25 kg/ha to kill the pupae in the soil. Spray dimethoate 30 EC 1.5 L or quinalphos 25 EC 2.0 L in 500-1000 L of water per ha.

❑ Top shoot borer: *Cydia hemidoxa* (Meyr.)

Common Name	:	Top shoot borer; Tortrix moth; leaf rollers
Scientific Name	:	*Cydia hemidoxa* (Meyr.)
Family	:	Eucosmidae
Order	:	Lepidoptera

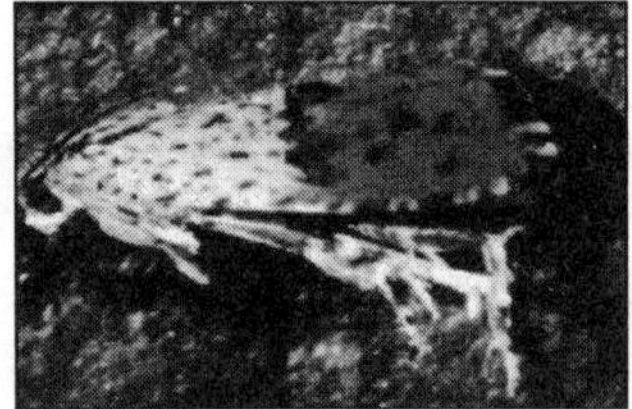

Source: *https://vikaspedia.in*

Distribution and Host Range

Its distribution is in India and found in different regions of the world with wide host range.

Nature and Symptoms of Damage

Serious pests of pepper in Kerala. The larva feeds on growing and young leaves causing drying and dying of terminal shoots.

Life History and Description

Larva greyish green, 12-14 mm long, larval period 10 -15 days. Pupates inside shoots, pupal period 8-10 days. Adult moth is tiny, forewing black with distal half red, hind wing greyish. Life cycle completed in a month.

Management:

Parasitoid: *Apanteles cypris*, *Eudederus* sp. (Hymenoptera), *Goniozus* sp.

Parasitic mite: *Clinotrombium* sp. (on larvae).

Entomopathogenic nematode: *Hexamermis* sp.

Chemical management: Spray quinalphos 25 EC 1.0 L in 500-1000 L water/ha.

❑ Marginal gall thrips: *Liothrips karnyi* (Bagnall)

Common Name	:	Marginal gall thrips
Scientific Name	:	*Liothrips karnyi* (Bagnall)
Family	:	Thysanoptera
Order	:	Thripidae

Source:*http://krishimala.com/catalogue/leaf-gall-thrips*

Distribution and Host Range

They are distributed across India and host plants include pepper.

Nature and Symptoms of Damage

Both nymphs and adults feed on leaves and cause formation of marginal folded galls on them. Presence of white or creamy white nymphs and adults inside the marginal galls is the typical symptom of attack. In severe cases of attack, whole plant becomes stunted and affects formation of spikes.

Both nymphs and adults feed on leaves and cause formation of marginal folded galls on them. Presence of white or creamy white nymphs and adults inside the marginal galls is the typical symptom of attack. In severe cases of attack, whole plant becomes stunted and affects formation of spikes.

Life History and Description

Eggs are laid in single within the marginal leaf folds or on the leaf surface, egg period 6-8 days. Nymphs whitish and sluggish, nymphal period 9-13 days, pupal period, 2 to 3 days adult longevity is 7-9 days.

Management

Parsitoids: *Aphytis* sp., *Pseudoscymcus* sp., *Chilocorus circumdatus*.

Predators: *Montandoniola moraguesi*, *Androthrips flavipes*, *Geogarypus* sp., *Lestodiplosis* sp., *Rhodesiella* sp, Predatory mites, Hoverflies, Thrips, Mirids. Spray monocrotphos 36 SL 750 ml or dimethaote 30 EC 1.0 L or chlorpyriphos 1.5 L in 500-1000 L water.

❑ Scale insects: *Aspidiotus destructor* Signoret, 1869

Common Name	:	Scale insects
Scientific Name	:	*Lepidosaphes piperis* (Green, 1908); *Aspidiotus destructor* Signoret, 1869
Family	:	Diaspididae
Order	:	Hemiptera

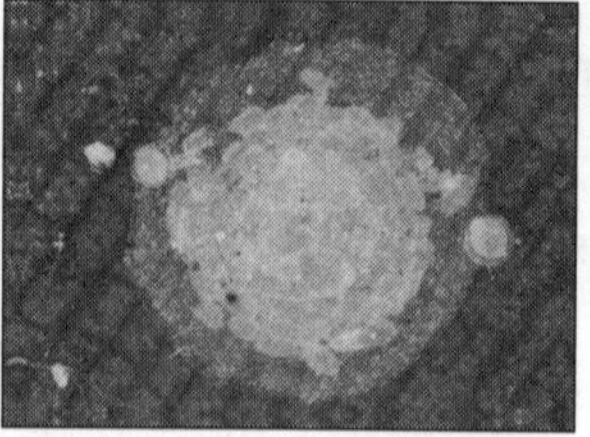

Source:*https://nrcb.icar.gov.in*

As Described in Mango

❑ Burrowing nematode: *Radopholus similis* (Cobb, 1893) Thorne, 1949

Common Name	:	Burrowing nematode
Scientific Name	:	*Radopholus similis* (Cobb, 1893) Thorne, 1949
Family	:	Pratylenchidae
Order	:	Tylenchida

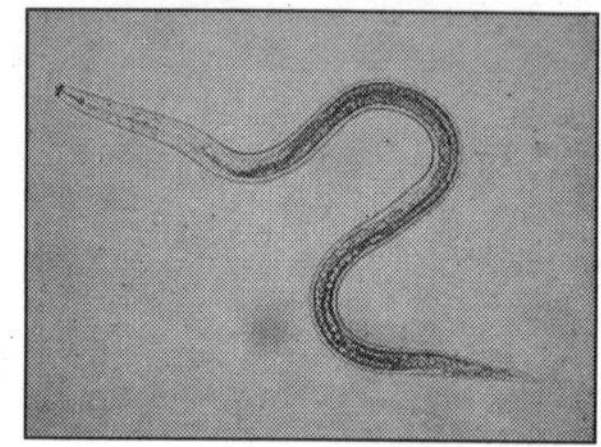

Source:*https://www.apsnet.org*

As Described in Banana

Resistant Varieties

Panniyur-1: Developed in India, Panniyur-1 is a high-yielding variety of pepper that is resistant to thrips and mites. It is known for its large berries and high piperine content.

Panniyur-2: Another variety developed in India, Panniyur-2 is resistant to thrips, mites, and mealybugs. It has a high yield potential and is characterized by its large, uniform berries.

Kuching: Developed in Malaysia, Kuching is a pepper variety that is resistant to thrips and has a high yield potential. It is known for its long, slender berries and pungent flavour.

Sarawak: Also developed in Malaysia, Sarawak is a pepper variety that is resistant to thrips, mites, and mealybugs. It has a high yield potential and is characterized by its small, round berries and strong flavor.

Tellicherry: Grown in India and named after the city of Thalassery (formerly known as Tellicherry), this variety is known for its large, aromatic berries and is resistant to thrips.

Lampong: Grown in Indonesia, Lampong is a variety of pepper that is resistant to mites and has a strong, pungent flavor. It is characterized by its long, thin berries and is often used in Indonesian cuisine.

Brazil: Grown in Brazil, this variety of pepper is resistant to thrips and has a high yield potential. It is known for its small, round berries and is often used in the production of pepper oil and oleoresins.

39 Pests of Cashew

Scientific Name	*Elettaria cardamomum*
Family	Zingiberaceae
Origin	Indian subcontinent and Indonesia
Chromosome Number	2n = 48

Cardamom, also known as *Elettaria cardamomum*, is a perennial herbaceous plant that belongs to the family Zingiberaceae. India is one of the major producers of cardamom in the world. The states of Kerala, Karnataka, and Tamil Nadu are the major cardamom-growing regions in the country. According to the latest statistics from the Ministry of Agriculture and Farmers Welfare, the total area under cardamom cultivation in India is around 110,000 hectares, and the total production is around 15,000 metric tonnes.

Insect pests are a major constraint to cardamom production in India, as they can cause significant yield losses and reduce the quality of the harvested produce. Insect pests on cardamom can cause significant economic damage, with cardamom thrips infestation causing 30-40%, shoot and capsule borer infestation causing 25-30%, root grub infestation causing 10-15%, and whitefly infestation causing 5-10% of the total yield loss. Some of the insect pests that affect cardamom in India and their economic importance are as follows:

Cardamom thrips: *Sciothrips cardamomi*

Common Name	:	Cardamom thrips
Scientific Name	:	*Sciothrips cardamomi*
Family	:	Thripidae
Order	:	Thysanoptera

Source: *https://keys.lucidcentral.org*

Distribution and Host Range

The cardamom thrips is found in Hawaii and India. It was first found in Hawaii on pink flowering ginger in 1986. Cardamom thrips are now found on the islands of Hawaii and Maui but are probably present on all the major islands due to inter island movement of flowering ginger. In Hawaii this thrips species has attacked red and pink ginger flowers. Outside of Hawaii this pest attacks cardamom and others in the family Zingiberaceae, edible ginger, and *Pancium longipes*.

Nature and Symptoms of Damage

Injury is caused by thrips feeding in young leaf sheaths and basal ends of unopened flower bracts. Nymphs and adults feed with their piercing-sucking mouth parts, which lacerate young tissues and suck the juices that ooze from ruptured cells. First the injured area develops a silvery sheen because of air occupying the emptied cell cavities. Due to oxidation, this area becomes a mixture of white, yellow, and brown splotches and streaks. Because of the secretive nature of feeding only within the sheaths and unopened bracts, its early presence usually goes undetected, until one actually looks down into the opened inflorescence and sees the feeding damage at the bottom of the flower bracts. This thrips is suspected to be a vector of a mosaic disease that effect cardamom in India.

Life History and Description

The life cycle (egg to adult) is 25 to 30 days. Reproduction is mostly sexual, though virgin females are able to lay viable eggs during the summer.

Egg: The white kidney shaped eggs are inserted in leaf sheaths or flower bracts by the sharp ovipositor of the adult. Eggs hatch in about a week.

Larvae: The transparent larvae are approximately 1/25 inch in length. The larval stage consists of three larval stages separated by moults in the course of 15 to 21 days.

Pupae: Pupae resemble the larvae except for the presence of wing pads (incompletely developed wings). There are 2 pupal stages, prepupa and pupa, neither of which are feeding stages. Pupae become adults in 10 to 15 days.

Adults: The head and abdomen of this thrips are dark grey brown and the thorax and legs are pale yellowish brown. Females measure approximately 1/4 inch in length; males are slightly smaller.

Management

General cultural practices involving sanitation, such as the removal of alternative hosts and plant debris within and outside the field. On cardamom, removal of dried shoot peels at the base of the stem resulted in a reduction of thrips populations by one-third. Chemical control is difficult because the thrips remain hidden under the cover of leaf sheaths and bracts. Insecticide trials for the cardamom thrips performed in India on cardamom demonstrated that synthetic pyrethroids gave adequate control. Of the different synthetic pyrethroids, permethrin was the most effective.

❑ Shoot, panicle and capsule borer: *Conogethes punctiferalis* (Guenée, 1854)

Common Name	:	Shoot, panicle and capsule borer
Scientific Name	:	*Conogethes punctiferalis* (Guenée, 1854)
Family	:	Crambidae
Order	:	Lepidoptera

Source:https://www.inaturalist.org

As Described in Guava

Hairy caterpillar: *Eupterote cardamom*

Common Name	:	Hairy caterpillar
Scientific Name	:	*Eupterote cardamomi*
Family	:	Bombycidae
Order	:	Lepidoptera

Source: http://www.nbair.res.in/insectpests/Eupterote.php

Distribution and Host Range

They are distributed across South India and their host is found to be cardamom.

Nature and Symptoms of Damage

These appear sporadically in enormous populations at intervals of several years and cause heavy damage to the foliage. Caterpillars are gregarious in habit and they congregate on the trunks of shade trees during day time and drop down on the cardamom plants during night time. They fed voraciously on leaves and defoliating the whole cardamom plants. Usually, the damage is observed during October-December.

Life History and Description

Eggs: Dome shaped and lay on under surface of the leaves of shade trees. **Larva:** Robust, bluish black with pale brown head, white hairs and dorsal conical tuff of hairs.

Pupa: Pupation takes place in soil.

Adult: Large moth, pale yellow with wavy lines and a series of spots near the outer margin of wings.

Management

Hairy caterpillar incidence can be checked by lopping off and burning branches of shade trees in which eggs are laid. Gradual elimination of shade trees favoured for egg laying will reduce the incidence. Caterpillars that congregate at the base of shade trees can be collected and killed. Moths can be attracted to light during night and by installing light traps, moths can be collected and killed.

Shoot fly: *Formosina flavipes*

Common Name	:	Shoot fly
Scientific Name	:	*Formosina flavipes*
Family	:	Chloropidae
Order	:	Diptera

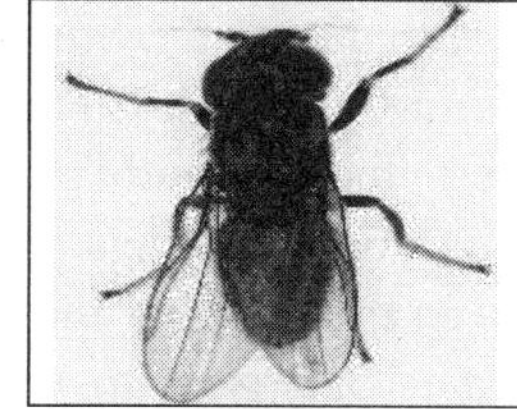

Source: https://agritech.tnau.ac.in/crop_protection/cardamom/

Nature and Symptoms of Damage

Larvae feed on the growing shoot of the young cardamom suckers and lead to dead heart.

Life History and Description

Eggs are cigar shaped and white colour and is laid in between leaf sheath and pseudostem on the whorl and **adult** is a dipteran fly.

Management

Remove the affected shoots at ground level and destroy them. Spray dimethoate or quinalphos (0.05% each).

❑ Cardamom aphid: *Pentalonia nigronervosa* (Coquerel, 1859)

Common Name	:	Cardamom aphid
Scientific Name	:	*Pentalonia nigronervosa* (Coquerel, 1859)
Family	:	Aphididae
Order	:	Hemiptera

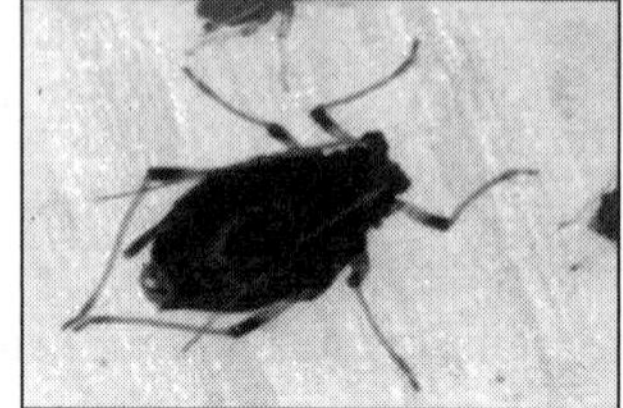

Source:https://nrcb.icar.gov.in/album/Banana*

Distribution and Host Range

Probably native to Southeast Asia, banana aphid is present just about everywhere banana is grown through the world. The banana aphid was first recorded in the state in 1924 from Honolulu, but was previously known in the Islands as an undetermined species. Although known to be on Oahu, Hawaii, and Kauai, it was not recorded on Maui, until 1989. The preferred host of this aphid is banana. However, it will also infest many tropical and subtropical food and ornamental plants, including *Alpinia purpurata* (floral red and pink ginger), *Xanthosoma* (ape), cardamom, Heliconia, tomatoes, taro, Calla, Costus, kahili ginger, torch ginger, and Zingiber.

Nature and Symptoms of Damage

Like most aphids, banana aphid is a phloem feeder that uses its long stylets to pierce plant tissues to suck the sap directly from the vessels. This can cause plants to become deformed; leaves become curled and shrivelled, and in some cases, galls are formed on the leaves. Young plants may be killed or their growth checked if there is sufficient feeding by the banana aphid. However, direct damage by this aphid is generally negligible. Like many other soft bodied insects, such as leafhoppers, mealybugs, and soft scales, aphids excrete honeydew. This sweet and watery excrement if fed on by bees, wasps, ants and other insects. The honeydew serves as a medium on which a sooty fungus, called sooty mold, grows. Sooty mold blackens the leaf, decreases photosynthetic activity, and decreases vigour of the host. Aphids vector many plant diseases that cause substantially greater losses than that caused by direct feeding injury. Both wingless (apterous) and winged (alate) aphids are able to transmit viruses. Transmission is usually in a nonpersistent manner where the virus is taken up into the aphids "mouth" while feeding on an infected plant and transferred to a healthy plant during subsequent feedings. In nonpersistent transmission, virus reproduces in the plant, and aphids simply aid in transporting the virus. With these types of virus-vector associations, aphid acquires the virus and is only able to transmit the virus temporarily. Banana aphid vectors bunchy top disease of bananas. Symptoms of the disease include dark green streaking of the leaves, midrib, and petioles; progressive leaf dwarfing; marginal chlorosis; and leaf curling. Fruits of diseased plants are unsaleable because they are small and distorted. In India, banana aphid vectors a mosaic virus of cardamom called "**katte**". The disease causes considerable losses to cardamom crops.

Life History and Description

Reproduction in the banana aphid is entirely parthenogenetic. Females give birth to live female young. Males are not known for this species. The life cycle is completed in 9 to 16 days. The adult life span ranges from 8 to 26 days; there could be as many as 30 generations produced per year in Hawaii.

Eggs: There is no egg stage. Young ones are born live.

Nymphs: Like most other aphid species, banana aphid has four nymphal stages. New-born nymphs are oval at first and become slightly elongated. They are reddish brown, with four segmented antennae, and measure 1/250 inch in length. The second stage nymphs are similar in appearance and measure approximately 7/250 inch long. The third nymphal stage individuals are light brown, measuring about 9/250 inch in length; the compound eyes are more noticeable beginning with this stage, and the nymphs have five-segmented antennae. The fourth stage nymphs have six-segmented antennae, are light brown in color, and are 1/25 inch long. The first, second, third, and fourth nymphal stages last 2 to 4, 3 to 4, 2 to 4, and 2 to 4 days, respectively.

Adults: Adult banana aphids are small to medium sized aphids (1/25 to 1/12 inch), shiny, reddish to dark brown or almost black. They have six-segmented antennae that are as long as the body. Alates have prominent, dark (brown or black) wing veins. Adults start producing young one day after reaching maturity. They can give birth to 4 aphids per day with an average production of 14 offspring per female.

Management

Bloated, tan coloured mummies are evidence that braconid wasps are parasitizing the colony. Other predators that have been successfully introduced to combat aphids are *Coelophora inaequalis, C. pupillata, Hippodamia convergens, Scymnodes lividigaster, Diomus notescens* (Coleoptera: Coccinelidae), and *Nesomicromus navigatorum* (Neuroptera: Hemerobiidae). Chlorpyrifos and acephate foliar sprays have been effective in reducing aphid populations and attending ants. Prewashing in a mild detergent or soap solution, opening tight bracts, followed by a 5-minute dip in an insecticidal soap or soap-pyrethroid combination at the label rate eliminates most aphids. Immersing flowers and foliage in hot water at 49°C. This treatment is safe for many commodities, but preconditioning may be required.

❑ Rhizome Weevil: *Prodioctes haematicus* L.A.A. Chevrolat, 1885

Common Name	:	Rhizome weevil
Scientific Name	:	*Prodioctes haematicus* L.A.A. Chevrolat, 1885
Family	:	Curculionidae
Order	:	Coleoptera

Source: *https://www.albemarlepestsolutions.com/grain-weevils*

Distribution and Host Range

Prodioctes haematicus, commonly known as **rhizome weevil**, is a species of weevil native to India and Sri Lanka. It is one of the common pests on cardamom and ginger.

Nature and Symptoms of Damage

Grubs tunnel and feed on the rhizome causing death of entire clumps of cardamom.

Life History and Description

Adult weevil lays eggs in the cavities made on rhizome. Egg period is about 8 to 10 days. Grub is usually found inside the rhizome where they make tunnels and feed on the rhizome causing death of entire clumps of cardamom. Grub period is about 21 days. Larvae become full fed within three weeks. Final grub starts to pupate in the feeding tunnels. Pupal period lasts for 21 days. Lifespan of the adult is about 7 to 8 months. Adult completes only one generation in a year. Grub infestation is severe in the secondary nursery during november to january. Grubs are also known to attack rhizomes of ginger where grubs bore into the pseudostem and cause dead hearts. This small weevil has a body length of 12 mm. Adult is brown in color.

Management

Adults and final grubs can be control by hand picking. Affected plants and seedlings can be destroyed and burn. Base of the clump can be treated with chlorpyriphos, malathion or carbaryl pesticides. Infected ginger plants can be treated with monocrotophos, fenitrothion, nimbicidine or carbofuran 3G granules immediately after mother rhizome extraction.

❑ White flies: *Dialeurodes cardamom*

Common Name	:	White flies
Scientific Name	:	*Dialeurodes cardamom*
Family	:	Aleyrodidae
Order	:	Hemiptera

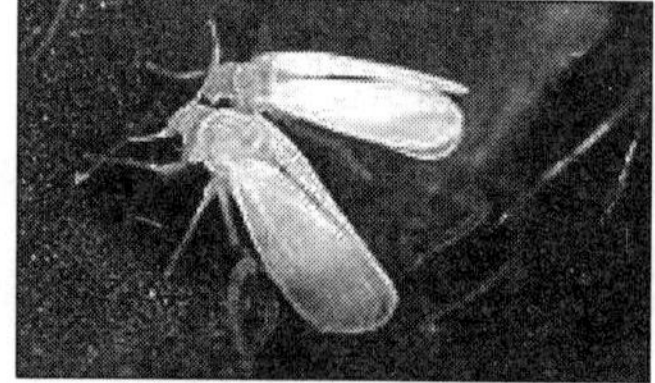

Source:*https://agritech.tnau.ac.in/crop_protection/cardamom/cardamom_7.html*

As Described in Potato

Resistant Varieties
Mysore cardamom (India): This variety is resistant to shoot borer and thrips. It is one of the most widely grown varieties in India and is known for its strong aroma.
Vazhukka (India): This variety is resistant to shoot borer and leaf roller. It is mainly grown in the Idukki district of Kerala.
Njallani (India): This variety is resistant to thrips, shoot borer, and leaf roller. It is mainly grown in the Wayanad district of Kerala.
Malabar cardamom (India): This variety is resistant to thrips and mealybugs. It is mainly grown in the Wynad, Nilgiris, and Palani hills of India.
Guatemala cardamom: This variety is resistant to thrips and is known for its strong aroma. It is mainly grown in the highlands of Guatemala.
Mysore-5 (India): This variety is resistant to thrips, shoot borer, and leaf roller. It is mainly grown in the Coorg and Wynad regions of India.
Tadong (India): This variety is resistant to thrips and shoot borer. It is mainly grown in Sikkim and Darjeeling.

40 Pests of Turmeric and Ginger

Common name	Turmeric	Ginger
Scientific Name	*Curcuma longa*	*Zingiber officinale*
Family	Zingiberaceae	Zingiberaceae
Origin	Indian subcontinent and Southeast Asia	Maritime Southeast Asia
Chromosome Number	2n = 63	2n = 30

Turmeric (*Curcuma longa*) and Ginger (*Zingiber officinale*) are rhizomatous plants belonging to the family Zingiberaceae. They both have tall leafy stems and produce underground rhizomes that are used as spices. Turmeric has dark green leaves and yellow flowers, while ginger has green leaves and white or yellow flowers.

India is the largest producer, consumer, and exporter of turmeric in the world. The major turmeric-growing states in India are Andhra Pradesh, Telangana, Tamil Nadu, Maharashtra, and Odisha. The total area under turmeric cultivation in India is around 550,000 hectares, and the total production is around 1.5-2 million metric tonnes. Ginger is also an important spice crop in India, with the major ginger-growing states being Kerala, Karnataka, Assam, and Arunachal Pradesh. The total area under ginger cultivation in India is around 135,000 hectares, and the total production is around 1.2-1.3 million metric tonnes.

Both turmeric and ginger are important cash crops in India, and they are used for a variety of purposes such as cooking, medicinal, and cosmetic applications. They are also exported to various countries around the world. Insect pests can cause significant economic damage to turmeric and ginger crops in India. Some of the most common insect pests affecting these crops include:

❑ Leaf roller: *Ancistroides folus* (Cramer, 1775)

Common Name	:	Leaf roller
Scientific Name	:	*Ancistroides folus* (Cramer, 1775)
Family	:	Hesperiidae
Order	:	Lepidoptera

***Source:**https://en.wikipedia.org/wiki/File:Udaspes_Folus.jpg*

Distribution and Host Range

Udaspes folus, the **grass demon**, is a small but prominent butterfly found in India and Nepal that belongs to the skipper family, **Hesperiidae**. It is regarded as an occasional pest of ginger and turmeric plants.

Nature and Symptoms of Damage

Leaves become folded or rolled longitudinally and leads to complete defoliation.

Life History and Description

The butterflies emerge in february or march and lay eggs before they die. The eggs remain dormant till the rains, that is, usually the month of may, when they hatch. The caterpillars pupate in september and october and the adults emerge four to six months later. In some cases, the caterpillars pupate later and in these cases the pupa remain dormant, throughout the dry season, till may when the rains begin.

Eggs: The female normally sits on the underside of the leaf of the host plant and lays a single egg. The egg is reddish and appears smooth and dome shaped. When about to hatch it turns white with a red top.

Larva: Soon after hatching, the caterpillar does not consume the eggshell completely and it makes itself a spacious cell and hides inside it. The caterpillar is sluggish and comes out to feed only at night. Even when disturbed it is reluctant to leave its cell. The caterpillar is a light uniform leaf green colour with a dark green pulsating line on the back and a relatively small, dark head. The full-grown larva has the habit of resting with the first three segments contracted, so as to give a humped appearance. It always lies closely applied to the leaf, by turning over a triangular piece from the edge onto the upper surface over itself. Specific host plants include *Zingiber zerumbet*.

Pupa: Pupation takes place on the same plant within a cell. The pupa is long and cylindrical, watery green in colour. It has a long conical projection in front of the head. The eyes are easily seen but do not protrude out of the outline of the pupa. The pupa broadens towards the shoulders and the abdomen gradually tapers to the last segment. The most striking characteristic of the pupa is its proboscis. It is long and thin generally extending up to and a little beyond the tip of the abdomen. The pupa is the same colour of the caterpillar and unmarked. It is covered in a thin layer of white powder. The body band is neither too tight nor too loose and allows the pupa to wriggle if disturbed.

Management

A spray with carbaryl (0.1%) or dimethoate (0.05%) may be undertaken when the severe infestation. Spray the following dissolved in 1 lit of water, bavisitin 2 g +mancozeb 2 g + teefol 1 ml.

Other Important Pests				
Common Name	**Scientific Name**	**Family**	**Order**	**Remarks**
Shoot borer	*Conogethes punctiferalis*	Cambidae	Lepidoptera	As Described in Cardamom
Rhizome scale	*Aspidiella hartii*	Diaspididae	Hemiptera	As Described in Pepper
Thrips	*Panchaetothrips indicus*	Thripidae	Thysanoptera	As Described in Bulb Crops
Rhizome	*Cosmopolites sordidus*	Curculionidae	Coleoptera	As Described in Banana

Resistant Varieties

Lakadong Turmeric: It is a popular variety of turmeric grown in Meghalaya, India. It is known for its high curcumin content and strong aroma. It is also resistant to insect pests like rhizome scale insects and root knot nematodes.

Salem Turmeric: It is a popular variety of turmeric grown in Tamil Nadu, India. It is known for its high oleoresin content and resistance to insect pests like rhizome scale insects.

Maran Turmeric: It is a variety of turmeric grown in Tamil Nadu, India. It is known for its high curcumin content and resistance to insect pests like rhizome scale insects.

Suprabha Ginger: It is a variety of ginger grown in India, Indonesia, and Thailand. It is known for its high yield and resistance to insect pests like shoot borer and root knot nematodes.

Rio de Janeiro Ginger: It is a variety of ginger grown in Brazil. It is known for its high yield and resistance to insect pests like shoot borer and root knot nematodes.

Varada Ginger: It is a variety of ginger grown in Kerala, India. It is known for its high yield and resistance to insect pests like shoot borer and root knot nematodes.

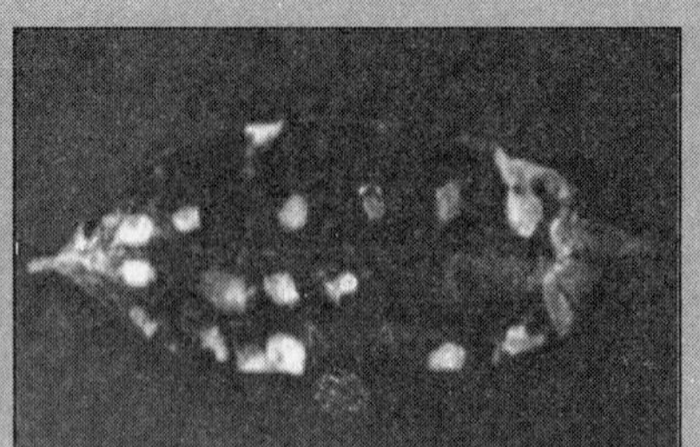

41 Pests of Cinnamon

Scientific Name	*Cinnamomum verum; C. zeylanicum*
Family	Lauraceae
Origin	India, Sri Lanka, Bangladesh and Myanmar
Chromosome Number	2n = 24

Cinnamon is a tropical evergreen tree belonging to the Lauraceae family. Cinnamon is mainly grown in the southern states of India, particularly in Kerala and Tamil Nadu. The total area under cinnamon cultivation in India is around 16,000 hectares, and the total production is around 18,000 metric tonnes. India is one of the major producers and exporters of cinnamon in the world. Insect pests can cause significant economic damage to cinnamon plantations in India. Some of the most common insect pests affecting cinnamon crops include:

❑ Cinnamon butterfly: *Papilio clytia* Linnaeus, 1758

Common Name	:	Cinnamon butterfly
Scientific Name	:	*Papilio clytia* Linnaeus, 1758
Family	:	Papilionidae
Order	:	Lepidoptera

Source:*http://butterfliesvietnam.blogspot.com*

Distribution and Host Range

Chilasa clytia, a tailless swallowtail butterfly, was first described by Linnaeus in *Systema Naturae* (1758). They are distributed across Nepal to Thailand and Malaysia (Other subspecies are found in Sri Lanka, India to South China, Philippines and the Lesser Sunda Islands of Indonesia). **Host plants**: Cinnamon, Camphor Tree, Leather-Leaf Litsea, large-flowered bay tree and *Nelthare*.

Nature and Symptoms of Damage

Larvae feed on tender and slightly mature leaves. In severe cases of infestation, the entire plant is defoliated and only midribs of leaves with portions of veins are left.

Life History and Description

Eggs: Pale yellow in colour.

Larva: Undergoes various changes of colour pattern. Grown up caterpillar are shaded with deep yellow on sides.

Adult: The upper side of adult is rich velvety brown.

Fore wing: The upper side has marginal series of spots and terminal series of spots between the veins.

Hind Wing: The upper side bears a series of long arrow shaped streaks, yellow and white spots between the veins. *Chilasa clytia* is a black-bodied swallowtail butterfly with a wing span of 79.3 (±11.16) mm. It serves as an excellent example of a batesian mimicry among the Indian butterflies. They have the habit of puddling on wet grounds.

Management

Spraying quinalphos 0.05% on tender and partly mature leaves.

❑ Leaf miner: *Conopomorpha civica*

Common Name	:	Leaf miner
Scientific Name	:	*Conopomorpha civica*
Family	:	Gracillaridae
Order	:	Lepidoptera

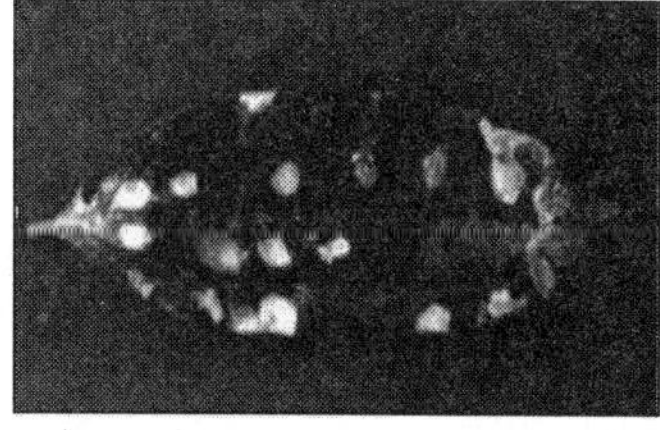

Source:https://vikaspedia.in/agriculture/crop-production/

Nature and Symptoms of Damage

Larvae feed on the tissues between the upper and lower epidermis of tender leaves resulting in linear mines that end in **'blister'** like patches. The infested leaves become crinkled and the mined areas dry up leading to the formation of large holes on the leaves.

Life History and Description

Infestation by the leaf miner is more common during the monsoon period and generally nursery seedlings are seriously affected. The adults are a minute silvery grey moth.

Larva: Larvae are pale creamy white and are generally seen at the centre of the mine. The larvae become pinkish red when fully grown measuring about 5 mm in length. The larvae are pale grey initially and later become pink measuring about 10 mm in length.

Pupa: Pupation generally occurs outside the larval mines on the leaf.

Adult: Adults are minute silvery grey moths with narrow fringed wings with a wing span of about 5 mm.

Management

Spraying quinalphos 0.05% during emergence of new flushes is effective in preventing the pest infestation. Many other leaf feeding caterpillars and beetles also occur sporadically on cinnamon feeding on tender flushes. Application of quinalphos 0.05% would keep them under check.

Resistant Varieties	
World	**India**
Cinnamomum cassia: Also known as Chinese cinnamon, this variety is the most widely used type of cinnamon. It has been reported to have some level of resistance to the cinnamon bark beetle (*Coccotrypes dactyliperda*), which is a major pest of cinnamon bark. **Cinnamomum verum:** Also called true cinnamon or Ceylon cinnamon, this variety is grown primarily in Sri Lanka, but also in other parts of South Asia and Madagascar. It has been reported to be resistant to the cinnamon bark beetle and the cinnamon shoot borer (*Pempelia palumbella*). **Cinnamomum loureiroi:** This variety, also known as Saigon cinnamon or Vietnamese cinnamon, is primarily grown in Vietnam. It has been reported to have resistance to the cinnamon bark beetle.	**Indian Cinnamon (*Cinnamomum tamala*):** Also known as Tejpat, this variety is native to India and is commonly used as a spice in Indian cuisine. It is resistant to many insect pests, including the cinnamon bark beetle and the shoot borer. **Malabar Cinnamon (*Cinnamomum verum*):** This variety is native to Sri Lanka but is also grown in India. It is resistant to many insect pests, including the cinnamon bark beetle and the leaf roller. **Java Cinnamon (*Cinnamomum burmannii*):** This variety is native to Indonesia but is also grown in India. It is resistant to many insect pests, including the cinnamon bark beetle and the leaf roller.

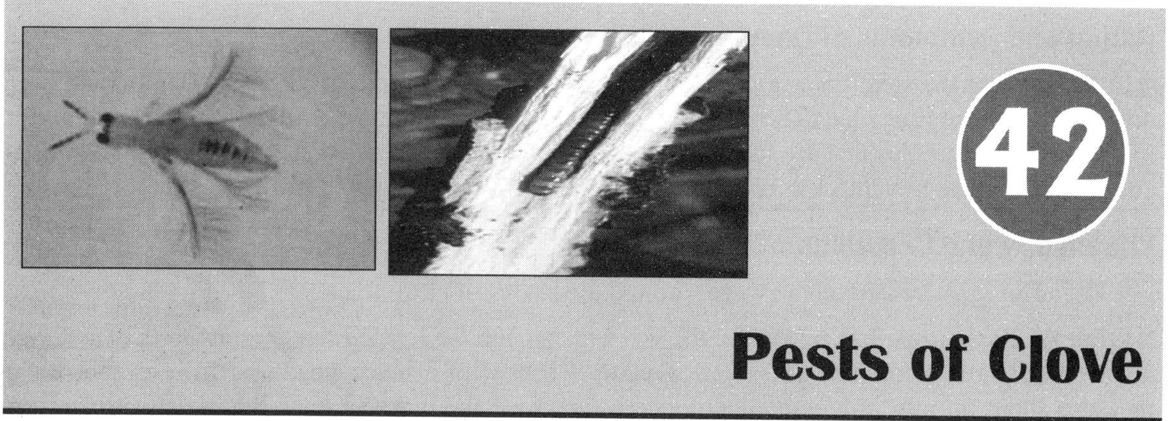

42 Pests of Clove

Scientific Name	*Syzygium aromaticum*
Family	Myrtaceae
Origin	Maluku Islands in Indonesia
Chromosome Number	2n= 22

Clove is an aromatic spice that comes from the dried flower buds of the clove tree, which belongs to the family Myrtaceae. Clove is mainly grown in the southern state of Kerala in India. The total area under clove cultivation in India is around 10,000 hectares, and the total production is around 2,000 metric tonnes. India is not a major producer of clove, and most of the clove is imported to meet the domestic demand.

The economic damage caused by these insect pests can vary depending on the severity of infestation and the crop stage. In severe cases, the damage can result in up to 50% yield loss, which can have a significant impact on the livelihoods of farmers and the overall economy. Insect pests can cause significant economic damage to clove plantations in India. Some of the most common insect pests affecting clove crops include:

Stem borer: *Sahyadrassus malabaricus* Moore

Common Name	:	Stem borer
Scientific Name	:	*Sahyadrassus malabaricus* Moore
Family	:	Hepialidae
Order	:	Lepidoptera

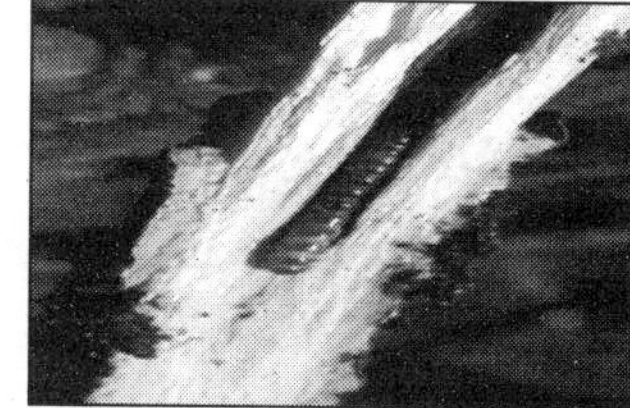

Source: *https://agritech.tnau.ac.in/crop_protection/clove/clove_1.html*

Distribution and Host Range

The stem borer is the most serious pest of clove in India and is generally seen in clove plantations grown near forest clearings. The pest has a wide host range and has been recorded on more than 40 species of woody plants and trees.

Nature and Symptoms of Damage

The larva of the stem borer girdles the stem of young clove trees at the basal region and bores downward into the root zone. The girdled region and the bore-hole are covered with frass consisting of coarse wood particles that are formed as a mat-like structure. The infested trees wilt and defoliate and succumb to the pest attack subsequently.

Life History and Description

Egg: The eggs are laid on the weeds around the basins of clove trees.

Larva: Early instar larvae feed on the weed plants and the later instars migrate to the clove trees and bore into the stem. The larvae are creamy white with a black head and fully grown larvae measure about 90 mm in length. The dorsal sclerites of the thoracic and abdominal segments are brown.

Pupa: Pupation occurs within the larval tunnel.

Adult: The adult is a large sized moth with a wing span of about 110 mm with greyish-brown mottled forewings.

Management

The base of clove trees is to be inspected regularly for symptoms of pest infestation. In case the pest infestation is noticed on the stem, the mat-like frass has to be removed and quinalphos 0.1% sprayed around and injected into the bore hole. Swabbing the basal region of the main stem of young clove trees with carbaryl paste and keeping the basins of clove trees free of weeds are prophylactic measures for preventing the pest infestation.

❑ Scale insects: *Pulvinaria psidii* Maskell, 1893

Common name	:	Guava scale; green shield scale; guava mealy scale
Scientific name	:	*Pulvinaria psidii* Maskell, 1893
Family	:	Coccidae
Order	:	Hemiptera

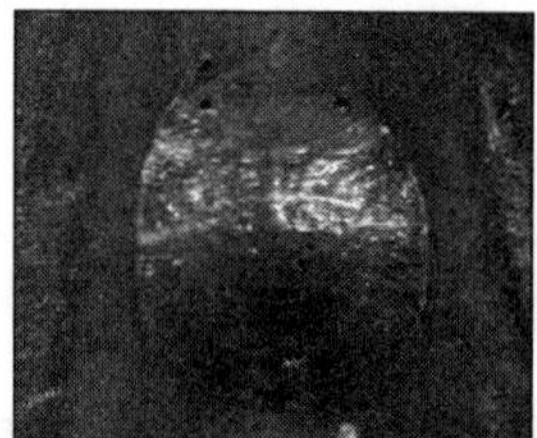

Source: *https://www.google.co.in/imgres?imgurl=https%3A%2F%2Fbugwoodcloud.org%2Fimages%2F768x512%2F5112036.jpg&tbnid*

Distribution and Host range

A few species of scale insects infest clove seedlings in the nursery and sometimes young plants in the field. The scale insects generally seen on clove include wax scale (*Ceroplastes floridensis* Com.), shield scale (*Pulvinaria psidii* Mask.), masked scale (*Mycetaspis personata* Com.) (Hemiptera: Diaspididae) and soft scale (*Kilifia accuminata* (Sign.) (Hemiptera: Coccidae).

Nature and Symptoms of Damage

Scale insects are generally seen clustered together on tender stems and lower surface of leaves. Scale insects feed on plant sap and cause yellow spots on leaves, defoliation and wilting and drying of shoots.

Life History and Description

Female adults are elliptical, flattened and shiny black.

Management

Spraying of dimethoate (0.05%) is recommended for the management of various species of scale insects. Very few insects have been recorded on nutmeg in the field in India; however, a few species of scale insects infest seedlings in the nursery and sometimes young plants in the field.

❑ Chilli thrips: *Scirtothirps dorsalis* Hood, 1919

Common Name	:	Chilli thrips; Yellow tea thrips
Scientific Name	:	*Scirtothrips dorsalis* Hood, 1919
Family	:	Thripidae
Order	:	Thysanoptera

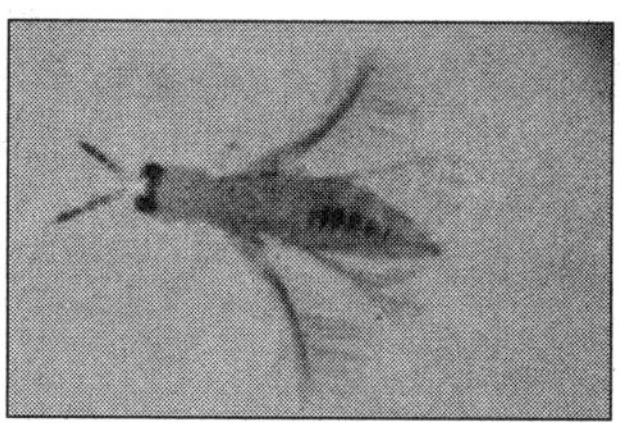

Source:*https://en.wikipedia.org/wiki/Scirtothrips_dorsalis#/media/File:Sd_adult_spread.jpg*

As Described in Chilli

Resistant Varieties	
World	**India**
Zanzibar clove: This variety of clove is grown primarily in Tanzania and is known for its resistance to clove stem borers. **Pemba clove:** Grown on the island of Pemba in Tanzania, this variety is also resistant to clove stem borers and has a high oil content. **Madagascar clove:** Grown in Madagascar, this variety is resistant to pests like root-knot nematodes and clove stem borers. **Sri Lankan clove:** This variety of clove is grown in Sri Lanka and is known for its resistance to the clove bud mite, which can cause significant damage to clove crops. **Java clove:** Grown in Indonesia, this variety is resistant to pests like the black twig borer and clove stem borer. **Philippine clove:** Grown in the Philippines, this variety is resistant to pests like the clove bud borer and clove shoot borer.	**PKN-1:** This is a high-yielding variety of clove that is commonly grown in the South Indian states of Kerala and Tamil Nadu. It is known to be moderately resistant to the clove shoot borer insect (*Leucinodes orbonalis*) and the clove scale insect (*Aspidiotus destructor*). **PKM-1:** This is another high-yielding variety of clove that is grown in the same regions as PKN-1. It is also moderately resistant to clove shoot borer and clove scale insect. **PBC-1:** This is a clove variety that is commonly grown in the Northeastern state of Assam. It is known to be tolerant to the root borer insect (*Indarbela* spp.) and the stem borer insect (*I. tetraonis*). **Indian clove:** Grown in India, this variety is known for its resistance to the clove stem borer and is often used for the production of clove oil.

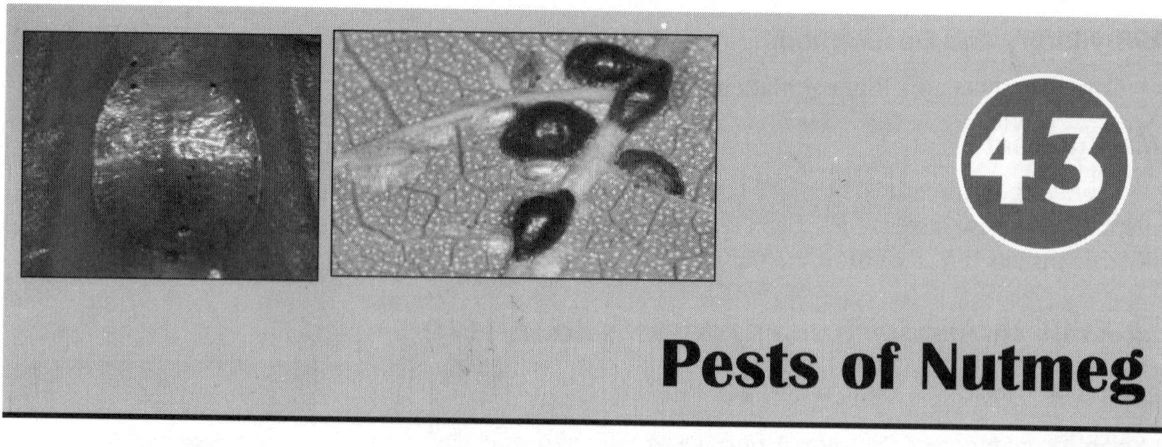

43 Pests of Nutmeg

Scientific Name	*Myristica fragrans* Houtt
Family	Myristicaceae
Origin	A small cluster of islands in Indonesia, the Banda Islands
Chromosome Number	2n = 38

Nutmeg is a spice that comes from the seeds of the nutmeg tree, which belongs to the family Myristicaceae. Nutmeg is mainly grown in the southern state of Kerala and the western state of Goa in India. The total area under nutmeg cultivation in India is around 1,000 hectares, and the total production is around 500 metric tonnes. India is not a major producer of nutmeg, and most of the nutmeg is imported to meet the domestic demand.

The economic damage caused by these insect pests can vary depending on the severity of infestation and the crop stage. In severe cases, the damage can result in up to 50% yield loss, which can have a significant impact on the livelihoods of farmers and the overall economy. Insect pests can cause significant economic damage to nutmeg plantations in India. Some of the most common insect pests affecting nutmeg crops include:

❑ Scale insects: *Pulvinaria psidii* Maskell, 1893; *Mycetaspis personata* (Comstock, 1883)

Common name	:	Guava scale; green shield scale; guava mealy scale
Scientific name	:	*Pulvinaria psidii* Maskell, 1893
Family	:	Coccidae
Order	:	Hemiptera

Source: *https://www.google.co.in/imgres?imgurl=https%3A%2F%2Fbugwoodcloud.org%2Fimages%2F768x512%2F5112036.jpg&tbnid=ZarP_xMuudIBqM&vet=12ahUKEwiF99H5rdv-*

As Described in Clove

Some other Pests of Nutmeg

Common Name	Scientific Name	Family	Order
Nutmeg fruit fly	*Bactrocera* spp.	Tephritidae	Diptera
Shoot borers	*Various* sps.	—	—
Nutmeg weevil	*Curculio* spp.	Curculionidae	Coleoptera
Mites	Red spider mite: *Tetranychus urticae*	Acari	Arachnida
Root-knot nematode	*Meloidogyne* spp.	Heterodoidae	Eylenchida

Resistant Varieties	
World	**India**
Banda Nutmeg: This variety of nutmeg is native to the Banda Islands of Indonesia and is known for its resistance to pests and diseases. It is also valued for its high oil content and strong flavour. **Grenada Nutmeg:** This variety is grown in the Caribbean Island of Grenada and is known for its resistance to pests and diseases. It is also valued for its high oil content and strong flavour. **Papua New Guinea Nutmeg:** This variety is grown in Papua New Guinea and is known for its resistance to pests and diseases. It has a slightly different flavour profile compared to other nutmeg varieties. **Sri Lanka Nutmeg:** This variety is grown in Sri Lanka and is known for its resistance to pests and diseases. It has a milder flavour compared to other nutmeg varieties.	**Vellarikundu:** This variety of nutmeg is mainly cultivated in the Wayanad district of Kerala and is known for its high yield and good quality nutmeg. **Arambagh:** This variety of nutmeg is mainly cultivated in West Bengal and is known for its high yield and good quality nutmeg. **Myristica fragrans:** This is the most common variety of nutmeg grown in India, and is mainly cultivated in Kerala, Tamil Nadu, and Karnataka. **Malabar Nutmeg:** This variety is grown in parts of India and is known for its resistance to pests and diseases. It has a milder flavour compared to other nutmeg varieties.

44 Pests of Saffron

Scientific Name	*Crocus sativus* L.
Family	Iridaceae
Origin	Iran
Chromosome Number	2n = 24

Saffron is a spice that is derived from the stigmas of the *Crocus sativus* flower. It belongs to the family Iridaceae and is a perennial herb that grows up to 30 cm in height. Saffron is mainly grown in the northern state of Jammu and Kashmir in India. The total area under saffron cultivation in India is around 5,700 hectares, and the total production is around 2.5 metric tonnes. India is a small producer of saffron, and most of the world's saffron is produced in Iran, Spain, and Afghanistan.

Insect pests can cause significant economic damage to saffron production in India. Some of the most common insect pests affecting saffron crops include:

Corm fly: This pest attacks the corms of saffron plants, causing reduced growth and yield.

Aphids: These insects feed on the sap of the saffron plants, causing wilting, yellowing, and reduced yields.

Thrips: These pests cause damage by feeding on the flowers and developing buds, leading to reduced yields and quality.

Spider mites: These pests suck the sap of the leaves, causing them to turn yellow and die prematurely.

The economic damage caused by these insect pests can be severe, resulting in yield losses of up to 40-50%. Additionally, saffron is a high-value crop, and any reduction in yield or quality can have a significant impact on the income of farmers and the overall economy. Farmers often use integrated pest management strategies to minimize the impact of insect pests, including cultural, biological, and chemical control methods.

❑ Saffron bulb mite: *Rhizoglyphus robini* Claparede

Common Name	:	Saffron bulb mite
Scientific Name	:	*Rhizoglyphus robini* Claparede
Family	:	Acaridae
Order	:	Acari

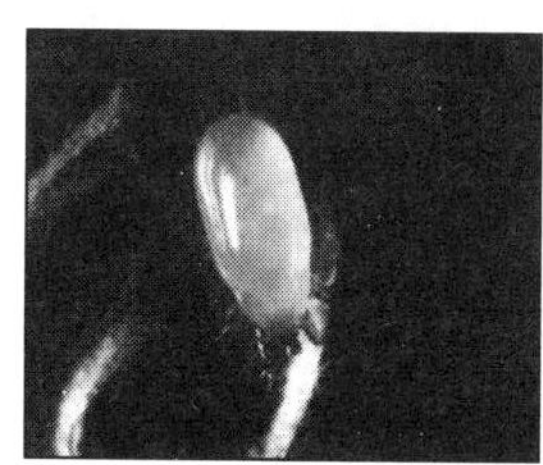

***Source:**https://www.uvm.edu/~saffron/Old/Workshops/Saffron*

Distribution and Host Range

This mite infesting crop such as saffron corms, onions, garlic, leeks and lilies. Bulb mites were observed associated with diseased saffron corms in Vermont research sites, confirming their pest status in New England.

Nature and Symptoms of Damage

They attack saffron corms through wounds. By producing tunnels and cavity in corms the mite starts reproduction within this cavity. Infested plants: shorter and thinner leaves, yellow leaves.

Life History and Description

On an average, the life cycle duration (egg to adult) on saffron corm: 13-14 days, 15 generation per year. Life cycle of male on saffron corm: 80 days. Life cycle of female on saffron corm: 60 days. Adult mite is around 0.6-0.8 mm long.

Management

Do not irrigate saffron during the summer. Weed control must be done with care. Choose healthy and uninform corms for planting. Treat the corms with fungicide – miticide before planting. The depth of planting more than 5 inches can help.

❑ Onion thrips: *Thrips tabaci* Lindeman, 1889

Common Name	:	Onion thrips
Scientific Name	:	*Thrips tabaci* Lindeman, 1889
Family	:	Thripidae
Order	:	Thysanoptera

***Source:**https://academic.oup.com/jipm/article/6/1/6/2936974*

As Described in Tomato

Resistant Varieties
Kashmiri saffron: Kashmiri saffron is considered one of the best varieties of saffron in the world. It is grown in the Kashmir valley and is known for its high-quality aroma, flavour, and color. Kashmiri saffron is resistant to many pests and diseases, which makes it a popular choice among farmers.

Iranian saffron: Iranian saffron is another popular variety that is grown in India. It is known for its high-quality aroma and flavour, and is resistant to many pests and diseases.

Spanish saffron: Spanish saffron is also grown in India. It is known for its distinct aroma and flavour and is used in many dishes. Spanish saffron is resistant to many pests and diseases, which makes it a good choice for farmers.

Afghan saffron: Afghan saffron is a rare variety that is grown in India. It is known for its distinct aroma and flavour and is used in many dishes. Afghan saffron is resistant to many pests and diseases, which makes it a good choice for farmers.

Italian Saffron: Grown in the Abruzzo and Sardinia regions of Italy, this variety is known for its delicate flavour and aroma. It is resistant to the corm rot disease and is also less susceptible to damage from the saffron fly.

45 Pests of Cumin

Scientific Name	*Cuminum cyminum*
Family	Apiaceae; Umbelliferae
Origin	Asia, Africa, and Europe
Chromosome Number	2n = 14

Cumin (*Cuminum cyminum*) is an annual herbaceous plant belonging to the Apiaceae family. India is one of the largest producers of cumin in the world, with the majority of its cultivation concentrated in the western states of Gujarat and Rajasthan. The total area under cumin cultivation in India is around 4,00,000 hectares, and the total production is around 3,50,000 metric tonnes per year. Insect pests are a major constraint in the production of cumin crops in India, and their damage can result in significant economic losses for farmers. Some of the most common insect pests affecting cumin crops include:

Cigarette beetle: *Lasioderma serricorne* (Fabricius, 1792)

Common Name	:	Cigarette beetle
Scientific Name	:	*Lasioderma serricorne* (Fabricius, 1792)
Family	:	Ptinidae
Order	:	Coleoptera

Source:*https://www.cabidigitallibrary.org/doi/10.1079/cabicompendium.29882*

Distribution and Host Range

The cigarette beetle is pan-tropical but can be found worldwide – especially wherever dried tobacco in the form of leaves, cigars, cigarettes, or chewing tobacco is stored.

Nature and Symptoms of Damage

Larval feeding causes direct damage to foodstuffs and non-food items. These products are contaminated by the presence of beetles, larvae, pupae, cocoons, frass, and insect parts. Beetles chewing through cardboard boxes, containers, and packaging cause indirect damage. Cocoons are often attached to a solid substrate and in severe infestations form large clusters. Larvae will sometimes bore their way through cardboard boxes and other packaging in search of a place to pupate.

Life History and Description

Egg: An egg is pearly white, and is not easily seen with the naked eye. When fully grown, beetle larvae are C-shaped (grub-like) and about 3/16-inch long. Female lays about 30 eggs in a period of 3 weeks. Eggs hatch in 6 to 10 days.

Larva: Larvae are creamy white and covered with long, yellowish-brown hairs. They have a brown head and legs. The larval stage lasts from 5 to 10 weeks. Pre-pupa and **pupa**: The pre-pupal and pupal periods last 2 to 3 weeks and are passed in a cell.

Adult: Adults are yellowish- to reddish-brown, oval-shaped, and about 1/10-inch long. The head is bent downward sharply, nearly at right angles to the body, giving a humpbacked appearance when viewed from the side. The wing covers (elytra) are smooth, and the antennal segments are uniform and saw-like (serrate). Adults are strong flyers and active in subdued light at temperatures above 65°F. Adult beetles may live from 23 to 28 days. In temperate climates, beetles begin swarming in may and again in august. Overwintering may be passed in the larval stage, with some adults not too resistant to cold hibernating in crevices. There may be 5 to 6 overlapping generations per year in warm localities with only one generation in the more temperate regions. In warehouses, the life cycle may be completed in 52 days.

Management

Cigarette beetle predators include *Tenebriodes* sp. (F: Tenebrionidae), *Thaneroclerus* sp. (F: Cleridae) and several carabids. Eggs may be eaten by predatory mites. Female sex pheromone is vital to cigarette beetle mating success. Laboratory assays in one study determined that the active fraction of female extract that elicited the most activity in males is **serricornin** (4, 6-dimethyl-7-hydroxy-nonan-3-one).

❑ Drugstore beetle: *Stegobium paniceum* (Linnaeus, 1758)

Common Name	:	Drugstore beetle
Scientific Name	:	*Stegobium paniceum* (Linnaeus, 1758)
Family	:	Ptinidae
Order	:	Coleoptera

Source:*https://extension.okstate.edu/programs/digital-diagnostics*

Distribution and Host Range

Drugstore beetles have a worldwide distribution, but are more abundant in warmer regions or in heated structures in more temperate climates. They are less abundant in the tropics than the cigarette beetle.

Nature and Symptoms of Damage

Stored product pests cause tremendous damage and economic losses to post-harvest and stored grains and seeds, packaged food products, and animal and plant-derived items and products. Besides causing direct damage by feeding, they elicit disgust, annoyance, and anger in many of those who find them infesting these products.

Life History and Description

Females lay up to 75 eggs in the food or substrate. The larval period ranges from four to 20 weeks. Larvae tunnel through the substrate and when fully grown build a cocoon and pupate. Pupation takes from 12 to 18 days. Adult females live approximately 13 to 65 days. The entire life cycle is generally less than two months but can be as long as seven months. The duration of the life cycle is highly dependent on the temperature and food source. Development occurs between 60 to 93°F (~15 to 34°C) but is optimal at about 85°F (~30°C) and 60 to 90% relative humidity.

Adults: The beetles are cylindrical, 2.25 to 3.5 mm (1/10 to 1/7 inch) long, and are a uniform brown to reddish brown. They have longitudinal rows of fine hairs on the elytra (wing covers). Drugstore beetles are similar in appearance to the cigarette beetle; however, two physical characters can be used to tell the difference between them. The antennae of the cigarette beetle are serrated (like the teeth on a saw) while the antennae of the drugstore beetle are not and end in a 3-segmented club. The other difference is that the elytra (wing covers) of the drugstore beetle have rows of pits giving them a striated (lined) appearance while those of the cigarette beetle are smooth. **Larvae**: Small, white grubs; the later instars are scarab-like. They are similar to cigarette beetle larvae, but have shorter hairs and the marking on the head ends in a straight line across the frons just above the mouthparts.

Management

To prevent reinfestation, clean up spilled flour, mixes, crumbs, etc. and thoroughly vacuum and clean areas where the contaminated items were stored. Store foods in airtight glass, metal or plastic containers. Clear containers make it easier to check for infestation. Chemical treatment using commercially available insecticides or insect growth regulators is usually not necessary but if used, be sure to follow the label. The drugstore beetle is attacked by a variety of generalist natural enemies. Predators include *Tenebriodes* sp. (Tenebrionidae), *Thaneroclerus* sp. (Cleridae) and several carabids. Eggs may be eaten by predatory mites. Parasitoids include wasps in the families Pteromalidae, Eurytomidae and Bethylidae. The drugstore beetle sex pheromone, stegobinone (2, 3-dihydro-2,3,5-trimethyl-6-(1-methyl-2-oxobutyl)-4H-pyran-4-one) is used in commercially available traps and lures. **Stegobinone** has also been identified as the sex pheromone of a wood-feeding anobiid, common furniture beetle, *Anobium punctatum*.

Some Other Important Pests of Cumin				
Common Name	**Scientific Name**	**Family**	**Order**	**Remarks**
White flies	*Bemisia tabaci*	Aleyrodidae	Hemiptera	As Described in Potato
Leaf eating caterpillar	*Spodoptera litura*	Noctuidae	lepidoptera	As Described in Potato
Aphids	*Aphis gossipy*	Aphididae	Hemiptera	As Described in Chilli
Root-knot nematode	*Meloidogyne incognita*	Heteroderidae	Tylenchida	As Described in Tomato

Resistant Varieties	
World	**India**
Syrian Cumin: Syrian cumin is known for its high yield and resistance to insect pests. It is characterized by its large seed size and strong, sweet aroma. **Iranian Cumin:** Iranian cumin is another variety that is resistant to insect pests. It is known for its high essential oil content and strong aroma. **Turkish Cumin:** Turkish cumin is also known for its resistance to insect pests. It is characterized by its small seed size and strong, bitter flavour. **Moroccan Cumin:** Moroccan cumin is known for its high yield and resistance to insect pests. It is characterized by its strong, slightly bitter flavour and aroma.	**Gujarat Cumin:** Gujarat is one of the major producers of cumin in India, and the Gujarat variety is known for its resistance to insect pests. It is also characterized by its high essential oil content and strong aroma. **Rajasthan Cumin:** Rajasthan is another major cumin-producing region in India, and the Rajasthan variety is also resistant to insect pests. It is known for its large seed size and strong aroma. **GC-4:** This variety of cumin has shown good resistance to aphids and thrips, which are common insect pests that attack cumin crops. **RZ-209:** This variety of cumin has shown good tolerance to whitefly and jassid, two insect pests that can cause significant damage to cumin crops. **GC-5:** This variety of cumin has shown good resistance to stem fly, a serious pest that can cause damage to the stems of cumin plants. **Rajendra jeera-1:** This variety of cumin has shown good resistance to thrips and aphids. **Gujarat jeera-1:** This variety of cumin has shown good resistance to stem fly and jassid.

Pests of Vanilla

Scientific Name	*Vanilla planifolia*
Family	Orchidaceae
Origin	Mesoamerica, including parts of modern-day Mexico
Chromosome Number	2n = 32

Vanilla (*Vanilla planifolia*) is a perennial vine belonging to the Orchidaceae family. The fruits of vanilla are elongated pods containing numerous tiny seeds that are used as a flavouring agent in various food products. Vanilla is a minor crop in India, and its cultivation is mainly restricted to the states of Kerala, Karnataka, and Tamil Nadu. The total area under vanilla cultivation in India is around 500 hectares, and the total production is around 10-20 metric tonnes per year. Insect pests are a significant threat to vanilla crops and can cause significant economic losses. Some of the most common insect pests affecting vanilla crops include:

Some Important Pests of Vanilla				
Common Name	**Scientific Name**	**Symptoms**	**Control Measures**	**Image**
Vanilla bug	*Halyomorpha* spp., *Picus* spp.	Sucks the sap from the vegetative bud and inflorescence leading to rotting	Collect the egg masses at nymph stage in Nov-Feb	**Source:**https://en.wikipedia.org/wiki/Halyomorpha

Vanilla vine weevil	*Sipalus* sp.	Black coloured weevil bores into and eats tender stem and leaves	Collect and destroy the weevils during adult stage during Nov-Feb	***Source:***https://www.theguardian.com/lifeandstyle/2012/jun/22/alys-fowler-vine-weevil
Caterpillar	*Plusia aurifera*	Light greenish caterpillars feed on vegetative shoots and first leaf forming a web in between	Collect and destroy the caterpillars	***Source:***https://www.papua-insects.nl/insect%20orders/Lepidoptera/Noctuidae/Plusiinae
Beetle	*Saula ferruginea*	Adults cut through the leaf from the lower surface eating the entire leaf tissue except the thick translucent cuticle of epidermis	Collect and destroy or spray 0.1 per cent malathion	***Source:***https://www.forestryimages.org/browse/detail.cfm?imgnum=5073020

Resistant Varieties

Bourbon Vanilla: Bourbon vanilla is one of the most commonly cultivated varieties of vanilla. It is grown mainly in Madagascar, Reunion, and the Comoros Islands. Bourbon vanilla beans are known for their sweet, creamy flavour and strong aroma. Bourbon vanilla is resistant to many common insect pests, including thrips and spider mites.

Tahitian Vanilla: Tahitian vanilla is grown mainly in French Polynesia, although it is also cultivated in other parts of the world. Tahitian vanilla beans are smaller than Bourbon vanilla beans and have a fruity, floral flavour. Tahitian vanilla is resistant to some insect pests, including thrips and scale insects.

Mexican Vanilla: Mexican vanilla is grown mainly in Mexico and Central America. It is known for its earthy, spicy flavour and strong aroma. Mexican vanilla is resistant to some insect pests, including spider mites.

Ugandan Vanilla: Ugandan vanilla is grown mainly in Uganda and other parts of East Africa. It has a strong, rich flavour and aroma. Ugandan vanilla is resistant to some insect pests, including thrips and spider mites.

Indian Vanilla: Indian vanilla is grown mainly in the Indian state of Kerala. It is known for its deep, complex flavour and strong aroma. Indian vanilla is resistant to some insect pests, including mealybugs.

*Vanilla is not commonly grown in India due to unsuitable climate and soil conditions. Therefore, there are no varieties of vanilla that are resistant to insect pests specifically grown in India.

47 Pests of Bay Leaf

Scientific Name	*Cinnamomum tamala*
Family	Lauraceae
Origin	India, Bhutan, Bangladesh, Nepal and China
Chromosome Number	2n = 24

Bay Leaf (*Laurus nobilis*) is an evergreen tree that belongs to the family Lauraceae. Bay Leaf is cultivated in different parts of India, including the states of Himachal Pradesh, Uttar Pradesh, Bihar, Maharashtra, and Karnataka. However, Uttar Pradesh is the major producer of bay leaves in India. The total area under bay leaf cultivation in India is around 5,000 hectares, and the total production is around 10,000 metric tonnes per year.

Insect pests are a significant threat to bay leaf crops and can cause significant economic losses. Some of the most common insect pests affecting bay leaf crops include:

Bay Leaf Thrips: These pests damage the leaves and can cause yellowing, wilting, and stunting of the plants, ultimately leading to reduced growth and yield.

Bay Leaf Mealybugs: These insects feed on the plant sap, causing wilting, stunting, and discoloration of the leaves and stems, ultimately leading to reduced growth and yield.

Leaf Eating Caterpillars: These pests consume the leaves, leading to defoliation and reduced growth and yield.

Shoot Borers: These pests bore into the stem and shoots of the plant, leading to wilting, stunting, and ultimately reduced yield and quality.

The economic damage caused by these insect pests can be severe, resulting in yield losses of up to 50%. Additionally, bay leaf is a valuable spice, and any reduction in yield or quality can have a significant impact on the income of farmers and the overall economy.

❑ Bay leaf sucker/Bay psyllid: *Trioza alacris* Flor, 1861

Common Name	:	Bay leaf sucker/Bay psyllid
Scientific Name	:	*Trioza alacris* Flor, 1861
Family	:	Triozidae
Order	:	Hemiptera

***Source:**https://www.biodiversidadvirtual.org/insectarium/Trioza-alacris-img913689.html*

Distribution and Host Range

T. alacris is a sap-sucking hemipteran bug in the family *Triozidae* which creates galls on the leaves of *Laurus* species. It is found in Europe. Found on bay trees – no other psyllid is likely to be found on bay.

Nature and Symptoms of Damage

T. alacris causes the edges of leaves to thicken and roll downwards forming pale, elongated pouches.

Life History and Description

The galls can house two generations in a summer, of up to thirty pale-green nymphs, which are covered in a white wax. Adults can also be found in the gall. The adults usually overwinter in leaf litter but can also spend the winter in the gall. Species of *Laurus* galled include the Azores laurel, bay tree and Canary Avocado.

Adult length 3.5 to 4 mm. *Lauritrioza alacris* has long, sharply pointed wings, the outermost vein is short and curved, and only the last two antennal segments are dark. Its colouring varies dramatically with age, dorsal surfaces darkening to black, with slightly paler longitudinal and transverse lines. The pink-yellow nymphs form leaf-roll galls on bay leaves, in which they produce thick waxy secretions. The galls are seen more often than the adults.

Management

Not clear

Resistant Varieties

Bay leaves are primarily grown for their culinary use and are not considered a major commercial crop. However, there are several varieties of bay leaf that are known for their resistance to insect pests. Some of these include:

California Bay Leaf: This variety of bay leaf is native to California and is known for its strong, spicy flavour. It is also resistant to pests such as mites and aphids.

Indian Bay Leaf: Also known as Tej Patta, this variety of bay leaf is commonly used in Indian cuisine. It is resistant to pests such as whiteflies, thrips, and mites.

Turkish Bay Leaf: This variety of bay leaf is native to the Mediterranean region and is known for its strong, sweet flavour. It is resistant to pests such as spider mites and thrips.

Indonesian Bay Leaf: This variety of bay leaf is native to Indonesia and is commonly used in Indonesian and Malaysian cuisine. It is resistant to pests such as mites and aphids.

Mexican Bay Leaf: This variety of bay leaf is native to Mexico and is known for its strong, slightly bitter flavour. It is resistant to pests such as spider mites and whiteflies.

Pests of Curry Leaf

Scientific Name	*Murraya koenigii*
Family	Rutaceae
Origin	Tarai region of Uttar Pradesh, India
Chromosome Number	2n = 18

Curry Leaf (*Murraya koenigii*) is a small, bushy tree that belongs to the Rutaceae family. It is native to India and is widely used in Indian cuisine as a seasoning. Curry Leaf is widely cultivated in different parts of India, including the states of Tamil Nadu, Karnataka, Andhra Pradesh, Maharashtra, and Kerala. Tamil Nadu is the major producer of curry leaves in India. The total area under curry leaf cultivation in India is around 30,000 hectares, and the total production is around 250,000 metric tonnes per year. Insect pests are a significant threat to curry leaf crops and can cause significant economic losses. Some of the most common insect pests affecting curry leaf crops include:

❑ Citrus butterfly: *Papilio demoleus* Linnaeus, 1758

Common Name	:	Swallow tail butterfly; Lime butterfly; Lemon butterfly; Chequered swallowtail
Scientific Name	:	*Papilio demoleus* Linnaeus, 1758
Family	:	Papilionidae
Order	:	Lepidoptera

Source: *https://www.cabidigitallibrary.org/doi/10.1079/cabicompendium.38758*

Distribution and Host Range

The butterfly is native to Asia and Australia, and can be considered an invasive pest in other parts of the world. The butterfly has spread to Hispaniola Island (Dominican Republic) in the Western Hemisphere, and to **Mahé**, Seychelles. The larval food plants of *P. demoleus* in Asia are from the family Rutaceae, while in Australia and Papua New Guinea, the butterfly also feeds on host plants of family Fabaceae.

Nature and Symptoms of Damage

Due to its capability for rapid population growth under favourable circumstances and its having been recorded to have five generations in a year in temperate regions of China, it is considered a serious potential threat. The caterpillars can completely defoliate young citrus trees (below 2 feet) and devastate citrus nurseries. In mature trees, caterpillars may prefer young leaves and leaf flush.

Life History and Description

Eggs: Yellowish white, round, smooth eggs are laid singly on tender leaves and shoots by *P. demoleus*. Egg hatches in about 3-8 days.

Larva: Freshly hatched caterpillars are dark brown and soon develop irregular white markings on their body resembling bird's drop. The caterpillars feed voraciously on tender leaves right up to the mid ribs and defoliate the entire seedlings or the tree leaving behind the only midribs.

Adults: *Papilio demoleus* is a big beautiful butterfly with yellow and black markings on all the four wings, having wing expanse of about 50-60 mm. Its hind wings have a brick red oval patch near the anal margin and there is no tail like extension behind though common in Papilionidae. *Papilio polytes* males are black and females vary in form. *Papilio helenus* has black wings with three white distal spots.

Management

Hand-picking of caterpillars. Natural enemies are listed below:

Egg parasites	*Ooencyrtus malayensis* Ferriere (Hymenoptera: Encyrtidae) *Tetrastichus* sp. (Hymenoptera: Eulophidae)
Larval stage	*Erycia nymphalidophaga* Baronoff (Diptera: Tachinidae) (parasite) *Cantheconidea furcellata* (Wolff) (Pentatomidae predator Other natural enemies of larvae included reduviid bugs; birds; spiders; sphecid wasps; and chameleons
Pupal parasites	*Brachymeria* sp. (Hymenoptera: Chalcididae) *Pteromalus puparum* Linnaeus (Hymenoptera: Pteromalidae) *Ophiocordyceps*

Some other Pests of Curry Leaf			
Common Name	**Scientific Name**	**Family**	**Order**
Tortoise beetle	*Aspidomorpha miliaris* (Fabricius, 1775); *Cassida circumdata* Herbst, 1799; *Chiridopsis bipunctata* (Linnaeus, 1767)	Cassididae; Chrysomelidae	Coleoptera
Citrus psyllid	*Diaphorina citri* Kuwayama, 1908	Liviidae	Hemiptera

Resistant Varieties

Krishna Curry Leaf: This variety is known for its strong aroma and is commonly used in South Indian cuisine. It is also resistant to several insect pests, including whiteflies, aphids, and mealybugs.

Gamthi Curry Leaf: This variety is grown in Gujarat and is known for its large leaves and strong aroma. It is resistant to several insect pests, including whiteflies and aphids.

Surabhi Curry Leaf: This variety is grown in the southern part of India and is known for its long and narrow leaves. It is resistant to several insect pests, including whiteflies, aphids, and mites.

Rajapuri Curry Leaf: This variety is grown in Maharashtra and is known for its strong aroma and high oil content. It is resistant to several insect pests, including whiteflies and aphids.

Nimbkar Improved Curry Leaf: This variety is developed by Nimbkar Agricultural Research Institute in Maharashtra and is known for its high yield and resistance to several insect pests, including whiteflies and aphids.

PART E

PESTS OF MEDICINAL AND AROMATIC CROPS

D. Lava Kumar
(Ph.D. Scholar)
Division of Floriculture and Landscaping
ICAR- Indian Agricultural Research Institute
Pusa, New Delhi

Pests of Medicinal Crops

Medicinal crops refer to those plants that are used for their medicinal properties and are cultivated or collected for their therapeutic value. These crops are important for the healthcare sector and are in high demand in both domestic and international markets. Some of the commonly grown medicinal crops in India include aloe vera, neem, tulsi, ashwagandha, and guggul. India is one of the largest producers and exporters of medicinal plants in the world. The country has a rich biodiversity of medicinal plants, and it is estimated that around 8,000 species of medicinal plants are used in traditional medicine. The area under cultivation of medicinal plants in India is around 1.2 million hectares, and the annual production is estimated to be around 2.5 million metric tonnes. Here is a list of some medicinal crops grown in India with their botany, area, production, and therapeutic importance:

Common Name (Economic part)	Scientific Name	Family	Origin	Chromosom e Number
Ashwagandha (Root)	*Withania somnifera*	Solanaceae	India, Middle East, and parts of Africa	2n = 48
Guggal (Extrat)	*Commiphora wightii*	Burseraceae	India	2n = 26
Isabgol (Husk/Seed)	*Plantago ovata*	Plantaginaceae	Mediterranean region	2n = 8
Kalmegh (Whole Plant)	*Andrographis paniculata*	Acanthaceae	India and Sri Lanka	2n =50
Liquirice (Mulethi) (stem)	*Glycyrrhiza glabra*	Fabaceae	Western Asia, North Africa, and Southern Europe	2n =16
Sarpgandha (Root)	*Rauvolfia Serpentina*	Apocynaceae	Indian subcontinent and East Asia	2n = 22
Senna (Sanai) (Leaf)	*Cassia angustifolia*	Fabaceae	Upper Egypt	2n = 28
Tulsi (Whole Plant)	*Ocimum sanctum*	Lamiaceae	Indian subcontinent	2n = 32

Ashwagandha: Ashwagandha (*Withania somnifera*) is a perennial plant belonging to the family Solanaceae. It is commonly known as Indian ginseng, winter cherry, or poison gooseberry. The plant grows up to a height of 1.5 meters and has ovate leaves and greenish-yellow flowers. The plant is primarily cultivated for its roots, which are used for medicinal purposes. Ashwagandha is native to India and is widely cultivated in various parts of the country. It is also cultivated in other parts of the world, including the United States, China, and Nepal. According to the Food and Agriculture Organization (FAO), India is the largest producer of Ashwagandha, accounting for around 90% of the global production. The production of Ashwagandha has been steadily increasing in recent years, with an estimated 10,000-12,000 tons produced annually. The active ingredients in Ashwagandha are a group of compounds called withanolides. These compounds have been shown to have various pharmacological properties, including anti-inflammatory, immunomodulatory, and anti-tumor activities. Withanolides are found in the roots, leaves, and berries of the plant. Ashwagandha is susceptible to various pests and diseases, including root-knot nematodes, leaf spot, and Fusarium wilt. Root-knot nematodes are the most significant pest of Ashwagandha, causing significant yield losses in infected plants. Other pests that can attack Ashwagandha include spider mites, aphids, and whiteflies.

Ashwagandha
Resistant Varieties
Jawahar Ashwagandha-1: This variety is known for its high yield and resistance to pests and diseases.
Pratibha Ashwagandha-1: This variety is resistant to leaf spot disease and is suitable for cultivation in hot and dry regions.
K-1 Ashwagandha: This variety is resistant to root rot disease and is known for its high yield potential.
Anmol Ashwagandha: This variety is resistant to stem rot disease and is suitable for cultivation in northern India.
Poshita Ashwagandha: This variety is resistant to pests and diseases and is known for its high medicinal value.
RAU Ashwagandha-1: This variety is resistant to leaf spot disease and is suitable for cultivation in various agro-climatic regions.
Rishi Ashwagandha-1: This variety is resistant to pests and diseases and is known for its high yield potential.
Arka Ashwagandha: This variety is resistant to root knot nematodes and is known for its high root yield.
KWR-1: This variety of Ashwagandha has been developed by the Indian Institute of Horticultural Research (IIHR), Bangalore. It is resistant to several insect pests, including root knot nematodes and whiteflies.
HCU-1: This variety has been developed by the Horticultural College and Research Institute, Tamil Nadu. It is known for its resistance to root-knot nematodes and spider mites.
CO-1: This variety has been developed by the Tamil Nadu Agricultural University (TNAU) and is resistant to root-knot nematodes, whiteflies, and aphids.
RAU-1: This variety has been developed by the Rajasthan Agricultural University and is resistant to root-knot nematodes and whiteflies.
Anand-1: This variety has been developed by Anand Agricultural University in Gujarat. It is resistant to root-knot nematodes and spider mites.

Guggul: Guggul (*Commiphora wightii*) is a small tree or shrub belonging to the family Burseraceae. It is native to India and Pakistan and is commonly known as Indian bdellium-tree or Mukul myrrh. The tree has thorny branches and produces yellow flowers and red fruit. The gum resin obtained from the tree is used for medicinal purposes. Guggul is primarily found in the arid regions of India, particularly in the states of Rajasthan and Gujarat. The production of guggul has been steadily increasing in recent years, with an estimated 1,000 tons produced annually. The active ingredients in guggul are a group of compounds called guggulsterones. These compounds have been shown to have various pharmacological properties, including cholesterol-lowering, anti-inflammatory, and anti-tumor activities. Guggul is susceptible to various pests and diseases, including mealybugs, scale insects, and leaf spot. Mealybugs are the most significant pest of guggul, causing significant yield losses in infected trees. Other pests that can attack guggul include spider mites, aphids, and whiteflies.

Guggal
Resistant Varieties
Bikaneri Guggul: This variety of guggul is native to the Bikaner region of Rajasthan in India. It is known for its high yield of resin and its resistance to insect pests.
Mphashu Guggul: This variety is native to southern Africa and is known for its drought tolerance and resistance to insect pests.
Saurashtra Guggul: This variety of guggul is grown in the Saurashtra region of Gujarat in India. It is known for its high yield of resin and its resistance to insect pests.
Gum Guggul: This variety is native to the Middle East and is grown in countries such as Iran, Iraq, and Saudi Arabia. It is known for its medicinal properties and its resistance to insect pests.
Jafrabadi Guggul: This variety of guggul is native to the Kutch region of Gujarat in India. It is known for its high yield of resin and its resistance to insect pests.

Isabgol: Isabgol (*Plantago ovata*) is an annual herb belonging to the family Plantaginaceae. It is native to India, Pakistan, and Iran and is commonly known as psyllium or Indian plantain. The plant has narrow, elongated leaves and produces small, inconspicuous flowers. The seeds of the plant are used for medicinal purposes. Isabgol is primarily cultivated in India and Pakistan, with India being the largest producer. The production of Isabgol has been steadily increasing in recent years, with an estimated 200,000-250,000 tons produced annually. The active ingredient in Isabgol is a group of compounds called mucilage. This compound has been shown to have various pharmacological properties, including laxative and cholesterol-lowering activities. Isabgol is used as a natural remedy for constipation, diarrhea, and other digestive problems. Isabgol is susceptible to various pests and diseases, including powdery mildew, leaf spot, and root rot. Powdery mildew is the most significant pest of Isabgol, causing significant yield losses in infected plants. Other pests that can attack Isabgol include aphids and spider mites.

Isabgol
Resistant Varieties
Gujarat Isabgol 1: This variety of isabgol is known for its resistance to insect pests and diseases. It is mainly grown in the Gujarat region of India and is characterized by its high yield and good quality seeds.
Gujarat Isabgol 2: Another variety of isabgol grown in the Gujarat region of India, Gujarat Isabgol 2 is also known for its resistance to insect pests and diseases. It is a hardy crop that can withstand adverse weather conditions.
IC-308: Developed by the Indian Council of Agricultural Research (ICAR), IC-308 is a high-yielding variety of isabgol that is resistant to insect pests and diseases. It is characterized by its uniform seed size and good quality seeds.
PS-7: PS-7 is a variety of isabgol that is resistant to insect pests and diseases. It is mainly grown in the Rajasthan region of India and is characterized by its high yield and good quality seeds.
R-12: Developed by the Central Arid Zone Research Institute (CAZRI) in India, R-12 is a variety of isabgol that is resistant to insect pests and diseases. It is characterized by its high yield and good quality seeds.

Kalmegh: Kalmegh (*Andrographis paniculata*) is an annual herb belonging to the family Acanthaceae. It is native to India and Sri Lanka and is commonly known as green chireta or king of bitters. The plant has lanceolate leaves and produces small, white flowers. The aerial parts of the plant are used for medicinal purposes. Kalmegh is primarily cultivated in India, Thailand, and China. The production of Kalmegh has been steadily increasing in recent years, with an estimated 25,000-30,000 tons produced annually. The active ingredient in Kalmegh is a group of compounds called andrographolides. These compounds have been shown to have various pharmacological properties, including anti-inflammatory, immunomodulatory, and anti-tumor activities. Kalmegh is susceptible to various pests and diseases, including leaf spot, root rot, and powdery mildew. Leaf spot is the most significant pest of Kalmegh, causing significant yield losses in infected plants. Other pests that can attack Kalmegh include aphids and whiteflies.

Kalmegh
Resistant Varieties
Parvati: This variety of kalmegh is resistant to aphids, leafhoppers, and mites. It is known for its high andrographolide content, which is the main bioactive compound responsible for its medicinal properties.
Kalmegh-9: This variety is resistant to leafhoppers and aphids. It is known for its high andrographolide content and is used for the treatment of various respiratory ailments.
Kalmegh-10: This variety is resistant to aphids and is known for its high andrographolide content. It is used in the treatment of fever, cold, and cough.
Kalmegh-11: This variety is resistant to aphids and is known for its high andrographolide content. It is used in the treatment of various skin ailments.
Kalmegh-12: This variety is resistant to aphids and is known for its high andrographolide content. It is used in the treatment of liver disorders and digestive ailments.

Licorice: Licorice (*Glycyrrhiza glabra*) is a perennial plant belonging to the family Fabaceae. It is native to Asia and Europe and is commonly known as sweetwood or liquorice. The plant has pinnate leaves and produces small, purple flowers. The roots and underground stems of the plant are used for medicinal purposes. Licorice is primarily cultivated in China, Iran, Turkey, and Russia. The production of Licorice has been steady in recent years, with an estimated 250,000-300,000 tons produced annually. The active ingredient in Licorice is a group of compounds called triterpenoids and flavonoids. These compounds have been shown to have various pharmacological properties, including anti-inflammatory, antioxidant, and anti-tumor activities. Licorice is susceptible to various pests and diseases, including root rot, leaf spot, and powdery mildew. Root rot is the most significant pest of Licorice, causing significant yield losses in infected plants. Other pests that can attack Licorice include spider mites and aphids.

Licorice
Resistant Varieties
***Glycyrrhiza glabra*:** This is the most widely cultivated species of licorice, and is native to the Mediterranean and Middle Eastern regions. It is commonly grown in India, China, Spain, Italy, and Turkey, among other countries. This variety is known for its strong flavor and high glycyrrhizin content, which gives it its characteristic sweetness.

***Glycyrrhiza uralensis*:** This species of licorice is native to the steppes of central Asia, and is commonly grown in China, Mongolia, and Russia. It is known for its high quality, and is often used in traditional Chinese medicine.

***Glycyrrhiza inflata*:** This species of licorice is native to Iran and Afghanistan, and is commonly grown in these countries, as well as in China. It is known for its high yield and good quality, and is often used in the production of licorice extract.

***Glycyrrhiza echinata*:** This species of licorice is native to central and southwestern Asia, and is commonly grown in Iran, Afghanistan, and Pakistan. It is known for its high glycyrrhizin content, and is often used in traditional Ayurvedic medicine.

Sarpgandha: Sarpgandha (*Rauvolfia serpentina*) is a perennial plant belonging to the family Apocynaceae. It is native to the Indian subcontinent and is commonly known as Indian snakeroot. The plant has glossy, dark green leaves and produces small, fragrant white or pink flowers. The roots of the plant are used for medicinal purposes. Sarpgandha is primarily cultivated in India, Nepal, and Sri Lanka. The production of Sarpgandha has been steady in recent years, with an estimated 10,000-15,000 tons produced annually. The active ingredient in Sarpgandha is a group of compounds called alkaloids, including reserpine, yohimbine, and ajmalicine. These compounds have been shown to have various pharmacological properties, including antihypertensive, sedative, and antipsychotic activities. Sarpgandha is susceptible to various pests and diseases, including leaf spot, stem rot, and root knot nematodes. Root knot nematodes are the most significant pest of Sarpgandha, causing significant yield losses in infected plants.

Sarpagandha

Resistant Varieties

Indian Sarpagandha: This variety is native to India and is the most commonly grown variety of sarpagandha. It is a hardy plant that can tolerate a wide range of growing conditions and is known to be highly productive.

Sri Lankan Sarpagandha: This variety is native to Sri Lanka and is known for its high yield and superior quality roots. It is widely cultivated in Sri Lanka and has been introduced to other countries as well.

Chinese Sarpagandha: This variety is grown in China and is known for its high alkaloid content. It is used mainly for the production of antihypertensive drugs.

African Sarpagandha: This variety is grown in some parts of Africa and is used in traditional medicine to treat various ailments. It is known for its high alkaloid content and is also used for the production of antihypertensive drugs.

Senna: Senna (*Cassia angustifolia*) is a perennial plant belonging to the family Fabaceae. It is native to the Arabian Peninsula and is commonly known as senna or Indian senna. The plant has pinnate leaves and produces yellow flowers. The leaves and pods of the plant are used for medicinal purposes. Senna is primarily cultivated in India, Sudan, and Pakistan. The production of Senna has been steady in recent years, with an estimated 50,000-60,000 tons produced annually. The active ingredient in Senna is a group of compounds called anthraquinones, including sennosides A and B. These compounds have been shown to have various pharmacological properties, including laxative and antipyretic activities. Senna is susceptible to various pests and diseases, including leaf spot, root rot, and stem canker. Stem canker is the most significant pest of Senna, causing significant yield losses in infected plants. Other pests that can attack Senna include spider mites and aphids.

Senna
Resistant Varieties
***Cassia angustifolia*:** This variety is also known as Indian Senna or Tinnevelly Senna. It is a small shrub that grows up to 1.5 meters in height and is widely cultivated in India, Pakistan, and Sudan. It is resistant to various insect pests and is a rich source of anthraquinone glycosides, which are used in the production of laxatives.
***Cassia acutifolia*:** This variety is also known as Alexandrian Senna and is native to Egypt. It is a small shrub that grows up to 1 meter in height and is widely cultivated in Egypt and Sudan. It is also resistant to various insect pests and is a rich source of anthraquinone glycosides.
***Cassia obovata*:** This variety is also known as Senna Italica or Neutral Henna. It is a small shrub that grows up to 1.5 meters in height and is native to India and Pakistan. It is resistant to various insect pests and is used as a natural hair conditioner and colorant.
***Cassia tora*:** This variety is also known as Sickle Senna or Foetid Cassia. It is an annual plant that grows up to 1 meter in height and is native to India. It is resistant to various insect pests and is used in traditional medicine for its laxative and anti-inflammatory properties.

Tulsi: Botany: Tulsi (*Ocimum sanctum*) is a perennial plant belonging to the family Lamiaceae. It is native to the Indian subcontinent and is commonly known as holy basil. The plant has green, fragrant leaves and produces small, white or pink flowers. The leaves and flowers of the plant are used for medicinal purposes. Tulsi is primarily cultivated in India, Nepal, and Thailand. The production of Tulsi has been steady in recent years, with an estimated 50,000-60,000 tons produced annually. The active ingredient in Tulsi is a group of compounds called eugenol, carvacrol, and rosmarinic acid. These compounds have been shown to have various pharmacological properties, including anti-inflammatory, antioxidant, and antimicrobial activities. Tulsi is susceptible to various pests and diseases, including powdery mildew, downy mildew, and leaf spot. Downy mildew is the most significant pest of Tulsi, causing significant yield losses in infected plants. Other pests that can attack Tulsi include aphids and whiteflies.

Tulsi
Resistant Varieties
Rama Tulsi: Rama Tulsi is a green leaf variety that is highly valued for its medicinal properties. It is known to be relatively resistant to insect pests, although it may still be susceptible to certain types of fungi.
Krishna Tulsi: Krishna Tulsi is a purple-leaf variety that is also highly valued for its medicinal properties. Like Rama Tulsi, it is known to be relatively resistant to insect pests, although it may still be susceptible to certain types of fungi.
Kapoor Tulsi: Kapoor Tulsi is a green-leaf variety that is highly aromatic and is commonly used in cooking. It is also known to be relatively resistant to insect pests.
Vana Tulsi: Vana Tulsi is a wild variety of tulsi that is native to India and is known to have a higher resistance to insect pests than other varieties. It is also highly valued for its medicinal properties.

Insect pests can cause significant economic losses to medicinal crops, affecting both their yield and quality. Some of the most common insect pests affecting medicinal crops in India include:

COMMON PESTS ASSOCIATED WITH MEDICINAL CROPS

Common Name	Scientific Name	Family	Order	Remarks
Cut worm	*Agrotis* sp.	Noctuidae	lepidoptera	As Described in Potato
Fruit borer	*Helicoverpa armigera* (Hübner, [1808])	Noctuidae	lepidoptera	As Described in Tomato
Epilachna Beetle	*Henosepilachna vigintioctopunctata* (Fabricius, 1775)	Coccinellidae	Coleoptera	As Described in Potato
White flies	*Bemisia tabaci* (Gennadius, 1889)	Aleyrodidae	Hemiptera	As Described in Potato
Leaf eating caterpillar	*Spodoptera litura* (Fabricius, 1775)	Noctuidae	lepidoptera	As Described in Potato
Aphids	*Aphis gossypii* Glover, 1877	Aphididae	Hemiptera	As Described in Chilli
Ash weevil	*Myllocerus viridanus* Fabricius, 1775	Curculionidae	Coleoptera	As Described in Brinjal
Mealy bug	*Coccidohystrix insolita* (Green, 1908)	Pseudococcidae	Hemiptera	As Described in Brinjal

PESTS OF AROMATIC CROPS

Aromatic crops are those plants which have aromatic properties and are used for their essential oils, spices, and flavorings. In India, several aromatic crops are cultivated. Aromatic crops come from different plant families, including Lamiaceae, Apiaceae, Zingiberaceae, and Rutaceae. These plants are mainly herbs, but some are shrubs and trees. They have specialized glands in their leaves, stems, flowers, and roots, which produce essential oils and other aromatic compounds.

The major aromatic crops cultivated in India are mint, coriander, cumin, fennel, ajwain, dill, lemongrass, palmarosa, citronella, and vetiver. The area and production of these crops vary from region to region. For example, mint is grown in Uttar Pradesh, Punjab, Haryana, and Bihar, while coriander is mainly cultivated in Rajasthan, Gujarat, and Madhya Pradesh. In 2019-20, India produced about 47,000 metric tons of mint, 29,000 metric tons of coriander, and 22,000 metric tons of cumin.

Insect pests are a major threat to the production of aromatic crops. They can cause significant damage to the plants, reducing the yield and quality of the produce. Some of the major insect pests of aromatic crops in India are described here under accordingly:

Pests of Lemongrass

Scientific Name	*Cymbopogon flexuosus*
Family	Poaceae
Origin	India
Chromosome number	2n = 20

Lemon grass (*Cymbopogon citratus*) is a perennial grass native to India and tropical regions of Asia. It is mainly cultivated in the states of Kerala, Tamil Nadu, and Andhra Pradesh in India. India is the major producer of lemon grass oil in the world, with an annual production of about 250-300 tonnes. The essential oil of lemon grass contains citral, geraniol, and limonene, which are used in the manufacture of perfumes, cosmetics, and medicines. The major insect pests of lemon grass include shoot and stem borer (*Conogethes punctiferalis*), leaf roller (*Cnaphalocrocis medinalis*), and red spider mite (*Oligonychus biharensis*).

❑ Stem borer: *Chilo infuscatellus* Snellen, 1890

Common Name	:	Stem boring caterpillar, yellow top borer, sugarcane shoot borer
Scientific Name	:	*Chilo infuscatellus* Snellen, 1890
Family	:	Pyralidae
Order	:	Lepidoptera

Source: *https://www.indiamart.com/*

Distribution and Host Range

It is distributed in India, Malaysia, Afghanistan, Java, Myanmar, Tajikistan, Korea, Taiwan, the Philippines and Timor. The larvae attacks many grass family (Poaceae) members like citronella grass, rice, sugarcane, maize, oats, barley, Bermuda grass, Java grass, jungle rice, millet and pearl millet etc.

Nature and Symptoms of Damage

Chilo bores into the stem and feeds on the shoot portion. Stem borer is typically located at the base of the stem. The upper grass portion which is unaffected since the caterpillar is remained at the lower portions, the grass is chopped a few inches above the ground. The core leaf dries out as the first sign of an attack. As a result, the entire shoot dies, resulting in a considerable drop in grass output.

Life History and Identification

Chilo infuscatellus, lays the eggs in groups, which are creamish white and translucent initially and then turns yellowish with pin head size spots before hatching. These are seen on the lower surface of the leaves with an incubation period of 3 to 5 days. The hatch-out larvae, moult for 4 times and pass through 5 instars before becoming pre-pupa. The larval stage lasts for an average of 18 to 26 days. Larvae stops feeding, became sedentary and shrank during the pre-pupal stage, which lasts for 1 to 2 days. Then it enters pupal stage which lasts for 4 to 5 days. It is followed by adult stage. The adult moth measures 30 to 40 mm in length. The hindwings are creamy white with buff-coloured tips. Adult female moth longevity ranges from 3 to 5 days, with an average of 4.07 days, whereas adult male moth longevity ranges from 3 to 4 days, with an average of 3.24 days. *C. infuscatellus* had a total life span of 29 to 44 days for females and 29 to 42 days, in case of males.

Management

During the summer, *i.e.,* at the time of off-season, the dry stubbles are burnt off. So, that the larvae lurking in the stubbles are destroyed. Provide enough moisture to reduce soil heating and enhance humidity, which is unfavorable for the pest multiplication. Early plantation can help in prevention of severe damage from this pest. Deep ploughing during summer. The infected shoots are just pulled out and then destroyed. Egg masses are collected and destroyed. Prick the larvae by using an iron needle. On 35 and 50 DAP, apply granulosis virus 750 diseased larvae per hectare together with teepol or release of 125 gravid females of tachinid parasite (*Sturmiopsis inferens*) per acre. Use of egg parasites like *Trichograma* spp. and *Telenomus beneficious*, larval parasites like *Apanteles flavipes*, *Goniojus indicus*, *Melcha* sp, *Bracon* sp. and pupal parasites like *Tetrastichus ayyari*. Soil application of carbaryl and sevidol 4% G @ 12.5 kg or carbofuron 3G @ 33 kg and followed by irrigation.

❑ Termite: *Odontotermes obesus* (Rambur 1842)

Common Name	:	White ants, fungus-growing termites, Indian white termite.
Scientific Name	:	*Odontotermes obesus* (Rambur 1842)
Family	:	Scarabaeidae
Order	:	Blattodea

Source: *https://commons.wikimedia.org/*

As described in Mango

Mealy bugs: *Dysmicoccus brevipes* (Cockerell, 1893)

Common Name	:	Pineapple mealybug
Scientific Name	:	*Dysmicoccus brevipes* (Cockerell, 1893)
Family	:	Pseudococcidae
Order	:	Hemiptera

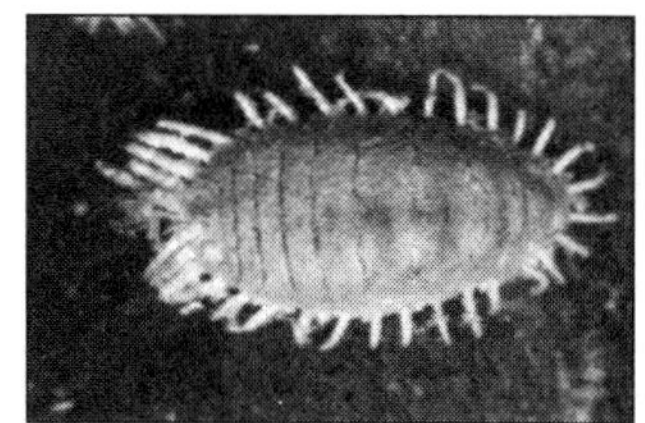

Source: *https://apps.lucidcentral.org/*

Distribution and Host Range

This pest is commonly seen in tropical, humid regions of the world and also found in Egypt, Israel, and Lebanon. Host plants includes lemongrass, sugar cane, pineapple, banana, avocado, coffee, cocoa, date palms and soybeans etc.

Nature and Symptoms of Damage

The nymphs and wingless females cause significant harm. They attack the leaves and tender shoots. Nymphs congregate along stems and on the undersides of leaves. Suck the sap from tender shoots and leaves. Mealybugs often create honeydew, a sticky, carbohydrate-rich material. The affected portions dry out and yield is significantly diminished.

Life History and Identification

The mealybug lives on roots all the year, but in late summer it climbs the plant to infest the leaves and tender shoots. It typically occupies plant bases, lower sections of stems and exposed roots of grasses and lower stalks. In various parts of the world, this mealybug contains both sexual and non-sexual populations. It is oviparous, and females can give birth to around 1000 crawlers, which are the primary mechanism of dissemination.

Management

In order to avoid the spread of mealybugs, carefully inspect purchased plants. Look for mealybugs or clusters of cottony wax on sensitive plants and clear them. Removal of crop stubbles which carries the inoculum for next season. Hand picking and scrap-out with a tooth brush is followed at low level of infections. Use of mealybug parasites like *Aenasius cariocus*, *A. colombiensis*, *Anagyrus ananatis*, *Euryhopauus propinquus*, *Hambletonia pseudococcina*, *Ptomastidae abnormis* and predators like *Cryptolaemus montrouzieri*, *Lobodiplosis pseudococci*, *Nephus bilucernarius*, *Scymnus unicatus* and *S. pictus etc*. Spray any following insecticides: phosphomidon 40 SL 2 ml/lit; chlorpriphos 20 EC 2 ml/lit; imidacloprid 80.5 SC 0.6 ml/lit; thiamethoxam 25 WSG 0.6 mg/lit; profenophos 2 ml/lit.

Spittle bug: *Clovia bipunctata* Kirby, 1891

Common Name	:	Spittle bug
Scientific Name	:	*Clovia bipunctata* Kirby, 1891
Family	:	Cercopidae
Order	:	Hemiptera

Source: *https://en.wikipedia.org/*

Distribution and Host Range

It is widely distributed in the Eastern half of the United States. A similar genus but distinct species can be seen throughout the Central America. Host plants includes lemongrass, jack fruit, sugarcane and rice etc.

Nature and Symptoms of Damage

In lemongrass, the tender leaves are infested by the nymphal stages of spittle bug. The infested leaves represent the characteristic markings and also the leaves will become crinkled, if there is a severe infection.

Life History and Identification

The matured beetle is straw-colored, with average length of 8.75 mm and a thorax width of 3 mm. On the anal edges of the forewings, there are two noticeable spots. The nymphs are seen in light cream color. Eggs generally hatch-out in may, which are overwintered. Nymphs are seen to be feed under a frothy, spittle like foam. Only one generation is seen per year.

Management

Spittlebugs can be controlled with a garden hose wipes (larvae and eggs are washed-off). Use of predators like assassin bugs, syrphid larvae, minute pirate bugs and spiders which feeds on nymphs. Use acetamiprid 20% SP @ 0.2 g per litre.

❑ Nematodes: *Helicotylenchus* spp. (Steiner)

Common Name	:	Spiral nematode
Scientific Name	:	*Helicotylenchus* spp. (Steiner)
Family	:	Hoplolaimidae
Order	:	Tylenchida

Source: *https://edis.ifas.ufl.edu/*

Distribution and Host Range

Spiral nematodes found all over the world because they can live and survive in a variety of environments. They are among the most prevalent plant parasitic nematodes, found in Poaceae members like lemongrass, corn, and other crops like bananas and soybeans etc.

Nature and Symptoms of Damage

Plants infected with the aggressive species seen to be stunted and yellowed, without a sign of infestation in crop. But the species *H. multicinctus*, harm the plant by causing enough root necrosis and represent the symptoms.

Life History and Identification

The majority are root-ectoparasites of plants. To feed, they stab their stylets into the root epidermis. Some species inhabit the tissue of the root while others pierce it and dwell inside. Within 2 or 3 days the young insects emerge to feed after they lay their eggs on, near, or inside the roots. The genus can be found on many different host plant taxa. Indicating that the worm frequently reproduces by parthenogenesis, males can be infrequent.

The female is a worm-like and are in straight or in spiral-shaped. The male look similar to female, but has little anterior end. The nematode body take a spiral shape immediately after the death.

Management

Use of crop rotation with non-host plants. Tilling or soil ploughing for 2 to 3 times in summer. Parasitic fungi like *Paecilomyces lilacinus* should be choosen. Use of nematicides like 1,3 Dichloropropene, fumigants like methyl isocyanate (dazomet).

Resistant Varieties

East Indian Lemongrass: This variety of lemongrass is native to India and is widely cultivated in tropical regions around the world. It is known for its lemony flavor and fragrance and is a popular ingredient in Asian cuisine. East Indian lemongrass is relatively resistant to insect pests and is easy to grow.

West Indian Lemongrass: Another variety of lemongrass that is resistant to insect pests is the West Indian lemongrass. This variety is native to South Asia and is commonly grown in the Caribbean and South America. It has a milder flavour and fragrance than East Indian lemongrass, but is still used in a variety of dishes and as an herbal tea.

Red Lemongrass: This variety of lemongrass is grown for its ornamental value, as well as its culinary and medicinal properties. It has red stems and leaves, which make it a popular choice for landscaping and garden decoration. Red lemongrass is also known to be resistant to insect pests, making it a low-maintenance option for gardeners.

African Lemongrass: Also known as *Cymbopogon afronardus*, this variety of lemongrass is native to Africa and is commonly used in African cuisine. It has a slightly sweet, lemony flavour and is also used in herbal medicine. African lemongrass is known to be relatively resistant to insect pests, making it a good choice for home gardens.

Cochin Lemongrass: This variety of lemongrass is native to Kerala, India, and is also known as Malabar grass. It has a distinct lemony flavour and fragrance and is commonly used in Indian and Southeast Asian cuisine. Cochin lemongrass is known to be resistant to insect pests and can be easily grown in home gardens.

51 Pests of Vetiver

Scientific Name	*Chrysopogon zizanioides*
Family	Poaceae
Origin	India
Chromosome number	2n = 20

Vetiver (*Vetiveria zizanioides*) is a perennial grass native to India and Southeast Asia. It is mainly cultivated in the states of Tamil Nadu, Karnataka, and Kerala in India. India is the major producer of vetiver oil in the world, with an annual production of about 200 tonnes. The essential oil of vetiver contains vetiverol, vetivone, and vetiverene, which are used in the manufacture of perfumes, cosmetics, and medicines. The major insect pests of vetiver include shoot borer (*Conogethes punctiferalis*) and leaf folder (*Marasmia patnalis*).

❑ Stem borer: *Chilo infuscatellus* Snellen, 1890

Common Name	:	Stem boring caterpillar, yellow top borer, sugarcane shoot borer
Scientific Name	:	*Chilo infuscatellus* Snellen, 1890
Family	:	Pyralidae
Order	:	Lepidoptera

Source: https://www.indiamart.com/

As Described in Lemon grass

❑ Termite: *Odontotermes obesus* (Rambur 1842)

Common Name	:	White ants, fungus-growing termites, Indian white termite.
Scientific Name	:	*Odontotermes obesus* (Rambur 1842)
Family	:	Scarabaeidae
Order	:	Blattodea

Source: https://commons.wikimedia.org

As Described in Mango

Resistant Varieties

Sunshine: This variety of vetiver is known for its high oil content and strong pest resistance, making it a popular choice for essential oil production. It is also able to tolerate a wide range of soils and weather conditions.

North Indian: This variety is commonly grown in India and is known for its high yields and resistance to pests and diseases. It is also able to withstand drought and flooding.

Khus Khus: This variety is commonly grown in the Middle East and Asia and is known for its strong fragrance and insect pest resistance. It is often used in perfumery and as a natural insect repellent.

Thai: This variety of vetiver is commonly grown in Thailand and is known for its high oil content and strong resistance to pests and diseases. It is often used for soil stabilization and erosion control.

Monto: This variety is commonly grown in Indonesia and is known for its high yields and strong resistance to pests and diseases. It is also able to withstand drought and flooding.

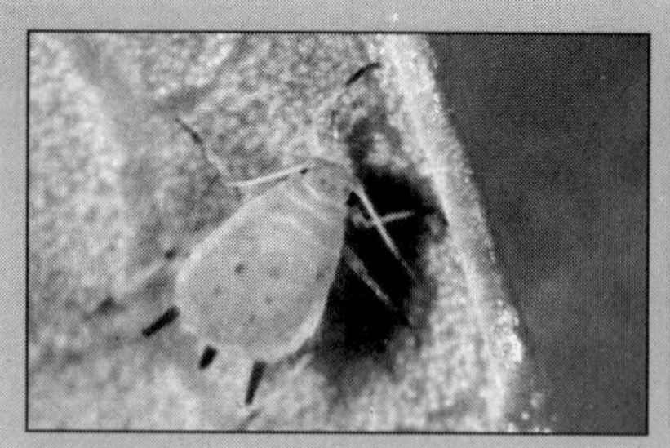

Pests of Palmarosa

Scientific Name	*Cymbopogon martinii*
Family	Poaceae
Origin	India
Chromosome number	2n = 20

Palmarosa (*Cymbopogon martinii*) is a perennial grass native to India and Southeast Asia. It is mainly cultivated in the states of Gujarat, Uttar Pradesh, and Madhya Pradesh in India. India is the major producer of palmarosa oil in the world, with an annual production of about 300 tonnes. The essential oil of palmarosa contains geraniol, geranyl acetate, and linalool, which are used in the manufacture of perfumes, cosmetics, and medicines. The major insect pests of palmarosa include shoot and stem borer (*Conogethes punctiferalis*) and leaf folder (*Marasmia patnalis*).

❑ Aphid: *Aphis gossypii* Glover, 1877

Common Name	:	Cotton aphid, melon aphid, melon and cotton aphid
Scientific Name	:	*Aphis gossypii* Glover, 1877
Family	:	Aphididae
Order	:	Hemiptera

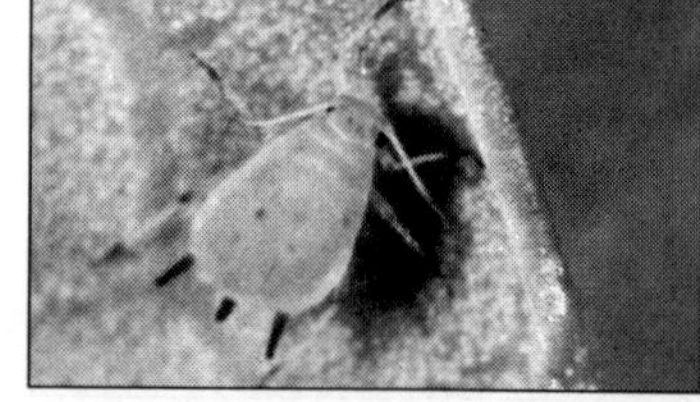

Source: https://entomologytoday.org/

As Described in Chilli

❑ Thrips: *Haplothrips* sp. (Amyot and Serville)

Common Name	:	Thrips
Scientific Name	:	*Haplothrips* sp. (Amyot and Serville)
Family	:	Phlaeothripidae
Order	:	Thysanoptera

Source: https://www.researchgate.net/

Distribution and Host Range

It is distributed all over the world and has approximately 240 species. Haplothrips feed and breed primarily in flowers. The Northern hemisphere species prefer Poaceae and Asteraceae blooms, while some associated with the leaves also.

Nature and Symptoms of Damage

Both the nymphs and adults suck the sap. Yellowish or silvery streaks are seen on the foliage, which may later turn brown.

Life History and identification

Adult female lays the eggs in groups, containing 4 to 8 eggs per group for about 25 to 35 days. Fecundity is about 13 to 30 eggs and the incubation period is for 6 to 11 days. The larval stages come after egg stage, known as nymphs. The larval emerges in spring from wintering. Then the adults arise in May-June and the metamorphosis period will be for a month. Eggs are oval, pale orange in colour with a size of 0.5 to 0.6 mm. Mature larva seen in bright red. Adults have an elongated body and are blackish brown to black colour. Females are slightly bigger than the males with an average size of 1.8 and 1.2 mm respectively.

Management

Use of crop rotations, early under winter ploughings. Install 4 to 5 blue sticky traps per acre. Predators such as ladybirds, ground beetles, bugs, lacewing larvae, staphilinids and robber flies are proficient of causing a drop in thrip count. Spray methyl demeton 25 EC @ 2 ml (or) phosalone @ 2 ml/lit or neem oil @ 3%.

❑ White grub: *Holotrichia consanguinea* Blanchard, 1850

Common Name	:	Sugarcane beetle
Scientific Name	:	*Holotrichia consanguinea* Blanchard, 1850
Family	:	Scarabaeidae
Order	:	Coleoptera

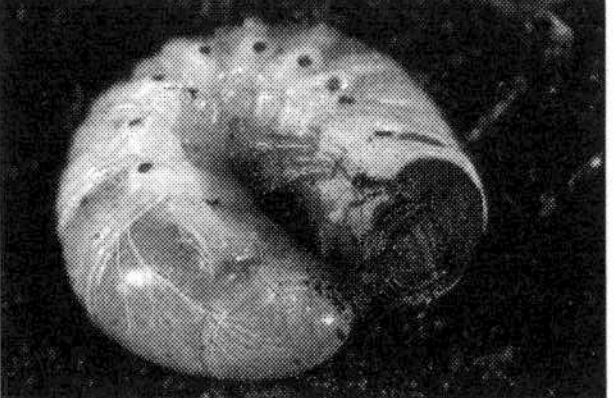

Source: *https://www.agriglobalmarket*

Distribution and Host Range

It is a devasting pest widely distributed all over India. Host crops ranges from sugarcane, other grass (Poaceae) members etc.

Nature and Symptoms of Damage

Grub stage is the destructive phase and affected plants shows leaves yellowing and wilting. Crown portion dries out and affected bushes come off easily when pulled.

Life History and Identification

The adult beetles return to the earth where they conceal and lay their eggs. The female lays 20-80 clusters of eggs. Eggs are white and spherical in shape. It takes 9 to 11 days to pass the egg phase. Larval stages are the grubs. Young grubs are seen translucent, whitish yellow in colour and fleshy 'C' shape. Mature larva pupates in the soil, where it stays till the next year as a pupa. During the start of the monsoon season, the adult beetles emerge. Adults are dark brown coloured beetles.

Management

During application of the compost to the crop, screen the grubs. Adult beetles are manually removed and destroyed during the monsoon. The pest invasion can be decreased highly by deep ploughing in the summer. Use of *Beauveria bassiana* a pathogenic fungus that infects a wide range of insect species, can be used. Use of carbaryl 10% @ 30 g per plant to treat the soil around the trunk. Spray malathion 50 EC or methyl parathion 50 EC at 2 ml per litre of water.

❑ Termite: *Odontotermes obesus* (Rambur 1842)

Common Name	:	White ants, fungus-growing termites, Indian white termite.
Scientific Name	:	*Odontotermes obesus* (Rambur 1842)
Family	:	Scarabaeidae
Order	:	Blattodea

Source: *https://commons.wikimedia.org/*

As Described in Mango

Resistant Varieties
Palmarosa V1: This variety of Palmarosa is highly resistant to insect pests, including the shoot fly and leaf spot.
Palmarosa V2: This variety of Palmarosa is also resistant to several insect pests, including the shoot fly and the whitefly.
Palmarosa V3: This variety of Palmarosa is resistant to the leaf spot disease, which is caused by the fungus *Drechslera* sp.
Palmarosa V4: This variety of Palmarosa is resistant to the leaf folder and the whitefly.
Palmarosa V5: This variety of Palmarosa is resistant to the red spider mite and the whitefly.
Palmarosa V6: This variety of Palmarosa is resistant to the shoot borer and the leaf folder.

Pests of Rosemary

Scientific Name	*Rosmarinus officinalis*
Family	Labiatae
Origin	Mediterranean region
Chromosome number	2n = 20, 24

Rosemary (*Rosmarinus officinalis*) is a woody perennial herb native to the Mediterranean region. It is mainly cultivated in the states of Tamil Nadu, Karnataka, and Maharashtra in India. India is a minor producer of rosemary oil in the world. The essential oil of rosemary contains camphor, cineole, and borneol, which are used in the manufacture of perfumes, cosmetics, and medicines. The major insect pests of rosemary include whitefly (*Bemisia tabaci*), spider mite (*Tetranychus urticae*), and aphids (*Aphis* spp.).

Common Name	Scientific Name	Family	Order	Remarks
Aphids	*Aphis gossypii* Glover, 1877	Aphididae	Hemiptera	As described in Palmarosa
Spider mites	*Tetranychus urticae* C. L. Koch, 1836	Tetranychidae	Trombidiformes	As described in Carnation
Mealybugs	*Dysmicoccus brevipes* Cockerell, 1893	Pseudococcidae	Hemiptera	As described in Lemongrass
White flies	*Bemisia tabaci* (Gennadius, 1889)	Aleyrodidae	Hemiptera	As Described in Potato

Resistant Varieties

Arp: This variety of rosemary is known for its resistance to cold weather and insect pests, making it a popular choice for gardeners in colder regions.

Salem: Salem is a rosemary variety that is resistant to drought and insect pests. It has dark green foliage and a strong, spicy aroma.

Tuscan Blue: Tuscan Blue is a large rosemary variety that is resistant to insect pests and has a strong, pine-like flavour. It is commonly used in Mediterranean cuisine and is popular for its ornamental value.

Blue Boy: Blue Boy is a compact rosemary variety that is resistant to insect pests and is suitable for growing in containers or small spaces. It has a strong, aromatic flavour and is commonly used in cooking.

Miss Jessup's Upright: This variety of rosemary has an upright growth habit and is resistant to insect pests and disease. It has a strong, herbal flavour and is commonly used in Mediterranean cuisine.

Spice Islands: Spice Islands is a rosemary variety that is resistant to insect pests and has a strong, pine-like flavour. It is commonly used in Italian and Mediterranean cuisine.

54 Pests of Patchouli

Scientific Name	*Pogostemon cablin*
Family	Lamiaceae
Origin	Tropical Asia
Chromosome number	2n = 32, 34, 64

Patchouli (*Pogostemon cablin*) is a perennial herbaceous plant belonging to the Lamiaceae family. It grows up to a height of 1 meter and has hairy stems with large leaves. Patchouli is cultivated mainly in the states of Tamil Nadu, Karnataka, Maharashtra, and Kerala in India. The total area under cultivation is about 15,000 hectares with an annual production of around 2,500 metric tonnes. Patchouli oil is the most valuable product obtained from the leaves of the plant. The oil contains a number of chemical constituents such as patchoulol, norpatchoulenol, bulnesene, and caryophyllene. The major pests of patchouli include stem borers (*Cleora anastomosis*), leaf rollers (*Hedylepta indicata*), and shoot and capsule borers (*Conogethes punctiferalis*). These pests cause significant yield losses by damaging the stems, leaves, and capsules of the plant.

❑ Root knot nematode: *Meloidogyne incognita* (Kofoid & White, 1919)

Common Name	:	Root knot nematode (RKN)
Scientific Name	:	*Meloidogyne incognita* (Kofoid & White, 1919)
Family	:	Heteroderidae
Order	:	Tylenchida

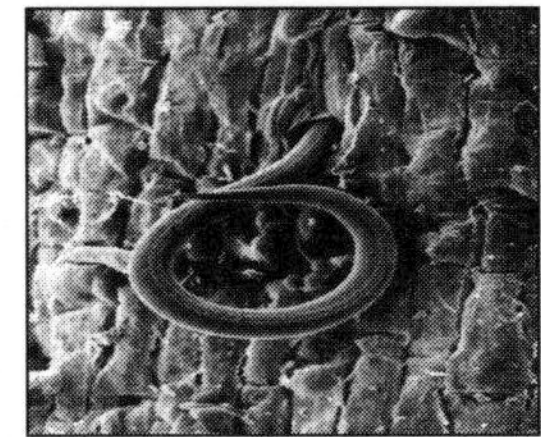

Source: *https://en.wikipedia.org/*

As Described in Tomato

Resistant Varieties

Pogostemon cablin: This is the most common variety of patchouli and is widely cultivated in India, China, and Southeast Asia. It has a strong, earthy aroma and is commonly used in perfumes and soaps.

Pogostemon heyneanus: This variety is native to India and is also cultivated in other tropical regions such as Brazil and Indonesia. It has a slightly milder aroma than Pogostemon cablin and is used primarily in traditional medicine.

Pogostemon patchouli: This variety is native to the Philippines and has a strong, woody aroma. It is also used in perfumes and aromatherapy.

Pogostemon hortensis: This variety is grown primarily in Indonesia and has a more floral aroma than other patchouli varieties. It is used in perfumes and in traditional medicine.

Pogostemon plectranthoides: This variety is native to India and has a citrusy, minty aroma. It is used primarily in traditional medicine.

55 Pests of Lavender

Scientific Name	*Lavandula angustifolia*
Family	Lamiaceae
Origin	Mediterranean region
Chromosome number	2n= 18

Lavender (*Lavandula angustifolia*) is a perennial flowering plant belonging to the Lamiaceae family. It has narrow, gray-green leaves and purple flowers arranged in spikes. It is mainly grown in the states of Jammu & Kashmir, Himachal Pradesh, and Uttarakhand in India. The total area under cultivation is around 1,000 hectares with an annual production of around 100 metric tonnes. The essential oil extracted from the flowers of lavender contains a number of chemical compounds such as linalool, linalyl acetate, and lavandulyl acetate. These compounds are responsible for the therapeutic properties of the plant, including its relaxing and soothing effects. The major pests of lavender include leafhoppers (*Empoasca* spp.), aphids (*Aphis* spp.), and spider mites (*Tetranychus* spp.). These pests can cause significant damage to the plant by feeding on the leaves and stems, and by transmitting viral diseases.

Common Name	Scientific Name	Family	Order	Remarks
White flies	*Bemisia tabaci* (Gennadius, 1889)	Aleyrodidae	Hemiptera	As Described in Potato
Aphids	*Aphis gossypii* Glover, 1877	Aphididae	Hemiptera	As described in Palmarosa
Spittle bug	*Clovia bipunctata* Kirby, 1891	Cercopidae	Hemiptera	As described in Lemongrass

Resistant Varieties

***Lavandula angustifolia* 'Hidcote'** – This compact, hardy lavender variety is known for its resistance to pests and diseases. It produces fragrant purple flowers and is commonly used in landscaping and as a culinary herb.

Lavandula × intermedia 'Grosso' – This hybrid lavender variety is known for its high oil content and strong insect-repellent properties. It has tall, sturdy stems and produces long, dense spikes of lavender-blue flowers.

Lavandula stoechas 'Pedunculata' – This Mediterranean species of lavender is known for its attractive flowers and strong fragrance. It is also resistant to pests and diseases, making it a popular choice for gardeners.

***Lavandula dentata* 'Royal Crown'** – This Spanish lavender variety has fragrant, grey-green foliage and produces spikes of deep purple flowers. It is known for its insect-repellent properties and is often used in landscaping and as a culinary herb.

Lavandula pinnata – This native South African species of lavender is known for its delicate, finely divided foliage and fragrant flowers. It is resistant to pests and diseases and is often used in rock gardens and as a ground cover.

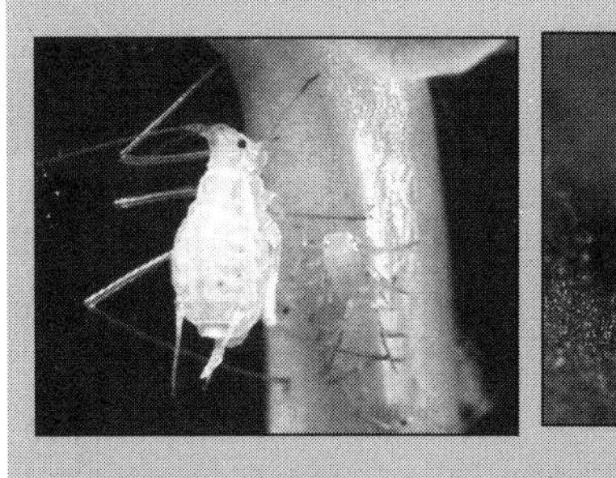

Pests of Geranium

Scientific Name	*Pelargonium graveolens*
Family	*Geraniaceae*
Origin	South Africa
Chromosome number	2n=28

Geranium (*Pelargonium graveolens*) is a perennial flowering plant belonging to the Geraniaceae family. It has small, velvety leaves and pink, red, or white flowers. It is mainly grown in the states of Tamil Nadu, Karnataka, Maharashtra, and Gujarat in India. The total area under cultivation is around 8,000 hectares with an annual production of around 2,000 metric tonnes. The essential oil extracted from the leaves and stems of geranium contains a number of chemical compounds such as citronellol, geraniol, and linalool. These compounds are responsible for the therapeutic properties of the plant, including its ability to reduce stress and anxiety. The major pests of geranium include spider mites (*Tetranychus* spp.), aphids (*Aphis* spp.), and thrips (*Thrips tabaci*). These pests can cause significant damage to the plant by feeding on the leaves and stems and by transmitting viral diseases.

Aphid: *Acyrthosiphon malvae* (Mosley, 1841)

Common Name	:	Geranium aphid, pelargonium aphid
Scientific Name	:	*Acyrthosiphon malvae* (Mosley, 1841)
Family	:	Aphididae
Order	:	Hemiptera

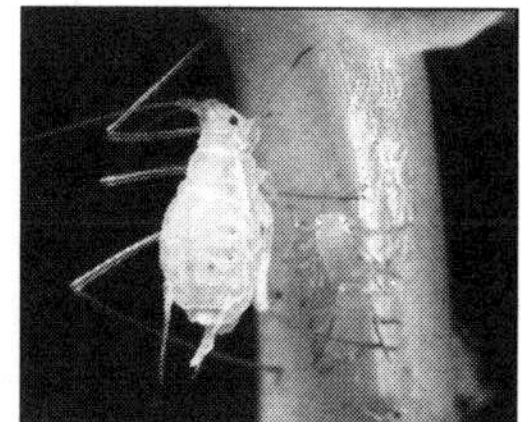

Source: *https//en.wikipedia.org*

Distribution and Host Range

This aphid is widespread throughout the entire world, with the exception of the coldest terrestrial environments. It has been observed on many species, at least of about 25 different plant families, including the herbaceous Rosaceae (Fragaria, Acaena, Alchemilla, Agrimonia, Poterium, and Potentilla), the Geraniaceae (Geranium, Erodium and Pelargonium), Malva and Alcea.

Nature and Symptoms of Damage

Adults and nymphs both feed by sucking plant sap from the underside of leaves or the growing tips of shoots. It may cause leaf chlorosis and premature death. There is a lot of leaf curling and deformation, which makes photosynthesis less effective. Aphids emit honeydew, which encourages the formation of sooty moulds and reduces crop production and quality. It has been concerned in virus transmission also.

Life History and Identification

Geranium aphids are the broad, spindle-shaped and short-haired aphids. They have long antennae, siphunculi, legs and the cauda. These aphids are usually seen in green but occasionally occur in pink, brown or yellow. Nymphs are similar to the adults, but lesser in size.

Management

As mentioned in Palmarosa.

Resistant Varieties

Lemon-Scented Geranium (*Pelargonium crispum*): This variety is known for its lemon-scented leaves and is often used in cooking and as a natural insect repellent. It is resistant to many insect pests, including spider mites and whiteflies.

Rose-Scented Geranium (*Pelargonium graveolens*): This variety is known for its sweet rose fragrance and is often used to make essential oils. It is also resistant to many insect pests, including spider mites and whiteflies.

Mint-Scented Geranium (*Pelargonium tomentosum*): This variety has a strong mint fragrance and is often used in cooking and to make herbal teas. It is resistant to many insect pests, including spider mites and whiteflies.

Citronella-Scented Geranium (*Pelargonium citrosum*): This variety is known for its citronella-like fragrance, which is said to repel mosquitoes. It is also resistant to many insect pests, including spider mites and whiteflies.

Nutmeg-Scented Geranium (Pelargonium × fragrans 'Nutmeg'): This variety has a spicy nutmeg fragrance and is often used in cooking and to make potpourri. It is resistant to many insect pests, including spider mites and whiteflies.

PART F

PESTS OF FLOWER CROPS

D. Lava Kumar
(Ph.D. Scholar)
Division of Floriculture and Landscaping
ICAR-Indian Agricultural Research Institute
Pusa, New Delhi

57 Pests of Rose

Scientific Name	*Rosa* spp.
Family	Rosaceae
Origin	Cooler regions of Norther Hemisphere
Chromosome Number	2n = 14

Rose (*Rosa* spp.) is a perennial flowering plant belonging to the family Rosaceae. It is one of the most widely cultivated ornamental plants and is native to various regions around the world. Roses are characterized by their prickly stems and fragrant flowers, which come in a range of colors and sizes. Roses are cultivated in many parts of the world, including Europe, Asia, and North America. The top producers of roses are Colombia, Ecuador, and Kenya. The global production of roses is estimated to be around 20 million tons per year. Rose production can be challenging due to the susceptibility of the plant to pests and diseases, which can result in significant yield losses if not managed properly. Some of the major pests that can affect roses include:

❑ Rose aphid: *Macrosiphum rosaeformis* (Das)

Common Name	:	Rose aphid
Scientific Name	:	*Macrosiphum rosaeformis* (Das)/ *M. rosae* (Linnaeus, 1758)
Family	:	Aphididae
Order	:	Hemiptera

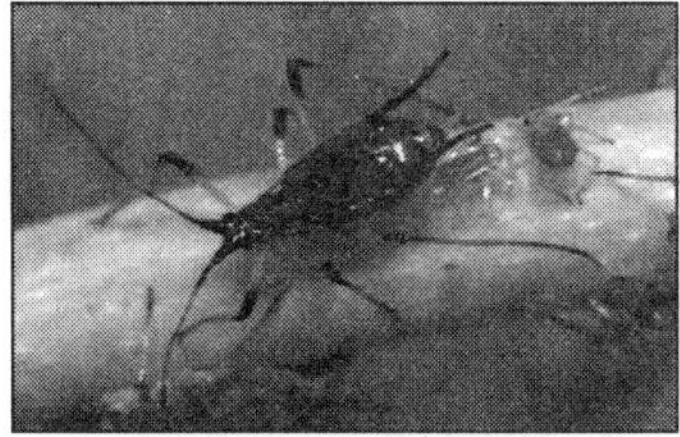

Source:*https://www.ozanimals.com/*

Distribution and Host Range

M. rosaeformis was originated and first described in Europe. But, nowadays, it is found distributed on cultivated roses practically everywhere, all over the world. There are about 208 genera and 794 species of aphids described from India, of which 385 are endemic. The Northern hemisphere experiences its highest population densities in June and July, right before the bushes bloom and then the populations start to drop.

Nature and Symptoms of Damage

Aphids are seen in clusters, both in **nymphal** and **adult** stages on the tender parts of shoots, flowers, buds and damages the aesthetic nature of rose plants by sucking the plant sap. This sap sucking by aphids, distorts the plant growth by withering of shoots and also results in flowers fadeout and premature bud fall. Aphids attracts the ants and wasps with its the honey dew excretions and also promotes the **sooty mould** disease.

Life History and Description

Aphids have a very short lifespan, on an average for a month. However, some aphids during that time were able to produce 12 nymphs every day. Aphids have simple metamorphosis with diapause egg, nymphs and adult (winged or wingless) or parthenocarpic multiplication. *i.e.*, these can reproduce either by sexually or asexually, namely by two different types of reproductive life cycles *i.e.*, **Holocyclic** and **Anholocyclic**. For many generations, the aphids will replicate asexually before developing winged forms that will reproduce sexually and lay eggs to overwinter in the former case with involvement of both male and females. Whereas, in the next case there is no involvement of males, instead of which wingless female reproduce the clones throughout the summer. Aphids have elongated, soft, pear shaped body with black cornicles and greenish or pink in colour. These are about the size of 1.7 to 3.6 mm long and found in clusters on tender parts of the plant. Winged individuals size ranges between 2.2 to 3.4 mm, with green to pinkish brown coloured body and distinctive lateral black markings.

Management

Use of sprinkler type of irrigation system to limit the infestation. To reduce the number of aphids on indoor plants, rinse them with water or wipe them down with a cloth. Install yellow sticky traps. Release aphid lions- *Chrysoperla carnea* (green lacewing larvae- first instar grubs) @ 10,000 per hectare. Ladybugs (*Coccinella septempunctata)* both at nymphal and adult stage are also the common predators to the aphids and other predators includes parasitic wasps, hoverfly larvae, aphid midge larvae and arachnids like spiders. Spray dimethoate 30 EC or methyl demeton 25 EC @ 2 ml/lit or neem oil @ 0.5%

❑ Thrips: *Rhipiphorothrips cruentatus* Hood, 1919

Common Name	:	Rose thrips, thunderflies, corn lice, Thunderbugs
Scientific Name	:	*Rhipiphorothrips cruentatus* Hood, 1919
Family	:	Thripidae
Order	:	Thysanoptera

Source: *https://keys.lucidcentral.org/*

Distribution and Host Range

Thrips are cosmopolitan in nature and are commonly seen in India, Sri Lanka, Pakistan, Bangladesh, Afghanistan, as well as Myanmar and Oman. Thrips are polyphagous and feed on various economically important crops like rose, grapes, pomegranate, other vegetable and ornamentals. Approximately 5800 species of thrips from 9 different families have been described.

Nature and Symptoms of Damage

Thrips attack results in severe damage in quantity and quality of the roses. These cause intense threat for the crops cultivated both in open fields and protected farms. Thrips found in bulk on lower side of green lush, lacerate the tissues and suck the oozed-out sap. Infested leaves show white or silvery streaks. On severe infection leaves get withered, distorted and eventually fall down. Economic parts like flowers, do not open and also cause premature bud fall.

Life History and Description

Thrips have very short life cycle which completes in about 12 to 20 days. Adult up to 15 days; egg is 2 to 7 days; nymph is 8 to 10 days; pupa 2 to 4 days. Multiple generations can be seen per year. Adult female *R. cruentatus* can lay about 50 to 100 eggs, which are small, oval to bean shaped and are inserted into the tender tissue of leaf in underside with a serrated sword like ovipositor. Eggs hatch out and produce nymphs and it consists of four instar larvae and these are similar to adults but are wingless. Next followed by pupal stages. It pupates in soil or on leaves itself and ultimately produces the adults.

Management

Regular cleaning of the field or polyhouse is required to remove weeds, pruned plant parts and other dropped leaves which serves as the infestation source. To eradicate the pest completely, it is preferable to burn the infected plant debris. Deep ploughing in summer or soil raking destroys the pupal stages and minimizes the incidence. Use of resistant varieties like gladiator, folklore, landora, skyline, confetti, tinike, grand gala and first red. Install 4 to 5 blue sticky traps per acre. Use of predatory mites like *Amblyseius swirskii,* effective in controlling the thrips. Spray methyl demeton 25 EC @ 2 ml (or) phosalone @ 2 ml/lit or neem oil @ 3%.

❑ Rose scales: *Aulacaspis rosae* (Bouché, 1833)

Common Name	:	Rose scales, Soft scales
Scientific Name	:	*Aulacaspis rosae* (Bouché, 1833)
Family	:	Coccoidea
Order	:	Hemiptera

Source: *https://ru.pinterest.com/*

Distribution and Host Range

Scales are seen all around the world. There are about 8000 thousand different types of scale species and the majority of them favor particular plant varieties. Rose scales feed on *Rosa* spp. and also on raspberries, blackberries, dewberries, hydrangeas and pear trees.

Nature and Symptoms of Damage

Rose scales with its piercing and sucking type of mouthparts, sucks up the plant sap. Canes may become weak or even die by severe infestations. Plants attacked by scales may exhibit yellowed foliage, fallen leaves, and diminished flowering and finally dies completely. The extra fluid they consume is released as honeydew, which is conducive to the growth of sooty mould.

Life History and Description

The egg, nymphal, and adult stages make up the life cycle of the rose scale. Each adult lays about

50 to 150 eggs and are deposited beneath under covered and this rose scale overwinters. The unprotected, mobile first instar nymphs known as orange crawlers choose a location to settle after the springtime when the temperatures rise. Then a waxy scale covering starts to be secreted by the older nymphs. Adult females size ranges about 3 mm which are stationary. Adult males, resemble small, winged flies, can move around in pursuit of females. In adult females, although the body is not clearly divided into segments, it is indicated by the presence of marginal bristles. In certain families, females lack legs altogether. When legs do exist, they can range from single-segment stubs to five-segment limbs.

In the summer, rose scale is most active. If scale populations are healthy, a second generation could emerge in August. Overall life cycle of a rose scale can be completed in a few weeks or months and overlapping generations can be seen in a year if the favourable conditions are available. Rose scales can be identified by the presence of white to light grey coloured bumps on the rose stems. These bumps are about one-fourth inch and the waxy shell is made on armoured scale which provide the insect with protection from the predators and any insecticidal spray. Nymphs are small orange coloured and are seen under the armour. They have a habit to live in colonies, which seen as the multiple scales on rose stems resembles a disease on rose shrubs.

Management

Pruning and destroying of all canes that are severely infested. Grow your roses in direct sunlight as in humid and shaded areas, scale infestations will be more severe. Rose canes that are lightly infested by scales gently scraped off with cotton or brush soaked in diesel or kerosene. Although this is unlikely to totally eradicate the infestation. Release of predatory insects like lady beetles and the parasitic wasps that attack scale insects by planting the nectar-producing ornamentals next to the plants that are susceptible to scale insects. Apply the carbofuran 3 G granules @ 5 g per plant or spray of fish oil rosin soap @ 25 g per litre.

❑ Red spider mite: *Tetranychus urticae* C.L. Koch, 1836

Common Name	:	Carmine spider mite, red spider mite, cotton spider mite and carnation mite.
Scientific Name	:	*Tetranychus urticae* C.L. Koch, 1836
Family	:	Tetranychidae
Order	:	Trombidiformes

Source: *https://www.cabidigitallibrary.org/doi/10.1079/cabicompendium.30965*

As Described in Tomato

❑ Leaf cutter bee: *Megachile anthracina* Smith, 1853

Common Name	:	Leaf cutter bee
Scientific Name	:	*Megachile anthracina* Smith, 1853
Family	:	Megachilidae
Order	:	Hymenoptera

Source: *https://www.colorado.edu*

Distribution and Host Range

Leaf cutter bees are commonly seen all over the world but, most widely distributed in the Southern Asian countries. Adults attack rose, azaleas, bougainvillea, red gram, alfalfa, clover, buckwheat, lamb's quarters, lilac, and plantain lilies.

Nature and Symptoms of Damage

Leaf cutter bees create distinctive damage to the rose foliage. The leaf margins are cut into precise circles or ovals of 0.25-to-0.5-inch size. Cut-up pieces of leaves are used to build the nest cells. These bees will attack only few leaves of a bush and does not affect any quality of the flowers and growth of the plant. But it damages the aesthetic look of the ornamentals.

Life History and Description

Leafcutter bees are only seen active for about 4-6 weeks, especially in the summer, 15 days to hatch out from eggs and 35 days to reach pupal stage. Rest of their lives were inside their nesting chambers, where they eat, grow, spin cocoons, overwinter as mature larvae, and eventually turn into adults when summer temperatures consistently reach 21°C. Leafcutter bees are cavity-nesters. The female bee constructs a protective leafy wall, which it fills with pollen and the nectar. Then it covers the chamber with another layer of protective leaf wall after laying a single egg. Females typically lay eggs that hatch into females at the back of the nest and males in the front. This behaviour adds an extra layer of defence to the female eggs. Under ideal conditions, a female bee may complete 2 to 4 tunnels in its lifespan, laying an average of 30 eggs. The hatched-out larva will consume the pollen loaf for about 20 days and start spinning cocoon around it. This dormant stage will be overwintered. Metamorphosis is seen and the pupa changes to adult bee in late spring or early winter. During metamorphosis, larva completely changes its shape, develops head, thorax legs and abdomen and eyes changes black in females and green in males. Adults are hairy, medium-sized dark coloured insects with a red-brown tinge base of the abdomen.

Management

If nesting places are removed, the population of leafcutter bees in a region can be decreased. Seal the exposed pith as the canes are clipped to stop leafcutter bees from boring into the rose canes. Since these cutter bees do not feed but just cut the leaves, insecticides are generally ineffective on them. To prevent leaf damage, cover susceptible plants with cheesecloth or loose netting. Sawdust application on tunnel or thick-stemmed plants with hollowed apertures. Many natural enemies are seen to attack the nests of leaf cutter bees which includes wasps of chrysididae and mutillidae, beetles of rhiphoridae, cleridae and meloidae family members. *Crematogaster* spp. of ants also known to attack the nests.

❑ Slug caterpillar: *Parasa lepida* (Cramer, 1799)

Common Name	:	Nettle caterpillar, blue-striped nettle grub, castor slug caterpillar
Scientific Name	:	*Parasa lepida* (Cramer, 1799)
Family	:	Limacodidae
Order	:	Lepidoptera

Source: https://metastudio.org/

Distribution and Host Range

It is a minor pest native to Indo-Malayan region, including India, Indonesia, Bangladesh, Vietnam, Burma, Sri Lanka, Malaysia and Thailand, China, Nepal, Hongkong, Japan, Laos, Kampuchea, and Pakistan. Coconut, castor, oil palm, cacao, coffee, mulberry, pineapple, mango, pomegranate, and tea are all targets to this slug caterpillar. It is seen mostly to attack at vegetative and flowering stage and parts affected are leaves and fruits.

Nature and Symptoms of Damage

Larva stages are the infective stage of the insect to the plants. They voraciously feed on leaves, leaving only the leaf midrib and the veins, resulting in severe defoliation. This ultimately affects the growth and yield of the crop.

Life History and Description

Parasa lepida life history consists of egg, larva, pupa and adult stages. The duration of the egg stage was six days, the larval stage was forty days and the pupal stage was twenty-two days. This may fluctuate based on climate changes also. The infective stage is the larva and this stage lasts for about more than a month which is a great disadvantage to the crop growers.

The female adult lay the eggs which are flat and they overlap each other. These eggs are covered by a thin transparent layer of cement type material. In a week, the hatched-out larvae are seen in pale green, white or brilliant yellowish green coloured on the dorsal side. There are 3 green stripes running through the body of the caterpillar. A sub-dorsal and sub-lateral series of short spinous tubercles with red-tipped spines on the anterior and posterior tubercles. A series of red tipped short spined tubercles are seen along the sub lateral and sub dorsal sides of the posterior and anterior tubercles. This larva feed voraciously on leaves and enter pupal stages which are purple brown in color. Then the adult comes out of the pupa after 3 weeks. The male has a greenish head with red brown color on the sides. The thorax is in green shade with a brown band on the vertex with brown abdomen. The forewings are pale green in color, which is similar to that of a pea plant. The costa has a red-brown basal area. The outer area is reddish brown and it is widest at the inner boundary. Hindwing is yellowish at the base and reddish brown near the border. Leg joints have whitish tips. The female has reddish-brown line on the thorax which is significantly larger compared to the male and the entire hindwing is nearly reddish brown in color.

Management

Collect and destroy the infested plant leaves along with the caterpillars. Installation of pheromone traps @ 15/ha to attract adult males. *Chrysis shanghaiensis*, a cuckoo wasp, is a recognized as a parasite on these caterpillars. Spray malathion 50% EC @ 1 ml per lire.

☐ Bud Borer: *Helicoverpa armigera* (Hübner, [1808])

Common Name	:	Cotton bollworm, corn earworm, old World bollworm, scarce bordered straw
Scientific Name	:	*Helicoverpa armigera* (Hübner, [1808])
Family	:	Noctuidae
Order	:	Lepidoptera

Source: *https://www.cabidigitallibrary.org/*

As Described in Tomato

Flower Chaffer beetle: *Gametis versicolor* (Fabricius, 1775)

Common Name	:	Flower chafer beetle, Flower beetle, Rose chafer
Scientific Name	:	*Gametis versicolor* (Fabricius, 1775)
Family	:	Scarabaeidae
Order	:	Coleoptera

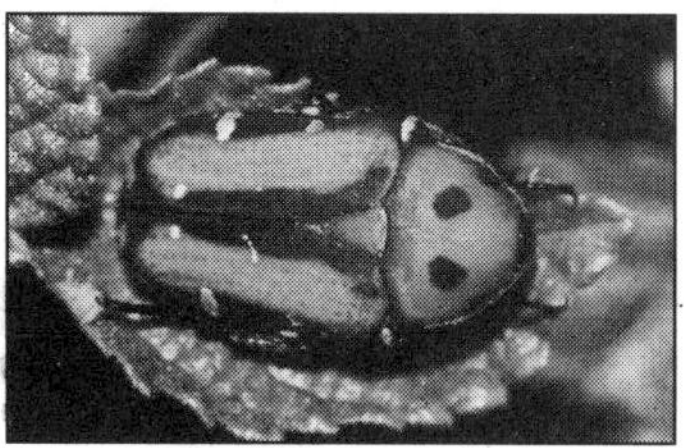

Source: *https://www.flickr.com/*

Distribution and Host Range

Flower chafer beetle is found in a number of locations around the world, including Samoa, India, China, Sri Lanka, Chagos, Madagascar, and South Africa. In India, the Indore (Madhya Pradesh) region was where the beetle was first discovered. But now it has become familiar to Andhra, Telangana, Tamil Nadu, Kerala and Punjab etc. This chafer beetle is found to cause damage in numerous crops along with rose, which includes honeysuckle, Viburnum, groundnut, okra, brinjal, cotton, pigeon pea, mungbean, sesamum, sorghum, maize and *Parthenium* etc.

Nature and Symptoms of Damage

These beetles have biting and chewing type of mouth parts that mainly attacks the buds and flowers, which results in great loss to the growers. They feed on the colourful petals and buds. This results in irregular feeding marks that can lessen the beauty of the flowering plants in gardens. Apart from this, they may also damage the leaves and shoots sometimes.

Life History and Description

The life cycle of chafers includes egg, grub stage, pupa and the adults. They deposit the eggs during early summer in the soil. Then the hatch out larvae feed on decaying plant material and rotting wood and grows about a size of 30 mm for two-three years. These grubs are distinguished from other by the presence of reddish head and legs and by few slanting rows of reddish hairs on body.

The adults have a dimension of 7-15 mm in length and 5-7 mm in width. Both sexes are similar. The body is tiny, oval, typically a little flattened, vividly coloured, mainly red, and marked with black. The smooth upper surface of body has a shiny sheen and eye-catching colour patterns. Elytra and the prothorax are brick red. On the prothorax, there are two black patches, and the lateral borders have a white border. Different white spot patterns can be seen on the elytra. All of the femora are fringed with yellow hairs and the front tibiae are tridentate.

Management

Screen the grubs during composting to the plants. Hand picking of the beetles. Deep ploughing in summer can reduce the pest infestation. Currently, no biological treatments are known to be exist. Apply carbaryl 10% dust at 30 g per plant to the soil around the trunk. Spray malathion 50 EC or methyl parathion 50 EC @2 ml per litre of water.

❑ Chafer beetle: *Anomala binotata* (Gyllenhaal, 1817)

Common Name	:	Shining leaf chafer
Scientific Name	:	*Anomala binotata* (Gyllenhaal, 1817)
Family	:	Scarabaeidae
Order	:	Coleoptera

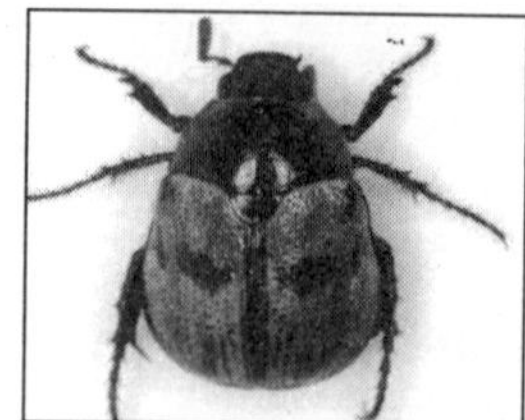

Source: *https://www.inaturalist.org/*

Distribution and Host Range

Leaf chafers majorly found in North America, especially East Rocky Mountains. *Anomala* genus consists of about 1200 different species. Now seen in Colombia, China, Japan, Korea, Philippines, Taiwan, India and Nepal. Found feeding on roots of grasses, maize, wheat and sorghum. Also act as foliage feeders at adult stage in rose, blueberries, cassava, coffee, eucalyptus, grapes, sugarcane, sweet potato and tobacco etc. Soft petals were also chopped sometimes in roses.

Nature and Symptoms of Damage

These species are regarded economically significant pests due to the harm caused primarily by the larval stage, which destroys the roots of cultivated plants while adults can feed on foliage and flowers.

Life History and Description

Adult female lay the eggs in the early spring. Eggs hatch out into the larva in a week. The larva (grub) feeds on the decaying matter and roots for about 80 to 85 days and enter the pupal stage. This stage lasts for about 16 days on average. Adults undergo transformation in the fall as they remain in their pupal cells until the following spring, thus completes a one life cycle.

Management

During application of compost to the plants screen the grubs. Chafer beetles are manually removed and destroyed during the day. The pest invasion can be decreased by deep ploughing in the summer. *Beauveria bassiana* is a pathogenic fungus that infects a wide range of insect species, can be used. Spray petroleum ether @ 0.1 to 0.5% extracted from *Acorus calamus* dried rhizomes. Use of carbaryl 10% @ 30 g per plant to treat the soil around the trunk. Spray malathion 50 EC or methyl parathion 50 EC at 2 ml per litre of water.

❑ Termite: *Odontotermes obesus* (Rambur, 1842)

Common Name	:	White ants, fungus-growing termites, Indian white termite.
Scientific Name	:	*Odontotermes obesus* (Rambur 1842)
Family	:	Scarabaeidae
Order	:	Blattodea

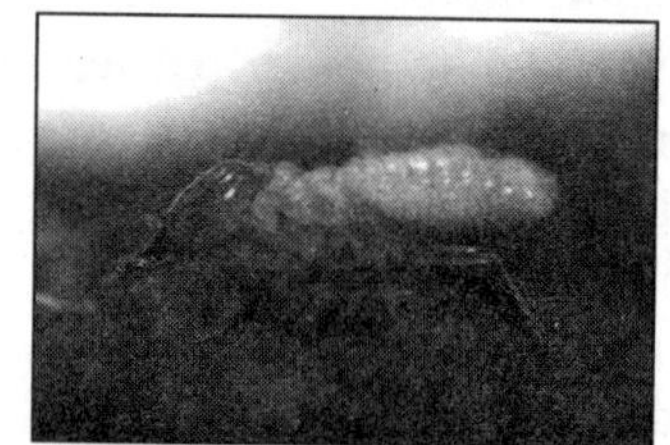

Source: *https://commons.wikimedia.org/*

As Described in Mango

❑ Blackfly: *Aleurocanthus spiniferus* (Quaintance, 1903)

Common Name	:	Blackfly
Scientific Name	:	*Aleurocanthus spiniferus* (Quaintance, 1903)
Family	:	Aleyrodidae

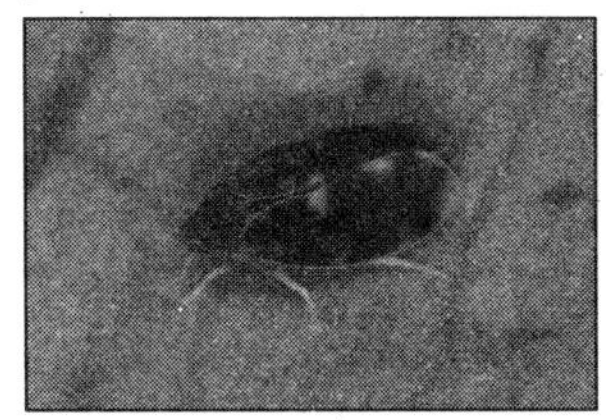

Source: *https://www.naturamediterraneo.com/*

Distribution and Host Range

It is one of the quarantined pests by many countries. Africa, Australia, Caribbean, and the Pacific Islands have all experienced the spread of the orange spiny whitefly. Gowdey (1922) noted orange spiny whiteflies as a sporadic citrus pest in Jamaica in the Caribbean Islands. In Guam, it was initially noted for the Pacific Islands in 1951, where it was shown on guava, grape, peach, rose, and grapefruit in addition to citrus. On rose foliage, the orange spiny whitefly was first discovered in Honolulu, Hawaii, in 1974. It was found on navel orange, lime, tangerine, and pear in later surveys, but infestation levels were deemed low. The first reports of this pest in Africa were made in 1988 in South Africa and 1987 in Swaziland. More recently, reports of orange spiny whiteflies came from Montenegro, Croatia, and Italy. These are also hosted by hibiscus, bay leaf, curry leaf, fig, grapes and other rosaceae fruit crops.

Nature and Symptoms of Damage

Both the adults and nymphs both suck the sap from the leaves. Wrinkling of leaves. On the underside of the leaves, black oval puparia can be seen. Due to sap loss and the growth of sooty mould, general weakness of infected plants is seen. Usually, sooty mould is seen on the leaves, hips, and branches of infected shrubs. The shifting of nursery stock and other materials that has been infected with orange spiny whitefly allows it to spread from one location to another. Additional potential threats to various attractive ornamentals can be caused by the blackflies.

Life History and Description

Six developmental phases are present in whiteflies: egg, crawler, two sessile nymphal instars, pupa and adult. Egg stage (11 to 22 days), 1st instar, (7 to 11 days), 2nd instar, (5 to 7 days), 3rd instar, (7 to 130 days), pupal stage (7 to 34 days). Pupal stage features are mostly used to identify the Aleyrodidae family members. The current environment has great influence on number of generations per year. Ideal circumstances for growth and development are provided by a moderate temperature and high relative humidity.

The egg is small (0.2 × 0.1 mm), yellowish, stalked, curled and polygonally marked. The stalk is very short and holds egg in an upright position of the leaf. The larva is brown to black, oval to elliptical in shape, and has a thin fringe of wax surrounding its body. The second instar of the orange spiny whitefly is about 0.4 × 0.3 mm and has a clearly crenulated marginal edge as it matures to the sessile nymphal stage. The marginal wax tubes between the second instar's incisions are additionally short and sharp. Additionally, the abdominal segments are more defined than the thoracic segments in the second and third instar stages. The fourth instar or oval-shaped pupa, is jet black, convex, 1.23 mm long and 1.88 mm wide. It has strong, dark dorsal spines. Due to their similar slate blue hues, the adult orange spiny whitefly and citrus blackfly cannot be distinguished from one another.

Management

Pruning and destroying of all canes that are severely infested. Use of yellow, pink, red and white coloured sticky traps. *Encarsia smithi* and coccinellid *Cryptognantha* sp. can be used as the biological control. Spray of Fish Oil Resin Soap @ 25 g per litre or profenofos 50% EC @ 2 ml per litre of water.

Resistant Varieties	
World	**India**
Knock Out Roses: Knock Out roses are a popular series of landscape roses that are highly resistant to many common rose pests, including aphids and black spot disease. They are easy to grow, bloom prolifically, and come in a variety of colors. **Carefree Wonder:** Carefree Wonder is a low-maintenance shrub rose that displays excellent resistance to insect pests and diseases. It produces clusters of pink flowers and has a mild fragrance. **Bonica:** Bonica is a hardy shrub rose that is highly resistant to insect pests and diseases. It features clusters of light pink flowers and has a lovely fragrance. **Earth Song:** Earth Song is a hybrid tea rose known for its resistance to insect pests and diseases. It produces large, fragrant blooms in deep pink or red tones. **Belinda's Dream:** Belinda's Dream is a disease-resistant rose that also exhibits good resistance to insect pests. It produces clusters of fragrant, pink blooms and is well-suited for warm climates. **Radrazz:** Radrazz, commonly known as the 'Knock Out Double Red,' is another member of the Knock Out rose series. It offers excellent resistance to pests and diseases and produces abundant double red flowers. **Morden Blush:** Morden Blush is a shrub rose with good resistance to insects and diseases. It features pale pink blooms with a delicate fragrance.	**Iceberg:** Iceberg is a popular white-flowering rose variety that is known for its strong resistance to insect pests. It produces clusters of small, double blooms and has a mild fragrance. **Dona:** Dona is a hybrid tea rose that exhibits good resistance to insect pests. It features large, double blooms in shades of pink and has a strong fragrance. **First Red:** First Red is a hybrid tea rose variety that is resistant to insect pests. It produces vibrant red blooms and has a pleasant fragrance. **Paradise:** Paradise is a disease-resistant rose variety that also displays good resistance to insect pests. It features large, fragrant blooms in shades of pink and is suitable for Indian climatic conditions. **Eiffel Tower:** Eiffel Tower is a tall-growing rose variety with good resistance to insect pests. It produces clusters of fragrant, pink flowers and is often used as a cut flower. **Golden Celebration:** Golden Celebration is an English rose variety that exhibits good resistance to pests. It features large, fragrant, golden-yellow blooms and has a classic rose fragrance. **Kardinal:** Kardinal is a shrub rose variety that shows resistance to insect pests. It produces clusters of deep red flowers and has a mild fragrance.

58 Pests of Gladiolus

Scientific Name	*Gladiolus* spp.
Family	Iridaceae
Origin	South Africa
Chromosome Number	n = 15

Gladiolus (*Gladiolus* spp.) is a perennial flowering plant belonging to the family Iridaceae. It is native to sub-Saharan Africa and is widely cultivated as an ornamental plant for its showy flowers, which come in a range of colors and sizes. Gladiolus is characterized by its long, sword-shaped leaves and tall flower spikes. Gladiolus is grown in many parts of the world, including Europe, Asia, and North America. The top producers of gladiolus are the Netherlands, South Africa, and Zimbabwe. The global production of gladiolus is estimated to be around 250,000 tons per year. Gladiolus is susceptible to various pests and diseases, which can cause significant damage to the plant and reduce flower production. Some of the major pests that can affect gladiolus include:

❑ Gladiolus thrips: *Thrips simplex* Morison, 1930

Common Name	:	Gladiolus thrips
Scientific Name	:	*Thrips simplex* Morison, 1930
Family	:	Thripidae
Order	:	Thysanoptera

Source: https://nathistoc.bio.uci.edu/

Distribution and Host Range

The gladiolus thrips attack the crops like gladiolus, freesia, lily, iris and crocus, but the damage is most significantly seen in glads. Probably introduced from Southern Africa to Northern Europe.

Nature and Symptoms of Damage

Infestation on gladiolus plants result in yellowish or silvery streaks on the foliage and stems, which may later turn brown. Corms attacked by thrips develop rough, greyish-brown surface patches.

Silvery flecks appear on the petals when feeding spreads to the flowers; if attacks are severe, the petals may also turn brown and perish.

Life History and Description

Thrips may show 2 to 3 generations per year. The adult female may deposit roughly one hundred eggs over the period of a few months. The eggs are placed on or in the plant tissues and after hatch out the larvae start ingesting on the sap. After passing through two larval stages, they become non-feeding prepupae and may fall to the ground. They undergo a short pupal stage before becoming winged adults. The wingless larvae are yellow or orange in colour. Adult is a small, brownish-black bug with a pale band at the base of its wings that measures 2 mm in length. These thrips, which typically occur in groups, dwell concealed inside the leaf and flower sheaths of their host plants where they ingest sap.

Management

Planting of clean corms without thrips infestation. Deep ploughing in summer or soil raking destroys the pupal stages and minimizes the incidence. The gladiolus thrips will also perish if exposed to winter frosts. So, it is better to harvest and store the corms between 35 and 40°F (2 and 4°C) for four months. Use of predatory mites like *Amblyseius swirskii,* effective in controlling the thrips. Spray methyl demeton 25 EC @ 2 ml (or) phosalone @ 2 ml/lit or neem oil @ 3%.

❑ Mirid bug: *Lygus lineolaris* (Palisot de Beauvois, 1818)

Common Name	:	Tarnished plant bug (TPB)
Scientific Name	:	*Lygus lineolaris* (Palisot de Beauvois, 1818)
Family	:	Miridae
Order	:	Hemiptera

Source: *https://bugguide.net/*

Distribution and Host Range

From Northern Canada to Southern Mexico, this insect can be found all over North America. It is a highly polyphagous species that consumes more than 50% of all crops grown for commercial purposes, but it prefers cotton, beans, alfalfa, stone fruits and other ornamentals like gladiolous.

Nature and Symptoms of Damage

This plant bug has a special type of feeding known as the "lacerate and flush" feeding strategy where it uses sucking mouthparts to inject saliva into the host plant. The saliva of the TPB contains an enzyme called polygalacturonase which degrades plant tissue and pectin in the plant cell wall allowing for faster digestion. Since the insect will travel from dried plants like weeds onto the nearby gladiolus crop during hot, dry conditions, harm may be more obvious. The insect transfers a toxin into the plant while it feeds. The toxin makes blooms drop off too soon and causes leaves to wilt and distort.

Life History and Description

The life cycle of the mirid bugs can be finished in about a month and two to three generations can occur during the progression of a growing season. The greater incidence of the bugs is generally seen in mid-August. The adult bug spends its winter months hiding out in plant leaves, stems, leaf mould, stones and tree bark. It targets the terminal buds in the spring as it becomes active. It moves to different weeds to lay eggs and appears to like weeds like dandelion and chickweed. Goldenrods, lamb's quarters, plantains, and pigweed are the plants that have the most first-generation adults. When these other hosts grow too mature, the bug arrives on glades.

The circular, flattened, little tarnished plant bug has piercing-sucking mouthparts. The nymphs have lengthy antennae and legs. The young nymphs are yellowish-green and roughly 1 mm long. The older nymphs have one black dot at the base of the abdomen and four black dots on the thorax. The adult is around 6 mm long, often copper colored, and mottled with tiny, asymmetrical spots of reddish-brown, white, yellow, and black. On its back, there is a distinct yellow triangle. There is a tiny, extremely black dot in the center of this triangle.

Management

The bug population can be greatly reduced by periodic leaf washing or overhead irrigation. Regular monitoring of weeds which serves as the alternative hosts. Installation of pink and white sticky traps. Sweep nets are effective in controlling the nymphs. Use of parasitic wasps like *Peristenus digoneutis*, and fungus *Beauvaria bassiana* for better control of mirid bugs. Spray of imidacloprid WG 70% @ 0.5 ml per litre or profenofos EC 50% @1.5-2 ml per litre.

Resistant Varieties	
World	**India**
Black Beauty: Black Beauty is a striking gladiolus variety with deep maroon to black flowers. It is known for its resistance to insect pests and is a popular choice for cut flower arrangements.	**Blue Isle:** Blue Isle is a stunning gladiolus variety with deep blue flowers. It is known for its resistance to insect pests and is a favorite among Indian gardeners for its vibrant color.
Canary Diamond: Canary Diamond is a yellow gladiolus variety that exhibits resistance to insect pests. It produces large, bright yellow flowers and is a delightful addition to gardens and floral displays.	**Carina:** Carina is a lovely gladiolus variety that showcases a blend of pink and white flowers. It exhibits resistance to insect pests and is prized for its delicate beauty.
Green Star: Green Star is a unique gladiolus variety with green flowers. It shows resistance to insect pests and adds a touch of elegance to bouquets and flower beds.	**Golden Sun:** Golden Sun is a yellow gladiolus variety that is resistant to insect pests. It produces large, golden-yellow flowers and adds a cheerful touch to gardens and floral arrangements.
Rose Supreme: Rose Supreme is a pink gladiolus variety that is known for its pest resistance. It features large, ruffled flowers in shades of pink and adds beauty to garden borders and containers.	**Indian Summer:** Indian Summer is a vibrant orange gladiolus variety that shows good resistance to insect pests. Its warm hues and pest resistance make it a popular choice for Indian gardens.
Purple Flora: Purple Flora is a vibrant purple gladiolus variety that exhibits resistance to insect pests. Its striking color and pest resistance make it a popular choice for floral arrangements and garden plantings.	**Snow Princess:** Snow Princess is a white gladiolus variety that exhibits resistance to insect pests. It features pure white flowers and creates an elegant display in Indian gardens.
White Prosperity: White Prosperity is a white gladiolus variety that shows good resistance to insect pests. It produces pristine white blooms and creates an elegant display in any garden setting.	**Star of India:** Star of India is a bi-colored gladiolus variety with pink and white flowers. It is known for its resistance to insect pests and adds a touch of grace to floral arrangements.
Salmon Pearl: Salmon Pearl is a salmon-colored gladiolus variety that exhibits resistance to insect pests. Its unique color and pest resistance make it a desirable choice for floral designs and landscape plantings.	**Violetta:** Violetta is a deep purple gladiolus variety that shows resistance to insect pests. Its rich color and pest resistance make it a sought-after choice for Indian gardens.

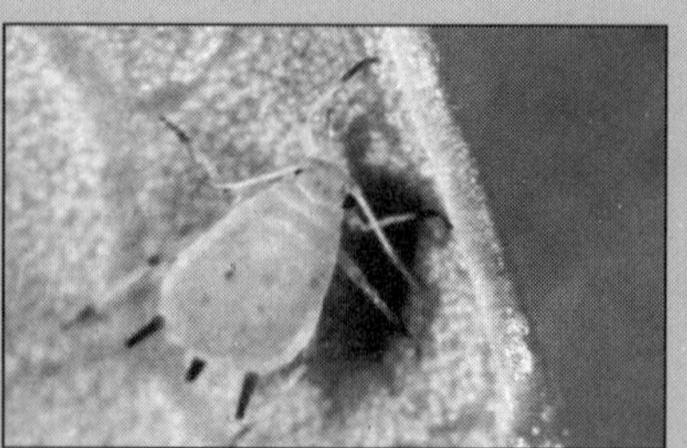

Pests of Carnation

Scientific Name	*Dianthus caryophyllus*
Family	Caryophyllaceae
Origin	Mediterranean region
Chromosome Number	2n = 30

Carnation (*Dianthus caryophyllus*) is a perennial flowering plant belonging to the family Caryophyllaceae. It is native to the Mediterranean region and is widely cultivated as an ornamental plant for its fragrant flowers, which come in a range of colors and sizes. Carnation is grown in many parts of the world, including Europe, Asia, and North America. The top producers of carnation are Colombia, Ecuador, and Kenya. The global production of carnation is estimated to be around 1.5 million tons per year. Carnation is susceptible to various pests and diseases, which can cause significant damage to the plant and reduce flower production. Some of the major pests that can affect carnation include:

❑ Red spider mite: *Tetranychus urticae* C.L. Koch, 1836

Common Name	:	Carnation mite; Red spider mite; Two-spotted spider mite; Carmine spider mite
Scientific Name	:	*Tetranychus urticae* C.L. Koch, 1836
Family	:	Tetranychidae
Order	:	Trombidiformes

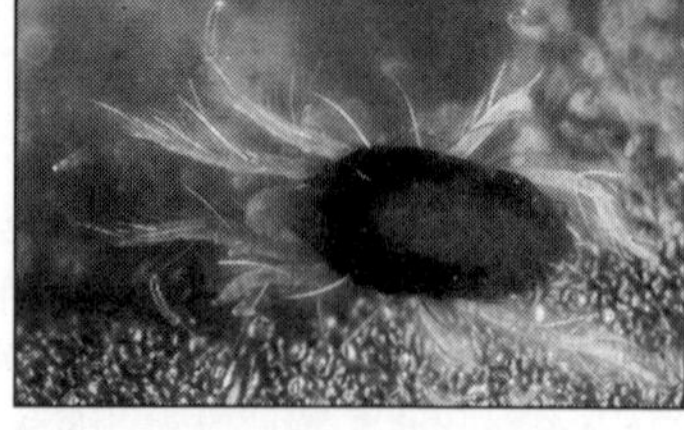

Source:*https://www.cabidigitallibrary.org/doi/10.1079/cabicompendium.30965*

As Described in Tomato

❑ Aphids: *Aphis gossypii* Glover, 1877

Common Name	:	Cotton aphid, melon aphid, melon and cotton aphid
Scientific Name	:	*Aphis gossypii* Glover, 1877
Family	:	Aphididae
Order	:	Hemiptera

Source: https://entomologytoday.org/

As Described in Tomato

❑ Thrips: *Thrips tabaci* Lindeman, 1889

Common Name	:	Onion thrips, potato thrips, tobacco thrips, Cotton seedling thrips.
Scientific Name	:	*Thrips tabaci* Lindeman, 1889
Family	:	Thripidae
Order	:	Thysanoptera

Source: https://onfloriculture.com/

As Described in Tomato

❑ Carnation tortrix moth: *Cacoecimorpha pronubana* (Hübner, 1799)

Common Name	:	Carnation tortrix, European carnation moth
Scientific Name	:	*Cacoecimorpha pronubana* (Hübner, 1799)
Family	:	Tortricidae
Order	:	Lepidoptera

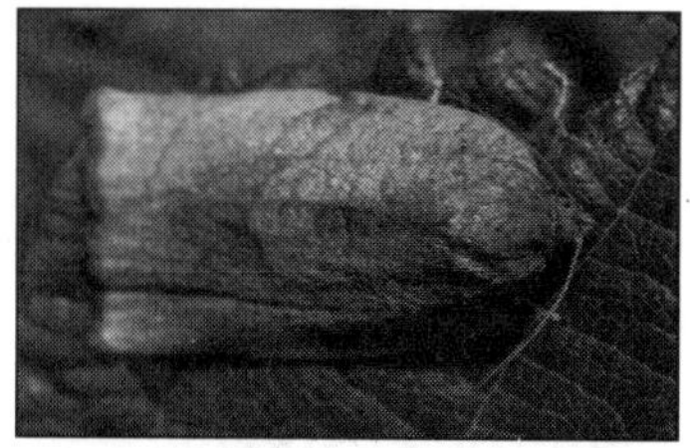

Source:https://www.koppert.com/

Distribution and Host Range

It is seen in the USA, Europe, the Balearic and Channel Islands, Madeira, Sicily, North Africa, the Middle East, and North Africa. It is a prominent pest in carnation crop throughout the Mediterranean region, especially in Israel, Italy, France, and Spain. It has been observed on 160 cultivated and wild plant species, including trees and herbaceous forms, from 42 plant families. It is most well-known for the damage it causes to strawberries and carnations in greenhouses.

Nature and Symptoms of Damage

Caterpillar feeds inside the shelter which is made by weaving silken threads into the leaves. Larvae will feed on the leaves and may burrow into the flower buds. They also found to damage the developing tips of the stems which ultimately affects the quality and quantity of the carnations.

Life History and Description

The number of generations may range from 2 to 6 based on the availability of the favorable conditions. About 700 eggs are laid by adult females in tiny groupings of 10 to 200, which are flattened oval to round in shape. The first instar larvae mine leaves or buds, but the later instar larvae roll or web leaves and terminals. These larvae are in green to dark green shades with yellow head. The larval stage overwinters in regions where there are no constant generations. Pupa is brownish black to black shade and 9-12 mm long. It consists of eight strong, hooked spines on the cremaster. Depending on the location, adults may wing from May to June and from August to September. For females, the wingspan is 18 to 22 mm, while for males, it is 15 to 17 mm. The ground color of the forewings is in light reddish ochreous with few darker lines. The costa of the forewing is rounded.

Management

Deep ploughing in summers is highly beneficial in controlling the pupal stages. Moths' occurrence can be decreased by hand-picking larvae. Pheromone traps were installed @12/ha to attract the male moths and installation of light traps @1/ha to catch the adults. Use of endoparasitoid *Elacherus lateralis* (Eulophidae) to control the pest the pest. Spray insecticides like chlorpyriphos 20 EC @1 lit/ha or neem oil @ 3%.

❑ Carnation fly: *Hylemya briennescens* (Bruneteau)

Common Name	:	Root-maggot flies
Scientific Name	:	*Hylemya briennescens* (Bruneteau)
Family	:	Anthomyiidae
Order	:	Diptera

Source: *https://en.wikipedia.org/*

Distribution and Host Range

These flies known to be distributed from Southern zone of North America to the South-Eastern parts of South America. It is known to attack a wide range of ornamentals along with some vegetables and fruits.

Nature and Symptoms of Damage

Maggots feed their way in tunnels made through the leaves and developing tips of young plants. Then the young plants are killed by tunnelling down the apical stalk.

Life History and Description

The carnation fly lays its eggs on the leaves and stems of carnations, in late summer or early autumn. When the eggs hatch, the larvae tunnel into the plant leaves and shoots, feeding on the tissue. Until the arrival of the first frosts, the larvae will continue to feed and then moves into the soil below to pupate that lasts for 8 weeks. Next, they will re-emerge as adults in the spring when the weather begins to warm up. The reproductive cycle restarts after the flies have lived for about four months. It consists of only one generation per year.

Eggs are white, elongated oval shape with one convex and one flattened side. The larva body is obliquely truncated behind, are about 9 mm long, creamy white, hefty, and rather slow. The adult measures about 6-7 mm in length. A strap-shaped abdomen with a thin black median stripe and thin black transverse bands on the front edges of the segments characterises males. Their heads are brownish, their thoraxes are blackish-brown in front and yellowish-grey behind them. Females have a greyish-yellowish head with two rows of post-orbital bristles and a bright yellowish patch above the lunule.

Management

Removal of the affected leaves and destroying them. The use of glue traps can be effective and also yellow sticky traps are also beneficial to certain point. Use of predators like lacewings, lady beetle, spiders, fire ants, dragonfly, robber fly, praying mantis etc. Add phorate granules 10G to the soil at a rate of 10 kg/ha, followed by mild irrigation or spray malathion 50 EC @ 2 ml/l.

Resistant Varieties	
World	**India**
Malmaison Carnation: Malmaison carnations are highly resistant to common insect pests. They are renowned for their large, double blooms in various colours, including pink, white, and red. This variety is cherished for its fragrance and is widely cultivated in many regions. **Cindy Carnation:** Cindy carnations are known for their resistance to insect pests and diseases. They produce elegant, ruffled blooms in shades of pink, white, and red. Cindy carnations are popular choices for cut flowers and garden displays. **Yellow Sunblaze Carnation:** Yellow Sunblaze is a compact carnation variety that displays excellent resistance to insect pests. It features bright yellow flowers and is commonly used in container gardening or as bedding plants. **Red Rocket Carnation:** Red Rocket carnations are prized for their pest resistance and vibrant red blooms. They are known for their durability and long-lasting flowers, making them popular for cut flower arrangements and garden borders. **Oscar Carnation:** Oscar carnations exhibit good resistance to insect pests and diseases. They produce large, fringed flowers in various colours, including white, pink, and purple. Oscar carnations are favored for their longevity and strong fragrance. **Grenadin Mix Carnation:** Grenadin Mix carnations are a series of cultivars that are bred for their resistance to pests and diseases. They come in a range of vibrant colors and produce abundant, long-lasting flowers. **Chabaud Carnation:** Chabaud carnations are known for their resistance to insect pests and diseases. They are characterized by their full, double blooms and strong, sweet fragrance. Chabaud carnations are commonly used in floral arrangements and garden borders.	**Serenade Carnation:** Serenade carnations are highly resistant to insect pests and diseases. They produce large, double blooms in various colours, including pink, red, white, and bi-colours. Serenade carnations are favored for their long-lasting flowers and sweet fragrance. **Pallas Carnation:** Pallas carnations are known for their pest resistance and are cultivated in India. They feature fringed petals and come in a range of colours, including pink, red, white, and bi-colours. Pallas carnations are popular choices for cut flower arrangements. **Angel Pink Carnation:** Angel Pink carnations display good resistance to insect pests and diseases. They have delicate, ruffled petals in shades of pink and are prized for their elegant appearance. Angel Pink carnations are commonly used in floral decorations and bouquets. **Indian Summer Carnation:** Indian Summer carnations are bred to be resistant to insect pests and diseases prevalent in India. They offer vibrant, warm-coloured blooms in shades of orange, yellow, and bronze. Indian Summer carnations are cherished for their exotic appearance and fragrance. **Safari Mix Carnation:** Safari Mix carnations are a series of cultivars that are specifically bred for their pest resistance. They produce compact plants with double blooms in a mix of colours, including red, pink, white, and bi-colours. Safari Mix carnations are suitable for container gardening and as bedding plants.

Pests of Chrysanthemum

Scientific Name	*Dendranthema grandiflora*
Family	Asteraceae
Origin	China
Chromosome Number	n = 9

Chrysanthemum (*Chrysanthemum* spp.) is a flowering plant belonging to the family Asteraceae. It is native to Asia and is widely cultivated as an ornamental plant for its colourful flowers, which come in a range of shapes and sizes. Chrysanthemum is characterized by its toothed leaves and flower heads that consist of many small flowers arranged in a disk shape. Chrysanthemum is grown in many parts of the world, including Asia, Europe, and North America. The top producers of chrysanthemum are China, Japan, and Korea. The global production of chrysanthemum is estimated to be around 200,000 tons per year. Chrysanthemum is susceptible to various pests and diseases, which can cause significant damage to the plant and reduce flower production. Some of the major pests that can affect chrysanthemum include:

❑ Chrysanthemum aphid: *Macrosiphoniella sanborni* (Gillette, 1908)

Common Name	:	Chrysanthemum aphid; Black aphid
Scientific Name	:	*Macrosiphoniella sanborni* (Gillette, 1908)
Family	:	Aphididae
Order	:	Hemiptera

Source: *https://www.biodiversidadvirtual.org/*

Distribution and Host Range

The distribution of chrysanthemum aphids is cosmopolitan. These aphids are seen on cultivated chrysanthemums, like Paris daisy, Indian chrysanthemum and florists daisy. Chrysanthemum aphids are of East Asian origin, but it also found on other Asteraceae members like Aster, Anthemis and Artemisia.

Nature and Symptoms of Damage

Chrysanthemum aphids feed by puncturing the plant surface with the mouthparts that resemble the threads and suck out the plant sap. They congregate towards the terminal buds and eat the fresh growth. Curling of leaves and withering of flowers are seen. Feeding results in deformed growth along with honeydew and cast skins seen on the leaves. The leaves and stems with honeydew may develop sooty mould, giving them a black look. Both the chrysanthemum vein mottle virus and the chrysanthemum virus B can also be spread by these chrysanthemum aphids.

Life History and Description

Adult female aphids reproduce by giving birth to more females, without mating. Chrysanthemum aphids spend the winter months feeding in greenhouses where they overwinter. They leave the greenhouses in the warmer months in search of new plants. The winged female stage typically begins eating and produces live nymphs as soon as it infests new plants. A female aphid can give birth to four to eight young each day. The new nymphs develop into wingless females in about a week, at which point they start having their own offspring. A single aphid on a plant can quickly increase the population to hundreds of creatures. When the plant gets congested, an increasing number of the young turn into winged females that may leave to infest neighbouring plants.

Winged adults are fragile, lustrous mahogany brown and about 1/16 inch long. Adults without wings are slightly smaller than those with wings. At the end of the body, there are a pair of tiny, robust, black cornicles. Nymphs resemble scaled-down versions of adults without wings. Nymphs feature relatively large legs and antennae, as well as dull, brick-red bodies. Short and black cornicles are seen. Young nymph antennae and the outer two-thirds of their legs are grey to dark grey. Cornicles on older nymphs are proportionately longer. Wing buds are seen in the latter stages of development in those which will become winged adults.

Management

As discussed earlier in Rose.

❑ Thrips: *Microcephalothrips abdominalis* (Crawford)

Common Name	:	Composite thrips
Scientific Name	:	*Microcephalothrips abdominalis* (Crawford)
Family	:	Thripidae
Order	:	Thysanoptera

Source: *https://keys.lucidcentral.org/*

Distribution and Host range

The cosmopolitan, *Microcephalothrips abdominalis* was first identified in Mexico. It is widely distributed in Africa, Asia, Central America and Caribbean, Europe, Middle East, North America, Oceania and South America. *M. abdominalis*, also referred to as composite thrips, as it tends to feed on plants in the composite family. It has been observed on hosts plants like mums, sunflower, Calendula, Dahlia, marigold and Tridax daisy, blue billy goat weed, Chinese wedelia, Bay Biscayne creeping-oxeye etc.

Nature and Symptoms of Damage

The nature of thrips is often cryptic. The flower heads are highly infected by these thrips. Abrasions are formed by lacerating the sepals and petals. Corolla and stamen damage by severe infection causes early flower wilting. It also spreads the necrotic spot virus and tomato spotted wilt virus to various floricultural crops along with chrysanthemums.

Life History and Description

M. abdominalis has a life cycle that lasts 9 to 12 days. Oviposition coincides with the emergence of the petals of the disc florets of host plants in their late bud stage. Oviposition and larval emergence are monitored and synchronised with anthesis and nectar production in the flowers of the host. This species typically lays eggs in the tissues of involucral bracts and on the upper side of the pedicles rarely.

Thrips are tiny, slender insects with fringed wings that occupy a variety of ecological niches. The adult range in colour from dark brown to brown. The third and perhaps the fourth of the seven antennal segments are faintly pigmented. Ocellar setae come in two pairs, with the interocellar pair either outside or close to the ocellar triangle. Adult thrips have a relatively small head that is narrower than their prothorax. Two pairs of postero-lateral setae and five to six pairs of postero-marginal setae can be found on the prothorax.

Management

Field sanitation by removal of weeds which harbour virus from outside and inside of the greenhouse. Use of resistant varieties like Bangalore Local, Chandrika, Yellow Double, Pankaj, M-7, and Yellow Star. Installation of 4 to 5 blue sticky traps per acre. Use of predatory mites like *Amblyseius swirskii*, effective in controlling the thrips. Spray methyl demeton 25 EC @ 2 ml (or) phosalone @ 2 ml/lit or neem oil @ 3%

❑ Flower feeder: *Helicoverpa armigera* (Hübner, [1808])

Common Name	:	Cotton bollworm, corn earworm, old World bollworm, scarce bordered straw
Scientific Name	:	*Helicoverpa armigera* (Hübner, [1808])
Family	:	Noctuidae
Order	:	Lepidoptera

Source: https://www.cabidigitallibrary.org/

As Described in Tomato

❑ Serpentine leaf miner: *Liriomyza trifolii* (Burgess, 1880)

Common Name	:	American serpentine leafminer, celery leafminer
Scientific Name	:	*Liriomyza trifolii* (Burgess, 1880)
Family	:	Agromyzidae
Order	:	Diptera

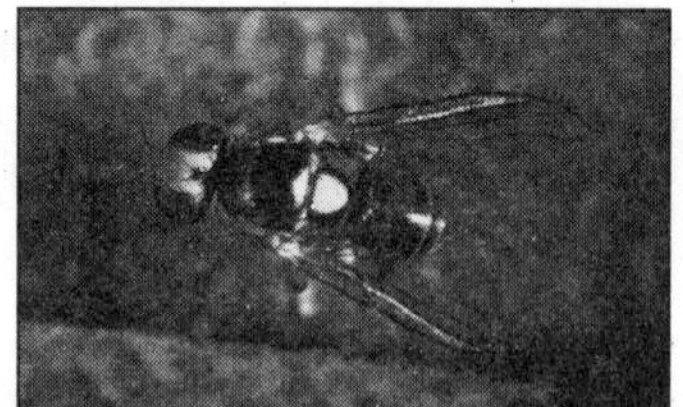

Source: https://www.cabidigitallibrary.org/

As Described in Tomato

Resistant Varieties	
World	**India**
Mammoth Series: The Mammoth Series of chrysanthemums includes varieties that are bred for their strong resistance to pests and diseases. They produce large, fully-double flowers in various colours, such as yellow, pink, red, and bronze. The Mammoth Series is valued for its vigorous growth and robust performance.	**Jyoti:** Jyoti is a widely grown chrysanthemum variety in India that exhibits good resistance to insect pests. It produces large, semi-double to double flowers in various colours, including white, yellow, pink, and purple. Jyoti chrysanthemums are valued for their vibrant blooms and are often used in flower arrangements.
Charm Series: The Charm Series features chrysanthemum varieties that are resistant to common insect pests. They produce medium-sized flowers with a range of colours, including shades of pink, purple, and white. The Charm Series is favored for its compact habit and long-lasting blooms.	**Nandini:** Nandini is another popular chrysanthemum variety in India that is known for its resistance to insect pests. It produces medium to large-sized flowers in shades of yellow, pink, and orange. Nandini chrysanthemums are sought after for their attractive colours and long-lasting blooms.
Ice Series: The Ice Series of chrysanthemums is known for its resistance to insect pests and diseases. These varieties produce daisy-like flowers with a distinctive white or cream-colored center, surrounded by petals in various shades of pink, lavender, and yellow. The Ice Series is appreciated for its elegant appearance and ability to withstand pest pressure.	**Raksha:** Raksha is a pest-resistant chrysanthemum variety commonly grown in India. It produces fully-double flowers with petals in shades of white, yellow, and pink. Raksha chrysanthemums are favored for their robust growth and ability to withstand pest infestations.
Yuri Series: The Yuri Series consists of chrysanthemum varieties that exhibit resistance to insect pests and diseases. They produce fully-double flowers with a button-like appearance and come in a range of colors, including white, yellow, pink, and bronze. The Yuri Series is valued for its compact growth habit and abundant blooms.	**Pratima:** Pratima is a chrysanthemum variety that exhibits resistance to insect pests and diseases. It produces large, semi-double to fully-double flowers in a range of colors, such as white, yellow, and pink. Pratima chrysanthemums are known for their graceful appearance and prolonged blooming period.
Anastasia Series: The Anastasia Series features chrysanthemum varieties that possess resistance to pests and diseases. They produce large, fully-double flowers with fringed petals in vibrant colors, such as pink, orange, and red. The Anastasia Series is sought after for its eye-catching blooms and reliable performance.	**Ravi:** Ravi is a pest-resistant chrysanthemum variety grown in India. It produces medium-sized flowers with a mix of single and semi-double blooms in colors like white, yellow, and pink. Ravi chrysanthemums are appreciated for their compact growth habit and resistance to pest damage.

Pests of Marigold

Scientific Name	*Tagetes* sps.
Family	Asteraceae
Origin	Mexico
Chromosome Number	n = 12

Marigold (*Tagetes* spp.) is a flowering plant belonging to the family Asteraceae. It is native to the Americas and is widely cultivated as an ornamental plant for its bright, colorful flowers. Marigold is characterized by its pinnate leaves and flower heads that consist of many small flowers arranged in a flat or rounded shape. Marigold is grown in many parts of the world, including Asia, Europe, and North America. The top producers of marigold are India, China, and Ethiopia. The global production of marigold is estimated to be around 17,000 tons per year. Marigold is susceptible to various pests and diseases, which can cause significant damage to the plant and reduce flower production. Some of the major pests that can affect marigold include:

❑ Cut worms: *Spodoptera litura* (Fabricius, 1775)

Common Name	:	Tobacco cutworm, cotton leafworm
Scientific Name	:	*Spodoptera litura* (Fabricius, 1775)
Family	:	Noctuidae
Order	:	Lepidoptera

Source: https://en.wikipedia.org/

As Described in Potato

❑ Flower feeder: *Helicoverpa armigera* (Hübner, [1808])

Common Name	:	Cotton bollworm, corn earworm, old World bollworm, scarce bordered straw
Scientific Name	:	*Helicoverpa armigera* (Hübner, [1808])
Family	:	Noctuidae
Order	:	Lepidoptera

Source: https://www.cabidigitallibrary.org/

As Described in Tomato

Mealy bug: *Drosicha* spp. (Walker)

Common Name	:	Mealy bugs
Scientific Name	:	*Drosicha* spp.
Family	:	Pseudococcidae
Order	:	Hemiptera

Source: https://www.yates.co.nz/

As Described in Mango

Aphids: *Lipaphis erysimi* (Kaltenbach, 1843)

Common Name	:	Mustard aphid, turnip aphid
Scientific Name	:	*Lipaphis erysimi* (Kaltenbach, 1843)
Family	:	Aphidideae
Order	:	Hemiptera

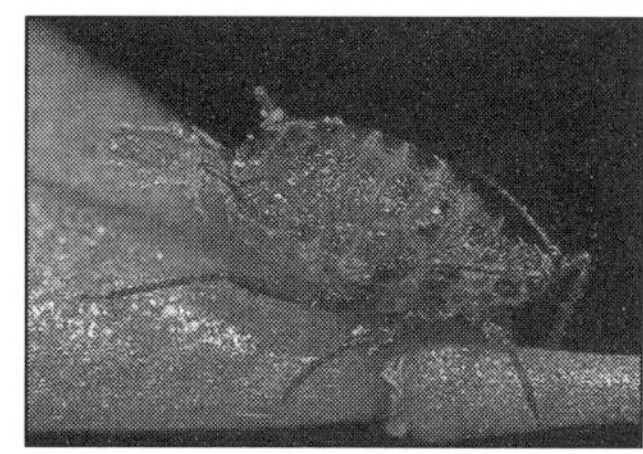

Source: https://influentialpoints.com/

Distribution and Host Range

This aphid species was originally discovered in Europe, but now present in many regions of the world, both tropical and temperate. Along with marigold and other ornamentals it prefers cole crops like cabbage, cauliflower, broccoli, Brussels sprouts, kale, kohlrabi, radish, turnip, wild mustard and other cruciferous weeds etc.

Nature and Symptoms of Damage

Both the nymphal and adult stages are destructive. They are usually found in clusters and cause damage the growing tip regions of the plant by sucking the sap. Plants that have been infected become feeble and unproductive.

Life History and Description

This aphid is exclusively viviparous, although eggs have been seen occasionally. It is highly prolific, with a maximum of 35 generations per year observed in warm climates such as Texas. Over a period of 20 to 40 days, the wingless females can generate up to 6 offspring per day, for a total of 80 to 100 young. Winged females can disperse to other plants, but they produce fewer offspring.

The adult wingless female is seen pale greenish or whitish green color with presence of two rows of dark stripes on the thorax and the abdomen that merge into a single band towards the abdomen tip. The antennae are dark, legs are pale with dark joints and cornicles with dark tips. The body surface is a little powdery, measures from 1.4 and 2.4 mm long. The winged female is of about the same size as the male and has a black head and thorax, as well as a pale green abdomen with black bands towards the tip and black spots on the sides. The antennae and legs are black, while the cornicles are black at the base and yellowish at the tips. Wingless males are seen occasionally and these are smaller in size than females. Seen in olive green to light brown in colour.

Management

Use of sprinkler type of irrigation system to limit the infestation. Adjusting the planting layout; adjusting the sowing time and harvest time; deep ploughing and winter turning over; appropriate use of crop fertilizers and timely drainage. Use silver grey film nets to cover field crops that can inhibit aphid landing and settlement. Use of lady beetles, soldier beetles, hoverflies, acalyptrate flies, gall midges, flower bugs, leaf bugs, damsel bugs, stink bugs, lacewings, parasitic wasps, mites, fungal pathogens as well as other aphids. Spray dimethoate 30 EC or methyl demeton 25 EC @ 2 ml/lit or neem oil @ 0.5%.

❑ Leaf miner: *Liriomyza sativae* Blanchard, 1938

Common Name	:	Vegetable leaf minor
Scientific Name	:	*Liriomyza sativae* Blanchard, 1938
Family	:	Agromyzidae
Order	:	Diptera

Source: *https://www.cabidigitallibrary.org/*

Distribution and Host Range

L. sativae is found in the Southern United States, Central America, and South America. It is occasionally seen in more Northern portions of the United States after being transferred there in plant debris. It cannot survive in cold temperatures (apart from glasshouses). Along with marigolds other members of Cucurbitaceae, Fabaceae, and Solanaceae plants are frequently infested.

Nature and Symptoms of Damage

Continuous mines are produced by larvae in leaves and young tender stems. Mined regions are whitish or greenish in appearance, with noticeable black thread-like streaks of frass on alternate sides of the channel. Individual mines are insignificant; however, when larval populations are huge, entire leaves may be mined. Feeding injury can severely weaken or even destroy mature and young plants in large quantities. Plants that have been severely harmed appear to have been burned by fire. Wind damage and plant pathogen infection are more likely in infested leaves.

Life History and Identification

The female lays eggs inside the leaf tissues of a sensitive plant by puncturing them. As the larva develops, it feeds on the leaf tissue, forming a tunnel between the upper and bottom surfaces. This begins small but expands as the larva grows in size. After three instars phases, the larva makes a slit in the upper surface of the leaf and falls to the ground to pupate. The larval stage lasts around 8 days at 25 to 30°C. Then the pupal stage is seen. The entire cycle takes 25 days at 15 °C. Throughout the course of a month, a female may lay several hundred eggs. *L. sativae* eggs are transparent and pale, measuring roughly 0.12 mm. The larvae are maggots with no legs and no head capsule. They are translucent at first, but later instars turn yellowish-orange. When the adults are nearly ready to emerge, the pupae are oval and slightly flattened, ranging in colour from yellowish-orange to a darker golden brown are represented. The adults can grow to be up to 1.7 mm long, with females being little larger than males; the head, frons, third segment of the antenna, scutellum is yellow, the mesothorax and abdomen are black, with the exception of the borders of several plates on the abdomen, which are yellow. This unique feature mesonotum is helpful in distinguishing the *L. sativae* from close relatives like *L. trifolii*.

Management

The accumulation of the pest in endemic areas can be decreased by the judicial application of nitrogenous fertiliser. Leaves with severe infestations need to be removed and destroyed. Encourage larval and pupal parasitoids like *Semielacher petiolatus*. Spray of triazophos @ 0.15% or imidacloprid @ 0.0075% or deltamethrin @ 0.0028%.

❑ Thrips: *Thrips tabaci* Lindeman, 1889

Common Name	:	Onion thrips, Potato thrips, tobacco thrips, Cotton seedling thrips.
Scientific Name	:	*Thrips tabaci* Lindeman, 1889
Family	:	Thripidae
Order	:	Thysanoptera

Source: https://keys.lucidcentral.org/

As Described in Tomato

❑ Red spider mite: *Tetranychus urticae* C.L. Koch, 1836

Common Name	:	Carnation mite, Red spider mite; Two-spotted spider mite, Carmine spider mite,
Scientific Name	:	*Tetranychus urticae* C.L. Koch, 1836
Family	:	Tetranychidae
Order	:	Trombidiformes

Source:https://www.cabidigitallibrary.org/doi/10.1079/cabicompendium.30965

As Described in Tomato

❑ Leaf Hoppers: *Empoasca kerri* (Pruthi)

Common Name	:	Green leaf hopper
Scientific Name	:	*Empoasca kerri* (Pruthi)
Family	:	Cicadellidae
Order	:	Hemiptera

Source:https://plantwiseplusknowledgebank.org

As Described in Potato

Resistant Varieties	
World	**India**
French Marigold (*Tagetes patula*): French marigolds are compact plants that produce an abundance of small, single or double flowers. They come in various colours such as yellow, orange, and red. French marigolds emit a strong fragrance that repels many insect pests, including aphids, whiteflies, and nematodes. **African Marigold (*Tagetes erecta*):** African marigolds are tall, robust plants that produce large, fully-double flowers. They are available in shades of yellow, orange, and red. African marigolds have a strong scent that helps repel insect pests like aphids, whiteflies, and spider mites. **Signet Marigold (*Tagetes tenuifolia*):** Signet marigolds have fine, lacy foliage and small, single flowers. They are available in colors such as yellow, orange, and red. Signet marigolds are known for their strong aroma and pest-repellent properties. They can deter aphids, whiteflies, and spider mites. **Inca Marigold (*Tagetes minuta*):** Inca marigold is a tall, bushy variety that produces small, single flowers in yellow or white. It has a strong scent and is known for its ability to repel insects like aphids, whiteflies, and nematodes. Inca marigold is often used as a companion plant to protect other crops from insect pests. **Mexican Marigold (*Tagetes lucida*):** Mexican marigold, also known as Mexican tarragon, is valued for its culinary and medicinal uses. It has attractive, fern-like foliage and small, yellow flowers. Mexican marigold has insect-repellent properties and can deter pests like mosquitoes and aphids.	**Pusa Narangi Gainda:** Pusa Narangi Gainda is a popular marigold variety in India that exhibits resistance to insect pests. It produces large, double flowers in shades of orange and gold. The variety is valued for its strong fragrance and robust growth habit. **Pusa Basanti Gainda:** Pusa Basanti Gainda is a pest-resistant marigold variety grown in India. It produces medium-sized flowers in a beautiful combination of red, orange, and yellow hues. Pusa Basanti Gainda is known for its long-lasting blooms and resistance to pests and diseases. **African Marigold (*Tagetes erecta*):** African marigold is a common variety grown in India and is known for its robust growth and resistance to insect pests. It produces large, fully-double flowers in vibrant shades of yellow, orange, and red. African marigolds are often used in decorative plantings and flower arrangements. **French Marigold (*Tagetes patula*):** French marigold is another variety that exhibits resistance to insect pests and is grown in India. It produces smaller-sized flowers with a mix of single and double blooms in colours like yellow, orange, and burgundy. French marigolds are valued for their colourful blooms and ability to repel pests. **Signet Marigold (*Tagetes tenuifolia*):** Signet marigold is a unique variety known for its fine, lacy foliage and small, single flowers. It is generally more tolerant of pest infestations compared to other marigold varieties. Signet marigolds come in various colours such as yellow, orange, and red, and they are often used as edging plants or in container gardening.

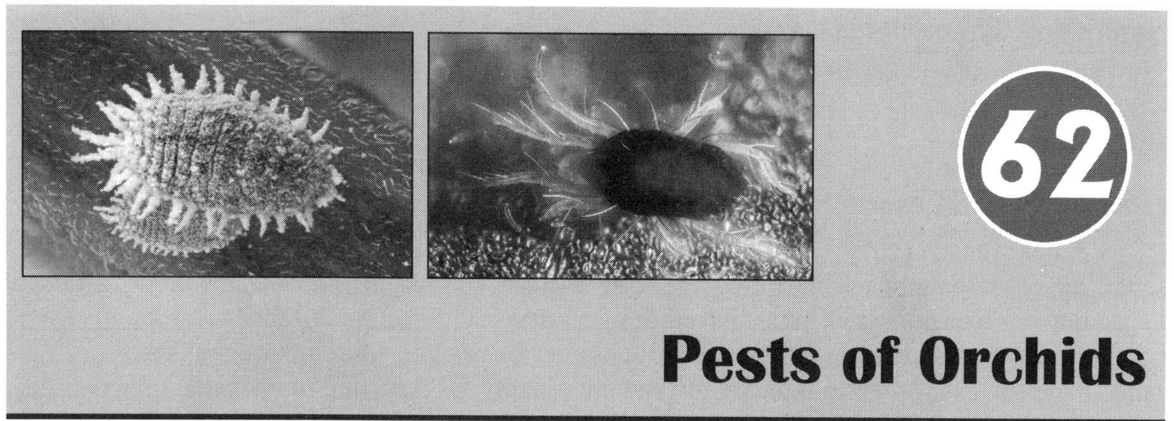

62

Pests of Orchids

Scientific Name	*Orchid* sps.
Family	Orchidaceae
Origin	Mexico
Chromosome Number	n = 12

Orchids are a diverse family of flowering plants with over 25,000 species found worldwide. Orchids are grown in a wide range of environments, from tropical rainforests to temperate zones. They can be grown indoors or outdoors, in pots or in the ground. Orchids are highly prized for their ornamental value and are grown commercially for use in the floral industry. They are also grown for their medicinal properties and as a source of food. Pests can have a significant economic impact on the production of orchids. Common pests of orchids include mealybugs, spider mites, thrips, and scale insects. These pests can damage the plants, reduce flower production, and spread diseases. In addition, the use of pesticides to control these pests can be costly and may have negative environmental impacts. Some of the major pests that can affect orchids include:

❑ Scales: *Diaspis boisduvali* Signoret

Common Name	:	Boisduval scale
Scientific Name	:	*Diaspis boisduvali* Signoret
Family	:	Diaspididae
Order	:	Hemiptera

Source: *https://www.insectimages.org/*

Distribution and Host Range

The boisduval scale is a greenhouses pest in temperate regions and occurs throughout the tropics. Boisduval scale is an economically important pest of orchids. In Florida alone, this species has been identified in over 15 families and 65 genera, however it is most frequently seen on palms (Arecaceae) and orchids (Orchidaceae).

Nature and Symptoms of Damage

This scale seems to prefer the midrib of the leaf and the sheathed section of the petiole on orchids. Boisduval scale can also infest all aerial parts of the plant, including the pods as well as the pseudobulbs.

Life History and Description

A mature female can lay up to 200 eggs and have a lifespan of seven months. Within five to seven days, the eggs hatch into crawlers. Egg colours can range from clear yellow to orange depending on ripeness. Males take an average of 33 days and females take an average of 50 days to mature from egg to adult stage. Females are flat, circular or oval, white-transparent shed skins that range in colour from white to light yellow and are roughly 1.2-2.25 mm in diameter. One horn-like projection on both sides of the body, close to head and thorax, will be seen when the scale cover is removed. Males have an oval to elongated shape with a white covering and shed skin on the margins. Male scale has a length of about 1 mm.

Management

The first step in preventing a boisduval scale infestation is exclusion. Before making a purchase, carefully inspect all plants and propagation supplies. Make sure planting material is pest-free by placing the new plants apart from collections and nursery stock for at least two weeks. Scrap the scales with the use of toothbrush dipped in kerosene. Use of green lace wing (*Chrysoperla carnea)* larvae or *Coccidencyrtus* sp. (Hymenoptera) as a parasite of boisduval scale. Spray of malathion 50 EC or methyl demeton 25 EC or phosalone 35 EC @ 1 ml per litre.

❑ Mealy bugs: *Planococcus citri* Risso, 1813

Common Name	:	Citrus mealy bugs
Scientific Name	:	*Planococcus citri* Risso, 1813
Family	:	Pseudococcidae
Order	:	Hemiptera

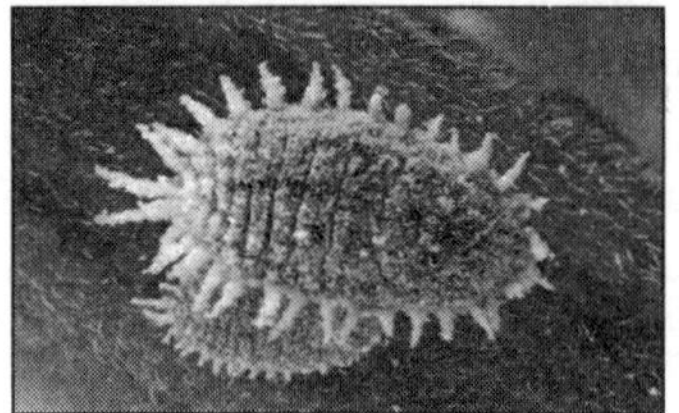

Source: *https://antropocene.it/*

As Described in Citrus

❑ Mites: *Tetranychus urticae* C.L. Koch, 1836

Common Name	:	Carnation mite, Red spider mite; Two-spotted spider mite, Carmine spider mite,
Scientific Name	:	*Tetranychus urticae* CL. Koch, 1836
Family	:	Tetranychidae
Order	:	Trombidiformes

Source:*https://www.cabidigitallibrary.org/doi/10.1079/cabicompendium.30965*

As Described in Tomato

❑ Giant African snail: *Lissachatina fulica* (Férussac, 1821)

Common Name	:	Giant African snail, Giant African land snail
Scientific Name	:	*Lissachatina fulica* (Férussac, 1821)
Family	:	Achatinidae
Order	:	Stylommatophora

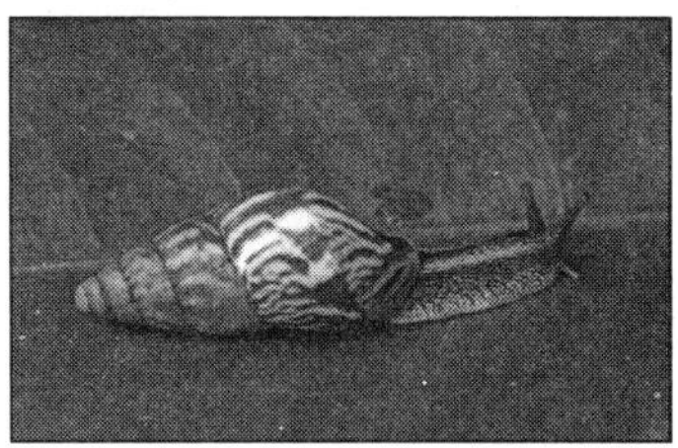

Source:*https://commons.wikimedia.org/*

Distribution and Host Range

The species is endemic to East Africa, but it has spread widely over the world through accident by the pet trade and as a source of food. Now it is found throughout India, China, Taiwan, Soth-east Asia and West Indies. Orchids along with a wide variety of plant matter, including fruit, vegetables, lichens, fungi, paper, and cardboard are all consumed by it.

Nature and Symptoms of Damage

The giant African land snail is a macro-phytophagous herbivore. They consume open flowers as well as young leaves, roots, and flower buds. Slugs typically hide during the day and come out at night. Slimy liquid is seen on the foliage.

Life History and Identification

Incubation time for the eggs range from a few hours to 17 days. Depending on the temperature, snails reach adulthood at 5 to 15 months. It can live up to 9 years, however the average lifespan is 5 to 6 years. The giant African land snails are one of the largest extant land snails. The mature snail is around 7 cm in diameter and 20 cm or more in length. The shell is roughly twice as long as it is wide, giving it a conical appearance. The coiling of the shell can be seen going either in a dextral (clockwise) or sinistral (counter-clockwise) direction, however the dextral cone is more typical. Shell coloration varies greatly and is influenced by nutrition. The shell is typically banded and predominately brown.

Management

Earlier inspection of snails before planting. Collect and destroy, if the count of the pest is very low. Use of parasitodal nematode like *Angiostrongylus cantonensis*, (rat lungworm). Apply metaldehyde dust or metaldehyde liquid @ 15% and 20% respectively.

Resistant Varieties

Cattleya Orchids: Cattleya orchids are popular for their large, showy flowers and delightful fragrance. They come in a wide range of colours and exhibit some resistance to common orchid pests such as aphids, scale insects, and mealybugs.

Dendrobium Orchids: Dendrobium orchids are a diverse group of orchids known for their abundant blooms and long-lasting flowers. They have a reputation for being relatively resistant to common orchid pests like aphids, thrips, and scale insects.

Vanda Orchids: Vanda orchids are highly prized for their vibrant colours and large, waxy flowers. They are generally more resistant to pests compared to some other orchid varieties. However, they can still be susceptible to pests like spider mites and mealybugs, so proper care and vigilance are necessary.

Phalaenopsis Orchids: Phalaenopsis orchids, also known as moth orchids, are popular for their elegant, long-lasting blooms. While they can attract certain insect pests like aphids and scale insects, they generally have a good level of resistance and are relatively easier to manage in terms of pest control.

Oncidium Orchids: Oncidium orchids, often referred to as "dancing lady" orchids, are known for their numerous small flowers and delicate appearance. They are generally resistant to many common orchid pests but may occasionally attract aphids and spider mites.

Cymbidium Orchids: Cymbidium orchids are valued for their long-lasting flowers and suitability for cooler climates. They are known to be relatively resistant to pests but can occasionally encounter issues with aphids, mealybugs, and spider mites.

63 Pests of Jasmine

Scientific Name	*Jasminum* sps.
Family	Oleaceae
Origin	India
Chromosome Number	n = 13

Jasmine is a genus of flowering plants in the olive family, with over 200 species found in tropical and subtropical regions around the world. Jasmine flowers are often white or yellow and are highly fragrant, making them popular for use in perfumes, teas, and as ornamental plants. Jasmine is grown in a wide range of environments, including tropical and subtropical regions, and can be grown both indoors and outdoors. Jasmine is grown commercially for its essential oil, which is used in perfumes and aromatherapy. It is also grown for its ornamental value, with many different varieties cultivated for their attractive flowers. Pests can have a significant economic impact on the production of jasmine. Common pests of jasmine include spider mites, aphids, scale insects, whiteflies, and mealybugs. Some of the major pests that can affect jasmine include:

❑ Budworm: *Hendecasis duplifascialis* (Hampson, 1891)

Common Name	:	Jasmine budworm, Jasmine bud borer
Scientific Name	:	*Hendecasis duplifascialis* (Hampson, 1891)
Family	:	Crambidae
Order	:	Lepidoptera

Source: https://lepiforum.org/

Distribution and Host Range

Jasmine budworm is commonly seen in India, Sri Lanka, Philippines, Cambodia, The Comoros, China, Japan and Thailand. It is found to show its infestation in Jasmine flower crop.

Nature and Symptoms of Damage

The tiny caterpillar bores holes in the flower bud and feeds on the bud's interior contents. It emerges from a circular hole in the corolla tube and burrows into neighbouring buds on the same stem. Each larva attacks 2 to 3 flower buds. Flowers that have been infested turn violet and fall off. With extreme infestations, adjacent flower buds are webbed by silken thread together.

Life History and Identification

Bud worm eggs are spherical and creamy white when first laid, then turn yellow. Eggs are placed singly and glued to immature buds, calyx, and occasionally bud stalk. They hatch in 3 to 4 days. The neonatal larva is creamy yellow in colour with a dark black head and prothoracic shield. It has five instars. Pupation occurs primarily within the soil and occasionally on the leaves, near the intersection of petioles and leaf blades. The adult moth is a tiny, creamy white moth with wavy wing markings and black patches on the wing border. The moths have scaly proboscis and a pair of well-developed black palpi.

Management

Soil raking or deep ploughing in summer or soil raking destroys the pupal stages and minimizes the incidence of budworm. Collection and destruction of the injured pinkish blossoms once a week to prevent further multiplication. Proper pruning and maintenance of hygienic bushes and plots. Setting a light trap during the peak emergence of adult moths. Conserve the larval parasitoids like *Phanerotoma* sp. *Perilampus* sp., and *Mesochrous* sp. In the late hours, spray 5% neem seed kernel extract or endosulfan 750 ml or chlorpyriphos 20 EC @ 750 ml or cypermethrin 25 EC @ 200 ml or dimethoate 30 EC @ 500 ml in 500-750 litres of water per hectare.

❑ Gallery worm: *Elasmopalpus jasminophagus*

Common Name	Jasmine gallery worm
Scientific Name	*Elasmopalpus jasminophagus*
Family	Pyralidae
Order	Lepidoptera

Source: *http://arentolib.blogspot.com*

Distribution and Host Range

Gallery worm is seen from the Southern US to Mexico, South America, Central America, and Southern Asia. This insect causes severe affect in the flower crop Jasmine.

Nature and Symptoms of Damage

Elasmopalpus genus includes the snout mouth moths. Caterpillars make tunnels and feed on the terminal leaves, shoots and the flower heads that they weave together with web. The silky web has faecal matter of the pest adhering to it. Great damage is seen to the economical part *i.e.,* the flower buds.

Life History and Description

Adults live on average for 10 days and each female lays approximately about 125 eggs. Eggs are usually laid singly on the upper and lower surfaces of the leaves or at any point on inflorescence. Eggs hatch within a week and Larvae start constructs a radiating tube-like silk shelter. Larval stage lasts for 15 to 21 days and pupates in the web itself. The pupa overwinters and adults emerge in summer. The caterpillar seen in green colour with a red head and prothorax. It also consists of lateral brown streaks on the body, whereas the moth is tiny and dark grey.

Management

Collection and destruction of plant debris, that may carry the source of infection Collection and destruction of the damaged buds along with the silken tunnels. Maintenance of plots clean with proper pruning. Installation of light traps to attract adults. Use of the larval parasitoids like *Phanerotoma* sp. and *Perilampus* sp. Spray of cypermethrin 25 EC @ 2 ml or dimethoate 30 EC @ 1 ml in 1 litre of water.

❑ Leaf web worm: *Nausinoe geometralis* (Guenée, 1854)

Common Name	:	Jasmine web worm
Scientific Name	:	*Nausinoe geometralis* (Guenée, 1854)
Family	:	Crambidae
Order	:	Lepidoptera

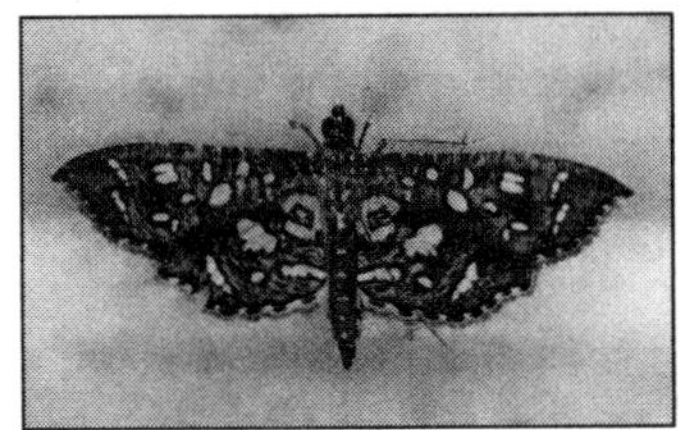

Source: *https://www.inaturalist.org/guide*

Distribution and Host Range

It is seen commonly in Eastern, Western, and Southern Africa, various Indian Ocean islands, Australia, Pakistan, China as well as India. Oleaceae members along with *Jasminum* species are the known hosts of this pest.

Nature and Symptoms of Damage

Larval stages are destructive forms to the plant. Caterpillars primarily attack the lower, bushy, and shaded sections of plant. The leaves are loosely and openly webbed. On the surface of the leaves, the silk threads resemble a cobweb. Larvae skeletonize the leaves by consuming the parenchyma. The severely infected bush shows a 'burnt appearance' as the affected and dried out leaves remain attached and entrapped in the web itself. This results in the reduction of vitality which reflects in the bush growth and ultimately the production of flower buds in the subsequent years.

Life History and Identification

The leaf web worm life cycle lasts for about 22 to 24 days. On the leaf lamina, the adult female lays 15 to 30 greenish yellow-coloured eggs. Eggs will hatch out in about 3-4 day incubation period. The larval and pupal stages last for 12 to 15 and 6 to 7 days, respectively. Larvae pupates within the web. Caterpillars are green in colour with dark warts that give rise to thin hairs. Adult moth is characterized as a medium-sized moth with light brownish wings and white dots on it.

Management

Collection and destruction of plant debris, that may carry the source of infection. Collecting and eradication of damaged buds and silken tunnels. Proper pruning is necessary to keep plots tidy. Adults will be attracted by the installation of light traps. Ladybird beetles and green lace wings have been observed feeding on eggs and caterpillars. Spiders, carnivorous arthropods, consume a vast number of jasmine ecosystem larvae, including the leaf webworm. Spray of dimethoate 30 EC @ 1 ml per 1 L of water.

❑ Leaf roller: *Glyphodes unionalis* (Hubner)

Common Name	:	Jasmine moth
Scientific Name	:	*Glyphodes unionalis* (Hubner)
Family	:	Crambidae
Order	:	Lepidoptera

Source: *https://sites.ju.edu.jo*

Description and Host Range

A migratory species found in Asia, Africa, and southern Europe. This species is a non-resident migrant and rare that is not recognized as a pest in places like the British Isles. In oleaceous plants like jasmine (*Jasminum* spp.), damage to the new branches is occasionally noticed. Infestations are occasionally seen on ornamentals like container-grown olive (*Olea europaea*).

Nature and Symptoms of Damage

Caterpillars are the destructive phase. The leaves are rolled by caterpillars and feed on the leaves. Growth and development of the bush is highly reduced. This ultimately hampers the flower production also.

Life History and Description

Usually, the eggs (200-600/female) are laid on young leaves, flowers and branches. The hatch-out larvae stay together in groups at first, then disperse out, within its own web. Elder larvae frequently weave multiple leaves together to pupate. The moth in the Middle East has 6 to10 partially overlapping generations every year and lives for 2 to 3 weeks. Caterpillars are green in colour and the adult is a coloured white moth with a brown line at costal margins of the forewings.

Management

Same as Jasmine web worm.

❑ Jasmine eriophyid mite: *Aceria jasmini*

Common Name	:	Jasmine eriophyid mite
Scientific Name	:	*Aceria jasmini*
Family	:	Eriophyidae
Order	:	Acarina

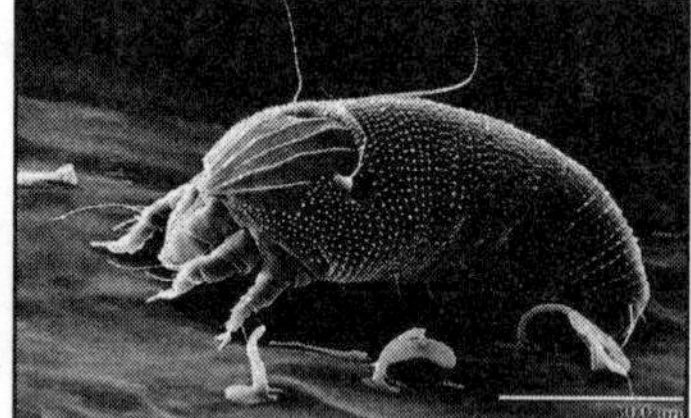

Source: *https://en.wikipedia.org/wiki/*

Distribution and Host Range

Widely distributed in India. Host plants ranges from *Jasminum* species and *Jatropha intergrima*.

Nature and Symptoms of Damage

On the leaf surface, tender stem and the flower buds, feeding by mite results in the creation of a felt-like, hairy outgrowth known as Erineum. It produces a felt-like webs that resemble the white hairy growths and are visible on the surface of leaves, fragile stems and the flower buds. Stunted growth of the plants and reduction of flower production is seen in affected plants.

Life History and Description

Females are cylindrical, vermiform, and have two pairs of legs. They are about 44 microns thick and between 150 and 160 microns long. Life cycle includes; egg, protonymph, followed by deuteronymph and finally the adult. Here all the life phases have 2 pairs of legs.

Management

Removal of the alternate hosts near the jasmine plots. Use of resistant variety like Parimullai (TNAU). Removal and destruction of the affected parts. Use of predaceous insects like, *Scolothrips indicus* and *Scymnus gracilis*. Repeated spray of triazophos 40 EC @ 1.5 ml per litre in combination with the neem oil @ 5 ml per litre for twice or thrice or spray of wettable sulphur 40 WP @ 3.75 kg or malathion 50 EC @ 1 litre or dimethoate 30 EC @ 625 ml in 500 -750 litre of water per hectare.

❑ Red spider mite: *Tetranychus cinnabarinus* (Boisduval)

Common Name	:	Carnation mite, red spider mite; Two-spotted spider mite, Carmine spider mite,
Scientific Name	:	*Tetranychus cinnabarinus* (Boisduval)
Family	:	Tetranychidae
Order	:	Trombidiformes

Source: https://www.cabidigitallibrary.org/doi/10.1079/cabicompendium.30965

As Described in Tomato

❑ Tingid bug: *Corythauma ayyari* (Drake, 1933)

Common Name	:	Lace bug, Tingid bug
Scientific Name	:	*Corythauma ayyari* (Drake, 1933)
Family	:	Tingidae
Order	:	Hemiptera

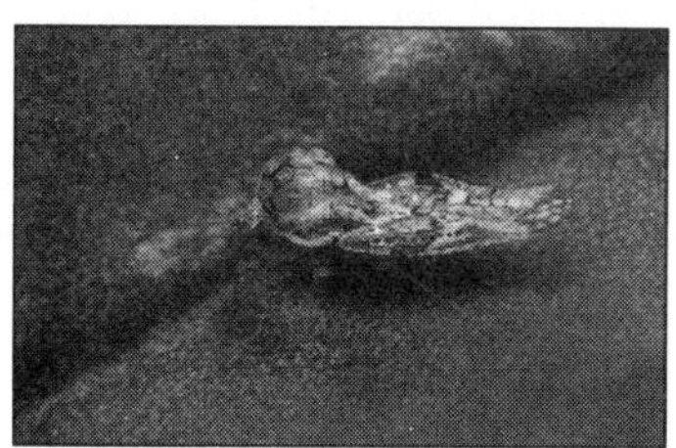

Source: https://indiabiodiversity.org/

Distribution and Host Range

This invasive pest is native to the Asia region. But has been imported to a number of nations, mostly in the Mediterranean region. This species has widely distributed from India, Laos, Indonesia, Malaysia and Thailand. This lace bug has been observed on a wide range of plant species from various families, and it is considered to be a serious pest for cultivated and ornamental plants, including like several species of Jasmine (Oleaceae) which includes *J. azoricum, J. grandiflorum, J. multiflorum, J. officinale, J. sambac*, and others like *Eranthemum pulchellum* (Acanthaceae), *Ocimum* and *Volkameria inermis* (Lamiaceae), *Trachelospermum* sp. (Apocynaceae), *Althaea officinalis* (Malvaceae), Lantana (Verbenaceae), *Musa* (Musaceae) and Hedychium (Zingiberaceae).

Nature and Symptoms of Damage

Both the nymphs and adults of tingid bug feed on the sap of *Jasminum sambac* leaves. Infected leaves show chlorotic spots, turn yellow. As a result of the excrements, the leaf undersides turn dark brown or black and develop spots, and the photosynthesis is decreased. They eventually dry out and drop.

Life History and Description

Jasmine lace bug is a small, non-hairy, Tinginae bug. Both the males and female bugs are short-lived and may live up to 10 and 12 days respectively. Overlapping generations are seen. The eggs incubate for 9 to 11 days. The species *C. ayyari* is highly unusual, with an elongated oval body measuring 2.5 to 3.0 mm long and being distinguished by the presence of a subspherical pronotal hood that is sharply elevated above the medial carina.

Management

Collection and destruction of infested leaves along with various life stages of the insects. Spray of dimethoate 30 EC @ 2 ml per litre or methyl demeton 25 EC @ 2 ml per litre.

❑ Whitefly: *Dialeurodes kirkaldyi* (Kotinsky)

Common Name	:	Jasmine whitefly
Scientific Name	:	*Dialeurodes kirkaldyi* (Kotinsky)
Family	:	Aleyrodidae
Order	:	Hemiptera

Source: *https://www.cabidigitallibrary.org/*

Distribution and Host Range

The most preferred hosts of *D. kirkaldyi* are *Jasminum* spp. and *Morinda citrifolia*. It is also seen to attack the members of Apocynaceae, Combretaceae, Loganiaceae, Lythraceae, Malvaceae, Rubiaceae, Verbenaceae and Malpighiacea.

Nature and Symptoms of Damage

Nymphs and adults suck the sap from the under surface of the leaves. Yellowing occurs on infected leaves.

Life History and Description

Eggs are laid on underside of the leaves in groups. Eggs has an incubation period of 1-4 weeks, based on temperature. The immature stages are scale like and feed for 3-4 weeks on the underside portion of leaves, then they enter a dormant pupal stage that lasts for about 2 to 42 weeks. Then pupa overwinters and under the favorable condition adult emerges. Shows four generations per year. Eggs are oval, pale yellow and 0.2-0.3 mm length with a pedicel. Nymphs are up to 1.5 mm long, flat, oval and scale-like in colour. Pseudo-pupa is flat, oval and resembles scale with a size of 1.2 to 1.5 mm. Adult are creamy white in colour (1.2-1.4 mm long) covered in white wax.

Management

Manipulation of planting dates and crop rotation with non-host plants. Collection and destruction of infested leaves along with various life stages of the insects. Use of biological control agents like *Encarsia* and *Eretmocerus*. Spray of methyl demeton 25 EC @ 2 ml per litre or dimethoate 30 EC @ 2 ml per litre.

❑ Jasmine bug: *Antestia cruciata* (Fabricius)

Common Name	:	Jasmine bug
Scientific Name	:	*Antestia cruciata* (Fabricius)
Family	:	Pentatomidae
Order	:	Hemiptera

Source: *https://www.flickr.com/*

Distribution and Host Range

Widely distributed in Sikkim, Kolkata, Nilgiri hills, Sri Lanka, Malayan archipelago, Thailand, Malaysia. Antestia bugs are found on forest jasmine and other commercial species of Jasmine (Oleaceae) along with on charcoal-tree, blume (Cannabaceae) and some Rubiaceae members.

Nature and Symptoms of Damage

Adults and nymphs consume the sap from young shoots and buds, which hinders the development of flowers.

Life History and Description

Adults are tiny (7-9 mm), with dorsal colour range from pale greenish to orange yellow colour with two central black lines on the head. A black spot in front of each eye, ten black dots on the pronotum, four on the scutellum and three on the corium. Antennae are greenish in colour with deflected head. The biology of *Antestia* species has rarely been discussed because of its secondary relevance due of their limited distribution and minimal impact on Jasmine.

Management

Same as mentioned in the tingid bug.

❑ Flower thrips: *Thrips orientalis* (Bagnall, 1915)

Common Name	:	Flower thrips
Scientific Name	:	*Thrips orientalis* (Bagnall, 1915)
Family	:	Thripidae
Order	:	Thysanoptera

Source: *http://www.ozthrips.org/*

Distribution and Host Range

Thrips orientalis has a widespread distribution from Asian tropics including India to Japan, Hawaii, Tanzania, Trinidad, New Caledonia, Florida and Australia. Flower thrips are mostly allied with the scented flowers like Jasmine, Plumeria and Gardenia.

Nature and Symptoms of Damage

T. orientalis are the polyphagous flower dwelling thrips. Thrips species generally feed on pollen and can be a serious agricultural pest. Both the adults and the nymphs attack the blossoms. Brown striations can be detected on the affected flower petals. There is a possibility of mechanical transmission of the phytopathogenic bacteria and fungi.

Life History and Description

The life cycle from egg to adult, is temperature-dependent, just like the other thrips species. A full cycle can be completed from 15 days to more than a month. Depending on the season, adults may live longer than one month and give birth to numerous generations in a single year. Breeding of these flower thrips occurs in white and the scented flowers. Flower thrips body colour mostly ranges from light brown to dark brown. The head, pronotum and foreleg surfaces are inconspicuous or sparsely reticulate sculpture. Presence of both the fore and hind wings which are macropterous (*i.e.*, more than the half and as long as abdomen)

Management

As discussed earlier in Rose thrips.

Resistant Varieties	
World	**India**
Arabian Jasmine (*Jasminum sambac*): This is one of the most popular varieties of jasmine, which is native to Asia. It is widely cultivated for its fragrant flowers and essential oil. Arabian jasmine is relatively resistant to insect pests and can be grown in tropical and subtropical regions. **Winter Jasmine (*Jasminum nudiflorum*):** This variety of jasmine is native to China and is known for its bright yellow flowers that bloom in winter. Winter jasmine is also relatively resistant to insect pests and can be grown in a wide range of soil types. **Italian Jasmine (*Jasminum humile*):** This variety of jasmine is native to the Mediterranean region and is known for its sweet-smelling yellow flowers. Italian jasmine is also relatively resistant to insect pests and can be grown in dry and sandy soil. **Carolina Jasmine (*Gelsemium sempervirens*):** This variety of jasmine is native to the south-eastern United States and is known for its yellow trumpet-shaped flowers. Carolina jasmine is relatively resistant to insect pests and can be grown in a wide range of soil types. **Pink Jasmine (*Jasminum polyanthum*):** This variety of jasmine is native to China and is known for its fragrant pink or white flowers that bloom in winter. Pink jasmine is also relatively resistant to insect pests and can be grown in well-draining soil. **Angel Wing Jasmine (*Jasminum nitidum*):** This variety of jasmine is native to Southeast Asia and is known for its glossy evergreen leaves and fragrant white flowers. Angel Wing jasmine is also relatively resistant to insect pests and can be grown in tropical and subtropical regions.	**Mogra Jasmine (*Jasminum sambac*):** Also known as Arabian jasmine, Mogra jasmine is one of the most popular varieties grown in India. It is known for its intensely fragrant white flowers. Mogra jasmine has good resistance to common insect pests and is a suitable choice for cultivation in different parts of India. **Madurai Malli Jasmine (*Jasminum grandiflorum*):** Madurai Malli, also called Spanish jasmine or Poet's jasmine, is another widely cultivated variety in India. It features large, white, highly fragrant flowers. While it is not completely immune to insect pests, Madurai Malli jasmine has good resistance and is a favored choice for jasmine cultivation in South India. **Parijat Jasmine (*Nyctanthes arbor-tristis*):** Although not a true jasmine, Parijat jasmine is a highly revered flowering plant in India. It has small white flowers that turn orange as they age and emit a beautiful fragrance. Parijat jasmine is known for its resilience against insect pests and is grown in various regions of India. **Chameli Jasmine (*Jasminum officinale*):** Chameli jasmine, also known as Common jasmine or Poet's jasmine, is a hardy variety grown in India. It produces small, white, highly fragrant flowers and has good resistance to insect pests. Chameli jasmine is commonly cultivated in North India. **Kunda Jasmine (*Jasminum multiflorum*):** Kunda jasmine is a vining variety with clusters of white, fragrant flowers. It is native to India and is known for its resistance to insect pests. Kunda jasmine is often grown in gardens and as an ornamental plant in different parts of the country.

Pests of Anthurium

Scientific Name	*Anthurium andreanum*
Family	Araceae
Origin	Central and South America
Chromosome Number	2n = 30

Anthuriums are a genus of flowering plants in the Araceae family, with over 1000 species found in tropical regions around the world. Anthurium flowers are typically heart-shaped and come in a range of colors, including red, pink, orange, and white. Anthuriums are grown in tropical regions around the world, including Central and South America, the Caribbean, and Southeast Asia. They are also grown as indoor houseplants in many other regions. Anthuriums can be susceptible to a range of pests that can have a significant economic impact on production. Common pests of anthuriums include spider mites, thrips, mealybugs, scale insects, and whiteflies. Some of the major pests that can affect anthuriums include:

❑ Aphid: *Neomyzus circumflexus* (Buckton, 1876)

Common Name	:	Crescent-marked lily aphid or Mottled arum aphid
Scientific Name	:	*Neomyzus circumflexus* (Buckton, 1876)
Family	:	Aphididae
Order	:	Hemiptera

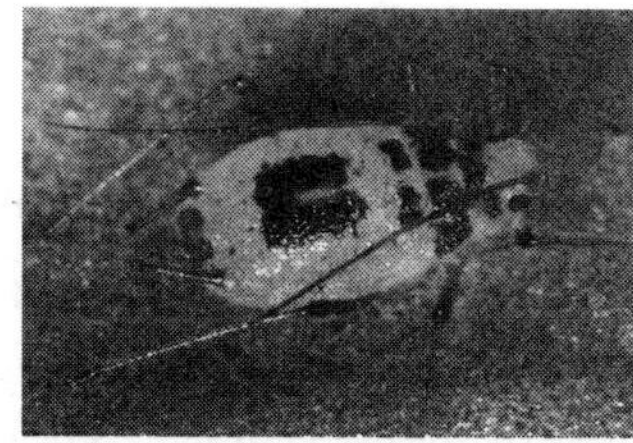

Source: https://influentialpoints.com/

Distribution and Host Range

With the exception of the temperate terrestrial habitats, this aphid is widespread throughout the world. Generally found host plants are Anthuriums, *Zantedeschia*, *Asparagus*, *Begonia*, *Cineraria*, *Fuchsia*, *Cyclamen*, *Adiantum*, *Viola tricolor*.

Nature and Symptoms of Damage

Aphids ingest sap from their hosts to obtain food. Due to this, plants frequently develop deformities, including curled, shrivelled and occasionally gall-forming leaves.

Life History and Description

There is no sex exchange or egg-laying during reproduction. Live female nymphs are born to females. Because of this mode of reproduction, populations are entirely made up of females. Overlapping generations are seen. The *N. circumflexus* apterae size ranges from 1.2 to 2.6 mm. These aphids are glossy white to yellowish green colour with few black crisscross bands on the thoracic segments, which is broken along the middle and a giant horse shoe-shaped mark on the abdomen. The antennae are 1 to 1.5 times the length of the body. The siphunculi looks dusky by a darker flange. The cauda is in pale shade, which is elongated with 4 to 6 lateral hairs like structures along with a single dorsal preapical hair. The juvenile, nymphs are pale greenish white and lacks the dark stripes.

Management

Same as discussed in Rose.

❑ Thrips: *Chaetanaphothrips orchidii* (Moulton, 1907)

Common Name	:	Anthurium thrips, Orchid thrips
Scientific Name	:	*Chaetanaphothrips orchidii* (Moulton, 1907)
Family	:	Thripidae
Order	:	Thysanoptera

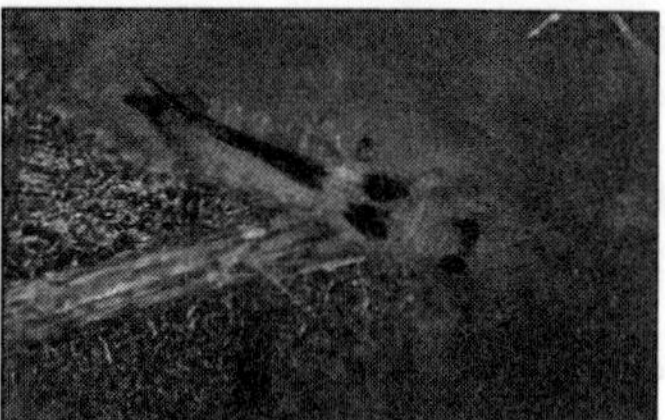

Source: https://www.anthura.nl/

Distribution and Host Range

A cosmopolitan insect that restricted to glasshouses in temperate zones and occurs outside in subtropical and tropical climates. Host plants includes Anthurium (Araceae), Orchids (Orchidaceae), *Citrus* (Rutaceae), *Musa* (Musaceae) and some other greenhouse plants.

Nature and Symptoms of Damage

Adults and nymphs both consume the sap from leaves. Effect of mottling on flowers and foliage is seen. *Anthurium* bracts do not open its leaves and also can develop bronzing, striping. Growth is also slowed down.

Life History and Description

Anthurium thrips lays 50-140 eggs per adult female in the leaf epidermis, where the developing nymphs feed. They typically dwell among unopened leaves and blossoms, keeping hidden for the most of their existence. They "jump" to the ground when they finish the juvenile period, where they complete their development and pupate. Life cycle takes around 5 weeks at 24°C. Almost all the adults have a similar lifespan. The fully grown-up nymphs are about 1 mm long and yellow-pink in colour. The adult thrips is yellow, similar in size of matured nymphs except with the presence of dark-banded wings.

Management

Eradication of weeds, pruning of plant parts and other leaves that serve as the infestation source. Requires regular sanitation. Burning the affected plant waste is advised to entirely get rid of the thrips. Install 4 to 5 blue sticky traps per acre. Release of predatory mite like *Amblyseius cucumeris*

@ 500,000 per hectare. Foliar spray of dimethoate 30 EC or cyfluthrin 2.0 EC @ 1 ml per litre reduce the count of injured flowers.

Whitefly: *Aleurotulus anthuricola* (Nakahara)

Common Name	:	Anthurium whitefly
Scientific Name	:	*Aleurotulus anthuricola* (Nakahara)
Family	:	Aleyrodidae
Order	:	Hemiptera

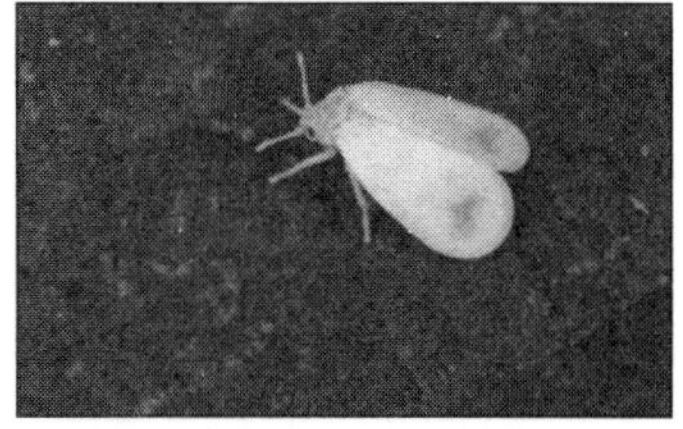

Source: *https://housing.com/news*

Distribution and Host Range

Colombia and the Lesser Antilles are the native habitats of Anthurium whitefly. Barbados, Guadeloupe, Trinidad and Tobago, Dominica, Martinique, as well as the Caribbean and Oceania's Hawaii, have reported to occurrence of it. *Aleurotulus anthuricola* is described to be restricted to the *Anthurium* species only. Hosts include species includes mostly Flamingo Lily and *A. palmarum*.

Nature and Symptoms of Damage

Nymphs and adults both ingest the sap from the underside of leaves. It causes a decrease in plant vigour, which finally causes blooms to fall off of the plant. Due to the secretion of honey dew, sooty mould grows on infected leaves and inhibits photosynthetic activity.

Life History and Description

A. anthuricola, completes its life sequence with-in the innermost surface of the anthurium sheaths. The entire life cycle of anthurium whitefly from egg to adult finish in 35 to 37 days. Adults are the minute insect with yellowish coloured body and the whitish wings. Whereas the nymphs are oval and resembles scales and are in yellowish color.

Management

Manipulation of planting dates and crop rotation with non-host plants. Use of yellow sticky traps and reflecting mulch covers to monitor the whitefly population. Release of parasitic wasp like *Encarsia formosa* @ 3/m2 is effective. Spray of dimethoate 4.0 EC @ 2 ml per litre significantly reduces the count of eggs, nymphs, pupae and the adult whiteflies. Malathion 50 EC @ 2 ml per litre was effective against adults and pupae of white flies.

Red spider mite: *Tetranychus urticae* C.L. Koch, 1836

Common Name	:	Carnation mite, red spider mite; Two-spotted spider mite, Carmine spider mite,
Scientific Name	:	*Tetranychus urticae* C.L. Koch, 1836
Family	:	Tetranychidae
Order	:	Trombidiformes

Source: *https://www.cabidigitallibrary.org/doi/10.1079/cabicompendium.30965*

As described in Tomato

Resistant Varieties

***Anthurium andraeanum*:** This is one of the most common and widely cultivated Anthurium varieties. It features heart-shaped leaves and vibrant spathes in various colours, including red, pink, and white. *Anthurium andraeanum* is known for its tolerance to pests and diseases, making it a suitable choice for both indoor and outdoor cultivation.

Anthurium clarinervium: Known for its striking velvety leaves with prominent white veins, *Anthurium clarinervium* is a unique and visually appealing variety. It has good resistance to pests and diseases, making it a favored choice among Anthurium enthusiasts.

Anthurium crystallinum: This variety is prized for its large, dark green, velvety leaves with prominent white veins. Anthurium crystallinum is known to have relatively better resistance to pests, and with proper care, it can thrive and produce stunning foliage.

***Anthurium jenmanii*:** *Anthurium jenmanii* is a compact variety that is characterized by its glossy, dark green leaves and attractive, elongated spathes. It is known to have good resistance to pests and diseases, making it a suitable choice for indoor cultivation.

***Anthurium warocqueanum*:** This variety, also known as Queen Anthurium or Bird's Nest Anthurium, is highly valued for its large, deeply veined leaves that have a leathery texture. *Anthurium warocqueanum* is known for its resilience against pests and diseases, making it a desirable choice for collectors and enthusiasts.

65 Pests of Tuberose

Scientific Name	*Polianthes tuberosa*
Family	Agavaceae
Origin	Mexico
Chromosome Number	n = 30

Tuberose (*Polianthes tuberosa*) is a perennial plant native to Central America, with fragrant white flowers that are highly valued for their aroma. The flowers grow on tall spikes and are typically used in perfumes and as cut flowers. Tuberose is grown in tropical and subtropical regions around the world, including India, Mexico, and Hawaii. Tuberose can be susceptible to a range of pests that can have a significant economic impact on production. Some of the major pests that can affect tuberose include:

❑ Bud Borer: *Helicoverpa armigera* (Hübner, [1808])

Common Name	:	Cotton bollworm, corn earworm, old World bollworm, scarce bordered straw
Scientific Name	:	*Helicoverpa armigera* (Hübner, [1808])
Family	:	Noctuidae
Order	:	Lepidoptera

Source: https://www.cabidigitallibrary.org/

As Described in Tomato

❑ Aphids: *Aphis craccivora* C.L. Koch, 1854

Common Name	:	Cowpea aphid, Groundnut aphid, Black legume aphid.
Scientific Name	:	*Aphis craccivora* C.L. Koch, 1854
Family	:	Aphididae
Order	:	Hemiptera

Source: https://bugguide.net/

Distribution and Host Range

Aphis craccivora is thought to have originated in the Palearctic region but has now spread to became cosmopolitan. Its distribution has recently expanded to North regions like Siberia and Canada and further South into Chile and Argentina. It is prolific in the Mediterranean region and the subtropics. It is one of the most frequent aphid species in the tropical regions. Commonly found in India, Thailand, the Philippines, the Southern United States, tropical Africa and South America.

This aphid is a highly polyphagous pest. Asteraceae, Brassicaceae, Cucurbitaceae, Caryophyllaceae, Chenopodiaceae, Malvaceae, Rosaceae, Ranunculaceae and Solanaceae are some of the plant families that can act as hosts. Crops infected by this cowpea aphid include tuberose, cowpeas, peanut, chickpeas, beetroot, brassicas, cucurbits, cotton and cardamom.

Nature and Symptoms of Damage

A. craccivora, adults and nymphal stages suck the sap and damage the plants by causing stunting and distort growth. The honeydew secretions produced is deposited on plant surfaces and this encourages the progress of sooty mould by restricting the photosynthesis. Even this aphid is also a vector for a number of viral diseases.

Life History and Description

A. craccivora overwinter as eggs. Early in the spring, the eggs hatch-out and develops into the first larval stage are known as fundatrix (stem mothers). These aphids are completely female and reproduce through parthenogenesis, generating nymphs that moult 4 times in 8 to 12 days. Winged females will disperse to other host plants by the end of april. A female aphid can live for 9 to 25 days and give birth to 25 to 125 young. The year may have up to 20 generations. Winged forms have formed by november, and eggs are laid before winter arrives. Parthenogenetic reproduction occurs throughout the year in warmer areas.

A. craccivora is a tiny aphid species. The female has a shiny black or dark brown coloured body with large cauda and brown or yellow legs. The antennae comprise six segments, which are pale proximally and dark distally. The adults have no wax on their dorsal side, while the nymphs have a little coating of wax. Females with wings are up to 2.2 mm long and have **cross-bearing** on the abdomen. Wingless females are slightly smaller in size.

Management

Use of sprinkler type of irrigation system to limit the infestation. If the number of aphids is low, then rinse them with water or wipe them down with a cloth. Install yellow sticky traps. Release aphid lions- *Chrysoperla carnea* (green lacewing larvae-first instar grubs) @ 10,000 per hectare. Ladybugs (*Coccinella septempunctata*) both at nymphal and adult stage are also the common predators to the aphids and other predators includes parasitic wasps, hoverfly larvae, aphid midge larvae and arachnids like spiders. Spray dimethoate 30 EC or methyl demeton 25 EC @ 2 ml/lit or neem oil @ 0.5%.

❑ Grasshoppers: *Atractomorpha crenulata* Fabricius, 1793

Common Name	:	Tobacco grasshopper
Scientific Name	:	*Atractomorpha crenulata* Fabricius, 1793
Family	:	Pyrgomorphidae
Order	:	Orthoptera

Source: *https://in.pinterest.com/*

Distribution and Host Range

India, Sri Lanka, Myanmar, Bangladesh, southern Vietnam and Northwestern Sumatra are all the places that well distributed by *A. crenulata*. But now it is also to be found in North American midwestern states such as Kansas, Nebraska and others. This preferrable host plants of this pest are tobacco, tuberose, mint and brinjal etc.

Nature and Symptoms of Damage

Young leaves and blossom buds are preferred by these grasshoppers and feed on them. Plants with damaged leaves and blossoms lose their elegance. This not also lowers the aesthetic value of the plant but also leads to a greater economic loss to the growers.

Life History and Description

The life cycle of *A. crenulata* is finished in a half to one month duration. Adult female lays the eggs singly on leaf ventral surface. Pupation occurs on the leaf surface itself. Adult grasshopper has a greenish coloured body with well-developed tegmina and rosy wings. They have medium-sized bodies and short antennae. Nymphal stages are similar to the adults but little pinkish in color, smaller in size compared to adults.

Management

Use of screens like net can avoid the hoppers damage to nurseries. Installation of bird perches. Encourage the birds like Brazilian cardinal and English sparrow that feed on grasshoppers. Spray of carbaryl 50% WDP @ 0.2% or quinalphos 25% @ 0.05% or malathion 50% EC 0.1% protects the foliage.

❑ Red spider mite: *Tetranychus urticae* C.L. Koch, 1836

Common Name	:	Carnation mite, red spider mite; Two-spotted spider mite, Carmine spider mite,
Scientific Name	:	*Tetranychus urticae* C.L. Koch, 1836
Family	:	Tetranychidae
Order	:	Trombidiformes

Source: https://www.cabidigitallibrary.org/doi/10.1079/cabicompendium.30965

As Described in Tomato

❑ Weevils: *Myllocerus discolor* Schoenherr, 1826

Common Name	:	Gray weevil, ash weevil
Scientific Name	:	*Myllocerus discolor* Schoenherr, 1826
Family	:	Curculionidae
Order	:	Coleoptera

Source: https://inaturalist.ca/

Distribution and Host Range

Ash weevils are distributed throughout the India, Sri Lanka and Myanmar. It is a polyphagous pest, along with tuberose, it is known to attack cocoa, mango, maize, sugarcane, sorghum etc.

Nature and Symptoms of Damage

Plants wilt in patches as the leaf margins are notched. Grubs chew away at the roots, causing plants to come-off easily when pulled. Adults feed on the leaves.

Life History and Description

The adult weevil is brown with a white mark on the elytra. Grub is a tiny, white apodous grub that feeds on roots. The weevil emerges in the summer season and lays ovoid, light yellow-coloured eggs in the soil. Throughout the course of 24 days, the female lays an average of 360 eggs. The eggs hatch-out in three to five days. The grub period lasts 1-2 months, pupation occurs in soil inside the earthen cells, and the pupal period lasts 7-10 days. The life cycle is finished in 6 to 8 weeks, resulting in 3 to 4 generations per year. Adults live for about 4 to 5 months in winter.

Management

Grubs can be controlled by deep ploughing in summer, harrowing, flooding, hoeing and fallowing. Use of crop rotations and trap crops like sorghum, maize can avoid the adults as well. Installation of light trap @ 1/ha to catch adults. Hand picking of adults can also be done. Use of parasitic fungus like *Metarhizium anisopilae*, entomopathogenic fungus like *Beauveria brogniartii* to control grubs. Adults and pupa are also controlled by *Heterorhabditis indica*, *H. bacteriophora*. Before planting, apply 10% carbaryl dust to the soil to reduce larvae. Use of quinolphos 5% @ 25 kg/ha or phorate granules etc.

❑ Root knot nematode: *Meloidogyne incognita* (Kofoid & White, 1919)

Common Name	:	Root knot nematode (RKN)
Scientific Name	:	*Meloidogyne incognita* (Kofoid & White, 1919)
Family	:	Heteroderidae
Order	:	Tylenchida

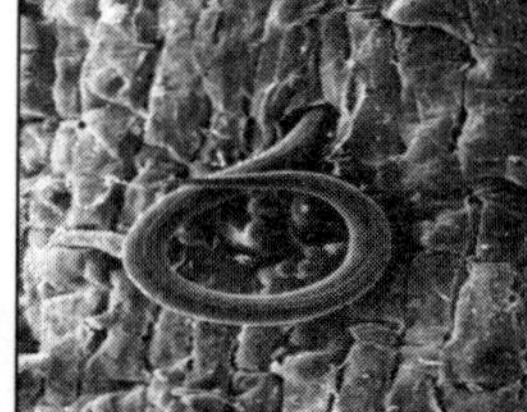

Source: *https://en.wikipedia.org/*

As Described in Tomato

Resistant Varieties
Single Mexican Tuberose (*Polianthes tuberosa*): This is the most commonly cultivated Tuberose variety. It produces long-lasting, highly fragrant white flowers on tall stems. Single Mexican Tuberose is known for its resistance to pests and diseases, making it a suitable choice for gardens.
Double Tuberose (*Polianthes tuberosa*): The Double Tuberose variety features densely packed, multiple layers of white petals, giving it a fuller appearance. It is also known for its strong fragrance. While it may be slightly more susceptible to pests compared to the Single Mexican Tuberose, it still exhibits good resistance overall.

Pearl Tuberose (Polianthes tuberosa 'Pearl'): This variety is a selected form of Tuberose that produces large, double flowers with a pearl-like sheen. Pearl Tuberose is known for its strong resistance to pests and diseases, making it a reliable choice for cultivation.

The Pearl Double Tuberose (Polianthes tuberosa 'The Pearl'): This is a popular variety that produces large, double flowers with a creamy white color. It is highly fragrant and exhibits good resistance to pests, making it a preferred choice for Tuberose enthusiasts.

Rajat Rekha Tuberose: This is an Indian variety of Tuberose that produces white, highly fragrant flowers. Rajat Rekha Tuberose is known for its resistance to pests and diseases, making it suitable for cultivation in various regions.

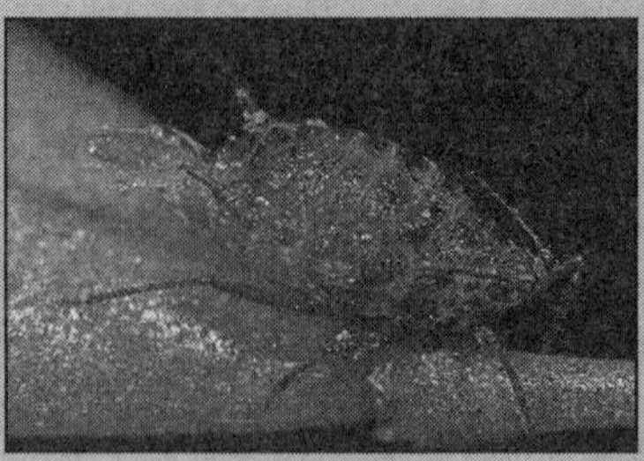

Pests of China Aster

Scientific Name	*Callistephus chinensis*
Family	Asteraceae
Origin	China
Chromosome Number	2n = 18

China aster (*Callistephus chinensis*) is an annual flowering plant that belongs to the Asteraceae family. It is native to China and is widely cultivated for its attractive flowers. China aster is widely cultivated as an ornamental plant in many parts of the world, including Asia, Europe, and North America. Some of the major pests that can affect China aster include:

❑ Aphids: *Lipaphis erysimi* (Kaltenbach, 1843)

Common Name	:	Mustard aphid, turnip aphid
Scientific Name	:	*Lipaphis erysimi* (Kaltenbach, 1843)
Family	:	Aphidideae
Order	:	Hemiptera

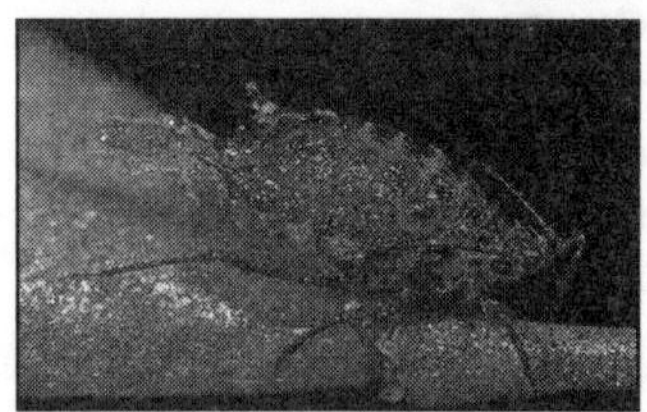

Source: *https://influentialpoints.com/*

As Described in Marigold

❑ Red spider mite: *Tetranychus urticae* C.L. Koch, 1836

Common Name	:	Carnation mite, red spider mite; Two-spotted spider mite, Carmine spider mite,
Scientific Name	:	*Tetranychus urticae* C.L. Koch, 1836; *Tetranychus cinnabarinus* Boisduval
Family	:	Tetranychidae
Order	:	Trombidiformes

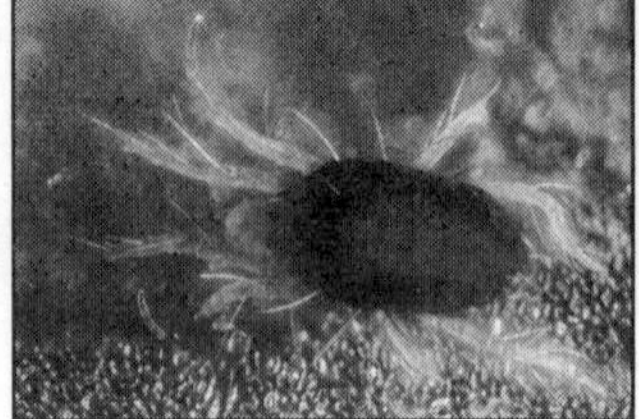

Source: *https://www.cabidigitallibrary.org/doi/10.1079/cabicompendium.30965*

As Described in Tomato

❑ Leaf Hoppers: *Empoasca kerri* (Pruthi)

Common Name	:	Green leaf hopper
Scientific Name	:	*Empoasca kerri Pruthi, E. binotata, E. flavescens* (Fabricius, 1794)
Family	:	Cicadellidae
Order	:	Hemiptera

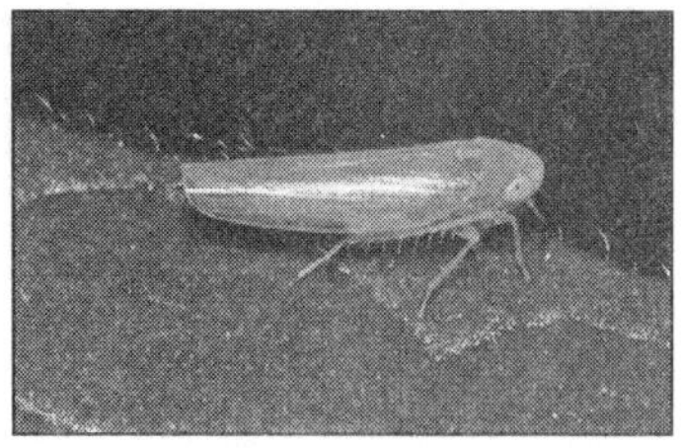

Source: *https://plantwiseplusknowledgebank.org*

As Described in Marigold

Resistant Varieties	
World	**India**
Lady Coral China Aster: Lady Coral is a variety known for its large, fully double flowers in a beautiful coral color. It exhibits good resistance to common insect pests, making it a reliable choice for gardeners.	**Milady China Aster:** Milady is a dwarf variety of China Aster that produces compact plants with double flowers in various colours, including pink, purple, red, and white. It is known for its resistance to pests and diseases, making it suitable for cultivation in Indian gardens.
Duchess China Aster: Duchess China Aster is a versatile variety that produces large, double flowers in a wide range of colors, including pink, purple, red, and white. It shows good resistance to insect pests and can thrive in various growing conditions.	**Dwarf Princess China Aster:** This variety features compact plants with double blooms in shades of pink, lavender, red, and white. It exhibits good resistance to pests and diseases, making it a reliable choice for Indian gardeners.
Queen China Aster: Queen is a robust variety with large, semi-double to double flowers in vibrant colours like pink, purple, and white. It exhibits good resistance to pests and diseases, making it a popular choice for cut flower production.	**Peony China Aster:** Peony China Aster is characterized by its large, fully double flowers that resemble peonies. The flowers come in a wide range of colors, including pink, purple, red, and white. This variety shows good resistance to pests and diseases, making it a popular choice among gardeners in India.
Viceroy China Aster: Viceroy is a tall-growing variety that produces large, fully double flowers in an array of colours, including pink, purple, and white. It shows good resistance to common insect pests, making it suitable for garden beds and borders.	**Serenade China Aster:** Serenade is a variety known for its abundant blooms and resistance to pests. It produces large, double flowers in a wide range of colors, including purple, pink, and white. The flowers are held on sturdy stems, making them suitable for cut flower arrangements.
Imperial China Aster: Imperial is a compact variety with double flowers in shades of pink, purple, red, and white. It exhibits good resistance to pests and diseases, making it an excellent choice for containers and smaller garden spaces.	**Comet China Aster:** Comet is a tall-growing variety that produces large, semi-double flowers in vibrant colours such as pink, purple, red, and white. It exhibits good resistance to pests and diseases and is well-suited for garden beds and borders in India.

Pests of Crossandra

Scientific Name	*Crossandra infundibuliformis*
Family	Acanthaceae
Origin	Indo-Malayan region
Chromosome Number	2n = 40

Crossandra (*Crossandra infundibuliformis*) is a tropical evergreen shrub native to India. It belongs to the Acanthaceae family and is prized for its attractive flowers, which come in shades of orange, yellow, and red. Crossandra is grown in tropical regions around the world, including India, Southeast Asia, and Africa. Crossandra can be susceptible to a range of pests that can have a significant economic impact on production. Common pests of Crossandra include mealybugs, spider mites, whiteflies, and thrips. Some of the major pests that can affect crossandra include:

❑ Scales: *Parasaissetia nigra* (Nietner, 1861)

Common Name	:	Black scale
Scientific Name	:	*Parasaissetia nigra* (Nietner, 1861)
Family	:	Coccidae
Order	:	Hemiptera

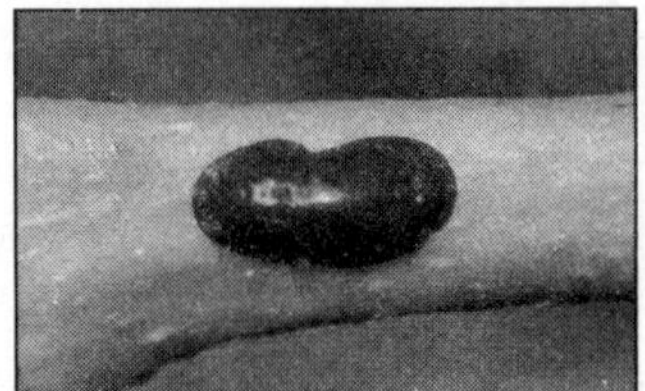

Sourcehttps://www.brisbaneinsects.com/

Distribution and Host Range

This scale is native to Africa, yet it is found all around the world. Host plants of nigra scale include crossandra, anthurium, croton, bamboo, cotton, coffee, edible ginger, guava, eggplant, macadamia, fig and pineapple.

Nature and Symptoms of Damage

The black scale feeds on the sap of the host plant and can be found on chlorophyll-containing leaves or twigs. The damage caused by feeding an individual scale is minor. When substantial populations are present, yellowing, defoliation, along with reduction of flower yield and plant vigour is seen.

Life History and Description

This scale is known to reproduce non-sexually or parthenogenetically. Females can deposit fertile eggs without male fertilisation. Only females are seen in a population without males. The eggs are oval, translucent with a shiny surface when they are laid and turn pink in a few hours. Then eggs change to bright orange colour before hatching, with two black specks that correspond to the eyes. Eggs are located under protected adult body and hatch-out in 4 days. There are three stages of larvae. The first, second, and third phase, which last 16, 13 and 12 days respectively.

Mature females range in hue from dark brown to lustrous black and can grow to be 1/5 inch long. Adults, those have not been weathered are fragile, have flat plates of wax laid in a row over their bodies. On the leaves, their general form is widely oval and little convex. On twigs, however, they become narrower, longer, and more convex. The shape, size and colour of pest vary depending on the host.

Management

Pruning and destroying of all canes that are severely infested. Scrap off with cotton or brush soaked in diesel or kerosene. Use of parasites like *Microterys flavus*, *Encyrtus kotinskyi*, *Encyrtus infelix*, *Encyrtus barbatus*, *Tomocera californica*, *Scutellista cyanea*, *Coccophagus hawaiiensis*, *Aneristus ceroplastae*, *Quaylea whittieri* and predators like beetles, moths, butterflies, flies, mites and thrips. The black scale is attacked even by a fungus, *Entomophthora pseudococci*. Apply the carbofuran 3G granules @ 5g per plant or spray of fish oil rosin soap @ 25 g per litre.

❑ White fly: *Bemisia tabaci* (Gennadius, 1889)

Common Name	:	White fly, sweet potato white fly or Silvery leaf white fly
Scientific Name	:	*Bemisia tabaci* (Gennadius, 1889)
Family	:	Aleyrodidae
Order	:	Hemiptera

Source:https://www.eurekalert.org/

As Described in Potato

❑ Gram borer: *Helicoverpa armigera* (Hübner, [1808])

Common Name	:	Cotton bollworm, corn earworm, old World bollworm, scarce bordered straw
Scientific Name	:	*Helicoverpa armigera* (Hübner, [1808])
Family	:	Noctuidae
Order	:	Lepidoptera

Source:https://www.cabidigitallibrary.org/

As Described in Tomato

Root knot nematode: *Meloidogyne incognita* (Kofoid & White, 1919)

Common Name	:	Root knot nematode (RKN)
Scientific Name	:	*Meloidogyne incognita* (Kofoid & White, 1919)
Family	:	Heteroderidae
Order	:	Tylenchida

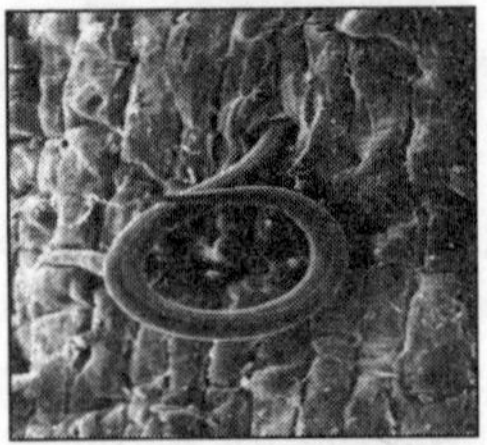

Source: https://en.wikipedia.org/

As Described in Tomato

Resistant Varieties

***Crossandra Infundibuliformis* 'Firecracker':** Firecracker Crossandra is a popular variety with bright orange-red flowers. It is known for its pest resistance and can tolerate a range of growing conditions, including heat and humidity.

***Crossandra Infundibuliformis* 'Orange Marmalade':** Orange Marmalade is another variety of Crossandra with stunning orange flowers. It exhibits good resistance to pests and can add a pop of color to garden beds or containers.

***Crossandra Infundibuliformis* 'Apricot Shower':** Apricot Shower is a variety that produces apricot-colored flowers. It is known for its pest resistance and can be a beautiful addition to tropical gardens or as a cut flower.

***Crossandra Infundibuliformis* 'Sundance':** Sundance is a compact variety with bright yellow-orange flowers. It exhibits good resistance to pests and can be grown in containers or used as a bedding plant.

***Crossandra Infundibuliformis* 'Tropic Flame':** Tropic Flame is a variety with fiery red-orange flowers. It shows good resistance to common insect pests and can be grown as an accent plant or in mass plantings.

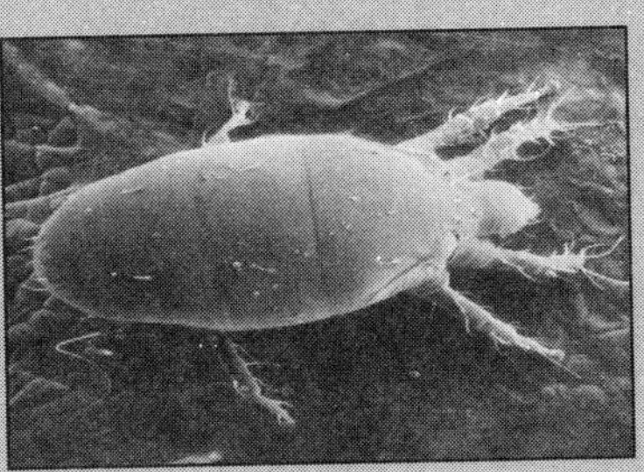

68 Pests of Gerbera

Scientific Name	*Gerbera jamesonii*
Family	Asteraceae
Origin	Africa
Chromosome Number	2n = 50

Gerbera (*Gerbera jamesonii*) is a popular flowering plant that belongs to the Asteraceae family. It is native to South Africa and is widely cultivated for its attractive, daisy-like flowers. Gerbera flowers come in a range of colors, including white, pink, yellow, orange, and red. Gerbera is grown commercially in many parts of the world, including Europe, South America, and Asia. Gerbera can be susceptible to a range of pests that can have a significant economic impact on production. Some of the major pests that can affect gerbera include:

❑ Greenhouse whitefly: *Trialeurodes vaporariorum* Westwood, 1856

Common Name	:	Glasshouse whitefly, greenhouse whitefly
Scientific Name	:	*Trialeurodes vaporariorum* Westwood, 1856
Family	:	Aleyrodidae
Order	:	Hemiptera

Source: *https://www.biolib.cz/en*

Distribution and Host Range

Trialeurodes vaporariorum, the greenhouse whitefly, is a native of tropical and subtropical America, most likely Brazil or Mexico. This whitefly is suited to hundreds of plant species from many families. Many crops, such as roses, gerbera, poinsettias, aubergines, cucumber, beans, sweet pepper and tomatoes are affected by it.

Nature and Symptoms of Damage

They have piercing-sucking mouthparts and shortly after developing, they start to feed on plant sap. *Trialeurodes vaporariorum* adults and nymphs harm plants in three different ways: by sucking up plant sap directly, covering them in honeydew from copious sugar secretions, and spreading plant viruses. When whitefly populations is high, there is a risk of serious damage by sucking sap from plant tissue. Plants can eventually die if whiteflies feast heavily on them. The usual photosynthetic activities are hampered by sugary excretions and honeydew, which also encourage the development of fungi. As result of sooty mould lower the quality of the harvest is obtained.

Life History and Description

The life cycle of whiteflies is finished in about 25 to 30 days. The greenhouse whitefly has six developmental phases: namely egg, first, second, third, and fourth larval stages, and the adult stage. Eggs are pale yellow colour when hatched and later turns to greyish colour. The oval-shaped larvae are found on the underside of young leaves. While other larval stages remain flattened on the leaf, first instar larvae (crawlers) are mobile. An upright circulation of waxy sticks surrounds the fourth larva stadium forms the white, round casing. These are located on oldest leaves and are known as the pupa stadium. The adult whitefly emerges out from the pupa through a 'T' shaped fissure. Adult flies can be seen top and bottom surfaces of the leaves, but lays eggs in under surface. A white waxy material coats the insect body.

The nymphs of greenhouse whiteflies have an oval, flattened shape with perpendicular sides and prominent long waxy filaments on top. Adult whiteflies consist of wings with zig- zag patterns. The greenhouse whitefly spreads its wings flat, which gives it a triangular look from top.

Management

Removal of crop residues for complete eradication of white flies before planting. Installation of yellow sticky traps. Use of predators like *Chrysoperla* species larvae (lace wings) or *Orius* species and parasaitoids like *Encarsia sp* or *Eretmocerus spp*. etc. Spray of lambda-cyhalothrin 5% EC 0.5 ml per litre.

❑ Serpentine leaf miner: *Liriomyza trifolii* (Burgess, 1880)

Common Name	:	American serpentine leafminer, celery leafminer
Scientific Name	:	*Liriomyza trifolii* (Burgess, 1880)
Family	:	Agromyzidae
Order	:	Diptera

Source:https://www.cabidigitallibrary.org/

As Described in Tomato

❑ Mites: *Polyphagotarsonemus latus* (Banks, 1904)

Common Name	:	Broad mite
Scientific Name	:	*Polyphagotarsonemus latus* (Banks, 1904)
Family	:	Tetranychidae
Order	:	Trombidiformes

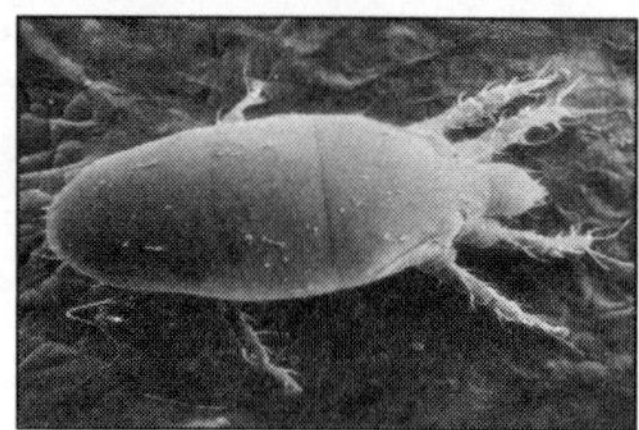

Source:https://www.google.com/

As Described in Chilli

❑ Aphid: *Myzus persicae* (Sulzer, 1776)

Common Name	:	Green peach aphid, green fly or Peach-potato aphid
Scientific Name	:	*Myzus persicae* (Sulzer, 1776)
Family	:	Aphididae
Order	:	Hemiptera

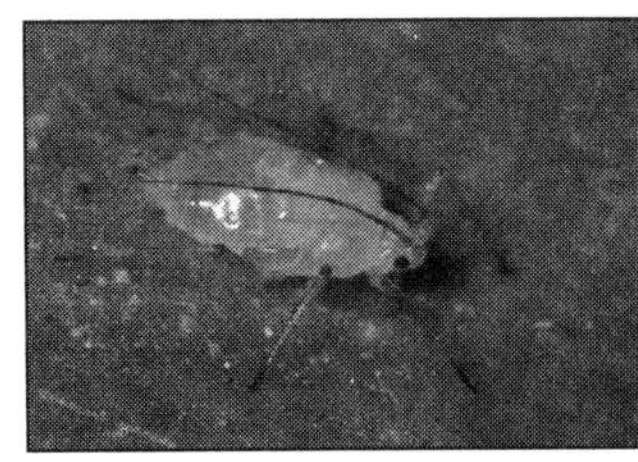

Source: *https://inpn.mnhn.fr/*

As Described in Potato

Resistant Varieties
***Gerbera jamesonii* 'Mega Revolution':** Mega Revolution is a variety known for its large, vibrant flowers. It exhibits good resistance to insect pests and is a popular choice among growers for its pest tolerance.
***Gerbera jamesonii* 'Patio':** Patio Gerbera is a compact variety that is well-suited for container gardening. It is known to have good resistance to pests and can be grown on balconies, patios, or small gardens.
***Gerbera jamesonii* 'Festival'**: Festival Gerbera is a variety that produces a range of vibrant colors, including red, orange, pink, and yellow. It is relatively resistant to insect pests and can be grown in gardens or used as cut flowers.
***Gerbera jamesonii* 'Essence'**: Essence Gerbera is a variety with a wide color range, from pastel shades to bold and bright hues. It exhibits good resistance to pests and is suitable for both garden beds and containers.
***Gerbera jamesonii* 'Terra'**: Terra Gerbera is a variety that produces large, double flowers in various shades of red, pink, and yellow. It shows good resistance to pests and can be grown as a focal point in garden borders or containers.

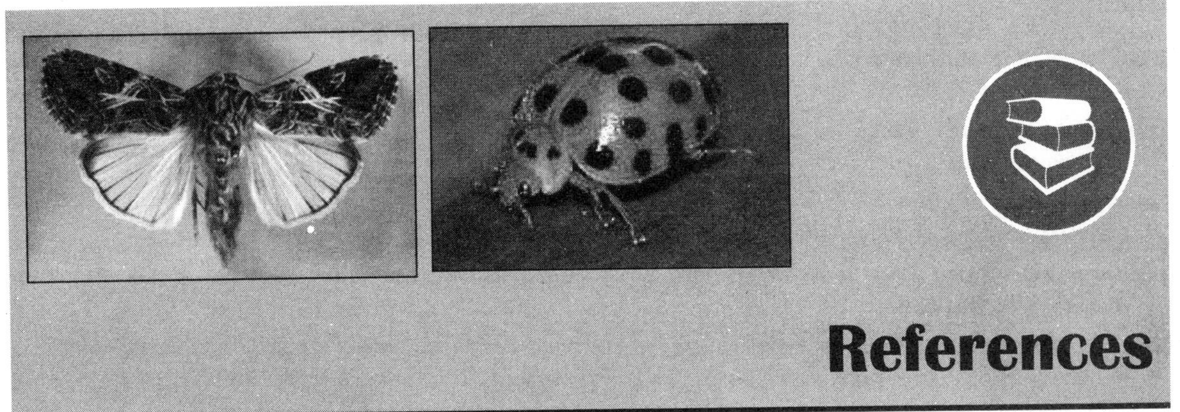

References

Agboton, C., Onzo, A., Ouessou, F. I., Goergen, G., Vidal, S., & Tamo, M. (2014). Insect Fauna Associated with *Anacardium occidentale* (Sapindales: Anacardiaceae) in Benin, West Africa. Journal of Insect Science, 14(1).

Anathakrishnan, T.N. (1971). Thrips (Thysanoptera) in Agriculture, Horticulture and Forestry - Diagnosis, Bionomics and Control. J. Scien. Ind. Res., 30(3), 113-146.

Anonymous. (2023). Horticulture in India: Its Growth and Future. Retrieved from https://www.geeksforgeeks.org/horticulture-in-india-its-growth-and-future/

Anonymous. (2023a). Chapter VI: Insect Management. In Texas Vegetable Growers Handbook. Retrieved from https://aggie-horticulture.tamu.edu/vegetable/guides/texas-vegetable-growers-handbook/chapter-vi-insect-management/

Balaji Rajkumar, M., Gundappa, B., Tripathi, M. M., & Rajan, S. (2018). Pests of jackfruit. Pests and Their Management, 587-602.

Balikai, R. A. (2008). Insect pest status of ber (*Ziziphus mauritiana* Lamarck) in India and their management strategies. In I International Jujube Symposium 840 (pp. 461-474).

Biological Records Centre - Database of Insects and their Food Plants. (2017). March 24). *Leptinotarsa decemlineata* (Say). Retrieved from https://www.brc.ac.uk/dbif/invertebratesresults.aspx?insectid=2386

Butani, D.K. (1978). Pests and diseases of jackfruit in India and their control. Fruits, 33(5), 351-357.

CABI. (2017). *Spodoptera litura* (taro caterpillar). Retrieved from https://www.cabi.org/isc/datasheet/52743

Cho, J.R., Hong, K.J., & Yoo, J.K. (1997). Comparative toxicity of selected insecticides to *Aphis citricola, Myzus malisuctus* (Homoptera: Aphididae), and the predator Harmonia axyridis (Coleoptera: Coccinellidae). Journal of Economic Entomology, 90(1), 11-15.

Cramer, H. H. (1967). Plant protection and world crop production. Pflanzenschutz-Nachrichten Bayer.

Cui, L., & Francis, F. (2012). The functional significance of E-β-Farnesene: does it influence the populations of aphid natural enemies in the fields? Biological Control, 60(2), 108-112.

Dadmal, S.M., Ghuge, P. A., Khadakkar, S.S., & Khodke, S. W. (2013). Occurrence of Holotrichia serrata (Scarabaeidae: Melolonthinae) in Vidarbha. Indian Journal of Entomology, 75(4), 354

Daneel, M. S., & De Waele, D. (2017). Nematode pests of banana. Nematology in South Africa: A view from the 21st century, 359-371.

Distant, R. (2019). Rostratus (Distant) on *Garcinia xanthochymus*. Indian Journal of Entomology, 81, 567. https://doi.org/10.5958/0974-8172.2019.00120.2

EFSA Panel on Plant Health (PLH), Bragard, C., Dehnen-Schmutz, K., Di Serio, F., Gonthier, P., Jacques, M. A., & MacLeod, A. (2018). Pest categorisation of Sternochetus mangiferae. EFSA Journal, 16(10), e05439.

Entnemdept.ufl.edu. (2017, October 25). Potato tuberworm. Retrieved from http://entnemdept.ufl.edu/creatures/veg/potato_tuberworm.htm

FAO/WHO. (2014). The international code of conduct on pesticide management. Retrieved from http://www.fao.org/fileadmin/templates/agphome/documents/CODE_2014Sep_ENG.pdf

Gundappa, B., Balaji Rajkumar, M., Singh, S., & Rajan, S. (2018). Pests of guava. Pests and their management, 491-516.

Gupta, R., & Tara, J. S. (2013). Biological studies of *Lymantria obfuscata* Walker (Lepidoptera: Lymantridae) on apple plantations (*Malus domestica* Borkh.) in Jammu region of J & K, India. Munis Entomology & Zoology, 8(2), 749-755.

Halder, J., Dey, D., & Rai, A.B. (2019). New host record of *Rastrococcus iceryoides* (Green, 1908) (Hemiptera: Pseudococcidae), an emerging pest of Arecanut from West Bengal, India. National Academy Science Letters, 42, 1-3.

Kallekkattil, S., Krishnamoorthy, A., & Venkatesha, M. G. Biology and Incidence of the Jackfruit Bud Weevil *Ochyromera artocarpi* Marshall (Coleoptera: Curculionidae). Indian Journal of Agricultural Research, 1, 5.

Kumar, A., Kumar, P., Mishra, P.K., Rajpoot, P.K., & Mishra, R. Integrated Approach for Management of Hadda/Epilachna Beetle (Henosepilachna vigintioctopunctata Fabricius).

Kumar, A., Pandey, S.K., & Kumar, R. (2009). Population dynamics of mango mealy bug, *Drosicha mangiferae* Green from Jhansi, Uttar Pradesh. In Biol. Forum. Int. J (Vol. 1, pp. 77-79).

Landolt, P. J., Guedot, C., & Zack, R.S. (2011). Spotted cutworm, *Xestia c-nigrum* (L.) (Lepidoptera: Noctuidae) responses to sex pheromone and blacklight. Journal of Applied Entomology, 135(8), 593-600.

Marlatt, C. L. (1904). The annual loss occasioned by destructive insects in the United States. U.S.

Maruthadurai, R., & Karuppaiah, V. (2014). Managing menace of insect pests on custard apple.

McMenemy, L. S., Mitchell, C., & Johnson, S. N. (2009). Biology of the European large raspberry aphid (*Amphorophora idaei*): its role in virus transmission and resistance breakdown in red raspberry. Agricultural and Forest Entomology, 11(1), 61-71.

McSorley, R., & Parrado, J. L. (1983). The spiral nematode, *Helicotylenchus multicinctus*, on bananas in Florida and its control. In Proceedings of the Florida State Horticultural Society (Vol. 96, pp. 201-206).

Metcalf, R. (1996). Applied entomology in the twenty-first century: needs and prospects. American Entomologist, 42(1), 10-16.

Mifsud, D., Falzon, A., Malumphy, C., Lillo, E. D., Vovlas, N., & Porcelli, F. (2012). On some arthropods associated with *Ficus* species (Moraceae) in the Maltese Islands.

Morstatt, H. (1929). Die jährlichen Ernteverluste durch Pflanzenkrankheiten und Schädlinge und ihre statistische Ermittlung. Berüber Landw, 9, 433-477.

Neiswander, R. B. (1944). Insect pests of strawberries in Ohio.

Oerke, E. C., & Dehne, H. W. (2004). Safeguarding production – losses in major crops and the role of crop protection. Crop Protection, 23, 275-285.

Ordish, G. (1952). Untaken Harvest: Man's loss of crops from pest, weed and disease: An introductory survey. Faber and Faber.

Perry, C., Smith, H., Deng, Z., & Lahiri, S. (2022). Common Arthropod Pests in Blackberries and Pomegranates in Florida: ENY2084/IN1376, 12/2022. EDIS, 2022(6).

Pests of fruit trees (Citrus, Banana, Mango, Pomegranate and Sapota)- E-Pest Surveillance and Pest Management Advisory.

Pimentel, D. (1976). World food crisis: energy and pests. Bulletin of the Entomological Society of America, 22(1), 20-26.

Plantwise Knowledge Bank. (2021, July 15). Species Page: white grub (Holotrichia serrata). Retrieved from https://www.plantwise.org/knowledgebank/datasheet/42794

Rasib, K. Z., Ashraf, H., & Afzal, M. (2014). Feeding preferences of *Odontotermes obesus* (Rambur) (Isoptera: Termitidae) on different commercial and non-commercial woods from Lahore, Pakistan, under laboratory and field conditions. Zoology and Ecology, 24(4), 369-379.

Revathy, V. S., & Mathew, G. (2014). Identity, biology and bionomics of the Common Mime Chilasa clytia Linnaeus (Lepidoptera: Papilionidae). Journal of Threatened Taxa, 6(14), 6719-6722. https://doi.org/10.11609/JoTT.o3808.6719-22.

Rota, J., Aguiar, A., & Karsholt, O. (2014). Choreutidae of Madeira: review of the known species and description of the male of *Anthophila threnodes* (Walsingham, 1910) (Lepidoptera). Nota lepidopterologica, 37(1), 91-103.

Sankaranarayanan, C., Somasekhar, N., & Singaravelu, B. (2006). Biocontrol potential of entomopathogenic nematodes Heterorhabditis and Steinernema against pupae and adults of white grub Holotrichia serrata F. Sugar Tech, 8(4), 268-271.

Satyagopal, K., *et al.* (2014). AESA based IPM package for Cumin (pp. 34).

Shrestha, S., Chaudhary, M., Upadhyaya, N., & Khanal, D. (2022). Mango Leaf Webber (*Orthaga euadrusalis* Walker, (Pyralidae: Lepidoptera); A Potential Threat in Tropical Plains of Nepal. Nepalese Horticulture, 16(1), 55-62.

Sosa, M. R., Zamar, M. I., & Torrejon, S. E. (2017). Ciclo de vida y reproducción de *Caliothrips phaseoli* (Thysanoptera: Thripidae) sobre Fabaceae y Solanaceae (Plantae) en condiciones de laboratorio. Revista de la Sociedad Entomológica Argentina, 76(3-4), 1-10.

Srikanth, J., & Santhalakshmi, G. (2012). Effect of Media Additives on the Production of Beauveria brongniartii, an Entomopathogenic Fungus of Holotrichia serrata. Sugar Tech, 14(3), 284-290.

Srinivasan, R. (2014). Insect and mite pests on vegetable legumes: a field guide for identification and management. AVRDC – The World Vegetable Center. AVRDC Publication No. 14-778.

Stojanović, D. V., Jerinić-Prodanović, D., Keresi, T., Graora, D., & Marković, M. (2020). *Choreutis nemorana* (Hübner, 1799) (Lepidoptera: Choreutidae) in Serbia. Topola, (206), 29-34.

Thamarai Chelvi, C., Richard Thilagaraj, W., & Nalini, R. (2011). Field efficacy of formulations of microbial insecticide Metarhizium anisopliae (Hyphocreales: Clavicipitaceae) for the control of sugarcane white grub Holotrichia serrata F (Coleoptera: Scarabidae). Journal of Biopesticides, 4(2), 186-189.

TNAU Agritec Portal. (2021, July 15). Crop Protection: Oil Seeds: Pest of Groundnut. Retrieved from https://agritech.tnau.ac.in/crop_protection/oil_seeds_pest%20of_groundnut.html

Varela, L. G., & Bernays, E. A. (1988). Behaviour of newly hatched potato tuber moth larvae, *Phthorimaea opercula.*

Wohlfarter, M., & Venter, E. (2010, August). Thrips spp. recorded from commercial figs, *Ficus carica* (Moraceae), in the Western Cape Province of South Africa. In XXVIII International Horticultural Congress on Science and Horticulture for People (IHC2010): International Symposium on the 940 (pp. 393-395).

WEBSITES

CABI. (n.d.). Rhizome fly. Retrieved from https://www.cabidigitallibrary.org/doi/10.1079/cabicompendium.

Central Agricultural University, Imphal. (n.d.). Pests of vanilla. Retrieved from http://www.celkau.in/crops/spices/Vanilla/pests.aspx

Department of Agriculture and Fisheries. (n.d.). Pumpkin beetle. Retrieved from https://apps.lucidcentral.org/pppw_v10/text/web_full/entities/pumpkin_beetle_040.htm

Directorate of Economics and Statistics, Ministry of Agriculture and Farmers Welfare, Government of India. (n.d.). Retrieved from http://eands.dacnet.nic.in/

Eagri.org. (n.d.). Amaranthus stem weevil: *Hypolixus truncatulus*. Retrieved from http://eagri.org/eagri50/ENTO331/lecture26/Amaranthus/001.html#:~:text=Amaranthus%20stem%20weevil%3A%20Hypolixus%20truncatulus,leafy%20vegetables%20with%20large%20leaves.

Food and Agriculture Organization (FAO) of the United Nations. (n.d.). Retrieved from http://www.fao.org/faostat/

Indian Agricultural Statistics Research Institute. (n.d.). Module 10: Insect morphology and systematic. Retrieved from http://ecoursesonline.iasri.res.in/mod/page/view.php?id=16712

Indian Council of Agricultural Research (ICAR). (n.d.). Retrieved from http://www.icar.org.in/

Ministry of Agriculture and Farmers Welfare, Government of India. (n.d.). Retrieved from http://agricoop.nic.in/

National Horticulture Board, India. (n.d.). Retrieved from https://nhb.gov.in/

National Research Centre for Soil Salinity and Water Quality. (n.d.). Management of banana rhizome weevil. Retrieved from https://nrcss.icar.gov.in/Upload/637876999594373935.pdf

Oklahoma State University Extension. (n.d.). Drugstore beetle (*Stegobium paniceum*) and cigarette beetle (*Pasioderma serricorne*). Retrieved from https://extension.okstate.edu/programs/digital-diagnostics/insects-and-arthropods/drugstore-beetle-stegobium-paniceum-cigarette-beetle-pasioderma-serricorne/

University of Florida Department of Entomology and Nematology. (n.d.). Coconut scale. Retrieved from https://entnemdept.ufl.edu/creatures/FRUIT/TROPICAL/coconut_scale.htm

University of Florida Department of Entomology and Nematology. (n.d.). *Ferrisia virgata*. Retrieved from https://entnemdept.ufl.edu/creatures/orn/mealybug/ferrisia_virgata.htm

University of Florida Department of Entomology and Nematology. (n.d.). *Radopholus similis*. Retrieved from https://entnemdept.ufl.edu/creatures/NEMATODE/Radopholus_similis.htm#:~:text=Infection%20by%20burrowing%20nematode%20causes,up%20water%20and%20translocate%20nutrients.

University of Florida Mid-Florida Research and Education Center. (n.d.). Mite pests of ornamental plants. Retrieved from https://mrec.ifas.ufl.edu/lso/entomol/ncstate/mite2.htm

University of Hawaii at Manoa. (n.d.). Cardamom shoot and capsule borer. Retrieved from http://www.extento.hawaii.edu/kbase/crop/Type/s_cardam.htm

University of Hawaii at Manoa. (n.d.). Pentalonia nigronervosa. Retrieved from http://www.extento.hawaii.edu/kbase/crop/Type/pentalon.htm

Wikipedia. (n.d.). *Amrasca biguttula*. Retrieved from https://en.wikipedia.org/wiki/Amrasca_biguttula